Borland® C++ 4

Developer's Guide

$53.60 GST
Jy 5/p

Borland® C++ 4 Developer's Guide

Nabajyoti Barkakati, Ph.D.

A Division of Prentice Hall Computer Publishing
201 West 103rd Street, Indianapolis, Indiana 46290

This book is dedicated to:
My wife Leha, and daughters
Ivy, Emily, and Ashley

FIRST EDITION

International Standard Book Number: 0-672-30441-4

Library of Congress Catalog Card Number: 93-086955

97 96 95 94 4 3 2 1

Interpretation of the printing code: the rightmost double-digit number is the year of the book's printing; the rightmost single-digit, the number of the book's printing. For example, a printing code of 94-1 shows that the first printing of the book occurred in 1994.

Composed in AGaramond and MCPdigital by Prentice Hall Computer Publishing

Printed in the United States of America

Trademarks

Publisher
Richard K. Swadley

Associate Publisher
Jordan Gold

Acquisitions Manager
Stacy Hiquet

Managing Editor
Cindy Morrow

Acquisitions Editor
Gregory S. Croy

Development Editor
Phillip W. Paxton

Software Development Editors
Wayne Blankenbeckler
Keith Davenport

Production Editor
Carolyn Linn

Copy Editors
Mitzi Foster Gianakos
Matthew Usher

Editorial and Graphics Coordinator
Bill Whitmer

Editorial Assistants
Sharon Cox
Lynette Quinn

Technical Reviewer
Jim Gershfield

Marketing Manager
Greg Wiegand

Cover Designer
Karen Ruggles

Book Designer
Michele Laseau

Illustrator
Kathy Harley

Director of Production and Manufacturing
Jeff Valler

Imprint Manager
Kelli Widdifield

Manufacturing Coordinator
Paul Gilchrist

Production Analyst
Mary Beth Wakefield

Proofreading/ Indexing Coordinator
Joelynn Gifford

Graphics Image Specialists
Tim Montgomery
Dennis Sheehan
Sue VandeWalle

Production
Ayrika Bryant
Lisa Daughtery
Karen Dodson
Rich Evers
Kim Hannel
Stephanie J. McComb
Jamie Milazzo
Shelly Palma
Juli Pavey
Ryan Rader
Kim Scott
Tonya R. Simpson
Alyssa Yesh

Indexers
Jeanne Clark
Jennifer Eberhardt
Suzanne Snyder

Overview

Overview

Contents

Contents

Contents

Contents

Contents

Contents

Contents

Contents

Contents

Contents

Contents

Contents

Preface

For years, C has been the language of choice among programmers, especially those developing software for MS-DOS systems and Microsoft Windows. More recently though, C++ has started to gain popularity because it supports object-oriented programming (OOP)—the current method of choice for software design. Because C++ is based on C, C compilers for MS-DOS systems, such as Borland C++, are capable of compiling both C and C++ programs. If you are a C programmer, you can use the Borland C++ compiler to learn OOP techniques and migrate to C++.

The combination of OOP, C++, and the comprehensive class libraries (container classes and the ObjectWindows Library) that come with Borland C++ gives you all the tools you need to create applications for MS-DOS and Microsoft Windows. OOP techniques help you organize software into modules based on real-world objects. Although you could apply OOP techniques in any language (C, for instance), C++ provides the language constructs that make it easier to implement the OOP techniques. The class and function libraries are needed because both C and C++ provide only a small set of keywords for controlling program execution and defining new data types—all other tasks such as input and output, string manipulations, and mathematical computations are relegated to a library of functions.

To harness the full capabilities of the Borland C++ programming environment, you have to become knowledgeable in three distinct subjects: OOP concepts and techniques, C++, and the tools and libraries that accompany Borland C++. Further, you have to gain some experience in the synergistic use of OOP, C++, and the libraries to create complete applications. A large number of books have been published on these topics. However, most of the books suffer from one or more drawbacks:

- Books that cover object-oriented design principles do not pay much attention to C++.
- Books designed to teach C++ do not adequately describe how to implement OOP techniques in C++.
- Books designed as reference guides to the Borland C++ class libraries do not cover C++ and OOP.
- The documentation that accompanies Borland C++ has all the information you need—many thousands of pages—but is too extensive to be of use as an easy-to-use tutorial.

Due to these shortcomings, there is a definite need for a comprehensive source of information for all three topics: OOP, C++, and the Borland C++ class libraries.

Borland C++ 4 Developer's Guide is intended to answer the needs of intermediate to advanced level C programmers learning C++ and OOP and developing Windows applications using the Borland C++ 4 compiler. This book teaches OOP and C++, and provides a tutorial introduction to Windows programming with Borland C++ and the ObjectWindows Library (OWL). Because OOP and C++ are likely to be new to a C programmer, the book includes in-depth tutorials that gently introduce OOP concepts and show how to apply these techniques in C++.

Borland C++ 4 Developer's Guide features the following:

- Descriptions of the Borland C++ 4 Interactive Development Environment and the program development tools that accompany the Borland C++ compiler, including TLINK, TLIB, and MAKE
- A quick overview of ANSI standard C
- Extensive tutorials on the basic concepts of object-oriented programming
- Discussion of data abstraction, inheritance, and polymorphism
- A step-by-step introduction to the features of C++, such as classes and virtual functions, that support OOP
- Discussion of how C++ differs from ANSI standard C
- Detailed examples showing how to use OOP techniques
- Descriptions of the different approaches to building a library of reusable classes in C++
- Tutorial coverage of the ObjectWindows library
- A diskette with source code for all example programs appearing in the book
- Real-world examples of using C++ and OOP techniques in DOS and Microsoft Windows applications

Instead of going through a litany of syntactical details, *Borland C++ 4 Developer's Guide* illustrates the OOP techniques through many short example programs. Features of C++ are always presented in the context of an OOP concept that the feature supports.

Borland C++ 4 Developer's Guide also includes coverage of the class libraries that are necessary for building real-world applications. Specifically, the book covers application development for the Microsoft Windows environments using the ObjectWindows library—an extensive collection of over 140 classes designed to make Windows programming easier. The last part of the book includes sample graphics and imaging applications built using OWL.

To make it easier for you to use the programs appearing in the book, *Borland C++ 4 Developer's Guide* includes a bound-in disk that contains the source code for all example programs appearing in the book.

It is easy to get overwhelmed by the new syntax of C++, the details of how everything fits together in a program that uses an object-oriented design, and the large number of tools, functions, and classes that Borland C++ 4 offers. However, with a grasp of the fundamentals of OOP and with the help of the ObjectWindows library, you will find it relatively easy to employ OOP techniques in your Windows applications. I sincerely hope that *Borland C++ 4 Developer's Guide* will get you started on your way to harnessing the full power of object-oriented techniques, C++, and the ObjectWindows libraries.

Acknowledgments

I am grateful to Greg Croy for giving me the opportunity to write this book—a tutorial guide to Windows programming with Borland C++ 4 and the ObjectWindows library. Thanks to Greg for getting me started on this project and seeing it through to its successful completion.

Thanks to Nan Borreson of Borland International for providing me the beta copies of the Borland C++ 4 compiler. Thanks to everyone at Sams Publishing for a job well-done. In particular, thanks to Wayne Blankenbeckler and Keith Davenport for taking care of the companion disk, Phil Paxton for overseeing the book's development, and Carolyn Linn for managing the production of the book.

Finally, my greatest thanks go to my wife Leha and my daughters Ivy, Emily, and Ashley—this book would not have been possible without their love and understanding.

Acknowledgments

Introduction

What This Book Is About

Borland C++ 4 Developer's Guide is an intermediate-level book that introduces you to the basic concepts of object-oriented programming (OOP) and shows you how to apply OOP techniques using the C++ programming language. Additionally, the book is designed to serve as a tutorial to the extensive class libraries that accompany Borland C++ 4. This book assumes that you already know the C programming language. The goal is to get you, the C programmer, familiar with the terminology of OOP, describe how various features of C++ support OOP, and show you how to use the ObjectWindows library to develop Windows applications.

To this end, *Borland C++ 4 Developer's Guide* focuses on the basic concepts of OOP, how OOP helps you handle changes in software requirements easily, and how C++ supports OOP. It also covers programming with the *iostream* I/O library and shows how to call C functions from C++, organize C++ class libraries, and use Borland's template-based Container Class library and the ObjectWindows library (OWL). Once you have mastered the basics of OOP, C++, and OWL, *Borland C++ 4 Developer's Guide* moves on to the subject of developing Windows applications in C++. It includes sample graphics and imaging applications for Microsoft Windows. Figures are used extensively to illustrate concepts and show the inheritance hierarchies of classes.

What You Need

To make the best use of this book, you should have access to a reasonably powerful computer with the Borland C++ 4 compiler. At a minimum, you need an 80386 or 80486 system with a clock speed of 33 MHz with a large disk (at least 200M) and enough memory (at least 8M) to run Microsoft Windows 3.1 efficiently. You also need a large disk because the Borland C++ compiler with all of its libraries and sample codes takes up more than 80M of disk space.

All example programs in this book were tested on the author's system, a 486DX2/66 with 16M of RAM, a 17-inch 1024x768 resolution 256-color display, a SoundBlaster board, and a 450-megabyte hard disk, running MS-DOS 6 and Windows 3.1. Most programs were built with the Borland C++ 4 integrated development environment (IDE), but I compiled many small programs using the DOS command-line version of the compiler in a Windows DOS box.

Conventions Used in This Book

Borland C++ 4 Developer's Guide uses a simple notational style. All listings are typeset in a monospace font for ease of reading. All function names, variable names, and keywords appearing in text are are also in the same monospace font. The first occurrence of new terms and concepts is in *italic*. Notes, typeset in boxes, are used to explain terms and concepts that appear in the text nearby.

How To Use This Book

If you are a newcomer to Borland C++, you should browse through Chapters 1 through 4 to see what Borland C++ 4 offers and how to set it up in your MS-DOS system. If you are starting to learn C++, you should read Chapters 5 through 16 in sequence. These chapters teach object-oriented programming (OOP), C++, and how to apply OOP techniques. If you already know OOP and C++ and you want to learn how to develop Windows applications with Borland C++ and OWL, then you would be interested in Chapters 16 through 25.

There are six parts in the book. The first four parts are tutorials with a total of sixteen chapters. Part I includes four chapters that describe the Borland C++ 4 programming environment and give an overview of the C programming language. Part II has two chapters that explain the basic concepts of object-oriented programming (OOP). Part III comprises seven chapters that describe how to use the features of C++ that support OOP. Part IV includes three chapters that show how to organize C++ class libraries and use the Borland C++ container classes.

The next two parts of the book constitute a tutorial guide to Windows programming with Borland C++ 4 and OWL. Part V has six chapters that cover the OWL classes and their use in a variety of Windows programming tasks. Chapter 17 gives an overview of Windows programming, and Chapter 22 briefly describes how to generate sound under Windows.

The three chapters in Part VI show you how to develop Windows applications capable of drawing graphics and animating images. Chapter 23 describes how to read, interpret, and display images while Chapter 24 shows a technique for animating images. Chapter 25 presents a complete Windows application capable of animating a script-driven demo.

From this quick overview, you can decide how you want to use the book. For example, if you are already familiar with Borland C++ 4, you can skip Part I and go straight to Part II to learn the basic terminology of OOP. If you are a newcomer to C++, consult the chapters in Part III. On the other hand, if you know how C++ supports OOP and want to start using C++ in Windows applications, you can skip Parts I through III and read Chapters 17 through 25.

How To Contact the Author

If you have any questions or suggestions, or if you want to report any errors, please feel free to contact me either by mail or through electronic mail. Here is how:

- Write to: LNB Software Inc., 7 Welland Court, North Potomac, MD 20878-4847.
- If you have access to an Internet node, send e-mail to:

  ```
  naba@access.digex.net
  ```

- If you use CompuServe, specify the following as **SEND TO**: address:

  ```
  >INTERNET:naba@access.digex.net
  ```

- From MCIMAIL, specify the following when sending mail:

  ```
  EMS: INTERNET
  MBX: naba@access.digex.net
  ```

Please do not phone, even if you happen to come across my telephone number. Instead, drop me a letter or send an e-mail message and you are guaranteed a reply.

I

Getting Started with Borland C++

1

The Borland C++ Programming Environment

This book's major goal is to help you, the C programmer, learn the basic concepts of object-oriented programming (OOP) and C++ using the Borland C++ 4 compiler. At the same time, this book also serves as a tutorial guide to developing Windows applications using the C++ class library and the ObjectWindows Library 2.0 (OWL 2.0) that accompany Borland C++ 4. However, before you get into OOP, C++, and the OWL classes, you need to know what tools Borland C++ 4 offers to help you carry out the essential programming tasks of editing, compiling, linking, and debugging. To help familiarize you with the Borland C++ 4 environment, this chapter provides an overview of the Borland C++ 4 product, including what components it contains and how to set up and use it on a PC running Microsoft Windows. This chapter covers the Integrated Development Environment (IDE), the interactive environment; and BCC, the command-line interface to the compiler and linker. Chapter 2, "Program Development Tools in Borland C++ 4," further describes the rest of the program development tools such as TLIB, TLINK, MAKE, and TDW that help you manage the "edit-compile-link-debug" cycle of building applications.

Chapter 3, "An Overview of ANSI Standard C," and Chapter 4, "Borland C++ Extensions to Standard C," summarize the features of the C programming language. Although this book assumes that you already know C, you may want an overview of the C language as a refresher, especially to review the features of ANSI Standard C and the extensions to the language that are specific to Borland C. Another reason for reviewing ANSI C is that familiarity with ANSI C will help you learn the syntax of C++ because of the similarity between the two. Chapter 3 offers an overview of ANSI C, and Chapter 4 describes how Borland augments ANSI C with certain keywords that are necessary to fully utilize the capabilities of the Intel 80x86 microprocessors used in MS-DOS PCs running Microsoft Windows.

A Quick Tour of Borland C++ 4

Borland C++ 4 is many products in one. It provides a complete programming environment for C and C++ and contains all the supporting tools and libraries necessary to write MS-DOS and Microsoft Windows applications. As a programmer, you will primarily use the following tools:

- BCW, the Integrated Development Environment (IDE) for editing, compiling, linking, and debugging programs.
- TDW, the Turbo debugger for Windows.
- BCC, the C and C++ compiler for translating source files into object files. BCC is a 16-bit application that generates 16-bit code. BCC32 is the corresponding 32-bit application that compiles C and C++ source files and generates 32-bit code. Both BCC and BCC32 also provide access to the linker.
- TLINK, the linker for combining one or more object modules into an executable file.
- BRCC, the Borland resource compiler for converting resource files (.RC) into a binary form (.RES) suitable for linking into the executable file (.EXE).
- RLINK, the resource linker for linking a binary resource file (.RES) with an executable file (.EXE).
- TLIB, the library manager for managing collections of object modules in a single file.
- MAKE, the make utility for automating program development.

Utilities that you may not normally use, but are handy when you need what they do, include the following:

- WinSight, a Windows application for viewing information about windows and messages being sent to the windows.
- TDUMP, a utility for displaying information contained in an .EXE file, an .OBJ file, or an .LIB file.
- TDSTRIP, for removing the symbol table from an executable file or the debugging information from an object file.
- TDMEM, for displaying information about your computer's memory.
- GREP, a text search utility derived from the UNIX utility of the same name.
- IMPLIB, the import librarian for creating a special type of library called import library from one or more dynamic link libraries. Import libraries are used in Microsoft Windows programs.
- TOUCH, a utility program that changes a file's creation time to the current time. This is useful when you want to force recompilation of a source file when building an executable with MAKE.

How you use Borland C++ 4 depends on your needs. You can compile and link your program with one or more of the following approaches:

- Accessing the compiler and linker from IDE
- Running the compiler and linker from the DOS command line
- Using MAKE to automate the compiling and linking process

The first two methods are suitable for quickly testing a small program. Whether you use the Windows IDE or run BCC (from a DOS window) to compile and link a program depends on your choice of an editor. If you prefer to use your own editor, prepare the source file with your editor and use BCC to create the executable file.

On the other hand, the Borland C++ IDE offers an excellent editor, which can be configured to your liking. Also, you can easily add your own text editor as a tool that can be accessed through the IDE. Thus, you will find the IDE an ideal environment for developing DOS and Windows applications. To use the IDE, run BCW under Microsoft Windows and access the compiler and linker interactively through the pull-down menus of BCW. BCW enables you to go through the entire cycle of preparing the source file, compiling and linking, running the program, and finding the bugs.

For a large software project involving many source modules, many programmers prefer to prepare a *makefile*—a file with directives for MAKE to compile and link all necessary modules—and run MAKE to go through the compile-and-link cycle. With a makefile, you edit one or more source files, then run MAKE to compile all affected files—for example, changing a header file requires compiling all source files that include the altered header file. As explained in Chapter 2, "Program Development Tools in Borland C++," the makefile describes the interdependence of source, object, and executable files. MAKE uses the knowledge of the interdependency to compile the appropriate files and build a new executable program.

The method you use to specify various options for the compiler and linker varies depending on whether you are using the Windows IDE or accessing the compiler directly from the DOS command line or through MAKE. Later in this chapter, summary descriptions demonstrate how to use the compiler and linker from the IDE and the DOS command line. But first, the next section briefly describes how to set up Borland C++ 4. Following that section is an overview of the Windows IDE and BCC, the command-line interface to the compiler and linker. Several other tools included with Borland C++ 4 are described in Chapter 2.

Installing Borland C++ 4

Installing Borland C++ 4 is straightforward with the INSTALL program included with the product. INSTALL, which must be run under Microsoft Windows, decompresses files from the distribution disks, which may be floppy disks or a CD-ROM, and copies them to specific directories on your hard disk. The steps for installing from a CD-ROM are identical to the ones for installing from floppy disks except that you do not have to keep changing disks when you install from a CD-ROM. You have the option to indicate the drive and the directory where you want Borland C++ 4 installed. The basic steps are as follows:

1. Start Microsoft Windows.
2. Insert the first disk into the appropriate disk drive—A: or B:, depending on the disk size and your system's configuration. For CD-ROM installation, place the CD-ROM in the CD-ROM drive.
3. Select the **R**un option from the Program Manager's **F**ile menu and enter the following as the command line:

```
A:INSTALL
```

Use a different drive letter if you have inserted the disk in a drive other than A. If you are installing from a CD-ROM, use the drive letter for the CD-ROM drive.

4. Once INSTALL runs, you should read and respond to the dialog box that INSTALL displays. Help is available at the beginning of the installation of process when you are prompted for the installation options. Through the dialog box displayed by INSTALL, you will

   - Select the drive and directory where you want to install Borland C++ 4.
   - Select the *memory models* (explained in Chapter 4) for which you want the libraries installed. If you aren't familiar with memory models, you can make the safe choice and install libraries for all memory models.
   - Decide whether you want sample programs copied to your hard disk.
   - Decide whether you want to install Win32s extensions to Microsoft Windows 3.1. (Win32s extensions let you run 32-bit applications under Windows 3.1. You do not need Win32s if you are installing under Windows NT.)

INSTALL also creates icons for several tools and utilities including Borland C++ 4, Turbo Debugger, the Borland Resource Workshop, and WinSpector.

After running INSTALL, you should modify the definition of the `PATH` environment variable in the AUTOEXEC.BAT file. You should add to `PATH` the full pathname of the BIN subdirectory where the executable versions of the Borland C++ programs reside. If you use the recommended default drive and directory when installing Borland C++ 4, you should include `C:\BC4\BIN` in `PATH`'s definition. With PATH modified in this way, you will be able to run the Borland C++ compiler and tools from DOS or from DOS running under Microsoft Windows.

Using the BCW Integrated Development Environment

Once you have successfully installed Borland C++ 4, you can try out the C and C++ compiler from the Windows IDE, an all-in-one C and C++ programming environment. Through BCW's Windows-based graphical user interface, you can

- Edit one or more source files.
- Browse the class hierarchies in an application.
- Build an executable file by compiling source files and linking one or more object files.
- Run the newly built program.
- Use the built-in debugger to find the offending code that causes an error (should one occur).

Additionally, Borland C++ 4 offers a voluminous amount of online help. In fact, the best way to learn BCW is to start using it and browsing through the online help. For your convenience, though, the next few sections briefly summarize some of the significant options offered in BCW's menus—especially the options that are important for C and C++ programming.

Getting Started with BCW

Start BCW from Microsoft Windows by double-clicking on the icon for BCW. This brings up BCW's graphical user interface. What appears on-screen depends on your last session with BCW. If you edited a source file during the last session, BCW automatically starts with that file in a window.

> **Exiting BCW**
>
> To exit BCW, press Alt+F4. Otherwise, bring up the **F**ile menu using the mouse or by pressing Alt+F, and then select the E**x**it option (use the mouse or press X).

Getting Help in BCW

BCW has so many features that it would take several chapters to document all of them. Borland C++ 4 does offer extensive online help, however, so you only need to know how to navigate the help system. Once you discover how to get help in BCW, you can learn the features as you need them.

There are three ways you can get help in BCW:

- Select the **H**elp menu item using the mouse or by pressing Alt+H.
- Press F1 to get help for the current context.
- Press Shift+F1 to call up the index of help topics.

Figure 1.1 shows the result of pressing Alt+H to drop down the **H**elp menu. As you can see, with the **H**elp menu you can see a table of contents or get help for a specific keyword. Notice the second menu item:

Keyword search F1

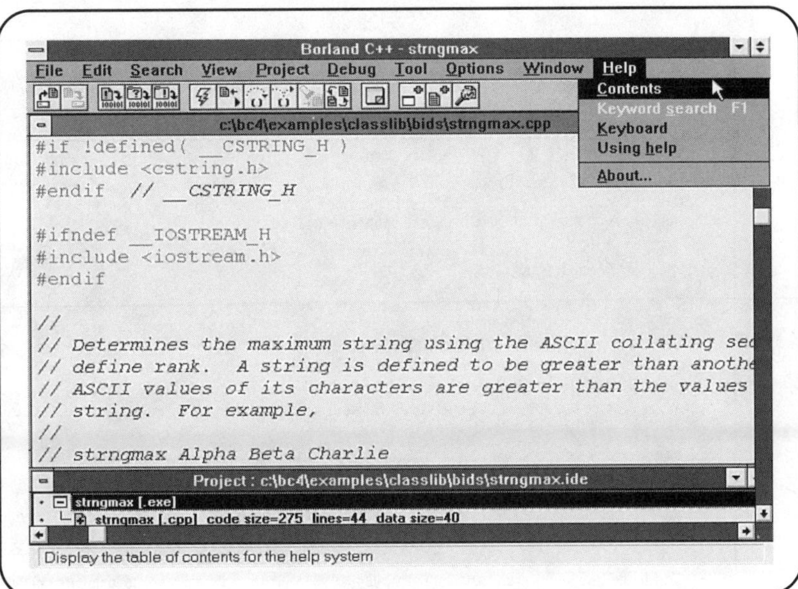

Figure 1.1. The Help menu in Borland C++ 4.

Here, the label F1 denotes the *short-cut* (or *accelerator*) key that you can use to select this menu item.

Keypress Notations

In the Borland C++ 4 documentation and in this book, you will often see references to key combinations such as Alt+F, Shift+F1, and

Ctrl+F4. This notation means that you have to press two keys simultaneously. Thus for Alt+F, keep the Alt key pressed down while you press the F key. Similarly, to get Ctrl+F4, keep the Ctrl (Control) key pressed down and press the F4 key. Notice that Alt+F is the same as Alt+f; you don't need to press the Shift key for an uppercase F when you want the Alt+F key combination.

If you select the **C**ontents option from the **H**elp menu you will see the screen shown in Figure 1.2.

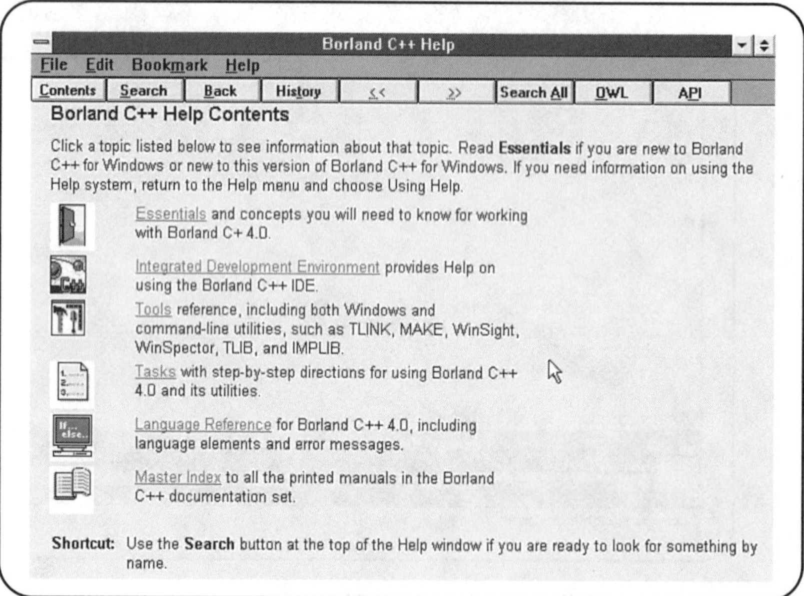

Figure 1.2. The table of contents in Borland C++ 4's Help system.

From this table of contents, you can select any topic of interest by bringing the mouse pointer to the topic and double-clicking the left button. Because this is the standard Microsoft Windows Help system and you are a Windows programmer and user, you will find the help system familiar and easy to navigate. Through this online help system, you can find information on all aspects of Borland C++ 4, from C++ syntax to details of the ObjectWindows Library.

Using the Menus

All your interaction with BCW occurs through menus. As you can see in Figures 1.1 and 1.2, the main menu options appear on a menu bar at the top of BCW's main window. A row of pushbuttons, collectively called the *speed bar*, appears underneath the menu bar. The bottom of the main window serves as a message area and a status bar. The rest of the BCW window acts as a *desktop* on which Borland C++ 4 displays multiple overlapping child windows, each serving a specific function such as editing a source file, displaying error messages, displaying class hierarchies, and displaying information on a project.

As you can see in Figure 1.3, BCW's menu bar has ten items: **F**ile, **E**dit, **S**earch, **V**iew, **P**roject, **D**ebug, **T**ool, **O**ptions, **W**indow, and **H**elp. Each of these items leads to a pull-down menu. Through these pull-down menus, you can perform tasks such as opening and editing files, compiling and linking programs, browsing through C++ class hierarchies, and debugging programs if necessary. Table 1.1 summarizes the options offered in BCW's pull-down menus.

The pushbuttons in the speed bar provide quick access to tasks that you perform often. You can modify the contents of the speed bar by selecting **E**nvironment... from the **O**ptions menu. Click the plus sign next to the SpeedBar item in the resulting dialog box. An item labeled Customize will appear; clicking that item will display the options to customize the contents of the speed bar.

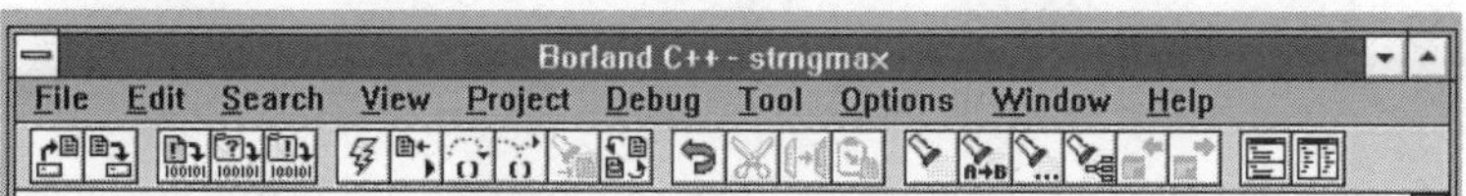

Figure 1.3. The menu bar in BCW.

> **Figuring out the speed bar**
>
> The speed bar gives you quick access to many functions in the Borland C++ 4 IDE, but it can be difficult to guess the meaning of the icons on the buttons. Luckily, Borland C++ 4 provides helpful hints that appear in the status area at the bottom of the main window. As you move the mouse cursor into a button on the speed bar, a one-line message in the status area tells you what that button does. Use this feature to find out what a button does before you click the button to initiate an action.

Table 1.1. Summary of BCW'S pull-down menus.

Title	Summary of Options
File	Create a new file or open an existing file for editing. Close and save files. Print a file. Exit the IDE.
Edit	Edit a file: cut, copy, and paste text; undo and redo the last editing command.
Search	Find and replace a text string or pattern. Locate a source line with errors in case building an executable file fails. (These errors are displayed in the message window.)
View	Switch to the project window or the message window. View the C++ class hierarchy. View all global variables. Display information on current breakpoints and watches (used for debugging). View the current contents of the microprocessor's registers. Obtain information about the current system such as the current version of the operating system and the amount of available memory.
Project	Set up and edit a project (a list of modules and their interdependencies). Compile a C or C++ source file. Build an executable program. Run the AppExpert application generator (described in Chapter 17, "Windows Programming with Borland C++").
Debug	Run and debug the current program. (Command-line arguments for the program can be specified through the Options menu.)
Tool	Run a tool such as Turbo Debugger for Windows, Resource Workshop, Grep, WinSight, WinSpector, and Key Map Compiler. You can add other tools to this menu through the **O**ptions menu.
Options	Customize the look and behavior of IDE (colors, contents of the speed bar). Specify the location of include files and libraries. Specify C and C++ compiler options. Specify options for the editor, linker, debugger, and the librarian. Specify the lists of tools that are available through the **T**ool menu.
Window	Manage the windows in the IDE's desktop. Reduce a window to an icon (minimize) and restore it back to normal size. Arrange the windows on the IDE's desktop. Bring a hidden window to the top.

Title	Summary of Options
Help	Display a table of contents for online help information. Search for information on a specific topic. Displays the compiler's version number and copyright notice.

Menu Selections with the Mouse

Because BCW is a Windows application, you will usually interact with BCW through the mouse. To activate a pull-down menu, move the mouse cursor to an item and click the left mouse button. The pull-down menu will appear and remain on-screen. Now you can move the mouse cursor to an item in the menu and click the left button to select it. To close a pull-down menu without making a selection, click anywhere outside the menu.

Mouse Actions

You can perform a number of actions with the mouse. Here are the six basic actions with which you can interact with Borland C++ 4 and most mouse-based user interfaces:

- *Press* a mouse button by holding the button down without moving the mouse.
- *Release* a mouse button that you have previously held down. This usually initiates some action.
- *Click* a mouse button by quickly pressing and releasing it.
- *Double-click* a mouse button by clicking it twice in rapid succession without moving the mouse.
- *Drag* the mouse cursor by pressing a mouse button and moving the mouse while keeping the button pressed.
- *Move* the mouse cursor by moving the mouse without pressing any button.

In response to certain menu selections, Borland C++ 4 displays dialog boxes. A *dialog box* is a window through which BCW solicits input from the user. Usually the dialog box has check boxes where you indicate your choices, lists from which you pick a selection, and text-entry fields where you enter text. When interacting with a dialog box using a mouse, you just move the mouse cursor to an item and click the left button. Clicking a check box turns on a selection. If you click a text-entry area such as a box for entering a filename, you will see another cursor in that area waiting for you to enter the requested information.

Menu Selections with the Keyboard

You don't need a mouse to use BCW; you can access all of BCW's functions from the keyboard. Here is a brief description of how to access BCW's menus using the keyboard.

Press the Alt key to activate the menu bar. The **F**ile menu is highlighted because this is the initial choice; if you press Enter, the **F**ile pull-down menu appears. You can activate the pull-down menu for a specific option in one of two ways:

- Use the left and right arrow keys to select a main menu option and then press Enter.
- Press the first character of the main menu option you want, displaying the pull-down menu for that option.

Once a pull-down menu is displayed, you can use the left and right arrows to switch to other pull-down menus. Within a pull-down menu, use the up and down arrows to indicate the selection. As you press the up or down arrow, the selected item will be highlighted. Pressing the Enter key activates the selection. If you do not want to make any selection from a pull-down menu, press the Alt key again or press the Esc key to get rid of the pull-down menu.

A faster way to access menu items is to press the Alt key and the first letter of one of the items on the menu bar. For example, to get the **H**elp menu, simultaneously press the Alt key and H—this is commonly written as Alt+H. Once the **H**elp menu appears (see Figure 1.1), you will notice an underlined character in some of the items in the menu. This character is called a *hot key* or *mnemonic key*. Pressing the underlined character activates that item. For instance, when the **H**elp menu is up, pressing A activates the **A**bout... menu item.

Next to some menu items, you will notice the names of keystrokes. In the **H**elp menu, shown in Figure 1.1, notice the F1 next to the Keyword **s**earch option. These are the *shortcut keys* or *accelerator keys*—pressing these key combinations activates that menu option even when the pull-down menu is not displayed. Thus, pressing F1 will always bring up the online Help system with help on a keyword determined by the current context. Table 1.2 summarizes the purposes of several shortcut keys and a number of other keys in BCW.

Table 1.2. Shortcut keys in IDE.

Keystroke	Function
Alt	Toggles the main menu bar.
Alt+Backspace	Undoes the effects of the last editing action.
Alt+Esc	Switches to the next application's window (applies to any application running under Microsoft Windows).
Alt+F4	Exits BCW.
Alt+F7	Moves to the line with the previous error.
Alt+F8	Moves to the line with the next error.
Alt+F9	Compiles the source files in the current project.
Alt+Shift+Backspace	Repeats the last editing action.
Alt+Tab	Switches to the next application (applies to any application running under Microsoft Windows).
Delete	Deletes (when editing a file).
Ctrl+End	Moves to the end of the file.
Ctrl+Esc	Switches to Windows Task Manager (applies to any application running under Microsoft Windows).
Ctrl+F1	Closes the current window.
Ctrl+F4	Provides help on a selected topic.
Ctrl+F6	Jumps to the next window, making it the topmost one on the desktop.
Ctrl+F9	Runs the current program, building it if necessary.
Ctrl+Home	Moves to the beginning of a file.
Ctrl+Insert	Copies selected text (removed to an internal buffer).
Ctrl+C	Copies selected text (removed to an internal buffer).

continues

Table 1.2. continued

Keystroke	Function
Ctrl+V	Pastes previously cut or copied text.
Ctrl+X	Cuts a text selection (removes it to an internal buffer).
Ctrl+Z	Undoes last editing operation.
End	Moves to the end of the current line.
Esc	Closes the help window or pull-down menu. This is equivalent to selecting the Cancel button in dialog boxes.
F1	Provides help on a selected topic. This is the same as selecting the Help button in a dialog box.
F3	Searches forward for a text string or pattern.
F7	Executes the next statement, stepping into function calls.
F8	Executes the next statement, stepping over function calls.
Home	Moves to the beginning of the current line.
Insert	Toggles between Insert and Overtype mode. In Insert mode, text is inserted into the file; in Overtype mode, each character replaces an existing character at the same position.
Shift+Delete	Cuts a text selection (removes it to an internal buffer).
Shift+Enter	Moves the cursor to a new line.
Shift+F1	Displays the table of contents of the online Help system.
Shift+F4	Tiles windows (arranges them in a nonoverlapping pattern).
Shift+F5	Cascades windows (arranges them in an overlapped pattern).
Shift+Insert	Pastes previously cut or copied text.

Keystroke	Function
Shift+Tab	Moves to the previous option in a dialog box.
Space	Toggles the current option in a dialog box.
Tab	Moves to the next option in a dialog box.

Some menu options end in an ellipsis (...). Selecting these menu items causes BCW to display dialog boxes in which you have to enter some information. In such dialog boxes, you must use some other keystrokes to navigate through the options. First of all, you can get rid of a dialog box—or just about anything in IDE—by pressing the Esc key. Pressing the Tab key moves the cursor from one group of options to another, while Shift+Tab moves the cursor from option to option in the reverse order. Once the cursor is on the item you want, you can select it by pressing Enter. In list boxes, you can select an item by using the up and down arrows. Most dialog boxes show three or four buttons, usually labeled OK, Cancel, and Help. You can get to these buttons by repeatedly pressing the Tab key. Navigating through a dialog box is tedious without a mouse, but it can be done.

Editing a Program

One of the first steps in writing a program is to prepare the source file. BCW includes a text editor that you can use to prepare the source files for your program. You can use BCW's editor as you would use any Windows word processor. The editor supports keyboard commands—you have the option to pick one from a set of predefined commands. There are four keyboard mappings available in Borland C++ 4: Default, IDE Classic, Brief, and Epsilon. You can also customize the keyboard mappings. The editing commands for each of these sets is listed in the online help. If you are in an editor window, you can get online help on the editor by pressing F1.

To create a new source file, start by selecting the **N**ew option from the **F**ile menu (see Figure 1.4). This creates a window named `noname000.cpp`. You can immediately start entering text in the window. To save the text in a file, select Save **a**s... from the **F**ile menu. BCW displays a dialog box and prompts you for the name of the file. When you select the OK button in the dialog box, BCW saves the text in the specified file.

To edit an existing source file, select **O**pen... from the **F**ile menu. BCW displays a dialog box with the list of files in the current directory (see Figure 1.5). You can either type the name of a file in the text-entry area labeled File **N**ame: or pick a file from the list of files. You can change the directory or drive by making a selection from the **D**irectories: list. Selecting a directory brings up the list of files in that directory in the list of files. After selecting a file, click the OK button to load the file.

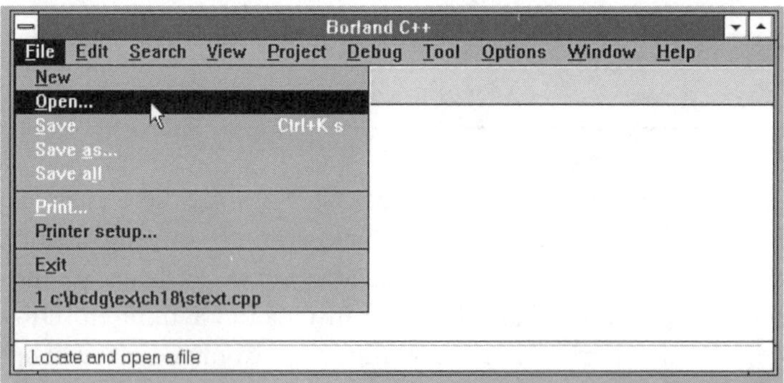

Figure 1.4. The File menu.

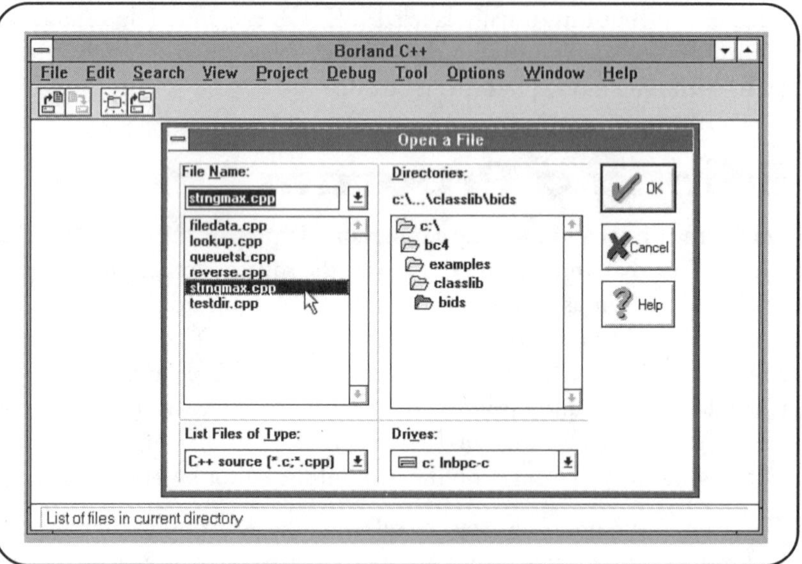

Figure 1.5. The Open File dialog box.

Editing a file is straightforward with a mouse. Move the mouse cursor to the desired position, click the left mouse button, and begin typing the new text. To select text for cut and paste operations, press the left mouse button at the starting location and drag the mouse cursor to the end of the text you want to select. You then can select **C**opy or Cu**t** from the **E**dit menu. Later, you can paste this text anywhere in the file (or in another file) by using the **P**aste option from the **E**dit menu.

Like the menu selections, you can edit with the keyboard only. For example, to select text, position the cursor at the start of the selection, press the Shift key, and use the arrow keys to move the cursor to the end of the selected text. Next press Ctrl+C or Ctrl+Insert to copy the text into an internal buffer called the *clipboard.* To paste, position the cursor where you want to insert the text and press Ctrl+V or Shift+Insert.

Adding Your Own Text Editor as a New Tool in the IDE

You can specify your own text editor as a tool in the Borland C++ IDE. Here are the basic steps to add a DOS text editor (C:\EMACS\EMACS.EXE) to edit source and header files in the IDE:

- Under Windows, use thee PIF editor to create a PIF file, C:\EMACS\EMACS.PIF, for the text editor's executable file C:\EMACS\EMACS.EXE. Mark the check box labeled "Windowed" so that the editor runs in a DOS window under Windows 3.1 (386 Enhanced mode).
- From the **O**ptions menu, select **T**ools… and click the **N**ew button in the resulting dialog window.
- Fill-in the fields of the Tool Options dialog box that appears. In particular, specify C:\EMACS\EMACS.PIF as the **P**ath and $EDNAME as the **C**ommand Line (this ensures that the editor loads the currently selected file in project window). The **M**enu Text field should be the text you want to appear as menu entry for the editor and the **H**elp Hint field is a one-line helpful hint that appears in the IDE's status window when the user selects this tool from the menu.
- Click the **A**dvanced button in the **T**ool Options menu. Select the **V**iewer toggle button and mark the check boxes: Place on T**o**ols Menu and Place on S**p**eedMenu (the menu that pops up when you press the right mouse button in the project window). Also fill in the field labeled **A**pplies To: with the following string:
  `.c;.cpp;.h;.def;.rc;.hpj;`
  The IDE will apply the newly-defined tool on files with these filename extensions.
- Close the dialog boxes one by one.

After going through these steps, the editor will appear in the **T**ool menu as well as in the **V**iew submenu of the S**p**eedMenu that pops up when you press the right mouse button anywhere in the Project window of the IDE. You can then select your editor from one of these menus to edit the currently selected source file from the project window. A quick way to start the editor and edit a file is to double-click that file's name in the project window.

Compiling, Linking, and Running a Program

Once the source files are ready, you have to compile and link the source files to create an executable program. In BCW, the best way to build a program is to define a project. Start by selecting **N**ew Project… from the **P**roject menu (see Figure 1.6). This brings up the New Project dialog box (see Figure 1.7). Enter a name up to eight characters long for the project or click the **B**rowse… button to locate and specify the full pathname of a project file. BCW suggests a default .IDE extension for the name and treats that file as the project.

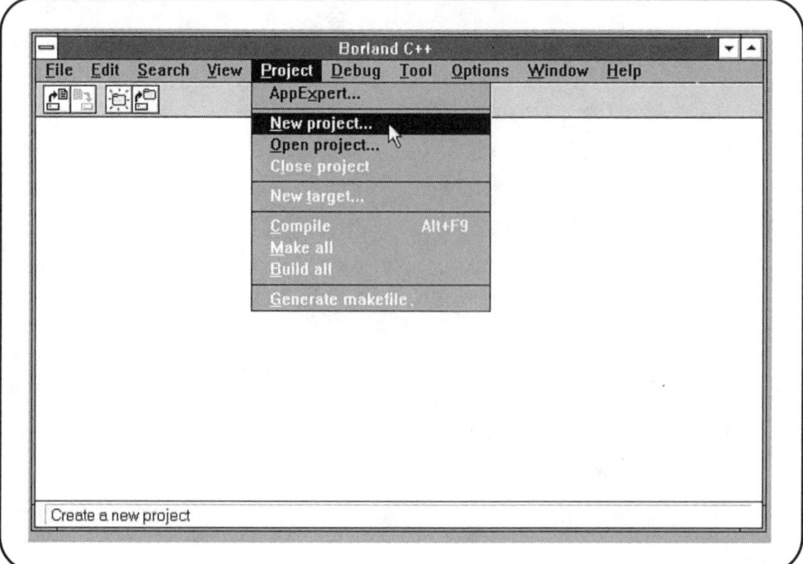

Figure 1.6. The Project menu.

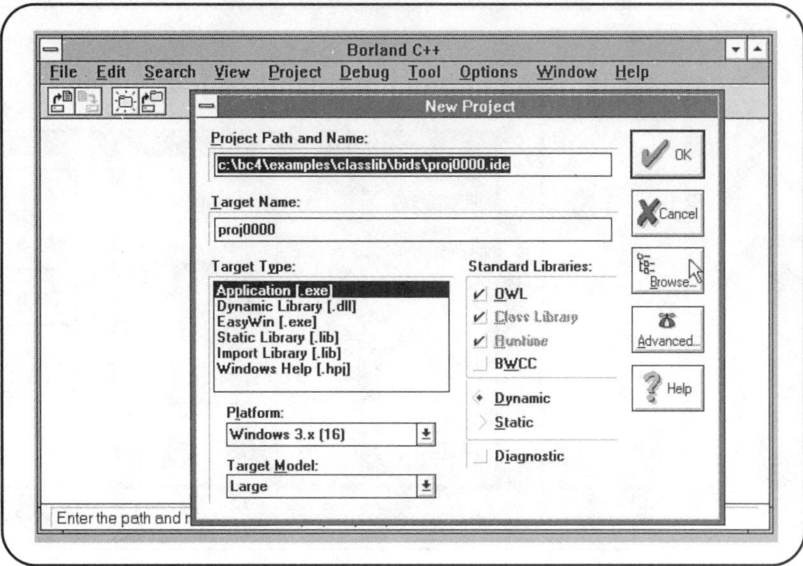

Figure 1.7. The New Project dialog box.

In the New Project dialog, BCW displays the New Project dialog box (see Figure 1.8) and also prompts for the name of the target—the name of the executable program that you want to build. You can enter a name and press OK. To illustrate the process of using a project, I selected the STRNGMAX.CPP example program that appears in the EXAMPLES\CLASSLIB\BIDS subdirectory of the directory where you installed Borland C++ 4. In addition to showing how to create a project and build an executable, this example illustrates another interesting feature of Borland C++ 4—the ability to create a simple Windows program out of text-oriented programs that use C `stdio` functions (`printf`) or C++ iostream classes to accept user input and display output.

Once the project is defined, BCW displays a project window (see Figure 1.9) where the project appears as a tree structure that shows the interdependencies of the source modules and libraries that make up the executable. In this case, BCW provides a set of modules by default: a source file (.CPP), a resource file (.RC), and a module definition file (.DEF). Because this example is not a Windows program, there is no resource file or definition file. To delete the names of these unneeded modules from the project, click the resource file's name to highlight it. Then press the right mouse button while the cursor is in the project window. This brings up a pop-up menu as shown in Figure 1.9. From that pop-up menu, select the **D**elete node item to get rid of the resource file's name from the project. You can get rid of the definition file's name by following similar steps.

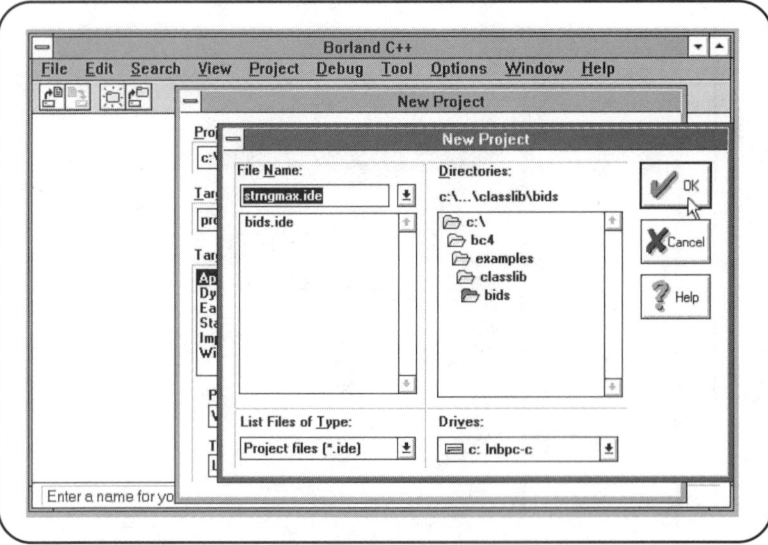

Figure 1.8. Specifying a new project filename in BCW.

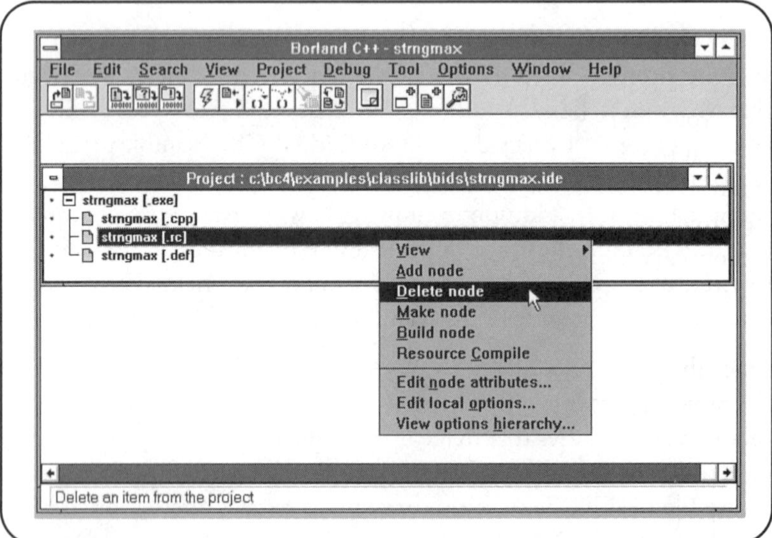

Figure 1.9. The project window in BCW.

To add a new item to the project, select the **Add** node option from the pop-up menu that you can get by pressing the right mouse button while the cursor is in the project window. This displays a dialog box (see Figure 1.10) from which you can add other source and libraries to the project.

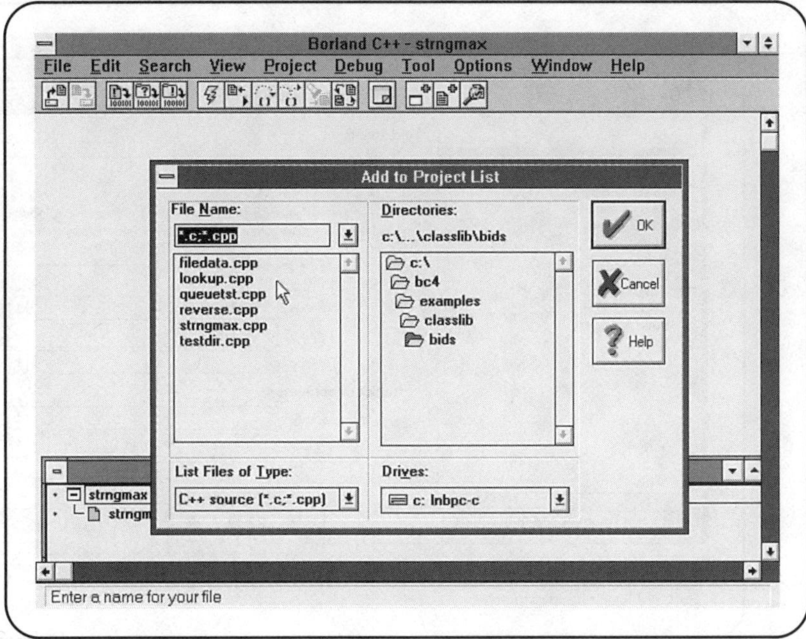

Figure 1.10. Adding items to a project in BCW.

Once you define a project, select the **P**roject... item from the **O**ptions menu and make sure that the names of the directories for the include files and libraries are correct (see Figure 1.11). Then, you can build the executable program by selecting **M**ake all from the **P**roject menu (see Figure 1.6). BCW will invoke the compiler and linker with the appropriate options and build the executable program. In case of any errors, BCW will display the error and warning messages in a separate message window. You can then examine the source statement that caused the error or warning and decide how to fix the problem.

Location of Header Files and Libraries

When building an executable file with BCW, if an error message appears saying that one your include files was not found, select **P**roject... from the **O**ptions menu and click the Directories topic to make sure that the pathnames indicating the locations of the include and library files are correct (see Figure 1.11).

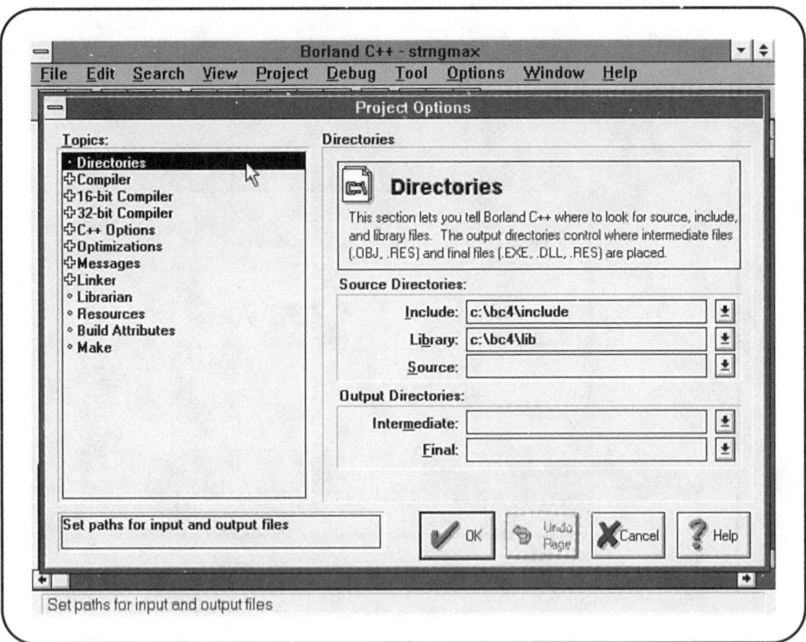

Figure 1.11. The Directories options in BCW.

Once the executable file is successfully built, you can run it by selecting the **R**un option from the **D**ebug menu. However, this particular program was designed to run under DOS and it accepts a number of command-line arguments—the program displays the "largest" (in a lexicographic sense) of the strings that you provide on the command-line. BCW automatically converts the program to use a predefined window where the output appears, but you still need to provide the command-line arguments for the program.

To specify the command-line arguments, select **E**nvironment... from the **O**ptions menu. A dialog box appears (see Figure 1.11) through which you can specify settings that control many aspects of BCW. The dialog box shows a list of topics on the left-hand side and the current topic's options on the right-hand side.

Click the Debugger topic that appears on the left-hand side of the Environment Options dialog box. The right-hand side of the dialog changes to show the settings for debugging (see Figure 1.12). Now you can enter the command-line arguments in the text input area labeled Run arguments. Suppose you enter the following as arguments:

```
Firmware Hardware Software
```

After exiting the dialog box, run the program by selecting **R**un from the **D**ebug menu; it will display a window with the result—the largest of the three strings:

```
Software
```

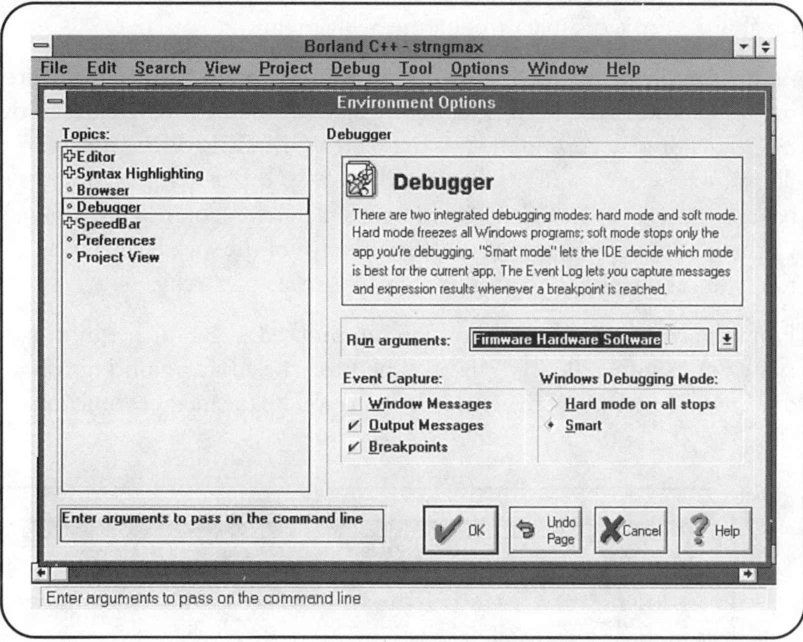

Figure 1.12. The Debugger options dialog.

When you compile and link a DOS program—one that uses C `stdio` function calls or C++ iostream classes for input and output—you have to use the EasyWin library to convert the program to work under Windows. The EasyWin library provides a window where the programs output appears and through which the program can read keyboard input from the user. To use the EasyWin library, select the EXE file's name in the project window and press the right mouse button. Select **T**argetExpert… from the resulting pop-up menu. From the TargetExpert dialog, select EasyWin[.exe] as the Target Type.

Browsing

A useful feature of BCW is that it enables you to see how your program is organized; you can see information such as the order in which functions call each other, where a function or variable is defined, and the hierarchy of classes in C++ programs. These capabilities are accessible through the **View** menu.

As an example, select the **C**lasses option from the **V**iew menu (see Figure 1.13). Figure 1.14 shows the resulting graphical display of the class hierarchies. activated dialog box. This display corresponds to the STRNGMAX.EXE example that was used to illustrate how to compile and link with BCW. Notice that the contents of the speed bar changes when you are viewing the class hierarchy. For instance, now a button with a printer's icon appears towards the right edge of the speed bar. By clicking this button, you can print the graph that shows the class hierarchy.

From the class hierarchy display, you can proceed to get further information about a class. For example, double-clicking the box labeled `string` brings up another window (see Figure 1.15) with detailed information on the member functions of the `string` class.

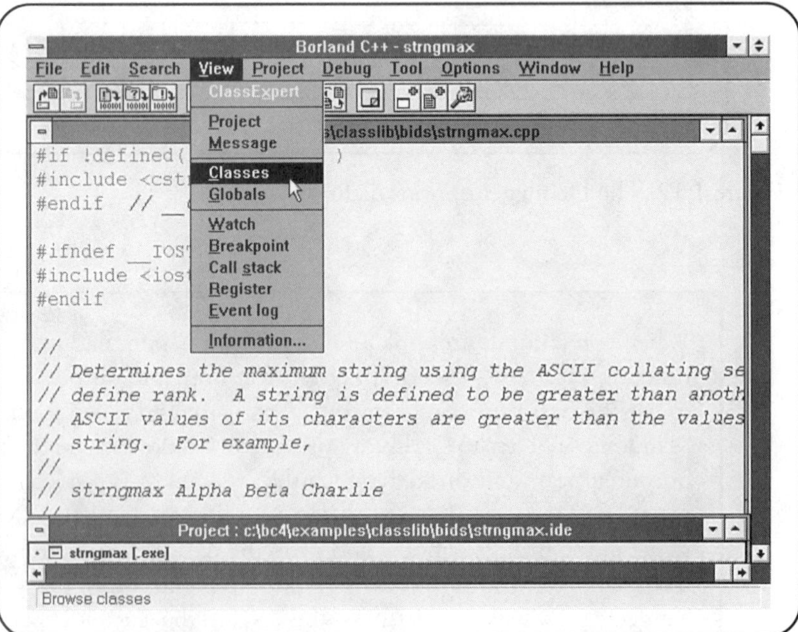

Figure 1.13. The View menu in BCW.

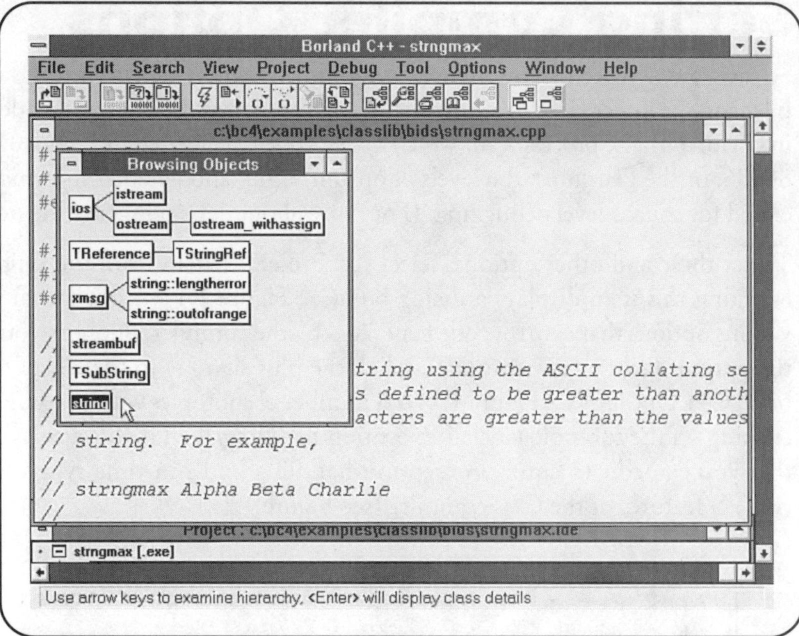

Figure 1.14. The class hierarchy for a sample program.

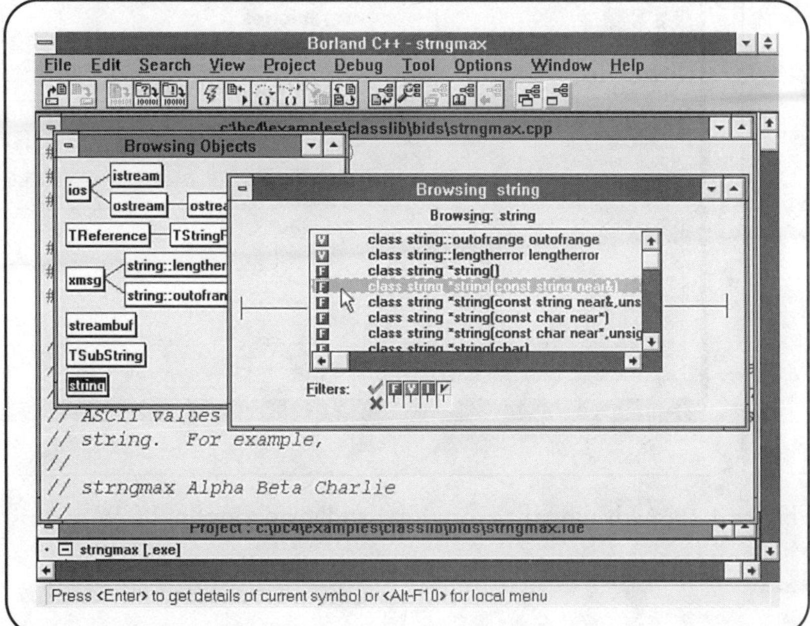

Figure 1.15. Details of the `string` class.

Setting Compiler Options

So far, you have seen how to compile and link using the default settings of the compiler and the linker. These settings include items such as the memory model (described in Chapter 4), the processor for which object code is generated (80186, 80286, 80386, 80486, or the Pentium), the levels of optimization, and whether information is generated for source-level debugging. (For more about debugging, see the next section.)

To set these and other options, select the **P**roject... item from the **O**ptions menu. Selecting this item displays a dialog box (see Figure 1.11) from which you can set various options that control code generated by the compiler. Suppose you want to set the options for the C++ compiler. Click the plus sign (+) to the left of the topic labeled C++ Options (see Figure 1.11). A number of subtopics will appear. For instance, clicking on the subtopic labeled Exception handling/RTTI, will display the settings that you can edit to control exception-handling and run-time type identification (RTTI) features of the C++ compiler (see Figure 1.16).

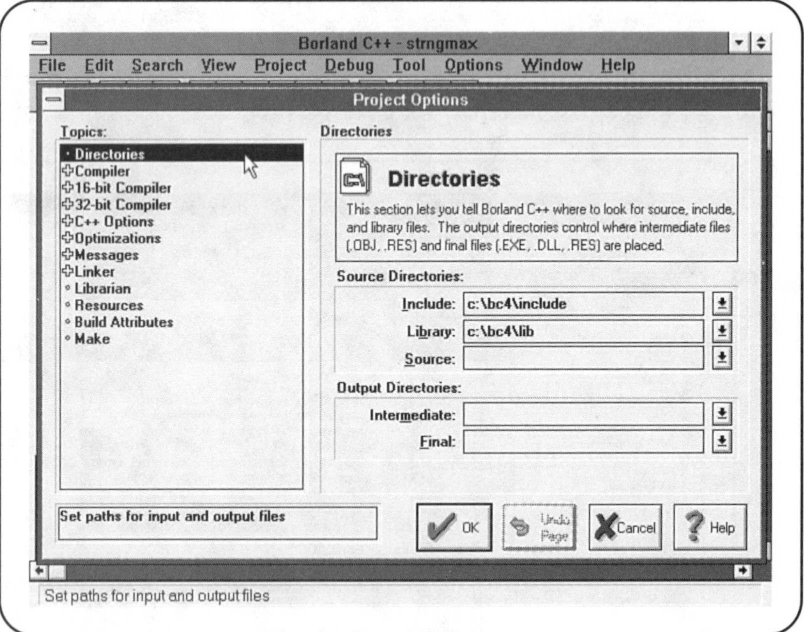

Figure 1.16. Activating the exception-handling options in BCW.

Debugging

In addition to compiling, linking, and running a program, you can also debug your program in BCW. If you want to debug at the source code level—to see lines of the source file as you step through your program—you need to enable the generation of information for the debugger. By default, BCW embeds information for the debugger into object files and creates an executable that can be used for source-level debugging.

To prepare an executable file for debugging, first select the **P**roject... item from the **O**ptions menu. Click the plus sign next to the Compiler topic and then click the Debugging subtopic. Enable the generation of debug information by clicking the check box labeled **D**ebug information in OBJs. Next, click the plus sign next to the Linker topic to view the list of subtopics. From the list, select General to bring up a number of check boxes on the right-hand side of the dialog box. From these check boxes, enable the one labeled Include debu**g** information.

Typically, you will set a breakpoint near the suspect source lines where you want the debugger to stop so that you can examine values of variables and look for clues. To designate a line of code as a breakpoint, position the cursor on that line and select Add breakpoint... from the **D**ebug menu. BCW highlights the designated line to indicate it as a breakpoint. After setting a breakpoint, if you select **R**un from the **D**ebug menu (or press Ctrl+F9), the debugger will start the program and run up to the line designated as the breakpoint. Once the debugger stops at a breakpoint, you can use the **I**nspect... option of the **D**ebug menu to check the values of variables.

Sometimes you may want to execute the program one statement at a time to pinpoint an erroneous statement. Press F7 to run the program in this manner by stepping into each function as your program calls it. Pressing F8 works similarly, but it treats each function call as a single statement and does not step through the statements in the function.

Using BCC

Although BCW's interactive environment is convenient, sometimes you may prefer to invoke the compiler and linker directly from the DOS command line. One reason might be that you are developing your application under MS-DOS. The BCC.EXE program provides a command-line interface to the 16-bit C++ compiler and linker. The BCC32.EXE program is the corresponding interface for the 32-bit compiler and linker. Both BCC.EXE and BCC32.EXE accept similar command-line options.

The rest of this chapter briefly describes how to use BCC and lists the options it offers.

Compiling and Linking with BCC

Using BCC to compile and link a program with a small number of source files is simple. You can compile and link the C++ source files FORMFILL.CPP and FORMPACK.CPP and create the executable program named FORMFILL.EXE with the following command issued at the MS-DOS prompt:

```
BCC -W FORMFILL.CPP FORMPACK.CPP
```

This command runs the C++ compiler with the `-W` option, links the resulting object files, and creates a Windows executable program named FORMFILL.EXE. The `-W` option to ensure that the compiler generates the code necessary to run the resulting executable under Windows.

BCC determines how to process a file based on the filename extension. Table 1.3 lists the extensions BCC understands.

Table 1.3. Interpretation of file extensions by BCC.

Extension	How BCC Processes a File
.C	C source file. Compile using C compiler.
.CPP	C++ source file. Compile using C++ compiler.
.ASM	Assembly language file. Assemble using TASM (Turbo Assembler) if you have it installed in your system.
.OBJ	Object file. Pass to linker for use during linking.
.LIB	Library file. Pass to linker for use in linking.
.DEF	Module definition file (used in Microsoft Windows programs). Pass name to linker.
No file extension	C++ source file. Compile using C++ compiler.
Other extensions	C source file. Compile using C compiler.

However, more often than not, you will want to use BCC with certain options—each option is a combination of letters and numbers preceded by a minus sign (`-`) that instructs BCC to take some specific action. For instance, you may want to build a Windows executable, use a large memory model, generate code for an 80286 processor, disable optimizations (because you want to debug), and include information for the debugger. To do this, you have to run BCC with the command:

```
BCC -W -ml -2 -Od -v FORMFILL.CPP FORMPACK.CPP
```

where `-W` generates code needed to run under Windows, `-ml` selects the large memory model, `-2` generates 80286 code, `-Od` disables optimizations, and `-v` ensures inclusion of information needed for source-level debugging.

> **Options are Case-Sensitive**
>
> All BCC options are case-sensitive. At the DOS command line, type `BCC` to view a short summary of the BCC options.

Using Configuration Files and Response Files

If you run BCC to compile and link several times, you may find it tedious to type the long command line every time. Besides, you can only enter a maximum of 128 characters at the DOS prompt. A long list of BCC options can exceed the 128-character limit. One way to avoid the repetitive typing and this character limit is to place the list of options in a configuration file. By default, BCC looks for a configuration file by the name TURBOC.CFG (so named because Borland's first C compiler was called Turbo C). BCC looks for this configuration file first in the current working directory, then in the directory where BCC.EXE is installed. For instance, here is a typical TURBOC.CFG file:

```
-W
-IC:\BC4\INCLUDE
-LC:\BC4\LIB
```

With this file in place, entering the command:

```
BCC -Od FORMFILL.CPP FORMPACK.CPP
```

would be the equivalent of typing

```
BCC -W -IC:\BC4\INCLUDE -LC:\BC4\LIB -Od FORMFILL.CPP FORMPACK.CPP
```

This way, you get all the options that were already set in the configuration file followed by anything else that you entered when invoking BCC from the command line.

If you save compiler options in a different file, you can get BCC to read those options by specifying that file's name prefixed with a + on the command-line. For instance, if you wanted to use a configuration file named AWIPS.CFG and compile the file AWIPSWIN.CPP, you could use the following command:

```
BCC +AWIPS.CFG AWIPSWIN.CPP
```

Another way to provide long command-lines to BCC is to save the command-lines in a file and specify the filename with a `@` prefix when starting BCC. This file is referred to as a response file. To compile a number of source files, specify the names of the source files as well as any compiler options in the response file. For instance, to compile and link a program with the modules FORFILL.CPP and FORMPACK.CPP with the option `-Od`, create a response file, FORMFILL.RSP, with the following lines in it:

```
-Od
FORMFILL.CPP
FORMPACK.CPP
```

Now you can build the FORMFILL.EXE program by entering the following command at the DOS prompt:

```
BCC @FORMFILL.RSP
```

Note that in this case BCC reads the options from the default configuration file TURBOC.CFG as well as the lines from the response file.

BCC Options

BCC accepts more than 150 command-line options so that it may offer you, the programmer, complete control over building an executable program or Windows Dynamic Link Library (DLL). Of course, you don't need to explicitly specify every option when using BCC; the options have default settings adequate for most programming tasks. However, if you ever need them, the options are there.

To familiarize you with the kind of operations that the command-line options control, Table 1.4 summarizes the commonly used BCC options according to category. Table 1.5 provides a complete alphabetical listing of all the options that BCC accepts. Note that a number of options are meant for BCC32, the 32-bit version of the compiler. BCC also has a large number of error and warning reporting options that start with a `-w`. These are summarized in Table 1.6.

Notice that within the list of options items, angular brackets (`<...>`) signify required parameters, while those in square brackets (`[...]`) denote optional parameters.

Table 1.4. Summary of commonly used BCC options by category.

Category	Options
Memory models	`-ms` small model (default). `-mc` compact model. `-mm` medium model. `-ml` large model.
Floating-point library	`-f` uses the floating-point emulation library. `-f-` implies program does not need any floating-library. `-f287` uses inline 80287 instructions.
Optimization	`-O` optimizes jumps. `-O1` generates smallest size code. `-O2` generates fastest possible code. `-Oa` ignores pointer aliasing. `-Ob` eliminates dead code. `-Oc` eliminates duplicate subexpressions. `-Od` disables all optimizations. `-Oe` allocates global registers. `-Og` eliminates duplicate expressions in functions. `-Oi` expands common functions inline for speed. `-Ol` compacts loops. `-Om` moves invariant code out of loops. `-Op` remembers and uses copies of expressions. `-Ov` enables loop induction variables and strength reduction. `-OW` disables generation of Windows prolog and epilog code. `-Ox` generates fastest code.
Preprocessor	`-D<name>[=text]` defines a macro. `-I<pathname>` searches the specified directories when including files. `-U<name>` removes a predefined macro.
Code generation	`-2` generates 80286 instructions (default for 16-bit compilation). `-3` generates 80386 instructions (default for 32-bit compilation).

continues

Table 1.4. continued

Category	Options
	-4 generates 80486 instructions. -5 generates Pentium instructions. -a aligns all integer data types on machine-word boundary. -d merges duplicate strings. -Ff=<number> sets the data size threshold for separate segments. -G generates fast code at the expense of code size. -p generates Pascal-style function calls. -pr uses the fastcall convention for passing arguments on the stack. -N generates calls to function that checks for stack overflow. -r uses register variables. -R includes browser information in object files. -u generates underscore prefixes for external symbols. -v places in object files information necessary for source debugging. -W generates code for a Windows executable making all functions exportable (default). -WD generates code for a Windows DLL making all functions exportable (default).
Output files	-e<file> names the executable file. -H<file> names the precompiled header file. -o<file> names the object file.
Language extensions	-A allows ANSI C keywords only. -AT enables Borland-specific extensions (default). -AK allows Kernighan & Ritchie style code only. -AU allows UNIX System V style code only. -b causes enum variables to be the same size as int. -C allows nested comments. -i<n> causes compiler to recognize only first <n> characters of identifier names.
Miscellaneous	-c compiles only, does not link. -g<n> stops after <n> warning messages.

Category	Options
	-j<n> stops after <n> error messages. -K default char type is unsigned. -w<xxx> turns on the warning messages identified by .<xxx> (see Table 1.6).
Assembly language	-B calls the assembler to process inline assembly language code. -E<filename> specifies <filename> as the assembler to be used. -T<options> passes options to the assembler.
Linking	-l<linker_options> passes options to the linker. -M instructs linker to create a map file.
C++ specific options	-Jg generates definitions for all templates and merges. duplicates (default). -P performs a C++ compilation regardless of source file's extension. -P-<ext> performs a C or C++ compilation depending on source file's extension and makes <ext> the default extension for C++ files. -po uses a fast register-based calling convention for passing the this argument to C++ member functions. -RT enables generation of runtime type information. -vi enables expansion of inline functions. -V uses smart C++ virtual tables (default). -Vo enables backward compatibility with C++ libraries written using earlier versions of Borland C++ compiler.

Table 1.5. Alphabetic list of BCC options.

Option	Interpretation by BCC
@<filename>	Reads commands from the specified response file.
+<filename>	Uses specified file as a configuration file.
-1	Generates 80186 and real-mode 80286 instructions.

continues

Table 1.5. continued

Option	Interpretation by BCC
-2	Generates protected-mode 80286 instructions (default for 16-bit compilation).
-3	Generates protected-mode 80386 instructions (default for 32-bit compilation).
-4	Generates protected-mode 80486 instructions.
-5	Generates protected-mode Pentium instructions.
-A	Allows ANSI C keywords only.
-AT	Allows Borland C++ keywords (same as -A-).
-AK	Allows only Kernighan and Ritchie-style code.
-AU	Allows UNIX System V keywords only.
-a<*n*>	Aligns structures to multiples of <*n*> bytes where <*n*> is 1, 2, or 4.
-a-	Does not align at byte boundaries (default).
-B	Compiles via an intermediate assembly language step by calling the assembler to process inline assembly code.
-b	Makes enum variables the same size as integers (default).
-b-	Makes enum variables byte-sized if the value is small enough.
-C	Allows nested comments. (Default is to turn them off.)
-c	Compiles and generates object file but does not link.
-D<*name*>*[=string]*	Defines a macro.
-d	Merges duplicate strings. (Default is -d-, meaning that duplicate strings are not merged.)
-dc	Moves string literals from data segment to code segment (for 16-bit compilation only).
-E<*name*>	Uses <*name*> as the assembler when assembling inline assembly language statements.
-e<*filename*>	Uses <*filename*> as the name of the executable file.

Option	Interpretation by BCC
-Fc	Generates COMDEF records in object files (16-bit compilation only). These records allow sharing of uninitialized global variables.
-Ff	Automatically places global data with size exceeding a threshold (the default is 32,767 bytes) in its own segment (16-bit only).
-Ff=<*size*>	Sets the threshold used by the -Ff option to <*size*> bytes (16-bit only).
-Fm	Enables the -Fc, -Ff, and -Fs options (16-bit only).
-Fs	Assumes that the DS and SS registers are set to the same value in all memory models (16-bit only).
-f	Uses the floating-point emulation package (default).
-f-	Does not link with floating-point package. (Use this option only if your program does not use any floating-point computations.)
-ff	Optimizes floating-point operations by disregarding certain type conversions.
-ff-	Follows strict ANSI conventions for floating-point conversions.
-f287	Generates code for the 80287 coprocessor (16-bit only).
-G	Generates code that is optimized for speed.
-G-	Generates code optimized for smaller size (default).
-g<*n*>	Stops after <*n*> warnings (default). The default value of <*n*> is 255.
-H	Generates and uses precompiled headers. (Default is -H-, meaning precompiled headers are not used.)
-Hu	Uses but does not generate precompiled headers.
-H=<*filename*>	Uses the specified filename to store the precompiled header.

continues

Table 1.5. continued

Option	Interpretation by BCC
`-h`	Uses fast huge-pointer arithmetic (16-bit only).
`-I<pathname>`	Searches named directory for include file. Here `<pathname>` is a semicolon-separated list of directories.
`-i<n>`	Sets `<n>` as the number of significant characters in an identifier (default). The default value for `<n>` is 32.
`-Jg`	Generates definitions for all templates and merges duplicates (default).
`-Jgd`	Generates definitions for all templates and displays errors indicating any duplicates.
`-Jgx`	Generates external references for all templates.
`-j<n>`	Stops after `<n>` errors (default). The default value of `<n>` is 255.
`-K`	Assumes that char type is unsigned. (The default is `-K-`, meaning char is signed.)
`-K2`	Allows only two types of char variables: signed and unsigned.
`-k`	Generates a standard stack frame (default).
`-L<pathname>`	Searches named directory for libraries during linking. Here `<pathname>` is a semicolon-separated list of directories.
`-l<linker_option>`	Passes the specified option string to the linker.
`-l-<linker_option>`	Disables specified option for the linker.
`-M`	Causes the linker to generate a map file.
`-mc`	Uses the compact memory model (16-bit compilation only).
`-ml`	Uses the large memory model (16-bit compilation only).
`-mm`	Uses the medium memory model (16-bit compilation only).

Option	Interpretation by BCC
`-mm!`	Uses the medium memory model but assumes SS != DS (16-bit compilation only).
`-ms`	Uses the small memory model (16-bit compilation only). This is the default.
`-ms!`	Uses the small memory model but assumes DS != SS (16-bit compilation only).
`-N`	Checks for stack overflow.
-n<*pathname*>	Saves output files in the specified directory.
`-O`	Optimizes jumps.
`-O1`	Generates smallest size code possible.
`-O2`	Generates fastest possible code.
`-Oa`	Optimizes, assuming that pointer expressions are not aliased. Aliasing occurs when two pointer expressions evaluate to the same address—thus pointing to the same location in memory.
`-Ob`	Eliminates dead code.
`-Oc`	Eliminates duplicate expressions in blocks of code.
`-Od`	Disables all optimizations.
`-Oe`	Allocates global registers.
`-Og`	Eliminates duplicate expressions within functions.
`-Oi`	Expands common string and buffer manipulation functions inline.
`-Ol`	Compacts loops.
`-Om`	Moves invariant code (expressions whose values do not change) out of loops.
`-Op`	Remembers and uses copies of constants and expressions.
`-Ov`	Enables loop induction variables (creates variables from expressions used in a loop) and performs strength

continues

Table 1.5. continued

Option	Interpretation by BCC
	reduction (reduces computational complexity).
`-OW`	Suppresses Windows prolog and epilog code (16-bit compilation only).
`-Ox`	Generates fastest code (compatible with same option in Microsoft Visual C++).
`-o<filename>`	Saves object code in file named `<filename>`.
`-P`	Compiles source file with the C++ compiler regardless of the source file's extension. (Default is `-P-` meaning C or C++ compiler is used based on file's extension.)
`-P<ext>`	Compiles source file with C++ compiler and changes the default extension of C++ source files to `<ext>`.
`-P-<ext>`	Compiles as a C or C++ file depending on file's extension and sets the default extension of C++ files to `<ext>`.
`-p`	Uses Pascal calling convention. (The default is `-p-`, which means C calling convention is used.)
`-pc`	Uses C calling convention (default). This is same as the option `-p-`.
`-po`	Uses a fast register-based convention for passing the `this` argument to C++ member functions.
`-pr`	Uses a fast register-based convention for passing function arguments.
`-ps`	Uses the stdcall-calling convention (32-bit compilation only). This option generates faster and smaller code for function calls.
`-r`	Uses register variables (default).
`-rd`	Allows only declared register variables to be stored in registers.
`-R`	Includes browser reference information in the object file.

Option	Interpretation by BCC
-Rp	Includes browser reference information in the object file.
-RT	Enables runtime-type identification.
-S	Generates assembly language output.
-T<*string*>	Passes the <*string*> as an option to TASM or the assembler specified with the -E option.
-tW	Generate a Windows executable with all functions exportable (default).
-tWD	Creates a Windows DLL with all functions exportable.
-tWDE	Creates a Windows DLL with explicit functions exportable.
-tWE	Builds a Windows executable exporting only those functions that are explicitly specified as exportable.
-tWS	Builds a Windows executable that uses smart callbacks (16-bit compilation only).
-tWSE	Creates a Windows executable that uses smart callbacks with only explicitly specified functions exportable (16-bit compilation only).
-U<*name*>	Undefines the macro specified by <*name*>.
-u	Assumes that all external variable names begin with an underscore (default).
-v	Includes information in the object file to allow source level debugging.
-vi	Enables inline expansion in C++ programs.
-V0	Generates external C++ virtual tables.
-V1	Generates public C++ virtual tables.
-V	Uses smart C++ virtual tables (default).
-Va	Passes class values to functions via references to temporary instances of the class (16-bit compilation only).

continues

Table 1.5. continued

Option	Interpretation by BCC
`-Vb`	Makes virtual base class pointer the same size as the this pointer of the class (16-bit compilation only). This is the default.
`-Vc`	Makes the class instance layout the same as that generated by the previous version (3.1) of Borland C++ (16-bit compilation only).
`-Vf`	Generates far C++ virtual tables (16-bit compilation only).
`-Vmd`	Uses the smallest representation for member pointers.
`-Vmm`	Enables member pointers to point to instances of classes with multiple inheritance.
`-Vmp`	Uses the declared precision for all member pointer types.
`-Vms`	Restricts member pointers to support classes with single inheritance only.
`-Vmv`	Removes any restrictions on member pointers (default).
`-Vo`	Sets the options `-Va -Vb -Vc -Vp -Vt -Vv` (16-bit compilation only).
`-Vp`	Passes the `this` argument to Pascal member functions as the first argument on the stack (16-bit compilation only).
`-Vs`	Generates local C++ virtual tables.
`-Vt`	Places the virtual table pointer after the non-static data members in a class instance (16-bit compilation only).
`-Vv`	Does not change the layout of any classes (16-bit compilation only).
`-W`	Generates code for a Windows executable with all functions exportable (default).
`-WD`	Generates code for a Windows DLL with all functions exportable.

Option	Interpretation by BCC
-WDE	Generates code for a Windows DLL with explicitly defined functions exportable.
-WE	Generates code for a Windows executable with explicitly defined functions exportable.
-WS	Generates code for a Windows executable that uses smart callbacks (16-bit compilation only).
-WSE	Generates code for a Windows executable that uses smart callbacks with explicitly defined functions exportable.
-w	Displays warnings (default).
-w<*xxx*>	Enables warning messages identified by the three letter name <*xxx*> (see Table 1.6).
-w-<*xxx*>	Disables warning messages identified by the three letter name <*xxx*> (see Table 1.6).
-X	Disables the generation of autodependency information.
-x	Enables C++ exception handling (default).
-xd	Enables destructor cleanups during exception handling.
-xds	Allows throwing exceptions from a DLL.
-xp	Enables generation of exception location information.
-y	Embeds line number information for use by debugger.
-Z	Suppresses redundant loading of registers.
-zA<*name*>	Changes name of code segment class to <*name*>. The default is CODE.
-zB<*name*>	Changes name of uninitialized data segment class to <*name*>. The default name is BSS.
-zC<*name*>	Changes the name of the code segment to <*name*>. The default name is _TEXT.
-zD<*name*>	Changes the name of the uninitialized data segment to <*name*>. The default is _BSS.

continues

Table 1.5. continued

Option	Interpretation by BCC
`-zE<name>`	Changes the name of the segment where far data is stored to <*name*>. The default name is the name of the source file with a _DATA suffix.
`-zF<name>`	Changes the name of the class for far data to <*name*>. The default name is FAR_DATA.
`-zG<name>`	Changes the name of the uninitialized data segment group to <*name*>. The default name is DGROUP.
`-zH<name>`	Places all far data into the group named <*name*>.
`-zP<name>`	Uses <*name*> as the name of any code segment group.
`-zR<name>`	Changes the name of the initialized data segment to <*name*>. The default is _DATA.
`-zS<name>`	Changes the name of the initialized data segment group to <*name*>. The default is DGROUP.
`-zT<name>`	Changes the name of the initialized data segment class to <*name*>. The default name is `DATA`.
`-zV<name>`	Sets the name of the far virtual table segment to <*name*>. By default is CODE (16-bit compilation only).
`-zW<name>`	Changes the name of the far virtual table class segment to <*name*>. The default is CODE (16-bit compilation only).

In the `-z` options, if <*name*> is a *, the default segment name is used.

Table 1.6. Error and warning reporting options of BCC. (Options that are on by default are so indicated with a legend next to the message.)

Option	Message from BCC
Violations of ANSI standard for C	
`-wbbf`	Bit fields must be signed or unsigned int.
`-wbig`	Hexadecimal value contains more than three digits. (ON)

Option	Message from BCC
`-wdpu`	Declare type prior to use in prototype. (ON)
`-wdup`	Redefinition of macro is not identical. (ON)
`-weas`	Type assigned to enumeration. (ON)
`-wext`	Identifier is declared as both external and static. (ON)
`-wpin`	Initialization is only partially bracketed.
`-wret`	Both return and return with a value are used. (ON)
`-wstu`	Undefined structure. (ON)
`-wsus`	Suspicious pointer conversion. (ON)
`-wvoi`	Void functions cannot return a value. (ON)
`-wzdi`	Division by zero. (ON)
Potential Portability Problems	
`-wcln`	Constant is long.
`-wcpt`	Nonportable pointer comparison. (ON)
`-wrng`	Constant out of range in comparison. (ON)
`-wrpt`	Nonportable pointer conversion. (ON)
`-wsig`	Conversion might lose significant digits.
`-wucp`	Mixing pointers to signed and unsigned char.
Potential C and C++ Errors	
`-wamb`	Ambiguous operators need parentheses.
`-wccc`	Condition is always true/false. (ON)
`-wdef`	Possible use of identifier before definition.
`-wnod`	No declaration for function.
`-wpia`	Possibly incorrect assignment. (ON)
`-wpro`	Call to function with no prototype. (ON)
`-wrvl`	Function should return a value. (ON)

continues

Table 1.6. continued

Option	Message from BCC
Inefficient C and C++ Coding	
`-waus`	Identifier is assigned a value that is never used. (ON)
`-weff`	Code has no effect. (ON)
`-wpar`	Parameter is never used. (ON)
`-wrch`	Unreachable code. (ON)
`-wstv`	Structure passed by value.
`-wuse`	Identifier is declared but never used.
Obsolete C++ Features	
`-wobi`	Base initialization without a class name is now obsolete. (ON)
`-wofp`	Style of function definition is now obsolete. (ON)
`-wovl`	Overload is now unnecessary and obsolete. (ON)
`-wpre`	Overloaded prefix operator ++/- - used as a postfix operator.
Potential C++ Errors	
`-wnci`	Constant member identifier is not initialized. (ON)
`-wbei`	Assigning type to enumeration. (ON)
`-whid`	*<Function1>* hides virtual function *<Function2>*. (ON)
`-wncf`	Non-const function called const object.
`-wibc`	Base class *<base1>* is inaccessible because also in *<base2>*. (ON)
`-wdsz`	Array size for “delete” ignored. (ON)
`-wnst`	Use qualified name to access nested type. (ON)
Inefficient C++ Coding	
`-winl`	Functions containing identifier are not expanded inline. (ON)
`-wlin`	Temporary used to initialize identifier. (ON)
`-wlvc`	Temporary used for parameter in call to identifier. (ON)

Option	Message from BCC
Miscellaneous Errors	
`-wasm`	Unknown assembler instruction.
`-will`	Ill-formed pragma. (ON)
`-wias`	Array variable is near. (ON)
`-wamp`	Superfluous `&` with function or array.

Summary

Borland C++ 4 is a combination of program development tools and utilities. Its most visible component is the Windows-hosted interactive development environment (BCW) through which you can edit, compile, link, and debug a program. This chapter briefly described how to use BCW, summarized BCW's features, and pointed out that the best way to learn about all of the tools is through the extensive online help. The last part of this chapter described BCC, the command-line interface to the C and C++ compiler and linker.

Although you can perform all the edit-compile-link-debug chores from BCW, it is helpful to be familiar with the individual program development tools. That way, you can set up makefiles that invoke these tools and access them using MAKE. Chapter 2 covers a number of the tools: LINK, LIB, and MAKE.

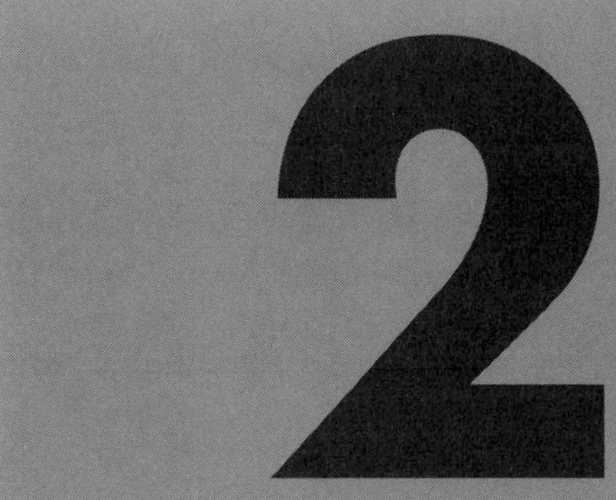

Program Development Tools in Borland C++ 4

Chapter 1, "Borland C++ 4 Programming Environment," provided you with an overview of the Borland C++ 4 product—the tools it offers and how the Borland C++ compiler typically is used. Chapter 1 also describes the interactive development environment (IDE) and BCC, the command-line version of the compiler. This chapter describes how to use a number of other program development tools: TLINK, TLIB, MAKE, and TDW—the Turbo Debugger for Windows. Notice that BCC also invokes TLINK to create executable programs, but Chapter 1 does not show TLINK's options.

Briefly, the TLINK tool combines a number of object modules to create an executable file (an .EXE file), whereas TLIB enables you to store many object modules in a single library file (a .LIB file). MAKE automates the use of the compiler, linker, and other tools. TDW is the Turbo debugger that enables you to find errors in your programs. This chapter presents a short description of how to use each of these tools and lists the options each offers. This chapter does not cover the programming tools in great detail because all of these tools provide complete and, more importantly, up-to-date online help.

> **Getting Help**
>
> Use the online help facility to find out more about the program development tools in Borland C++ 4—the tools described in this chapter (TLINK, TLIB, MAKE, and TDW) as well as others, such as TDUMP, GREP, and IMPLIB, that are not covered in this chapter. You can use one of the following tips to see the command-line options of most program development tools in Borland C++ 4:
>
> - Run the tool without any options from a DOS prompt. This displays a list of all command-line options.
> - For MAKE, enter `MAKE -h` to see a list of command-line options accepted by MAKE.
>
> Some tools, such as TDW, stand alone and provide help through menus in their user interface.

TLINK, the Linker

The job of TLINK, the Turbo Link, is to combine one or more object files (.OBJ files) into an executable file (.EXE file). The linker is necessary because Microsoft Windows cannot execute .OBJ files, even if there is only a single source file for a program. The resulting .OBJ file must be converted to an .EXE format before Windows can load it into memory and run it. TLINK performs this conversion from .OBJ format to .EXE.

Additionally, when a software project is broken down into a number of modules or source files, one source file might call functions that are defined in another file. When the compiler translates each source file into an object file, it embeds information about external functions and variables referenced in that source file. The linker then blends all the object files and ensures that all external functions and variables are found and referenced correctly in the executable program that it generates. TLINK can also search through libraries (.LIB files) to resolve these references to external functions and variables.

Using TLINK

Most of the time you will invoke TLINK indirectly through BCC, but TLINK is often invoked directly in makefiles, described later in this chapter. First, source files are compiled into object files, then TLINK is invoked to link the object files together with the required libraries. You can invoke TLINK in two different ways:

- Enter the TLINK command with options and filenames on the command line. The syntax is

  ```
  TLINK [opt] <objfiles>,[exefile],[mapfile],[libs],[deffile],[resfile]
  ```

  where *[opt]* refers to one or more optional TLINK options (see Table 2.1) and *<objfiles>* denotes the required object filenames. The other fields in the command are optional except for the separating commas—they are required. You can, however, enter a semicolon anywhere after the names of the object files to end the command line. In this case, TLINK uses default values for the remaining filenames.

- Place all TLINK options and filenames in a text file and invoke TLINK as follows:

  ```
  TLINK @<response_file>
  ```

  where *<response_file>* is the name of the file containing the input commands meant for TLINK. Notice that TLINK does not assume any specific filename extension for the response file; you should provide the complete filename for the response file.

The simplest way to link a few object files to build a Windows executable file is to invoke TLINK as follows:

```
TLINK /Tw c0ws test,test,,cws import
```

In this case, TLINK looks for the file C0WS.OBJ and TEST.OBJ and searches the libraries CWS.LIB and IMPORT.LIB to complete the linking process and create an executable file named TEST.EXE. The /Tw option directs TLINK to build a

Windows executable program. The COWS.OBJ file contains start-up code for a small memory model Windows program. TEST.OBJ is the object file created by compiling your C or C++ source file using BCC with the default small memory model option.

This example of TLINK usage relies on the presence of a TLINK configuration file, TLINK.CFG, in the current directory or the directory where TLINK resides. In my system, the text file TLINK.CFG contains the single line:

```
-LE:\BC4\LIB
```

which specifies the pathnames that TLINK will search to locate any library file such as CWS.LIB and IMPORT.LIB.

Filenames for TLINK

TLINK uses or generates several types of files. TLINK's command syntax also shows these filenames:

```
TLINK [opt] <objfiles>,[exefile],[mapfile],[libs],[deffile],[resfile]
```

You already know about the `<objfiles>` field, which contains the names of the object files that TLINK combines to create the executable file.

The `[exefile]` field refers to the name of the executable file. If you do not specify a name, TLINK takes the name of the first object file, changes the extension to .EXE, and uses that as the name of the executable file.

The `[mapfile]` field in the TLINK command line refers to the name of the map file created by TLINK. The map file usually contains a list of segments, but you can use the `/m` option to generate a list of all global variables and functions. If you do not provide the name of the map file, TLINK does not create it. However, if you specify the `/MAP` option, TLINK creates a map file with the same name as the executable file but with a .MAP extension.

The `[libs]` field in the TLINK command is a list of library files (.LIB) that should be searched to locate external functions and variables. If you do not specify the extensions of the library files, TLINK assumes a .LIB extension.

The `[deffile]` field denotes the name of a module definition file—something that TLINK needs when creating Windows applications or Dynamic Link Libraries (DLLs).

The `[resfile]` field specifies the name of a binary resource file (.RES) that should be linked into the executable file. The resource file contains the menus, dialog boxes, and icons used by a Windows program. TLINK invokes RLINK, the resource linker, to link the resource file into the executable file.

TLINK Options

TLINK accepts a number of options. When you compile and link using BCC, you can pass these options to TLINK through BCC's `-l` option. Table 2.1 lists TLINK's command-line options and their meanings.

Table 2.1. TLINK options.

Option	Interpretation by TLINK
`/?`	Displays the list of command-line options.
`/3`	Enables linking 32-bit code for 80386 or 80486 processors.
`/A=<size>`	Aligns the segments in the executable file at the boundaries specified by `<size>`, which is in bytes. The default is to align along 512-byte boundaries. For instance, the option `/A=16` specifies alignment at 16-byte boundaries.
`/c`	Treats public and external symbols as case-sensitive. This option is turned off by default—TLINK normally ignores case when looking for global variables and functions.
`/C`	Assumes that symbols in the EXPORTS and IMPORTS sections of a module definition file are case-sensitive. By default, TLINK ignores the case of these symbols.
`/d`	Warns if there are duplicate symbols in the libraries. Normally, TLINK does not warn if a symbol appears in more than one library.
`/e`	Does not search extended dictionaries when searching a library for a module. The extended dictionary is a list of symbols and their locations in libraries created by TLIB with TLIB's `/E` option.
`/E`	Processes extended dictionaries when locating symbols.
`/f`	Inhibits optimization of far calls to near.
`/Gn`	Discards nonresident name table.

continues

Table 2.1. continued

Option	Interpretation by TLINK
/Gr	Transfers names from resident name table to the nonresident name table.
/i	Initializes and outputs all segments to the executable file.
/l	Includes source line numbers in the map file. To use this option, you must have used the -y or -v option with BCC.
/L<pathnames>	Searches the semicolon-separated list of directories in <pathname> when trying to locate libraries. TLINK also searches for the start-up object files, such as COWS.OBJ, in these directories.
/m	Creates a map file with a list of all public symbols.
/M	Creates a map file with a list of all public symbols including mangled public names from C++ programs (mangling refers to the transformation of public names by the C++ compiler).
/n	Does not search the default libraries specified by the compiler in the object file.
/P=<num>	Packs as many adjacent code segments as possible into a single segment. The optional numeric parameter with a value between 1 and 65,536 specifies the maximum size of a packed code segment. The default is 8K or 8,192 bytes. By default, TLINK packs code segments.
/R[mpekv]	Specifies options for RLINK.
/s	Generates a map file with detailed information about the segments.
/Tw	Creates a Windows executable file.
/Twd	Creates a Windows DLL.
/Twe	Creates a Windows executable file.
/v	Generates an executable file with embedded information that will be used by the debugger.
/x	Inhibits generation of the map file.
/ye	Uses expanded memory for swapping during linking.
/yx	Uses extended memory for swapping during linking.

TLIB, the Library Manager

TLIB, the Turbo Librarian, organizes one or more object modules into a single library file (with a .LIB extension). Instead of keeping a large number of object files and providing their names to the linker, you can use TLIB to keep all the object files in a single library file and make the linker search the library file for any required object files. You also can use TLIB to create a new library and modify an existing library file.

Using TLIB

Like TLINK, you can invoke TLIB in two ways:

- Enter a complete `TLIB` command at the DOS prompt. The full syntax is

  ```
  TLIB <library> [options] [commands] [,listfile]
  ```

  where *<library>* is the name of the library file (.LIB extension) being created or modified, and `[options]` denotes one or more optional TLIB command-line options (see Table 2.2). The optional `[commands]` field indicates what operations, if any, TLIB should perform on the *<library>*. If you do not specify any commands, TLIB checks that the specified library is a valid one and exits. If you provide a filename in the `[listfile]` field, TLIB places an alphabetic list of symbols and modules in that file.

- Place all TLIB options and filenames in a text file and invoke TLIB as follows:

  ```
  TLIB @<response_file>
  ```

  where *<response_file>* is the name of the file containing the input commands meant for TLIB. Notice that TLIB does not assume any specific filename extension for the response file; you should provide the complete filename for the response file.

The simplest example of using TLIB is to create a new library. To create a library named TXTWIN.LIB, enter the following command:

```
TLIB TXTWIN
```

TLIB assumes the extension .LIB and creates an empty library file named TXTWIN.LIB. Now you can add object files to this library. For example, to add the modules TVIDEO.OBJ and TWINDOW.OBJ to the library TXTWIN.LIB, you would enter

```
TLIB TXTWIN +TVIDEO +TWINDOW
```

The plus signs (+) preceding the names of the object modules are commands to TLIB to add those modules to the specified library (TXTWIN.LIB). TLIB automatically selects the filename extensions. Later, if you want to remove the TWINDOW module from the TXTWIN library, you enter

```
TLIB TXTWIN -TWINDOW
```

TLIB Options and Commands

The command line for TLIB has the following syntax:

```
TLIB <library> [options] [commands] [,listfile]
```

Here, the `[options]` field can be any one of the options listed in Table 2.2. You can view this list by entering `TLIB` without any arguments at the command prompt.

Table 2.2. Options for TLIB.

Option	Interpretation by TLIB
/0	Purge comment records.
/C	Treats symbols as case sensitive. Normally, TLIB ignores case when comparing symbols.
/E	Builds an extended dictionary of cross references between modules.
/P<n>	Sets the page size to <n> bytes. The page size refers to the alignment of modules within the library files; modules start at locations that are multiples of the page size from the beginning of the file. The default page size is 16; you can specify any value that is an integer power of 2 and is from 16 to 32,768.

You specify the operations to be performed on a library in the `[commands]` field in the TLIB command line. Table 2.3 lists the operations that TLIB supports.

Table 2.3. Commands supported by TLIB.

Command	Action by TLIB
+<name>	Adds the object file or library specified by <name>. If <name> has no extension, TLIB assumes that <name> refers to an .OBJ file. In this case <name> can be a library that explicitly indicates the .LIB extension. For example, to add the contents of the CHART.LIB library to GRAPH.LIB, you would enter: `TLIB GRAPH +CHART.LIB`
-<name>	Deletes the module specified by <name>.
-+<name>	Replaces the specified object file (deletes the module from the library and then adds the new object file).
*<name>	Extracts the specified module into an object file with the same name. The module still remains in the library.
-*<name>	Extracts the specified module and then deletes it from the library.

MAKE, the Program Maintenance Utility

MAKE is a program maintenance utility patterned after the UNIX utility of the same name. The following sections provide an overview of MAKE. You should consult the online help or the *Borland C++ Tools and Utilities Guide* for a detailed description of MAKE.

The Makefile

MAKE works by reading and interpreting a *makefile*—a text file that you have to prepare according to a specified syntax. By default, MAKE expects the makefile to be named MAKEFILE, literally. In fact, if you invoke MAKE by entering

```
MAKE
```

at the DOS prompt, MAKE will search for a text file named MAKEFILE. If the file exists, MAKE will interpret its contents and act upon the commands contained in that file.

The makefile describes how MAKE should maintain your program—how it should create the object files and which object files should be linked to create the executable program.

For a program that consists of several source and header files, the makefile indicates which items will be created by MAKE—these are usually the .OBJ and .EXE files—and how these files depend on other files. For example, suppose you had a C++ source file named FORM.CPP containing the following statement:

```
#include "form.h"  // Include header file
```

FORM.OBJ clearly depends on the source file FORM.CPP and the header file FORM.H.

In addition to these dependencies, you must also specify how MAKE should convert the FORM.CPP file into FORM.OBJ. In this case, suppose you want MAKE to use BCC with the options `-c -W -ml -v -Od`. This fact can be expressed by the following lines in the makefile:

```
# This is a comment in the makefile
# The following lines indicate how FORM.OBJ depends
# on FORM.CPP and FORM.H and how to build FORM.OBJ.

FORM.OBJ: FORM.CPP FORM.H
          BCC -c -W -ml -v -Od FORM.CPP
```

Here, FORM.OBJ is the *target* and FORM.CPP and FORM.H are the *dependent* files. The line following the dependency indicates how to build the target from its dependents.

The biggest advantage of using MAKE is that it avoids unnecessary compilations. After all, you could invoke BCC in a DOS batch file to compile and link all the modules in your program, but the batch file will compile everything even if the compilations are unnecessary. MAKE, on the other hand, only builds a target if one or more of its dependents has changed since the last time the target was built. It verifies this by examining the time of last modification stamped on the files.

One curious aspect of MAKE is that it treats the target as the name of a goal to be achieved—the target does not have to be a file. For example, you can have a target such as:

```
clean:
        erase form.exe
        erase form.obj
```

which specifies an abstract target named `clean` that does not depend on anything. This dependency statement says that to make `clean`, MAKE should invoke two commands: `erase form.exe` and `erase form.obj`. Thus, the net effect of creating the target named `clean` is to delete the files FORM.EXE and FORM.OBJ. Note that the command `make clean` performs the actions necessary to build the target named `clean`, which, in effect, deletes the files `form.exe` and `form.obj`.

Macros

In addition to the basic service of building targets from dependents, MAKE provides many nice features that make it easy for you to express the dependencies and rules for building a target from its dependents. For example, if you need to compile a large number of C++ files with the same BCC options, it would be tedious to type the options for each file. You can avoid this by defining a symbol or *macro* in MAKE as follows:

```
# Define macros for standard options for BCC
BCCFLAGS=-c -W -ml -v -Od
# Define macro used to invoke BCC
BCC=bcc $(BCCFLAGS)
# Now define the rule for building FORM.OBJ
FORM.OBJ: FORM.CPP FORM.H
        $(BCC) FORM.CPP
```

Notice how the BCC options are defined as a macro named `BCCFLAGS` and this symbol is used to define another macro named `BCC` that uses `BCCFLAGS`. To use a macro elsewhere in the makefile, start with a `$` followed by the macro within parentheses. In this example, MAKE replaces all occurrences of `$(BCCFLAGS)` with the definition of the macro `BCCFLAGS`.

MAKE has a number of predefined macros as well as some macros with special meaning (see Table 2.4). You can view a list of all MAKE macros by entering the `-p` option when you run MAKE. When you see the list of predefined macros that MAKE displays, you will notice that MAKE considers all environment variables to be predefined macros.

Table 2.4. Some predefined macros in MAKE.

Macro	Meaning
`$*`	Pathname of the target file without the extension.
`$@`	Complete pathname of the target.
`$**`	All names appearing in the list of dependents.
`$<`	Name of a dependent file that is out of date with respect to the target.
`$?`	All dependent files that are out of date with respect to the target.
`MAKE__`	MAKE's version number in hexadecimal form.
`MAKE`	MAKE's executable file name.

Inference Rules

MAKE also supports the definition of rules—known as *inference rules*—that define how a file with one extension is created from a file with another extension. Consider, for example, the rule for generating an object file (.OBJ file) from a C++ source file (.CPP file). Because this involves running BCC with a specified set of options, this is a good candidate for an inference rule. You only have to define an inference rule once in a makefile. For example, to instruct MAKE to build an .OBJ file from a .CPP file by using BCC with the `-c -W` option, you would write the following inference rule:

```
# Inference rule to make .OBJ file from .CPP file
.CPP.OBJ:
        BCC -c -W $<
```

Notice the use of the macro `$<` in this rule; you can also write this as `$(<)`. As you can see from Table 2.4, this predefined macro represents the name of a dependent file that is out of date with respect to the target.

To help you set up makefiles, MAKE already defines a number of inference rules, including the one that builds .OBJ files from .CPP files.

A Sample Makefile

You can easily write a makefile if you use MAKE's predefined macros and its built-in inference rules. Consider, for example, a makefile that creates the executable WINDRAW.EXE from three C++ source files (WINDRAW.CPP, SHAPES.CPP, and WINVIEW.CPP) and a header file (WINDRAW.H). Assume that each source file includes the header file. Given this, MAKE will create WINDRAW.EXE if you use the following makefile with MAKE:

```
####################################################################
#  Sample makefile for MAKE
#  Comments start with '#'
#
#  Macro to define memory model

MODEL=s

# Define flags for the C++ compiler

CPPFLAGS=-m$(MODEL) -Od -v -W

# Define the target "all" — the first target (MAKE builds this
# one by default).

all: windraw.exe

# Compile the files

windraw.obj: windraw.cpp windraw.h

winview.obj: winview.cpp windraw.h

shapes.obj: shapes.cpp windraw.h

# Invoke TLINK to create the executable with support for debugging

windraw.exe:  windraw.obj shapes.obj winview.obj
     TLINK /Tw /v c0ws $**,$@,,cws import
```

Notice that this makefile relies heavily on MAKE's built-in inference rules. The conversion of .CPP files to .OBJ files uses the built-in rule. The flags to the C++ compiler are passed by defining the macro CPPFLAGS. The target named `all` is defined as the first target for a reason—if you invoke MAKE without specifying any targets on the command line (see the syntax presented in the next section), it builds the first target it finds. By defining the first target as WINDRAW.EXE, you can ensure that MAKE builds this executable file even if you do not explicitly specify it as a target. UNIX programmers traditionally use `all` as the name for the first target, but the target's name is immaterial—all that matters is that it is the first target in the makefile.

Running MAKE

You may run MAKE from the DOS command prompt. Invoke MAKE by using the following syntax:

```
MAKE [options] [-fmakefile] [macrodefs] [targets]
```

Where `[options]` is one or more options from Table 2.5, `[macrodefs]` is a macro definition of the form `MACRO=STRING` that is passed to MAKE, and `[targets]` is the name of a target from the makefile you want built. The `-f` option is explicitly shown because this option requires you to provide a filename—you must provide the name of a makefile for the `-f` option.

If you save the sample makefile from the previous section in a file named MAKEFILE, all you have to do is type `MAKE` and press Enter to build the target—in this case, WINDRAW.EXE. However, if the makefile has a different name—WINDRAW.MAK, for example—you must use a command-line option to indicate this to MAKE as follows:

```
MAKE -fwindraw
```

where, by default, MAKE assumes a .MAK extension for the makefile.

MAKE accepts many more options on the command line, as shown in Table 2.5.

Table 2.5. Options for MAKE.

Option	Interpretation by MAKE
-a	Updates an .OBJ file if any of the related include files and nested include files have changed.
-B	Builds all targets in the makefile, including those with dependents that are not out of date with respect to the target.
-D<*macro*>	Defines a macro.
-d<*swapdir*>	Writes MAKE's swap files to the specified directory.

Option	Interpretation by MAKE
`-e`	Overrides macro definitions in the makefile with definitions of environment variables of the same name.
`-f<file>`	Designates `<file>` as the name of the makefile. If you omit the extension from `<file>`, MAKE assumes a .MAK extension.
`-I<dirname>`	Searches for include files in the named directory.
`-i`	Ignores errors returned by commands in the makefile.
`-K`	Keeps the temporary files that MAKE creates.
`-m`	Displays the time stamp of each file.
`-n`	Displays but does not execute the makefile's commands. Use this option to find out what a makefile might cause MAKE to do before actually doing it.
`-N`	Enables compatibility with Microsoft's NMAKE.
`-p`	Displays all macro definitions and implicit rules.
`-q`	Returns zero if target is up to date; nonzero otherwise. This command is useful when MAKE is invoked from a batch file.
`-r`	Ignores predefined macros and implicit rules defined in the file BUILTINS.MAK.
`-s`	Suppresses the display of commands listed in the makefile.
`-S`	Swaps MAKE out of memory to execute commands.
`-U<macro>`	Undefines a previously defined macro.
`-W`	Saves current options to MAKE as defaults.
`-?`	Displays a brief summary of MAKE's command-line syntax and its list of options.

TDW, the Turbo Debugger for Windows

When you debug a program in Borland C++ 4, you can use the debugger built into the integrated development environment. You can also run TDW, the Turbo Debugger for Windows, by clicking its icon in a Program Manager window. TDW is a source-level debugger, which means that if you write a C or C++ program and compile and link it with the appropriate options, you will be able to trace the program's execution under TDW one source line at a time. The capability to view the source code as you debug the program is helpful in tracking down the cause of errors. In fact, you will often notice the erroneous statement as soon as the program fails under TDW.

Even though TDW is a Windows application, it provides a full-screen text-mode interface. You interact with TDW through pull-down menus and by pressing function keys. Once you finish debugging and exit from TDW, the old Windows display reappears.

Using TDW

You can start TDW by clicking its icon, but if you want to provide command-line options to TDW, start it by selecting Run… from the Program Manager's File menu. When the Program Manager prompts for a command-line to start a program, you can enter a command of the following form:

```
tdw [options] [file [arguments]]
```

where *[file]* is the name of the executable file (with the extension .EXE by default) to be loaded for debugging, and *[options]* is one or more of the CV options listed in Table 2.6. The *[arguments]* are passed to the program being debugged as its command-line arguments.

For example, if you start TDW by selecting Run from the Windows Program Manager's File menu and entering `TDW -?` as the command line, TDW displays a summary of the command-line options in a window (see Figure 2.1).

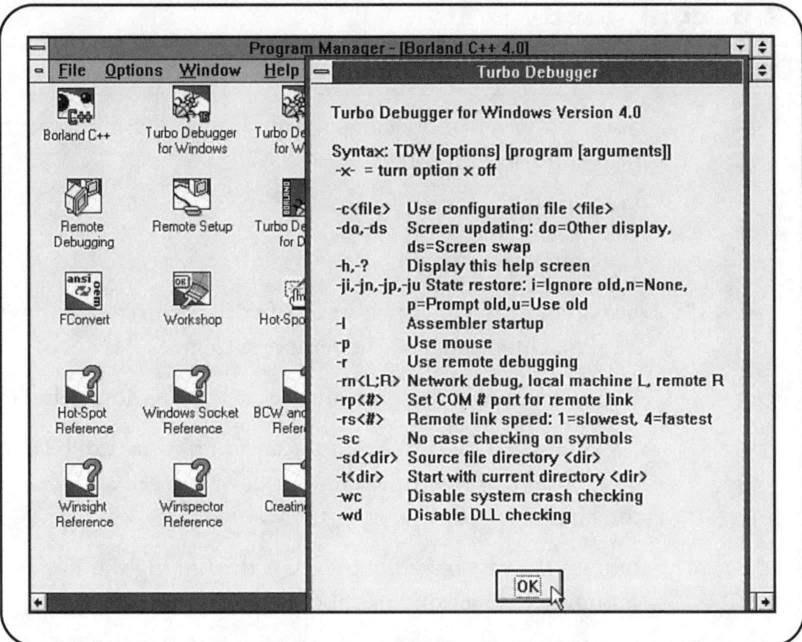

Figure 2.1. TDW's command-line options.

Table 2.6. Options for TDW.

Option	Interpretation by TDW
`-?`	Displays the command-line options in a window.
`-c<file>`	Uses <*file*> as the configuration file.
`-do`	Runs on a secondary display.
`-ds`	Uses screen-swapping. TDW uses a memory buffer to save the screen's contents while you watch the output of your program.
`-h`	Displays the command-line options in a window (same as `-?`).
`-ji`	Ignores old state.
`-jn`	Does not restore the states.
`-jp`	Asks if old state should be used.
`-ju`	Uses old state.

continues

Table 2.6. continued

Option	Interpretation by TDW
`-l`	Starts up in Assembly language mode and does not execute the program's startup code.
`-p`	Uses the mouse.
`-r`	Uses remote debugging.
`-rn<L>;<R>`	Uses remote debugging over a network with `<L>` denoting the local machine and `<R>`, the remote system.
`-rp<n>`	Uses communication port number `<n>` for remote debugging.
`-rs<n>`	Sets the speed for the communication link; `<n>` can be one of 1, 2, 3, or 4, where 1 denotes the slowest speed and 4 denotes the highest speed.
`-sc`	Ignores the case of symbols even if the linking was done assuming case-sensitive symbol names.
`-sd<dirname>`	Looks for source files in the specified directory.
`-t<dirname>`	Makes the specified directory the current directory.
`-wc`	Does not check for system crashes.
`-wd`	Does not check for existence of DLLs before starting a program.

TDW Start-Up

If you want to debug the C++ program named SHAPETST.EXE that appears in Chapter 6, "C++ and Object-Oriented Programming," build the executable file with support for debugging. (See Chapter 1 for a discussion of these options in BCW.) Then start TDW by clicking its icon. You will see that the TDW start-up screen has a main menu bar and a blank area that serves as a "desktop." The menu bar enables your interaction with TDW through the pull-down menus that appear when you select items from the menu bar.

To start debugging the program, click the File item in the menu bar and select Open... from the pull-down menu that appears. Click the box labeled Browse and navigate through the directories until you find the .EXE file that you want to debug. Click the OK box to load the executable file into TDW.

Debugging the Program

When you find that your program is not working correctly, you usually will run it under TDW. Your first goal should be to locate the offending code that is causing the program to fail. You can gather this information in several ways.

For some errors, such as dividing by zero, you can load the program into TDW and press the F9 function key to let TDW begin executing the program. When the error occurs, TDW will stop and the source window will display the line where the error occurred.

However, for many errors you must step through your program one statement at a time. TDW tells you how to do this with a message on the status line—the last line in the TDW start-up screen. This line shows the meanings of a number of function keys. The comment `F7-Trace` means that you can step through the program one line at a time by pressing the F7 function key. The term *trace* means that TDW will step into each function as your program calls it. Pressing F8 works similarly, but it steps over function calls—that is, it treats each function call as a single step. Table 2.7 lists a number of keys you can use to navigate through TDW's user interface and control how TDW steps through your program.

Table 2.7. Shortcut keys in TDW.

Keystroke	Interpretation by TDW
Alt+*n*	Makes window number *n* visible and sends all keypresses to that window. Here, *n* is a number that appears next to a window's title in the **W**indow menu.
Alt+B	Displays the Breakpoints menu.
Alt+D	Displays the Data menu.
Alt+E	Displays the Edit menu.
Alt+F	Displays the File menu.
Alt+H	Displays the Help menu.
Alt+O	Displays the Options menu.

continues

Table 2.7. continued

Keystroke	Interpretation by TDW
Alt+R	Displays the Run menu.
Alt+V	Displays the View menu.
Alt+W	Displays the Windows menu.
Alt+X	Exits TDW.
Ctrl+F2	Resets the program.
Ctrl+F5	Resizes the window.
Ctrl+F8	Toggles a breakpoint.
Ctrl+F9	Runs the program.
Ctrl+F10	Displays local pop-up menu for the current window.
F1	Displays context-sensitive help in a window. The information displayed is determined by the location of the mouse cursor.
F2	Sets or clears a breakpoint on the line containing the cursor.
F3	Allows selection of a new module for viewing in a window.
F4	Executes up to the line on which the cursor rests.
F5	Maximizes (zooms) the current window.
F6	Moves the cursor to the next window (used to move from one window to another).
F7	Executes the next statement, stepping into function calls.
F8	Executes the next statement, stepping over function calls.
F9	Executes up to the next breakpoint or to the end of the program if there are no breakpoints.
F10	Selects the menu bar.

Keystroke	Interpretation by TDW
Up arrow	Moves the cursor up one line.
Down arrow	Moves the cursor down one line.
PgUp	Scrolls up one page.
PgDn	Scrolls down one page.
Home	Jumps to the beginning of the buffer associated with the current window.
End	Jumps to the end of the buffer associated with the current window.
Shift+F1	Displays the index of online help information.

Breakpoints and Watches

A smart way to locate errors with TDW is to set a *breakpoint* at a statement near the suspect code and press the F9 key to begin executing the program. TDW will stop, or "break," when it reaches a breakpoint. The easiest way to set a breakpoint is to click at the left edge of a line of source code. When you do, you will notice that the line with the breakpoint is highlighted. Another way is to move the cursor to the line and press F2. If you want to set the breakpoint on a line in a different module than the one with the main function, press F3 to see a list of source modules from which you can pick the module you want. Once the breakpoint is set, you can run the program up to the breakpoint by pressing the F9 key.

In addition to breakpoints, you can watch the value of any expression involving variables in the program. For example, suppose you want to see the value of the expressions `2*i+1` and `shapes[0]` as your program executes. You can set up these watch expressions by entering the following in the prompt window that appears when you select Add Watch... from the Data menu:

```
2*i+1
shapes[0]
```

After adding these watch expressions, if you step through the program (by pressing the F8 key), the current value of the expressions will appear in the watch window. If you need to, use the mouse or the options in the Window menu to resize the watch window.

Summary

In addition to the C and C++ compilers, Borland C++ 4 includes a large assortment of programming tools and utilities. This chapter provided an overview of the following program development tools: TLINK, the linker; TLIB, the library manager; MAKE, the program maintenance utility; and TDW, the Turbo debugger. By reading this chapter, you have gained an understanding of how to use each of these tools for program development. Consult the extensive online help to access fully detailed information on these tools as well as others such as the Resource Workshop, GREP, WinSpector, and WinSight that were not described in this chapter.

An Overview of ANSI Standard C

In late 1989, the C programming language went through a significant transition. That's when the American National Standards Institute (ANSI) adopted a standard for C, referred to as the ANSI X3.159 1989, which defines not only the C language but also the standard header files, standard libraries, and the behavior of the C preprocessor. Prior to the ANSI standard, the C language as defined by Kernighan and Ritchie's 1978 book was the de facto standard—one that often goes by the name K&R C. As for the library, the de facto standard was the C library in UNIX. ANSI C changes this by clearly specifying all aspects of C: the language, the preprocessor, and the library.

One goal of this book is to provide you with complete details of the C++ programming language—explaining its syntax and showing how to use its features to write object-oriented programs. However, before getting into C++ in earnest, you should become familiar with the ANSI standard for the C programming language, because certain seemingly new features of C++ are already in ANSI C. Because C++ existed and continued to evolve as C was being standardized during the period from 1983 through 1989, many features that appeared in C++ also found their way into ANSI C. Therefore, if you know ANSI C, you will find many C++ constructs familiar. This chapter briefly describes ANSI C.

The Structure of a C Program

As Figure 3.1 shows, a typical C program is organized into one or more *source files*, or *modules*. Each file has a similar structure with comments, preprocessor directives, declarations of variables and functions, and their definitions. You will usually place each group of related variables and functions in a single source file.

Some files are simply a set of declarations that are used in other files through the `#include` directive of the C preprocessor. These files are usually referred to as *header files* and have names ending with the .H extension. In Figure 3.1, the file SHAPES.H is a header file which declares common data structures and functions for the program. Another file, SHAPES.C, defines the functions. A third file, SHAPETST.C, implements the `main` function—this is the function in which the execution of a C program begins. These files with names ending in .C are the source files where you define the functions needed by your program. Although Figure 3.1 shows only one function in each source file, in typical programs there are many functions in a source file.

shapes.h

```
/* File: shapes.h
 * Header file for data structures
 */
#ifndef _SHAPES_H
#define _SHAPES_H

enum shape_type(T_CIRCLE, T_RECTANGLE);
typedef struct RECTANGLE
{
    double x1, y1, c2, y2;
} RECTANGLE;
typedef struct CIRCLE
{
    double xc, yc, radius;
} CIRCLE;
typedef struct SHAPE
{
    enum shape_type type;
    union
    {
        RECTANGLE r;
        CIRCLE    c;
    } u;
} SHAPE;

/* Function prototypes */
double compute_area(SHAPE *p_s);
#endif
```

shapes.c

```
/* File: shapes.c
 * Compute area of shapes
 */
#include <math.h>
#include <shapes.h>

double compute_area(SHAPE *p_s)
{
    switch(p_s->type)
    {
        case T_CIRCLE:
        {
            CIRCLE *p_c = &(p_s->u.c);
            return M_PI * p_c->radius * p_c->radius;
        }
        case T_RECTANGLE:
        {
            RECTANGLE *p_r = &(p_s->u.r);
            return fabs((p_r->x2 - p_r->x1) *
                         p_r->y2 - p_r->y1));
        }
    }
}
```

shapetst.c

```
/* File: shapetst.c
 * Main program to test shapes.c
 */
#include <stdio.h>
#include <shapes.h>

int main(void)
{
    SHAPE s;
    CIRCLE *p_c = &(s.u.c)
    s.type = T_CIRCLE;
    p_c->radius = 50.0;
    p_c->xc = p_c->yc = 100.0;
    printf("Area of circle = %f\n",
        compute_area(&s));
    return 0;
}
```

Figure 3.1. Source files of a C program.

You must compile and link the source files to create an executable program. The exact steps for building programs from C source files depend on a number of details, such as whether you are building a Windows program or a DOS program. Chapters 1 and 2 provide an overview of the compiler and linker in Borland C++ and describe tools such as MAKE that you can use to automate the process of building an executable program from source files. Chapter 17, "Windows Programming with Borland C++," covers the topic of Windows programming with Borland C++ and the ObjectWindows library.

Declaration Versus Definition

A *declaration* determines how the program interprets a symbol. A *definition*, on the other hand, actually creates a variable or a function. Definitions cause the compiler to set aside storage for data or code, but declarations do not. For example,

```
int x, y, z;
```

is a definition of three integer variables, but

```
extern int x, y, z;
```

is a declaration indicating that the three integer variables are defined in another source file.

Within each source file, the components of the program are laid out in a standard manner. As Figure 3.2 shows, the typical components of a C source file are as follows:

1. The file starts with some comments that describe the purpose of the module and that provide some other pertinent information, such as the name of the author and revision dates. In ANSI C, comments start with `/*` and end with `*/`.
2. Commands for the preprocessor, known as *preprocessor directives*, follow the comments. The first few directives typically are for including header files and defining constants.
3. Declarations of variables and functions that are visible throughout the file come next. In other words, the names of these variables and functions may be used in any of the functions in this file. Here, you also define variables needed within the file. Use the `static` keyword as a prefix when you want to confine the visibility of the variables and functions to this module only. On the other hand, the `extern` keyword indicates that the items you declare are defined in another file.
4. The rest of the file includes definitions of functions. Inside a function's body, you can define variables that are local to the function and that exist only while the function's code is being executed.

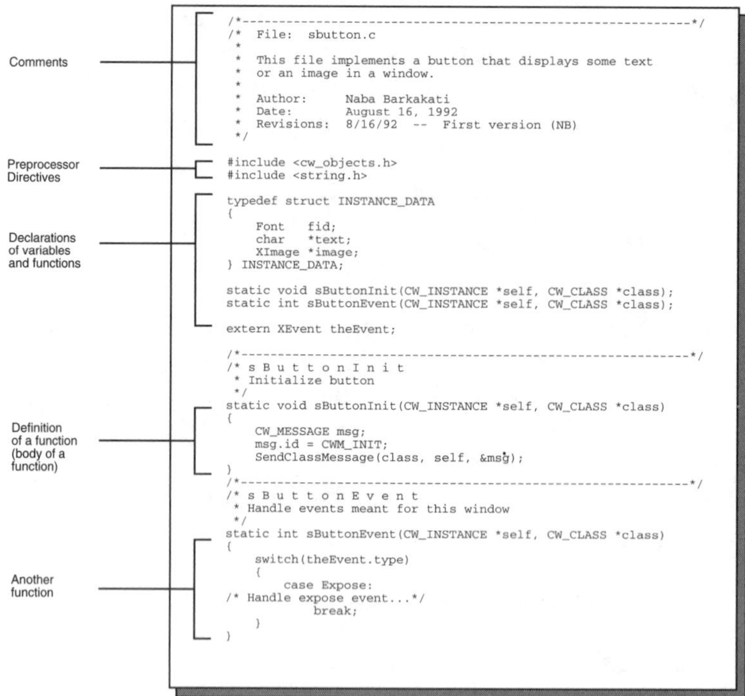

Comments
Preprocessor Directives
Declarations of variables and functions
Definition of a function (body of a function)
Another function
/*--*/
/* File: sbutton.c
 *
 * This file implements a button that displays some text
 * or an image in a window.
 *
 * Author: Naba Barkakati
 * Date: August 16, 1992
 * Revisions: 8/16/92 -- First version (NB)
 */
#include <cw_objects.h>
#include <string.h>
typedef struct INSTANCE_DATA
{
    Font   fid;
    char   *text;
    XImage *image;
} INSTANCE_DATA;
static void sButtonInit(CW_INSTANCE *self, CW_CLASS *class);
static int sButtonEvent(CW_INSTANCE *self, CW_CLASS *class);
extern XEvent theEvent;
/*--*/
/* s B u t t o n I n i t
 * Initialize button
 */
static void sButtonInit(CW_INSTANCE *self, CW_CLASS *class)
{
    CW_MESSAGE msg;
    msg.id = CWM_INIT;
    SendClassMessage(class, self, &msg);
}
/*--*/
/* s B u t t o n E v e n t
 * Handle events meant for this window
 */
static int sButtonEvent(CW_INSTANCE *self, CW_CLASS *class)
{
    switch(theEvent.type)
    {
        case Expose:
/* Handle expose event...*/
            break;
    }
}

Figure 3.2. Layout of a typical C source file.

ANSI C Keywords

Here is a list of all the ANSI C keywords:

`auto`	`double`	`int`	`struct`
`break`	`else`	`long`	`switch`
`case`	`enum`	`register`	`typedef`
`char`	`extern`	`return`	`union`
`const`	`float`	`short`	`unsigned`
`continue`	`for`	`signed`	`void`
`default`	`goto`	`sizeof`	`volatile`
`do`	`if`	`static`	`while`

The keywords `const`, `enum`, `void`, and `volatile` are new in ANSI C.

ANSI C Escape Sequences and Trigraphs

In C, you can insert nonprintable characters, such as a tab, in strings by using an *escape sequence*—a sequence of characters that starts with a backslash (\). For example, a tab and a newline character are represented by \t and \n respectively. ANSI C has enlarged the set of escape sequences. Table 3.1 lists the escape sequences supported in ANSI C.

Table 3.1. ANSI C escape sequences.

Sequence	Name	Interpretation or Action
\a	Alert	Rings bell
\b	Backspace	Moves backward one space
\f	Form feed	Moves to the beginning of the next page
\n	Newline	Moves to the beginning of the next line
\r	Carriage return	Moves to the beginning of the current line
\t	Horizontal tab	Moves to the next tab position on this line
\v	Vertical tab	Moves to the next vertical tab position
\\	Backslash	\
\'	Single Quote	'
\"	Double Quote	"
\?	Question Mark	?
\<octal digits>	Octal Constant	Depends on the printer or terminal
\x<hexadecimal digits>	Hexadecimal	Depends on the printer or terminal

ANSI C also introduces the concept of *trigraph sequences,* enabling programmers to enter certain important characters from their keyboard, even if their keyboards do not have that feature—for instance, non-English keyboards may not have some characters that English keyboards have. Each three-character trigraph sequence begins with a pair of question marks (`??`) followed by a third character. For example, if a keyboard does not have a backslash (`\`), a programmer can use the trigraph `??/` to enter it in a C program. Table 3.2 lists the nine trigraph sequences available in ANSI C.

Table 3.2. ANSI C trigraph sequences.

Trigraph	Translation
`??(`	[
`??/`	\
`??)`	]
`??'`	^
`??<`	{
`??!`	¦
`??>`	}
`??-`	~
`??=`	#

Preprocessor Directives

Preprocessing refers to the first step in translating or *compiling* an ANSI C file into machine instructions. Traditionally, the C preprocessor has been used for this task. Although the ANSI standard does not require a separate preprocessor, most C compilers provide a distinct preprocessor.

The preprocessor processes the source file and acts on the commands, called *preprocessor directives,* embedded in the program. These directives begin with the pound sign (`#`). Usually, the compiler automatically invokes the preprocessor before beginning compilation, but most compilers give you the option of invoking the preprocessor alone. You can utilize three major capabilities of the preprocessor to make your programs modular, more readable, and easier to customize:

1. You can use the #include directive to insert the contents of a file into your program. With this, you can place common declarations in one location and use them in all source files through file inclusion. The result is a reduced risk of mismatches between declarations of variables and functions in separate program modules.
2. Through the #define directive, you can define macros that enable you to replace one string with another. You can use the #define directive to give meaningful names to numeric constants, thus improving the readability of your source files.
3. With directives such as #if, #ifdef, #else, and #endif, you can compile only selected portions of your program. You can use this feature to write source files with code for two or more systems, but compile only those parts that apply to the computer system on which you compile the program. With this strategy you can maintain multiple versions of a program using a single set of source files.

Including Files

You can write modular programs by exploiting the #include directive. This is possible because the C preprocessor enables you to keep commonly used declarations in a single file that you can insert in other source files as needed. ANSI C supports three forms of the #include directive. As a C programmer, you should be familiar with the first two forms:

```
#include <stdio.h>
#include "winobj.h"
```

You use the first form of #include to read the contents of a file—in this case, the standard C header file STDIO.H from the default location where all the header files reside. You can use the second form, which displays the filename within double quotation marks, when the file being included (WINOBJ.H) is in the current directory. For locating the file that is being included, the exact conventions depend on the compiler.

ANSI C provides a third way of specifying the name of the file in the #include directive. You can now specify the name of the file through a macro. The following example illustrates how this might be done:

```
/* The following was introduced in ANSI C */
```

```
#ifdef WINDOWS
    #define  SYSTEM_DEFINES  "windef.h"
#else
    #define  SYSTEM_DEFINES  "dosdef.h"
#endif

#include SYSTEM_DEFINES
```

This example uses the `#ifdef` and `#define` directives (described in the section titled "Conditional Directives") to set the symbol `SYSTEM_DEFINES` to the name of the file to be included, depending on the definition of the symbol `WINDOWS`.

Defining Macros

By defining a macro, you can define a symbol (a *token*) to be equal to some C code. You can then use that symbol wherever you want to use that code in your program. When the source file is preprocessed, every occurrence of a macro's name is replaced with its definition. A common use of this feature is to define a symbolic name for a numerical constant and then use the symbol instead of the numbers in your program. This improves the readability of the source code because with a descriptive name you are not left guessing why a particular number is being used in the program. You can define such macros in a straightforward manner using the `#define` directive as follows:

```
#define PI          3.14159
#define GRAV_ACC    9.80665
#define BUFSIZE     512
```

Once these symbols are defined, you can use `PI`, `GRAV_ACC`, and `BUFSIZE` instead of the numerical constants throughout the source file.

The capabilities of macros, however, go well beyond replacing a symbol for a constant. A macro can accept a parameter and replace each occurrence of that parameter with the provided value when the macro is used in a program. Thus, the code that results from the expansion of a macro can change depending on the parameter you use when running the macro. For example, here is a macro that accepts a parameter and expands to an expression designed to calculate the square of the parameter:

```
#define square(x) ((x)*(x))
```

If you use `square(z)` in your program, it becomes `((z)*(z))` after the source file is preprocessed. This macro is essentially equivalent to a function that computes the square of its arguments, except that you don't call a function—the expression generated by the macro is placed directly in the source file.

Side Effects of Macros

When the preprocessor expands a macro, it replaces each parameter with the one you provide when using the macro. If you are not careful when you define the macro, you may end up with code that does something completely different from what you intended. For example, if you define `square(x)` as `x*x`, a macro invocation of the form `square(a+b)` would expand to `a+b*a+b`, which is certainly not the square of `a+b`. However, with `square(x)` defined as `((x)*(x))`, `square(a+b)` results in `((a+b)*(a+b))`, which gives you the correct result. So, as a general rule, you should use parentheses liberally when defining a macro with parameters.

An interesting new feature of the ANSI C preprocessor is the *token-pasting* operator denoted by a pair of pound signs (`##`). With this operator, you can append one token to another and create a third valid token. The following scenario provides an example of where you might use this. Suppose you have two types of data files, and an integer at the beginning of each file identifies each type. File type 1 uses the hexadecimal constant `0x4d4d`, while type 2 uses `0x4949` in the first two bytes. To read these files in your program, you want to refer to the type with a macro of the form `Type(n)` where `n` is either `1` or `2`. Here is how you can use the token-pasting operator `##` to define the `Type(n)` macro:

```
#define TYPE1    0x4d4d
#define TYPE2    0x4949
#define Type(n) TYPE##n
```

With this definition, when the preprocessor expands the macro `Type(2)`, it replaces `n` with `2` and generates the string `TYPE##2` that, upon interpretation of the "token-pasting" operator, becomes the token `TYPE2`. The preprocessor finds that `TYPE2` is defined as `0x4949` and uses that as the replacement for the macro `Type(2)`.

Another new feature of the ANSI C preprocessor is the *string-izing* operator, which creates a string out of any parameter with a `#` prefix by putting that parameter in quotes. Suppose you want to print the value of certain variables in your program. Instead of calling the `printf` function directly, you can define a utility macro that will do the work for you. Here is how you might write the macro:

```
#define Trace(x)        printf(#x" = %d\n", x)
```

Then, to print the value of a variable named current_index for instance, you can write

```
Trace(current_index);
```

When the preprocessor expands this, it generates the statement:

```
printf("current_index"" = %d\n", current_index);
```

At this point, another new feature of ANSI C becomes relevant. ANSI C also stipulates that adjacent strings will be concatenated. Applying this rule, the macro expansion becomes

```
printf("current_index = %d\n", current_index);
```

This is exactly what you would write to print the value of the current_index variable.

Conditional Directives

You can use the *conditional directives,* such as #if, #ifdef, #ifndef, #else, #elif, and #endif, to control which parts of a source file are compiled and under what conditions. With this feature, you maintain a single set of source files that can be selectively compiled with different compilers and in different environments. Another common use is to insert printf statements for debugging that are compiled only if a symbol named DEBUG is defined. Conditional directives start with either #if, #ifdef, or #ifndef and may be followed by any number of #elif directives (or none at all). Next comes an optional #else, followed by an #endif directive that marks the end of that conditional block. Here are some common ways of using conditional directives. To include a header file only once, you can use the following:

```
#ifndef __PROJECT_H
#define __PROJECT_H
/*  Declarations to be included once */
/* ... */

#endif
```

The following prints a diagnostic message during debugging (when the symbol DEBUG is defined):

```
#ifdef DEBUG
    printf("In read_file: bytes_read = %d\n", bytes_read);
#endif
```

The following example shows how you can include a different header file depending on the version number of the software. To selectively include a header file, you can use

```
#if CPU_TYPE == 80286
    #include <mode_16.h>
#elif CPU_TYPE == 80386
    #include <mode_32.h>
#else
    #error Unknown CPU type.
#endif
```

The `#error` directive is used to display error messages during preprocessing.

Other Directives

Several other preprocessor directives perform miscellaneous tasks. For example, you can use the `#undef` directive to remove the current definition of a symbol. The `#pragma` directive is another special purpose directive that you can use to convey information to the C compiler. You can use pragmas to access special features of a compiler, and as such they vary from one compiler to another.

ANSI standard C compilers maintain several predefined macros (see Table 3.3). Of these, the macros `__FILE__` and `__LINE__` respectively refer to the current source filename and the current line number being processed. You can use the `#line` directive to change these. For example, to set `__FILE__` to `"file_io.c"` and `__LINE__` to `100`, you would say

```
#line 100 "file_io.c"
```

Table 3.3. Predefined macros in ANSI C.

Macro	Definition
`__DATE__`	This is a string containing the date when you invoke the C compiler. It is of the form `MMM DD YYYY` (for example, `Oct 26 1992`).
`__FILE__`	This expands to a string containing the name of the source file.
`__LINE__`	This is a decimal integer with a value that is the line number within the current source file.
`__STDC__`	This macro expands to the decimal constant `1` to indicate that the C compiler conforms to the ANSI standard.
`__TIME__`	This string displays the time when you started compiling the source file. It is of the form "`HH:MM:SS`" (for example, "`21:59:45`").

Declaration and Definition of Variables

In C, you must either define or declare all variables and functions before you use them. The definition of a variable specifies three things:

- Its *visibility*, which indicates exactly where the variable can be used; for example, is it defined for the whole file or only in a function?
- Its *lifetime*, which determines whether the variable exists temporarily (for example, a local variable in a function) or permanently (as long as the program is running).
- Its *type* and, where allowed, its *initial value*. For example, an integer variable `x` initialized to `1` is defined as:

  ```
  int  x = 1;
  ```

If a variable that you are using is defined in another source file, you declare the variable with an `extern` keyword like this:

```
extern int message_count;
```

You must define this variable without the `extern` qualifier in at least one source file. When the program is built, the linker resolves all references to the `message_count` variable and ensures that they all use the same variable.

Basic Types

C has four basic data types: `char` and `int` are for storing characters and integers, and `float` and `double` are for floating-point numbers. The ANSI standard specifies only the minimum range of values that each type must be able to represent. The exact number of bytes used to store each data type may vary from one compiler to another. For example, ANSI C requires that the size of an `int` be at least two bytes, which is what most 16-bit MS-DOS C compilers provide. Most UNIX C compilers and 32-bit MS-DOS C compilers, on the other hand, use four bytes for an `int`. Most systems use a single byte for a `char`. Common sizes for `float` and `double` are four and eight bytes, respectively. You can define variables for these basic data types in a straightforward manner:

```
char   c;
int    i, j, bufsize;
float  volts;
double mean, variance;
```

With C, you can expand the basic data types into a much larger set by using the long, short, and unsigned qualifiers as prefixes. The long and short qualifiers are size modifiers. For example, in ANSI C a long int is at least four bytes long, whereas a short int has a minimum size of only two bytes. The size of an int is system-dependent, but it will definitely be at least as large as a short.

The unsigned qualifier is reserved for int and char types only. Normally, each of these types holds negative as well as positive values. This is the default signed form of these data types. You can use the unsigned qualifier when you want the variable to hold positive values only. Here are some examples of using the short, long, and unsigned qualifiers:

```
unsigned char  mode_select, printer_status;
short          record_number; /* Same as "short int"          */
long           offset;        /* Same as "long int"           */
unsigned       i, j, msg_id;  /* Same as "unsigned int"       */
unsigned short width, height; /* Same as "unsigned short int" */
unsigned long  file_pos;      /* Same as "unsigned long int"  */
long double    result;
```

Notice that when the short, long, and unsigned qualifiers are used with int types, you can drop the int from the declaration. Also, ANSI C enables you to extend the double data type with a long prefix.

The exact sizes of the various data types and the ranges of values they can store depend on the C compiler. ANSI C requires that these limits be defined in the header files limits.h and float.h. You can examine these files in your system to determine the sizes of the basic data types that your C compiler supports.

Enumerations

ANSI C introduces the enum data type, which you can use to define your own *enumerated list*—a fixed set of named integer constants. For example, you can declare a Boolean data type named BOOLEAN using enum as follows:

```
/* Declare an enumerated type named BOOLEAN */
     enum BOOLEAN {false = 0, true = 1, stop = 0, go = 1,
                   off = 0, on = 1};

/* Define a BOOLEAN called "status" and initialize it */
     enum BOOLEAN status = stop;
```

This example first declares BOOLEAN to be an enumerated type. The list within the braces shows the *enumeration constants* that are valid values of an enum BOOLEAN variable. You can initialize each constant to a value of your choice, and several constants can use the same value. In this example, the constants false, stop, and off are set to 0, while true, go, and on are initialized to 1. The example then defines an enumerated BOOLEAN variable named status, which is initially set to the constant stop.

Structures, Unions, and Bit Fields

In C, you use struct to group related data items together, and refer to that group by a name. For example, the declaration of a structure to hold variables of a queue might look like this:

```
/* Declare a structure */
struct QUEUE
{
    int  count;     /* Number of items in queue     */
    int  front;     /* Index of first item in queue */
    int  rear;      /* Index of last item in queue  */
    int  elemsize;  /* Size of each element of data */
    int  maxsize;   /* Maximum capacity of queue    */
    char *data;     /* Pointer to queued data       */
};

/* Define two queues */
struct QUEUE rcv_q, xmit_q;
```

The elements inside the QUEUE structure are called its *members*. You can access these members by using the member selection operator (.). For instance, rcv_q.count refers to the count member of the rcv_q structure.

A union is like a struct, but instead of grouping related data items together as struct does, a union allocates storage for several data items starting at the same location. Thus, all members of a union share the same storage location. You can use unions to view the same data item in different ways. Suppose you are using a compiler that supports four-byte longs, and you want to access the four individual bytes of a long integer. Here is a union that lets you accomplish this:

```
union
{
    long  file_type;
    char  bytes[4];
} header_id;
```

With this definition, header_id.file_type refers to the long integer, while header_id.bytes[0] is the first byte of that long integer.

In C, you also can define structures that contain groups of bits that are packed into an int. These *bit fields* are useful for manipulating selected bits of an integer and are often used when accessing hardware devices such as disk drive controllers and serial ports. Think of a bit field as a structure with bits as members. The declaration of a bit field is like any other structure except for the syntax used to indicate the size of each group of bits. For example, in the IBM PC, the text display memory uses a 16-bit cell for each character: the least significant eight bits for the character's ASCII code and the other eight bits for attributes such as foreground and background colors. A 16-bit bit field describing this layout might be as follows:

```
struct TEXT_CELL
{
    unsigned  c:8, fg_color:4, bg_color:3, blink_on:1;
};
```

This bit field definition assumes that the compiler packs the bit fields from the least significant bit to the most significant bit. The exact order of the bits in a bit field depends on the compiler.

Arrays

An *array* is a collection of one or more identical data items. You can declare arrays of any type of data, including structures and types defined by typedef. For example, to define an array of 80 characters, you would write the following:

```
char    string[80];
```

The characters in the string array occupy successive storage locations, beginning with location 0. Thus in this example, string[0] refers to the first character in this array, while string[79] refers to the last one. You can define arrays of other data types and structures similarly:

```
struct Customer                   /* Declare a structure       */
{
    int  id;
    char first_name[40];
    char last_name[40];
};

struct Customer customers[100]; /* Define array of structures */
int             index[64];      /* An array of 64 integers    */
```

You also can define multidimensional arrays. For example, to represent an 80-column by 25-line text display, you can use a two-dimensional array as follows:

```
unsigned char text_screen[25][80];
```

Each item of text_screen is an array of 80 unsigned chars, and text_screen contains 25 such arrays. In other words, the two-dimensional array is stored by laying out one row after another in memory. You can use expressions such as text_screen[0][0] to refer to the first character in the first row and text_screen[24][79] to refer to the last character of the last row of the display screen. Higher dimensional arrays are defined similarly:

```
float coords[3][2][5];
```

This example defines coords as a three-dimensional array of three data items: each item is an array of two arrays, each of which, in turn, is an array of five float variables. Thus, you interpret a multidimensional array as an "array of arrays."

Pointers

A *pointer* is a variable that can hold the address of any type of data except a bit field. For example, if p_i is a pointer to an integer variable, you can define and use it as follows:

```
/* Define an int pointer and an integer */
   int *p_i, count;

/* Set pointer to the address of the integer "count" */
    p_i = &count;
```

In this case, the compiler will allocate storage for an int variable count and a pointer to an integer p_i. The number of bytes necessary to represent a pointer depends on the underlying system's addressing scheme. You should not use a pointer until it contains the address of a valid object. The example shows p_i being initialized to the address of the integer variable count using the & operator, which provides the address of a variable. Once p_i is initialized, you can refer to the value of count with the expression *p_i, which is read as "the contents of the object with its address in p_i."

Pointers are useful in many situations; an important one is the dynamic allocation of memory. The standard C libraries include functions such as malloc and calloc, which you can call to allocate storage for arrays of objects. After allocating memory, these functions return the starting address of the block of memory. Because this address is the only way to reach that memory, you must store it in a variable capable of holding an address—a pointer.

Suppose you allocated memory for an array of 50 integers and saved the returned address in p_i. Now you can treat this block of memory as an array of 50 integers with the name p_i. Thus, you can refer to the last element in the array as p_i[49], which is equivalent to *(p_i+49). Similarly, ANSI C treats the name of an array as a pointer to the first element of the array. The difference between the name of an array and a pointer variable is that the name of the array is a constant without any explicit storage necessary to hold the address of the array's first element, whereas the pointer is an actual storage location capable of holding the address of any data.

In addition to storing the address of dynamically allocated memory, pointers are also commonly used as arguments to functions. When a C function is called, all of its arguments are *passed by value*—that is, the function gets a copy of each argument, not the original variables appearing in the argument list of the function call. Thus, a C function cannot alter the value of its arguments. Pointers provide a way out. To change the value of a variable in a function, you can pass it a pointer to the variable and the function can alter the value through the pointer.

Type Definitions

Through the typedef keyword, C provides you with a convenient way of assigning a new name to an existing data type. You can use the typedef facility to give meaningful names to data types used in a particular application. For example, a graphics application might declare a data type named Point as follows:

```
/* Declare a Point data type */
    typedef struct Point
    {
        short x;
        short y;
    } Point;

/* Declare PointPtr to be pointer to Point types */
    typedef Point *P_PointPtr;

/* Define some instances of these types and initialize them */
    Point     a = {0, 0};
    PointPtr  p_a = &a;
```

As shown by the Point and PointPtr types, you can use typedef to declare complex data types conveniently.

Type Qualifiers: *const and volatile*

ANSI C introduces two new keywords, `const` and `volatile`, that you can use as qualifiers in a declaration. The `const` qualifier in a declaration tells the compiler that the particular data object must not be modified by the program. This means that the compiler must not generate code that might alter the contents of the location where that data item is stored. On the other hand, `volatile` specifies that the value of a variable may be changed by factors beyond the program's control. You can use both keywords on a single data item to mean that, while the item must not be modified by your program, it may be altered by some other process. The `const` and `volatile` keywords always qualify the item that immediately follows (to the right). The information provided by the `const` and the `volatile` qualifiers is supposed to help the compiler optimize the code it generates. For example, suppose the variable `block_size` is declared and initialized as follows:

```
const int block_size = 512;
```

In this case, the compiler does not need to generate code to load the value of `block_size` from memory. Instead, it can use the value 512 wherever your program uses `block_size`. Now suppose you added `volatile` to the declaration and changed the declaration to

```
volatile const int block_size = 512;
```

This says that the contents of `block_size` may be changed by some external process. Therefore, the compiler cannot optimize away any reference to `block_size`. You may need to use such declarations when referring to an I/O port or video memory because these locations can be changed by factors beyond your program's control.

Expressions

An *expression* is a combination of variables, function calls, and operators that results in a single value. For example, here is an expression with a value that is the number of bytes needed to store the null-terminated string `str` (an array of `char`s with a zero byte at the end):

```
(strlen(str) * sizeof(char) + 1)
```

This expression involves a function call, `strlen(str)`, and the multiplication (*), addition (+), and `sizeof` operators.

ANSI C has a large number of operators that are an important part of expressions. Table 3.4 provides a summary of the operators in ANSI C.

Table 3.4. Summary of ANSI C operators.

Name of Operator	Syntax	Result
		ARITHMETIC OPERATORS
Addition	x+y	Adds x and y
Subtraction	x-y	Subtracts y from x
Multiplication	x*y	Multiplies x and y
Division	x/y	Divides x by y
Remainder	x%y	Computes the remainder that results from dividing x by y
Preincrement	++x	Increments x before use
Postincrement	x++	Increments x after use
Predecrement	—x	Decrements x before use
Postdecrement	x—	Decrements x after use
Minus	-x	Negates the value of x
Plus	+x	Maintains the value of x unchanged
		RELATIONAL AND LOGICAL OPERATORS
Greater than	x>y	Value is 1 if x exceeds y; otherwise, value is 0
Greater than or equal to	x>=y	Value is 1 if x exceeds or equals y; otherwise, value is 0
Less than	x<y	Value is 1 if y exceeds x; otherwise, value is 0
Less than or equal to	x<=y	Value is 1 if y exceeds or equals x; otherwise, value is 0
Equal to	x==y	Value is 1 if x equals y; otherwise, value is 0
Not equal to	x!=y	Value is 1 if x and y are unequal; other wise, value is 0
Logical NOT	!x	Value is 1 if x is 0; otherwise, value is 0
Logical AND	x&&y	Value is 0 if either x or y is 0
Logical OR	x¦¦y	Value is 0 if both x and y are 0

continues

Table 3.4. continued

Name of Operator	Syntax	Result
		ASSIGNMENT OPERATORS
Assignment	x=y	Places the value of y into x
Compound assignment	x O=y	Equivalent to x = x O y, where O is one of the following operators: +, -, *, /, %, <<, >>, &, ^, or ¦
		DATA ACCESS AND SIZE OPERATORS
Subscript	x[y]	Selects the yth element of array x
Member selection	x.y	Selects member y of structure (or union) x
Member selection	x->y	Selects the member named y from a structure or union with x as its address
Indirection	*x	Contents of the location with x as its address
Address of	&x	Address of the data object named x
Size of	sizeof(x)	Size (in bytes) of the data object named x
		BITWISE OPERATORS
Bitwise NOT	~x	Changes all 1s to 0s and 0s to 1s
Bitwise AND	x&y	Result is the bitwise AND of x and y
Bitwise OR	x¦y	Result is the bitwise OR of x and y
Bitwise exclusive OR	x^y	Result contains 1s where corresponding bits of x and y differ
Left shift	x<<y	Shifts the bits of x to the left by y bit positions. Fills 0s in the vacated bit positions.
Right shift	x>>y	Shifts the bits of x to the right by y bit positions. Fills 0s in the vacated bit positions.

Name of Operator	Syntax	Result
	MISCELLANEOUS OPERATORS	
Function call	`x(y)`	Result is the value returned (if any) by function `x`, which is called with argument `y`
Type cast	`(type)x`	Converts the value of `x` to the `type` named in parentheses
Conditional	`z?x:y`	If `z` is not `0`, evaluates `x`; otherwise, evaluates `y`
Comma	`x,y`	Evaluates `x` first and then `y`

Operator Precedence

Typical C expressions consist of several operands and operators. When writing complicated expressions, you must be aware of the order in which the compiler evaluates the operators. For example, a program uses an array of pointers to integers defined as follows:

```
typedef int *IntPtr;  /* Use typedef to simplify declarations */
IntPtr  iptr[10];     /* An array of 10 pointers to int       */
```

Now, suppose that you encounter the expression `*iptr[4]`. Does this refer to the value of the `int` with the address in `iptr[4]`, or is this the fifth element from the location with the address in `iptr`? In other words, is the compiler going to evaluate the subscript operator (`[]`) before the indirection operator (`*`), or is it the other way around? To answer questions such as these, you need to know the *precedence* or order in which the program applies the operators.

Table 3.5 summarizes ANSI C's precedence rules. The table shows the operators in order of decreasing precedence. The operators with highest precedence—those that are applied first—are shown first. The table also shows the *associativity* of the operators—this is the order in which operators at the same level are evaluated.

Table 3.5. Precedence and associativity of ANSI C operators.

Operator Group	Operator Name	Notation	Associativity
Postfix	Subscript	`x[y]`	Left to right
	Function call	`x(y)`	
	Member selection	`x.y`	
	Member selection	`x->y`	
Unary	Postincrement	`x++`	
	Postdecrement	`x—`	
	Preincrement	`++x`	Right to left
	Predecrement	`—x`	
	Address of	`&x`	
	Indirection	`*x`	
	Plus	`+x`	
	Minus	`-x`	
	Bitwise NOT	`~x`	
	Logical NOT	`!x`	
	Sizeof	`sizeof x`	
	Type cast	`(type)x`	
Multiplicative	Multiply	`x*y`	Left to right
	Divide	`x/y`	
	Remainder	`x%y`	
Additive	Add	`x+y`	Left to right
	Subtract	`x-y`	
Shift	Left shift	`x<<y`	Left to right
	Right shift	`x>>y`	
Relational	Greater than	`x>y`	Left to right
	Greater than or equal to	`x>=y`	
	Less than	`x<y`	
	Less than or equal to	`x<=y`	
Equality	Equal to	`x==y`	Left to right
	Not equal to	`x!=y`	
Bitwise AND	Bitwise AND	`x&y`	Left to right
Bitwise XOR	Bitwise exclusive OR	`x^y`	Left to right

Operator Group	Operator Name	Notation	Associativity
Bitwise OR	Bitwise OR	`x¦y`	Left to right
Logical AND	Logical AND	`x&&y`	Left to right
Logical OR	Logical OR	`x¦¦y`	Left to right
Conditional	Conditional	`z?x:y`	Right to left
Assignment	Assignment	`x=y`	Right to left
	Multiply assign	`x *= y`	
	Divide assign	`x /= y`	
	Remainder assign	`x %= y`	
	Add assign	`x += y`	
	Subtract assign	`x -= y`	
	Left shift assign	`x <<= y`	
	Right shift assign	`x >>= y`	
	Bitwise AND assign	`x &= y`	
	Bitwise XOR assign	`x ^= y`	
	Bitwise OR assign	`x ¦= y`	
Comma	Comma	`x,y`	Left to right

Getting back to the question of interpreting `*iptr[4]`, a quick look at Table 3.5 tells you that the `[]` operator has precedence over the `*` operator. Thus, when the compiler processes the expression `*iptr[4]`, it evaluates `iptr[4]` first, and then it applies the indirection operator, resulting in the value of the `int` with the address in `iptr[4]`.

Statements

You use statements to represent the actions C functions will perform and to control the flow of execution in the C program. A *statement* consists of keywords, expressions, and other statements. Each statement ends with a semicolon.

A special type of statement, the *compound statement*, is a group of statements enclosed in a pair of braces (`{...}`). The body of a function is a compound statement. Also known as *blocks*, such compound statements can contain local variables.

The following alphabetically arranged sections describe the types of statements available in ANSI C.

break Statement

You use the `break` statement to jump to the statement following the innermost `do`, `for`, `switch`, or `while` statement. It is also used to exit from a `switch` statement. Here is an example that uses `break` to exit a `for` loop:

```
for(i = 0; i < ncommands; i++)
{
     if(strcmp(input, commands[i]) == 0) break;
}
```

case Statement

The `case` statement marks labels in a `switch` statement. Here is an example:

```
switch (interrupt_id)
{
     case XMIT_RDY:
          transmit();
          break;

     case RCV_RDY:
          receive();
          break;
}
```

Compound Statement or Block

A compound statement or block is a group of declarations followed by statements, all enclosed in a pair of braces (`{...}`). The body of a function and the block of code following an `if` statement are some examples of compound statements. In the following example, the declarations and statements within the braces constitute a compound statement:

```
if(theEvent.xexpose.count == 0)
{
     int i;
/* Clear the window and draw the figures
 * in the "figures" array
 */
     XClearWindow(theDisplay, dWin);
     if(numfigures > 0)
```

```
        for(i=0; i<numfigures; i++)
            draw_figure(theDisplay, dWin,
                        theGC, i);
}
```

continue Statement

The `continue` statement begins the next iteration of the innermost `do`, `for`, or `while` statement in which it appears. You can use `continue` when you want to skip the execution of the loop. For example, to add the numbers from 1 to 10, excluding 5, you can use a `for` loop that skips the body when the loop index (`i`) is `5`:

```
for(i=0, sum=0; i <= 10, i++)
{
        if(i == 5) continue;    /* Exclude 5 */
        sum += i;
}
```

default Label

You use `default` as the label in a `switch` statement to mark code that will execute when none of the `case` labels match the `switch` expression.

do Statement

The `do` statement, together with `while`, forms iterative loops of the kind

```
do
  statement
  while(expression);
```

where the statement (usually a compound statement) executes until the expression in the `while` statement evaluates to `0`. The expression is evaluated after each execution of the statement. Thus, a `do-while` block always executes at least once. For example, to add the numbers from 1 to 10, you can use the following `do` statement:

```
sum = 0;
do
{
    sum += i;
    i++;
}
while(i <= 10);
```

Expression Statements

Expression statements are evaluated for their side effects. Some typical uses of expression statements include calling a function, incrementing a variable, and assigning a value to a variable. Here are some examples:

```
printf("Hello, World!\n");
i++;
num_bytes = length * sizeof(char);
```

for Statement

Use the `for` statement to execute a statement any number of times based on the value of an expression. The syntax is as follows:

```
for (expr_1; expr_2; expr_3) statement
```

where the `expr_1` is evaluated once at the beginning of the loop, and the statement is executed until the expression `expr_2` evaluates to 0. The third expression, `expr_3`, is evaluated after each execution of the statement. All three expressions are optional and the value of `expr2` is assumed to be 1 if it is omitted. Here is an example that uses a `for` loop to add the numbers from 1 to 10:

```
for(i=0, sum=0; i <= 10; sum += i, i++);
```

In this example, the actual work of adding the numbers is done in the third expression, and the statement controlled by the `for` loop is a null statement (a lone ;).

goto Statement

The `goto` statement transfers control to a statement label. Here is an example that prompts the user for a value and repeats the request if the value is not acceptable:

```
ReEnter:
    printf("Enter offset: ");
    scanf(" %d", &offset);
    if(offset < 0 || offset > MAX_OFFSET)
    {
        printf("Bad offset: %d Please reenter:\n",
                offset);
        goto ReEnter;
    }
```

if Statement

You can use the `if` statement to test an expression and execute a statement only when the expression is not zero. An `if` statement takes the following form:

```
if ( expression )  statement
```

The statement following the `if` is executed only if the expression in parentheses evaluates to a nonzero value. That statement is usually a compound statement. Here is an example:

```
if(mem_left < threshold)
{
     Message("Low on memory! Close some windows.\n");
}
```

if-else Statement

The `if-else` statement is a form of the `if` statement together with an `else` clause. The statement has the syntax:

```
if ( expression )
     statement_1
else
     statement_2
```

where `statement_1` is executed if the expression within the parentheses is not zero. Otherwise, `statement_2` is executed. Here is an example that uses `if` and `else` to pick the smaller of two variables:

```
if ( a <= b)
     smaller = a;
else
     smaller = b;
```

Null Statement

The null statement, represented by a solitary semicolon, does nothing. You use null statements in loops when all processing is done in the loop expressions rather than in the body of the loop. For example, to locate the zero byte marking the end of a string, you might use the following:

```
char str[80] = "Test";
int i;

for (i=0; str[i] != '\0'; i++)
                              ;  /* Null statement */
```

return Statement

The return statement stops executing the current function and returns control to the calling function. The syntax is

```
return expression;
```

where the value of the expression is returned as the value of the function.

switch Statement

The switch statement performs a multiple branch, depending on the value of an expression. It has the following syntax:

```
switch (expression)
{
     case value1:
          statement_1
          break;
     case value2:
          statement_2
          break;
             .
             .
             .
     default:
          statement_default
}
```

If the expression being tested by switch evaluates to value1, statement_1 is executed. If the expression is equal to value2, statement_2 is executed. The value is compared with each case label and the statement following the matching label is executed. If the value does not match any of the case labels, the block statement_default following the default label is executed. Each statement ends with a break statement that separates the code of one case label from another. Here is a switch statement that calls different routines depending on the value of an integer variable named cmd:

```
switch (cmd)
{
     case 'q':
          quit_app(0);

          case 'c':
```

```
          connect();
          break;

     case 's':
          set_params();
          break;

     case '?':
     case 'H':
          print_help();
          break;

     default:
          printf("Unknown command!\n");
}
```

while Statement

The `while` statement is used in the form:

```
while (expression) statement
```

where the statement is executed until the expression evaluates to 0. A `while` statement evaluates the expression before each execution of the statement. Thus, a `while` loop executes the statement zero or more times. Here is a `while` statement for copying one array to another:

```
i = length;
while (i >= 0)  /* Copy one array to another */
{
     array2[i] = array1[i];
     i—;
}
```

Functions

Functions are the building blocks of C programs. A *function* is a collection of declarations and statements. Each C program has at least one function: the `main` function. This is the function where the execution of a C program begins. The ANSI C library also comprises mostly functions, although it contains quite a few macros.

Function Prototypes

In ANSI C, you must declare a function before using it. The function declaration tells the compiler the type of value that the function returns and the number and type of arguments it takes. Most C programmers are used to declaring functions only when they return something other than an `int` because that is how Kernighan and Ritchie's definition of C works. For example, in the old UNIX C library, the memory allocation function `calloc` would return a pointer to a `char` (as you will see soon, the ANSI C version of `malloc` returns a `void` pointer). Thus, an old-style C program that uses `calloc` includes the declaration:

```
char *calloc();
```

You can continue to use this in ANSI C, but you also can declare a function as a complete *function prototype*, showing the return type as well as a list of arguments. The `calloc` function in the ANSI C library returns a `void` pointer and accepts two arguments, each of type `size_t`, which is an unsigned integer type of sufficient size to hold the value of the `sizeof` operator. Thus, the ANSI C prototype for `calloc` is

```
void *calloc(size_t, size_t);
```

which shows the type of each argument in the argument list. You also can include an identifier for each argument and write the prototype as follows:

```
void *calloc(size_t num_elements, size_t elem_size);
```

In this case, the prototype looks exactly like the first line in the definition of the function, except that you stop short of defining the function and end the line with a semicolon. With well-chosen names for arguments, this form of prototype can provide a lot of information about the function's use. For example, one look at the prototype of `calloc` should tell you that its first argument is the number of elements to allocate, and the second one is the size of each element.

Prototypes also help the compiler check function arguments and generate code that may use a faster mechanism for passing arguments. From the prototype, the compiler can determine the exact number and type of arguments to expect. Therefore, the prototype enables the compiler to catch any mistakes you might make when calling a function, such as passing the wrong number of arguments (when the function takes a fixed number of arguments) or passing a wrong type of argument to a function.

The *void* Type

What do you do when a function doesn't return anything nor accept any parameters? To handle these cases, ANSI C provides the `void` type, which is useful for declaring functions that return nothing and for describing pointers that can point to any type of data. For example, you can use the `void` return type to declare a function such as `exit` that does not return anything:

```
void exit(int status);
```

On the other hand, if a function doesn't accept any formal parameters, its list of arguments is represented by a `void`:

```
FILE *tmpfile(void);
```

The `void` pointer is useful for functions that work with blocks of memory. For example, when you request a certain number of bytes from the memory allocation routine `malloc`, you can use these locations to store any data that fits the space. In this case, the address of the first location of the allocated block of memory is returned as a `void` pointer. Thus, the prototype of `malloc` is

```
void *malloc(size_t numbytes);
```

Functions with a Variable Number of Arguments

If a function accepts a variable number of arguments, you can indicate this by using an ellipsis (`...`) in place of the argument list; however, you must provide at least one argument before the ellipsis. A good example of such functions is the `printf` family of functions defined in the header file STDIO.H. The prototypes of these functions are as follows:

```
int fprintf(FILE *stream, const char *format, ...);
int printf(const char *format, ...);
int sprintf(char *buffer, const char *format, ...);
```

As you can see, after a list of required arguments, the variable number of arguments is indicated by an ellipsis.

The ANSI C Library

The ANSI standard for C defines all aspects of C: the language, the preprocessor, and the library. The prototypes of the functions in the library, as well as all necessary data structures and preprocessor constants, are defined in a set of standard header files. Table 3.6 lists the standard header files, including a summary of their contents. (See Appendix A, "ANSI C Headers" for a list of macros and declarations in each header.)

Table 3.6. Standard header files in ANSI C.

Header File	Purpose
assert.h	Defines the `assert` macro. Used for program diagnostics.
ctype.h	Declares functions for classifying and converting characters.
errno.h	Defines macros for error conditions, `EDOM` and `ERANGE`, and the integer variable `errno` where library functions return an error code.
float.h	Defines a range of values that can be stored in floating-point types.
limits.h	Defines the limiting values of all integer data types.
locale.h	Declares the `lconv` structure and the functions necessary for customizing a C program to a particular locale.
math.h	Declares math functions and the `HUGE_VAL` macro.
setjmp.h	Defines the `setjmp` and `longjmp` functions that can transfer control from one function to another without relying on normal function calls and returns. Also defines the `jmp_buf` data type used by `setjmp` and `longjmp`.
signal.h	Defines symbols and routines necessary for handling exceptional conditions.
stdarg.h	Defines macros that provides access to the unnamed arguments in a function that accepts a varying number of arguments.
stddef.h	Defines the standard data types `ptrdiff_t`, `size_t`, `wchar_t`; the symbol `NULL`; and the macro `offsetof`.

Header File	Purpose
stdio.h	Declares the functions and data types necessary for input and output operations. Defines macros such as BUFSIZ, EOF, NULL, SEEK_CUR, SEEK_END, and SEEK_SET.
stdlib.h	Declares many utility functions, such as the string conversion routines, random number generator, memory allocation routines, and process control routines (such as abort, exit, and system).
string.h	Declares the string manipulation routines such as strcmp and strcpy.
time.h	Defines data types and declares functions that manipulate time. Defines the types clock_t and time_t and the tm data structure.

Summary

One quick way to grasp C++'s seemingly new syntax is to learn ANSI standard C, because many features of C++ have been incorporated into ANSI standard C (officially known as ANSI X3.159 1989). For instance, function prototypes, as well as void and enum types, appear in both ANSI C and C++. Because many syntactical details of C++ are similar to those of ANSI C, a knowledge of ANSI C is helpful when you write programs in C++. This chapter provided a quick overview of ANSI C.

4

Borland C++ Extensions to Standard C

As its title indicates, Chapter 3 provides an "Overview of ANSI Standard C." Borland C++, however, adds a number of keywords, global variables, and predefined macros to support the unique needs of the Intel 80x86 microprocessor family and the MS-DOS operating system. In particular, the unique memory-addressing scheme of the Intel 80x86 microprocessors has resulted in a number of *memory models* that specify how a program's code and data are organized in memory. In addition to the compiler options summarized in Chapter 1, "The Borland C++ 4 Programming Environment," Borland C++ also includes many keywords and compiler directives (called *pragmas*) to support these memory models. This chapter describes the keywords, pragmas, and preprocessor macros unique to Borland C++ 4. Other compiler-specific information, such as limits on the values of various data types, is also described in this chapter.

Unique to Borland C++ 4

This chapter describes the keywords, pragmas, and preprocessor macros that are unique to the Borland C++ 4 compiler and not part of ANSI standard C. The C++ language itself can be thought of as an extension of ANSI standard C, but C++ is not covered in this chapter. Chapters 5 through 13 teach C++ from the viewpoint of object-oriented programming.

Keywords Unique to Borland C++ 4

In Chapter 3, you saw the reserved keywords of ANSI C. In addition to the ANSI C keywords, Borland C++ 4 defines 20 additional reserved words, each with one or two leading underscores. Table 4.1 summarizes these Borland-specific reserved words. The sections following this table briefly describe some of these keywords.

Table 4.1. Borland-specific keywords.

Keyword	Purpose
`_AH`	Used to refer to the AH register.
`_AL`	Used to refer to the AL register.
`_AX`	Used to refer to the AX register.
`_BH`	Used to refer to the BH register.
`_BL`	Used to refer to the BL register.
`_BX`	Used to refer to the BX register.
`_CH`	Used to refer to the CH register.
`_CL`	Used to refer to the CL register.
`_CX`	Used to refer to the CX register.
`_DH`	Used to refer to the DH register.

Keyword	Purpose
`_DL`	Used to refer to the DL register.
`_DX`	Used to refer to the DX register.
`_CS`	Used to refer to the CS register.
`_DS`	Used to refer to the DS register.
`_ES`	Used to refer to the ES register.
`_SS`	Used to refer to the SS register.
`_SI`	Used to refer to the SI register.
`_DI`	Used to refer to the DI register.
`_SP`	Used to refer to the SP register.
`_BP`	Used to refer to the BP register.
`_FLAGS`	Used to refer to the FLAGS register.
`__asm`	Used to insert assembly language code in a C or C++ source file.
`__cdecl`	Used to indicate that the function or variable that follows uses the C naming and calling conventions. (During function calls, arguments are pushed on the stack from right to left; names are case-sensitive and an underscore prefix is added to each name.) The function's caller is responsible for removing the arguments that were pushed on to the stack prior to the function call.
`__cs`	Used to specify a near pointer as an offset from the segment address in the CS register.
`__ds`	Used to specify a near pointer as an offset from the segment address in the DS register.
`__es`	Used to specify a near pointer as an offset from the segment address in the ES register.
`__except`	Used to specify the action that has to be taken when a given exception occurs.

continues

Table 4.1. continued

Keyword	Purpose
`__export`	Indicates that a function or data item is exported from an executable file or a dynamic link library (DLL).
`__far`	An address qualifier indicating that full 32-bit segment:offset addressing is used for a function or a variable.
`__fastcall`	Indicates that a function uses a calling convention that passes arguments in the registers for faster function calls.
`__huge`	Used to indicate that a data item must be addressed using 32-bit segment:offset address and that it may exceed 64K in size. Huge addresses are maintained in a normalized form so that pointer comparisons are always correct. This is not the case for `far` pointers.
`__loadds`	Used to force the compiler to load the data segment register (the DS register) with an appropriate value before calling a function. The previous value of DS is restored just before the function returns.
`__near`	An addressing modifier indicating that a function or data item should be accessed using its 16-bit offset address only.
`__pascal`	Used to indicate that a function or variable uses the FORTRAN and Pascal naming and calling conventions. (During function calls, arguments are pushed on the stack from left to right and names are converted to all uppercase.) The function is responsible for removing the arguments that were pushed on to the stack during the function call.
`__rtti`	A qualifier for a `class` or `struct` that adds support for run-time type identification for C++ objects.
`_saveregs`	Forces the compiler to generate code to save and restore all CPU registers when entering and exiting a function, respectively.
`__ss`	Used to specify a near pointer as an offset from the segment address in the SS register.
`__stdcall`	Used to indicate that a function follows a standard calling convention similar to `__cdecl`, except that the function is responsible for popping the arguments off the stack.

Keywords to Support Memory Models

C programmers who work on UNIX systems generally do not need to think about the memory-addressing scheme of their underlying system's central processing unit (CPU). On Intel 80x86 microprocessor-based MS-DOS PCs, the memory-addressing scheme is not so transparent to programmers—at least not if you want to write realistic applications that manipulate large amounts of textual or graphical information.

Intel 80x86 Processors

The term *Intel 80x86 processors* refers to the entire family of Intel microprocessors including the 8088, 8086, 80186, 80286, 80386SX, 80386DX, 80486SX, 80486DX, and most recently the Pentium. It is common to use the term *80x86* to refer to these binary-compatible microprocessors that power most MS-DOS PCs. Individual models are often referred to by their last three digits, such as *186*, *286*, *386*, or *486*. The 8086, 186, and 286 are 16-bit microprocessors, meaning that they can handle units of data as large as 16 bits. The 8088, used in the original IBM PC and XT, is like the 8086, but its data path to the outside world is only 8 bits wide—that is, the 8088 can retrieve only 8 bits of information at a time. The more modern 386DX, 486SX, and 486DX are 32-bit processors that can process 32-bit data internally and access memory in 32-bit units. The 386SX is a version of the 386DX that can process 32-bit data internally, but it can only retrieve information from memory in 16-bit units. The 486SX and 486DX are both full 32-bit microprocessors—the difference between the two is that the 486DX has a built-in 80487 math coprocessor (also called the floating-point unit or FPU) but that coprocessor is defective in the 486SX. Thus, the 486SX is a 486DX with a broken FPU. Another new breed of 486DX microprocessors is the 486DX2 that operates internally at double the clock speed used for all external operations such as memory access. A popular version of these "clock-doubled" 486DX2 processors is the 66MHz 486DX2 that operates internally at a 66MHz clock speed.

Segment:Offset Addressing in 80x86 Processors

The memory-addressing scheme used by the 80x86 microprocessors brings up the concept of *segments.* Under the MS-DOS operating system, all 80x86 processors—including the 80386 and 80486 that are capable of 32-bit processing—run in *real mode.* In real mode, all 80x86 processors behave like the 8086; they use 16-bit internal registers and can address up to a megabyte of physical memory using a 20-bit value as the address of any 8-bit byte in memory.

The concept of segments arises because a single 16-bit register cannot hold the entire 20-bit physical address. Intel's solution is to break down each memory address into two parts, a segment address and an offset, each a 16-bit value. The *segment address* is simply the address of the first byte of a block of memory located anywhere in the 1M addressable locations. The *offset address* is the location of a byte with respect to the beginning of the segment—the first byte in the segment is at offset 0, the second at offset 1, and so on. With this segment:offset-addressing scheme, two registers—one containing the segment address and the other the offset—can hold the address of any byte in physical memory.

Because a 16-bit number can hold values from 0 to 65,535, the offset can be up to 65,536 or 64K in size. Also, a 16-bit segment address can represent as many as 65,536 segments. However, this does not mean that the MS-DOS PC can access 65,536 segments that are each 64K in size. With the segment:offset-addressing scheme, Intel also stipulates that you should compute the 20-bit physical address by applying the following formula:

```
20-bit physical address = (16-bit segment address) × 16 +
                          (16-bit offset address)
```

Thus, the processor is still limited to the amount of physical memory that it can access using a 20-bit address.

The advantage of segmented memory addressing is that if all of a program's data fits into a single segment (which can be up to 64K in size), the 80x86 processor can set up the segment address in a register and access any data item using only a 16-bit offset. This results in a speedier program because the processor does not need to manipulate the segment portion of the address.

The 640K Barrier Under MS-DOS

Although Intel 80x86 processors operating in real mode can address up to 1M or 1,024K of physical memory, 384K of addressable space above the lower 640K is normally reserved for adapter ROMs (read-only memory), video buffers, and other hardware. That is why only 640K of memory is available under MS-DOS.

Standard Memory Models

Because of the 80x86 processor's segmented memory addressing, the Borland C++ compiler organizes code and data into one or more segments. To begin with, Borland C++ gives you six predefined memory segmentation schemes called *memory models.* Table 4.2 summarizes these memory models.

Table 4.2. Standard memory models in Borland C++.

Model	Description
Small	Program size is limited to one segment of code and one segment of data. The compiler assumes the Small memory model by default. You can explicitly specify the Small memory model with the `-ms` option.
Medium	Program size is limited to only one segment of data, but many segments of code. All data addresses are 16-bit offsets, but code uses explicit segment and offset addresses. The `-mm` compiler option selects the Medium memory model.
Compact	The program can contain several data segments, but only one code segment. All data have full segment:offset addresses, whereas code addresses are offset only. Use the `-mc` compiler option to select the Compact model.
Large	The program can contain multiple segments of data and code. The total size of a program is limited only by the available memory under MS-DOS, but a single data item can be no larger than 64K. The `-ml` compiler option selects the Large memory model.

Near, Far, and Huge

It is common practice among MS-DOS and Windows programmers to use the terms *near* and *far* as adjectives that specify the addressing requirements for a function or a data. A *near address* is a 16-bit offset, whereas a *far address* requires the full 32-bit segment:offset address. The keywords `__near` and `__far` are used as qualifiers to indicate near and far addressing respectively.

In a similar vein, the term *huge array* refers to an array that can exceed the 64K segment limit and is declared with the `_huge` keyword.

Overriding Default Addressing Conventions

What if you wanted a small memory program for efficiency, but needed a single large array? Do you use the Medium model because your program has more than 64K of data? The answer is no. Borland C++ provides several keywords that you can use to declare explicitly the addressing convention for each individual variable or function. For instance, to declare a single far data item, you only need to add a `__far` prefix to the variable's name.

Borland C++ supports the following three keywords:

```
__near      __far    __huge
```

These keywords are used to indicate the addressing requirements of data and functions. You can use these three keywords to mix data items and function calls with an addressing convention that differs from the defaults used by the selected standard memory model. Table 4.3 summarizes the use of these keywords.

Table 4.3. The `__near`, `__far`, and `__huge` keywords.

Keyword	Description
`__near`	Both data and functions that are qualified with a `__near` keyword are accessed with 16-bit addresses. Pointers are 16-bit values and all address arithmetic is performed assuming 16-bit values.

Keyword	Description
`__far`	Data can be anywhere in memory, but a single data item cannot exceed 64K in size and must not cross any segment boundary. Both function and data are accessed through full 32-bit segment:offset addresses. All pointers are 32-bit values. However, pointer arithmetic is performed with the 16-bit offsets only because no data item is expected to extend beyond the boundary of a segment.
`__huge`	You can declare huge data only; the `__huge` keyword is not applicable to functions. Data can be anywhere in memory and individual arrays can exceed 64K in size. Data is accessed with 32-bit segment:offset addresses. Pointers to data are 32 bits and all pointer arithmetic is done using the full 32-bit addresses.

Other Special Keywords

As you can see from Table 4.1, there are many more Borland-specific keywords supported by Borland C++. These keywords serve a number of purposes from embedding assembly language statements in a C or C++ program to controlling events that occur when entering or leaving a function. The following sections describe some of these keywords.

Embedding Assembly Language Code in C and C++

The `__asm` keyword enables you to place assembly language statements directly inside a C or C++ program. You can place a single line of assembly language in your program by prefixing the statement with the `__asm` keyword like this:

```
// Assembly language statements—one per line
   __asm mov ah, 02h
   __asm mov dl, 7
   __asm int 21h
```

If you prefer, you also can place all three statements on a single line:

```
// Multiple __asm statements on a single line
   __asm mov ah, 02h;  __asm mov dl, 7;  __asm int 21h;
```

You also can embed a block of assembly language statements by enclosing them inside a pair of braces ({...}) and prefixing the block with the __asm keyword. For example, the preceding statements could be written as follows:

```
__asm    // An __asm block
{
    mov ah, 01h
    mov dl, 7
    int 21h
}
```

The inline assembler supports a large subset of assembly language statements and directives available under TASM, the Turbo Assembler and MASM, the Microsoft Macro Assembler. You can reference C and C++ symbols including constants, macros, variables, and function names inside __asm blocks.

Predefined Global Variables and Preprocessor Macros

Borland C++ includes a number of predefined global variables in the C library. These variables contain important information, such as the DOS version number, the current operating system (DOS or Windows), and a pointer to the environment variables. You can refer to these global variables if you include the header file where they are declared. These global variables are automatically initialized when your program starts up. Table 4.4 lists the predefined global variables in Borland C++.

Table 4.4. Predefined global variables in Borland C++.

Name	Type, Declaration, and Purpose
`_8087`	Type: `int` Declared in: DOS.H This variable is nonzero if the startup code detects the presence of a math coprocessor in the system.
`_argc`	Type: `int` Declared in: DOS.H This variable is set to the number of command-line arguments used when running the program.

Name	Type, Declaration, and Purpose
`_argv`	Type: `char**` Declared in: DOS.H This is an array of null-terminated strings containing the command-line arguments used when running the program.
`_ctype`	Type: `char*` Declared in: CTYPE.H This is an array of character attribute information indexed by one plus the ASCII value of each character.
`daylight`	Type: `int` Declared in: TIME.H This variable has a nonzero value if a daylight-saving time zone is specified in the `TZ` environment variable; otherwise, the variable has a zero value. This variable is used when converting local time to Greenwich Mean Time (also known as Universal Coordinated Time or by its French acronym, UTC).
`_doserrno`	Type: `int` Declared in: STDLIB.H This variable contains the MS-DOS error code returned by the last MS-DOS system call.
`environ`	Type: `char**` Declared in: STDLIB.H This is an array of null-terminated strings that constitute the environment of the current program. You can directly access the environment variables through this array. The library functions `getenv` and `putenv` use the `environ` array.
`errno`	Type: `int` Declared in: STDLIB.H This variable is set to an error code corresponding to the last error.

continues

Table 4.4. continued

Name	Type, Declaration, and Purpose
`_floatconvert`	Type: `int` Declared in: STDIO.H An external reference to this variable (with `#pragma extref _floatconvert`) forces the linking of floating-point format conversion code with the program.
`_fmode`	Type: `int` Declared in: STDLIB.H This variable controls the default file translation mode. The default value is 0, which means files are translated in the text mode.
`_new_handler`	Type: `typedef void (*pvf)();` `pvf _new_handler;` Declared in: STDLIB.H This variable holds a pointer to a function that is called by the C++ operator `new` when `new` fails to allocate memory.
`_osmajor`	Type: `unsigned char` Declared in: STDLIB.H This is the major version number of the operating system. For example, if you have MS-DOS 6.0, `_osmajor` is 6.
`_osminor`	Type: `unsigned char` Declared in: STDLIB.H This is the minor version number of the operating system. For MS-DOS 6.0, `_osminor` is 0; for MS-DOS 3.3, `_osminor` is 30 (decimal).
`_osmode`	Type: `unsigned char` Declared in: STDLIB.H This variable contains a constant that indicates what operating system is currently running. The value can be one of the defined constants, `_DOS_MODE`, `_WIN_MODE`, or `_OS2_MODE`, which respectively indicate that either MS-DOS, Windows, or OS/2 is the current operating system.

Name	Type, Declaration, and Purpose
_osversion	Type: unsigned Declared in: STDLIB.H This 2-byte value contains the complete version number of the underlying operating system. The least-significant byte contains the major version number and the most-significant byte (the "high" byte) contains the minor version number. Thus, for MS-DOS 3.1, _osversion is 0x0a03 (in hexadecimal); for DOS 5.0, _osversion is 5.
_stklen	Type: unsigned Declared in: DOS.H This variable indicates the size of the stack. The default is 4,096 bytes; the minimum allowed is 256 bytes.
sys_errlist	Type: char** Declared in: STDLIB.H This variable comprises an array of strings, each corresponding to a system error message.
sys_nerr	Type: int Declared in: STDLIB.H This variable is set to the total number of strings in the sys_errlist array.
_threadid	Type: long Declared in: STDDEF.H This refers to a long integer value that identifies the currently executing thread. It is implemented as a macro, so you have to include <stddef.h> to use _threadid.
__throwExceptionName	Type: char* Declared in: EXCEPT.H This variable is a string with the name of the last exception thrown.

continues

Table 4.4. continued

Name	Type, Declaration, and Purpose
`__throwFileName`	Type: `char*` Declared in: EXCEPT.H This variable is a string with the name of the file containing the code responsible for the last exception thrown.
`__throwLineNumber`	Type: `char*` Declared in: EXCEPT.H This variable is a string with the line number of the code that generated the last exception.
`_timezone`	Type: `long` Declared in: TIME.H This variable contains the difference in seconds between Greenwich Mean Time and the local time.
`_tzname`	Type: `char *tzname[2];` Declared in: TIME.H This is an array of two null-terminated strings with `tzname[0]` set to the three-letter time zone name (for example, EST or PST), and `tzname[1]` set to the name of the daylight saving time zone.
`_version`	Type: `unsigned` Declared in: STDLIB.H This variable contains the operating system's version number. The major version number is stored in the low byte and the minor version number is in the high byte. For example, if the operating system is MS-DOS 3.1, `_version` will be 0A03 in hexadecimal format.
`_wscroll`	Type: `int` Declared in: CONIO.H If this variable is zero, scrolling is disabled in programs that generate text output, including Windows programs that rely on the EasyWin library for text output in a window.

The Borland C++ preprocessor also defines a number of macros (symbols) that you can use in your source files without defining them. As explained in Chapter 3, ANSI C also contains a number of preprocessor macros that are predefined. In addition to these ANSI standard preprocessor macros, Borland C++ defines the additional macros listed in Table 4.5. You can use these macros to conditionally compile sections of code based on conditions, such as the processor type and the memory model being used.

Table 4.5. Borland-specific predefined preprocessor macros in Borland C++.

Symbol	Purpose
`__BCPLUSPLUS__`	Defined during C++ compilation.
`__BORLANDC__`	Set to the version number of the compiler.
`__CDECL__`	Defined if the function calling convention is set to the C convention.
`__cplusplus__`	Defined during C++ compilation.
`__DLL__`	Defined when the file is being compiled as a Windows DLL.
`__MSDOS__`	Defined when the operating system is MS-DOS.
`__PASCAL__`	Defined when the function calling convention is set to Pascal.
`__TCPLUSPLUS__`	Defined during C++ compilation. This is the same value as `__BCPLUSPLUS__`.
`__TURBOC__`	Set to the version number of the compiler. This is the same value as `__BORLANDC__`.
`_Windows`	Always defined in Borland C++ 4 because the compiler is meant for compiling Windows programs only.

Pragmas

You can use the `#pragma` preprocessor directive to instruct the compiler to turn on or off specific features. Pragmas vary from one compiler to another. The following is a list of pragmas supported by the Borland C++ 4 compiler:

- `#pragma argsused`
  Instructs the compiler to disable warning messages for unused arguments in the function that follows this pragma.

- `#pragma exit <func> [priority]`
  Sets up `<func>` as a function to be called just before the program exits by calling `_exit`. The function `<func>` should not take any arguments and should not return any value. The `[priority]` should be a number between 64 and 255 (the lower the value the higher the priority). The functions with higher priorities are called after those with lower priorities. If `[priority]` is unspecified, a default value of 100 is used.

- `#pragma hdrfile <filename>`
  Specifies the filename for storing precompiled header.

- `#pragma hdrstop`
  Disables precompilation of headers for any header files that appear after this pragma.

- `#pragma inline`
  Informs the compiler that there is inline assembly language code in the file. This causes the compiler to restart itself with the `-B` option (which is equivalent to this pragma).

- `#pragma intrinsic [-]<func>`
  When the minus sign is not present, this pragma instructs the compiler to use the intrinsic form of the function named `<func>`. Using the intrinsic form of a function implies inline placement of the function's code. This results in faster execution because you do not incur the overhead of a function call. If a minus sign precedes `<func>`, this pragma inhibits the inline placement of the function's code. This also is controlled by the `-Oi` option.

- `#pragma option [options...]`
  Here `[options...]` denotes one or more command line options of BCC (see Table 1.5). You cannot use the following compiler options in `[options...]`:

-B -c -d*name* -D*name=string* -e*filename* -E -Fx

-h -l*filename* -lexset -M -o -P -Q -S -T

-U*name* -V -X -Y

- `#pragma saveregs`
  Generates code to save all registers upon entering a function and restore them (except for the register with the return value) when exiting it. Applies to the function that follows this pragma.

- `#pragma startup <func> [priority]`
  Sets up *<func>* as a function to be called just before the program starts running by calling *main*. The function *<func>* should not take any arguments and should not return any value. The *[priority]* should be a number between 64 and 255 (the lower the value the higher the priority). The functions with higher priorities are called before those with lower priorities. If *[priority]* is unspecified, a default value of 100 is used.

- `#pragma warn +<xxx> or -<yyy> or .<zzz>`
  Turns on or off the generation of warning messages for a specific class of warnings. The tokens *<xxx>*, *<yyy>*, and *<zzz>* are names of warnings as they appear in the `-w` compiler option (see Table 1.6). This pragma overrides the `-w` option. In this case, the warning *<xxx>* will be turned on, *<yyy>* turned off, and *<zzz>* restored to the state it had when the compilation started.

Size and Capacity of Basic Data Types

The size and numerical limits of several standard C data types depend on the compiler. Following the ANSI standard requirement, Borland C++ provides the numerical limits of integer and floating-point variables in the header files LIMITS.H and FLOAT.H respectively. Table 4.6 provides a combined listing of the size and numerical limits of the standard C data types.

Table 4.6. Sizes and numerical limits of basic data types in Borland C++.

Type Name	Storage Size in Bytes	Range of Values
`char`	1	--128 to 127
`int`	2	--32,768 to 32,767
	4 (in 32-bit mode)	--2,147,483,648 to 2,147,483,647 (in 32-bit mode)
`short`	2	--32,768 to 32,767
`long`	4	--2,147,483,648 to 2,147,483,647
`unsigned char`	1	0 to 255
`unsigned`	2	0 to 65,535
	4 (in 32-bit mode)	0 to 4,294,967,295 (in 32-bit mode)
`unsigned short`	2	0 to 65,535
`unsigned long`	4	0 to 4,294,967,295
`enum`	2	--32,768 to 32,767
`float`	4	Approximately 1.2E --38 to 3.4E+38 with 7-digit precision
`double`	8	Approximately 2.2E --308 to 1.8E+308 with 15-digit precision
`long double`	10	Approximately 3.4E --4932 to 1.2E+4932 with 19-digit precision

Knowing the size and numerical limits of the data types can help you decide the type of variable you want for a specific purpose. For example, instead of using a 2-byte `short int` for a variable with values between 0 and 255, you can use an `unsigned char`. Similarly, 4-byte `float` variables might be sufficient where you might otherwise use an 8-byte `double` variable.

Also note that the size of the `int` data type can be a problem for C or C++ code that might otherwise be portable. Although `int` is a 2-byte data type in 16-bit mode MS-DOS, on almost all other systems (including 32-bit mode compilation in Borland C++), an `int` occupies 4 bytes and is the same as a `long`. This size difference can create subtle problems when you move Borland C++ code to other systems. One way to minimize these problems is to use `short` where you need 2-byte storage and `long` where you need a 4-byte data type.

Summary

To fully support MS-DOS and Microsoft Windows environments, Borland C++ includes a number of reserved keywords in addition to those required by ANSI standard C. Many of these keywords are necessary to support the segmented memory-addressing scheme used by the Intel 80x86 microprocessors in MS-DOS systems. The segmented memory architecture also brings up the concept of memory models—a number of standard ways to organize segments of code and data. Borland C++ supports four standard memory models: Small, Medium, Compact, and Large—each of which is activated by a specific compiler option. Additionally, you can mix and match data and functions that require addressing conventions other than those supported by the currently selected memory model.

This chapter also described a number of predefined global variables, preprocessor macros, and compiler directives or pragmas that let your programs take full advantage of the capabilities of Borland C++ 4.

Object-Oriented Programming

Basics of Object-Oriented Programming

Part I provides an overview of the tools that Borland C++ 4 provides for writing programs in C and C++. Part II covers object-oriented programming (OOP).

Object-oriented programming is not new; its underlying concepts—*data abstraction, inheritance,* and *polymorphism*—have been around for quite some time (for example, in languages such as Simula67 and Smalltalk). What's new is the increasing interest in OOP among programmers in general and C programmers in particular. One of the reasons for this growing appeal is the popularity of the C++ programming language, which improves C (the current language of choice among software developers) by introducing several new programming constructs that directly support object-oriented techniques. If you program in C, you will find it reasonably easy to learn the syntax of C++, but you will need to reorient your thinking if you want to use object-oriented techniques in your programs.

The best way to learn C++ is to understand the basic concepts of OOP and see how C++ supports OOP. This book uses this approach, explaining OOP through examples, and at the same time, teaching the C++ programming language—explaining its features and their relationship to OOP. This chapter begins by explaining the basic terminology of OOP. Examples show how you can apply object-oriented techniques in C. Chapter 6, "C++ and Object-Oriented Programming," furnishes you with an overview of C++ with an emphasis on OOP. Chapter 6 also revisits the examples of Chapter 5, "Basics of Object-Oriented Programming," rewritten in C++. Seeing the examples again illustrates how an object-oriented programming language such as C++ makes it easy to apply object-oriented methods.

What is Object-Oriented Programming?

The term *object-oriented programming* (OOP) is widely used, but experts do not agree on its exact definition. However, most of them agree that OOP involves defining *abstract data types* (ADTs), which represent complex real-world or abstract objects, and organizing your program around these ADTs with an eye toward exploiting their common features. The term *data abstraction* refers to the process of defining ADTs, whereas *inheritance* and *polymorphism* refer to the mechanisms that enable you to take advantage of the common characteristics of the ADTs (the *objects* in OOP). These terms are explored in this chapter.

The term *abstract data type* refers to a programmer-defined data type together with a set of operations that can be performed on that data. It is called *abstract* to distinguish it from the fundamental built-in C data types such as `int`, `char`, and `double`. In C, you can define an ADT by using `typedef` and `struct` and implementing the operations with a set of functions. As you will soon learn, C++ has much better facilities for defining and using ADTs.

Before jumping into OOP, you should take note of two points. First, OOP is only a method of designing and implementing software. Use of object-oriented techniques does not add anything to a finished software product that the user can see. However, as a programmer implementing the software, you can gain a significant advantage by using object-oriented methods, especially in large software projects. Because OOP enables you to remain close to the conceptual, higher-level model of the real-world problem you are trying to solve, you can manage its complexity better than with approaches that force you to map the problem to fit the features of the language. You can take advantage of the modularity of objects and implement the program in relatively independent units that are easier to maintain and extend. You can also share code among objects through inheritance.

Second, OOP has nothing to do with any programming language, although a programming language that supports OOP makes it easier to implement the object oriented techniques. As you will see shortly, with some discipline you can use objects in C programs.

Procedure-Oriented Programming

Before you get into OOP, take a look at conventional procedure-oriented programming in a language such as C. In the procedure-oriented approach, you view a problem as a sequence of things to do. You organize the related data items into C `struct`s and write the necessary functions (procedures) to manipulate the data. In the process, you complete the sequence of tasks that solves your problem. Although the data may be organized into structures, the primary focus is on the functions. Each C function transforms data in some way. For example, one function may calculate the average value of a set of numbers, another may compute the square root of a number, and another may print a string. You don't need to look far to find examples of this kind of programming—C function libraries are implemented this way. Each function in a library performs a well-defined operation on its input arguments and returns the transformed data as a return value. Arguments may be pointers to data that the function directly alters, or the function may display graphics on a video monitor.

An Example in C

For a better understanding of procedure-oriented programming, suppose that you want to write a computer program that works with geometric shapes, such as rectangles and circles. The program should be able to draw any shape and compute its area. This section takes a conventional approach to writing such a program.

As shown in Figure 5.1, you can break down the tasks of the program into two procedures: one to draw a shape and the other to compute its area. Call each function with a single argument: a pointer to a data structure that contains a shape's pertinent information, such as coordinates of a circle's center and its radius. For each geometric shape, it is easy to define an appropriate structure, but how do you reconcile these different structures into a single one? After all, the functions need a pointer to a single data structure. In such cases, a common technique is to combine the different structures into one using a C `union` with an additional integer flag to indicate the exact shape being handled by the `union`. In keeping with common C coding style, you should define these data types in a header file, CSHAPES.H, as shown in Listing 5.1. The resulting data type, `SHAPE`, is graphically illustrated in Figure 5.1.

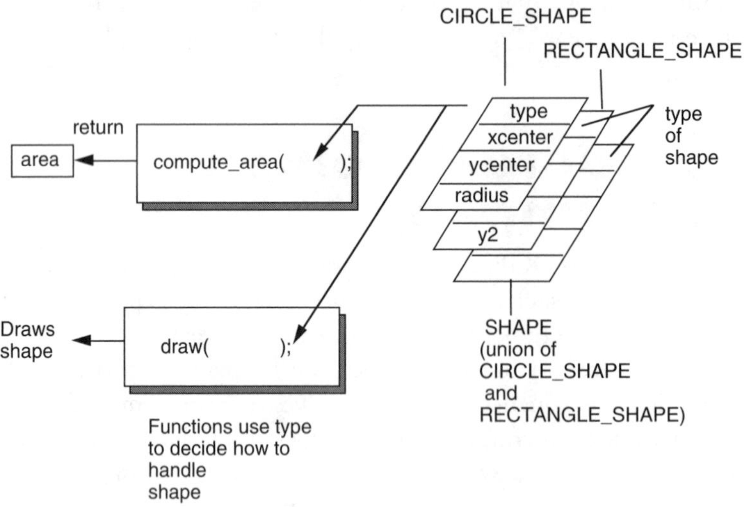

Figure 5.1. C data and procedures for handling geometric shapes.

Listing 5.1. CSHAPES.H. Definition of data types for shapes.

```
/*------------------------------------------------------------*/
/*  File:  cshapes.h
 *
 *  Defines data types for manipulating geometric shapes
 *  in C
 */
#ifndef CSHAPES_H      /* Used to avoid including file twice */
#define CSHAPES_H

#include <math.h>      /* For declaration of fabs and */
                       /* definition of M_PI ("pi")   */

#define T_CIRCLE    1
#define T_RECTANGLE 2
```

```
/* Define each individual shape's data structure      */

typedef struct CIRCLE_SHAPE
{
    short   type;      /* Type of shape (T_CIRCLE)      */
    double  x, y;      /* Coordinates of center         */
    double  radius;    /* Radius of circle              */
} CIRCLE_SHAPE;

typedef struct RECTANGLE_SHAPE
{
    short   type;      /* Type of shape (T_RECTANGLE)   */
    double  x1, y1;    /* Coordinates of the corners    */
    double  x2, y2;
} RECTANGLE_SHAPE;

/* Now define a union of the two structures */

typedef union SHAPE
{
    short            type;       /* type of shape      */
    CIRCLE_SHAPE     circle;     /* data for circle    */
    RECTANGLE_SHAPE rectangle;  /* data for rectangle*/
} SHAPE;

/* Function prototypes */

double compute_area(SHAPE *p_shape);
void   draw_shape(SHAPE *p_shape);

#endif  /* #ifndef CSHAPES_H  */
```

The data structure for each shape is essentially a block of memory. Because the members of a C `union` all share the same block of memory, you need a way to determine which member is valid at any time. This example does so by declaring the very first field in the `union SHAPE` as a `short` integer denoting the type of the shape. Knowing the type, you can access the right structure in the `union` to extract information about the shape. The code in Listing 5.2 shows how the structures in the `SHAPE union` are used.

Once the data structures are defined, you can start writing the functions that operate on the data. In fact, as required by ANSI standard C, the CSHAPES.H header file already includes the *prototypes* for the functions `compute_area` and `draw_shape`. Listing 5.2 shows the implementation of these functions. The functions are straightforward: a `switch` statement is used to handle each shape individually.

Listing 5.2. CSHAPES.C. Functions for geometric shapes.

```
/*-------------------------------------------------------------*/
/*  File: cshapes.c
 *
 *  C functions to operate on geometric shapes.
 */
#include <stdio.h>
#include "cshapes.h"

/*-------------------------------------------------------------*/
/*  c o m p u t e _ a r e a
 *
 *  Compute the area of the shape and return the area
 */
double compute_area(SHAPE *p_shape)
{
    double area;

/* Handle each shape according to its type */

    switch(p_shape->type)
    {
        case T_CIRCLE:
            area = M_PI * p_shape->circle.radius
                        * p_shape->circle.radius;
            break;

        case T_RECTANGLE:
            area = fabs(
               (p_shape->rectangle.x2 - p_shape->rectangle.x1) *
               (p_shape->rectangle.y2 - p_shape->rectangle.y1));
            break;

        default:  printf("Unknown shape in 'compute_area'!\n");
    }
    return area;
}
```

```
/*--------------------------------------------------------------*/
/*  d r a w
 *
 *  "Draw" a shape (print information about shape)
 */
void draw(SHAPE *p_shape)
{
/* Handle each shape according to its type */
    printf("Draw: ");
    switch(p_shape->type)
    {
        case T_CIRCLE:
            printf("Circle of radius %f at (%f, %f)\n",
                    p_shape->circle.radius,
                    p_shape->circle.x, p_shape->circle.y);
            break;

        case T_RECTANGLE:
            printf("Rectangle with corners:"
                   " (%f, %f) at (%f, %f)\n",
                    p_shape->rectangle.x1,
                    p_shape->rectangle.y1,
                    p_shape->rectangle.x2,
                    p_shape->rectangle.y2);
            break;

        default:  printf("Unknown shape in 'draw'!\n");
    }
}
```

To keep the program simple, this example does not proceed with the steps that actually display the shapes on a particular graphics device. Instead, the `draw` function simply prints the name, location, and size of the shape. The `compute_area` function uses a standard formula to compute the area and return the result.

You can test these functions with the simple program STEST1.C, shown in Listing 5.3. This program defines an array of two shapes and initializes them. It then computes the area of each shape and "draws" it. In a more realistic implementation, you might include utility functions such as `create_circle` and `create_rectangle` to dynamically allocate and initialize a `SHAPE union` and return a pointer to it.

Listing 5.3. STEST1.C. Program to test shape-manipulation functions.

```
/*-------------------------------------------------------------*/
/*  File:  stest1.c
 *
 *  Program to test shape-handling functions of Listing 5.2.
 *  Compile and link with the file shown in Listing 5.1
 */
#include <stdio.h>
#include "cshapes.h"

int main()
{
    int i;
    SHAPE s[2];

/* Initialize the shapes */

/* A 40x20 rectangle with lower left corner at (80,30) */
    s[0].type = T_RECTANGLE;
    s[0].rectangle.x1 = 80.0;
    s[0].rectangle.y1 = 30.0;
    s[0].rectangle.x2 = 120.0;
    s[0].rectangle.y2 = 50.0;

/* A circle at (200.0, 100.0) of radius 50.0 units */
    s[1].type = T_CIRCLE;
    s[1].circle.x = 200.0;
    s[1].circle.y = 100.0;
    s[1].circle.radius = 50.0;

/* Compute the areas... */
    for(i = 0; i < 2; i++)
        printf("Area of shape[%d] = %f\n", i,
                                   compute_area(&s[i]));

/* Draw the shapes... */
    for(i = 0; i < 2; i++) draw(&s[i]);
    return 0;
}
```

You can build the `stest1.c` program by compiling and linking the files shown in Listings 5.2 and 5.3. In BCW, create a new project and add the files STEST1.C and CSHAPES.C to the project. Then select the Make all option from the Project menu to create the executable file STEST1.EXE. (For more information on BCW, consult Chapter 1, "The Borland C++ Programming Environment.")

When you run `stest1.c` by selecting Run from the Debug menu in BCW, it displays a window with the following output:

```
Area of shape[0] = 800.000000
Area of shape[1] = 7853.981634
Draw: Rectangle with corners: (80.000000, 30.000000) at (120.000000,
50.000000)
Draw: Circle of radius 50.000000 at (200.000000, 100.000000)
```

Even though this example is somewhat contrived, it does embody the general style of procedure-oriented programming in C. Programmers design data structures first, and then write procedures to manipulate the data. The usual practice is to handle different types of related data (such as the geometric shapes circle and rectangle) by `switch` statements.

Adding a New Shape

Some problems do exist with conventional procedure-oriented programming. Consider what happens when you want your program to handle another type of geometric shape—say, a triangle. To do this, you must follow these steps:

1. Define a data structure for triangles. If you choose to represent the triangle by the coordinates of its vertices, you might add the following structure to the CSHAPES.H file (Listing 5.1):

   ```
   #define T_TRIANGLE  3

    typedef struct TRIANGLE_SHAPE
   {
       short   type;     /* Type of shape (T_TRIANGLE)   */
       double  x1, y1;   /* Coordinates of the corners   */
       double  x2, y2;
       double  x3, y3;
   } TRIANGLE_SHAPE;
   ```

2. Add a new member to the `SHAPE union` to reflect the addition of the new shape:

```
typedef union SHAPE
{
    short           type;       /* type of shape     */
    CIRCLE_SHAPE    circle;     /* data for circle   */
    RECTANGLE_SHAPE rectangle;  /* data for rectangle*/
    TRIANGLE_SHAPE  triangle;   /* data for triangle */
} SHAPE;
```

3. In the CSHAPES.C file (Listing 5.2), add code in the functions `compute_area` and `draw` to handle triangles. Specifically, you need to add additional case statements in the `switch` statement for each function, as in the following example:

```
/*  In the compute_area function  */

     double compute_area(SHAPE *p_shape)
    {
        double area;

    /* Handle each shape according to its type */
        switch(p_shape->type)
        {
            .
            .
            case T_TRIANGLE:
            {
                double x21, y21, x31, y31;

                x21 =  p_shape->triangle.x2 - p_shape->triangle.x1;
                y21 =  p_shape->triangle.y2 - p_shape->triangle.y1;
                x31 =  p_shape->triangle.x3 - p_shape->triangle.x1;
                y31 =  p_shape->triangle.y3 - p_shape->triangle.y1;

                area = fabs(y21 * x31 - x21 * y31) / 2.0;
            }

           break;
            .
            .
        }
```

```
/*-------------------------------------------------------------*/
/* In function: draw() */
void draw(SHAPE *p_shape)
{
    printf("Draw: ");
    switch(p_shape->type)
    {
        .
        .
        case T_TRIANGLE:
            printf("Triangle with vertices: "
                   "(%f, %f) (%f, %f) (%f, %f)\n",
                    p_shape->triangle.x1, p_shape->triangle.y1,
                    p_shape->triangle.x2, p_shape->triangle.y2,
                    p_shape->triangle.x3, p_shape->triangle.y3);
            break;
        .
        .
    }
}
```

4. Test operations on the triangle shape. For example, you can define a triangle shape and use it as follows:

```
    SHAPE s;
    s.type = T_TRIANGLE;
    s.triangle.x1 = 100.0;
    s.triangle.y1 = 100.0;
    s.triangle.x2 = 200.0;
    s.triangle.y2 = 100.0;
    s.triangle.x3 = 150.0;
    s.triangle.y3 = 50.0;
/* Compute the area... */
    printf("Area of triangle = %f\n", compute_area(&s));

/* Draw the triangle... */
    draw(&s);
```

This exercise illustrates the types of changes you must make when a new data type—a new *object*—is added to an existing program that is written in conventional procedure-oriented style. Notice that you have to edit working code—the switch statements in the compute_area and draw functions—when you want to handle triangles in addition to the rectangles and circles that the program was originally designed to accept. If this were a realistic program with many files, a change such as this would require you to edit switch statements in most of the files. As you will see next, the object-oriented approach avoids this problem by keeping data structures together with the functions that operate on them. This effectively localizes the changes that become necessary when you decide to add a new object to your program. This is one of the benefits of OOP.

Object-Oriented Programming Terminology

As mentioned earlier, there are three basic underlying concepts in OOP:

- Data Abstraction
- Inheritance
- Polymorphism

Individually, these concepts have been known and used before, but their use as the foundation of OOP is new.

Data Abstraction

To understand data abstraction, consider the file I/O routines in the C runtime library. With these routines, you can view the file as a stream of bytes, and you also can perform various operations on this stream by calling the file I/O routines. For example, you can call fopen to open a file, fclose to close it, fgetc to read a character from it, and fputc to write a character to it. This abstract model of a file is implemented by defining a data type named FILE to hold all relevant information about a file. The C constructs struct and typedef are used to define FILE. You will find the definition of FILE in the header file STDIO.H. You can think of this definition of FILE, together with the functions that operate on it, as a new data type just like C's int or char.

To use the FILE data type, you do not have to know the C data structure that defines it. In fact, the underlying data structure of FILE can vary from one system to another.

Yet, the C file I/O routines work in the same manner on all systems. This is possible because you never access the members of the FILE data structure directly. Instead, you rely on the functions and macros that essentially hide the inner details of FILE. This is known as *data hiding*.

Data abstraction is the process of defining a data type, often called an abstract data type (ADT), together with using data hiding. The definition of an ADT involves specifying the internal representation of the ADT's data as well as the functions that other program modules will use to manipulate the ADT. Data hiding ensures that you can alter the internal structure of the ADT without breaking the programs that call the functions operating on that ADT. Thus, C's FILE data type is an example of an ADT (see Figure 5.2).

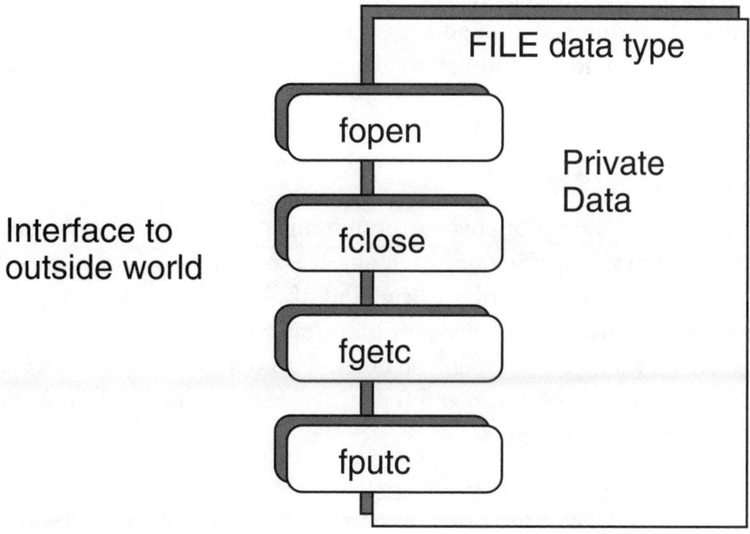

Figure 5.2. C's FILE type as an example of an ADT.

Objects, Classes, and Methods

In OOP, you create an *object* from an ADT. Essentially, an ADT is a collection of variables and the functions necessary to operate on those variables. The variables represent the information contained in the object, whereas the functions define the operations that can be performed on that object. You can think of the ADT as a template from which specific instances of objects can be created as needed. The term `class` is often used for this template; consequently, a class is synonymous with an ADT. In fact, C++ provides the `class` declaration precisely for defining an ADT—the template from which objects are created. The ADT is a template for objects in the sense that creating an object involves setting aside a block of memory for the variables of that object.

The functions that operate on an object are known as *methods.* This term comes from the object-oriented language Smalltalk. Methods define the behavior of an object. In C++, methods are called the *member functions* of the class.

Another common OOP concept also originated in Smalltalk: the idea of *sending a message* to an object which directs it to perform an operation by invoking one of the methods. In C++, you do this by calling the appropriate member function of the object. For objects implemented in C, you can send a message by calling a function that accepts a pointer to a data structure that represents the ADT's internal structure. Of course, the function must be capable of handling the operation you want. For instance, C's file I/O routines accept a pointer to the `FILE` structure as an argument. The file I/O routines then use that pointer to identify the file on which the I/O operation will be performed.

Inheritance

Data abstraction does not cover an important characteristic of objects: real-world objects do not exist in isolation. Each object is related to one or more other objects. In fact, you can often describe a new kind of object by pointing out how the new object's characteristics and behavior differ from that of a class of objects that already exists. This is what you do when you describe an object with a sentence such as "B is just like A, except that B has...and B does...." Here, you are defining objects of type B in terms of those of type A.

This notion of defining a new object in terms of an old one is an integral part of OOP. The term *inheritance* is used for this concept because you can think of one class of objects inheriting the data and behavior from another class. Inheritance imposes a hierarchical relationship on classes whereas a child class inherits from its parent. In C++ terminology, the parent class is the *base class,* and the child class is the *derived class.*

Multiple Inheritance

A real-world object often exhibits characteristics that it inherits from more than one type of object. For example, you could classify a lion as a carnivore on the basis of its eating habits, or as a mammal on the basis of its biological class. When modeling a corporation, you may want to describe a technical manager as someone who is an engineer as well as a manager. An example from the programming world is a full-screen text editor. It displays a block of text on-screen, and it also stores the text in an internal buffer so that you can perform operations (such as inserting a character, deleting a character, and so on). Thus, you may want to say that a text editor inherits its behavior from two classes: a *text buffer* class and a *text display* class that, for instance, manages an 80-character by 25-line text display area.

These examples illustrate *multiple inheritance*—the idea that a class can be derived from more than one base class. Many object-oriented programming languages do not support multiple inheritance, but C++ does.

Polymorphism

In a literal sense, *polymorphism* means the quality of having more than one form. In the context of OOP, polymorphism means that a single operation can behave differently in different objects. In other words, different objects can react differently to the same message. For example, consider the operation of addition. For two numbers, addition should generate the sum. In a programming language that supports OOP, you should be able to express the operation of addition with a single operator: a plus sign (+). When this is supported, you can use the expression `x+y` to denote the sum of `x` and `y` for many different types of `x` and `y`: integers, floating-point numbers, and complex numbers, to name a few. You can even define the + operation to mean the concatenation of two strings.

Similarly, suppose a number of geometric shapes all respond to the message `draw`. Each object reacts to this message by displaying its shape on a display screen. Obviously, the actual mechanism for displaying the object differs from one shape to another, but all shapes perform this task in response to the same message.

Polymorphism helps by enabling you to simplify the syntax that performs the same operation on a collection of objects. For example, by exploiting polymorphism, you can compute the area of each geometric shape in an array of shapes with a simple loop like this:

```
/* Assume "shapes" is an array of shapes (rectangles, circles,
 * etc.) and "compute_area" is a function that computes the
 * area of a shape
 */
for (i = 0; i < number_of_shapes; i++)
    area_of_shape = shapes[i].compute_area();
```

The program can do this because, regardless of the exact geometric shape, each object supports the `compute_area` function and computes the area in a way appropriate for that shape.

Object-Oriented Programming in C

Once you know the basic concepts of OOP, it isn't difficult to implement them in a C program, provided you have somehow identified the objects and what they do. Deciding how to organize your software around objects—physical or abstract—falls under the topic of object-oriented analysis and design. The remainder of this chapter uses the geometric shapes as an example and shows one way to handle these shapes using object-oriented techniques.

Defining Objects in C

To illustrate the use of OOP techniques in C, consider the example of the geometric shapes introduced earlier in this chapter to explain procedural programming. The task is to write a computer program that handles geometric shapes, such as rectangles and circles. The program should draw any shape and compute its area.

To implement the program using objects, you should first work out the details of how to support message-handling and inheritance. Figure 5.3 gives an overview of the data structures you can use to implement the objects.

An easy way to handle messages is to assign each message an identifier (ID). You can associate each message ID with the pointer to a function that handles the message. To maintain this association, you can use a data structure such as the `MESSAGE` structure shown below:

```
typedef struct MESSAGE
{
    int  message_id;            /* Message identifier        */
    int  (*message_handler)(); /* Function to handle message */
} MESSAGE;
```

With this definition of `MESSAGE`, a program can handle messages for a class by maintaining an array of `MESSAGE` structures (you can think of this as a table of messages). To exploit inheritance, each class data structure needs a pointer to the base class. This pointer will be `NULL` for any class not derived from anything. Thus, a possible declaration of the `CLASS` data structure is as follows:

```
typedef struct CLASS
{
```

```
    struct CLASS *base_class;   /* Pointer to "base" class */
    int          data_size;     /* Size of instance's data */
    int          num_messages;  /* Number of messages      */
    MESSAGE      *messages;     /* Table of messages       */
} CLASS;
```

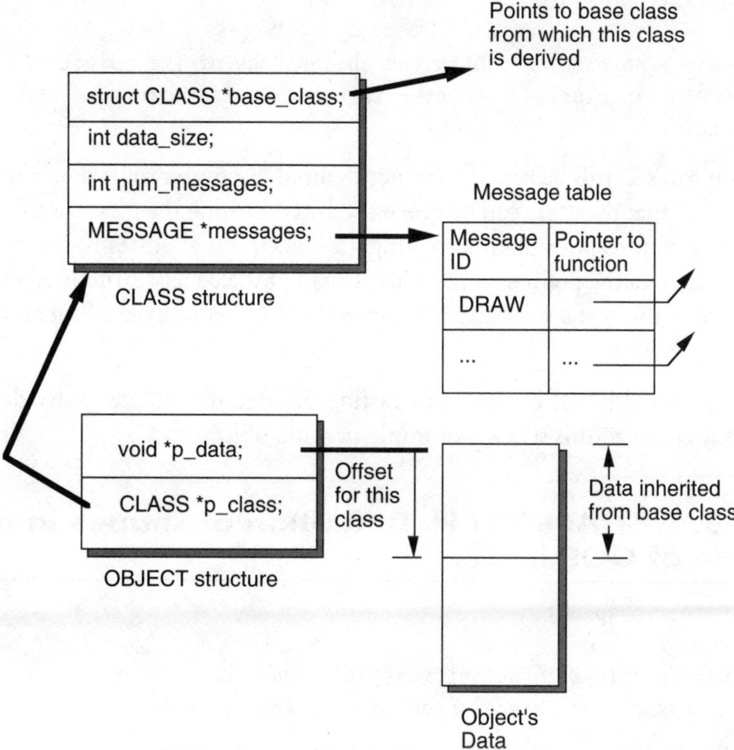

Figure 5.3. Data structures for OOP in C.

Later on, you will see a utility function that sends messages to objects. That function handles the messages by searching the `messages` array for an entry with a matching message ID and by calling the function with the pointer that is stored in that entry. You can implement inheritance by sending unprocessed messages to the base class through the `base_class` pointer.

Because the `CLASS` structure has only one base class, this implementation does not support multiple inheritance. If you want multiple inheritance, you must make room for more than one base class, perhaps through an array of pointers in place of the lone `base_class` pointer in the `CLASS` structure.

The CLASS structure can facilitate the handling of messages sent to an object, but it cannot accommodate the object's data. This is because each object has its own data. In other words, a single copy of the class structure can serve all the objects of that class, but each object must have room for its own data. You can handle this by defining a data structure specifically meant to hold the instance-specific data of an object:

```
typedef struct OBJECT
{
    void   *p_data;  /* Data for an instance of the object */
    CLASS  *p_class; /* Pointer to the class structure     */
} OBJECT;
```

As you can see, this OBJECT data structure holds a pointer to its data and a pointer to its class so that messages can be processed by consulting the message table in the class. The function responsible for creating an object also allocates room for the object's data and saves the pointer in the p_data field of the OBJECT structure. The data_size variable in the CLASS structure represents the number of bytes of memory needed for an object's data.

The file SHAPEOBJ.H shown in Listing 5.4 declares the necessary data structures and functions to this scheme of implementing objects in C.

Listing 5.4. SHAPEOBJ.H. Definition of shapes in an example of OOP in C.

```
/*  File:  shapeobj.h
 *
 *  Header file with definitions of shapes for
 *  an example of object-oriented programming in C.
 *
 */

#if !defined(SHAPEOBJ_H)
#define SHAPEOBJ_H

#include <stdio.h>
#include <stdlib.h>    /* For mem. alloc routines        */
#include <stdarg.h>   /* For variable no. of arguments */
#include <math.h>     /* For declaration of fabs and   */
                      /* definition of M_PI ("pi")     */
```

```
typedef struct MESSAGE
{
    int  message_id;          /* Message identifier        */
    int  (*message_handler)(); /* Function to handle message */
} MESSAGE;

typedef struct CLASS
{
    struct CLASS *base_class;  /* Pointer to "base" class */
    int          data_size;    /* Size of instance's data */
    int          num_messages; /* Number of messages      */
    MESSAGE      *messages;    /* Table of messages       */
} CLASS;

typedef struct OBJECT
{
    void   *p_data;  /* Data for an instance of the object */
    CLASS  *p_class; /* Pointer to the class structure     */
} OBJECT;

/* Define some messages */
#define  ALLOCATE_DATA 1
#define  DRAW          2
#define  COMPUTE_AREA  3

/* Functions to create objects */

OBJECT *new_circle(double x, double y, double radius);
OBJECT *new_rectangle(double x1, double y1,
                      double x2, double y2);

/* Utility functions to handle messages */

int send_message(OBJECT *p_obj, int msgid, ...);
int class_message(CLASS *p_class, OBJECT *p_obj, int msgid,
              va_list argp);
void *allocate_memory(size_t bytes);
int  get_offset(CLASS *p_class);

#endif /* #if !defined(SHAPEOBJ_H) */
```

Implementing Geometrical Shapes

To illustrate the use of these structures, implement two shapes: a circle and a rectangle. Because each shape must draw itself and compute its area, move these functions to a common base class called generic_shape. Figure 5.4 shows the inheritance hierarchy of shapes.

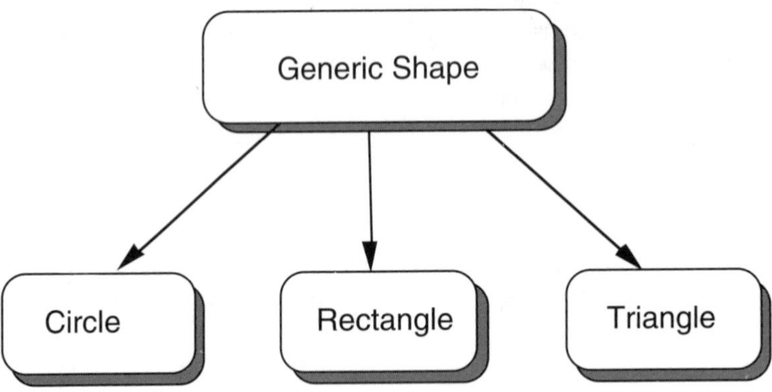

Figure 5.4. Inheritance hierarchy of geometric shapes.

Listings 5.5, 5.6, and 5.7 show the implementation of the generic shape, the circle, and the rectangle, respectively. If you study the listings, you will notice that each file includes a CLASS structure properly initialized with a message table, a pointer to the base class, if any, and the size of the data structure for each instance of that class. The circle and rectangle classes include functions that you can call to create an instance of each. For example, to create a circle, you call the new_circle function (see Listing 5.6) with the coordinates of the center and radius as arguments. This function allocates an OBJECT structure, sends a message to the base class for allocating the instance data, and returns a pointer to the newly allocated OBJECT structure.

Listing 5.5. ANYSHAPE.C. Implementation of a generic shape class.

```
/*  File:  anyshape.c
 *
 *  This is the generic "shape" class.
 *  Data and functions common to all shapes appear here.
 *
```

```
 */
#include "shapeobj.h"

static int allocate_data(OBJECT *p_obj, va_list argp);

static MESSAGE messages[] =
{
    ALLOCATE_DATA,  allocate_data
};

/* The "class" data structure */

CLASS generic_shape =
{
    NULL,                                /* No base class     */
    0,                                   /* No common data    */
    sizeof(messages)/sizeof(MESSAGE),    /* How many messages */
    messages                             /* Message table     */
};

/*--------------------------------------------------------------*/
/*  a l l o c a t e _ d a t a
 *
 *  Allocate memory for an object's data.
 */
static int allocate_data(OBJECT *p_obj, va_list argp)
{
    CLASS  *p_class;
    int    size = 0;

/* Determine sum of instance data sizes for each class in the
 * hierarchy of this object
 */
    for(p_class = p_obj->p_class, size = 0;
        p_class != NULL; p_class = p_class->base_class)
            size += p_class->data_size;

/* Allocate the necessary number of bytes */
    p_obj->p_data = allocate_memory(size);

    return 1;
}
```

Listing 5.6. O_CIRCLE.C Implementation of the `circle` class.

```
/*  File:  o_circle.c
 *
 *  This is the circle class of shapes
 */

#include "shapeobj.h"

typedef double *P_DOUBLE;

typedef struct CIRCLE_DATA
{
    double  x, y;    /* Coordinates of center */
    double  radius;  /* Radius of circle      */
} CIRCLE_DATA;

extern CLASS generic_shape; /* The base class */

static int compute_area(OBJECT *p_obj, va_list argp);
static int draw(OBJECT *p_obj, va_list argp);

static MESSAGE messages[] =
{
    COMPUTE_AREA,  compute_area,
    DRAW,          draw
};

/* The "class" data structure */

CLASS circle_class =
{
    &generic_shape,                    /* Ptr to base class   */
    sizeof(CIRCLE_DATA),               /* Data for circles    */
    sizeof(messages)/sizeof(MESSAGE), /* Number of messages */
    messages                           /* The message table   */
};

static int circle_offset = -1;  /* Offset to circle's data   */
/*-----------------------------------------------------------*/
/*  n e w _ c i r c l e
 *
 *  Create an instance of a circle and initialize it
 */
```

```
OBJECT *new_circle(double x, double y, double radius)
{
    OBJECT   *p_obj;
    CIRCLE_DATA *p_data;

    p_obj = (OBJECT *) allocate_memory(sizeof(OBJECT));
    p_obj->p_class = &circle_class;

/* Send message to allocate memory for data */
    send_message(p_obj, ALLOCATE_DATA, 0);

/* Get offset to circle-specific data */
    if(circle_offset < 0)
        circle_offset = get_offset(&circle_class);
    p_data = (CIRCLE_DATA *)((char *)p_obj->p_data +
                                     circle_offset);
    p_data->x = x;
    p_data->y = y;
    p_data->radius = radius;

    return(p_obj);
}
/*-------------------------------------------------------------*/
/*  c o m p u t e _ a r e a
 *
 *  Compute area of circle. Arguments expected:
 *      pointer to a double where answer is returned.
 */
static int compute_area(OBJECT *p_obj, va_list argp)
{
    int           status = 0;
    double        *p_area;
    CIRCLE_DATA   *p_data;

/* Set up the pointer to circle's data */
    p_data = (CIRCLE_DATA *)((char *)p_obj->p_data +
                                circle_offset);
/* Get pointer to double where answer is to be returned */
    p_area = va_arg(argp, P_DOUBLE);
    if(p_area != NULL)
    {
```

continues

Listing 5.6. continued

```
        *p_area = M_PI * p_data->radius * p_data->radius;
        status = 1;
    }
    return(status);
}
/*-------------------------------------------------------------*/
/*  d r a w
 *
 *  Draw the circle (for now, just print a message).
 *  Does not expect any arguments
 */
static int draw(OBJECT *p_obj, va_list argp)
{
    CIRCLE_DATA   *p_data;

/* Set up the pointer to circle's data */
    p_data = (CIRCLE_DATA *)((char *)p_obj->p_data +
                             circle_offset);
    printf("Draw: Circle of radius %f at (%f, %f)\n",
           p_data->radius, p_data->x, p_data->y);

    return 1;
}
```

Listing 5.7. O_RECT.C. Implementation of the `rectangle` class.

```
/*  File:  o_rect.c
 *
 *  This is the rectangle class of shapes
 */

#include "shapeobj.h"

typedef double *P_DOUBLE;

typedef struct RECTANGLE_DATA
{
    double  x1, y1;  /* Coordinates of the corners   */
    double  x2, y2;
```

```
} RECTANGLE_DATA;

extern CLASS generic_shape; /* The base class */

static int compute_area(OBJECT *p_obj, va_list argp);
static int draw(OBJECT *p_obj, va_list argp);

static MESSAGE messages[] =
{
    COMPUTE_AREA,  compute_area,
    DRAW,          draw
};

/* The "class" data structure */

CLASS rectangle_class =
{
    &generic_shape,                     /* Ptr to base class  */
    sizeof(RECTANGLE_DATA),             /* Data for rectangles*/
    sizeof(messages)/sizeof(MESSAGE),   /* Number of messages */
    messages                            /* The message table  */
};

static int rectangle_offset = -1; /* Offset to rectangle's data*/
/*-------------------------------------------------------------*/
/*  n e w _ r e c t a n g l e
 *
 *  Create an instance of a rectangle and initialize it
 */
OBJECT *new_rectangle(double x1, double y1, double x2, double y2)
{
    OBJECT   *p_obj;
    RECTANGLE_DATA *p_data;

    p_obj = (OBJECT *) allocate_memory(sizeof(OBJECT));
    p_obj->p_class = &rectangle_class;

/* Send message to allocate memory for data */
    send_message(p_obj, ALLOCATE_DATA, 0);

/* Get offset to rectangle-specific data */
    if(rectangle_offset < 0)
        rectangle_offset = get_offset(&rectangle_class);
```

continues

Listing 5.7. continued

```
    p_data = (RECTANGLE_DATA *)((char *)p_obj->p_data +
                                      rectangle_offset);

    p_data->x1 = x1;
    p_data->y1 = y1;
    p_data->x2 = x2;
    p_data->y2 = y2;

    return(p_obj);
}
/*--------------------------------------------------------------*/
/*  c o m p u t e _ a r e a
 *
 *  Compute area of a rectangle. Arguments expected:
 *      pointer to a double where answer is returned.
 */
static int compute_area(OBJECT *p_obj, va_list argp)
{
    int            status = 0;
    double         *p_area;
    RECTANGLE_DATA   *p_data;

/* Set up the pointer to rectangle's data */
    p_data = (RECTANGLE_DATA *)((char *)p_obj->p_data +
                                rectangle_offset);
/* Get pointer to double where answer is to be returned */
    p_area = va_arg(argp, P_DOUBLE);
    if(p_area != NULL)
    {
        *p_area = fabs((p_data->x2 - p_data->x1) *
                       (p_data->y2 - p_data->y1));
        status = 1;
    }
    return(status);
}
/*--------------------------------------------------------------*/
/*  d r a w
 *
 *  Draw the rectangle (for now, just print a message).
 *  Does not expect any arguments
 */
static int draw(OBJECT *p_obj, va_list argp)
```

```
{
    RECTANGLE_DATA   *p_data;

/* Set up the pointer to rectangle's data */
    p_data = (RECTANGLE_DATA *)((char *)p_obj->p_data +
                                rectangle_offset);
    printf("Draw: Rectangle with corners: "
           "(%f, %f) at (%f, %f)\n",
            p_data->x1, p_data->y1,
            p_data->x2, p_data->y2);
    return 1;
}
```

Allocating an Object's Data

When developing a framework for OOP in C, one tricky problem involves the allocation of an object's data. Suppose you are allocating the data structure for an object with a class that inherits data from a base class. In the current implementation, the data for the base class and the derived class is laid out in a single block with one following the other. Each class can access its data, provided it knows the offset for the start of its data in this block of memory. Figure 5.5 illustrates the layout of data for a derived class and a base class.

For the geometric shapes, the `allocate_data` function handles the allocation of the data block (see Listing 5.5) in the generic shape class. This function figures the amount of storage needed by adding the sizes of data blocks for all classes in the hierarchy and then allocates the data. When an object needs to access its data, for instance in the `new_circle` function of Listing 5.6, it obtains the offset to its data structure by calling a utility function named `get_offset`.

Utility Functions

Because C does not directly support sending messages to objects, you must devise your own means of doing so. For the messaging scheme used in our approach, you can accomplish this by writing a set of utility functions that invoke the appropriate function in response to a message. Listing 5.8 presents the file OOPUTIL.C, which defines a number of utility functions to help implement OOP in C. You may want to study the `send_message` function (see Listing 5.8) to see how messages are dispatched to an object's class and how any message not handled by a class is passed up the class hierarchy.

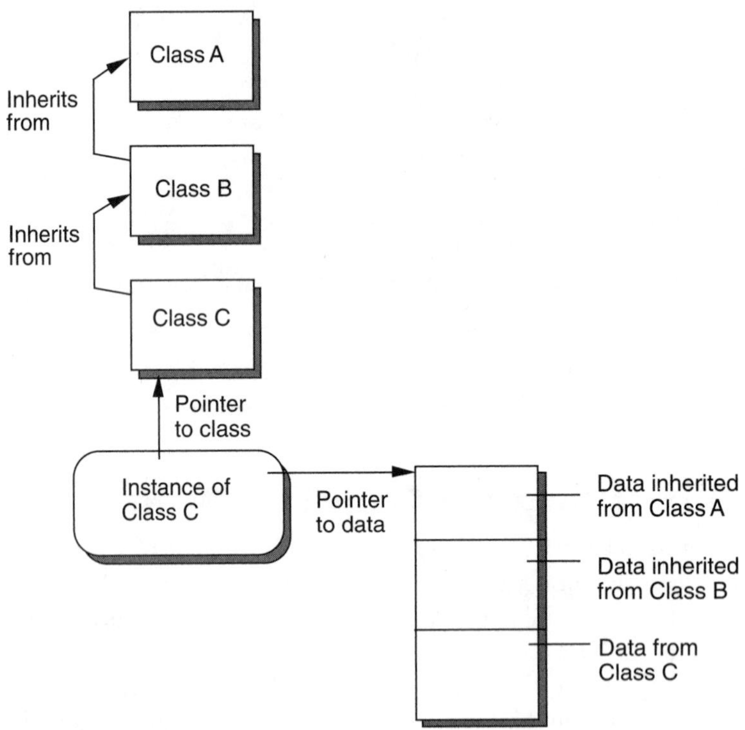

Figure 5.5. Layout of an object's data.

Listing 5.8. OOPUTIL.C. Utility functions for OOP in C.

```
/*-------------------------------------------------------------*/
/*  File: ooputil.c
 *
 *  Utility routines for example of OOP in C
 *
 */

#include "shapeobj.h"

/*-------------------------------------------------------------*/
/*  s e n d _ m e s s a g e
 *
 *  Process message sent to an object by passing it to its class
 */
int send_message(OBJECT *p_obj, int msgid, ...)
```

```
{
    int     status;
    va_list argp;
    va_start(argp, msgid);
    status = class_message(p_obj->p_class, p_obj, msgid, argp);
    va_end(argp);
    return(status);
}
/*-------------------------------------------------------------*/
/*  c l a s s _ m e s s a g e
 *
 *  Search through the message table for a specific message
 *  and call the "message handler" if found
 */
int class_message(CLASS *p_class, OBJECT *p_obj, int msgid,
                  va_list argp)
{
    int i, status;

    if(p_class == NULL) return 0;

    if(p_class->messages != NULL)
    {
        for(i = 0; i < p_class->num_messages; i++)
            if(p_class->messages[i].message_id == msgid)
            {
                return ((*p_class->messages[i].message_handler)
                                                (p_obj, argp));
             }
/* If the message is not handled, send it to the base class */
        status = class_message(p_class->base_class, p_obj,
                               msgid, argp);
    }
    return(status);
}
/*-------------------------------------------------------------*/
/*  a l l o c a t e _ m e m o r y
 *
 *  Allocate memory. Check for failure to allocate.
 */
void *allocate_memory(size_t numbytes)
{
    void *ptr;
```

continues

Listing 5.8. continued

```
    if((ptr = calloc(1, numbytes)) == NULL)
    {
     fprintf(stderr, "Error allocating %d bytes of memory."
          "Exiting...", numbytes);
        exit(1);
    }
    return(ptr);
}
/*---------------------------------------------------------------*/
/*  g e t _ o f f s e t
 *
 *  An instance's data is the concatenation of data of
 *  all classes in its hierarchy. This function computes
 *  the offset to the beginning of data for a specific class.
 */
int  get_offset(CLASS *p_class)
{
    CLASS *p_ct;
    int size = 0;
/* Traverse the class hierarchy up to the "root" class and add
 * up the sizes of data belonging to each class
 */
    for(p_class = p_class->base_class;
        p_class != NULL;
        p_class = p_class->base_class) size += p_class->data_size;

    return size;
}
```

Using the Shapes

Once the framework for C-based OOP is in place, you can easily create the shapes and use them. For example, to create a circle with a radius of 50 centered at the point (100,100), use the following:

```
    OBJECT *circle1;

/* Create a circle at (100, 100) with radius = 50 */
    circle1 = new_circle(100.0, 100.0, 50.0);
```

You can compute the area of this circle by sending it a COMPUTE_AREA message and passing it the arguments expected by this message as follows:

```
double area;
send_message(circle1, COMPUTE_AREA, &area);
printf("Area of circle = %f\n", area);
```

The file STESTOBJ.C in Listing 5.9 shows an example that uses the circle and rectangle shapes. To build the executable file for this example, you need to compile and link the following files:

- STESTOBJ.C (Listing 5.9)
- OOPUTIL.C (Listing 5.8)
- ANYSHAPE.C (Listing 5.5)
- O_CIRCLE.C (Listing 5.6)
- O_RECT.C (Listing 5.7)

Create a project with these files or prepare a makefile for MAKE to manage the compiling and linking operations.

Listing 5.9. STESTOBJ.C. Main function for testing the shape objects.

```
/*-------------------------------------------------------------*/
/*  File:  stestobj.c
 *
 *  Test C-based OOP implementation of geometric shapes.
 */

#include "shapeobj.h"

int main(void)
{
    int    i;
    double area;
    OBJECT *shapes[3];

/* Create some shapes */
    shapes[0] = new_circle(100.0, 100.0, 50.0);
    shapes[1] = new_rectangle(100., 150., 200., 100.);
```

continues

Listing 5.9. continued

```
/* Compute the area of the shapes */
    for(i = 0; i < 2; i++)
    {
     send_message(shapes[i], COMPUTE_AREA, &area);
        printf("Area of shape [%d] = %f\n", i, area);
    }

/* "Draw" the shapes */
    for(i = 0; i < 2; i++)
        send_message(shapes[i], DRAW);

    return 0;
}
```

Adding a New Shape Object

Earlier, this chapter discussed a procedural implementation of the geometric shapes, showing the steps needed to handle a new shape such as a triangle. To see how OOP helps reduce the ripple effect of change, consider the addition of a triangle shape to the shape objects. Here's what you do:

> Prepare a new file—call it O_TRIANG.C—that defines the data and functions for the triangle shape. Listing 5.10 shows a sample implementation of `o_triang.c`.

That's it! All you do is write a single module implementing the new object. Once you have done this, you can use the new shape in your programs (of course, you have to compile `o_triang.c` and link with it to build the program). For example, you can create a triangle, compute its area, and draw it as follows:

```
    OBJECT *t;
    double area;

/* Create a triangle */
    t = new_triangle(100.,100., 200.,100., 150.,50.);

/* Compute its area */
    send_message(t, COMPUTE_AREA, &area);
        printf("Area of triangle = %f\n", area);
    }
```

```
/* "Draw" the triangle */
    send_message(t, DRAW);
```

Clearly, OOP techniques make it easy to add new capabilities to the program because you don't need to modify existing code, only those new modules with code necessary to support the new objects.

Listing 5.10. O_TRIANG.C. Implementation of a triangle shape.

```
/*---------------------------------------------------------------*/
/*  File:  o_triang.c
 *
 *  This is the triangle class of shapes
 */

#include "shapeobj.h"

typedef double *P_DOUBLE;

typedef struct TRIANGLE_DATA
{
    double  x1, y1;   /* Coordinates of the corners   */
    double  x2, y2;
    double  x3, y3;
} TRIANGLE_DATA;

extern CLASS generic_shape; /* The base class */

static int compute_area(OBJECT *p_obj, va_list argp);
static int draw(OBJECT *p_obj, va_list argp);

static MESSAGE messages[] =
{
    COMPUTE_AREA,  compute_area,
    DRAW,          draw
};

/* The "class" data structure */

CLASS triangle_class =
{
```

continues

Listing 5.10. continued

```
    &generic_shape,                    /* Ptr to base class  */
    sizeof(TRIANGLE_DATA),             /* Data for triangles */
    sizeof(messages)/sizeof(MESSAGE), /* Number of messages */
    messages                           /* The message table  */
};

static int triangle_offset = -1;  /* Offset to triangle's data */
/*-------------------------------------------------------------*/
/*  n e w _ t r i a n g l e
 *
 *  Create an instance of a triangle and initialize it
 */
OBJECT *new_triangle(double x1, double y1, double x2, double y2,
                     double x3, double y3)
{
    OBJECT   *p_obj;
    TRIANGLE_DATA *p_data;

    p_obj = (OBJECT *) allocate_memory(sizeof(OBJECT));
    p_obj->p_class = &triangle_class;

/* Send a message to allocate memory for data */
    send_message(p_obj, ALLOCATE_DATA, 0);

/* Get the offset to triangle-specific data */
    if(triangle_offset < 0)
        triangle_offset = get_offset(&triangle_class);
    p_data = (TRIANGLE_DATA *)((char *)p_obj->p_data +
                                   triangle_offset);
    p_data->x1 = x1;
    p_data->y1 = y1;
    p_data->x2 = x2;
    p_data->y2 = y2;
    p_data->x3 = x3;
    p_data->y3 = y3;

    return(p_obj);
}
/*-------------------------------------------------------------*/
/*  c o m p u t e _ a r e a
 *
 *  Compute the area of triangle. Arguments expected:
```

```
 *      pointer to a double where answer is returned.
 */
static int compute_area(OBJECT *p_obj, va_list argp)
{
    int            status = 0;
    double         *p_area;
    TRIANGLE_DATA   *p_data;

/* Set up the pointer to triangle's data */
    p_data = (TRIANGLE_DATA *)((char *)p_obj->p_data +
                               triangle_offset);
/* Get the pointer to double where answer will be returned */
    p_area = va_arg(argp, P_DOUBLE);
    if(p_area != NULL)
    {
        double x21, y21, x31, y31;

          x21 =  p_data->x2 - p_data->x1;
          y21 =  p_data->y2 - p_data->y1;
          x31 =  p_data->x3 - p_data->x1;
          y31 =  p_data->y3 - p_data->y1;

        *p_area = fabs(y21 * x31 - x21 * y31) / 2.0;
        status = 1;
    }
    return(status);
}
/*-------------------------------------------------------------*/
/*  d r a w
 *
 *  Draw the triangle (for now, just print a message).
 *  Does not expect any arguments
 */
static int draw(OBJECT *p_obj, va_list argp)
{
    TRIANGLE_DATA   *p_data;

/* Set up the pointer to triangle's data */
    p_data = (TRIANGLE_DATA *)((char *)p_obj->p_data +
                               triangle_offset);
    printf("Draw: Triangle with vertices: "
                 "(%f, %f) (%f, %f) (%f, %f)\n",
```

continues

Listing 5.10. continued

```
                    p_data->x1, p_data->y1,
                    p_data->x2, p_data->y2,
                    p_data->x3, p_data->y3);
    return 1;
}
```

Problems with OOP in C

Although you can define data structures to implement objects in C, several problems occur when implementing OOP in C:

- As a basic tenet of OOP, you must access and manipulate the object's data by calling the functions provided by that object. This ensures that the internal implementation details of the object stay hidden from the outside world, thus enabling you to change these details without affecting other parts of the program. While object-oriented languages enforce this principle of data hiding, implementing object-oriented techniques in a C program requires discipline on the part of the programmer because C allows code that directly accesses members of an object's data structure.
- You are responsible for ensuring that the data structures of an object are laid out properly to support data inheritance from base classes. You must write utility functions to allow an object to access its data properly.
- The programmer must devise a scheme to invoke methods of objects in response to messages. Inheritance of behavior also requires support functions for properly dispatching messages.

In spite of these problems, the modularity and localization of change afforded by OOP is worth the trouble, even if you write your object-oriented programs in C. Of course, as you will see in Chapter 6, OOP becomes much easier if you use a programming language, such as C++, that supports the basic necessities of object-orientation: data abstraction, inheritance, and polymorphism.

Summary

Object-oriented programming, or OOP for short, relies on three basic concepts: data abstraction, inheritance, and polymorphism.

Data abstraction is the capability to define abstract data types, or ADTs (essentially, user-defined data types), that encapsulate some data and a set of well-defined operations. Such user-defined data types can represent objects in software. The term *class* refers to the template from which specific instances of objects are created. Objects perform specific actions in response to messages (which function calls may implement).

Inheritance is the mechanism that allows one object to behave like another one, except for some modifications. Inheritance implies a hierarchy of classes with derived classes inheriting behavior from base classes. In the context of software, inheritance promotes the sharing of code and data among classes.

Polymorphism occurs when different objects react differently to the same message. In particular, OOP is a new way of organizing your program using a collection of objects with classes that are organized in a predefined hierarchy with a view to sharing code and data through inheritance.

A comparison of two implementations of an example—one using a procedural approach and the other using OOP—shows that the object-based organization enhances the modularity of the program by placing related data and functions in the same module. Therefore, an object-based program can accommodate changes more easily than a procedural program. Although you can implement object-oriented techniques in a procedural programming language, such as C, you can do this more easily when the language has features that support OOP.

C++ and Object-Oriented Programming

Chapter 5, "Basics of Object-Oriented Programming," provided an overview of object-oriented programming (OOP) terminology and demonstrated how to implement the object-oriented techniques in a procedure-oriented language such as C. However, the example shown in Chapter 5 clearly illustrates several problems with using OOP in C:

- The language does not enforce information hiding.
- The programmer must implement message-passing.
- The programmer must devise clever schemes to implement inheritance.

Consider, for instance, C's `FILE` data type. Although you can think of it as an object, the file I/O functions are not closely tied to the `FILE` data type. Also, the internal details of the `FILE` data type are not really hidden because C has no way to prevent you from accessing the members of the `FILE` data structure. When writing object-oriented software in C, you can achieve information hiding only through self-discipline—you and others working on the software must agree not to directly access the contents of data structures that should be hidden.

Although it is possible to use OOP techniques in C, the lack of built-in support for OOP requires extra work to enforce the principles of data abstraction and to set up the mechanisms for inheritance and polymorphism. C++, on the other hand, was designed with OOP in mind. C++ was built by adding certain features to C that ease the task of implementing objects. This chapter describes these features and illustrates the ease of using OOP in C++ by reimplementing the first chapter's example of geometric shapes.

This chapter does not feature a complete description of all the C++ features. Instead, it provides an overview of the features necessary for object-oriented programming. In particular, this chapter does not delve into the syntactical details of C++. Part III, "Learning C++," covers all aspects of C++ in detail. Of course, you can supplement this book's coverage of C++ and OOP by consulting one or more of the references listed at the end of this book.

A Brief History of C++

C++ was developed in the early 1980s by Bjarne Stroustrup of AT&T Bell Laboratories. He created C++ while adding features to C to support efficient event-driven simulation programs. His inspiration came from the language Simula67, which supported the concept of a class. AT&T made many improvements to this initial language before releasing it commercially in 1985. Since then, C++ has continued to evolve with AT&T controlling the releases.

In the beginning, AT&T supplied a translator called *cfront* for converting C++ programs into C, which were then compiled using a C compiler. By the time Release 1.2 of AT&T's C++ came out, C++ compilers were becoming available for PCs and workstations. AT&T released C++ 2.0 in 1989 and followed it promptly with Release 2.1. Microsoft C/C++ 7.0 conforms to the specifications of AT&T C++ Release 2.1.

The X3J16 committee of the American National Standards Institute (ANSI) is currently in the process of drafting a standard specification for the C++ programming language based on the following documents:

- The ANSI C standard (*ANSI X3.159-1989— Programming Language C*).

- The *AT&T C++ Language System Release 2.1 Reference Manual* (also available as *The Annotated C++ Reference Manual* by Margaret A. Ellis and Bjarne Stroustrup, published by Addison-Wesley in 1990).

Object-Oriented Programming in C++

Chapter 5 mentioned three basic concepts that underlie OOP: *data abstraction, inheritance*, and *polymorphism.* To review, here is how these concepts help OOP:

- *Data abstraction* helps you tie data and functions together, which effectively defines a new data type with its own set of operations. Such a data type is called an *abstract data type (ADT)*, also referred to as a *class.*
- *Inheritance* helps you organize the classes in a hierarchy so you can place common data and functions in a base class from which other classes can inherit them (see Figure 6.1).
- *Polymorphism* helps you keep your programs conceptually simple by enabling you to call the same function to perform similar tasks in all classes of a hierarchy.

C++ includes features that support each of these concepts.

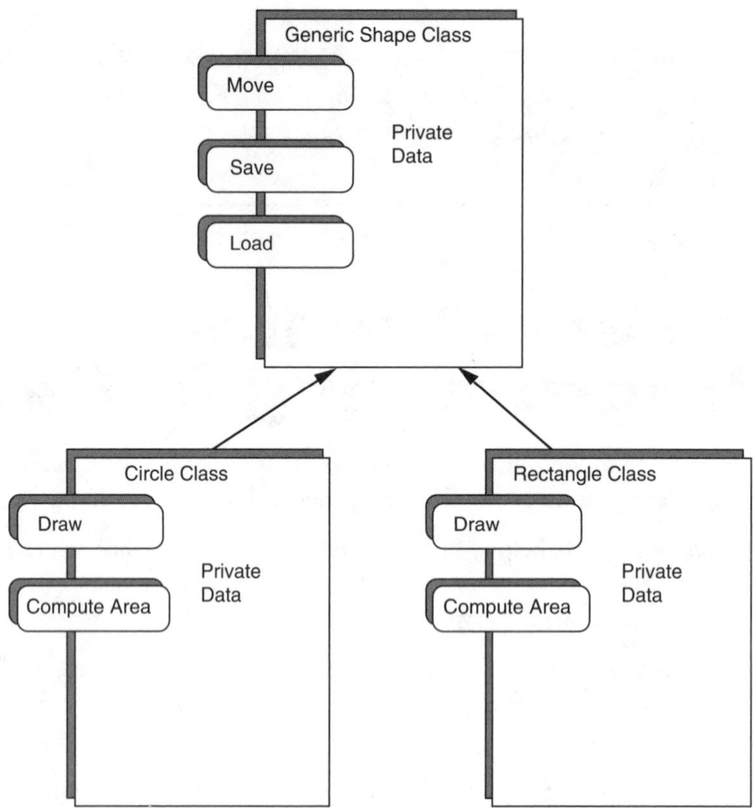

Figure 6.1. Data abstraction, inheritance, and polymorphism in OOP.

Data Abstraction in C++

In C, an abstract data type such as `FILE`, for instance, is declared with a construct such as this:

```
typedef struct
{
    char     *buf;   /* Buffer for file I/O        */
    unsigned flags;  /* Flags to indicate status   */
      .              /* Other internal variables   */
      .
} FILE;              /* This is the FILE data type */
```

The operations in FILE are separate functions which take a pointer to a FILE structure as an argument. C++ introduces the class construct to augment C's struct. Using class, you could define the FILE data type, equivalent to C's FILE, as shown in Listing 6.1.

Listing 6.1. FILE.H. A data type for file I/O.

```
/*  File: file.h
 *
 *  A File class for file I/O
 */
#if !defined(FILE_H)
#define FILE_H

#include <stdio.h>   // For C File I/O function declarations

class File
{
    FILE     *fp;    // C stream
//  ...              // Other internal variables

public:
    File(const char *name,                // Constructor
         const char *open_mode);
    ~File();                              // Destructor
    size_t read(const size_t howmany,     // Read from file
                const size_t elem_size,   //   into buffer
                void *buffer);
    size_t write(const size_t howmany,    // Write buffer to
                 const size_t elem_size, //  file
                 const void *buffer);
};                                        // Note the semicolon
#endif
```

C++ Comments

C++ recognizes the standard C comments which start with the /* characters and end after the */ characters. Additionally, C++ treats as a comment everything following the // characters up to the end of the line. You can use the C format for comments spanning multiple lines, and the new style is convenient for single-line comments.

The Meaning of `const`

The `const` keyword prefixing the name of a variable indicates that the variable is a constant and must not be modified by the program. Similarly, if a function's argument is a pointer and if that pointer is declared as a `const`, the function cannot modify the contents of the location referenced by that pointer.

As a C programmer (especially, if you know ANSI C), you should find most of Listing 6.1 familiar. Don't be concerned, however, if you understand little of this; the rest of this chapter explains much of it. Also, Part III of this book covers the C++ features again, in detail. In particular, Chapter 7, "C++ and ANSI Standard C," provides an overview of ANSI C and compares it to C++.

Listing 6.1 assumes the `File` class will provide a higher level abstraction for file I/O, but that it will use C's file I/O functions for the actual work. That is why a pointer to a `FILE` exists in the class. As you will see later, the constructor of the `File` class sets up this `FILE` pointer when an instance of the `File` class is created.

If you examine the declaration of the `File` class in Listing 6.1, you can see that it looks very similar to C's `struct`, except for the ANSI C-style declaration of several functions following the `public:` keyword. These functions, called *member functions*, operate on the data items being encapsulated in the class. The data items in the class declaration are called *member variables*. The `public:` keyword is significant because all member functions and variables appearing after the keyword are accessible to other parts of the program. The initial members of the class—those that appear before the `public:` keyword—are considered private. Such private variables and functions are not accessible to any function other than those declared within the class. The C++ compiler enforces this rule and displays an error message if any outside function refers to the private members of any class.

When you define a class in C++, you are defining a new, possibly complex, data type. The compiler hides the internal details of this data type from the outside world. The only way the outside functions can access the data is through the public member functions. Therefore, the `class construct` enables you to implement data abstraction and promotes modularity.

class Versus struct

C++ continues to support ANSI C's struct keyword. In fact, C++ expands the definition of struct by allowing the inclusion of member functions. In C++, the only difference between a class and a struct is that the struct's contents are always public.

Defining the Member Functions for *File*

When declaring a class, you declare its member functions, but you don't define them. Typically, you define the member functions in a separate file. That way, you can think of the header file with the class declaration as a specification of the interface to the class, whereas the module with the function definitions is its implementation. Ideally, if the interface is defined clearly enough, programmers using the class don't need to know the details of the implementation. For the File class, plan to call standard C file I/O functions to implement the member functions. You can do this in a straightforward manner as shown in Listing 6.2.

The C++ Filename Extension

This book uses .CPP as the filename extension for C++ source files. Header files have the .H extension, as they do in C.

Listing 6.2. FILE.CPP. Definition of member functions of the File class.

```
/*-------------------------------------------------------------*/
/*  File:  file.cpp
 *
 *  Illustrates data encapsulation in C++
 */
#include "file.h"
/*-------------------------------------------------------------*/
// Constructor — opens a file
File::File(const char *name, const char *open_mode)
```

continues

Listing 6.2. continued

```
{
    fp = fopen(name, open_mode);
}
/*-------------------------------------------------------------------*/
// Destructor — closes a file
File::~File()
{
    if(fp != NULL) fclose(fp);
}
/*-------------------------------------------------------------------*/
size_t File::read(const size_t howmany,    // Read from file
                  const size_t elem_size,  //   into buffer
                  void *buffer)
{
    if(fp != NULL)
        return(fread(buffer, elem_size, howmany, fp));
    else
        return 0;
}
/*-------------------------------------------------------------------*/
size_t File::write(const size_t howmany,    // Write buffer to
                   const size_t elem_size,  //  file
                   const void *buffer)
{
    if(fp != NULL)
        return(fwrite(buffer, elem_size, howmany, fp));
    else
        return 0;
}
```

You do need to be aware of one operator—the scope resolution operator, denoted by a pair of colons (::). When defining the member functions, you use the scope resolution operator to indicate the class with which the function is associated. Therefore, the notation `File::read` identifies `read` as a member function of the `File` class. You can also use the scope resolution operator without a class name to indicate a globally defined function or variable. For example, the following code illustrates how you can differentiate between a globally defined `int` variable and a local one with the same name:

```
int AllDone;        //Variable visible throughout file
```

```
void AnyFunction(void)
{
    int AllDone;  // Local variable with same name
    AllDone = 1;  // Refers to local variable

    if(::AllDone) // This refers to the global "AllDone"
        DoSomething();
}
```

The same approach can be used to call a global function in a member function of the same name.

Constructors and Destructors

Notice that the `File` class contains a member function named `File` and another named `~File`. The two member functions are called the *constructor* and the *destructor* of the class, respectively. The C++ compiler calls a constructor, if one is defined, whenever an instance of a class is created. You can use the constructor to handle any specific requirements for initializing objects of a class. For example, if an object needs extra storage, you can allocate memory in the constructor. In the `File` class, the constructor calls `fopen` to open the file. Notice that the constructor function always has the same name as the class.

You can also define a *destructor* function for a class, if any need exists to clean up after an object is destroyed (for example, if you want to free memory allocated in the constructor). The C++ compiler calls the destructor function of a class whenever it needs to destroy an instance of that class. The destructor has the same name as the class except for a tilde (~) prefix. Therefore, the destructor function for the `File` class is `~File()`. Notice that in the `File` class, you simply close the file that the constructor opened.

Using the *File* Class

You can define an instance of the `File` class and access its member functions just as you would define a C `struct`. For example, to define an instance of the `File` class named `f1` and call its read function, you would write the following:

```
// Open file named "test.dat" for reading
File   f1("test.dat", "rb");
char   buffer[128];
size_t bytes_read;
//...
bytes_read = f1.read(128, sizeof(char), buffer);
```

For a more meaningful example, consider the small program shown in Listing 6.3. It uses the `File` class to copy the contents of one file to another by reading from one and writing to the other.

Listing 6.3. Program to copy from one file to another.

```
/*-------------------------------------------------------------------*/
/*  Main function to copy file "test.dat" to "copy.out"
 */
void main(void)
{
// Open files...
    File f1("test.dat", "rb");
    File f2("copy.out", "wh");

    char   buffer[512];
    size_t count;

// Read a chunk from one file and write it to the other...
    while((count = f1.read(512, sizeof(char), buffer)) != 0)
    {
        f2.write(count, sizeof(char), buffer);
    }
}
```

Inheritance in C++ Classes

When declaring a class, you can also indicate whether it inherits from any other classes. On the first line of the `class` declaration, place a colon (:) followed by a list of base classes from which this class inherits. For example, suppose you want to declare the `circle_shape` class, which is derived from a generic shape class. In this case, the first line of the declaration of the `circle_shape` class looks like this:

```
class circle_shape: public shape
{

// Declare member variables and member functions...

}
```

Here, the shape class is the *base class* and `circle_shape` is the *derived class.* The `public` keyword preceding `shape` signifies that any public member variables and functions of `shape` will be accessible to the `circle_shape` class.

Polymorphism and Dynamic Binding

C++ provides a way to override a function defined in a base class with a function defined in a derived class. Another feature of C++ is that you can use pointers to a base class to refer to objects of a derived class. With these two features you can implement polymorphic behavior in C++ classes.

Suppose you have a base class called `shape` that encapsulates data and functions common to other classes of shapes, such as `circle_shape` and `rectangle_shape`, which are derived from the shape class. One of the functions is `draw`, which draws the shape. Because each shape is drawn differently, the base class defines the `draw` function with the `virtual` keyword:

```
class shape
{
public:
    virtual void draw(void) const{ }
// Other member functions...
};
```

The `virtual` keyword tells the C++ compiler that the `draw` function defined in the base class should be used only if the derived classes do not define it. In this case, the base class defines `draw` as a "do nothing" function.

In a derived class, you can override this definition by supplying a function with the same name, like this:

```
class circle_shape: public shape
{
// Private data...
public:
// Other member functions...
    virtual void draw(void) const;
};
```

Later, you must actually define the draw function for the `circle_shape` class. You can do the same for the `rectangle_shape` class. Once you do this, you can apply the same member function to instances of different classes and the C++ compiler will generate a call to the correct draw function:

```
// Create instances of circle_shape and rectangle_shape
circle_shape c1(100.,100.,50.);
rectangle_shape r1(10.,20.,30.,40.);

c1.draw();    // "draw" from "circle_shape" class is called
r1.draw();    // "draw" from "rectangle_shape" class is called
```

Although this is polymorphic behavior, it is not an interesting example because the C++ compiler (and you) can determine, by studying the code, exactly which function should be called. In fact, this case is referred to as the *static binding* of virtual functions because the compiler can determine the function to be called at compile time.

The more interesting case is that of *dynamic binding*, which happens when a virtual function is invoked through a pointer to an object and the type of the object is not known during compilation. This is possible because C++ enables you to use a pointer to a base class when referring to an instance of a derived class. For example, suppose you want to create a number of shapes, store them in an array, and draw them. Here is how you might do it:

```
    int i;
    shape *shapes[2];    // Array of pointers to base class

// Create some shapes and save the pointers
    shapes[0] = new circle_shape(100., 100., 50.);
    shapes[1] = new rectangle_shape(80., 40., 120., 60.);

// Draw the shapes
    for(i = 0; i < 2; i++) shapes[i]->draw();
```

Notice how you can loop through the pointers to the shapes and call the `draw` member function of each object. Because `draw` is a virtual function, the actual `draw` function that is called at runtime depends on the type of shape that the `shapes[i]` pointer references. If `shapes[i]` points to an instance of `circle_shape`, the `circle_shape::draw()` function is called. On the other hand, if `shapes[i]` points to an instance of `rectangle_shape`, the `draw` function of `rectangle_shape` is called. At runtime, the pointers in the shapes array can point to any instance of the classes derived from the `shape` base class. Therefore, the actual function being called varies according to the pointer's type determined at runtime. That is why this style of virtual function call is called *dynamic binding*.

Geometric Shapes in C++

To illustrate how C++'s object-oriented features help you write object-oriented programs, consider the example of geometric shapes from Chapter 5 that presented a C-based implementation of the shape objects. Here, that example is rewritten in C++. You will notice that the code is much more compact because you no longer need additional C utility routines to support the implementation of objects.

The Shape Classes

The first step in implementing the geometric shapes in C++ is to define the classes. As in the C version of the program (see Chapter 5), you start with an abstract base class called `shape`. This class is abstract because you never create any instance of this class. You use it to encapsulate data and functions common to all derived classes, thus promoting inheritance and polymorphism (through the `virtual` keyword, which is explained later). As shown in Figure 6.2, all other shapes are derived from this base class. See the SHAPES.H file (Listing 6.4) for the actual declaration of the classes.

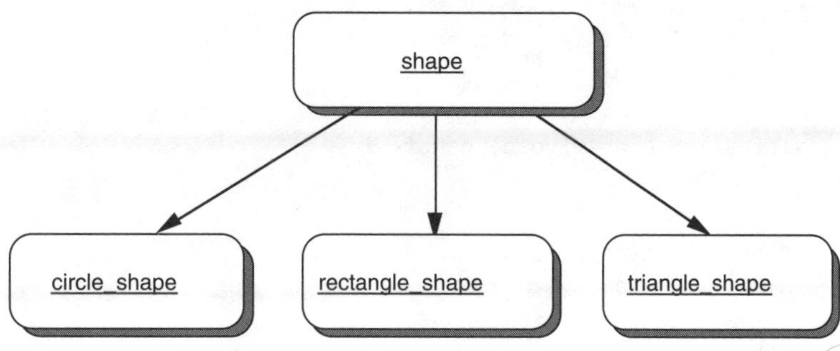

Figure 6.2. A class hierarchy for geometric shapes.

Listing 6.4. SHAPES.H. Classes of geometric shapes in C++.

```
/*--------------------------------------------------------------*/
/*  File:  shapes.h
 *
```

continues

Listing 6.4. continued

```
 *  C++ header file with definitions of geometrical shapes
 */

#if !defined(SHAPES_H)
#define SHAPES_H

#include <stdio.h>
#include <math.h>

// Define an abstract shape class_"abstract" because you
// do not create any instances of this class. It's there
// to encapsulate common data and functions that will be
// shared by all shapes

class shape
{
// In this case, you do not have any data,
// only member functions
public:
    virtual double compute_area(void) const
    {
        printf("Not implemented\n");
        return 0.0;
    }
    virtual void draw(void) const{ }
};

// Define the "circle" class

class circle_shape: public shape
{
private:
    double x, y;   // Coordinates of center
    double radius; // Radius of circle
public:
    circle_shape(double x, double y, double radius);
    virtual double compute_area(void) const;
    virtual void draw(void) const;
};

// Define the "rectangle" class
```

```
class rectangle_shape: public shape
{
private:
    double x1, y1;  // Coordinates of opposite corners
    double x2, y2;
public:
    rectangle_shape(double x1, double y1, double x2, double y2);
    double compute_area(void) const;
    void draw(void) const;
};

#endif  // #if !defined(SHAPES_H)
```

The SHAPES.H header file declares the member functions of the classes, but usually the definitions are placed in separate modules. For smaller functions, you can define a function directly in the body of the class as you have done for the `compute_area` function in the `shape` class.

> **`const` Member Functions**
>
> Use the `const` keyword after the arguments in the declaration of a member function if that member function does not modify any member variable. This tells the compiler that it can safely apply this member function to a `const` instance of this class. For example, the following is permissible because `compute_area` is a `const` member function:
>
> ```
> // Define a const circle
>    const circle_shape c1(100.0, 100.0, 50.0);
>    double area = c1.compute_area();
> ```

Circle and *Rectangle* Classes

Listings 6.5 and 6.6 show the implementation of the `circle_shape` and `rectangle_shape` classes, respectively. Implement each class in its own file just as you would for a larger project. You implement a class by defining its member functions. In this example, each class has two member functions: `draw` and `compute_area`. The definition of each member function resembles a standard C function, except for the scope resolution operator (`::`), which indicates the class to which that function belongs. For example, the `compute_area` function of the `circle_shape` class is defined as follows:

```
double circle_shape::compute_area(void) const
{
    return (M_PI * radius * radius);
}
```

Listing 6.5. CIRCLE.CPP. C++ implementation of the `circle_shape` class.

```
/*-------------------------------------------------------------------*/
/*  File:  circle.cpp
 *
 *  Definition of the "circle" class of shapes in C++
 */

#include "shapes.h"
/*-------------------------------------------------------------------*/
circle_shape::circle_shape(double xc, double yc, double r)
{
    x = xc;
    y = yc;
    radius = r;
}
/*-------------------------------------------------------------------*/
double circle_shape::compute_area(void) const
{
    return (M_PI * radius * radius);
}
/*------------------------------------------------------------------ */
void circle_shape::draw(void) const
{
    printf("Draw: Circle of radius %f centered at (%f, %f)\n",
            radius, x, y);
}$$
```

Listing 6.6. RECT.CPP. C++ implementation of the `rectangle_shape` class.

```
/*-------------------------------------------------------------------*/
```

```
/*  File:  rect.cpp
 *
 *  Definition of the "rectangle" class of shapes in C++
 */

#include "shapes.h"

rectangle_shape::rectangle_shape(double xul, double yul,
                                 double xlr, double ylr)
{
    x1 = xul;
    y1 = yul;
    x2 = xlr;
    y2 = ylr;
}
/*--------------------------------------------------------------------*/
double rectangle_shape::compute_area(void) const
{
    return fabs( (x1-x2) * (y1-y2) );
}
/*--------------------------------------------------------------------*/
void rectangle_shape::draw(void) const
{
    printf("Draw: Rectangle with corners (%f, %f) (%f, %f)\n",
            x1, y1, x2, y2);
}
```

Using the Shape Classes

Listing 6.7 shows a sample C++ program, SHAPETST.CPP, that creates instances of circle and rectangle shapes and tests their member functions. To build the executable file of this program, compile and link the following files in this order:

- SHAPETST.CPP (Listing 6.7)
- CIRCLE.CPP (Listing 6.5)
- RECT.CPP (Listing 6.6)

Each of these files needs the SHAPES.H header file shown in Listing 6.4.

Listing 6.7. SHAPETST.CPP. A C++ program to test the shape classes.

```
/*-------------------------------------------------------------*/
/*  File:  shapetst.cpp
 *
 *  Program to test the "shape" classes
 */

#include "shapes.h"

int main(void)
{
    int i;
    shape *shapes[3];

// Create some shapes
    shapes[0] = new circle_shape(100., 100., 50.);
    shapes[1] = new rectangle_shape(80., 40., 120., 60.);

// Compute the areas
    for(i = 0; i < 2; i++)
    {
        printf("Area of shape [%d] = %f\n", i,
               shapes[i]->compute_area());
    }

// Draw the shapes
    for(i = 0; i < 2; i++) shapes[i]->draw();

// Destroy the shapes
    delete shapes[0];
    delete shapes[1];

    return 0;
}
```

The sample program uses dynamic binding of the `virtual` function by storing pointers to different types of shapes in an array and invoking the member functions of the appropriate class through the pointer. This is a good example of how dynamic binding and polymorphism are used in C++ programs.

Adding a New Shape Class

How would you add a new shape such as a triangle to the classes that already exist? With an object-oriented program, it's easy to accomplish this. Here are the steps:

1. Insert the declaration of a `triangle_shape` class at the end of the SHAPES.H header file (Listing 6.4). Here is the definition:

```
// Define the "triangle" class

class triangle_shape: public shape
{
private:
    double x1, y1;  // Coordinates of the corners
    double x2, y2;
    double x3, y3;
public:
    triangle_shape(double x1, double y1,
                   double x2, double y2,
                   double x3, double y3);
    double compute_area(void) const;
    void draw(void) const;
};
```

2. Define the member functions of the `triangle_shape` class in a separate file. Listing 6.8 shows the file TRIANGLE.CPP that defines the functions.

Once you complete these two steps, you can begin using the `triangle_shape` class in your program. However, you do need to compile and link your program with the TRIANGLE.CPP file (Listing 6.8). For example, you can write code such as this:

```
    int i;
    shape *shapes[3];

// Create some shapes
    shapes[0] = new circle_shape(100., 100., 50.);
    shapes[1] = new rectangle_shape(80., 40., 120., 60.);
    shapes[2] = new triangle_shape(100.,100., 200.,100.,150.,50.);

// Compute the areas
    for(i = 0; i < 3; i++)
    {
        printf("Area of shape [%d] = %f\n", i,
               shapes[i]->compute_area());
    }
```

Listing 6.8. TRIANGLE.CPP. C++ implementation of the `triangle_shape` class.

```
/*-------------------------------------------------------------------*/
/*  File:  triangle.cpp
 *
 *  Definition of the "triangle" class of shapes in C++
 */

#include "shapes.h"

/*-------------------------------------------------------------------*/
triangle_shape::triangle_shape(double xa, double ya,
                     double xb, double yb, double xc, double yc)
{
    x1 = xa;
    y1 = ya;
    x2 = xb;
    y2 = yb;
    x3 = xc;
    y3 = yc;
}
/*-------------------------------------------------------------------*/
double triangle_shape::compute_area(void) const
{
    double area, x21, y21, x31, y31;
    x21 =  x2 - x1;
    y21 =  y2 - y1;
    x31 =  x3 - x1;
    y31 =  y3 - y1;
    area = fabs(y21 * x31 - x21 * y31) / 2.0;
    return (area);
}
/*-------------------------------------------------------------------*/
void triangle_shape::draw(void) const
{
    printf("Draw: Triangle with corners at\n"
           "      (%f, %f) (%f, %f) (%f, %f)\n",
            x1, y1, x2, y2, x3, y3);
}
```

Creating Objects at Runtime

I have not mentioned one important feature of C++: the capability to create instances of a class at runtime. In C, you use memory allocation routines such as `calloc` or `malloc` to dynamically allocate data. These functions return a pointer to the allocated data. When you no longer need the data, you can reclaim the memory by calling `free` with the pointer as the argument. C++ provides the operators `new` and `delete` to create and destroy objects, respectively.

Listing 6.7 illustrates how to use the `new` operator to create the geometric shapes and how to use `delete` to destroy them. Like `calloc` or `malloc`, `new` also returns a pointer to the newly created instance of the class. Unlike `malloc`, which returns a generic pointer (`void *`) that you must cast to the type of your data, `new` returns a pointer to the correct data type. Additionally, `new` automatically calls the constructor of the class to initialize the new instance.

Summary

Object-oriented programming is easier to practice if the programming language supports the basic necessities of OOP: data abstraction, inheritance, and polymorphism. C++ was developed from C by adding precisely the kind of features that support OOP. C++ provides the `class` construct to define abstract data types, supplies the `virtual` keyword to permit polymorphic functions, and includes the syntax necessary to indicate the inheritance relationship between a derived class and one or more base classes. C++'s `class` construct is similar to C's `struct`, but it has many more features. In particular, with `class` you can define the operations on the object—instances of a class—by member functions and operators. A C++ program manipulates objects by calling the member functions only. This enhances the modularity of programs because you are free to change the internal representation of objects without affecting other parts of a program.

III

Learning C++

7

C++ and ANSI Standard C

In Chapter 6, "C++ and Object-Oriented Programming," you encountered a small but important subset of C++ that specifically supports object-oriented programming. C++ possesses many more features that may not directly support OOP, but nevertheless, they are needed to write complete programs. Many of these features match what is in ANSI C, but some small differences exist between the two. This chapter describes some major features of C++ and demonstrates how C++ differs from ANSI C. If you are accustomed to ANSI standard C, knowing the differences between C++ and ANSI C can help you avoid potential problems when writing C++ programs. Consult Chapter 4, "Borland C++ Extensions to Standard C," for an overview of ANSI standard C.

Features of C++

The following sections provide a quick overview of C++ features that differ from those in ANSI C. The coverage of the topics in the following sections is sparse because these topics are covered again in Chapters 8 through 12.

New Features for Functions in C++

As with C, C++ programs contain functions. C++ introduces several new requirements that make functions efficient and safe to use. One helpful change is the use of prototypes for functions. Although you can use prototypes in ANSI C, they are not mandatory. You can use a prototype or define the function before it is called. In C++, you must declare a function before using it.

Default Arguments

As an additional improvement to functions in C++, you can specify the default values for the arguments when you provide a prototype for a function. For example, if you are defining a function named `create_window` that sets up a window (a rectangular region) in a graphics display and fills it with a background color, you may opt to specify default values for the window's location, size, and background color as follows:

```
// A function with default argument values
// Assume that Window is a user-defined type

Window create_window(int x = 0, int y = 0, int width = 100,
                     int height = 50, int bgpixel = 0);
```

When `create_window` is declared in this way, you can use any of the following calls to create new windows:

```
Window w;

// The following is same as: create_window(0, 0, 100, 50, 0);
w = create_window();

// This is same as: create_window(100, 0, 100, 50, 0);
w = create_window(100);

// Equivalent to create_window(30, 20, 100, 50, 0);
w = create_window(30, 20);
```

As you can see from these examples, it is impossible to give a nondefault value for the `height` argument without specifying the values for `x`, `y`, and `width`, because `height` follows them and the compiler can only match arguments by position. In other words, the first argument you specify in a call to `create_window` always matches `x`, the second one matches y, and so on. Therefore, you can leave only trailing arguments unspecified.

Overloaded Function Names

In C++ you can have several functions with the same name as long as their argument lists differ. When this happens, the function's name is *overloaded*. You can use overloading to give a meaningful name to related functions that perform the same task. For example, if you are evaluating the absolute value of numbers, the ANSI C library includes three functions for this purpose: `abs` for `int` arguments, `labs` for `long`, and `fabs` for the absolute value of a `double`. In C++, you can use the `abs` name for all three versions and declare them as follows:

```
int    abs(int x);
long   abs(long x);
double abs(double x);
```

Then, you can use the functions as follows:

```
int i, diff = -2;
long offset;
double x;

i = abs(diff);           // abs(int)    called
offset = abs(-21956L);   // abs(long)   called
x = abs(-3.55);          // abs(double) called
```

The C++ compiler selects the correct function by comparing the types of arguments in the call with those specified in the function's declaration.

When you overload functions in C++, you must ensure that the number and type of arguments of all overloaded versions are different. C++ does not permit overloading for functions that differ only in the type of return value. Thus, you cannot overload functions such as `double compute(int)` and `float compute(int)` because their argument lists are identical.

Inline Functions

Inline functions are like preprocessor macros because the compiler substitutes the entire function body for each inline function call. The inline functions are provided to support efficient implementation of OOP techniques in C++. Because the OOP approach requires the extensive use of member functions, the overhead of function calls can hurt the performance of a program. For smaller functions, you can use the `inline` specifier to avoid the overhead of function calls.

On the surface, inline functions look like preprocessor macros, but the two differ in a crucial aspect. Unlike macros, the compiler treats inline functions as true functions. To see how this can be an important factor, consider the following example. Suppose you define a macro named `multiply` as follows:

```
#define multiply(x,y) (x*y)
```

If you use this macro like this:

```
x = multiply(4+1,6);  // you want the product of 4+1 and 6
```

by straightforward substitution of the `multiply` macro, the preprocessor transforms the left side of this statement into the following code:

```
x = (4+1*6);
```

This evaluates to 10 instead of 30, the result of multiplying (4+1) and 6. Of course, you know that the solution is to use parentheses around the macro arguments, but consider what happens when you define an inline function exactly as you defined the macro:

```
#include <stdio.h>

// Define inline function to multiply two integers

inline int multiply(int x, int y)
{
    return(x * y);
}

// An overloaded version that multiplies two doubles

inline double multiply(double x, double y)
{
    return(x * y);
}

main()
{
    printf("Product of 5 and 6 = %d\n", multiply(4+1,6));
    printf("Product of 3.1 and 10.0 = %f\n",
         multiply(3.0+.1, 10.0));
}
```

When you compile and run this program, it correctly produces the following output:

```
Product of 5 and 6 = 30
Product of 3.1 and 10.0 = 31.000000
```

As you can see from this example, inline functions do not produce the kind of errors that plague poorly defined macros. Because inline functions behave like true functions, you can overload them and rely on the compiler to use the correct function-based argument types. However, because the body of an inline function is duplicated wherever that function is called, you should use inline functions only when the functions are small in size.

friend Functions

C++ introduces another new keyword to help you implement OOP techniques efficiently: the `friend` specifier. The rules of data encapsulation in a class are such that only member functions can access the private data of a class. Of course, a class can provide special member functions that can return the values of its private variables, but this approach may be too inefficient in some cases. In such instances, you may want to allow a function outside the class to directly access data that is private to the class. You can do this by declaring that outside function within the class with the `friend` access specifier. For example, suppose you want to define the nonmember function `add` to add two complex numbers. The following program illustrates how you might use `friend` functions to accomplish this. Note that this is a simplistic definition of a complex class; it is intended to show you how `friend` functions work.

```
#include <stdio.h>

class complex
{
    float real, imag;
public:
    friend complex add(complex a, complex b);
    friend void print(complex a);
    complex() { real = imag = 0.0;}
    complex(float a, float b) { real = a; imag = b;}
};

complex add(complex a, complex b)
{
    complex z;
    z.real = a.real + b.real;
    z.imag = a.imag + b.imag;
```

```
    return z;
}

void print(complex a)
{
    printf(" (%f + i %f)\n", a.real, a.imag);
}

main()
{
    complex a, b, c;
    a = complex(1.5, 2.1);
    b = complex(1.1, 1.4);

    printf("Sum of ");
    print(a);
    printf("and");
    print(b);

    c = add(a,b);

    printf(" = ");
    print(c);
}
```

This program uses the `friend` function `add` to add two complex numbers and the `friend` function `print` to display the results. When you execute this program, it generates the result:

```
Sum of  (1.500000 + i 2.100000)
and (1.100000 + i 1.400000)
 =  (2.600000 + i 3.500000)
```

Reference Types as Arguments

Unfortunately, the `add` function has a drawback stemming from the way C passes arguments to functions. C passes arguments by value—when you call a function with certain arguments, the values of the arguments are copied to a special area of memory known as the *stack*, and the function uses these copies for its operation. To see the effect of *call by value*, consider the following code:

```
void twice(int a)
{
    a *= 2;
```

```
    }
    .
    .
    int x = 5;

// Call the "twice" function
    twice(x);

    printf("x = %d\n", x);
```

Note that this program prints 5, not 10, as the value of x, even though the twice function multiplies its argument by 2. This result (5) happens because the twice function receives a copy of x and any change it makes to that copy is lost upon return from the function.

In C, the only way you can change the value of a variable through a function is by explicitly passing the address of the variable to the function. For example, to double the value of a variable, you can write the function twice as:

```
    void twice(int *a)
    {
        *a *= 2;    // Double the value
    }
    .
    .
    .
    int x = 5;

// Call "twice" with the address of x as argument
    twice(&x);

    printf("x = %d\n", x);
```

This time, the program prints 10 as the result. Therefore, you can pass pointers to alter variables through a function call, but the syntax is sloppy. In the function, you must dereference the argument with the * operator.

C++ provides a way of passing arguments by reference with the introduction of a *reference*, the defining of an alias or alternative name for any instance of data. Syntactically, you append an ampersand (&) to the name of the data type. For example, if you have:

```
int i = 5;
int *p_i = &i;  // a pointer to int initialized to point to i
int &r_i = i;   // a reference to the int variable i
```

you can use r_i anywhere you would use i or *p_i. In fact, if you write:

```
r_i += 10;  // adds 10 to i
```

i changes to 15 because r_i is simply another name for i.

Using reference types, you can rewrite the function named twice to multiply an integer by 2 in a much simpler manner:

```
    void twice(int &a)
    {
        a *= 2;
    }
    .
    .
    int x = 5;
// Call "twice" Argument automatically passed by reference
    twice(x);

    printf("x = %d\n", x);
```

As expected, the program prints 10 as the result, but it looks a lot simpler than trying to accomplish the same task with pointers.

When classes are passed by value, an overhead exists from copying objects to and from the stack—this is another reason for passing arguments by reference. Passing a reference to an object avoids this unnecessary copying and enables an efficient implementation of OOP. This brings us back to the example in the previous section. Now that you know about references, you can rewrite that small complex class as follows:

```
#include <stdio.h>

class complex
{
    float real, imag;
public:
    friend complex add(const complex &a, const complex &b);
    friend void print(const complex &a);
    complex() { real = imag = 0.0;}
    complex(float a, float b) { real = a; imag = b;}
};

complex add(const complex &a, const complex &b)
{
    complex z;
```

```
    z.real = a.real + b.real;
    z.imag = a.imag + b.imag;
    return z;
}

void print(const complex &a)
{
    printf(" (%f + i %f)\n", a.real, a.imag);
}
```

You can use the class in the same manner as its old version. If you look carefully, you can see that to pass arguments by reference, you simply add an ampersand (`&`) after the data type of the argument, thus changing all `complex` types to `complex&`. (You can add a space between the type and `&`.) I have also added a `const` prefix to the arguments to emphasize that the functions `add` and `print` must not alter their arguments.

Overloaded Operators

Just as C++ enables you to define several functions with the same name but with varying arguments, it also enables you to redefine the meaning of operators such as `+`, `-`, `*`, `/`, `%`, `+=`, and `-=` for any class. In other words, you can overload the meaning of operators. Because a class is a new abstract data type, such overloaded operators provide you with the ability to define operations on this data.

For example, instead of writing an `add` function to add two complex variables, you can define the `+` operator to perform addition for the complex class shown earlier. Using `friend` functions and `const` reference types, you might define the `+` operator as follows:

```
class complex
{
    float real, imag;
public:
    friend complex operator+(const complex &a, const complex &b);

    complex() { real = imag = 0.0;}
    complex(float a, float b) { real = a; imag = b;}
};

complex operator+(const complex &a, const complex &b)
{
    complex z;
    z.real = a.real + b.real;
```

```
    z.imag = a.imag + b.imag;
    return z;
}
```

As you can see from the example, defining the operator is just like defining a function, except for a special syntax for the name of the function. This syntax is the symbol of the operator with the `operator` keyword as a prefix.

After you define a + operator for the complex class, you can use it just as you would normally use the + operator for other data types:

```
complex a, b, c;
a = complex(1.5, 2.1);
b = complex(1.1, 1.4);

c = a+b;    // Add two complex numbers a and b
```

Data Declarations in C++

In ANSI C, you cannot mix declarations with the statements of a program. You must declare all variables at the beginning of a block. C++ does not distinguish between a declaration and other statements and it enables you to declare variables anywhere. Thus, in C++ you can write

```
#include <stdio.h>
#include <string.h>
.
.
void convert_string(char *s)
{
    if(str == NULL) return;
    int length = strlen(s);
    .
    .
    for(int i = 0; i <= length; i++)
    {
// Convert characters in the string...
    }
}
```

This feature of C++ is handy because you can declare a variable and initialize it immediately. The program is more readable because the variable is declared and initialized close to where it is actually used.

Another interesting feature of C++ enables you to start using the name of a struct as soon as its definition is started. In C, when you define structures containing pointers to its own type, you typically use constructs like this:

```
typedef struct node
{
    struct node *prev; /* Pointer to previous node */
    struct node *next; /* Pointer to next node     */
    void        *info; /* Other members of struct  */
} node;

node *top_node;        /* Define a node */
```

In C++, the same code becomes much simpler:

```
struct node
{
    node *prev; // Pointer to previous node
    node *next; // Pointer to next node
    void *info; // Other members of struct
} node;

node *top_node; // Define a node
```

As you can see, the name of a struct can be used inside the definition of the struct itself.

How C++ Differs from C

Although it is often casually stated that C++ is a superset of C, especially ANSI standard C, a small number of things in ANSI C do not work quite the same way in C++. A summary description of the differences follows.

New Reserved Keywords

To support object-oriented programming, C++ introduces 16 new keywords in addition to those reserved by ANSI C. You should watch out for any C program that might use these reserved words:

```
asm       friend     private    this
catch     inline     protected  throw
class     new        public     try
delete    operator   template   virtual
```

You will encounter most of these keywords in the rest of this book. Some of them, such as catch, template, and throw, are not yet in widespread use because they are used in new features that were recently added to the language. The template keyword is used to allow the definition of families for types or functions. A mechanism for handling exceptions uses the catch and throw and try keywords.

Function Prototypes

In ANSI C, if a function does not have a prototype, the compiler assumes that the function returns an integer. C++ strictly enforces the prototypes and generates an error if you use a function without first declaring it. Thus, C++ displays an error when compiling the following old-style C program:

```
main()
{
    printf("Hello, World!\n"); // Allowed in C, but not in C++
                               // C++ needs prototype before use
}
```

Of course, in ANSI C you can remedy this by simply including STDIO.H, which declares the printf function. You can also get another type of error from old-style C code where functions are declared only when they do not return an int. For example, many C programs declare and use malloc as follows:

```
char *malloc();
int  *raw_data;

raw_data = (int *) malloc(1024);
```

This code generates an error in C++ because C++ interprets empty argument lists differently than ANSI C. In ANSI standard C, an empty argument list in a function's declaration means that the function takes zero or more arguments, but C++ considers a function declaration with an empty argument list to be equivalent to the following:

```
char *malloc(void);
```

When C++ encounters the call malloc(1024), it produces an error message because it finds an argument where it expects none.

const Variables

C++ requires you to initialize `const` variables when you declare them; ANSI C does not. Thus, you have:

```
const buflen;       // OK in ANSI C, but not in C++
const buflen = 512; // OK in C++ as well as ANSI C
```

Another interesting property of `const` variables in C++ is that `const` integers can be used as subscripts in any constant expression. This is possible because C++ requires `const` variables to be initialized during declaration. Thus, the compiler always knows the value of a `const` integer. This enables the following:

```
const buflen = 512;
char  buffer[buflen];  // Allowed in C++, but not in ANSI C
```

Because `const` integers declared this way are full-fledged variables, you should use them wherever you need constants. In other words, in C++, instead of writing

```
#define  EOF    -1
#define  maxlen 128
#define  Pi     3.14159

char one_line[maxlen];   // Define an array to hold a line
```

you should write

```
const EOF = -1;              // This is a const int by default
const maxlen = 128;
const double Pi = 3.14159; // This is a floating-point constant


char one_line[maxlen];     // Define an array to hold a line
```

void Pointers

ANSI C permits pointers of the `void *` type to be assigned to any other pointer and vice versa—any pointer can be assigned to a pointer of the `void *` type. C++ does not permit the assignment of a pointer of the `void *` type to any other pointer without an explicit cast. The following example illustrates the difference:

```
void *p_void;
int  i, *p_i;

p_void = &i;          /* Allowed in both C and C++      */
```

```
p_i = p_void;          /* Allowed in C, but not in C++   */
p_i = (int *)p_void;   /* Cast makes it OK to use in C++ */
```

Initialization of Character Arrays

In ANSI C, you can initialize an array of three characters with the following:

```
char name[3] = "C++"; // Allowed in ANSI C, but not in C++
```

After the initialization, the array elements `name[0]`, `name[1]`, and `name[2]` are set, respectively, to C, +, and +. However, C++ does not allow this type of initialization because the array has no room for the terminating null character. In C++, if you need to set up the `name` array as you did in C, you must rewrite the initialization as follows:

```
char name[3] = {'C', '+', '+'}; // Allowed in both C and C++
```

Of course, the following initialization is valid in both C and C++, but this sets up a 4-byte array with the last byte set to a null character:

```
char name[] = "C++"; // Allowed in both C and C++
```

sizeof Operator

In ANSI C, the size of a character constant such as the expression `sizeof('Q')` evaluates to the same value as `sizeof(int)`. But C++ correctly evaluates this to `sizeof(char)`. Also in ANSI C, the size of an `enum` variable is the same as `sizeof(int)`. In C++, it is the size of an integral type, not necessarily `sizeof(int)`.

Scope of *enum*

In ANSI C, the list of constants appearing in an `enum` variable are known throughout the file. C++ considers the constants in an `enum` to be local to a `class` or a `struct` and known only to member and `friend` functions of the class. For example, the following code is allowed in C++, but not in ANSI C:

```
struct finite_state_machine
{
    enum state{init, reset, end};
// ...
}

int init(int state);  // Allowed in C++, but not in ANSI C
```

If a class declares an enum variable, functions outside the class can refer to the enumerated constants by explicitly qualifying the name with the scope resolution operator. For example, suppose you want to refer to the enumerated constant `scientific` that is defined in the class named `ios`. You must use the notation `ios::scientific` to access this constant.

Restriction on *goto*

With ANSI C, you can jump into a block of code, skipping over the declarations and initializations that may appear at the beginning of the block. You cannot do this in C++. Here is an example:

```
    goto Start;    // OK in ANSI C, but not in C++
// ...
    {
        int  x = 4, y = 8;
        Node t1;            // This could be a class
        char buf[10];

    Start:
// ...
    }  // Class destructors are called before leaving block
```

Although jumping into a block is a questionable practice in C, such jumps are almost always bound to be fatal in a C++ program because C++ calls constructors for any class objects created at the beginning of a block, and it calls the corresponding destructors when the block ends. Jumping into the middle of a block means that calls might go to destructors for which there are no matching calls to constructors. Typically, this produces a fatal error for the program.

Summary

C++ was created by extending C with features designed to support object-oriented programming. C++'s support for OOP comes through the `class` and `struct` constructs, the concepts of overloading functions and operators, and virtual functions. Many features of the C++ language such as function prototypes and the `void` and `enum` types have been incorporated into ANSI standard C. Although C++ compilers accept most ANSI C programs, certain constructs in ANSI C behave differently in C++. You should watch out for the new reserved keywords and for the strict enforcement of the function prototypes in C++.

C++ Classes for Standard I/O

Chapter 7, "C++ and ANSI Standard C," provided you with an overview of the C++ programming language and how it relates to ANSI standard C. Before you start using C++ to define your own classes, this chapter gets you started with the `iostream` class library, which comes with most C++ compilers, including Borland C++ 4. This library is C++'s equivalent to C's `stdio` library, which includes the `printf` and `scanf` family. This chapter explains the structure of the classes that form the basis of the `iostream` library and shows you how to use these classes for various types of I/O.

C++ I/O Library

Like C, C++ contains no built-in facilities for I/O. Instead, you must rely on a library of functions for performing I/O. In ANSI C, the I/O functions are a part of the standard library. (C++ does not yet have a standard library.) Of course, you can call the ANSI C library routines in C++, but for I/O, Borland C++ provides an alternative to `printf` and `scanf`. Borland C++ 4 includes the `iostream` library, which handles I/O through a class of objects. The following sections describe simple usage of the `iostream` library and explain the class hierarchy that constitutes the library.

Stream I/O in C++

As a programmer learning OOP, you may want to study the details of the classes in the iostream library, but you do not need to know much about these classes to use the library for simple I/O. To begin, you should be familiar with the concept of a stream and know the names of the predefined streams. The idea of a *stream*—a sequence of bytes—figures prominently in UNIX and C. As a C programmer, you have heard the term *stream* in connection with ANSI C's file I/O functions that are prototyped in the STDIO.H header file. A stream serves as an abstract model of I/O devices such as a disk file, the keyboard, the video display, or even a buffer in memory. In ANSI C, each stream has an associated FILE structure that holds the state of the stream and such data items as the buffer used for buffered I/O.

Buffered I/O

Buffered I/O refers to the use of a block of memory as a temporary storage area for the bytes being read from or written to the stream. ANSI C's stream I/O routines and C++'s iostream library use a buffer to hold data in transit to and from a stream. For example, in a buffered read operation from a disk file, a fixed-size byte chunk is read from the disk into a buffer of the same size. The routines requesting data from the file actually read from the buffer. When the buffer has no more characters left, it is automatically refilled by a disk read operation. A similar sequence occurs when writing to a file. Buffered I/O operations are efficient because they minimize time-consuming read/write operations with the disk. If needed, you can turn off the buffering.

Each ANSI C stream is identified by the pointer to its associated FILE structure. You get this pointer back when you open the stream by calling the fopen function. In OOP terminology, this is equivalent to creating the stream object. Not all streams need to be explicitly opened, however. When your C program starts up, three streams are already opened for you. These streams, identified as stdin, stdout, and stderr, are used to get input from the keyboard, display output, and display error messages, respectively. The scanf function reads from stdin, while the printf function sends its output to stdout. The fscanf and fprintf functions can handle I/O with streams that you open.

The C++ `iostream` library is an object-oriented implementation of a stream viewed as a flow of bytes from a source (producer) to a sink (consumer). As you will see later, the `iostream` library includes input streams (the `istream` class), output streams (the `ostream` class), and streams (the `iostream` class) that can handle both input and output operations. The `istream` class provides the functionality of `scanf` and `fscanf`, whereas the `ostream` class has capabilities similar to those of `printf` and `fprintf`. Like the predefined C streams `stdin`, `stdout`, and `stderr`, the `iostream` library includes four predefined streams:

- `cin`, an input stream connected to the standard input (analogous to `stdin` in C)
- `cout`, an output stream connected to the standard output (analogous to `stdout` in C)
- `cerr`, an output stream set up to provide unbuffered output to the standard error device (analogous to `stderr` in C)
- `clog`, a fully buffered stream like `cin` and `cout` (similar to `cerr`)

Later, you will see how to assign other streams to these identifiers so you can redirect I/O to a different file or device.

Using *iostream*

To use the `iostream` library, your C++ program must include the IOSTREAM.H header file. This file contains the definitions of the classes that implement the stream objects and provides the buffering. The IOSTREAM.H file is analogous to STDIO.H in ANSI C.

Instead of defining member functions that perform I/O, the `iostream` library provides an operator notation for input and output. It uses C++'s capability of overloading operators and defines << and >> as the output and input operators, respectively. Figure 8.1 illustrates how these operators work with the `cin` and `cout` streams.

When you see the << and >> operators in use, you realize their appropriateness. For example, consider the following program that prints some variables to the `cout` stream, which is usually connected to standard output:

```
#include <iostream.h>

void main()
{
    int    count = 2;
```

```
    double result = 5.4;
    char   *id = "Trying out iostream: ";

    cout << id;
    cout << "count = " << count << '\n';
    cout << "result = " << result << '\n';
}
```

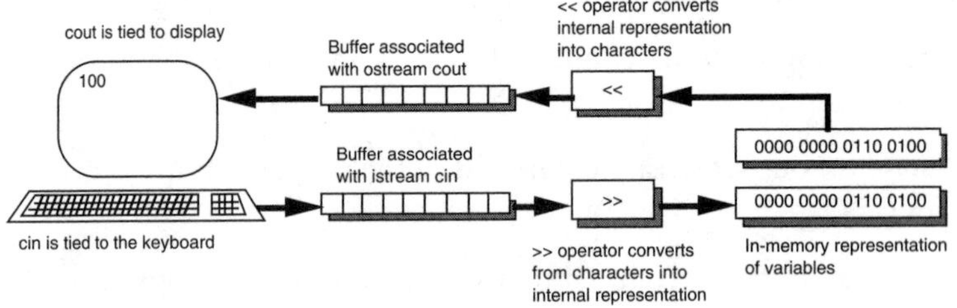

Figure 8.1. Buffered I/O with streams `cin` and `cout`.

When you run this program, it prints the following:

```
Trying out iostream: count = 2
result = 5.4
```

You can make three observations from this example:

- The << operator is a good choice to represent the output operation because it points in the direction of data movement that, in this case, is toward the `cout` stream.
- You can concatenate multiple << operators in a single line, all feeding the same stream.
- You can use the same syntax to print all the basic data types on a stream. The << operator automatically converts the internal representation of the variable into a textual representation. Contrast this with the need to use different format strings for printing different data types using `printf`.

Accepting input from the standard input is an easy process as well. Here is a small sample that combines both input and output:

```
#include <iostream.h>

void main()
{
```

```
    int   count;
    float price;
    char  *prompt =
          "Enter count (int) and unit price (float): ";

// Display the prompt string and flush
// to force it to be displayed
    cout << prompt << flush;

// Read from standard input
    cin >> count >> price;

// Display total cost
    cout << count << " at " << price << " will cost: ";
    cout << (price * count) << endl;
}
```

When you run the program and enter the input shown in boldface, the program interacts as follows:

```
Enter count (int) and unit price (float): 5 2.5
5 at 2.5 will cost: 12.5
```

Ignoring, for the moment, items that you do not recognize, notice how easy it is to read values into variables from the `cin` stream—simply send the data from `cin` to the variables using the >> operator. Like the << operator, you can also concatenate multiple >> operators. The >> operator automatically converts the strings into the internal representations of the variables according to their types. The simple syntax of input from `cin` is in sharp contrast with ANSI C's rather complicated `scanf` function, which serves the same purpose, but needs proper format strings and addresses of variables as arguments.

Using Manipulators

Among the new items in the last example, you may have noticed the identifiers flush (in the first cout statement) and endl (in the last cout statement). These are special functions known as manipulators, which are written so you can alter the state of the stream by placing a manipulator in the chain of << operators. The flush manipulator forces cout to display its output without waiting for its buffer to fill up; the buffer is flushed. The endl manipulator sends a newline to the stream and also flushes the buffer. Table 8.1 summarizes some of the manipulators available in the iostream package. (The manipulators that take arguments are declared in the file IOMANIP.H; the rest are in IOSTREAM.H.)

Table 8.1. C++ `iostream` manipulators.

Manipulator	Sample Usage	Effect
`dec`	`cout << dec << intvar;` `cin >> dec >> intvar;`	Converts integers into decimal digits; similar to the `%d` format in C
`hex`	`cout << hex << intvar;` `cin >> hex >> intvar;`	Hexadecimal conversion as in ANSI C's `%x` format
`oct`	`cout << oct << intvar;` `cin >> oct >> intvar;`	Octal conversion (`%o` format in C)
`ws`	`cin >> ws;`	Discards whitespace characters in the input stream
`endl`	`cout << endl;`	Sends a newline to `ostream` and flushes the buffer
`ends`	`cout << ends;`	Inserts a null character into a string
`flush`	`cout << flush;`	Flushes `ostream`'s buffer
`resetiosflags(long)`	`cout << resetiosflags (ios::dec);` `cin >> resetiosflags (ios::hex);`	Resets the format bits specified by the long integer argument
`setbase(int)`	`cout << setbase(10);` `cin >> setbase(8);`	Sets the base of conversion to the integer argument (must be 0, 8, 10, or 16). Zero sets the base to the default.
`setfill(int)`	`cout << setfill('.');` `cin >> setfill(' ');`	Sets the fill character used to pad fields to the specified width

Manipulator	Sample Usage	Effect
`setiosflags(long)`	`cout << setiosflags (ios::dec);` `cin >> setiosflags (ios::hex);`	Sets the format bits specified by the long integer argument
`setprecision(int)`	`cout << setprecision(6);` `cin >> setprecision(15);`	Sets the precision of floating-point conversions to the specified number of digits
`setw(int)`	`cout << setw(6) << var;` `cin >> setw(24) >> buf;`	Sets the width of a field to the specified number of characters

Using Manipulators for Formatted I/O

You can use manipulators for some simple formatted I/O. *Formatting* refers to the process of converting to and from the internal binary representation of a variable and its character string representation. For example, if a 16-bit integer variable holds the bit pattern `0000 0000 0110 0100`, its character string representation is `100` in the decimal number system and `64` in hexadecimal. If the base of conversion is octal, the representation is `144`. You can display all three forms on separate lines using the following output statements:

```
#include <iostream.h>

int i = 100;  // Integer initialized to 100 (decimal)

cout << dec << i << endl;  // Displays 100
cout << hex << i << endl;  // Displays 64
cout << oct << i << endl;  // Displays 144
```

This produces the output:

```
100
64
144
```

If you want to use a fixed field width of six characters to display each value, you can do this by using the `setw` manipulator as follows:

```
    #include <iostream.h>
    #include <iomanip.h>

    int i = 100;  // Integer initialized to 100 (decimal)

// Set field widths to 6
    cout << setw(6) << dec << i << endl;
    cout << setw(6) << hex << i << endl;
    cout << setw(6) << oct << i << endl;
```

This changes the output to:

```
100
 64
144
```

Here, each variable is displayed in a six-character field aligned at the right and padded with blanks at the left. You can change both the padding and the alignment. To change the padding character, use the `setfill` manipulator. For example, just before the `cout` statements shown above, insert the following line:

```
cout << setfill('.');
```

With that line in place, the output changes to:

```
...100
....64
...144
```

The spaces to the left are now padded with dots, the fill characters specified by the previous call to the `setfill` manipulator. The default alignment of fixed-width output fields pads on the left, resulting in right-justified output. The justification information is stored in a bit pattern called *format bits* in a class named `ios`, which forms the basis of all stream classes. (See the following discussion and Figure 8.2.) You can set or reset specific bits with the `setiosflags` and `resetiosflags` manipulators, respectively. Here is a sample of how these manipulators work:

```
    #include <iostream.h>
    #include <iomanip.h>

    int i = 100;  // Integer initialized to 100 (decimal)

    cout << setfill('.');

// Left-justified labels followed by right-justified values...
```

```
    cout << setiosflags(ios::left);
    cout << setw(20) << "Decimal";
    cout << resetiosflags(ios::left);
    cout << setw(6) << dec << i << endl;

    cout << setiosflags(ios::left);
    cout << setw(20) << "Hexadecimal";
    cout << resetiosflags(ios::left);
    cout << setw(6) << hex << i << endl;

    cout << setiosflags(ios::left);
    cout << setw(20) << "Octal";
    cout << resetiosflags(ios::left);
    cout << setw(6) << oct << i << endl;
```

This example generates the following output:

```
Decimal.................100
Hexadecimal.............64
Octal...................144
```

This output illustrates how the `setiosflags` and `resetiosflags` manipulators work and how they should be used. All you need to know are the names of the enumerated list of formatting flags so you can use them as arguments to the `setiosflags` and `resetiosflags` manipulators. Table 8.2 lists the format bit flags and their meanings.

To use any of the format flags shown in Table 8.2, insert the manipulator `setiosflags` with the name of the flag as the argument. Use `resetiosflags` with the same argument to revert to the format state prior to your using the `setiosflags` manipulator.

Table 8.2. Names of format flags in `iostream`.

Name of Flag	Meaning When Flag Is Set
`ios::skipws`	Skips whitespace on input
`ios::left`	Left-justifies output within the specified width of the field
`ios::right`	Right-justifies output
`ios::scientific`	Uses scientific notation for floating-point numbers (such as _1.23e+02)

continues

Table 8.2. continued

Name of Flag	Meaning When Flag Is Set
`ios::fixed`	Uses decimal notation for floating-point numbers (such as _123.45)
`ios::dec`	Uses decimal notation for integers
`ios::hex`	Uses hexadecimal notation for integers
`ios::oct`	Uses octal notation for integers
`ios::uppercase`	Uses uppercase letters in output (such as F4 in hexadecimal, 1.23E+02)
`ios::showbase`	Indicates the base of the number system in the output (a `0x` prefix for hexadecimal and a `0` prefix for octal)
`ios::showpoint`	Includes a decimal point for floating-point output (for example, .123)
`ios::showpos`	Shows a positive sign when displaying positive values
`ios::unitbuf`	Flushes all streams after inserting characters into a stream

Scope Resolution Operator (::)

The `ios::left` notation uses the scope resolution operator `::` to identify `left` as a member of the `ios` class. The names of the format flags are specified with an `ios::` prefix because they are defined in the `ios` class.

Controlling the Floating-Point Formats

You can control the floating-point format with the `setprecision` manipulator and three flags: `scientific`, `fixed`, and `showpoint`. To illustrate how these affect floating-point formatting, consider the following code that displays a floating-point value:

```
cout << "123.4567 in default format = ";
```

```
    cout << 123.4567 << endl;

    cout << "123.4567 in 2-digit precision = ";
    cout << setprecision(2) << 123.4567 << endl;

// Set the precision back to 6
    cout << setprecision(6);
    cout << "123.4567 in scientific notation = ";
    cout << setiosflags(ios::scientific) << 123.4567 << endl;
```

This code displays:

```
123.4567 in default format = 123.457
123.4567 in 2-digit precision = 1.2e+002
123.4567 in scientific notation = 1.234567e+002
```

The first line displays the value in the fixed format that is the default. The next line sets the precision to 2—that means you want no more than two digits after the decimal point. The floating-point number is rounded and printed. The last line shows the same number in the scientific notation. If you set the `ios::uppercase` flag, the `e` in the exponent appears in uppercase.

Overloading <<

If you define a class for complex numbers and want to use the << operator to display the objects of your class, you want code that looks like this:

```
    complex z(1.1, 1.2);
// ...
    cout << z;
```

You can do this easily by overloading the << operator. To redefine this operator, you need to define the function `operator<<` for your class. Because the << operator is used with an `ostream` object on the left and a complex class object on the right, the prototype for the `operator<<` function is

```
ostream& operator<<(ostream& s, const complex& x);
```

where the arguments are passed by reference for efficiency and the `const` prefix in the second argument directs the operator not to alter the complex number. When you learn more about references, you will see that the `operator<<` function must return a reference to the stream—this is the key to concatenating the << operators. To illustrate an actual overloading of the << operator, the following sample program uses an abbreviated definition of a complex class and follows the steps necessary to define and use the << operator:

```
#include <iostream.h>

class complex           // a simple class for complex numbers
{
    float real, imag;
public:
    complex() { real = imag = 0.0;}
    complex(float a, float b) { real = a; imag = b;}
    void print(ostream& s) const;
};

// Need this function so that operator<< can do its job
// by calling this one
void complex::print(ostream& s) const
{
    s << real << " + " << imag;
}

// Overload the operator << for use with complex class

ostream& operator<<(ostream &s, const complex& z)
{
    z.print(s);
    return s;
}

// Test the overloaded << operator...

void main()
{
    complex a(1.5, 2.1);
    cout << " a = " << a << endl;
}
```

When compiled, linked, and run, this program produces the expected output:

```
a = 1.5 + 2.1
```

Note the following key points:

1. Define a member function that prints the class members the way you want.

2. Define the `operator<<` function with a reference to an `ostream` and a reference to your class as its first and second arguments, respectively. The function's return type should be `ostream&`. In the body of the function, call your class member function to print and to return the first argument, which happens to be the reference to the stream.
3. Now you can use the << operator to print objects of your class on a stream.

The *iostream* Class Hierarchy

Now that you know how to use the `iostream` library for simple I/O, take a look at Figure 8.2, which graphically illustrates the hierarchy of classes in a typical implementation of the `iostream` library. As shown in the figure, the `streambuf` class provides the buffer used by the streams. All the stream classes are derived from the `ios` base class, which stores the state of the stream and handles errors. The `ios` class has an associated `streambuf` object that acts as the buffer for the stream. The `istream` and `ostream` classes, derived from `ios`, are intended for input and output, respectively. The `iostream` class uses multiple inheritance to acquire the capabilities of both `istream` and `ostream` classes and, therefore, supports both input and output. The `istream_withassign`, `ostream_withassign`, and `iostream_withassign` classes are derived from `istream`, `ostream`, and `iostream`, respectively, by adding the definition of the assignment operator (=) so that you can redirect I/O by assigning one stream to another. The predefined streams `cout`, `cerr`, and `clog` are of `ostream_withassign` class, whereas `cin` is an instance of `istream_withassign` class.

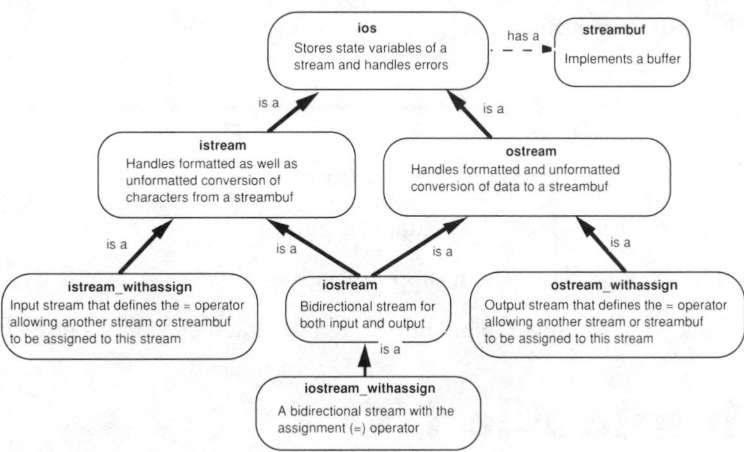

Figure 8.2. Classes in the C++ `iostream` library.

The iostream Classes and Multiple Inheritance

The classes declared in IOSTREAM.H use inheritance to organize the classes in the library. The iostream classes illustrate an interesting consequence of multiple inheritance. In C++, an instance of a derived class contains a copy of all members of its base class. Thus, a class like iostream that inherits from both istream and ostream, each with the same base class (ios), can end up with two copies of the members of ios. With C++, you avoid this by declaring istream and ostream with ios as a virtual base class, like so:

```
class istream : virtual public ios { /* ... */ };

class ostream : virtual public ios { /* ... */ };
```

You can find further details of virtual base classes in Chapter 11, "Using Inheritance in C++," and Chapter 12, "Virtual Functions and C++."

File I/O

In ANSI C, file I/O is handled by functions such as fopen to open a file, fclose to close it, fscanf to read from it, and fprintf to write to it. In the iostream package, the classes intended for file I/O are defined in the FSTREAM.H header file. Thus, for file I/O, you need to use:

```
#include <fstream.h>
```

There are three classes of interest in FSTREAM.H:

- The ifstream class, which supports input
- The ofstream class, which supports output
- The fstream class, which supports both

The following sections explain how to use the file I/O facilities in FSTREAM.H.

Simple File I/O

The easiest way to open a file for I/O is to create an instance of the ifstream or ofstream class as follows:

```
#include <fstream.h>     // Defines classes ifstream and ofstream

// Open file named "infile" for input operations only and
// connect it to the istream "ins"
ifstream ins("infile");

// Open file named "outfile" for output operations only and
// connect it to the ostream "outs"
ofstream outs("outfile");

//...
```

As you can see, you can open a file and connect it to a stream when you create the stream. Two distinct streams exist for input and output—`ifstream` for input and `ofstream` for output. The ANSI C equivalent of connecting a file to an `ifstream` is to call `fopen` with the `r` mode; using `ofstream` with a file is similar to calling `fopen` with the `w` mode.

Before using the stream connected to a file, you should check whether the stream was successfully created. The logical NOT operator `!` is overloaded for the stream classes so you can check a stream using a test like this:

```
// Open stream
   ifstream ins("infile");

// Check if stream has been opened successfully...
   if(!ins)
    {
        cerr << "Cannot open: infile\n";
        exit(1);
    }
```

You do not have need to attach an `ifstream` or `ofstream` to any file at the time of its creation. If you want, you can create the stream first, and then open the file later using the `open` member function of the stream, like this:

```
    ifstream ins;
//...
    ins.open("infile");
// Check if file opened successfully...
    if(!ins)  // Open failed...
//...
```

You can disconnect the file from the stream by closing it. To do this, call the stream's `close` member function:

```
// Close file
   ins.close();
```

This does not destroy the stream. You can reconnect it to another file by calling `open` again.

Controlling the Stream Operating Modes

When you open a stream by supplying the name of a file to the stream's constructor, you are taking advantage of C++'s allowance for default argument values. When you call

```
ifstream ins("infile");
```

the constructor invoked is declared as this:

```
ifstream(const char *, int = ios::in, int = filebuf::openprot);
```

The last two integer-valued arguments are used with the default values. The second argument to the constructor indicates the mode in which the stream operates. For `ifstream`, the default is `ios::in`, which means the file is open for reading. For an `ofstream` object, the default mode is `ios::out`, meaning that the file is open for writing. What if you want to open a file for output, but you want to append data to an existing file instead of destroying its current contents? You can do this by specifying an operating mode of `ios::app`. Like the format flags shown in Table 8.2, the stream operating modes are also defined in the `ios` class; hence, the `ios::` prefix for the names. Table 8.3 summarizes these modes.

Table 8.3. Stream operating modes.

Mode Name	Operation
`ios::app`	Appends data to the file.
`ios::ate`	When first opened, positions the file at the end of the file (`ate` stands for at end).
`ios::binary`	Opens the file in binary mode, which inhibits interpretation of carriage return and linefeed characters.
`ios::in`	Opens the file for reading.

Mode Name	Operation
`ios::nocreate`	Fails to open the file if it does not already exist.
`ios::noreplace`	If the file exists, trying to open it for output fails unless `ios::app` or `ios::ate` is set.
`ios::out`	Opens the file for writing.
`ios::trunc`	Truncates the file if it already exists.

Notice that you can specify more than one mode for a file simply by using a bitwise OR of the required modes. For example, to open a file for output and to position it at the end, use the `ios::out` and `ios::ate` modes as follows:

```
ofstream outs("outfile", ios::out | ios::ate);
```

Copying Files

As an example of file I/O in C++, consider a utility program that copies the contents of one file to another. Assume the utility is named `filecopy` and that when you type the command:

```
filecopy in.fil out.fil
```

`filecopy` copies the contents of the file named IN.FIL to a second file named OUT.FIL. Implementing such a program is straightforward: open the two files (one for input, another one for output), read characters from the input file, and write them to the output file. Listing 8.1 shows a sample implementation of the `filecopy` utility program.

Listing 8.1. FILECOPY.CPP. A utility program that copies the contents of one file to another.

```
//--------------------------------------------------------------
// FILE:  filecopy.cpp
// Copies contents of one file to another
//--------------------------------------------------------------

#include <stdlib.h>
#include <fstream.h>
```

continues

Listing 8.1. continued

```
void main(int argc, char **argv)
{
// Check if there are enough arguments
    if(argc < 3)
    {
        cerr << "Usage: filecopy infile outfile\n";
        exit(0);
    }

// Open the input file and connect it to stream "ins"
    ifstream ins(argv[1]);
    if(!ins)
    {
        cerr << "Cannot open: " << argv[1];
        exit(1);
    }

// Open the output file and connect it to stream "outs"
    ofstream outs(argv[2]);
    if(!outs)
    {
        cerr << "Cannot open: " << argv[2];
        exit(1);
    }

// Read from "ins" and write to "outs"
    char c;
    while(ins.get(c) && outs) outs.put(c);
}
```

Another way to implement the last `while` loop that does the actual copying between the files is to read and write one line at a time. To read a line, use the same `get` function but with the address of a buffer and the buffer's size as arguments:

```
const bufsize = 128;
char buf[bufsize];
//...
ins.get(buf, bufsize);
```

This call to `get` extracts up to `bufsize-1` characters (or until a newline character is encountered) from the input stream to the specified buffer. Then `get` places a terminating null character in the buffer. By default, the `get` function stops at the newline character, but you can specify another delimiter as a third argument to the get function. Notice that this call to get is similar to the fgets function in C, except that unlike fgets, get does not copy the newline character to the buffer, nor does get skip over the newline character. Therefore, to read lines repeatedly from a file, you must extract the newline separately after each line is read. Here is an example that does this:

```
#include <string.h>      // For prototype of "strlen"
#include <fstream.h>
//...
// Assume that streams "ins" and "outs" are already set up
// as shown in Listing 8.1

// Read lines from "ins" and write to "outs"

    const bufsize = 256;
    char buf[bufsize];
    char c;

    while(ins.get(buf, bufsize) && outs)
    {
// Write out buffer using the "write" function
        outs.write(buf, strlen(buf));

// Read leftover newline character and write that out also
        ins.get(c);
        outs.put(c);
    }
```

You can use this as the replacement for the last while loop of Listing 8.1. The actual writing of the buffer to the output file is done by the write function of the output stream. As shown, this function simply copies the specified number of characters from the buffer to the output stream.

Positioning in a File

Many times you have to read files containing binary data with a specific internal structure. For example, a 128-byte header might be followed by blocks of data. Information extracted from the header file might tell you that the data you need is at a specific location inside the file. To read this data, you need to position the stream properly before reading from it. In ANSI C, you can use functions such as fseek and ftell to position streams. With the iostream library, you can also reposition streams, and, as expected, classes provide member functions that accomplish this.

You can position a stream in the `iostream` library by calling the `seekg` or `seekp` member functions of that stream. Because the same stream can be used for both input and output, the stream classes work with the concept of a *get* position and a *put* position which, respectively, indicate the location from which the next read or write occurs. Set the *get* position using `seekg`; set the *put* position using `seekp`. For example, to position the stream at the 513th byte in the `ins` input stream, you can use `setg` as follows:

```
ins.seekg(512);     // next get will start at 513th byte
```

Specifying the Position: Relative Reference

You can also specify the position relative to some reference point such as the end of the file. For example, to move 8 bytes backward from the end of the stream, use:

```
ins.seekg(-8, ios::end);
```

Three reference points are identified by constants defined in the `ios` class:

- `ios::beg`, representing the beginning of the stream
- `ios::end`, representing the end of the stream
- `ios::cur`, representing the current position

Getting the Current Position

You can also retrieve the current *get* or *put* position in a file. The `tellg` function returns the current location in an input stream, whereas the `tellp` function returns the corresponding item for an output stream. Both functions return a variable of the `streampos` type. You can save the returned value and use it with `seekg` or `seekp` to return to the old location in a file:

```
    streampos saved_pos = tellg();
// Other operations on stream...
// ...
// Get back to old location
    seekg(saved_pos);
```

Detecting Errors in File I/O

The `iostream` library provides several functions for checking the status of a stream. The `fail` function tells you if something has gone wrong. Therefore, you can check for problems by calling `fail` for the stream as follows:

```
    ifstream ins("infile");
    if(ins.fail())
    {
// Stream creation has failed. Take appropriate action.
// ...
    }
```

In fact, the logical NOT operator `!` has been overloaded to call `fail` for a stream so that the `if` test can be written more simply as:

```
    if(!ins)
    {
// Handle error...
    }
```

Detecting the End of the File

When reading from or writing to a file, you will want to know if the program has reached the end of the file. The `eof` function returns a nonzero value if the stream is at the end of the file. Once a stream has reached the end of the file, it does not perform any I/O. (This is the case even if you attempt an I/O after moving the stream away from the end by using `seekg` or `seekp` because the stream's internal state remembers the encounter with the end of the file.) You have to call `clear` to reset the state before any further I/O can take place. Thus, sometimes `eof` and `clear` are used as follows:

```
// "ins" is an istream. If the stream reached eof, clear the
// state before attempting to read from the stream
    if(ins.eof()) ins.clear();
// Reposition stream and read again...
    ins.seekg(-16, ios::cur); // Move back 16 bytes
    ins.get(buf, 8);          // Read 8 bytes into buffer
```

Using Good and Bad Conditions

Two other member functions, `good` and `bad`, indicate the general condition of a stream. As the names imply, `good` returns true (a nonzero value) if no error has occurred in the stream, whereas `bad` returns true if an invalid I/O has been attempted or if the stream has an irrecoverable failure. You can use `good` and `bad` in tests such as:

```
    if(ins.bad())
    {
```

```
// Invalid operation...
    }

    if(ins.good())
    {
// Everything ok. Continue using stream...
    }
```

String I/O

When your application uses a windowing system for I/O, you cannot readily use the `cin` and `cout` streams for I/O. With most windowing systems, you display a *string* (a null-terminated array of characters) in a window by calling a designated function from the windowing system's library. This is easy to do with plain strings, but how do you display the value of a variable? What you need is a way to send the formatted output to a string that you can then display by using the windowing system's text output functions. In ANSI C, you can use the `sprintf` function to prepare a formatted string. Similarly, you can use `sscanf` to extract variables from a string. The C++ `iostream` package also includes these capabilities in the form of the `istrstream` and `ostrstream` classes for reading from and writing to a string, respectively. These classes are declared in the STRSTREA.H file.

> **Deviation from AT&T C++**
>
> In UNIX systems and in AT&T C++, the STRSTREA.H header file is named STRSTREAM.H. Because MS-DOS permits only eight characters to be used in a filename, this header file is named STRSTREA.H in Borland C++ 4.

Writing to a String

String I/O is commonly used to prepare formatted output to a string. You need an instance of an `ostrstream` class for this purpose. Typically, you have a buffer of fixed size in which to place the formatted output. To set up an `ostrstream` object connected to such a buffer, you can use the following code:

```
#include <strstrea.h>  // Defines the ostrstream class
```

```
// ...
    const buflen = 128;
    char buf[buflen];

// Set up an ostrstream connected to this buffer
    ostrstream s(buf, sizeof(buf));
```

This sets up an output stream connected to a buffer and assumes a stream operating mode of `ios::out`. As with file I/O, you can specify another mode, such as `ios::app`, to append data to an existing string. Sending output to this stream is as easy as writing to `cout`. Here is an example:

```
#include <strstrea.h>

void main()
{
    const buflen = 128;
    char buf[buflen];
    int   i = 100;
    float x = 3.1415;
// Open an output stream and connect to the buffer
    ostrstream s(buf, buflen);

// Write to the stream
    s << "i = " << i << " x = " << x << ends;

// Display the string on cout
    cout << buf << endl;
}
```

The program displays the following:

```
i = 100 x = 3.1415
```

Although here the program simply displays the buffer by sending it to `cout`, in practice, you prepare the output in a buffer because you need it for use by a function that cannot handle formatting.

Reading from a String

String I/O can also be used to convert characters from a string to internal representations of variables. The `istrstream` class is designed for reading from buffers. For example, if a string holds an integer and a floating-point number, you can extract the variables using the >> operator just as you would from `cin`. The following program illustrates the use of an `istrstream` class:

```
#include <strstrea.h>

void main()
{
    const buflen = 128;
    char  buf[buflen] = "120    6.432";  // A sample buffer
    int   i;
    float x;

// Open an input stream and connect to the buffer
    istrstream s(buf, buflen);

// Read from the stream
    s >> i >> x;

// Display the result on cout
    cout << "i = " << i << " x = " << x << endl;
}
```

The program displays:

```
i = 120 x = 6.432
```

This type of conversion from a string to variables is necessary when reading data from a text file to your program.

Summary

Although you can continue to use the ANSI C I/O routines (the `printf` and `scanf` family) in C++ programs, there is a better alternative. The `iostream` I/O library included in Borland C++ 4 provides a cleaner, object-based mechanism for I/O. Like ANSI C's `stdin`, `stdout`, and `stderr`, the `iostream` package includes the following predefined streams: `cin`, `cout`, `cerr`, and `clog`, a buffered version of `cerr`.

The stream classes use a simple syntax for I/O: the << and >> operators are used for output and input, respectively. The `iostream` library includes built-in support for I/O operations involving the basic data types such as `int`, `char`, `float`, and `double`. Additionally, you can overload the << and >> operators to handle I/O for your own classes. This enables you to use a consistent style for all I/O in your program.

The iostream package supports opening and closing files and performing I/O operations with files. The classes declared in fstream.h implement the file I/O capabilities similar to those provided by the C functions fopen, fclose, fscanf, and fprintf. Additionally, the I/O package includes several classes, declared in the strstrea.h header file, which can read from and write to arrays of characters just like C's sscanf and sprintf.

Using the iostream classes is easy, provided you know what classes are available and how to call their public member functions. Although you can learn some of this by browsing through the header files, to make proper use of the member functions, you need the documentation for the class. This chapter provides a reasonable amount of information about the iostream classes so you can begin using them for I/O in your C++ programs.

Apart from the I/O capabilities, the iostream package is also a good example of how C++'s support for OOP can be exploited in a class library. The classes in the library make extensive use of inheritance, including multiple inheritance and the virtual base class mechanism. Chapter 12 covers the details of these C++ language features.

Building Objects with Classes

Beginning with this chapter, you will learn the details of C++'s syntax and see how its constructs support OOP. Instead of going through a litany of seemingly unrelated features, Chapters 9 through 12 explain the syntax of most C++ features in light of some well-defined needs that arise when you use object-oriented techniques in your programs. Small examples illustrate the need for a feature and show how a particular construct fulfills that need. This chapter focuses on the `class` and `struct` constructs that enable you to define new types of objects. It also provides general guidelines for implementing and using classes.

Classes as Objects

Before you manipulate objects, you need a way to create them. Defining an object involves describing a new data type and the functions that can manipulate that data type. How do you represent a new data type? You must declare the new data type in terms of some existing types. For instance, you can express a point in a two-dimensional plane by an x,y coordinate pair. If each coordinate is represented by an integer type, such as `int`, you can declare a point as a structure:

```
struct Point          // Declare a Point structure
{
    int x, y;
};

struct Point ul, lr;  // Define two Points
```

These are facilities already existing in C. If you prefer calling the new type `Point` (without the `struct` prefix), you can do so with the `typedef` facility:

```
typedef struct Point  // Declare a Point type
{
    int x, y;
} Point;

Point ul, lr;         // Define two Points
```

With this code segment, you can use `Point` as the name of a type, but this is far from being a new data type. For example, you might want to define the addition operator (+) for `Point`. This is not possible with C's struct because C enables you to group data items into a single entity, but it does not provide any way to declare the functions and operators inside the structure. Therefore, it is not a complete data type with well-defined operations. Of course, you can write functions that manipulate `Point` structures, but you don't receive any support from the compiler to help associate these functions more closely with `Points`.

User-Defined Data Types

To support the definition of a full-fledged data type, C++ only needed to extend the syntax of struct by enabling you to include functions and operators as members of a struct. C++ also made the *structure tag* or *name*—the symbol following `struct`—a stand-alone name, meaning that you can use that name without the `struct` prefix. With these extensions to C's struct, C++ enables you to declare and use a `Point` type as follows:

```
struct Point     // Declare a Point type
{
    int x, y;

// Define operations on Point
    void operator+(const Point& p) const
    {
        return Point(x+p.x, y+p.y);
    }
//...
};

Point ul, lr;   // Define two Points
```

For now, ignore the definition of the {+} operator; it is covered in Chapter 10, "Defining Operations on Objects." Notice that you can place function definitions inside a `struct` and that the name of a `struct` serves as a data type.

As an example of another user-defined type, suppose you want to create a `String` data type that provides the functionality of C's null-terminated strings but uses an object-oriented approach. What you essentially want is a pointer to an array of characters and the ability to store C-style null-terminated strings in that array. Because the length of the string is needed often, you decide to store it as a member variable as well. Lastly, suppose you plan to use the strings to store lines of text that are being edited. Because the number of characters in each line can fluctuate as characters are added or removed, you decide to allocate a slightly larger array than necessary. To manage the string's storage properly, you also need to store the size of the allocated array. Allowing, for the moment, a lone function that returns the length of the string, you end up with a preliminary definition of the `String` as follows:

```
#include <stddef.h>   // For size_t type

struct String
{
    size_t length(void);
// Other member functions...

    char   *p_c;      // pointer to allocated space
    size_t _length;  // current length of string
    size_t _maxlen;  // number of bytes allocated
};
```

This appears clean enough, but a problem exists. By default, all members of the structure are accessible to any function that wants to use them. You don't want this because that goes against one of the basic principles of data abstraction, which advocates that you should define an abstract data type (a user-defined type) but hide the internal details of the new type. In particular, for String objects, you want to hide details, such as the way you decide to implement the string's internal storage. If programs come to rely on these details, you cannot change the implementation in the future, even if a change clearly makes manipulation of the String type more efficient.

Access Control for *Class* Members

For complete support of data abstraction, you need control over who can access what in a structure. C++ introduces a new keyword, class, which you can use exactly like struct. Unlike members of a struct, however, the members of a class are not accessible to any outside functions. In other words, a struct is wide open, but a class is totally hidden. Because neither of these is a good solution for all situations, C++ adds three new keywords to help specify access: private, public, and protected. You can explicitly mark sections of a class or a struct as private, public, and protected as follows:

```
#include <stddef.h>    // For size_t type

class String           // Declare the String class
{
public:
    size_t length(void);
// Other publicly-accessible member functions...

protected:
// Members accessible to derived classes only
// ...

private:
// Members accessible to other members of this class

    char   *p_c;      // pointer to allocated space
    size_t _length;   // current length of string
    size_t _maxlen;   // number of bytes allocated
};
```

The public section lists the members that are accessible to any function in the program. Only member functions of the class can access the private section. When you read about inheritance in Chapter 11, "Using Inheritance in C++," you will learn why the protected section is needed. For now, remember that the members in the protected section of a class are accessible to classes derived from that class. Figure 9.1 illustrates how the access control keywords work.

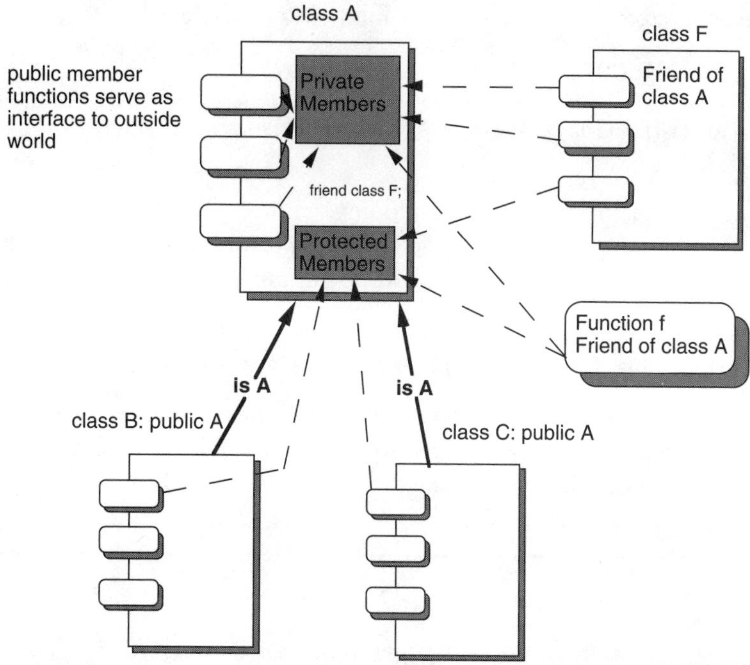

Figure 9.1. Access control in C++ classes.

Notice that you can include multiple public, private, and protected sections in a class. Each section label determines the access level of the members listed between that label and the next label or the closing right brace (}) that marks the end of the class declaration. If you don't provide any label at the very beginning of a class, the compiler considers all members up to the next access control label as private. On the other hand, everything before the first access specifier is public in a struct.

public Functions Can Return *private* Values

The public section of a class usually declares all the member functions that can be invoked from anywhere in the program. You can think of these functions as the interface to the outside world. If you need to provide the value of a private variable to the outside world, you can write a public member function that returns the value. A good example is the length member function of the rudimentary String class. The private variable _length holds the current length of the string. If you are working with a struct-based implementation of String without the private keyword, you might be tempted to access the length as follows:

```
    String this_line;
//...
    if(this_line._length > 0)  // this refers to length of string
// ...
```

But the principle of information hiding, enforced by the private keyword, prevents you from doing this. You can solve this problem by writing a length function that returns _length. In this case, any function can refer to the length of a string as follows:

```
if(this_line.length() > 0)  // this refers to length of string
```

This simple example illustrates what you encounter in all class-based designs: public member functions provide access to private variables of the class. This insulates the users of the class from any changes to its internal variables.

Leading Underscores in Names of Member Variables

You don't need the leading underscores in names of private member variables of a class; however, I have a reason for using names with leading underscores. Most private member variables require a corresponding public member function so that other classes can access the private variable. If you name the private member variable with a leading underscore, you can use the same name without the underscore for the access function. For instance, notice the private member variable named _length and the member function named length in the String class. By choosing the variable's name with a leading underscore (_length), you can provide an access function with a more logical name (length).

Note that many programmers favor an alternate approach of using an underscore suffix in the names of private member variables. In this approach, you would use length_ as the variable's name and provide an access function named length.

Member Functions

Member functions are designed to implement the operations allowed on the data type represented by a class. To declare a member function, place its prototype in the body of the `class` or `struct`. You don't need to define the function inside the class; the definition can be outside the class or even in a separate file.

Inline Member Functions

Defining a function inside the body of a class produces a special consequence. Such definitions are considered *inline*, and the entire body of an inline function is repeated whenever that function is called. Thus, if you have an inline function in a class and if you call that function often, you can use a large amount of memory for the program. The advantage of inline functions is that you avoid the overhead of a function call when executing the body of the function.

The previous argument implies that you should make a function inline only if the overhead of calling the function is a large proportion of the time needed to execute the body of the function. When you include a simple function such as length in the `String` class, you can safely define the entire function inside the body of the class, thus making it inline:

```
class String
{
public:
    size_t length(void) { return _length; }
// ...

private:
// ...
    size_t _length;
};
```

You don't need to define a function inside a class to make it inline. C++ provides the `inline` keyword that, when placed in front of a function's definition, makes it inline. Notice, however, that you can use an inline function only in the file in which it is defined. This is because the compiler needs the entire definition of an inline function so that it can insert the body of the function wherever the function is called. Therefore, you should place the definitions of inline functions in the same header file that declares a class to ensure that every program that uses the class can also use its inline functions.

Inline Functions and Preprocessor Macros

Inline functions are like preprocessor macros without the pitfalls. For example, the macro

```
#define  square(x)  x*x
```

provides the wrong answer when used to evaluate an expression such as `square(a+b)` because you didn't use parentheses around the macro's argument. However, if you define square as an inline function

```
inline double square(x) { return x*x; }
```

you can safely use `square(a+b)` to evaluate the square of `a+b` because inline functions work just like any C++ function.

Typical *public* Member Functions

The `public` member functions of a class are very important because they are the outside world's gateway to a class. For a class to be useful, it must include a complete set of `public` member functions. A minimal set should include the following categories of functions:

- *Class Management functions* are a standard set of functions that perform chores such as creating an instance of the class (*constructor*), destroying it (*destructor*), creating an instance and initializing it by copying from another instance (*copy constructor*), assigning one instance to another (`operator=` function), and converting an instance to some other type (*type conversion operator*). These functions have a standard declaration syntax. You will encounter these functions in this and the following chapter.

- *Class Implementation functions* implement the *behavior* of the data type represented by the class. They are the workhorses of the class. For a `String` class, these functions might include `operator+` for concatenating strings and comparison operators, such as `operator==`, `operator>`, and `operator<`. Chapter 10, "Defining Operations on Objects," explains how such functions are defined.

- *Class Access functions* return information about the internal variables of a class. The outside world can access the object's internal state through these functions. The length function in the `String` class is a good example of this type of member function.

- *Class Utility functions*, often declared to be private, are used internally within the class for miscellaneous tasks such as error handling.

const Member Functions

If a member function does not alter any data in the class, you should declare that member function as a `const` function. For instance, the `length` function of the `String` class simply returns the value of a member variable. It is definitely a `const` function because it doesn't change any data of the `String` class. You can declare it as such by appending a `const` to the usual function prototype like so:

```
size_t length(void) const;
```

This informs the compiler that the `length` function should not alter any variable in the class. The compiler generates an error message if the definition of the `length` function includes any code that inadvertently assigns a value to any variable in the `String` class.

Implementing Classes

The difficult part of writing object-oriented programs is deciding which classes or abstract data types you need to solve your problem. Once you know the classes, their inheritance hierarchy, and their desired behavior, implementing the classes is straightforward. The following sections offer some general guidelines.

Header Files Describe Interface

When implementing a class, think of the class as a provider of some service that other classes or functions need. In other words, the class is a server that acts upon the requests of its clients. This is the idea behind the client-server architecture, and it works well when implementing classes in object-oriented programs. The clients of a class make requests by calling the member functions of that class. The *interface* to the class refers to the information that a client must have in order to use the facilities of a class. At a minimum, the client must know:

- The names of the `public` member functions of the class
- The prototypes of the member functions
- The purpose of each member function

Ideally, if you want to use a class, you want a textual description of the class and how its facilities are intended for use. Without this information, you might have to manage with the header file that declares the class.

The header file describes the interface to a class. In fact, it shows you everything except the functions that are defined in another file, but your program can access only those members that appear in the `public` section. Because the public interface to the class is important to its clients, you should place these declarations at the very beginning of a class. The `protected` section can follow these declarations. The `private` members can come last because these members are visible only to the member functions of that class.

Assuming that a reasonable assortment of `public` member functions exists, a `String` class might include a header file STR.H as shown in Listing 9.1.

Listing 9.1. STR.H. Header file for the `String` class.

```
//----------------------------------------------------------------
//  File:  str.h
//  Declares a "String" data type
//
//  Note: Couldn't use String.h as name because we include
//        ANSI C's string.h and some systems (such as MS-DOS)
//        do not differentiate between uppercase and lowercase
//        letters in filenames
//----------------------------------------------------------------

#if !defined(__STR_H)  // Make sure the file is included only once
#define __STR_H

// Include any other required header files...
// NOTE: The header files from the ANSI C library must enclose
//       all function declarations inside a block like this:
//            extern "C"
//            {
//              ...
//            }
//       Borland C++ compiler's header files do this.

#include <stddef.h>      // For "size_t" type
#include <iostream.h>    // For stream I/O
#include <string.h>      // For ANSI C string library
```

```
typedef int Boolean;    // For return type of operators

class String
{
public:
// Constructors with a variety of arguments
    String();
    String(size_t len);
    String(const char *str);
    String(const String &s);

// Destructor
    ~String();

// Overloaded operators
//      Boolean operator==(const String &s) const;
//      Boolean operator<(const String &s) const;
//      Boolean operator>(const String &s) const;
//      Boolean operator<=(const String &s) const;
//      Boolean operator>=(const String &s) const;
//      Boolean operator!=(const String &s) const;

// Assignment operator
    void operator=(const String& s);

// Type conversion operator
    operator const char*() const;

// Access operator
     char& operator[](int index);
     char& char_at_pos(int index);

// The + operator concatenates strings
    friend String operator+(const String& s1, const String& s2);

// Function giving access to internal variable
    size_t length(void) const;

// Function to print a String
    void print(ostream& os) const;

private:
```

continues

Listing 9.1. continued

```
// Internal data members of this class

    char   *p_c;      // pointer to allocated space
    size_t _length;  // current length of string
    size_t _maxlen;  // number of bytes allocated
};

// Stream I/O operators for String class


ostream& operator<<(ostream& os, String& s);
istream& operator>>(istream& is, String& s);

//---------------------------------------------------------------
//     I N L I N E    F U N C T I O N S
//---------------------------------------------------------------
//  l e n g t h
//  Returns the length of the String

inline size_t String::length(void) const
{
    return _length;
}
//---------------------------------------------------------------
//  ~ S t r i n g
//  Destroys a String

inline String::~String()
{
    delete p_c;
}
//---------------------------------------------------------------
//  o p e r a t o r   c o n s t   c h a r   *
//  Converts from String to char pointer

inline String::operator const char*() const
{
    return p_c;
}
//---------------------------------------------------------------
//  o p e r a t o r = =
```

```
//  String equality operator. Returns nonzero if strings are
//  equal

inline Boolean String::operator==(const String &s) const
{
// Use ANSI C's strcmp function to compare the strings
// Remember strcmp returns 0 if the strings match, but this
//  function has to return nonzero (true) for a match
    return(strcmp(s.p_c, p_c) == 0);
}


#endif
```

Notice that the `#if !defined` directive is used to ensure that the header file is included only once in any file. It is also good practice to make your header file complete by including all other header files required by your class. For example, the `String` class uses the `size_t` type, which is defined in `<stddef.h>`. Instead of forcing users of the `String` class to include `<stddef.h>` whenever they use the class, you should include that file in the header file for the `String` class. This way, a user of the `String` class needs only to remember to include STR.H, the header file that defines the interface to the `String` class.

> **C++ File Naming Convention**
>
> The file suffix or extension—the characters following the period in a filename—used for header files and other source files varies among C++ compilers. In UNIX systems, C++ source files generally use the .C extension, whereas C uses the .C extension. In UNIX, header files end with .H for both C and C++ languages. Under MS-DOS, this is not possible because MS-DOS does not distinguish between lowercase and uppercase letters in filenames. C++ compilers under MS-DOS, including Borland C++ 4, use .CPP as the extension for C++ files. For header files, some C++ compilers use .HPP or . HXX as extensions instead of just .H. This book uses .H for header files and .CPP for C++ source files.

Separate Implementation from Interface

The clients of a class do not need the definition of a class's member functions, if they are adequately documented. Therefore, you can place the actual definitions of the member functions in a separate file. For a class like `String`, define the interface to the class in the STR.H file, whereas the member functions are implemented in a second file, such as STR.CPP. The general layout of STR.CPP looks like this:

```
//-------------------------------------------------------------
//  File:  str.cpp
//  Implements the member functions of the "String" class

#include "str.h"    // For declaration of String class

// Other header files, if needed...
// Header files needed by String class should be included
// in str.h

const chunk_size = 8;  // Allocation unit for Strings

//-------------------------------------------------------------
//  S t r i n g
//  Creates a String object and initializes it from a
//  from a null-terminated C string

String::String(const char *s)
{
    _length = strlen(s);
    _maxlen = chunk_size * (_length / chunk_size + 1);
    p_c = new char[_maxlen];
    strcpy(p_c, s);
}
//-------------------------------------------------------------
//  p r i n t
//  Outputs the String on a specified output stream

void String::print(ostream& os) const
{
    os << p_c;
}
//-------------------------------------------------------------
```

```
//  o p e r a t o r < <
//  Stream insertion operator for String class

ostream& operator<<(ostream& os, String& s)
{
    s.print(os);
    return os;
}
//-------------------------------------------------------------------
//  Definitions of other member functions...
//  ...
//-------------------------------------------------------------------
```

When defining a member function outside the body of a class, you must associate each function with the class by explicitly using the scope resolution operator (`::`). For the `String` class, use a `String::` prefix with each member function, as shown in the previous example. The implementation of the other parts of the `String` class is covered in Chapter 10, "Defining Operations on Objects," and the STR.CPP file is shown in its entirety in Listing 11.2.

Using Classes

A well-designed C++ class should behave like one of the basic data types, such as `int`, `char`, or `double`, except that a class is likely to permit a much larger variety of operations than those allowed for the basic types. This is because the operations defined for a class include all of its public member functions, which can be as diverse as the class's functionality warrants. Like the basic data types (such as `int` and `float`), to use a class in a program, you must proceed through the following steps:

1. Define one or more instances of the class. These are the objects of object-oriented programming. Just as you write

   ```
   double x, y, z;  // doubles named x, y, z
   ```

   to create three instances of double variables, you can create three `String` objects with

   ```
   String s1, s2, s3; // Strings named s1, s2, s3
   ```

   For a class that provides all required interface functions, you should be able to create and initialize instances in a variety of ways:

   ```
   String s1 = "String 1";
   ```

```
String s2("Testing.1..2...3");
String s3 = s1;
```

In each of these cases, the compiler calls the appropriate constructor and creates the `String`.

2. Call the member functions of the objects and use the available operators to manipulate the objects. For `String` objects, you can write code such as this:

```
#include "str.h"

void main()
{
    String title("Object-Oriented Programming in C++");

    cout << "title = " << title << endl;

    String first_name("Naba"), last_name("Barkakati");
    String full_name = first_name + " " + last_name;

    cout << "full_name = " << full_name << endl;

    cout << "Enter some text (end with a return):";
    String response;
    cin >> response;
    cout << "You typed: " << response << endl;
}
```

If you use this program with the full implementation of the `String` class shown in Listing 11.2, here is what you get when you run this program (user input is in boldface):

```
title = Object-Oriented Programming in C++
full_name = Naba Barkakati
Enter some text (end with a return):This is a test.
You typed: This is a test.
```

Creating Objects on the Fly

You can create instances of classes in two ways:

- Define the objects just as you define `int` or `double` variables.
- Create the objects dynamically as needed.

When you create objects through definition, the compiler can reserve storage space for the objects during compilation. To dynamically create objects, you need a way to acquire a chunk of memory for the object. In C, you can dynamically create variables or arrays by calling the functions, such as `malloc` or `calloc`, from the C library.

While you can often create objects by defining instances of classes, dynamic allocation of objects is more interesting because with this approach, you can use as much memory as is available in a system.

Allocating Objects in the Free Store

You may have encountered the term *heap* in reference to dynamic memory allocation in C. The *heap* is the pool of memory from which standard C functions such as `malloc` and `calloc` parcel out memory. C++ books and manuals refer to the heap with the term *free store*. In C++, you gain the functionality of `malloc` and `calloc` by using the new operator, which allocates enough memory to hold all members of a `class` or `struct`.

In C, if you define a structure such as

```
struct Opcode
{
    char   *name;
    void   (*action)(void);
};
```

you allocate space for an instance of this structure like so:

```
struct Opcode *p_code;
p_code = (struct Opcode *) malloc(sizeof(struct Opcode));
```

In C++, the equivalent code to create a new `Opcode` reduces to this:

```
Opcode *p_code;
p_code = new Opcode;
```

Apart from the cleaner syntax, the new operator also provides another advantage. If the Opcode structure contains a constructor that takes no arguments, the new operator automatically calls that constructor to initialize the newly created instance of Opcode.

In fact, you have the option of specifying other initial values for an object allocated by `new`. For example, you can write:

```
String *file_name = new String("cpphelp.doc");
int    *first_byte = new int(128);
```

to allocate and initialize a `String` and an `int` object. The `String` is initialized to `cpphelp.doc`, whereas the `int` is set to 128. The `String` is initialized by calling the `String(const char*)` constructor of the `String` class.

Destroying Objects in the Free Store

In C, when you no longer need memory that you had previously allocated in the heap, you call the `free` function to release the memory. In C++, the `delete` operator serves the same purpose as C's free. Like `free`, the `delete` operator expects a pointer to an object as its operand. Thus, if `p_code` is the pointer to an instance of `Opcode` created by the new operator, you can destroy it with the statement:

```
delete p_code;  // Frees storage pointed to by p_code
```

In addition to freeing up storage used by the object, if that object's class has a defined destructor, `delete` calls it to ensure proper cleanup.

Allocating Arrays of Objects in the Free Store

One use of `new` is to allocate an array of objects. The syntax for this is very much like the way you define arrays. For example, you can define an array of `String` objects by writing:

```
String edit_buf[128];
```

To create the same array on the free store, you use:

```
String *edit_buf = new String[128];
```

You can use the array of `Strings` as you would any other array. The first `String` is `edit_buf[0]`, the second one is `edit_buf[1]`, and so on.

A special syntax exists for deallocating the array of objects on free store. Use the following syntax to indicate that you are deleting an array of objects:

```
delete[] edit_buf;
```

This ensures that the destructor of the `String` class is called for each element of the array. Each `String` object maintains an internal pointer to a character array that is allocated by the constructor and freed by the destructor. So a call to the destructor of each `String` in the array takes care of properly deallocating the internal `char` arrays used by the `String` objects.

Handling Errors in Memory Allocation

If you allocate many objects dynamically, chances are that sooner or later the free space will be exhausted and the new operator will fail. In ANSI C, when malloc or calloc fails, they return a NULL pointer (a pointer set to zero). C++ provides a way to intercept allocation errors. In Borland C++, when the new operator fails, it calls a function that you install by calling the set_new_handler function. You can handle memory allocation errors in a central function by writing the error handler and calling set_new_handler with the pointer to the error handler as an argument. The advantage of handling errors this way is that you no longer need to test each use of the new operator for a return value of zero.

The set_new_handler function is declared in the NEW.H header file. In Borland C++, the pointer to the error handling function is of type new_handler, which is defined as a pointer to a function that does not take any argument and does not return anything. The error handler tries to allocate the requested amount of memory. If it succeeds, it returns the pointer to the allocated memory; otherwise, it returns zero. The set_new_handler function is provided for compatibility with older versions of C++. A better way is to override the new operator to handle error conditions that occur when memory allocation fails.

Calling Member Functions

In C++, you build object-oriented programs by creating instances of classes (the objects) as necessary. The program does its work by calling the member functions of the objects. The syntax for calling the member functions is similar to the syntax used to call any other function, except that you use the . and -> operators to identify the member function within the object. For example, to use the length function of a String object named s1, use the . operator to specify the function:

```
String s1;
size_t len;
len = s1.length();
```

Apart from the use of the . operator to identify the function, the calling syntax is like other function calls. As with any function, you must know the member function's return type as well as the number and type of arguments that it takes. For dynamically allocated objects, use the -> operator like so:

```
String *p_s = new String("Hello, World!");
size_t len;
len = p_s->length();
```

Using *static* Member Variables

When you define member variables for a class, each instance of that class obtains its own unique copy of the member variables. However, sometimes you want a single variable for all instances of a class. C++ makes use of the `static` keyword to introduce this type of member variable. Here, `static` member variables are introduced in the context of a rather useful class.

Most C programmers agree that at some point in time they have debugged their program by inserting calls to `printf` or `fprintf` and printing messages and values from variables of interest. These messages can help you pinpoint where a program fails. Often programmers enclose these calls to `fprintf` in a `#if` directive like this:

```
#if defined(DEBUG)
    fprintf(stderr, "Loop ended. Index = %d\n", i);
#endif
```

so that such messages are printed only when the DEBUG preprocessor macro is defined. In C++, you can use a similar strategy for debugging, but rather than insert calls to `fprintf`, you accomplish the work with a `Debug` class. The class is designed so that whenever an instance of the `Debug` class is created, it prints a message, properly indented to make the sequence of function calls easier to follow. The `Debug` class also provides a member function called `print`, which can be used just like `printf`. Listing 9.2 shows the DEBUG.H header file, which declares the interface to the class and defines the inline functions.

Listing 9.2. DEBUG.H. Interface to the `Debug` class.

```
//--------------------------------------------------------------
//  File:  debug.h
//
//  A class for debugging C++ programs
//
//--------------------------------------------------------------
#if !defined(__DEBUG_H)
#define __DEBUG_H

#include <stdio.h>
#include <stdarg.h>

class Debug
{
```

```
public:
    Debug(const char *label = " ");
    ~Debug();
    void print(const char *format, ...);
private:
    unsigned int indent();
    void draw_separator();

    static unsigned int debug_level;
    static unsigned int debug_on;
    static unsigned int indent_by;
    static unsigned int line_size;
    enum {off = 0, on = 1};
};

//-------------------------------------------------------------
//       I N L I N E   F U N C T I O N S
//-------------------------------------------------------------
//  ~ D e b u g
//  Destructor for the Debug class

inline Debug::~Debug()
{
    debug_level--;
    draw_separator();
}

#endif
```

At the end of the body of the `Debug` class, notice that a number of member variables are declared with the `static` keyword. These variables are static *member variables*, and the `Debug` class contains exactly one copy of them.

To understand the need for such static member variables, consider the `debug_level` member variable, which keeps track of how many instances of `Debug` class have been created up to that point. As you can see from Listing 9.3, this information is used to appropriately indent the messages printed by the `print` member function. You can't use `debug_level` to keep a count of the instances of the `Debug` class if each instance has its own copy of the `debug_level` variable. The solution is to have what you might call a *class-wide global variable*, which occurs when you place the `static` keyword in front of a member variable.

Listing 9.3. DEBUG.CPP. Implementation of the Debug class.

```
//---------------------------------------------------------------
// File: debug.cpp
//
// Implementation of the "Debug" class
//---------------------------------------------------------------
#include "debug.h"

//---------------------------------------------------------------
// D e b u g
// Constructor for Debug class

Debug::Debug(const char *label)
{
    if(debug_on)
    {
        int i;
        draw_separator();
        (void) indent();
        fprintf(stderr, "%s\n", label);
    }
    debug_level++;
}
//---------------------------------------------------------------
// p r i n t
// Uses ANSI C's vfprintf function to print debug message

void Debug::print(const char *format, ...)
{
    if(debug_on)
    {
        (void) indent();
        va_list argp;
        va_start(argp, format);
        vfprintf(stderr, format, argp);
    }
}
//---------------------------------------------------------------
// i n d e n t
// Indents line according to debug_level. Returns the
// number of spaces indented
```

```
unsigned int Debug::indent()
{
    int i;
    unsigned int num_spaces = debug_level*indent_by;
    for(i = 0; i < num_spaces; i++)
        fputc(' ', stderr);
    return(num_spaces);
}
//-------------------------------------------------------------------
//  d r a w _ s e p a r a t o r
//  Draws a separator using dashes (-) to identify debug levels

void Debug::draw_separator()
{
    if(debug_on)
    {
        unsigned int i;
        for(i = indent(); i < line_size; i++)
                               fputc('-', stderr);
        fputc('\n', stderr);
    }
}
//-------------------------------------------------------------------
```

Initializing Static Member Variables

Listing 9.4 shows a test program that illustrates how the `Debug` class of Listings 9.2 and 9.3 might be used. At the beginning of this program, you can see the syntax that refers to the static member variables of the `Debug` class. To refer to the static member variable of a class, use the name of the class (not the name of the instance) as prefix followed by the scope resolution operator (`::`). Therefore, you can set the `debug_level` member of the `Debug` class to zero by writing:

```
// Initialize static member "debug_level" of the Debug class
unsigned int Debug::debug_level = 0;
```

Except for the `Debug::` prefix, this looks like the definition of any other variable in the program.

Upon examination of Listing 9.3, you will notice that inside the member functions you can access the static member variables, such as `debug_level`, in the same way you would access any other member variable of the class. So, you need the scope resolution prefix (`Debug::`) for the static member variables only when referring to them outside the scope of the class.

Listing 9.4. DBGTST.CPP. Program to test the `Debug` class.

```
//-----------------------------------------------------------------------
//  File:  dbgtst.cpp
//
//  Test the "Debug" class
//-----------------------------------------------------------------------
#include "debug.h"

// Initialize the debug_level to 0 and debug_on to "on"
unsigned int Debug::debug_level = 0;
unsigned int Debug::debug_on = Debug::on;

// Set number of characters per line to 55
unsigned int Debug::line_size = 55;

// Indent by 4 spaces for each level
unsigned int Debug::indent_by = 4;
//-----------------------------------------------------------------------
//  f a c t o r i a l
//  Recursive function that evaluates factorial

unsigned long factorial(int n)
{
    Debug dbg("factorial");
    dbg.print("argument = %d\n", n);
    if(n == 1) return 1;
    else return n*factorial(n-1);
}
//-----------------------------------------------------------------------
//  m a i n
//  Main function to test 'Debug" class

void main()
{
```

```
    Debug dbg("main");
    unsigned long n = factorial(4);
    dbg.print("result = %ld\n", n);
}
```

The sample program defines and calls a `factorial` function, which is a recursive function that evaluates the factorial of its integer argument (to show the effects of `debug_level`). The `factorial` function creates an instance of the `Debug` class on each entry. The `Debug` class increases the indentation as the `debug_level` increases, and it draws dashed lines to show increases and decreases in `debug_level`. Therefore, you would expect to see an indented list of calls to `factorial` in the output of this program. Indeed, when you run the program built by compiling and linking the files shown in Listings 9.3 and 9.4, it displays the following output:

```
--------------------------------------------------------
main
    ----------------------------------------------------
    factorial
        argument = 4
        ------------------------------------------------
        factorial
            argument = 3
            --------------------------------------------
            factorial
                argument = 2
                ----------------------------------------
                factorial
                    argument = 1
                ----------------------------------------
            --------------------------------------------
        ------------------------------------------------
    ----------------------------------------------------
    result = 24
--------------------------------------------------------
```

Here, the indentation of the dashed lines clearly shows the sequence of function calls and returns.

Counting Class Instances

Declare a member variable `static` if you want a single copy of the variable for all instances of a class. You can count the number of instances of a class by incrementing a `static` member variable in the constructor of the class.

Using Static Member Functions

You can work with static member functions as well as static member variables. In C programs, programmers often define static functions to confine the visibility of a function to a specific file. With the `static` keyword, you can place more than one function with the same name in different files. C++ advances one step further and enables you to place functions that are static within a class. You can invoke such functions without creating any instance of the class. You only need to add the scope resolution operator to the class name. As an example, suppose you want a static member function of the `Debug` class that sets the `debug_on` variable. You can declare such a function inside the body of the class as follows:

```
class Debug
{
public:
//...
static void set_debug(int on_off);    // static member function
//...
private:
//...
}
```

The function is defined just like any other member function. Notice that you don't need the `static` keyword in the definition:

```
void Debug::set_debug(int on_off)
{
    if(on_off) debug_on = on;
    else       debug_on = off;
}
```

Once defined, you can call this function just like an ordinary function, but with a `Debug::` prefix as follows:

```
// Turn debugging off
    Debug::set_debug(0);
//...
// Turn debugging on
    Debug::set_debug(1);
```

Notice that you don't need an instance of the `Debug` class to call the `set_debug` function. The scope resolution prefix (`Debug::`) is necessary to indicate which `set_debug` function you are calling. After all, another class also might have defined a static member function named `set_debug`.

Using Pointers to Class Members

Because of encapsulation of data and functions in a class, C++ includes a pointer to a class member in addition to ordinary pointers to class and functions. A pointer *to a class member* is actually the offset of the member from the beginning of a particular instance of that class. In other words, it is a relative address, whereas regular pointers denote the absolute address of an object. The syntax for declaring a pointer to a class member is `X::*`, where `X` is the name of the class. So, if you declare a class as follows:

```
class Sample
{
public:
    short step;                // Member variable
    void set_step(short s); // Member function
//...
private:
};
```

you can define and initialize a pointer to a `short` member variable of the `Sample` class like this:

```
short Sample::*p_s;  // Pointer to short in class Sample
p_s = &Sample::step; // Initialize to member "step"
```

Notice that to define and even initialize the pointer, you do not need an instance of the `Sample` class. Contrast this with the way you initialize a regular pointer to a `short` variable. With the regular pointer you have to define a `short` variable before you can assign its address to the pointer.

With pointers to class members, you need a concrete instance of the class only when using the pointers. Thus, you have to define an instance of the `Sample` class before you can use the pointer p_s. A typical use of p_s might be to assign a new value to the class member through the pointer:

```
Sample s1;
s1.*p_s = 5;
```

The syntax for dereferencing the pointer is of the form x.*p, where x is an instance of the class and p is a pointer to a class member. If, instead of a class instance, you have a pointer to an instance of a Sample class, the syntax for using p_s changes to:

```
Sample s1;
Sample *p_sample1 = &s1;
p_sample->*p_s = 5;
```

Pointers to Member Functions

The syntax for declaring a pointer to a member function of the class is similar to the syntax used for declaring a pointer to ordinary functions. The only difference is that you use the class name together with the scope resolution operator (::). Here is an example that defines a pointer to a member function of the class Sample. The definition says that the member function to which p_func points returns nothing but requires a short as argument.

```
void (Sample::*p_func)(short) = Sample::set_step;
```

The sample definition also initializes the pointer p_func to the address of the set_step function of the Sample class. You can call the function through the pointer:

```
Sample s1;
(s1.*p_func)(2);  // Call function through pointer
```

Here is another small program that illustrates how pointers to member functions are used:

```
//-------------------------------------------------------------
//  Illustrates use of pointer to member function of a class

#include <iostream.h>

class CommandSet
{
public:
    void help(){cout << "Help!" << endl;}
    void nohelp(){cout << "No Help!" << endl;}
private:
```

```
//...
};

//  Initialize pointer to member function "f_help"

void (CommandSet::*f_help)() = CommandSet::help;

main()
{
    CommandSet set1;

// Invoke a member function through the "f_help" pointer
    (set1.*f_help)();

// Redefine the "f_help" pointer and call function again
    f_help = CommandSet::nohelp;
    (set1.*f_help)();
}
```

The example makes two calls to the function with the pointer. Between calls, it changes the pointer's value. When run, the program displays two messages:

```
Help!
No Help!
```

Pointers to Static Members

Static members of a class are not covered by the syntax used for defining and using pointers to other members of a class. A pointer to a static member is treated just like a regular pointer. For example, if you declare the class:

```
class Clock
{
public:
//...
    static double ticks_per_sec;
private:
//...
};
```

you can define a pointer to its static member variable as follows:

```
double *p_tick = &Clock::ticks_per_sec;
```

This is just a regular pointer to double that has been initialized to the ticks_per_sec static member variable of the Clock class. Notice that you must use the class name with the scope resolution operator to identify the static variable ticks_per_sec. Use the p_ticks pointer like an ordinary pointer to double. For instance, the following statement sets the ticks_per_sec static variable of the Clock class to 18.2:

```
*p_tick = 18.2; // Set 'ticks_per_sec' through pointer
```

Summary

C++ extends the syntax of C's struct and introduces the class construct. These enhancements enable the creation of user-defined data types that you can use just like the built-in types such as int, char, float, and double. In the terminology of object-oriented programming, the class and struct mechanisms support data abstraction, which is one of the basic requirements for creating objects. The class declaration indicates how the object should behave, and the instances of the class refer to the objects being manipulated by the program.

A C++ class can include both data and functions as members. The data members represent the internal state of an object of that class, whereas the functions define the behavior of the object. By grouping the members into sections labelled public, private, and protected, you can control which members are accessible to the functions outside the class. The data members usually become private, and all interactions with the class are made through a set of public member functions. To implement a class, you must declare the class and define all its member functions. A good strategy for modular implementation is to declare the class in a header file and define the member functions in a separate implementation file.

Once a class is defined, you can create and use objects of that class just as you would use built-in data types such as int, char, and double. You can either define the objects like any other variable or create them dynamically by calling the new and delete operators, which are analogous to the C library's malloc and free functions.

10

Defining Operations on Objects

Chapter 9, "Building Objects with Classes," focused on the use of `class` and `struct` constructs to encapsulate data with functions when defining a new data type with its own operators. That chapter explained the general strategy for implementing and using a class. The implementation includes two components: a header file with the declaration of the class and a source file with the actual definition of the member functions of the class.

This chapter shows you how to define the member functions and the operators for a class. While the concept of creating objects with `class` is straightforward, many small details become important when implementing classes in C++. For example, you need to know when to pass arguments by reference and how to ensure that objects are initialized properly. This chapter addresses these questions.

Arguments and Return Values

In C++, you manipulate objects using member functions and operators defined for the class of which the object is an instance. As a C programmer, you know that functions accept one or more arguments and return a value. C employs the *pass-by-value* mechanism for providing a function with its arguments.

In pass-by-value, functions receive their argument in a special area of memory called the *stack*, a last-in-first-out (LIFO) data structure. Before calling a function, the calling program copies each argument's value to the stack and passes control to the function. The function retrieves the arguments from the stack and uses them in the body of the function. If necessary, the function can return a single value to the calling program. The net effect of this mechanism of passing arguments is that the function never accesses the actual storage locations of the arguments that its caller provides. Instead, it always works with local copies of the arguments, and the local copies are discarded from the stack when they are returned from the function.

This pass-by-value approach is a good choice for argument passing because it guarantees that a function never alters its arguments. However, as you will see next, pass-by-value is not always beneficial when you need to pass objects around.

Understanding Pointers and References

Although a function that receives its arguments by value cannot alter the arguments, what if an argument is the address of a variable or, in other words, a *pointer* to the variable? In this case, the function can clearly alter the value of the variable through that pointer. For example, if you want to swap the contents of two integer variables, one way to do this is to write a function that accepts pointers to the two `int` variables:

```
void swap_int(int *p_a, int *p_b)
{
    int temp;
    temp = *p_a;
    *p_a = *p_b;
    *p_b = temp;
}
```

You can use this function to swap integer variables as follows:

```
int x = 2, y = 3;

swap_int(&x, &y);  /* Now x = 3 and y = 2 */
```

Although you can continue to use this type of function in C++ programs, C++ introduces a reference that makes it much easier to write this type of function. A *reference* is an alternate name for an object that you can use just as you would the object itself. Think of a reference as the address of an item. Unlike a pointer, however, a reference is not a real variable. A reference is initialized when it is defined, and you cannot modify its value later. The syntax of a reference mimics that of a pointer, except a reference requires an ampersand (&) and the pointer declaration requires an asterisk (*). Thus,

```
int *p_i;  // An uninitialized pointer to integer
```

defines an `int` pointer, whereas

```
int &r_i = i;  // Reference to i (an int variable)
```

is a reference to an `int` variable named `i`.

As a practical example of the use of a reference, here is the `swap_int` function with arguments passed by a reference:

```
void swap_int(int &a, int &b)
{
    int temp;
    temp = a;
    a = b;
    b = temp;
}
```

Compare this version of the function with the one that uses pointers. You can see that the version that uses references looks cleaner—you no longer need to dereference pointers in each expression. The new version of the function is simpler to use because you do not need to provide the address of the integers being swapped as arguments. Instead, you call the function as if the arguments are being passed by value:

```
void swap_int(int&, int&);  // Prototype of function

int x = 2, y = 3;

swap_int(x, y);             // Now x = 3 and y = 2
```

The compiler knows from the function's prototype that it must pass references to the x and y variables.

As you can see from the examples in this section, you can think of a reference as a pointer with a constant value that the C++ compiler automatically dereferences whenever you use it. In other words, given the following:

```
int i;           // An integer variable
int &r_i = i;    // A reference to "i"
int *p_i = &i;   // A pointer to "i"
```

you can think of r_i as equivalent to p_i, except that wherever you use the expression r_i, the compiler substitutes *p_i. Because the value of a reference cannot change from its initial assignment, the C++ compiler does not need to allocate storage for a reference. It only needs to implement the semantics of each reference.

Passing by Value Versus Passing by Reference

From the example of swapping integers, you might surmise that references are good for writing functions that need to alter the values of their arguments. While this is certainly one of the uses of passing arguments by reference, there is another important reason for providing the reference mechanism in C++.

Consider what happens when an object is passed to a function by value. To implement the pass-by-value semantics, the compiler must copy the object to the stack before the function is called. For large class objects, copying involves a space and time penalty. You can avoid the overheads of copying by using a reference to the object (instead of the object itself) as an argument. If the function does not modify an argument, you can indicate this with the const qualifier for that reference argument. Thus, passing arguments by reference enhances the efficiency of object-based programming in C++.

Returning a Reference

Just as passing arguments by reference prevents unnecessary copying to the stack, you can return an object by reference to avoid copying the returned object. Watch what happens when you return an object by value. Suppose you return a String object from an add_strings function that returns the concatenation of two strings:

```
String add_strings(const String& s1, const String& s2)
{
// In function's body
    String s;
// Append s1 and s2 to s
//...
    return s;
}
```

In this case, the `return` statement must copy `String` `s` to an area of memory provided by the calling program. To do so properly, the `return` statement calls a special constructor, called the *copy constructor*, which can create and initialize a new instance of an object from an existing one. After creating the copy, the `return` statement calls the destructor of the `String` class to destroy `String` `s` before returning to the calling program. This is a good example of the work done by the C++ compiler behind the scenes. You probably didn't realize that so much extra work was going into an innocuous `return` statement.

The example you have just seen illustrates what happens when a function returns an object. Although returning by reference would save the time spent in copying the object, you cannot return a reference to `String` `s` because `s` is a temporary object that exists only within the `add_strings` function (`s` is destroyed when the function returns). Therefore, you should be careful what you return by reference. Because a reference is like a pointer, you cannot return a reference to anything that is temporary.

The Significance of `const` Arguments

By qualifying an argument to a function with the `const` keyword, you can inform the C++ compiler that the function should not modify the argument. The compiler generates an error message if the function inadvertently tries to alter that argument. The `const` qualifier is significant only for arguments that are pointers or that are passed by reference because changes made by a function to arguments passed by value cannot be seen in the calling program.

A common use of returning by reference is in an *access function*—a function that provides access to an internal element of an existing object. For example, if you want to write a member function named `char_at_pos` for the `String` class that provides access to the character at a specified location in an instance of `String`, you can safely return a reference to the character at the specified location. Thus, you might write the char_at_pos function as follows:

```
//--------------------------------------------------------------------
//  c h a r _ a t _ p o s
//  Access a character in a String

char& String::char_at_pos(int index)
{
// Check if index goes beyond allocated length.
// Return last element, if it does
    if(index > _maxlen-1) return p_c[_maxlen-1];
    else  return p_c[index];
}
```

Here is a typical use of the function:

```
    String s1 = "Test";
// ...

// Print the second character of String s1
    cout << "3rd char = " << s1.char_at_pos(2) << endl;

// Change the first character of s1
    s1.char_at_pos(0) = 'B';  // Now s1 = "Best"
```

Although you may expect the first use of the char_at_pos function to retrieve the character at a specific position in the string, you may not realize that you can even set a character to a new value. The second use of char_at_pos is possible only because the function returns a reference to a char. Because a reference is exactly like the variable itself, you can assign a new value to the returned reference.

If you already know C++, you may realize that a better solution for accessing a character in String would be to overload the [] operator. A little later in this chapter you will see how to define such operators for a class.

Using References: The Guidelines

You can follow several rules of thumb when deciding where to use references. You should pass arguments to a function by reference when:

- You want the function to modify the arguments.
- The function will not modify the arguments, but you want to avoid copying the objects to the stack. In this case, use the `const` qualifier to indicate that the argument being passed by reference should not be altered by the function.

As for return values, you should return a reference to an object whenever you want to use that return value as the left side of an assignment. Of course, you should return a reference to an object only when the object is guaranteed to exist after the function returns.

Creating and Destroying Objects

Because basic data types, such as `int` and `float`, are simply chunks of memory that hold a single value, a user-defined class can contain many more components, some of which may require additional work during creation besides setting aside a number of bytes of storage. Take, for instance, the `String` class. Internally, it stores a pointer to an array of characters that holds the null-terminated string. To function properly, a newly created `String` object must set this pointer to a properly allocated array of `chars` and, quite possibly, initialize that array to a specific string. After all, if you treat `String` like any other type of variable, you must be able to handle statements such as

```
String this_os = "MS-DOS";
String new_os = this_os;
```

For proper handling of this type of initialization, C++ allows each class a special function called the *constructor*, which has the same name as the class and does not have any return type. Thus, the constructor for the `String` class is a function named `String`. Of course, as with other functions, you can have more than one constructor, each with a unique list of arguments and each intended for a specific type of initialization.

A constructor for a class like `String` allocates extra memory for the null-terminated string. This means that there must be a way to release this memory when the `String` is no longer needed. C++ handles this need through a *destructor*, a function with the same name as the class but with a tilde (~) as a prefix. Thus, the destructor of the `String` class is named `~String`. Destructors do not take any argument—you cannot overload a destructor.

Constructors and Destructors for the *String* Class

Chapter 9 provided you with a brief description and the declaration of a `String` class that represents a text string data type with its own operators and string manipulation functions. The idea is to hold a pointer to an array of bytes that can hold a null terminated array of characters, the standard way of representing strings in C and C++. The variables `_maxlen` and `_length` denote, respectively, the size of the allocated array and the length of the string stored in the array. To allow for character insertion into the `String`, the size of the `char` array is rounded up to the next highest multiple of a specified chunk of bytes. For example, if the chunk is 8 bytes, the allocated size of the array to hold a 10-character string will be 16 bytes—the nearest multiple of 8 that exceeds 10. This idea is useful, for example, if you plan to use the `String` objects in a text editor where you must allow for the insertion of characters into a `String`.

Listing 9.1 shows the STR.H header file, which declares the `String` class. To refresh your memory, here is a skeleton declaration of the `String` class showing the private members, the constructors, and the destructor:

```
class String
{
public:
// Constructors with a variety of arguments
    String();
    String(size_t len);
    String(const char *str);
    String(const String &s);

// Destructor
    ~String();

// ...

private:
// Internal data members of this class

    char   *p_c;      // pointer to allocated space
    size_t _length;   // current length of string
    size_t _maxlen;   // number of bytes allocated

};
```

Which Constructor Is Called?

If a class defines constructors, the C++ compiler calls an appropriate constructor to initialize each instance of a class. The way you define the class instances controls the constructor that is called. The constructor with no arguments is called when you define an instance but do not specify any initial value. For other cases, the type of initial value determines the constructor that the C++ compiler calls. You can define and initialize a class instance in three ways:

- Use the C-style syntax as illustrated by the following example for an instance of the `String` class:

  ```
  String operating_system = "MS-DOS";
  ```

- Use a function call syntax, such as:

  ```
  String operating_system("MS-DOS");
  ```

- Use the `new` operator to allocate on the free store:

  ```
  String *lines = new String[25];
  ```

In the first two cases, the C++ compiler calls the `String(const char*)` constructor because you are initializing the `String` object with a null-terminated character array. Thus, the compiler calls the constructor that takes as an argument the type of value you are using to initialize the class instance. In the last case, the compiler calls the constructor that takes no arguments, and it calls this constructor for each of the 25 `String` objects being created.

Because the `String` class defines a constructor that accepts a string length as an argument, here is an initialization that is appropriate to use with the `String` class (even though this may look strange to C programmers):

```
String eight_blanks = 8;  // A string with 8 blanks
```

Based on the description of the `String(size_t)` constructor, this statement creates a `String` initialized with eight blank spaces.

Default Constructor

The *default constructor* is a constructor that takes no arguments. For the `String` class, you can define the default constructor as a function that allocates a single chunk of bytes and initializes it to a zero-length string:

```
//----------------------------------------------------------------
//  S t r i n g
//  Creates a String and stores a zero-length string in it.

String::String()
{
    _maxlen = chunk_size;    // const chunk_size = 8;
    p_c = new char[_maxlen];
    _length = 0;
    p_c[0] = '\0';
}
```

In lieu of a constructor with no arguments, the upcoming ANSI standard for C++ plans to allow the compiler to use any constructor (with default values specified for all of its arguments) as a default constructor. For a `Point` class that represents a point in the x,y plane, such a default constructor might appear as follows:

```
Point::Point(int x = 0, int y = 0)
{
// Copy x and y coordinates into internal variables of Point
}
```

The default constructor is called whenever you define an instance of the class without providing any explicit initial value. Here is an example where the default constuctor is called:

```
String s1;  // s1 is initialized by calling default constructor
```

The default constructor also plays an important role when you allocate an array of class instances. Here, the C++ compiler automatically calls the default constructor for each element of the array. If you write

```
String edit_buf[24];  // Create an array of 24 Strings
```

the default constructor of `String` is called to initialize each element of the `edit_buf` array.

Define a Default Constructor for Each Class

If you define constructors for a class, you should always define a default constructor (a constructor that requires no arguments) as well. When you define an array of instances for a class, the C++ compiler initializes each instance in the array by calling the default constructor.

Defining Other *String* Constructors

The `String` class contains a few other constructors besides the default constructor. One of them takes a number of bytes as the argument and creates a blank string with that many bytes. Here is the definition of that constructor:

```
//--------------------------------------------------------------------
//  S t r i n g
//  This version creates a blank string of size "len"

String::String(size_t len)
{
    _length = len;
// NOTE: const chunk_size = 8;
    _maxlen = chunk_size*(_length / chunk_size + 1);
    p_c = new char[_maxlen];
    int i;
    for(i = 0; i < len; i++) p_c[i] = ' ';
    p_c[i] = '\0';
}
```

First, the constructor computes `_maxlen`, the number of bytes to allocate. It then uses the `new` operator to allocate the array of `chars` and initialize the array to a null-terminated string that contains the specified number of space characters.

Another useful constructor for the `String` class is one that accepts a null-terminated character array and creates a `String` from it. You might define this constructor as follows:

```
//--------------------------------------------------------------------
//  S t r i n g
//  Creates a String object and initializes it from a
//  null-terminated C string

String::String(const char *s)
{
    _length = strlen(s);
// NOTE: const chunk_size = 8;
    _maxlen = chunk_size*(_length / chunk_size + 1);
    p_c = new char[_maxlen];
    strcpy(p_c, s);
}
```

String Destructor

The destructor reverses anything done in the constructor. Usually, this means releasing memory that the constructor allocated when creating the object. For the String class, the constructor allocates the array that holds the null-terminated string. The pointer to this array is stored in the p_c private member variable. Thus, the ~String destructor frees up the memory allocated for the character array:

```
//--------------------------------------------------------------------
//  ~ S t r i n g
//  Destroys a String

String::~String()
{
    delete[] p_c;
}
```

Copy Constructor

Another special type of constructor is the *copy constructor*, which is capable of creating a replica of an object. To understand why a copy constructor is necessary, consider the following example. If you decide to pass a String object by value to an append_space function, which, presumably, adds a space to the end of the string, the function would be declared and used as follows:

```
void append_space(String s);  // expects argument by value
String s1 = "Result is";
append_space(s1);             //  a sample call
```

To implement the call to append_space, the C++ compiler must make a copy of the String s1 on the stack. As shown in Figure 10.1, the body of a String object contains a pointer to the actual null-terminated string. The constructor of the String class takes care of allocating and initializing this memory.

To make a copy of String s1 on the stack, the compiler, by default, copies each member of String s1 to the stack. This, however, results in the situation shown in Figure 10.2. Both the copy and the original String point to the same null-terminated string because the character pointers are identical.

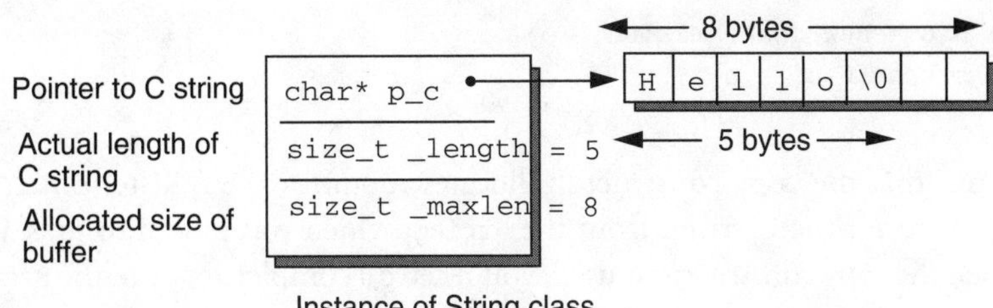

Figure 10.1. An instance of the `String` class.

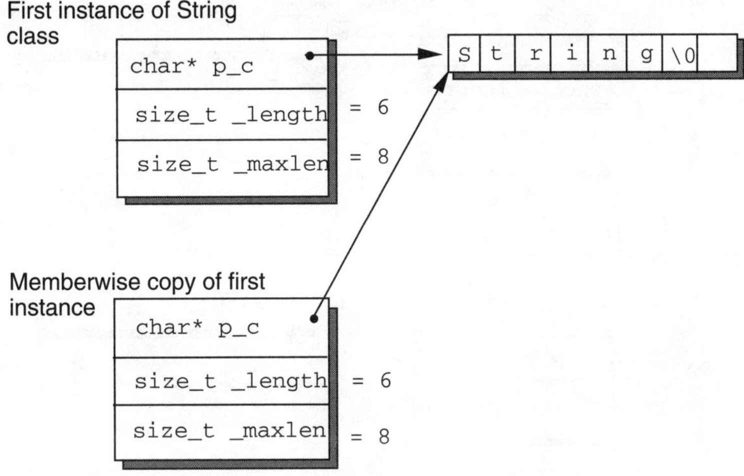

Figure 10.2. Memberwise copy of one `String` to another.

To create a complete copy, you must define a constructor for `String` that takes a `String` reference as the argument; in other words, a constructor that can create a copy of a `String`. For the `String` class, you might implement this copy constructor as follows:

```
#include "str.h"   // Header file that declares the String class

//---------------------------------------------------------------
//  S t r i n g  ( c o n s t  S t r i n g & )
//  Creates a new String as a copy of another String
//  This is called the "Copy Constructor"

String::String(const String &s)
{
    _length = s._length;
    _maxlen = s._maxlen;
```

```
    p_c = new char[_maxlen];
    strcpy(p_c, s.p_c);
}
```

Notice that the copy constructor allocates room for the null-terminated string and copies into it the C string from the `String`, which was passed to it as an argument. When the copy constructor is used, you receive a complete copy of the `String` as shown in Figure 10.3.

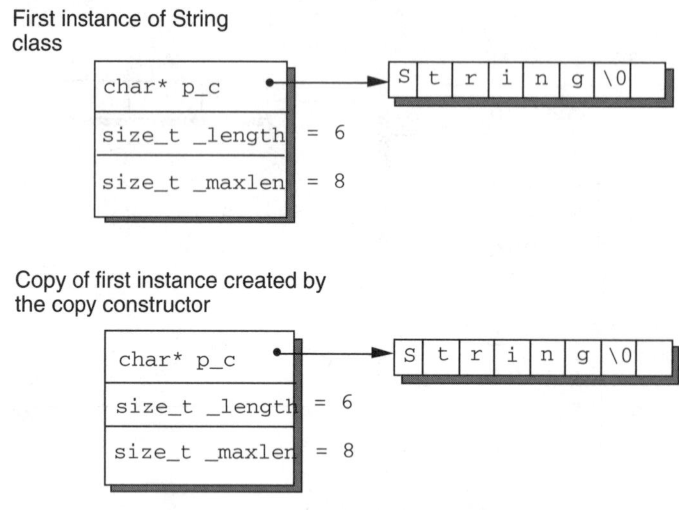

Figure 10.3. Copying with the copy constructor.

The copy constructor also comes into play when you write

```
String s1 = "Hello!";
String s2 = s1;
```

In this case, the C++ compiler must initialize `s2` with the value of another `String s1`. To do this, the compiler looks for a copy constructor for the `String` class. The copy constructor for `String` is declared as follows:

```
String(const String&);
```

Because of the form of the declaration, books and manuals on C++ often refer to this as the `X(const X&)` constructor, where `X` denotes any class.

When to Provide a Copy Constructor

If your class does not include any pointers that need to be properly initialized, you do not need to provide a copy constructor. The C++ compiler uses a default copy constructor that performs a memberwise copy of one class instance to another. You must provide a copy constructor only for classes with a pointer variable, such as the `String` class for example. If you do not, the result of copying is as shown for the `String` objects in Figure 10.2. Both copies hold pointers to a single array of characters.

Even if you can accept the memberwise copy, you will run into another problem because of the destructor. If a `String` object created by a memberwise copy operation is no longer needed, the `String` destructor is called. The destructor frees the storage with the address in the character pointer of that `String`. This leaves the remaining copy of `String` with a *dangling pointer*—a pointer that does not point to any valid block of memory. When that remaining copy of `String` has to be destroyed, the `delete` operator is called with the address of memory that has already been freed. Worse yet, if that memory has been allocated to some other object, the destructor inadvertently frees memory belonging to some other object. To avoid such problems, you should always provide a copy constructor for any class that includes dynamically allocated members.

> **Copy Constructor**
>
> Provide a copy constructor of the `X::X(const X&)` form for any class that allocates memory in its constructor. The copy constructor ensures that instances of that class are copied correctly.

Member Initializer List

How do you initialize a class that contains an instance of another class? If you decide to implement a `Line` class, which contains two instances of the `Point` class, each representing an endpoint of the line, your class declaration might look like this:

```
class Point
{
public:
```

```
    Point(double _x=0.0, double _y=0.0)
    {
        x = _x;
        y = _y;
    }
    Point(const Point& p) { x = p.x, y = p.y;}

private:
    double x,y;     // Coordinates of point
};

class Line
{
public:
    Line(const Point& b, Point& e) : p1(b), p2(e) {}
// ...
private:
    Point p1, p2;  // End-points of line
};
```

Notice the curious way of defining the constructor for the `Line` class. The constructor takes two `Point` references as arguments. It needs only to copy the points to the internal points `p1` and `p2`. Of course, the obvious way is to write

```
Line::Line(const Point& b, Point& e)
{
    p1 = b;
    p2 = e;
}
```

This works, but it sets up points `p1` and `p2` using the default constructor of the `Point` class and then performs a memberwise copy of `b` to `p1` and `e` to `p2`. A more efficient approach is to initialize `p1` and `p2` with the copy constructor. However, by the time you are inside the constructor of `Line`, the `Point` instances `p1` and `p2` are already constructed. C++ solves this problem by allowing the *member initializer list*—a list of member variable initializations of the form:

```
variable_name(value)
```

separated by commas. Here, `variable_name` refers to a member variable of the class, and the `value` within parentheses denotes the value with which that variable is initialized. The member initializer list appears between the function's argument list and its body and is guaranteed to be processed before the statements in the function's body are executed.

Restrictions on Initializer List

In the initializer list of a class's constructor, you can initialize only immediate base classes and member variables that are not inherited from a base class. This restriction ensures that base classes and inherited member variables are not initialized more than once.

Initializer List Versus Assignment

For another example of a member initializer list, consider a `Name` class that has two `String` members as follows:

```
class Name
{
public:
    Name(const char *first, const char *last);
// Other public member functions...
private:
    String first_name;
    String last_name;
};
```

How do you define the constructor for this class? Most C programmers define it as follows:

```
Name::Name(const char *first, const char *last)
{
    first_name = first;
    last_name = last;
}
```

Although this looks straightforward, a lot of behind-the-scenes work is done to initialize the `first_name` and `last_name` members of the `Name` class. To be specific, the compiler takes the following steps:

1. The compiler calls the default constructor of the `String` class to create the strings `first_name` and `last_name`. Note that the default constructor allocates some space for a character array.

2. The compiler creates two temporary `String` objects from the `first` and `last` character arrays.

3. The compiler calls the copy constructor of the String class to initialize first_name and last_name with the temporary Strings of the preceding step. The copy constructor also allocates storage for the character array.

4. The compiler generates code that destroys the temporary Strings created in Step 2.

Consider what happens if you rewrite the Name constructor using a member initializer list. The definition changes to

```
Name::Name(const char *first, const char *last)
        : first_name(first), last_name(last) {}
```

Now the compiler can construct an instance of Name in a single step by simply processing the initializer list. The compiler calls the String(const char*) constructor of the String class to create the String first_name out of first and the String last_name out of last. In this case, storage for character arrays is allocated only once for each String and no unnecessary temporary objects exist. For reasons of efficiency, you should use initializer lists to initialize member variables. Note that you can use the initializer list syntax for built-in types such as int, double, and char* as well.

Initialization of *const* Member Variables and References

Even if you ignore the efficiency of initializer lists, some occasions occur when you must use member initializers to create an instance of a class. This occurs when the class in question has either:

- A const member variable
- A reference member variable

Both of these, according to the rules of C++, must be initialized when defined. In other words, these member variables must contain a constant value as soon as the class instance is created. The following fictitious class illustrates how to do this:

```
class SampleClass
{
public:
// Constructor uses member initializer list
    SampleClass(int id) : obj_id(id), r_i(i) {}
//...
private:
    const int obj_id;
    int       i;
```

```
    int&        r_i;
};
```

Here, the integer argument to the constructor is used to initialize the `const` variable `obj_id`, whereas the `int` reference `r_i` is set to another integer variable within the class.

> **Efficient Initialization with Member Initializer Lists**
>
> Use member initializer lists to efficiently initialize class members that are instances of other classes. You must use member initializers to initialize nonstatic `const` and reference members of a class.

Nested Class Declarations

C++ allows you to nest one class declaration inside the body of another class. The name of such a nested class is local to the enclosing class. You can use nested classes to declare items with the same name but different types in several classes. For instance, you might declare a nested class named `Attribute` in several different classes as follows:

```
class A
{
public:
    int command;
//    ...
    class Attribute
    {
    public:
        Attribute() : _id(0) {}
        id() { return _id;}
    private:
        int _id;
    };
private:
    int opcode;
};

class B
{
public:
```

```
    float speed;
//    ...
    class Attribute
    {
    public:
        Attribute() : _range(0) {}
    private:
        float _range;
    };
private:
    float fuel;
};
```

First thing you should note is that declaring a class nested in another does not create an instance of the nested class. You have to explicitly define instances of the nested class to create the objects.

When you refer to a nested class outside the enclosing class, you have to qualify the nested class's name with a scope resolution operator. Thus, to define and use an instance of the nested class `Attribute`, declared in class `A`, you would write

```
A::Attribute attrib_a;
// ...
cout << "ID = " << attrib_a.id() << endl;
```

A nested class has to follow the usual access rules when accessing members of its enclosing class. Thus the `Attribute` class, which is nested in `A`, cannot access `A`'s private member variable `opcode`. Member functions of the enclosing class obey similar rules; they can access only the public members of the nested class. In the example, `A` cannot access the `_id` member variable of `Attribute` except through `Attribute`'s public function `id`.

Exploiting the Side Effects of Constructor and Destructor

You know that whenever an instance of a class is created, the C++ compiler automatically calls the constructor of that class. If the class instance is an automatic variable, the destructor is called when the instance goes out of scope and must be destroyed. This means that you can have classes that do all their work in the constructors and destructors.

There is nothing wrong with using classes only for the side effects of their constructors and destructors. In fact, they sometimes lead to an elegant solution of a problem.

As an example, consider the dilemma of estimating the time taken to execute a block of code. Typically, you would obtain the time at the start of the computation and perform the computation many times so that you could measure the elapsed time accurately. The ANSI C library includes functions such as `time` to obtain the current time and `clock` to get the clock ticks elapsed since the program started running; (`time` has an accuracy of seconds, whereas `clock` is somewhat more accurate—each *clock tick* lasting approximately 55 milliseconds on MS-DOS systems).

A *Timer* Class

To perform the timing in a C++ program, write a `Timer` class with a constructor that calls `clock` to obtain the current clock ticks. In the destructor, call `clock` again and compute the difference of the starting and ending clock ticks. Report the elapsed time in seconds between construction and destruction of an instance of `Timer`. You can convert clock ticks to seconds using the preprocessor macro `CLOCKS_PER_SEC`, which supplies the number of clock ticks per second. This macro, as well as the prototype of the `clock` function, appears in the TIME.H ANSI C header file. Listing 10.1 shows the TIMER.H header file, which is a typical implementation of the `Timer` class.

Listing 10.1. TIMER.H. Implementation of a `Timer` class.

```
//-------------------------------------------------------------------
//  File:  timer.h
//
//  Implements a timer that works solely through its
//  constructor and destructor.  Uses the "clock" function
//  of the ANSI standard C library.  The "clock" function
//  returns the number of clock ticks used by the current
//  process.  The preprocessor macro CLOCKS_PER_SEC tells us
//  how to convert clock ticks to seconds.
//-------------------------------------------------------------------
#if !defined(__TIMER_H)
#define __TIMER_H

#include <time.h>      // For definition of the clock_t type
                       // and the CLOCKS_PER_SEC macro

#include <iostream.h> // For output to "cerr" stream

class Timer
{
```

continues

Listing 10.1. continued

```
public:
    Timer() { start = clock();}  // Constructor

    ~Timer()  // Destructor (compute and display elapsed time)
    {
        clock_t stop = clock();
        cerr << "Elapsed time = ";
        cerr << (stop - start)/CLOCKS_PER_SEC;
        cerr << " seconds" << endl;
    }
private:
    clock_t start;    // Store starting clock tick count
};

#endif
```

Using the *Timer* Class

Listing 10.2 shows the C++ program TIMERTST.CPP, which uses the `Timer` class to estimate the time taken to execute a set of computations. In Listing 10.2, the compute function performs all the work. It defines an instance of `Timer` that starts the clock ticking, so to speak. Then the function repeatedly executes the computations in a loop. When the loop ends and the function returns, the `Timer` object is destroyed. The C++ compiler automatically calls the destructor of the `Timer` class, and the destructor prints out the elapsed time.

Listing 10.2. TIMERTST.CPP. Sample use of the `Timer` class.

```
//-------------------------------------------------------------------
//  File:  timertst.cpp
//
//  Use the Timer class to time a function
//-------------------------------------------------------------------
#include "timer.h"

//-------------------------------------------------------------------
//  c o m p u t e
//  A function that performs some computations
```

```
static void compute(unsigned long count)
{
    unsigned long i;
    double a, b, c, d;
    Timer t;                      // Create Timer to time function
    for(i = 0; i < count; i++)
    {
        a = (double)(i-1);
        b = (double)(i+1);
        c = (double)(i+i);
        d = a*b - c;
    }
}
//-------------------------------------------------------------
//  m a i n
//  Main function that times the "compute" function

void main()
{
    unsigned long count;
    cout << "How many times? ";
    cin >> count;
    compute(count);
}
```

After building the TIMERTST program with optimizations turned off (`-Od` option for the Borland C++ compiler), a typical output under Microsoft Windows on a 66MHz Intel 80486DX2 PC-AT compatible system (user's input is in boldface) is as follows:

```
How many times? 1000000
Elapsed time = 6.81 seconds
```

As you can see from this example, you can have perfectly useful classes with instances used only for the side effects of their construction and destruction.

Defining Functions and Operators

The member functions and operators model the behavior of a class and define how you use the objects represented by a class. The functions are defined like any other functions, except that you must indicate the association of a function with a class by using the scope resolution operator (`::`). You have already seen the definition of several constructors for the `String` class. The following sections present a few other functions for the `String` class and describe how to define operators for a class.

The *this* Pointer

Before describing how member functions and operators are defined, you should know about the `this` keyword. Although a unique copy of member variables exists for each instance of a class, all instances share a single set of member functions. However, none of the member functions that you have seen so far have any way of indicating the class instance with member variables that are being used in the function. Take, for instance, the `length` function of the `String` class. If you write

```
String s1 ("Hello"), s2("Hi");
len1 = s1.length();  // len1 = 5
len2 = s2.length();  // len2 = 2
```

each call to `length` returns a unique answer, yet the `length` function is defined as

```
inline size_t String::length(void) const
{
    return _length;
}
```

where `_length` is a member variable of the `String` class. How did the function know to return the correct length for each string? The answer is in `this`.

this Points to Instance of Class

The C++ compiler alters each member function in a class by making two changes:

1. It passes an additional argument named `this`, a pointer to the specific object for which the function is being invoked. Thus, the `s1.length()` call includes a `this` argument set to the address of the `String` instance `s1`.

2. It adds the `this->` prefix to all member variables and functions. Thus, the `_length` variable in the `length` function becomes `this->_length`, which refers to the copy of `_length` in the class instance with an address in `this`.

Typically, you do not need to use `this` explicitly in a member function, but you can refer to `this` if needed. For example, if you need to return the object to a calling program, you can use the following statement to do the job:

```
return *this;
```

You can return a reference to the object with the same statement. As you will see in the following sections, you must return references when defining certain operators such as the assignment operator (=).

If you are still wondering about the `this` keyword and its use, you may want to revisit the example of object-oriented programming in C that appears in Chapter 5, "Basics of Object-Oriented Programming." In that chapter, you were shown that the C functions implementing the OOP techniques need a pointer to the object as an argument. That need remains in C++, but the syntax of writing member functions is now more palatable to programmers by the behind-the-scenes handling of the pointer to the object through the `this` keyword.

Operators as Functions

Defining operators for a class is easy once you know how the application of an operator is translated to a function call. For a unary operator, such as `&`, when you write

```
&X
```

where `X` is an instance of some class, the C++ compiler applies the operator by calling the function:

```
X.operator&()
```

The compiler automatically passes a pointer to the class instance to binary operators such as `+`. For an expression such as

```
X + Y
```

where `X` and `Y` are class instances, the compiler calls the function:

```
X.operator+(Y)
```

As you can see, the C++ compiler reduces the application of operators to function calls. Consequently, you can overload an operator by defining a function with a name that begins with the operator keyword followed by the symbolic notation of that operator.

Arguments to Operator Functions

Like all member functions, operator functions receive a pointer to the class instance in the hidden argument named `this`. Because this argument is implicit, unary operator functions are defined with no arguments at all. Binary operator functions that are members of the class take a single argument that is the right side of the operator expression. However, you can define an operator function as a `friend` instead of a member function of the class. As you will see next, sometimes you need to define `friend` operator functions. When declared as a `friend`, the operator function requires all arguments explicitly. This means, to declare `operator+` as a friend function of class `X`, you write

```
friend X operator+(X&, X&);   // Assume X is a class
```

Then, to evaluate the expression `x1 + x2` for two instances of class `X`, the C++ compiler will call the function `operator(x1, x2)`.

Significance of the `this` Pointer

Every member function of a class implicitly receives a pointer to the current instance of the class in a pointer named `this`. Inside the body of a member function, you can use `this` to refer to the address of the class instance upon which the function is to operate. If a function must return the instance or a reference to it, you can write

```
return *this;
```

However, you do not need to explicitly use the `this` pointer in the member functions. The C++ compiler automatically uses it behind the scenes when accessing members of that instance of the class.

Operators You Can Overload

Table 10.1 lists the C++ operators that you can overload. As you can see, you can overload almost all predefined operators in C++. The only ones you cannot overload are the following:

Member access operator	`x.y`
Dereferencing a pointer to member	`x.*y`
Scope resolution operator	`x::y`
Conditional operator	`x?y:z`

Note that you can only overload the predefined operators. You cannot introduce any new operator notations. For example, FORTRAN uses ** to denote exponentiation. In FORTRAN, `X**Y` means `X` raised to the power `Y`. However, even with operator overloading, you cannot define a similar ** operator in C++ because C++ lacks a predefined ** operator.

Table 10.1. C++ operators that you can overload.

Type	Name	Notation	Comments
Unary	Preincrement	++x	Use operator++ for both
	Postincrement	x++	pre- and postincrement
	Predecrement	--x	Use operator-- for both
	Postdecrement	x--	pre- and postdecrement
	Address of	&x	
	Indirection	*x	
	Plus	+x	Define as operator+()
	Minus	-x	Define as operator-()
	Bitwise NOT	~x	
	Logical NOT	!x	
	Type cast	(type)x	Define as operator type()
Arithmetic	Multiply	x*y	
	Divide	x/y	
	Remainder	x%y	
	Add	x+y	Define as operator+(y) or as friend operator+(x,y)
	Subtract	x-y	Define as operator-(y) or as friend operator -(x,y)
Shift	Left shift	x<<y	
	Right shift	x>>y	
Relational	Greater than	x>y	
	Greater than or equal	x>=y	

continues

Table 10.1. continued

Type	Name	Notation	Comments
	Less than	x<y	
	Less than or equal	x<=y	
	Equal to	x==y	
	Not equal to	x!=y	
Bitwise	Bitwise AND	x&y	
	Bitwise exclusive OR	x^y	
	Bitwise OR	x¦y	
Logical	Logical AND	x&&y	
	Logical OR	x¦¦y	
Assignment	Assignment	x=y	
	Multiply assign	x *= y	
	Divide assign	x /= y	
	Remainder assign	x %= y	
	Add assign	x += y	
	Subtract assign	x -= y	
	Left shift assign	x <<= y	
	Right shift assign	x >>= y	
	Bitwise AND assign	x &= y	
	Bitwise XOR assign	x ^= y	
	Bitwise OR assign	x ¦= y	
Data Access	Subscript	x[y]	
	Member selection	x->y	
	Dereference Member Pointer	x->*y	
Function call	Function call	x(y)	

Type	Name	Notation	Comments
Comma	Comma	`x,y`	
Storage	`new`	`X *p=new X` or `X *q=new X[10]`	
	`delete`	`delete p` or `delete[] q`	

Operator Precedence Remains Unchanged

Although C++ enables you to redefine the meaning of most built-in operator symbols for a class, you cannot change the precedence rules that dictate the order in which operators are evaluated. C++ operators follow the same precedence as those of their ANSI C counterparts as shown in Table 3.5. Even if, for some class, you were to define + and * operators as something entirely different from addition and multiplication, in an expression such as

```
a + b * c    // a, b, c are some class instances
```

the C++ compiler would still invoke the `operator*` function to evaluate `b * c` before calling `operator+`.

Defining *operator+* for the *String* Class

As an example of operator overloading, consider the + operator—the binary version—for the `String` class. A good interpretation of this operator for the `String` class is to concatenate two `String` objects. In other words, a typical use of the + operator for `String` might be

```
String s1("This "), s2("and that"), s3;
s3 = s1+s2;  // Now s3 should contain "This and that"
```

You can get this functionality by defining the following function as a member of the `String` class:

```
//----------------------------------------------------------------
//  o p e r a t o r +
//  Member function to concatenate two String objects

String String::operator+(const String& s)
{
```

```
    size_t len = _length + s._length;
    char *t = new char[len+1];
    strcpy(t, p_c);
    strcat(t, s.p_c);
    String r(t);
    delete[] t;
    return (r);
}
```

Because this version of operator+ is a member function of the String class, it takes only one argument—a reference to the String on the right side of the + operator. The function returns a new String object that is a concatenation of the two Strings being added. As you can see from the body of this operator+ function, if you use new to allocate temporary storage, you are responsible for freeing the storage by using the delete operator.

While the operator+ member function works fine when adding Strings, it cannot handle another type of use for the operator. Because a String is intended to model a dynamic array of characters, it is natural to allow the use of the operator in expressions such as

```
String s1 = "World!";
String s2 = "Hello," + s1; // s2 should be "Hello, World!"
```

In this case, the C++ compiler interprets the right side of the expression as

```
"Hello".operator+(s1)
```

This is an error because "Hello" is not an instance of a class, and, therefore, contains no member operator+ function that can be applied to it. You might think that a solution would be to convert "Hello" to a String and then apply the operator+ function of the String class. However, this does not happen because the C++ compiler does not automatically convert the left operand of any member operator functions. However, if you define a nonmember friend operator+ function in the String class:

```
friend String operator+(const String& s1, const String& s2)
```

the compiler converts the expression "Hello" + s1 to the function call:

```
operator+(String("Hello"), s1)
```

which automatically converts the left side of the + operator to a String. The definition of the friend operator+ function is similar to the member function, except that it takes two String arguments, and the body of the function must refer to each argument explicitly. Here is a definition of the function:

```
//-------------------------------------------------------------------
//  o p e r a t o r +
//  Nonmember function that concatenates two String objects
//  (Declare as "friend" in String class)

String operator+(const String& s1, const String& s2)
{
    size_t len = s1._length + s2._length;
    char *t = new char[len+1];
    strcpy(t, s1.p_c);
    strcat(t, s2.p_c);
    String s3(t);
    delete[] t;
    return (s3);
}
```

The `friend` version of the `operator+` function does not require the `String::` scope resolution prefix because it is not a member function of the `String` class.

Testing Strings for Equality

Another interesting operator is ==. You can use this operator with the `String` class to compare two `String` instances for equality. Because the `String` class internally maintains a C string, the easiest way to implement this operator is to call the `strcmp` function from the C library as shown here:

```
#include "str.h"  // Includes <string.h>
//...

//-------------------------------------------------------------------
//  o p e r a t o r = =
//  String equality operator. Returns nonzero if strings are
//  equal

inline Boolean String::operator==(const String &s) const
{
// Use ANSI C's strcmp function to compare the strings
// Remember strcmp returns 0 if the strings match, but this
//  function has to return nonzero (true) for a match
    return(strcmp(s.p_c, p_c) == 0);
}
```

(You can similarly define other relational operators such as `operator!=`, `operator >`, and `operator<`.)

Accessing and Altering Individual Characters in a *String*

Earlier in this chapter, you encountered a char_at_pos function that returned a reference to a character at a specific position in the character array inside an instance of a String. A better way to provide the functionality of the char_at_pos function is to overload the [] operator for the String class. Knowing the implementation of the char_at_pos function, you can define the operator[] function as follows:

```
//---------------------------------------------------------------
//  o p e r a t o r [ ]
//  Access a character in a String

char& String::operator[](int index)
{
// Check if index goes beyond allocated length.
// Return last element, if it does
    if(index > _maxlen-1) return p_c[_maxlen-1];
    else  return p_c[index];
}
```

With the [] operator defined in this way, you can use it in statements such as

```
String s = "hello";
char c = s[4];      // c = 'o', the 5th character of "hello"
s[0] = 'H';         // Now String s contains "Hello"
```

Defining the Type Conversion Operator

The String class is an abstraction of a character string and suitable for use in places where C-style, null-terminated strings are required. Suppose you want to allow String instances to be used in calls to the C library's string manipulation functions—the ones defined in the STRING.H header file. An example might be an expression such as

```
#include <string.h>
//...
String command;
//...
if(strcmp(command, "quit") == 0) exit(0);
```

Because the strcmp function is declared to accept two const char* arguments, the C++ compiler successfully makes this call, provided it can convert the String command to a const char*. You can help the C++ compiler do this by defining a *type conversion operator* of the form

```
String::operator const char*()
```

Of course, for the String class, you need only return the private char pointer member p_c. Because this function is so simple, you may want to define it as inline like this:

```
//------------------------------------------------------------------
//  o p e r a t o r   c o n s t   c h a r   *
//  Converts from String to char pointer

inline String::operator const char*() const
{
    return p_c;
}
```

Once this conversion operator is defined, calls to functions such as strcmp work even with a String as an argument.

Defining the Assignment Operator for the *String* Class

The = assignment operator is similar to the copy constructor, except that the copy constructor works with an uninitialized copy of an object whereas the assignment operator copies an object to another that is already initialized. Thus, for a String object, the assignment operator must eliminate the existing character array and set up a new one with the new value. A typical implementation of this operator function looks like this:

```
//------------------------------------------------------------------
//  o p e r a t o r =
//  Assigns one String object to another

String& String::operator=(const String& s)
{
// Do nothing if left and right sides are the same
    if(this != &s)
    {
```

```
        _length = s._length;
        _maxlen = s._maxlen;
        delete[] p_c;
        p_c = new char[_maxlen];
        strcpy(p_c, s.p_c);
    }
    return *this;
}
```

If you compare this function with the copy constructor, you will find the two to be very similar. One crucial difference, however, is the `if` statement at the beginning of the `operator+` function. This test ensures that the assignment operator works properly even when the left and right sides of the assignment operator are identical. When this happens, the variables `p_c` and `s.p_c` refer to the same pointer. You cannot indiscriminately delete `p_c` and expect `strcpy(p_c, s.p_c)` to work. The correctness of the assignment operation is ensured by comparing the `this` keyword with the operator's right side, which is the argument of the `operator=` function.

Why *operator=* Returns a Reference

You may have noticed that the `operator=` function for the `String` class returns `String&`, and you might have wondered why this is so. This is to allow assignments such as

```
String s1, s2, s3;
s1 = s2 = s3 = "None";
```

where the second statement initializes all three strings to the same value. This statement is possible only because the `operator=` function of the `String` class returns a reference to a `String` object and thereby can be the left side of further assignments.

Assignment and Initialization in C++

In C++, assignment and initialization are often denoted by very similar statements. Consider the following definitions of `String` objects:

```
String s1 = "This is initialization";
String s2;
s2 = "This is assignment"
```

This defines `String s1` and `String s2`. `String s1` is initialized by calling the `String(const char*)` constructor, whereas `String s2` is initially constructed by the default constructor `String()`. The third statement assigns a value to `String s2`. The definition of a class instance followed by an equal sign indicates *initialization*, whereas a previously defined class instance name appearing on the left side of an equal sign denotes *assignment.*

Overloading the Input and Output Operators

In Chapter 8, "C++ Classes for Standard I/O," you saw the `iostream` class, which defines the >> `operator` for input and the << `operator` for output. As defined in the IOSTREAM.H header file, these operators work with all predefined types such as `int`, `long`, `double`, and `char*`. When you define your own classes such as the `String` class, you might want to overload the definitions of the << and >> operators so that they work with your classes. For example, once you overload the >> operator, you can read characters from an input stream to a `String` by writing

```
String user_input;
cin >> user_input;  // Accept user's input
Similarly, to display a String, you would write:

String greetings = "Hello, World!";
cout << greetings << endl;
```

The Output Operator

These operators are easy to define. To overload the output operator <<, you need a public member function for the class that can handle the actual output. For the `String` class, you can define a `print` function that performs the output as follows:

```
#include "str.h"   // This includes <iostream.h>
//...
//-----------------------------------------------------------------
//  p r i n t
//  Outputs the String on a specified output stream
```

```
void String::print(ostream& os) const
{
    os << p_c;
}
```

Once the print function is defined, you can overload the << operator for a String argument as follows:

```
//---------------------------------------------------------------
// o p e r a t o r < <
// Stream insertion operator for String class

ostream& operator<<(ostream& os, String& s)
{
    s.print(os);
    return os;
}
```

As you can see, this operator function does its work by calling the member function named print from the String class. Note that the ostream class declares operator<< as a friend function.

The Input Operator

The stream extraction operator >> is also easy to implement. The following version assumes a maximum string length of 256 characters, including the null byte, and uses the get function of the input stream to read the characters into an internal array. Then it creates a new String object from that character array and returns the String.

```
//---------------------------------------------------------------
// o p e r a t o r > >
// Stream extraction operator for String class

istream& operator>>(istream& is, String& s)
{
    const bufsize = 256;
    char buf[bufsize];

    if(is.get(buf, bufsize)) s = String(buf);
    return is;
}
```

Overloading Operators *new* and *delete*

The dynamic storage allocation operators new and delete are two more interesting operators that you can also overload. You can overload the new operator to use another method for allocating storage. For instance, it is inefficient to allocate many small objects on the free store using the new default operator. One way to improve the efficiency is to obtain a large chunk of memory and use that as the pool of memory from which an overloaded version of the new operator doles out storage for the objects. Like other operators, overriding new and delete for any class involves defining the functions operator new and operator delete.

Some Rules for *new* and *delete*

You should follow these rules when overriding new and delete:

- The first argument of operator new must be of the size_t type (as defined in the STDDEF.H ANSI C header file), and it must return a void*. Consequently, a prototype for operator new is as follows:

  ```
  void* operator new(size_t numbytes);
  ```

- The first argument to operator delete must be of the void* type, and it must not return a value. You also can have a second argument of the size_t type. Typical prototypes for operator delete are as follows:

  ```
  void operator delete(void *p);

  void operator delete(void *p, size_t n);
  ```

Whenever you define the operator new and operator delete functions for a class, the C++ compiler automatically treats them as static member functions of that class. This is true even if you do not explicitly declare them as static. The C++ compiler must call new before the constructor and delete after the destructor. In other words, the compiler must be able to call these operators even when no instance of the class exists. To make this possible, the compiler treats operator new and operator delete as static.

The Placement Syntax for *operator new*

There is an intriguing way of using the new operator to initialize objects in preallocated memory. This is done with the placement syntax of the new operator. The following example shows how you might initialize a buffer in place with instances of a fictitious my_widget class:

```
//-------------------------------------------------------------------
//  Illustrates placement syntax of operator "new"

#include <iostream.h>
#include <stddef.h>

class my_widget
{
public:
    my_widget(int x, int y) : _x(x), _y(y){}

// Define default new operator.
// NOTE: This simply calls global copy of "operator new"
    void* operator new(size_t sz) { return ::operator new(sz);}

// Define "new" invoked with placement syntax
    void* operator new(size_t sz, void* p)
    {
        return (my_widget*)p;
    }

// Another member function
    int& getx(){ return _x;}

private:
    int _x, _y;
};

//-------------------------------------------------------------------
// Test program

main()
{
    char buf[10*sizeof(my_widget)];
    int i=1;

// Initialize chunks of buf with instances of "my_widget"
    for(char *b=buf; b < buf+10*sizeof(my_widget);
        b += sizeof(my_widget), i++)
    {
        (void) new(b) my_widget(i, i);  // placement syntax
    }
```

```
// See if it worked...
    my_widget* widget = (my_widget*) buf;

    for(i=0; i<10; i++)
        cout << widget[i].getx() << " ";

    cout << endl;
}
```

When run, this sample program generates the following output:

```
1 2 3 4 5 6 7 8 9 10
```

which is what you would expect because of the way the instances of `my_widget` are initialized.

This approach of placing a new object in a predefined area of memory has a purpose. Some environments such as Microsoft Windows and Apple Macintosh have their own memory-management scheme that good programs are supposed to follow. If you happen to use C++ to write application programs for such environments, you can allocate a block of memory by calling an environment-specific function, and you can use the placement syntax of `operator new` to initialize instances of objects in that block of memory.

Using *friend* Classes

Sometimes data-hiding rules of C++ classes can be too restrictive. If, for reasons of efficiency, you want to provide an `A` class access to all members of a `B` class, you can do so by embedding the following statement in the declaration of class `B`:

```
class A;
class B
{
    friend A;  // A can access all members of this class
//...
};
```

To see how `friend` classes are used, consider the example in the next section.

Using a File as an Array

If you want to treat a file as an array of characters, to be specific, you should create a `File` class and then use it as follows:

```
File f("sample.dat");  // Open a file
char c = f[10];        // Get byte at index 10
f[128] = ']';          // Store ']' into a byte in the file
```

This tells you that you need a `File` constructor that takes a file's name as an argument. In the constructor, you must open the file and remember the `FILE` pointer, assuming that you use the standard C file I/O functions to the actual I/O operations with the file. Additionally, you must overload `operator[]` to read from and write to the file. With the `File` class alone, it is difficult to define this operator. You can do this, however, by using a helper class called `FileLoc`. The idea is to define `operator[]` for the `File` class so that applying the operator to a `File` implies creation of a `FileLoc` object—as the name implies, this object keeps track of the position within the file. The `FileLoc` object positions the stream and defines appropriate operators to read from and write to the disk file. The `File` and `FileLoc` classes are declared as friends of each other so that the I/O operations can be as efficient as possible. Listing 10.3 shows the actual declarations of the classes as well as a small test program.

Listing 10.3. FARRAY.CPP. An illustration of classes that treat a disk file as an array of characters.

```
//-------------------------------------------------------------
//  File:  farray.cpp
//  Treats a file as an array of bytes
//-------------------------------------------------------------

#include <stdio.h>
#include <iostream.h>

//-------------------------------------------------------------
//  Declare the "FileLoc" class_the helper of File class

class File;

class FileLoc
{
public:
    friend File;

    void operator=(char c);
    void operator=(const char* str);
    operator const char();
```

```
private:
    File* p_file;
    fpos_t file_loc;
    FileLoc(File& f, fpos_t loc): p_file(&f), file_loc(loc){}
};
//-----------------------------------------------------------------------
//  Now declare the "File" class

class File
{
public:
    friend FileLoc;

// Constructor open file for read and write operations
    File(const char* name)
    {
        fp = fopen(name, "r+");  // open for read and write
    }

// Destructor closes file
    ~File() { fclose(fp);}

// operator[] positions file and creates an instance of FileLoc
    FileLoc operator[](fpos_t loc)
    {
        fseek(fp, loc, SEEK_SET);
        return FileLoc(*this,loc);
    }

private:
    FILE* fp;  // ANSI C stream pointer
};
//-----------------------------------------------------------------------
//      M e m b e r   F u n c t i o n s
//-----------------------------------------------------------------------
//  o p e r a t o r = ( c h a r )
//  Handles assignments of the form:
//       f[n] = c, where f[n] is a FileLoc and c is a char
//  by storing the character in the file

void FileLoc::operator=(char c)
{
```

continues

Listing 10.3. continued

```
    if(p_file->fp != NULL)
    {
        putc(c, p_file->fp);
    }
}
//-------------------------------------------------------------------
//  o p e r a t o r = ( c h a r * )
//  Handles assignments of the form:
//       f[n]="string", where f[n] is a FileLoc object
//  This stores the string into the file

void FileLoc::operator=(const char* str)
{
    if(p_file->fp != NULL)
    {
        fputs(str, p_file->fp);
    }
}
//-------------------------------------------------------------------
//  o p e r a t o r   c o n s t   c h a r ( )
//  Handles assignments of the form:
//       c = f[n], where f[n] is a FileLoc and c is a char
//  This reads a character from the file.

FileLoc::operator const char()
{
    if(p_file->fp != NULL)
    {
        return getc(p_file->fp);
    }
    return EOF;
}
//-------------------------------------------------------------------
//  m a i n
//  A program to test the File and FileLoc classes
//  Before running program, create a file "test.dat"
//  with the following line:
//
//       Testing: File and FileLoc classes

void main()
{
```

```
    File f("test.dat");
    int i;
    char c;
    cout << "First 14 bytes = " << endl;
    for(i=0; i<14; i++)
    {
        c = f[i];
        cout << c;
    }
    cout << endl;

// Change first 7 bytes to ' ' (blank space)
    for(i=0; i<7; i++) f[i] = ' ';

// Display the first 14 characters again
    cout << "Now the first 14 bytes = " << endl;
    for(i=0; i<14; i++)
    {
        c = f[i];
        cout << c;
    }
    cout << endl;

// Store a string in the file
    f[0] = "Creating";

    cout << "After string insert: the first 25 bytes = " << endl;
    for(i=0; i<25; i++)
    {
        c = f[i];
        cout << c;
    }
    cout << endl;
}
```

If you prepare a file named TEST.DAT with the following line:

```
Testing: File and FileLoc classes.
```

and run the program shown in Listing 10.3, you should see the following output:

```
First 14 bytes =
Testing: File
```

```
Now the first 14 bytes =
       : File
After string insert: the first 25 bytes =
Creating File and FileLoc
```

When you write

```
char c = f[i];  // f is a File, i an integer
```

the expression `f[i]` results in a `FileLoc` object, which positions the file to the character at location `i`. The C++ compiler then applies `FileLoc::operator const char()` to this `FileLoc` object. As you can see from the definition of `FileLoc::operator const char()`, this reads a character from the file. On the other hand, when you write

```
f[i] = c;  // f is a File, i is an integer, c, a char
```

the expression `f[i]` again creates a `FileLoc` object that positions the file to the position `i`. The C++ compiler then invokes the function `FileLoc::operator=(char)`, which writes the character to the file. This operator is overloaded for a string argument as well, so that an entire string can be written to a file.

This is a good example of using a friend class as an intermediary when implementing a desired syntax of usage for a class. Here, as the sole purpose of the `FileLoc` class, you can use the `File` class to not only view a disk file as an array of characters, but you can even use the array-access syntax to read from and write to a file.

Summary

The `class` construct forms the basis of object-oriented programming in C++. The member functions of a class control how the class can be used. To make a class as easy to use as the built-in data types, you must define a complete assortment of member functions for each class. Constructors that the C++ compiler calls to initialize a newly created instance of a class are very important. At a minimum, you should provide the default constructor, which takes no arguments, and the copy constructor, which initializes a new instance of a class from an existing instance. When initializing a class that includes instances of other classes as members, you should use member initializer list syntax to initialize these class instances. The initializer list is the only way to initialize constant member variables.

To make classes easy to use, C++ enables you to redefine most operators so that they can be used with instances of a class to perform meaningful operations. For example, for a `String` class, the + operator can be defined to concatenate two `String`s. Overloading operators involves defining functions with names that begin with the `operator` keyword followed by the symbol used for the operator.

Although C++ supports strict data hiding, you can use the `friend` keyword to declare one class or a function as a friend of another class. A friend can access all members of a class: `public` as well as `private` and `protected`. An example illustrates how you can use a `friend` class to implement a convenient syntax of usage for a class that lets you treat a file as an array of bytes.

Using Inheritance in C++

The last two chapters focused on data abstraction. This is only one ingredient, albeit an important one, of object-oriented programming. The other two components of OOP are *inheritance* and *polymorphism*. Although data abstraction helps you define a new data type, you need inheritance to exploit the common features of related data types or to extend the functionality provided by one or more existing classes.

Inheritance enables you to

- Classify objects. For example, with inheritance you can categorize circles, rectangles, and triangles as different types of shapes and share everything the shapes have in common.
- Express the differences between related classes while sharing the functions and member variables that implement the common features.
- Reuse existing code from one or more classes simply by deriving a new class from them.
- Extend an existing class by adding new members to it.

This chapter explains how to use inheritance in C++ classes.

Derived Classes

Suppose you have a C++ class that implements a specific data type and you need another data type that is similar to the first but has some additional member variables or functions. Rather than create the new data type from scratch, OOP techniques suggest that you inherit from the existing type and add the necessary capabilities to the inherited type. In C++, you can do this by deriving the new class from the existing class. You can add capabilities to the derived class by

- Defining new member variables
- Defining new member functions
- Overriding the definition of inherited member functions

Inheritance Can Represent the "is a" Relationship

One common use of inheritance is to express the *is a* relationship among various types of objects. The geometric shapes discussed in Chapter 6, "C++ and Object-Oriented Programming," are based on this idea. Because a circle *is a* shape and a rectangle *is a* shape, the `circle_shape` and `rectangle_shape` classes inherit from the `shape` class. In some object-oriented languages, such as Smalltalk, `circle_shape` is called a *subclass* of `shape`, which in turn is the *superclass* of `circle_shape`. In C++, the `circle_shape` and `rectangle_shape` classes are derived from the `shape` class, which is their *base class.* Figure 11.1 illustrates this concept. Notice that you may further specialize the `rectangle_shape` class by deriving from it a `rounded_rectangle_shape` class that represents rectangles with rounded corners.

As you can see, a base class can have more than one derived class, and a derived class can serve as the base class for others. Thus, you end up with a tree-structured hierarchy of classes in which the classes near the bottom (the leaves) are more specialized versions of the classes at the top.

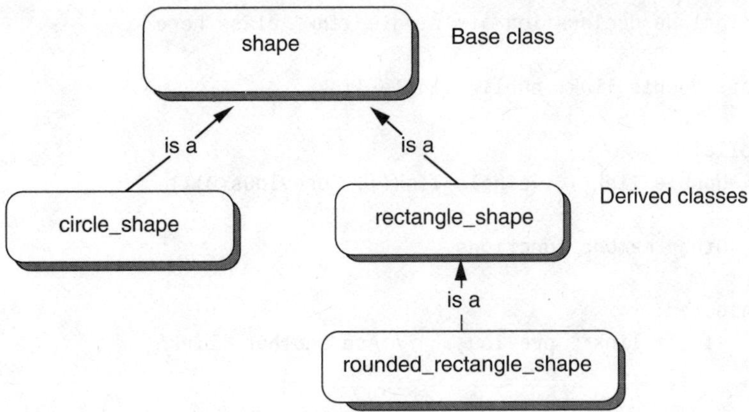

Figure 11.1. Inheritance in C++.

Inheritance Can Extend a Class

In addition to seeing inheritance as a mechanism for implementing the "*is a*" relationship among types of objects, you can also use inheritance to extend the functionality provided by one or more classes. Suppose you have a class named `single_link` that maintains a pointer to another instance of the same class. You plan to use the `single_link` objects in a linked list. You might declare the `single_link` as follows:

```
class single_link
{
public:
    single_link(): _next(0) {}

    single_link(single_link& sl) : _next(sl._next) {}

// Other member functions...

protected:
    single_link* _next;  // link to next "single_link"
};
```

Later, you might want a doubly-linked list for which you would need a `double_link` class with instances capable of holding two pointers—one to the next instance and the other to the previous one. Instead of defining from scratch, you can create the `double_link` class simply by deriving it from `single_link` and adding a new member variable like this:

```
// Include declaration of "single_link" class here

class double_link: public single_link
{
public:
    double_link() : single_link(), _previous(0){}

//  Other member functions...

protected:
    single_link* _previous;  // Add another "link"
};
```

As you will soon learn, making the `_next` data item in the `single_link` class `protected` allows derived classes, such as `double_link`, to directly access the `_next` pointer. This improves the speed with which a program can manipulate the items in linked lists that use these classes. Later in this chapter, you will see an example that uses these link classes to construct linked list data structures.

Syntax of a Derived Class

The `class` construct of C++ already includes the syntax necessary to indicate that a class is derived from another. For a base class, you declare the `class` exactly like a `struct`:

```
class shape
{
public:
// ...
};
```

For a derived class, you must list the name of its base class:

```
class circle_shape: public shape  // circle is derived from shape
{
public:
// ...
private:
    double x_center, y_center;
    double radius;
};
```

Access to the Base Class

The public keyword preceding the name of the base class indicates how circle_shape is derived from shape. In this case, circle_shape is publicly derived from shape; in other words, shape is a public base class of circle_shape. This means all public and protected members of shape are also public and protected members of circle_shape.

You can also specify a private keyword in front of the base class name. In this case, all public and protected members of the base class become private members of the derived class. As illustrated in Figure 11.2, the net effect is that if rectangle_shape is privately derived from shape, the rounded_rectangle_shape class derived from rectangle_shape can no longer access the public and protected members of shape. In effect, a privately derived class blocks any further access to members of its base class.

When you use the class keyword to define object types, the default derivation is private. In other words, if you forget the access specifier and write

```
class rectangle_shape: shape
{
// rectangle_shape is privately derived from shape
// ...
};
```

you get a private derivation of shape. On the other hand, with the struct keyword, all derivations are public by default. Thus, the following code declares a rectangle_shape class with a public base class named shape:

```
struct rectangle_shape: shape
{
// rectangle_shape is publicly derived from shape
// ...
};
```

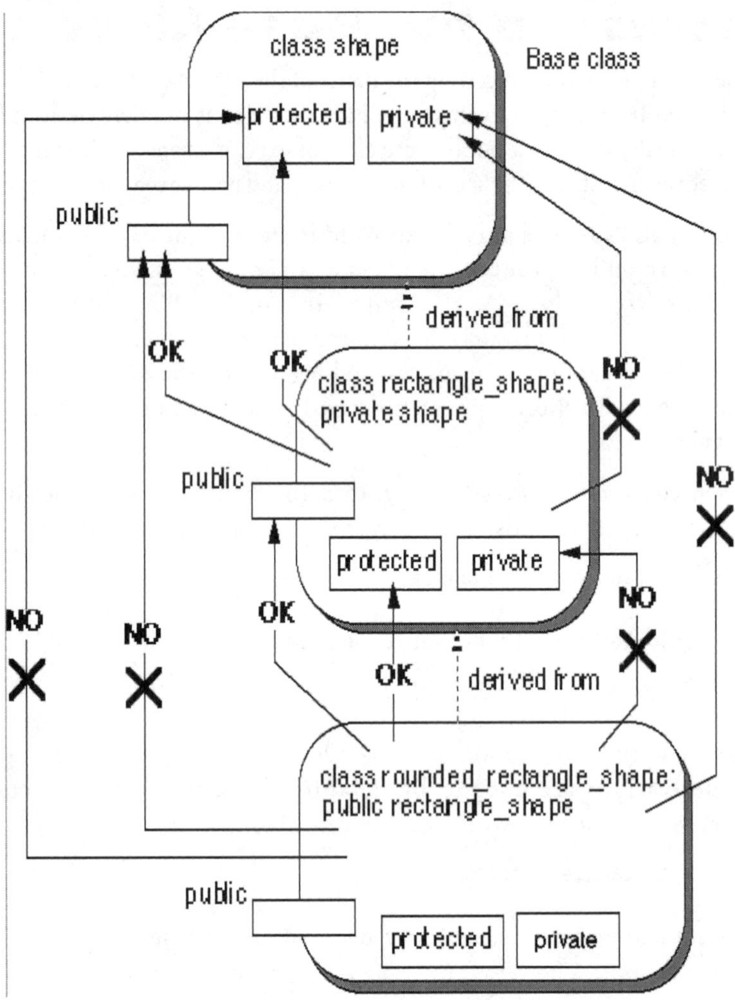

Figure 11.2. Controlling access to members of the base class.

Using Inheritance to Build a *Substring* Class

Chapter 9, "Building Objects with Classes," and Chapter 10, "Defining Operations on Objects," use a `String` class as an example. Suppose you want to create a new class called `Substring` with which you can access a part of a `String` object. The following code should accomplish this:

```
String path_name(32); // 32-character string, set to all blanks
path_name(0,4) = "/bin"; // Replace substring with "/bin"
```

One way to make this work is to overload the `operator()` for the `String` class so that it returns a `Substring`. The C string `/bin` is then copied into the substring. The net result of this code should be to set the first four characters of `String path_name` to `/bin`.

Deriving *Substring* from *String*

Because a `Substring` is a `String`, an easy way to define `Substring` is to derive it from `String`. As a benefit of deriving it from the `String` class, all operations defined for the `String` class are immediately available for the `Substring` class. A `Substring` is a full-fledged `String`, but it holds a reference to the `String` from which it was derived. This is necessary so the original `String` can be altered through a statement like the following:

```
String path_name(32);
path_name(0,4) = "/bin";
```

This `path_name(0,4)` expression creates a `Substring` class and the `Substring::operator=(const char*)` function replaces four characters, starting at the first character of `path_name` with the `/bin` string.

Listing 11.1 shows a revised STR.H header file that declares both the `String` and `Substring` classes. Before defining the `Substring` class, change the `private` members of `String` to `protected` so that `Substring` objects can access the internal variables of the `String`.

Initializing the Base Class

As you can see from Listing 11.1, declaring the `Substring` class is a straightforward process. Notice how you initialize a base class from the constructor of the derived class. In Chapter 10, you learned how member initializer lists are used to initialize static members and member classes; that is, class instances that appear as a member of another class. You can use the same technique to initialize the base class in the constructor of a derived class. As an example, consider the following `Substring` constructor:

```
// Substring constructor
    Substring(String& s, const char *cs, size_t pos, size_t len) :
        String(cs, len), s_original(s), _pos(pos) { }
```

This creates a `Substring` by copying `len` characters starting at position `pos` of the specified `String`. As you can see, the body of this constructor is empty. All initializations are done through the initializer list, which invokes an appropriate `String` constructor and initializes the members of the newly created `Substring`.

Listing 11.1. Revised STR.H file with declaration of `String` and `Substring` classes.

```
//------------------------------------------------------------------
//  File:  str.h
//  Declares a "String" class and a "Substring" class derived
//  from the "String" class
//------------------------------------------------------------------

#if !defined(__STR_H) // Be sure file is included only once
#define __STR_H

// Include other required header files...
// The ANSI C headers work because they are already enclosed
// in an extern "C"{...}
// Be sure your compiler does this.

#include <stddef.h>     // For "size_t" type
#include <iostream.h>   // For stream I/O
#include <string.h>     // For ANSI C string library

typedef int Boolean;    // For return type of operators

class Substring;

class String
{
public:
// Constructors with a variety of arguments
    String();
    String(size_t len);
    String(const char *str);
    String(const char *str, size_t len);
    String(const String &s);

// Destructor
    ~String() { delete[] p_c;}

// Overloaded operators
```

```
    Boolean operator==(const String& s) const
    {
        return(strcmp(s.p_c, p_c) == 0);
    }

// Assignment operator
    String& operator=(const String& s);

// Type conversion operator
    operator const char*() const { return p_c;}

// Access operator
    char& operator[](int index);

// Replace a portion of a string with another
// Used to insert or delete parts of a string
   String& replace(size_t pos, size_t len, const char* s);

//  o p e r a t o r ( )
//  Overload the function call operator to return a Substring

    Substring operator()(size_t pos, size_t len);

// The + operator concatenates strings
    friend String operator+(const String& s1, const String& s2);

// Function giving access to internal variable
    size_t length(void) const { return _length;}

// Function to print a String
    void print(ostream& os) const;

protected:   // so that derived classes can access these data

    char   *p_c;      // pointer to allocated space
    size_t _length;   // current length of string
    size_t _maxlen;   // number of bytes allocated

};

// Stream I/O for String class
```

continues

Listing 11.1. continued

```
#include <iostream.h>

ostream& operator<<(ostream& os, String& s);
istream& operator>>(istream& is, String& s);

//-----------------------------------------------------------------
//  Declare the "Substring" class

class Substring: public String
{
public:
    friend String;  // Give the String class access to this one

// Substring operators...
    String& operator=(const char* str)
    {
        return s_original.replace(_pos, _length, str);
    }
    String& operator=(Substring& s)
    {
        return s_original.replace(_pos, _length, s.p_c);
    }

private:
    String& s_original;  // Reference to original String
    size_t  _pos;        // Position of Substring in String

// Substring constructor
    Substring(String& s, const char *cs, size_t pos, size_t len) :
        String(cs, len), s_original(s), _pos(pos) { }

// Substring copy constructor

    Substring(const Substring& s) : String(s),
        s_original(s.s_original), _pos(s._pos) { }

};

#endif
```

Modifying the Original *String* Through a *Substring*

As I mentioned earlier, one reason to introduce the `Substring` class is to use it in statements such as the following that modify a portion of a `String` through an intermediate `Substring` created by the `String::operator()`:

```
String hello = "Hello......";
hello(5,6) = " there";    // Now hello = "Hello there..."
```

To make this work, you must define `Substring::operator=(const char*)` and have a way to replace a number of characters in a `String`. To this end, I added a `String::replace` function, shown toward the end of Listing 11.2, which shows the STR.CPP file, an implementation of the `String` class. With the `String::replace` function in place, you can implement the `operator=` function for the `Substring` class simply by calling `String::replace` as follows:

```
String& operator=(const char* str)
{
// Invoke the original String's "replace" function
    return s_original.replace(_pos, _length, str);
}
```

The *String::operator()*

Substrings are created through the `operator()` function of the `String` class. This operator is invoked with two `size_t` arguments, the first denoting the starting position of the substring and the second indicating the substring's length. Once you have defined a constructor for the `Substring` class that can create a `Substring` from a `String`, you can define the `String::operator()` as follows:

```
Substring String::operator()(size_t pos, size_t len)
{
    return Substring(*this, &(p_c[pos]), pos, len);
}
```

This function simply returns a new `Substring` by calling the `Substring` constructor.

Listing 11.2. STR.CPP. Implementation of the String class.

```
//--------------------------------------------------------------
//  File:  str.cpp
//  Implements the member functions of the "String" class

#include "str.h"    // For declaration of String class

const chunk_size = 8;

//--------------------------------------------------------------
//  S t r i n g
//  Creates a String object and initializes it
//  from a null-terminated C string

String::String(const char *s)
{
    _length = strlen(s);
    _maxlen = chunk_size*(_length / chunk_size + 1);
    p_c = new char[_maxlen];
    strcpy(p_c, s);
}
//--------------------------------------------------------------
//  S t r i n g
//  Creates a String object and initializes it using a
//  specified number of characters from a null-terminated
//  C string

String::String(const char *s, size_t len)
{
    _length = len;
    _maxlen = chunk_size*(_length / chunk_size + 1);
    p_c = new char[_maxlen];
    p_c[len] = '\0';
    strncpy(p_c, s, len);
}
//--------------------------------------------------------------
//  S t r i n g
//  Creates a String and stores a zero-length string in it.

String::String()
{
    _maxlen = chunk_size;
    p_c = new char[_maxlen];
```

```
    _length = 0;
    p_c[0] = '\0';
}
//------------------------------------------------------------------------
//  S t r i n g
//  This version creates a blank string of size "len"

String::String(size_t len)
{
    _length = len;
    _maxlen = chunk_size*(_length / chunk_size + 1);
    p_c = new char[_maxlen];
    int i;
    for(i = 0; i < len; i++) p_c[i] = ' ';
    p_c[i] = '\0';
}
//------------------------------------------------------------------------
//  S t r i n g
//  Creates a new String as a copy of another String
//  This is often called the "Copy Constructor"

String::String(const String &s)
{
    _length = s._length;
    _maxlen = s._maxlen;
    p_c = new char[_maxlen];
    strcpy(p_c, s.p_c);
}
//------------------------------------------------------------------------
//  o p e r a t o r +
//  Concatenates two String objects

String operator+(const String& s1, const String& s2)
{
    size_t len = s1._length + s2._length;
    char *t = new char[len+1];
    strcpy(t, s1.p_c);
    strcat(t, s2.p_c);
    String s3(t);
    delete[] t;
    return (s3);
}
```

continues

Listing 11.2. continued

```
//--------------------------------------------------------------------
//  o p e r a t o r =
//  Assigns one String object to another

String& String::operator=(const String& s)
{
    if(this != &s)
    {
        _length = s._length;
        _maxlen = s._maxlen;
        delete[] p_c;
        p_c = new char[_maxlen];
        strcpy(p_c, s.p_c);
    }
    return *this;
}
//--------------------------------------------------------------------
//  p r i n t
//  Outputs the String on a specified output stream

void String::print(ostream& os) const
{
    os << p_c;
}
//--------------------------------------------------------------------
//  o p e r a t o r < <
//  Stream insertion operator for String class

ostream& operator<<(ostream& os, String& s)
{
    s.print(os);
    return os;
}
//--------------------------------------------------------------------
//  o p e r a t o r > >
//  Stream extraction operator for String class

istream& operator>>(istream& is, String& s)
{
    const bufsize = 256;
    char buf[bufsize];
```

```
    if(is.get(buf, bufsize)) s = String(buf);
    return is;
}
//------------------------------------------------------------------
//  o p e r a t o r [ ]
//  Access a character in a String

char& String::operator[](int index)
{
// Check if index goes beyond allocated length.
// Return last element , if it does
    if(index > _maxlen-1) return p_c[_maxlen-1];
    else  return p_c[index];
}
//------------------------------------------------------------------
//  r e p l a c e
//  Replace a portion of a string with another C string

String& String::replace(size_t pos, size_t len, const char* s)
{
    size_t new_len = strlen(s);

// Check if there is enough room
    if(_length + new_len - len < _maxlen)
    {
// Move bytes around using ANSI C function "memmove"
        memmove(&(p_c[pos+new_len]), &(p_c[pos+len]),
                _length-pos-len);
        memmove(&(p_c[pos]), s, new_len);
    }
    else
    {
// Must reallocate string
        _maxlen = chunk_size * ((_length+new_len-len) /
                                        chunk_size + 1);
        char *t = new char[_maxlen];
// Copy strings over...
        memmove(t, p_c, pos);
        memmove(&(t[pos]), s, new_len);
        memmove(&(t[new_len+pos]),
                &(p_c[pos+len]), _length-pos-len);
        delete[] p_c;
```

continues

Listing 11.2. continued

```
        p_c = t;
    }
// Adjust the length of the String
    _length += new_len - len;

// Terminate the new C string
    p_c[_length] = '\0';

    return *this;
}
//-------------------------------------------------------------------
//  o p e r a t o r ( )
//  Overload the function call operator to return a Substring

Substring String::operator()(size_t pos, size_t len)
{
    return Substring(*this, &(p_c[pos]), pos, len);
}
```

Testing the *Substring* Class

Here is a short program that tries out the `Substring` class through `operator()` applied to a `String` variable named `hello`.

```
// Test Substring class
#include "str.h"

void main()
{
    String hello = "Hello......";
    cout << "Before: " << hello << endl;

    hello(5,3) = " there";
    cout << "After: " << hello << endl;

    hello(11,1) = " C++ Programmer";
    cout << "After another 'replace': " << hello << endl;
}
```

```
    void insert(size_t pos, char c);
    void insert(size_t pos, char* str);

protected:
//...
}
```

After deriving the `Substring` class from `String`, you decide to add another version of the `insert` function, this one to insert the formatted representation of a `float` variable into a `Substring`. With this in mind, you declare the new `insert` function as follows:

```
class Substring: public String
{
public:
//...
    void insert(size_t pos, float x);
private:
//...
};
```

The rule for overriding member functions of the base class says that the function `Substring::insert` hides the functions `String::insert`. In other words, once you define the new `insert` function for `Substring`, you lose access to the `insert` function that the `Substring` class inherits from the `String` class. Keep this in mind when overloading inherited member functions in a derived class.

Order of Initialization of Classes Under Single Inheritance

Another detail worth knowing is the order in which the C++ compiler initializes the base classes of a derived class. When the C++ compiler initializes an instance of a derived class, it must initialize all the base classes first. If you are working with a hierarchy of classes, it helps to know how C++ initializes the base classes so you can track down problems that may occur from improper initialization of a class instance. For single inheritance, the C++ compiler uses the following basic rules during initialization:

1. Initialize the base class, if any.
2. Within the base class, initialize the member variables in the order in which they are declared in the class.

The only catch is that the compiler applies these rules recursively. Also, notice that the order in the initializer list does not affect the order in which member variables of

You must compile this program, as well as the STR.CPP file shown in Listing 11.2, and link them to create the executable file. When run, the program generates the following output:

```
Before: Hello......
After: Hello there...
After another 'replace': Hello there C++ Programmer..
```

Other Issues for Derived Classes

Now that you have seen how the `Substring` class is created by deriving from `String`, you should be aware of a few more details about derived classes that were not illustrated by the `Substring` class. The following sections briefly cover these issues.

Overriding Inherited Member Functions

Presumably, your reason for declaring a derived class is to model a new type of object in terms of one or more existing types or to extend the functionality of an existing class. Usually, this means that you will be adding new member variables and member functions to complete the functionality of the derived class. Adding new members is a straightforward process: simply place any new member you want to add to the definition of the derived class. Apart from adding new members, you can also redefine member functions that already appear in a base class. You can do so to improve efficiency or to alter the functionality of an existing function. Whatever the reason, you can redefine member functions of the base class freely, provided you keep in mind the following rule:

> An overloaded member function in the derived class hides all inherited member functions of the same name.

This means that, if a base class provides one or more versions of a member function, overloading that function in a derived class hides all inherited versions of the function. The following example clarifies this.

Suppose the `String` class defines two versions of a member function called `insert`, one to insert a single character at a specific position and the other to insert a C string. You could declare the functions as follows:

```
class String
{
public:
//...
```

a class are initialized. The best way to see the order of initialization is to run a simple example. The following example has a class hierarchy in which class `C` is derived from `B`, and `B` in turn is derived from `A`. Another class named `Data` is a member of `A` and `B`. Here is a sample implementation of the classes:

```
// Illustrate order of initialization
#include <iostream.h>

class Data
{
public:
    Data(int x = 0): _x(x)
    { cout << "Data::Data(" << x << ") ";}
private:
    int _x;
};

class A
{
    Data d1;
public:
    A(int x): d1(x-1) { cout << "A::A(" << x << ") ";}
};

class B: public A
{
    Data d2;
public:
    B(int x): d2(x-1), A(x-2)
    { cout << "B::B(" << x << ") ";}
};

class C: public B
{
public:
    C(int x): B(x-1) { cout << "C::C(" << x << ") ";}
};

void main()
{
    C(5);
}
```

When run, this program generates the following output:

```
Data::Data(1) A::A(2) Data::Data(3) B::B(4) C::C(5)
```

If you trace through the program's code, you will see that the C++ compiler first initializes the `Data` member of class `A`, followed by class `A` itself. Then it initializes the `Data` member of class `B`, then class `B`, and finally class `C`. All the base classes are initialized before the derived classes.

As discussed in the following sections, the order of initialization is more complicated when you use multiple inheritance.

Multiple Inheritance

The examples thus far show a derived class with a single base class. This is known as *single inheritance*. C++ also supports the notion of *multiple inheritance*, in which you can derive a class from several base classes. Support for multiple inheritance was introduced in C++ Release 2.0 to enable implementation of classes that needed to share the data and function members of several classes at once. As you will see in the following sections, multiple inheritance is often used to reuse code from several base classes. Of course, you can also use multiple inheritance when you feel that a particular class truly manifests the characteristics of more than one class of objects. For example, suppose you have two classes: `CollectorsItem` and `Cars`. Perhaps the `CollectorsItem` class has member functions that can estimate the value of an object based on its age and rarity. You might decide to define a new class, `AntiqueCars`, that inherits from both `Cars` and `CollectorsItem`. In C++, you can do so by deriving `AntiqueCars` from two base classes in the following manner:

```
class Cars;
class CollectorsItem;

class AntiqueCars: public Cars, public CollectorsItem
{
//...
};
```

Now the `AntiqueCars` class can use all public members of both `Cars` and `CollectorsItem` classes. If necessary, the `AntiqueCars` class can also add new member functions and variables. Additionally, the member functions of `AntiqueCars` can access all `protected` members of its base classes.

iostream Uses Multiple Inheritance

The iostream class library, included with AT&T C++ Release 2.0, uses multiple inheritance. As discussed in Chapter 8, "C++ Classes for Standard I/O," and illustrated in Figure 8.2, the iostream library contains the istream class for input, the ostream class for output, and a bidirectional iostream class derived from both istream and ostream. Therefore, multiple inheritance allows the iostream class to support both input and output operations on a stream.

Virtual Base Class

A problem with inheriting from multiple base classes is that you may end up with more than one instance of a base class. As a concrete example, consider the following hierarchy of classes:

```
// Illustrates need for "virtual base class"

#include <iostream.h>

class device
{
public:
    device()
    { cout << "device: constructor" << endl;}
};

class comm_device: public device
{
public:
    comm_device()
    { cout << "comm_device: constructor" << endl;}
};

class graphics_device: public device
{
public:
    graphics_device()
    { cout << "graphics_device: constructor" << endl;}
};
```

```
class graphics_terminal: public comm_device,
                         public graphics_device
{
public:
    graphics_terminal()
    { cout << "graphics_terminal: constructor" << endl;}
};

void main()
{
    graphics_terminal gt;
}
```

Here, the `device` class models a generic UNIX-style device with functions to open and close the device and control it. The `comm_device` class models a communication device: it adds functions to set the communications parameters. The `graphics_device` class models a device capable of drawing graphics. Finally, the `graphics_terminal` class is derived from both `comm_device` and `graphics_device` classes. Notice what happens when an instance of the `graphics_terminal` class is created. The program prints the following:

```
device: constructor
comm_device: constructor
device: constructor
graphics_device: constructor
graphics_terminal: constructor
```

The constructor for the `device` base class is called twice because it appears twice in the inheritance hierarchy: once as the base class of `comm_device` and another time as the base class of `graphics_device`.

Because the `graphics_terminal` class models a physical device, you would not want two instances of the `device` base class in every instance of `graphics_terminal`. You need a way to create a `graphics_terminal` class that inherits from both `comm_device` and `graphics_device` but has only one instance of the device class. You can do this with the virtual base class. Simply add the `virtual` keyword wherever the `device` class name appears in the inheritance list of a class. The new class definitions are as follows:

```
// Illustrates how "virtual base class" works

#include <iostream.h>
```

```
class device
{
public:
    device()
    { cout << "device: constructor" << endl;}
};

class comm_device: public virtual device
{
public:
    comm_device()
    { cout << "comm_device: constructor" << endl;}
};

class graphics_device: public virtual device
{
public:
    graphics_device()
    { cout << "graphics_device: constructor" << endl;}
};

class graphics_terminal: public comm_device,
                         public graphics_device
{
public:
    graphics_terminal()
    { cout << "graphics_terminal: constructor" << endl;}
};

void main()
{
    graphics_terminal gt;
}
```

This version of the test program produces the following output:

```
device: constructor
comm_device: constructor
graphics_device: constructor
graphics_terminal: constructor
```

Notice that the `device` class is constructed only once.

Restrictions on Virtual Base Classes

The virtual base class mechanism fills an important need, but beware of the following restrictions when you use virtual base classes:

- You cannot initialize a virtual base class with an initializer list. For an example, look at the constructor of the `Substring` class in Listing 11.1. There, the `String` class is initialized through the initializer list. You can't do the same with a virtual base class. This implies that a class you plan to use as a virtual base class should have a *default constructor*, which is a constructor that takes no arguments.
- You cannot cast a virtual base class pointer as a pointer to any class that is derived from it. Therefore, in the example, you cannot cast a `device*` pointer to a `graphics_terminal*` pointer.

Order of Initialization of Classes Under Multiple Inheritance

The rules for initializing classes in the presence of multiple inheritance are rather complicated. Generally speaking, the C++ compiler follows this order of initialization:

1. All virtual base classes are initialized. The constructor of each virtual base class is called exactly once.
2. Nonvirtual base classes are initialized by the order in which they appear in a class declaration.
3. Member variables are initialized, again by the order in which they appear in the class declaration.

The C++ compiler applies these rules recursively, just as it does under single inheritance. For further details on this topic, consult *The Annotated C++ Reference Manual,* by Margaret Ellis and Bjarne Stroustrup.

Using Inheritance

You can use inheritance to create specialized versions of a general-purpose class. Suppose you have a class named `plain_window` that displays a rectangular area of screen wherein you can show text and graphics output. Typical members of such a class might include foreground and background colors, the font for text display, and a member function that refreshes the contents of the window.

Given the `plain_window` class, you can create a window that displays a text *label* in a window—a static_text_window—by deriving it from the `plain_window` class and adding a new member variable to store the text for the label. Furthermore, you can derive from `static_text_window` a `pushbutton_window` that displays a label. Unlike a `static_text_window`, though, it performs some action when a user selects the pushbutton with a pointing device such as a mouse. Figure 11.3 illustrates the inheritance hierarchy of these window classes. This is an example of specializing classes through inheritance.

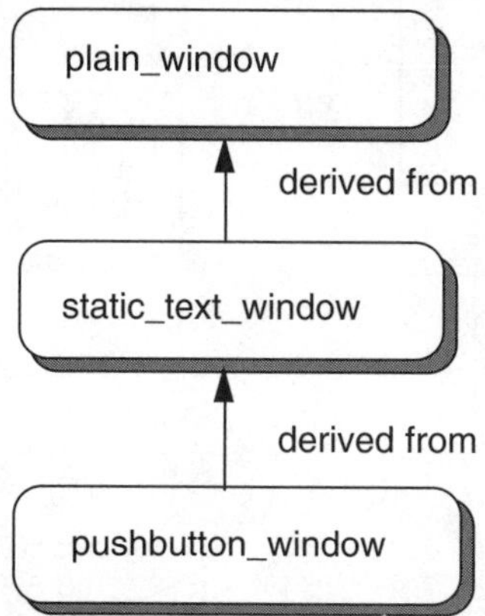

Figure 11.3. Inheritance hierarchy of window classes.

On the other hand, inheritance can extend the functionality of a `class`. Instead of specializing, use inheritance for even broader functionality than before. You can view the `class` construct in two ways:

- As a means for defining new data types
- As a module for packaging data and functions

When you use `class` to define a data type, inheritance is useful in creating more specialized types. When you think of a class as a means of packaging functions, you can use inheritance to add new functions, thus extending the capabilities of the module.

Linked Lists

Basic data structures, such as linked lists, queues, stacks, and trees, are popular targets for implementation as abstract data types because they can be easily implemented in the object-oriented style. Inheritance is often useful when defining such classes. A linked list, for example, can be the basis of several types of data structures, including queues, stacks, and trees. I'll begin with an example of a single-linked list and show how you can use inheritance to create such a data structure.

Figure 11.4 represents a singly-linked list of elements. The list consists of a number of data items, each capable of holding a pointer to another such item. In the single-linked list, each item points to the next one in the list so that you can start at the beginning of the list and reach every element in the list by following these pointers.

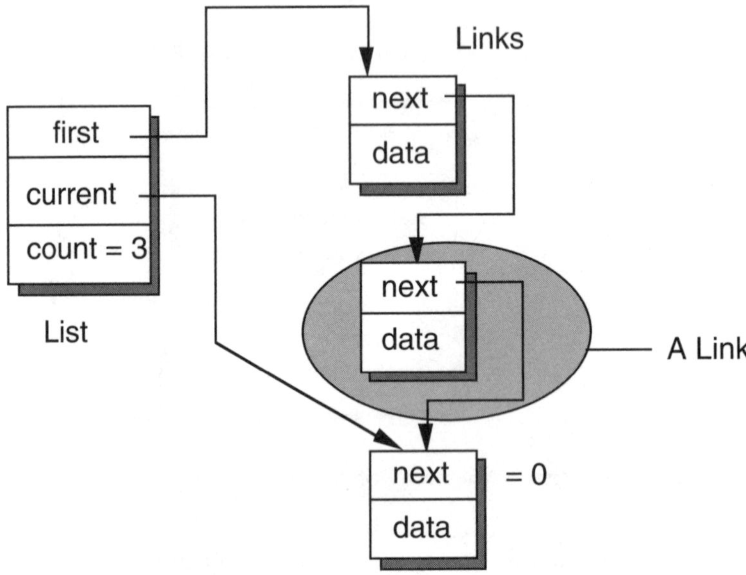

Figure 11.4. A single-linked list data structure.

In addition to these items, the list needs a pointer to the first element so you know where to start looking for data stored in the list. Sometimes you may also want to maintain a pointer to what you might call the current element, which is the element being accessed at that time. Another item of interest is the number of elements in the list.

The Link and the List

As Figure 11.4 illustrates, one of the basic objects in a linked list is the link—an object with some data and a pointer to another link. The other object is the *list*, which holds information about the linked list, such as a pointer to the first item and the number of items. Having identified the basic objects, you can proceed to declare the C++ classes for them.

Making a Generic List

Before declaring the classes for the linked list, I'll digress a bit to consider an important issue. You define data structures such as linked lists to store objects. What you really want is a linked list that can hold any type of object. If you could define a parameterized class with a parameter denoting the data type stored in each link, you could easily create linked lists capable of holding different data types by substituting an appropriate type for the parameter. As explained in Chapter 13, "Advanced Topics in C++," the `template` keyword of C++ is used to provide such a facility, but at this point, C++ does not support parameterized classes.

All is not lost, however, because you can simulate generic lists through inheritance. The idea is to create a list that can hold links of a class named `single_link`, for example. A `single_link` object does not contain any data other than a pointer to the next `single_link` object. Later, if you want a single-linked list of `String` objects, you can create a new type. I'll call it `slink_string`, which inherits from both `single_link` and `String`. Objects of the `slink_string` class should then be able to reside in the single-linked list you designed to hold `single_link` objects. Figure 11.5 illustrates this idea, and the following sections demonstrate how it works. The major drawback of this approach, however, is that you cannot have a list of built-in data types such as `int`, `char`, and `double` because they are not defined as classes. Therefore, you cannot create derived classes from these types.

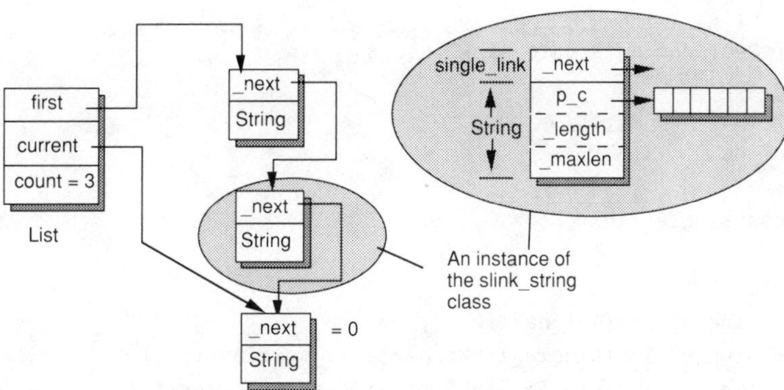

Figure 11.5. A single-linked list capable of holding `String` objects.

The *single_link* Class

Listing 11.3 shows the SLINK.H header file, which declares the `single_link` class. The class has only one `protected` data member named `_next`, which is a pointer to the next `single_link` object. Therefore, you can string together instances of `single_link` class through their `_next` pointers.

Apart from the constructors, the `single_link` class also provides the `next` member function, which returns its `_next` pointer, and the `set_next` function, which sets the `_next` pointer to a new value.

The class also includes two virtual functions: `clone` and `destroy`. These functions ensure that you can correctly create and destroy instances of a class derived from `single_link`. The `clone` function makes a duplicate copy of an object, while `destroy` properly deletes objects derived from `single_link`. As you will learn in Chapter 12, "Virtual Functions and C++," these functions are declared as *pure virtual*. This is what the `=0` assignment following the function's declaration does. As a side effect of this declaration, you can't create instances of the `single_link` class until you have derived another class from it and defined the functions `clone` and `destroy`.

Listing 11.3. SLINK.H. Declares the `single_link` class.

```
//-------------------------------------------------------------
//  File: slink.h
//  Declares a "single link" class

#if !defined (__SLINK_H)
#define __SLINK_H

class single_link
{
public:
    single_link(): _next(0) {}
    single_link(single_link* next) : _next(next) {}
    single_link(single_link& sl) : _next(sl._next) {}

    single_link* next() { return _next; }

    void set_next(single_link *next) { _next = next;}

    virtual single_link* clone() = 0;
    virtual void destroy() = 0;
```

```
protected:
    single_link* _next;
};

#endif
```

The *singly_linked_list* Class

Now that you have defined the links, proceed to the list itself. Listing 11.4 shows the SLLIST.H header file, which declares the `singly_linked_list` class, while Listing 11.5 has the actual implementation of some of the member functions. As expected, the `singly_linked_list` class provides member functions to traverse the list and to insert and remove elements from the list.

Listing 11.4. SLLIST.H. Declares the `singly_linked_list` class.

```
//---------------------------------------------------------------------
//  File: sllist.h
//  Declares a "singly linked list" class

#if !defined (__SLLIST_H)
#define __SLLIST_H

#include "slink.h"

class singly_linked_list
{
public:
// Constructors
    singly_linked_list() : _first(0), _current(0), _count(0){}

    singly_linked_list(single_link& sl)
    {
     _first = sl.clone();
     _count = 1;
     _current = _first;
    }

// Destructor
```

continues

Listing 11.4. continued

```
    ~singly_linked_list();

//  Member-access functions...
    single_link* current() { return _current;}

    single_link* first()
    {
        _current = _first;
        return _current;
    }

    single_link* next()
    {
        single_link* t = _current->next();
        if(t != 0) _current = t;
        return t;
    }

    unsigned count(){ return _count;}

// List insertion and deletion
    void insert(single_link& sl);
    void remove();

protected:
    single_link *_first;
    single_link *_current;
    unsigned    _count;
};

#endif
```

The `insert` function in Listing 11.5 shows how the virtual function `clone` is used. Suppose you are inserting a `slink_string` object into the list. Remember that the `slink_string` class is derived from `String` and `single_link`. The `insert` function requires a reference to a `single_link` object as an argument. With C++, you can call `insert` with a reference to an instance of any class derived from `single_link`. When you call `insert` with a `slink_string` reference, `insert` calls the `clone` function through the reference to the `slink_string` object. Because `clone` is a virtual function, this invokes the `clone` function of the `slink_string` class, which, as you will see shortly, returns a pointer to a copy of that instance of `slink_string`. Consequently, you can obtain a proper copy of an object by using this mechanism. Chapter 12 provides further details on virtual functions.

Listing 11.5. SLLIST.CPP. Member functions of the `singly_linked_list` class.

```
//-----------------------------------------------------------------
//  File: sllist.cpp
//  Implements a singly linked list

#include "sllist.h"

//-----------------------------------------------------------------
//  ~ s i n g l y _ l i n k e d _ l i s t
//  Destructor for the list

singly_linked_list::~singly_linked_list()
{
    int         i;
    single_link *p_sl = _first, *t;
    if(_count > 0)
    {
        for(i = 0; i < _count; i++)
        {
            t = p_sl->next();
            p_sl->destroy();
            p_sl = t;
        }
    }
}
//-----------------------------------------------------------------
//  i n s e r t
//  Insert a new item into the list

void singly_linked_list::insert(single_link& sl)
{
// Clone the element passed to the function and
// hook it up in the linked list
    single_link *t = sl.clone();
    if(_current != 0)
```

continues

Listing 11.5. continued

```
    {
        t->set_next(_current->next());
        _current->set_next(t);
    }
    else
    {
        _first = t;
    }

// Make this one the current item in the list
    _current = t;

// Increment of count of elements on the list
    _count++;
}
//----------------------------------------------------------------------
//  r e m o v e
//  Removes the current element from the list

void singly_linked_list::remove()
{
// Locate element that points to current
    single_link *p_sl;
    int         i;

    if(_current == 0) return;

    for(i = 0, p_sl = _first;
        p_sl->next() != _current && i < _count;
        i++, p_sl = p_sl->next()) ;

    if(i != _count)
    {
        p_sl->set_next(_current->next());
        _current->destroy();
        _current = p_sl;
        _count—;
    }
}
```

The remove function uses the virtual function destroy in a similar manner to properly delete an item from the linked list.

A Linkable *String* Class

You have already seen the String class in Listings 11.1 and 11.2. If you want to store String objects in a singly_linked_list, you must create a new type of String that might be called a *linkable* String. To do this, simply use multiple inheritance to derive from String and from single_link. Listings 11.6 and 11.7 show this new class, which is called slink_string because these are String objects to which a single_link is added.

Notice how the clone and destroy functions are defined in Listing 11.6. The clone function simply creates a "clone" of the current slink_string and returns a pointer to the new copy. The destroy function calls the delete operator for the current slink_string. These functions ensure that objects stored in the singly-linked list are properly initialized and destroyed.

Listing 11.6. SLSTR.H. Declares the slink_string class.

```
//--------------------------------------------------------------
//  File: slstr.h
//  Singly linkable string class

#if !defined(__SLSTR_H)
#define __SLSTR_H

#include "str.h"        // String class
#include "slink.h"      // single_link class

class slink_string: public single_link, public String
{
public:
    slink_string(const char *s): String(s), single_link(0){}

    slink_string(const slink_string& s) :
        String(s.p_c), single_link(s._next) {}

    slink_string(const String& s):
        String(s), single_link() {}
```

continues

Listing 11.6. continued

```
    slink_string& operator=(const slink_string& s);

    void destroy() { delete this;}

    single_link* clone()
    {
        slink_string* t = new slink_string(*this);
        return t;
    }

};

#endif
```

Listing 11.7. SLSTR.CPP. Implements the assignment operator for the `slink_string` class.

```
//--------------------------------------------------------------------
//  File:  slstr.cpp

#include "slstr.h"

//--------------------------------------------------------------------
//  o p e r a t o r =
//  Assign one "slink_string" to another

slink_string& slink_string::operator=(const slink_string& s)
{
    if(this != &s)
    {
        _next = s._next;
        _length = s._length;
        _maxlen = s._maxlen;
        delete[] p_c;
        p_c = new char[_maxlen];
        strcpy(p_c, s.p_c);
    }
    return *this;
}
```

A *String* List Iterator Class

Now you possess all the equipment necessary to create a linked list of `String` objects, but one problem still exists. Specifically, the `singly_linked_list` class maintains a list of `single_link` objects. It knows nothing about `slink_string` objects. So how do you traverse the list and process the `slink_string objects` in the list? You could use the `first`, `current`, and `next` member functions of the `singly_linked_list` class to traverse the list, but these return pointers to `single_link` objects. To treat them as pointers to `slink_string` objects, you must use an explicit cast. Instead of getting into details like this, it's best to create a helper class, commonly known as an *iterator* class, that provides access to the linked list of `String` objects. The class is called an iterator because it lets you *iterate* or "loop over" the list.

Listing 11.8 shows the SLSITER.H header file, which implements the `sllist_iterator` class that acts as an iterator for the linked list of `Strings`. The `sllist_iterator` class is quite simple. It holds a reference to the list over which it iterates, and it provides the same interface to the list as `singly_linked_list` does, but its member functions always return pointers to `slink_string` objects instead of to `single_link` objects.

Listing 11.8. SLSITER.H. An iterator for a single-linked list of `String` objects.

```
//--------------------------------------------------------------
//  File: slsiter.h
//  Iterator for single-linked list of strings

#if !defined(__SLSITER_H)
#define __SLSITER_H

#include "slstr.h"
#include "sllist.h"

class sllist_iterator
{
public:
    sllist_iterator(singly_linked_list& sl): sllist(sl){}

    slink_string* current()
    {
        return (slink_string*) sllist.current();
    }
```

continues

Listing 11.8. continued

```
    slink_string* next()
    {
        return (slink_string*) sllist.next();
    }

    slink_string* first()
    {
        return (slink_string*)sllist.first();
    }

private:
    singly_linked_list& sllist;
};

#endif
```

Trying Out a Single-Linked List of *Strings*

With all the equipment in place for working with single-linked lists of `slink_string` objects, you need only to try one out. Listing 11.9 shows a sample program that does this. It creates a linked list of `slink_string` objects and an iterator for the list. Then it inserts several `slink_string` objects into the list and displays what the list contains. Notice that you can display `slink_string` objects using the << operator because this operator is defined for the `String` class and the `slink_string` is derived from `String`. Finally, the program removes an item from the list and again displays the contents of the list.

Listing 11.9. A program to test a single-linked list of `String`s.

```
//--------------------------------------------------------------
// File:  tstsls.cpp
// Test linked list of strings

#include "slsiter.h"
//--------------------------------------------------------------
```

```
//  m a i n
//  Program that exercises a singly linked list of Strings
void main()
{
// Create a String with a single link
    slink_string s1("One");

// Create a singly linked list with s1 as first element
    singly_linked_list strlist(s1);

// Create an iterator for this linked list
    sllist_iterator si(strlist);

// Insert another copy of s1 into the list
    strlist.insert(s1);

// Change the string value of s1 and insert it again
    s1 = "Two";
    strlist.insert(s1);
    strlist.insert(s1);
    s1 = "Three";
    strlist.insert(s1);

// Display what the list contains
    cout << "------------------------------------" << endl;
    cout << "List contains:" << endl;
    slink_string* x;
    for(x = si.first(); x != 0; x = si.next())
        cout << *x << endl;

// Remove the current element from the list
// At this point, current element is the last element
    strlist.remove();

// Display the final contents of the linked list
    cout << "------------------------------------" << endl;
    cout << "Now list contains:" << endl;
    for(x = si.first(); x != 0; x = si.next())
        cout << *x << endl;
}
```

To build this program, you need to compile and link the files from Listings 11.2, 11.5, 11.7, and 11.9. When run, the program displays the following output:

```
----------------------------------
List contains:
One
One
Two
Two
Three
----------------------------------
Now list contains:
One
One
Two
Two
```

A Double-Linked List

Now that I've created a single-linked list, I can extend this design to create a double-linked list. This data type is important because you can use it as the basis of other higher-level data structures such as queues and stacks. As Figure 11.6 illustrates, a double-linked list is like a single-linked list except each link can point to both the previous and the next link on the list. The list also contains a pointer to the last element because you can go backward and forward on the list.

A *double_link* Class

You can create a class with two links by deriving from a class with a single link. Listing 11.10 shows the DLINK.H header file, which declares the `double_link` class, derived from the `single_link` class. This serves as the base for a doubly-linked list.

The `clone` and `destroy` virtual functions are still declared as purely virtual. This means that the `double_link` is still an abstract class with its only purpose being to provide two links to some other data class so that the instances of the newly derived class can reside in a doubly-linked list.

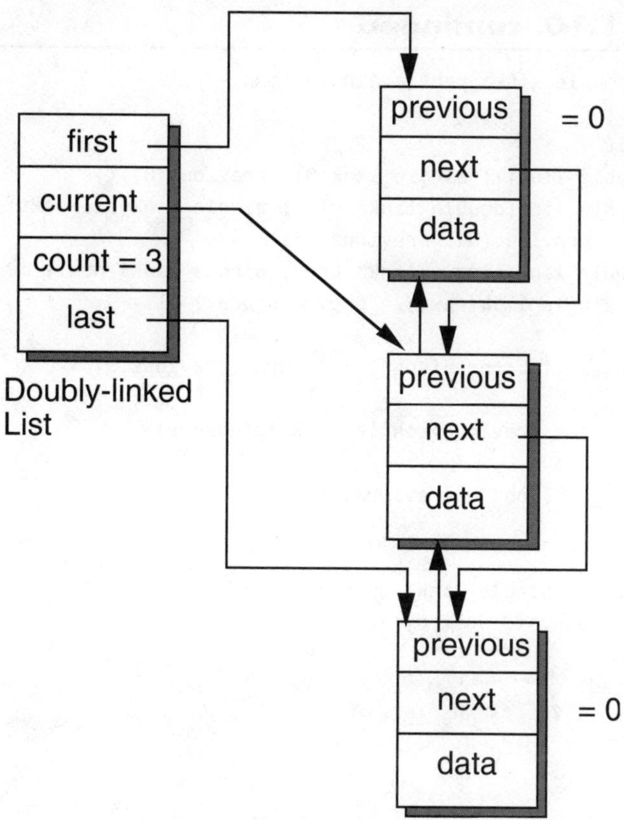

Figure 11.6. A double-linked list.

Listing 11.10. DLINK.H. Declares the `double_link` class.

```
//--------------------------------------------------------------------
//  File: dlink.h
//  Declares a "double link" class

#if !defined (__DLINK_H)
#define __DLINK_H

#include "slink.h"
```

continues

Listing 11.10. continued

```
class double_link: public single_link
{
public:
    double_link(): single_link(0),_previous(0) {}
    double_link(double_link& dl) : single_link(dl._next),
        _previous(dl._previous) {}
    double_link(single_link* prev, single_link* next) :
       single_link(next), _previous(prev) {}

    single_link* previous() { return _previous; }

    void set_previous(single_link *previous)
    {
        _previous = previous;
    }

    virtual single_link* clone() = 0;
    virtual void destroy() = 0;

protected:
    single_link* _previous;
};

#endif
```

The *doubly_linked_list* Class

You can also exploit the existing `singly_linked_list` class (see Listings 11.4 and 11.5) when defining the `doubly_linked_list` class. As Listings 11.11 and 11.12 illustrate, you can derive the `doubly_linked_list` from the `singly_linked_list`.

The `doubly_linked_list` class provides the `insert_last` and `remove_first` functions for inserting and removing elements from the list. The insertion occurs at the front of the list, while the `remove_last` function always returns the last item in the list. I include only these two functions because I plan to use the `doubly_linked_list` as a queue. To use it as a stack, you must provide two more insert and remove functions, `insert_first` and `remove_last`, because a stack inserts at the top and removes from the bottom.

Listing 11.11. DLLIST.H. Declares the `doubly_linked_list` class.

```
//--------------------------------------------------------------------
//  File: dllist.h
//  Declares a "doubly linked list" class

#if !defined (__DLLIST_H)
#define __DLLIST_H

#include "dlink.h"
#include "sllist.h"

class doubly_linked_list: public singly_linked_list
{
public:
// Constructor
    doubly_linked_list(double_link& dl) : singly_linked_list(dl)
    {
        _last = (double_link*)_current;
    }

    single_link* previous()
    {
        double_link* cur = (double_link*)_current;
        single_link* t = cur->previous();
        if(t != 0) _current = t;
        return t;
    }

    double_link* last() { return _last; }

// New list insertion and deletion functions
    void insert_last(double_link& sl);
    double_link* remove_first();

protected:
    double_link *_last;
};

#endif
```

If you examine the remove_last function in Listing 11.12, you'll notice that the function "unhooks" the last element from the list and returns a pointer to that element to the calling program. Because every item in the list is created on the free store, you need to somehow destroy the item when it is no longer needed. The idea is to have a queue class that provides the final interface to the programmer. The queue class calls remove_last to get an item, copies that item into a programmer-supplied variable, and then discards the item by calling its destroy function. The get function of the string_queue class, defined in Listing 11.15, illustrates how this is done.

Listing 11.12. DLLIST.CPP. Implements the doubly_linked_list class.

```
//-----------------------------------------------------------------
//  File: dllist.cpp
//  Implements "insert_last" and "remove_first" functions for a
//  doubly linked list

#include "dllist.h"

//-----------------------------------------------------------------
//  i n s e r t _ l a s t
//  Insert a new item at the end of the list

void doubly_linked_list::insert_last(double_link& dl)
{
// Clone the element passed to the function and
// hook it up in the linked list
    double_link *t = (double_link*)dl.clone();

    if(_last != 0)
    {
        _last->set_next(t);
        t->set_previous(_last);
        t->set_next(0);
    }
    else
    {
        _first = t;
        _current = t;
    }
```

```
// Make this one the last element in the list
    _last = t;
// Increment of count of elements on the list
    _count++;
}
//---------------------------------------------------------------------
//  r e m o v e _ f i r s t
//  Removes the element from the beginning of the list

double_link* doubly_linked_list::remove_first()
{
    if(_count == 0) return 0;

    double_link* cp = (double_link*)_first;
    if(_current == _first) _current = _first->next();
    _first = _first->next();

    double_link* t = (double_link*)_first;
    if(t != 0) t->set_previous(0);

    if(_last == cp) _last = 0;
    _count—;

    return cp;
}
```

A Double-Linkable *String*

To show a real use of the `doubly_linked_list` class, you need a data item that can be stored in the list. Like the `slink_string` class of Listings 11.6 and 11.7, you can create a `dlink_string` class that is derived from `String` and `double_link`. Examples of this class include a `String` object with two links, `_previous` and `_next`, that come from the `double_link` class. Listings 11.13 and 11.14 show the DLSTR.H and DLSTR.CPP files, which implement the `dlink_string` class.

Listing 11.13. DLSTR.H. Declares the `dlink_string` class.

```
//--------------------------------------------------------------------
//  File: dlstr.h
//  Doubly linkable string class

#if !defined(__DLSTR_H)
#define __DLSTR_H

#include "str.h"        // String class
#include "dlink.h"      // double_link class

class dlink_string: public double_link, public String
{
public:
    dlink_string() : String(), double_link(0,0) {}
    dlink_string(const char *s): String(s), double_link(0,0){}

    dlink_string(const dlink_string& s) :
        String(s.p_c), double_link(s._previous, s._next) {}

    dlink_string(const String& s):
        String(s), double_link() {}

    dlink_string& operator=(const dlink_string& s);

    void destroy() { delete this;}

    single_link* clone()
    {
        dlink_string* t = new dlink_string(*this);
        return t;
    }
};

#endif
```

Listing 11.14. DLSTR.CPP. Implements the assignment operator for the `dlink_string` class.

```
//------------------------------------------------------------------
//  File:  dlstr.cpp

#include "dlstr.h"

//------------------------------------------------------------------
//  o p e r a t o r =
//  Assign one "dlink_string" to another

dlink_string& dlink_string::operator=(const dlink_string& s)
{
    if(this != &s)
    {
        _next = s._next;
        _previous = s._previous;
        _length = s._length;
        _maxlen = s._maxlen;
        delete[] p_c;
        p_c = new char[_maxlen];
        strcpy(p_c, s.p_c);
    }
    return *this;
}
```

A Queue of *String* Objects

In place of the iterator class used for the singly-linked list, I'll create a class that maintains a queue of `dlink_string` objects. This class, named `string_queue`, is defined in the SQUEUE.H file, which appears in Listing 11.15. With the `string_queue`, you can create a queue—actually a `doubly_linked_list`, for which `string_queue` provides a queue-like interface. The `get` and `put` functions, respectively, enable you to store `dlink_string` objects into the queue and retrieve them.

Think of `string_queue` as a class that knows how to use a `doubly_linked_list` class and that provides a first-in, first-out (FIFO) interface appropriate for a queue. It inserts objects at the end of the list and returns items from the front. You could similarly construct a stack class that provides a last-in, first-out (LIFO) interface to the `doubly_linked_list` class. In this case, the queue grows dynamically, but you could easily limit the size of the queue with some added code.

Listing 11.15. SQUEUE.H. Defines the `string_queue` class.

```
//--------------------------------------------------------------------
//  File: squeue.h
//  Interface for a queue of doubly linkable String objects

#if !defined(__SQUEUE_H)
#define __SQUEUE_H

#include "dlstr.h"
#include "dllist.h"

class string_queue
{
public:
    string_queue(dlink_string& ds)
    {
        my_queue = new doubly_linked_list(ds);
        created_here = 1;
    }

    string_queue(doubly_linked_list& q) :
        my_queue(&q), created_here(0) {}

    ~string_queue() { if(created_here) delete my_queue;}

    int get(dlink_string& dl)
    {
     dlink_string *p;
        p = (dlink_string*)my_queue->remove_first();

        if(p)
        {
// Copy the item and then destroy it
            dl = *p;
            p->destroy();
            return 1;
        }
        else
            return 0;
    }

    void put(dlink_string& dl)
```

```
    {
        my_queue->insert_last(dl);
    }

private:
    doubly_linked_list* my_queue;
    int                 created_here;
};

#endif
```

Testing the Queue

Listing 11.16 shows a small program that tests the queue of `dlink_string` objects defined by the `string_queue` class. The program first creates a queue and inserts three `dlink_string` objects into it. It then retrieves the items one-by-one and displays them. Because the `dlink_string` objects are also of the `String` type, you can use the << operator with the `dlink_string` objects.

The program generates the following output:

```
-----------------------------------
Queue contains:
One
Two
Three
```

Listing 11.16. Sample program to exercise the `string_queue` class.

```
//--------------------------------------------------------------------
// File:  tstsq.cpp
// Test queue of strings

#include "squeue.h"
//--------------------------------------------------------------------
//  m a i n
//  Program that exercises a queue of Strings
```

continues

Listing 11.16. continued

```
void main()
{
// Create a String with a double link
    dlink_string ds1("One");

// Create a queue with ds1 as first element
    string_queue strq(ds1);

    ds1 = "Two";
    strq.put(ds1);

    ds1 = "Three";
    strq.put(ds1);

// Get entries from the queue and display them

    cout << "Queue contains:" << endl;
    cout << "--------------" << endl;

    while(strq.get(ds1))
    {
        cout << ds1 << endl;
    }
}
```

Summary

The first major component of OOP—data abstraction—enables you to introduce new data types from which you can create instances of objects. The second component, inheritance, defines new specialized data types in terms of existing ones or for extending the functionality of an existing type. C++'s `class` construct handles both of these needs: you can encapsulate data and functions with it and you can derive a class from one or more base classes. A derived class inherits all `public` and `protected` members of its base classes. Furthermore, you can differentiate the derived class from its base classes by one of the following methods:

- Adding new member variables
- Adding new member functions
- Overriding the definition of functions inherited from the base classes

When the `class` construct is used to define an abstract data type, inheritance enables you to create specialized subtypes. On the other hand, when a class is simply a module that encapsulates some data and functions, you can use inheritance to extend the capabilities offered by the module. When defining functions in a derived class, be aware that any overloaded function hides all inherited versions of the same name.

C++ supports single and multiple inheritance. In single inheritance, each derived class has exactly one base class; multiple inheritance enables you to derive a class from more than one base class. You can use multiple inheritance to simulate generic classes, such as linked lists and queues. This works by making the data structures capable of storing a link, for example, and then creating a linkable data type by inheriting from the link class as well as from your data type.

Another interesting feature of inheritance is that a pointer to an instance of the base class can hold the address of any of its derived class instances. The next chapter explains how this feature allows you to exploit polymorphism in C++ programs.

12

Virtual Functions and C++

This chapter focuses on polymorphism, the third basic component of object-oriented programming. Chapter 10, "Defining Operations on Objects," and Chapter 11, "Using Inheritance in C++," cover the other components of OOP—data abstraction and inheritance. Polymorphic functions work with many different argument types. C++ supports this kind of polymorphism through function overloading. The other type of polymorphism simplifies the syntax of performing the same operation with a hierarchy of classes. This is what enables you to use the same function name (`draw`, for example) to draw all types of `shape` objects, whether they are `circle_shapes`, `rectangle_shapes`, or `triangle_shapes`. You can therefore use polymorphism to maintain a clean interface to the classes because you don't need to define unique function names for similar operations on each derived class. This type of polymorphism goes hand in hand with inheritance and *late* or *dynamic binding*. This chapter explains the terminology and describes how the `virtual` keyword supports polymorphism.

Dynamic Binding

The term *binding* refers to the connection between a function call and the actual code executed as a result of the call. The following sections explain how binding is determined and how it affects the style of code you write.

Static Binding

Like any new concept, the best way to explain binding is through an example. Suppose you want to process a one-character command and you have defined a number of functions that perform the tasks requested by various commands. Using a `switch` statement, you might handle the commands as follows:

```
#include <ctype.h>
#include <iostream.h>
//...
static void quit(), newparams() showparams();
char ch;
//...
// Respond to user command
// Assume 'ch' holds the command character

    int code = toupper(ch);
    switch (code)
    {
        case 'Q': quit();
        case 'P': newparams();
                  break;
        case '?': showparams();
                  break;
        default:  cout << "Unknown command:" << ch << endl;
    }
```

Of course, in this case the function invoked in response to each command is known when the program is compiling because each function is explicitly called by name. This is known as *static binding* because the compiler can figure out the function to be called before the program ever runs.

Function Call Through a Pointer

Now consider an alternate implementation of this command-processing code. Start with a table of commands that can be implemented as an array of structures, each of which holds a command character and a pointer to the function to be called when the user types that character. The processing loop simply compares the input command character with the entries in the table and, if a matching entry is found, calls the function with the pointer that appears in that slot of the table. Here is a sample implementation of this scheme:

```
#include <ctype.h>
#include <iostream.h>

// Command-processing functions...
static void quit(), newparams(), showparams();

struct command
{
    char cmdchar;      // Each command is a character
    void (*action)(); // Function called to process command
};

command cmdtable[] =  // This is the table of commands
{
    'Q',  quit,
    'q',  quit,
    'P',  newparams,
    'p',  newparams,
    '?',  showparams
};

// Number commands in the command-table
int cmdcount = sizeof(cmdtable) / sizeof(command);

char ch;
int  i;

//...
// Sample command-processing loop:
// Assume character 'ch' holds input character
// Search the command table for matching command
```

```
    for(i = 0; i < cmdcount; i++)
    {
        if(cmdtable[i].cmdchar == ch)
        {
// Found command...call the corresponding function
            (*cmdtable[i].action)();
            break;
        }
    }

    if(i == cmdcount)
        cout << "Unknown command: " << ch << endl;
```

Notice that this version of the command-processing loop differs from the previous one in two respects:

- The `switch` statement is no longer needed.
- A function call via a pointer is used to invoke the function that performs the task requested by each command. The content of the pointer determines the actual function called.

This is known as *dynamic binding*. The term *dynamic* is used because the actual function called at runtime depends on the contents of the function pointer, which in turn depends on the character in the `char` variable `ch`. Dynamic binding is also known as *late binding* because the connection between the function call and the actual code executed by the call is determined late—that is, during runtime instead of compile time.

Incidentally, the lack of a `switch` statement is a characteristic feature of dynamic binding. By using the indirection afforded by the function pointer, you can forgo the tests required in a `switch` statement. Instead, you can call a different function by simply altering the content of the function pointer.

C++ compilers usually implement dynamic binding through function pointers. Like most other features of C++, this happens behind the scenes. You only need to use the `virtual` keyword, which I explain next.

Virtual Functions

Most of the examples you have seen thus far include classes with one or more virtual member functions. Consider, for example, the geometric shape classes introduced in Chapter 6, "C++ and Object-Oriented Programming." As you may recall, the `shape` class is the base class from which you derived several other classes, such as `rectangle_shape`, `circle_shape`, and `triangle_shape`. For a sample implementation, each shape needed to be able to compute its area and draw itself. In this case, the `shape` class declares the following virtual functions:

```
class shape
{
public:
    virtual double compute_area(void) const;
    virtual void draw(void) const;

// Other member functions that define an interface to all
// types of geometric shapes
};
```

Here, the `virtual` keyword preceding a function signals the C++ compiler that, if the function is defined in a derived class, the compiler may need to call the function indirectly through a pointer. Qualify a member function of a class with the `virtual` keyword only when there is a possibility that other classes may be derived from this one.

The `shape` class is an example of an *abstract base class*—a class that embodies a standard interface to a group of classes but does not provide a concrete implementation for any of the member functions. A common use of virtual functions is in defining such an abstract base class.

Pure Virtual Functions

One problem in defining a base class with virtual functions is that you may not be able to provide appropriate implementation for all the functions. For example, you can't define a `draw` or a `compute_area` function for a generic shape. Programmers often solve this problem by providing a dummy function that prints an error message. For the `compute_area` function of the `shape` class, you might write the following:

```
virtual void draw()
{
    cerr << "Derived class must implement!" << endl;
}
```

In this case, if you forget to implement `draw` in a derived class such as `circle_shape` and the program calls `draw` for a `circle_shape`, it prints an error message. This is not so bad, but the situation could be worse if you decided to call `exit` after printing the error message. A better way to handle this is to let the C++ compiler detect an unimplemented instance of a virtual class. That way, the error is detected before it's too late.

Pure virtual functions are virtual functions that the base class cannot implement. You can indicate a pure virtual function by adding the `=0` initializer following the declaration of the function. You gain two error-checking capabilities from pure virtual functions:

- The C++ compiler does not allow creation of instances of a class containing pure virtual functions. Thus, if you write

  ```
  shape s1;
  ```

  the compiler flags this as an error. This is good because you don't want anyone to create instances of an abstract base class anyway.

- The compiler checks to be sure the pure virtual functions of a base class are implemented by one of its derived classes. If an immediate derived class cannot provide an implementation, it can simply pass the problem on to one of its derived classes by also declaring the function as pure virtual.

C++ includes the notion of pure virtual functions that you can use to indicate that certain member functions of an abstract base class are not implemented. For example, in the `shape` class you can make `draw` and `compute_area` pure virtual functions as follows:

```
class shape
{
public:
// Make these "pure virtual functions"
    virtual double compute_area(void) const = 0;
    virtual void draw(void) const = 0;

// Other member functions
};
```

Concrete Implementation of Virtual Functions

An abstract base class uses the `virtual` keyword to qualify the member functions that constitute the interface to all the classes derived from that class. Each specific derived class must define its own concrete versions of the functions that have been declared `virtual` in the base class. Therefore, if you derive the `circle_shape` and `rec-`

tangle_shape classes from the shape class, you must define the compute_area and draw member functions in each class. For instance, the definitions for the circle_shape class might appear like this:

```
class circle_shape: public shape
{
public:
    virtual double compute_area(void) const;
    virtual void draw(void) const;
// ...
private:
    double xc, yc;  // Coordinates of center
    double radius;  // radius of circle
};

#define M_PI 3.14159 // value of "pi"
// Implementation of "compute_area" function
circle_shape::compute_area(void) const
{
    return (M_PI * radius * radius);
}

// Implementation of "draw" function
circle_shape::draw(void) const
{
//...
}
```

When declaring the draw and compute_area functions in the derived class, you can optionally add the virtual keyword to emphasize that these are indeed virtual functions. The function definitions do not need the virtual keyword.

Dynamic Binding Through Virtual Functions

You don't need to do anything special to use virtual functions. Treat them like any other member function of a class. As an example, consider the following calls to the virtual functions draw and compute_area:

```
circle_shape    c1;
rectangle_shape r1;
double area = c1.compute_area(); // Compute area of circle
r1.draw();                       // Draw a rectangle
```

When used in this manner, these functions are like any other member functions. In this case, the C++ compiler can determine that you want to call the `compute_area` function of the `circle_shape` class and the `draw` function of the `rectangle_shape` class. In fact, the compiler makes direct calls to these functions, and the function calls are bound to specific code at link time. This is static binding.

An interesting case occurs when you make the function calls through a pointer to a shape like so:

```
shape*   s[10];  // Pointers to 10 shape objects
int      i, numshapes=10;
//... create shapes and store pointers in array "s"
// Draw the shapes
    for(i = 0; i < numshapes; i++) shape[i]->draw();
```

Because the individual entries in the array of `shape` pointers can point to any type of shape derived from the `shape` class, the C++ compiler cannot determine which specific implementation of the `draw` function to call. This is where dynamic binding and the `virtual` keyword come in.

Pointer to a Derived Class Is also a Pointer to the Base

In C++, you can use a reference or a pointer to any derived class in place of a reference or a pointer to the base class without an explicit type cast. So, if both `circle_shape` and `rectangle_shape` are derived from the `shape` class, you can call a function that requires a pointer to `shape` with a pointer to a `circle_shape` or a `rectangle_shape` as well. The opposite is not true; hence, you cannot use a reference or a pointer to the base class in place of a reference or a pointer to an instance of a derived class.

Virtual Function Call Mechanism

As explained previously, an indirect function call (a function call through a pointer) provides dynamic binding. C++ compilers use this idea when calling virtual functions. The `virtual` keyword is a signal to the compiler that the member function qualified by the keyword may need to be called through a pointer.

A typical C++ compiler constructs an array of virtual function pointers for each class. This array goes by the name of *virtual table* or *vtable* for short. Each instance of the class has a pointer to its class-wide virtual table. Figure 12.1 illustrates the situation for the `circle_shape` class. Given this arrangement, the C++ compiler can achieve dynamic binding by transforming a call to a virtual function into an indirect call through a pointer in the class virtual table. For example, if the virtual table is laid out as shown in Figure 12.1, the compiler can implement the call

```
circle_shape *c1 = new circle_shape(100.,100.,50.);
c1->draw();
```

by generating code for

```
(*(c1->vtable[1]))(c1);  // c1 is "this"
```

where the second entry in the virtual table holds the pointer to the `draw` function of the `circle_shape` class. The pointer to the object is passed as the first argument of the function just as it is done implicitly for every member function of a class. This is the `this` pointer that a member function can use to refer to the current instance of the class.

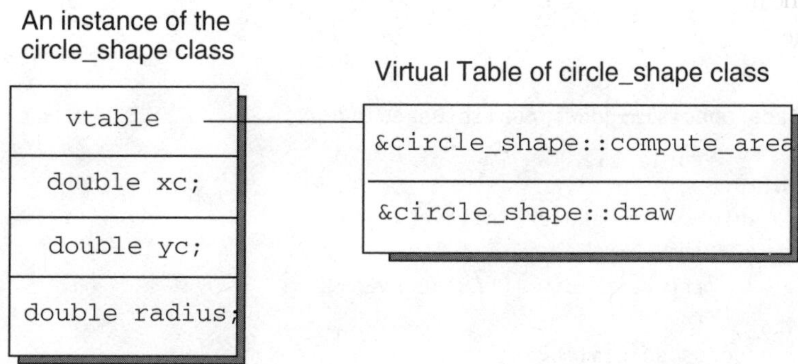

Figure 12.1. Virtual function implementation under single inheritance.

As a C++ programmer, you don't need to know how the compiler takes care of calling the correct virtual function, but you may find the knowledge helpful in understanding why a C++ program behaves the way it does. Also, C++ compilers are not required to implement the virtual function call mechanism exactly as illustrated in Figure 12.1. However, most C++ compilers do follow the same techniques, partly because these ideas are outlined in *The Annotated C++ Reference Manual* by Margaret Ellis and Bjarne Stroustrup, which is the basis of the ongoing standardization of C++ by the ANSI X3J16 committee. If you are curious, you may want to consult this book for further information on how various features of C++ can be implemented. For example, with multiple inheritance, implementing a virtual function call is somewhat more complicated. For more information on this, see *The Annotated C++ Reference Manual.*

Suppressing Virtual Function Calls

The virtual call mechanism is quite useful for implementing polymorphism, but occasions may arise when you want to call the function from the base class instead of the one from the derived class. For example, suppose you have a base class called BaseWindow with a virtual function called event_handler, which presumably processes events in a user interface. You are happy with the function, but you want a derived class called SpecialWindow with an event_handler that augments the processing done in the event-handling function of its base class. In the event_handler of the SpecialWindow class, you want to catch a special type of event and process it there. For all other types of events, you want to call the event_handler of the BaseWindow class. You can do this as follows:

```
class BaseWindow
{
public:
    virtual void event_handler(int event_id);
// Other members...
};

class SpecialWindow: public BaseWindow
{
public:
    void event_handler(int event_id)
    {
        if(event_id == SPECIAL_EVENT)
        {
// process special event...
        }
        else
        {
// Call BaseWindow's event_handler
            BaseWindow::event_handler(event_id);
        }
    }

// Other members...
};
```

You can suppress the virtual call mechanism by explicitly qualifying a function with its class name. In this example, you can call the event_handler of the BasicWindow class by explicitly qualifying the function name with the BasicWindow:: prefix.

Using Polymorphism

As you have seen from the examples in this chapter and Chapter 6, polymorphism eliminates the `switch` statement and generally simplifies the interface to a hierarchy of classes. The geometric shapes of Chapter 5, "Basics of Object-Oriented Programming," and Chapter 6 provide a good example of the use of polymorphism. Suppose you have a collection of `shape` objects in a storage structure, such as an array or a linked list. The array simply stores pointers to `shape` objects. These pointers could point to any type of shape, provided they are derived from the `shape` class. When operating on these shapes, you can simply loop through the array and invoke the appropriate member function via the pointer to the instance. Of course, for this to work, the member functions must be declared as `virtual` in the `shape` class, which happens to be the base class for all geometric shapes.

As you might gather from the examples, you must do the following to use polymorphism in C++:

1. Create a class hierarchy with the important operations defined by member functions declared as virtual in the base class. If the base class is such that you cannot provide implementations for these functions, you can declare them to be purely virtual. The `draw` function of the `shape` class is an example:

   ```
   virtual void draw() const = 0;
   ```

2. Provide concrete implementations of the virtual classes in the derived classes. Each derived class can have its own version of the functions. For example, the implementation of the `draw` function varies from one shape to another.

3. Manipulate instances of these classes through a reference or a pointer. This is what causes the C++ compiler to use dynamic binding and call the functions using the virtual function mechanism described earlier.

The last item—invoking member functions through a pointer—is the essence of polymorphic use in C++. This is because you get dynamic binding only when virtual member functions are invoked through a pointer to a class instance and when you need dynamic binding for polymorphism.

Implications of Polymorphic Use of Classes

Because polymorphic use of class instances requires that you manipulate objects through pointers or references, you should be aware of certain problems that you may encounter when programming this way. The following sections briefly discuss some pitfalls.

Virtual Destructors

When you manipulate objects through pointers, you often tend to create them dynamically through the new operator and later destroy them with the `delete` operator. A typical situation might be as shown in the following example:

```
//  Illustrates why "virtual destructor" is needed

#include <iostream.h>

class Base
{
public:
    Base() { cout << "Base: constructor" << endl; }

//*** The destructor should be "virtual"
    ~Base() { cout << "Base: destructor" << endl; }
};

class Derived: public Base
{
public:
    Derived() { cout << "Derived: constructor" << endl; }
    ~Derived() { cout << "Derived: destructor" << endl; }
};

void main()
{
    Base* p_base = new Derived;

// Use the object...

// Now delete the object
    delete p_base;
}
```

This is a case where the `main` function creates a copy of a derived class using the `new` operator and later destroys that instance using `delete`. When you compile and run this program, it displays:

```
Base: constructor
Derived: constructor
Base: destructor
```

The first two lines indicate the order in which the class constructors are called: the constructor for the base class followed by that for the derived class. This keeps with the order of initialization explained in Chapter 11, "Using Inheritance in C++." The third line of output, however, seems odd. Why isn't there a call to the destructor of the derived class?

The reason is that when you called the constructor, you used the derived class name with the `new` operator. Therefore, the C++ compiler correctly created the right type of object. You saved the pointer in a `p_base` variable, which is declared as a pointer to the base class. Subsequently, when you write

```
delete p_base;
```

the compiler can't tell that you are destroying a derived class instance.

Because `delete` does its job by calling the destructor for the class, you can solve the problem by declaring the destructor of the base class `virtual`. That way the destructor is invoked through the virtual function table and the correct destructor is called. Indeed, if you use the following for the base class destructor:

```
virtual ~Base() { cout << "Base: destructor" << endl; }
```

and rerun the program, you get the correct output as follows:

```
Base: constructor
Derived: constructor
Derived: destructor
Base: destructor
```

Notice that the order of calls to the destructors is the opposite order in which the constructors were called. Therefore, the virtual destructor ensures that the object is properly destroyed.

How do you decide whether to declare a destructor virtual? If a class has any virtual function, then chances are that instances of classes derived from this one will be manipulated through pointers to attain polymorphic behavior. In this case, you should declare a virtual destructor for the class.

Calling Virtual Functions in a Base Class Constructor

Another pitfall of using virtual functions is that at certain times they do not work as expected. One place where calling a virtual function may produce undesired results is in the constructor of a base class. You can see the problem from the following example program:

```
//  Illustrates what happens when a virtual function
//  is called from the constructor of a base class

#include <iostream.h>

class Base
{
public:
    Base()
    {
        cout << "Base: constructor. Calling clone()" << endl;
        clone();
    }
    virtual void clone()
    {
        cout << "Base::clone() called" << endl;
    }
};

class Derived: public Base
{
public:
    Derived()
    {
        cout << "Derived: constructor" << endl;
    }

    void clone()
    {
        cout << "Derived::clone() called" << endl;
    }
};

void main()
{
```

```
    Derived x;
    Base *p = &x;

// Call "clone" through pointer to class instance
    cout << "Calling 'clone' through instance pointer";
    cout << endl;
    p->clone();
}
```

When you run this program, you get the following output:

```
Base: constructor. Calling clone()
Base::clone() called
Derived: constructor
Calling 'clone' through instance pointer
Derived::clone() called
```

You can go over the output to see what happened. When you create an instance of the derived class, as expected, the C++ compiler first calls the constructor of the base class. At this point, the derived class instance is only partially initialized. Therefore, when the compiler encounters the call to the `clone` virtual function, it cannot bind it to the version of `clone` for the derived class. Instead, the compiler calls the version of `clone` from the base class.

The last two lines of output show that, once the object is created, you can correctly invoke the `clone` function for the derived class instance through a base class pointer as is common in polymorphic use of virtual functions.

If you call a virtual function in a class constructor, the compiler invokes the base class's version of the function, not the version defined for the derived class.

Summary

The three features of object-oriented programming—data abstraction, inheritance, and polymorphism—go hand in hand. For realistic object-oriented programs, you need to use all of these concepts in tandem. The data and functions are encapsulated into an object by a `class` or a `struct`. Inheritance enables you to implement the *is a* relationship among objects, as in *a circle is a shape.* Finally, polymorphism enables you to use the same functional interface such as member functions named `draw` and `compute_area` to work with all kinds of shapes.

Several features of C++ work in concert to support polymorphism:

- You can use a pointer to a derived class anywhere a pointer to the base class is expected. The same rule applies to references.
- If a base class declares a member function with the `virtual` keyword, the compiler places the function in the class-wide virtual function table and uses the base class's implementation of the function as a default, which is used only if a derived class does not define the function.
- If a derived class redefines a `virtual` function and you call that function through a pointer to the class instance, the compiler invokes the function through the pointer stored in the virtual table, thereby invoking the version of the function from the derived class. This is known as dynamic binding.

Dynamic binding makes polymorphism possible. With polymorphism, you can control a particular behavior of a whole group of objects by calling the same member function. The draw function of shape classes provides a good illustration of polymorphic usage.

When you use virtual functions in C++, you need to watch out for some pitfalls. For example, if you call a virtual function from the constructor of a class, the compiler calls the version from itself or one of the bases, but not a version defined by derived classes. Also, for correct destruction of objects, you may need to declare the destructor of the base class as virtual.

13

Advanced Topics in C++

The previous chapters have shown you how C++ supports object-oriented programming. Despite its well-known capabilities, C++ is relatively young. (It was released commercially in late 1985.) In fact, features such as multiple inheritance and the `iostream` library were not introduced until AT&T C++ Release 2.0 became available in 1989. The current release of AT&T C++ is 3.0, which includes a relatively new feature: templates (also known as parameterized types). AT&T is already working on the next release of C++, which is expected to include another new feature: exception handling.

Another ongoing development that affects the future of C++ is the work being done by the American National Standards Institute (ANSI) C++ Technical Committee, X3J16. The X3J16 committee is developing a draft proposal to standardize the C++ programming language. The committee is starting with the following documents as the basis for its proposal:

- The ANSI C standard (ANSI X3.159-1989—Programming Language C)
- *The Annotated C++ Reference Manual* by Margaret A. Ellis and Bjarne Stroustrup, published by Addison-Wesley Publishing Company, 1990

Already, the X3J16 committee has decided to include templates and exceptions in the C++ draft standard. The template mechanism is based on the experimental design presented in Chapter 14 of *The Annotated C++ Reference Manual*, or *ARM*, as it is popularly known. For exception handling, the design is derived from the material in Chapter 15 of *ARM*.

This chapter gives you an overview of templates and exception handling based on information available in *ARM* and some recent articles in the *C++ Report* and the *Journal of Object-Oriented Programming* (published by SIGS Publications, New York, USA). Templates enable you to define generic classes, and exception handling provides a uniform way to cope with errors in C++ programs. Borland C++ 4 supports both templates and exception handling. The examples in this chapter that illustrate how you might use these features are based on the proposed syntax for templates and the proposed mechanism for exception handling, but these proposals may change in the future when a C++ standard emerges.

Templates

When it becomes available in C++, a template will define a family of classes or functions. For example, with a class template for a `Stack` class, you can create stacks of various data types such as `int`, `float`, and `char*`. Similarly, with a function template for a `sort` function, you can create versions of the `sort` function that will sort an array of `int`, `float`, or `char*` data. When you create a class or function template, you essentially want to define a class or a function with a parameter—for example, a data type that you would specify when the class or function is being used. For this reason, templates are often referred to as *parameterized types*.

Stacks for *int* and *float*

As an example of a class declaration with a parameter, consider the following simple declaration of a stack class, named `intStack`, that is capable of holding `int` variables:

```
const int MAXSIZE = 128;
```

```
class intStack            // Define a stack for int variables
{
public:
    intStack() { _stackptr = 0;}
    int push(int x) {return _array[_stackptr++] = x;}
    int pop() { return _array[__stackptr];}
    int empty() const { return (_stackptr == 0);}
private:
    int _array[MAXSIZE]; // Internally, an array stores the data
    int _stackptr;
};
```

The `intStack` class uses an array of `int` variables as the internal storage for the stack. You might use the `intStack` class in this way:

```
    intStack i_stack;

// Push an integer value
    i_stack.push(301);

// Pop a number off the stack
    int last_val = i_stack.pop();
```

If you want to define a stack of `floats` (a `floatStack` class) that uses the same internal mechanism as `intStack`, simply replace every `int` in the `intStack` class declaration with `float`. This tells you that, if you were able to define a single `Stack` class that accepted a data type as a parameter, and if the C++ compiler enabled you to create new class definitions by invoking `Stack`'s definition with any data type, you could use a single definition to create stacks for any type of data. In other words, what you need is a way to define parameterized classes. With the C++ template mechanism, you can define classes and functions with parameters.

Generic Classes Using Macros

An alternate way of defining generic classes is to use the macro facility of the C preprocessor. After all, a preprocessor macro can take parameters, so it should be possible to use the `#define` directive to create a class definition that is parameterized. You can indeed use macros to define generic classes. In fact, Borland C++ comes with a header file named GENERIC.H that defines two macros to simplify the declaration of generic classes:

- The macro `_Paste2(a,b)` takes two arguments and "pastes" them together to create a new macro, `ab`. With ANSI standard C preprocessors, the `_Paste2` macro can be defined using the token-pasting operator `##` as follows:

  ```
  #define _Paste2(a,b) a##b
  ```

  With this macro, if you write

  ```
  _Paste2(int,Stack)
  ```

  the preprocessor expands it to the symbol `intStack`.

- The `declare` macro takes two arguments and is defined as follows:

  ```
  #define declare(x,y) _Paste2(x,declare)(y)
  ```

  The `declare` macro pastes the string `declare` to the first argument and passes the second argument to the resulting macro. Thus, if you were to write

  ```
  declare(Stack,int)
  ```

  the preprocessor would expand it and invoke the macro with

  ```
  Stackdeclare(int)
  ```

To use the `_Paste2` and `declare` macros to define a generic stack class, you can follow these steps:

1. Define a macro `Stack` with a data type as an argument. Let this macro create a new macro name by concatenating the symbol `Stack` with the type. You can use the `_Paste2` macro from `generic.h` to define the `Stack` macro like this:

   ```
   #include <generic.h>
   #define Stack(TYPE) _Paste2(TYPE,Stack)
   ```

   With this definition, `Stack(int)` will result in the symbol `intStack`.

2. Define another macro, `Stackdeclare(TYPE)`, that takes a data type as an argument and defines the class named `Stack(TYPE)`. Listing 13.1 shows how the `Stackdeclare(TYPE)` macro is defined.

Listing 13.1. GSTACK.H. A generic stack implemented using macros.

```
//--------------------------------------------------------------
// File: gstack.h
//
// Macro to declare a generic stack using macros declared
```

```
// in the <generic.h> header file

#if !defined(__GSTACK_H)
#define __GSTACK_H

#include <generic.h> // Define the macros "_Paste2" and "declare"

const int MAXSIZE = 128;

#define Stack(TYPE) _Paste2(TYPE,Stack)

// Skip the ending semicolon in the class declaration embedded
// in the following macro definition. The semicolon will be
// added when the macro is invoked. Also, every line must end
// with a backslash followed by a newline so that the
// preprocessor treats this as a single macro definition

#define Stackdeclare(TYPE)                                  \
class Stack(TYPE)                                           \
{                                                           \
public:                                                     \
    Stack(TYPE)() { _stackptr = 0;}                         \
    TYPE push(TYPE x) {return _array[_stackptr++] = x;}     \
    TYPE pop() { return _array[—_stackptr];}                \
    int empty() const { return (_stackptr == 0);}           \
private:                                                    \
    TYPE _array[MAXSIZE];                                   \
    int  _stackptr;                                         \
}

#endif
```

After defining the macros, `Stack(TYPE)` and `Stackdeclare(TYPE)`, as shown in Listing 13.1, you can declare and use a stack for `int` variables as follows:

```
// Declare a Stack for int types
declare(Stack,int);

main()
{
    Stack(int) id_stack;      // Define an instance of the stack
```

```
    id_stack.push(100);       // Push a value onto the stack
    int val = id_stack.pop(); // Pop a value from the stack
// . . .
}
```

Here is what happens. The invocation of the `declare(Stack,int)` macro expands to a call to `Stackdeclare(int)`, which declares a class named `intStack`—the name created by the macro `Stack(int)`. After this declaration, the statement

```
Stack(int) id_stack;
```

creates an instance of `intStack` named `id_stack`. You can then use the stack in the usual manner by calling its `push` and `pop` functions.

Listing 13.2 shows the file GSTACK.CPP, which is a complete program for testing the generic stack.

Listing 13.2. GSTACK.CPP. A test program for the generic stack.

```
//--------------------------------------------------------------
// File: gstack.cpp
// Main program to test the "generic stack."

#include "gstack.h"
#include <iostream.h>

// Declare a Stack for int types
declare(Stack,int);

int main()
{
    Stack(int) id_stack;

// Push some integers
    cout << "Pushing: " << endl;
    cout << id_stack.push(1) << endl;
    cout << id_stack.push(2) << endl;

// Pop one by one and display
    cout << "Popping: " << endl;
    cout << id_stack.pop() << endl;
    cout << id_stack.pop() << endl;
```

```
    if(id_stack.empty())
        cout << "Stack is now empty." << endl;

    return 0;
}
```

When compiled and run, this program correctly displays the following output:

```
Pushing:
1
2
Popping:
2
1
Stack is now empty.
```

Now if you need a stack for `float` variables, you can declare and use one as follows:

```
#include "gstack.h"
// Declare a stack for floats
    declare(Stack,float);
// . . .

// Create an instance of a stack of floats
    Stack(float) v_stack;

// Use the stack
    v_stack.push(39.95);
```

From this example, you can see that it is possible to create parameterized class definitions with the help of the C preprocessor, but the process is somewhat convoluted. Also, some preprocessors may not be able to handle the large macro definitions needed by some generic classes. Clearly, a simpler way of declaring parameterized classes would be a welcome addition to the C++ language.

Class Templates

In C++, the reserved `template` keyword is used to define class and function templates. With the proposed syntax, the template for a generic `Stack` class looks like this:

```
const int MAXSIZE = 128;
```

```
template<class T> class Stack
{
public:
    Stack() : _stackptr(0) {}
    T push(const T x)
    {
        if(_stackptr < MAXSIZE)
            return _array[_stackptr++] = x;
        else
            return (T)0;
    }

    T pop()
    {
        if(_stackptr >0)
            return _array[—_stackptr];
        else
            return (T)0;
    }

    int empty() const { return (_stackptr == 0);}
private:
    T    _array[MAXSIZE];
    int  _stackptr;
};
```

If you compare this with the approach based on the macros defined in GENERIC.H, you will find that the class definition is similar. The `template<class T>` prefix in the class declaration states that you will declare a class template and that you will use `T` as a class name in the declaration. Thus, `Stack` is a parameterized class with the `T` type as its parameter. With this definition of the `Stack` class template, you can create stacks for different data types like this:

```
Stack<int>    istack;   // A stack for int variables
Stack<float>  fstack;   // A stack for float variables
```

You can similarly define a generic `Array` class as follows:

```
template<class T> class Array
{
public:
    Array(int n=16) { _pa = new T(_size = n);}
    ~Array() { delete[] _pa;}
    T& operator[](int i);
//...
```

```
private:
    T*   _pa;
    int  _size;
};
```

You can then create instances of different Array types in the following manner:

```
Array<int>   iArray(128);  // A 128-element int array
Array<float> fArray(32);   // A 32-element float array
```

Function Templates

Like class templates, function templates define a family of functions parameterized by a data type. For example, you could define a parameterized sort function for sorting any type of array like this:

```
template<class T> void sort(Array<T>)
{
// Body of function (do the sorting)
// ...
}
```

This example essentially declares a set of overloaded sort functions, one for each type of Array. When defining the sort function, you will need a comparison operator for the class T. One restriction on using the sort function template is that the class you provide in place of T must define a comparison operator.

You can invoke the sort function as you would any ordinary function. The C++ compiler analyzes the arguments to the function and calls the proper version of the function. For example, given iArray and fArray, the arrays of int and float, respectively, you can apply the sort function to each as follows:

```
sort(iArray);  // Sort the array of int
sort(fArray);  // Sort the array of float
```

Member Function Templates

When declaring the Array class template, I left the operator[] member function undefined. Each member function in a class template is also a function template. When defined inline, no special syntax is necessary for the member functions of a template class—just use the template parameters as necessary in the function's body and in its argument list. When the member function of a class template is defined outside the body of the class, you must follow a specific syntax. For example, you can define the operator[] function of the Array class template like this:

```
template<class T> T& Array<T>::operator[](int i)
{
    if(i < 0 || i >= _size)
    {
// Handle error condition. Assume that there is a function
// named "handle_error" available for this purpose.
        handle_error("Array: index out of range");
    }
    else
        return _pa[i];
}
```

Advantages of Templates

Templates help you define classes that are general in nature (generic classes). Even though generic classes already can be defined using macros, templates make the process simpler and safer.

So far, I have shown you two ways to define generic classes. Early in this chapter you saw how the macros defined in the GENERIC.H header file can be used to declare parameterized classes. Although these macros work, they are cumbersome to define and use. The proposed syntax for templates will greatly simplify the process of defining parameterized classes.

Another approach to generic classes, explained in Chapter 11, "Using Inheritance in C++," presents a way of creating a generic `singly_linked_list` class starting with a singly-linked list of a base class called `single_link`, making sure that any data type that needs to be stored in the list is also derived from the `single_link` class. The only problem with this approach is that the member functions of the `singly_linked_list` class return pointers to `single_link`, but not to the type of objects actually stored in the list. Thus, you must cast each pointer returned by the `singly_linked_list` class to your data type before using it. Such type casts defeat the type-checking facilities of C++ and increase the potential for errors. With class templates, you can eliminate the need for any type casts and define parameterized classes in a safe manner.

Exception Handling

Exceptions refer to unusual conditions in a program. They can be outright errors that cause the program to fail or conditions that can lead to errors. Typically, you can always detect when certain types of errors are about to occur. For instance, when implementing the subscript function (`operator[]`) of the `Array` class, you can detect if the index is beyond the range of valid values. Such errors are called *synchronous exceptions* because they occur at a predictable time; an error caused by the array index going out of bounds occurs only after executing a statement in which that out-of-bounds index is used. Contrast this with *asynchronous exceptions*, which are caused by events beyond the control of your program; therefore, your program cannot anticipate their occurrence. The proposed exception-handling mechanism for C++ is intended to cope with synchronous exceptions only.

Benefits of Exception Handling

Although it is easy to detect synchronous exceptions such as failing to allocate memory or an array index going out of bounds, it is difficult to decide what to do when the exception occurs. Consider the `malloc` function in the ANSI C library. When you call `malloc` to allocate a block of memory, you get back a pointer to the allocated block. If `malloc` fails, it returns a NULL pointer (a zero address). The caller carries the burden of checking for this exceptional condition. As a C programmer, you are probably quite familiar with blocks of code like this:

```
#define MAXCHR 80
char *line;


if((line = (char *) malloc(MAXCHR)) == NULL)
{
/* Failed to allocate memory. Print message and exit. */
    fprintf(stderr, "Failed to allocate memory.\n");
    exit(1);
}
```

Whenever you call `malloc` in your program, you essentially repeat similar blocks of code again and again.

Now consider an alternative. Suppose `malloc` is written so that whenever it fails, it jumps (ANSI C's setjmp and longjmp functions provide the capability to jump from one function to another) to a function that you specify, perhaps with an error code—a code that indicates what went wrong—as an argument. Such a function is typically called a *handler* or an *exception handler*. If you do not provide an exception handler, `malloc` could jump to a default handler that prints a message and exits. If you do provide a handler, you could handle the error condition any way you wish. In certain applications, you may not even need to terminate the application. Best of all, with such an exception handler installed, you could call `malloc` without worrying about an error return. You know that, in case of any allocation failure, malloc will jump to the exception handler. Thus, if you know there is an exception handler, you can eliminate all those extra lines of code that check if malloc has returned a NULL pointer.

Like malloc, C++ class libraries have many functions that detect and handle error conditions. If *exception handling* is an integral part of C++, all class libraries will be able to cope with all "exceptional conditions" uniformly; thus the ongoing effort to provide exception handling in C++.

The Trouble with *setjmp* and *longjmp*

In ANSI C, the functions setjmp and longjmp enable you to jump back from many levels of function calls to a specific location in your program—you can abort what you were doing and return to your starting point. The setjmp function saves the "state" or the "context" of the process, and longjmp uses the saved context to revert to a previous point in the program. The terms *context* or *state* of a process refer to the information with which you can reconstruct the way the process is at a given point in its flow of execution. In ANSI C, an array data type named jmp_buf is available for storing information needed to restore a calling environment. This data type is defined in the SETJMP.H header file.

To understand the exact mechanics of setjmp and longjmp, look at the following lines of code:

```
#include <setjmp.h>
jmp_buf saved_context;

main()
{
    if (setjmp(saved_context) == 0)
    {
// This is executed the first time set_jmp is called.
        process_commands();
    }
    else
    {
// This block is executed when longjmp is called.
        handle_error();
    }
}
```

```
process_commands()
{
    int error_flag = 0;
// When an error occurs, error_flag is set to 1
// ...
    if(error_flag) longjmp(saved_context, 1);
}
```

When you call the setjmp function, it will save the current context in the jmp_buf variable named saved_context and return a zero. In this case, the first if statement in main is satisfied, and the process_commands function is called. If any error occurs in process_commands, the error_flag will be set to a nonzero value, and you will call longjmp with these arguments:

- The first argument is the jmp_buf variable, which contains the context to which longjmp should return.
- The second argument specifies the return value to be used during this return.

The longjmp function will revert the calling environment to this saved state. This amounts to *unrolling* or *unwinding* the stack to where it was when setjmp was originally called. After reverting to the saved context, longjmp returns. When the return statement in longjmp is executed, it will be like returning from the call to setjmp, which originally saved the saved_context buffer, except that the returned value will be provided by you as the second argument to longjmp. Calling longjmp causes the program to jump to the else block of the first if statement in main. In this way, setjmp and longjmp enable you to jump unconditionally from one C function to another without using conventional return statements. Essentially, setjmp marks the destination of the jump and longjmp acts as a nonlocal goto that executes the jump.

When you first look at it, the combination of setjmp and longjmp appears to be the ideal way to handle exceptions in C++. This is indeed true, and the proposed exception-handling mechanism (to be described later) can be implemented using setjmp and longjmp, but only because the proposed design also provides a solution to another problem. In C++, class instances must be initialized by calling class constructors and are destroyed by calling the corresponding destructors. Because longjmp abruptly jumps back to a previous point in the execution of the program, situations will occur where a constructor has been called, but a jump occurs before calling the destructor. In such cases, any memory allocated by a constructor will not be freed because the call to the destructor is skipped. Other problems may crop up as well because the internal state of some objects may be left in an unknown condition. Thus, if setjmp and longjmp are used to handle exceptions, there must be a way to call the destructors of all relevant objects before calling `longjmp`. Although I do not provide the details in this chapter, this is precisely what a `setjmp/longjmp`-based implementation of the exception-handling mechanism must do in practice.

Proposed Exception-Handling Mechanism for C++

Andrew Koenig and Bjarne Stroustrup have proposed an exception-handling mechanism for C++ that they describe in their recent paper "Exception Handling for C++" (*Journal of Object-Oriented Programming,* Vol.3, No.2, July/August 1990, pages 16-33). In this paper, they even outline a portable implementation of the proposed design based on C's `setjmp/longjmp` mechanism. In particular, they describe a scheme to solve the problem of ensuring that the destructors are called correctly before "unwinding" the stack. The following sections summarize how you, as a programmer, will see the proposed exception-handling features.

An Example

Consider a Forms software package that uses a `Form` class to represent a form. `Form` has a member function, `read`, to read the definition of a form from a file. Suppose you are rewriting `read` so it uses the proposed exception-handling mechanism to cope with the exception caused by the failure to open a specified file. Here is how you would add exception handling to the `read` function of the `Form` class:

1. Define a class with a descriptive name, `FormIOException` for example, representing the exception that can occur when the program is trying to read or write forms. You might declare it as follows:

```
class FormIOException
{
public:
        FormIOException(char* filename) :
                _filename(filename) {}
private:
        char* _filename;
}
```

2. In the `Form::read` function, when the file cannot be opened, throw a `FormIOException` like this:

```
void Form::read(const char* filename)
{
```

```
// Open an input stream on the specified file
        ifstream fs1(filename);
        if(!fs1)
        {
// Throw exception if file could not be opened
            throw FormIOException(filename);
        }
// Continue with normal processing
// ...
}
```

That's how you would throw the exception. Using the `Form` class, the programmer provides the code that catches the exception. It would look like this:

```
// Create a form and read in its definition from a file
    Form invoice;

// Be prepared to catch any exceptions
    try
    {
// If an exception is "thrown" control will transfer to the
// catch block.
        invoice.read("invoice.def");
    }
    catch(FormIOException fio)
    {
// You can display a message or display a dialog box informing
// the user that the file could not be opened.
        cout << "Error opening " << fio._filename << endl;
    }
```

This example illustrates the essential features of the proposed exception-handling mechanism. A few other important points are summarized next.

Summary of the Exception Handling Mechanism

The general syntax of exception handling can be illustrated as follows:

```
// Exception classes
    class IOException;
    class MemAllocException;
    class MathError;
```

```
// Place inside a "try" block code that may throw exceptions
    try
    {
        process_commands();
    }

// Place the exception handling code inside "catch" blocks_one
// for each type of exception.

    catch(IOException io)
    {
// Errors in I/O
//...
    }
    catch(MemAllocException mem)
    {
// "Out of memory" errors
//...
    }
    catch(MathError math)
    {
// Handle math errors
//...
    }
    catch(...)  // Use ... to mean any exception
    {
// Handle all other exceptions here
//...
    }
```

As you can see, each `try` block can contain several associated `catch` blocks, which establish handlers for various exceptions. The `catch` blocks are executed in the order of appearance. You should place `catch(...)` at the very end because this block is meant for any type of exception.

A function that detects errors and throws exceptions can indicate the specific exceptions that it might throw. Suppose a function named `setup_data` throws the exceptions `IOException` and `MemAllocException`. The function's declaration can indicate this as follows:

```
void setup_data() throw(IOException, MemAllocException);
```

The list of possible exceptions is called the *exception specification* of the function.

Special Functions

Two special functions are reserved for handling exceptions that occur during the exception handling itself:

- `void terminate();` is called when you do not provide an exception handler for a thrown exception or when an error occurs during the stack unwinding. The `terminate` function, by default, calls the `abort()` function from the ANSI C library. You can, however, direct `terminate` to call a function that you can set up by calling the `set_terminate` function, which is declared as follows:

  ```
  typedef void (*terminate_function)();
  terminate_function set_terminate(terminate_function);
  ```

  If you write a function named `handle_termination` to handle the termination, `terminate()` can call it with the following:

  ```
  PtrFuncVoid old_term_handler; // To save old handler
  void handle_termination();     // New handler
  old_term_handler = set_terminate(handle_termination);
  ```

- `void unexpected();` is called if a function throws an exception that is not in its *exception* specification—the list of exceptions that the function is supposed to throw. As the default action of `unexpected()`, it calls `terminate()`, which in turn calls `abort()` to exit the program. Like `set_terminate`, a `set_unexpected` function enables you to specify a function that `unexpected()` should call. You use `set_unexpected` in the same manner as `set_terminate`:

  ```
  typedef void (*unexpected_function)();
  unexpected_function old_unexpected;  // To save old handler
  void handle_unexpected();     // New handler
  old_unexpected = set_unexpected(handle_unexpected);
  ```

In Borland C++ 4, the header file `<except.h>` declares the prototypes of the functions `set_terminate` and `set_unexpected`.

Summary

Even though C++ is already proving to be useful in many practical problems, it is still evolving, as evidenced by the recent additions of new features such as *exception handling* and *templates.* Exception handling provides a uniform way to handle errors in C++ class libraries and programs, whereas templates support the definition of parameterized classes and functions. The American National Standards Institute's (ANSI)

X3J16 committee, which is developing a draft standard for the C++ programming language, has added exception handling and templates to the C++ language. The X3J16 committee has defined these features using the experimental designs presented in Chapters 14 and 15 of *The Annotated C++ Reference Manual* (*ARM*) by Margaret Ellis and Bjarne Stroustrup (Addison-Wesley, 1990). This chapter provided an overview of templates and exception handling based on the designs presented in the *ARM*. Borland C++ 4 supports both templates and exception handling.

IV

Applying OOP Techniques in C++

14

Using C Libraries in C++

The first three parts of this book, Chapters 1 through 13, describe the Borland C++ compiler, explain the terminology of object-oriented programming, and introduce you to the C++ programming language. Chapters 7 through 12, in particular, focus on the features of C++ that support data abstraction, inheritance, and polymorphism—the concepts that form the basis of object-oriented programming.

This section of the book, Chapters 14 through 16, focuses on building and using C++ class libraries. Because there are no standard C++ libraries yet, standard C libraries are still important functionality sources for C++ programmers. This chapter describes how you can use C libraries (both the standard one and your own) in C++ programs. It also provides a summary description of the functions in the ANSI standard C library and shows some examples of these functions in C++ programs. Chapter 15, "Building Class Libraries in C++," shows you how to build (and design) C++ class libraries. Chapter 16, "Using the Borland C++ Class Libraries," details the Borland container class library that comes with Borland C++ 4.

Linkage Between C and C++

Suppose you have a library of functions that have been compiled into object code and stored in the library object code form. When you call a function from such a library in your program, the compiler will mark the name of the function as an unresolved symbol in the object code of your program. To create an executable program, you must use a linker and make sure the linker searches the right library for the code of that function. If the linker finds the function's object code in the library, it will combine that code with your program's object code to create an executable file. To use C functions in C++ programs, you must be able to complete this process of linking. The following sections explain how you can do this by using the linkage specifier syntax of C++.

Type-Safe Linkage

To understand how C++ programs link with C functions, you must know how C++ resolves the names of functions. You can overload a function name in C++ so you can declare the same function with different sets of arguments. To help the linker, the C++ compiler uses an encoding scheme that creates a unique name for each overloaded function. The general idea of the encoding algorithm is to generate a unique signature for each function by combining the following components:

- The name of the function
- The name of the class in which the function is defined
- The list of argument types accepted by the function

You don't need to know the exact details of the encoding algorithm because they differ from one compiler to another. But knowing that a unique signature is generated for each function in a class should help you understand how the linker can determine which of the many different versions of a function to call.

Effect of Function Name Encoding

How does function name encoding affect C++ programs? To see one benefit of name encoding, consider the following C program:

```
//  Illustrates effect of wrong argument type

#include <stdio.h>

void print(unsigned short x)
{
    printf("x = %u", x);
}

void main(void)
{
    short x = -1;
    print(x);
}
```

The `print` function expects an `unsigned short` integer argument, but `main` calls print with a `signed short` integer argument. You can see the result of this type mismatch from the output of the program:

```
x = 65535
```

Even though `print` was called with a `-1`, the printed value is `65535` because the program was run on a system that uses a 16-bit representation for `short` integers. The bit representation of the value `-1` happens to be `0xffff` (all 16 bits are `1`); when treated as an `unsigned` quantity, `0xffff` produces the value `65535`. In C++, you can avoid problems like this by defining overloaded functions—one version of `print` for `unsigned short` type and another version for `short`. With this modification, the C++ version of the C program looks like this:

```
// C++ version avoids problem by overloading function

#include <stdio.h>

void print(unsigned short x)
{
    printf("x = %u", x);
}

void print(short x)
{
    printf("x = %d", x);
}

void main(void)
```

```
{
    short x = -1;
    print(x);
}
```

When you run this C++ program, the output is

```
x = -1
```

This time, the result is correct because the C++ compiler uses function name encoding to generate a call to the version of `print` that takes a `signed short` argument. This feature of C++, the capability to distinguish between overloaded functions based on argument types, is known as *type-safe* linkage because you cannot inadvertently call a function with the wrong types of arguments.

C Linkage Directive

Now that you know that C++ encodes all function names, you can understand the main problem with calling C functions from C++ programs. If a C++ program calls the C function `strlen` to get the length of a null-terminated string of characters as follows:

```
// C++ program

#include <stddef.h>            // for definition of "size_t"

size_t strlen(const char* s); // prototype of "strlen"

//...
char str[] = "Hello";
size_t length = strlen(str);
```

and then compiles and links the program containing this C++ code with the C library, the linker will complain that the function named `strlen` is unresolved, even though you are linking with the C library that contains the code for `strlen`. This happens because the C++ compiler uses the function prototype `strlen(const char*)` to create a name that is very different from `strlen`, the name the C library uses to store the object code of the `strlen` function.

To successfully link C object code with C++ programs, you need some mechanism to prevent the C++ compiler from encoding the names of C functions. The linkage directive of C++ provides this escape mechanism. You can successfully link the C++ program that uses `strlen`, for example, if you qualify `strlen` as a C function by declaring it as:

```
// Specify "C" linkage for the strlen function

extern "C" size_t strlen(const char* s);
```

Other Forms of Linkage Directive

To declare a number of functions with the "C" linkage, you can use the compound form of the linkage directive:

```
// Compound form of linkage directive

extern "C"
{
    int printf(const char* format, ...);
    void exit(int status);

/* Other functions... */
}
```

Typically, header files contain such linkage directives because that is where the functions are declared.

Sharing Header Files Between C and C++ Programs

Because of the close ties between C++ and C, you will often find the need to use C functions in C++ programs. In C++ programs, you need to declare the C functions with an extern "C" linkage. You can do this easily with the compound form of the linkage directive, but that leaves the declarations unacceptable to the C compiler because the extern "C" directive is not a standard C construct. You can solve this problem by using a conditional compilation directive of the C preprocessor as follows:

```
/* Header file shared between C and C++ */

#ifdef _ _cplusplus
extern "C" {      /* if it's C++, use linkage directive */
#endif

/* Declare C functions here */
void clearerr(FILE *f);
FILE* fopen(const char* name, const char* mode);
int fclose(FILE* f);
```

```
/* ... */

#ifdef _ _cplusplus
}
#endif
```

The _ _cplusplus macro is predefined in every C++ compiler. Compilers that can handle C and C++ programs define this symbol when compiling a C++ program. Usually, these compilers provide header files that use the #ifdef _ _cplusplus construct to declare the C library functions with extern "C" linkage (you only need to include the header file in your C++ program). The programs in this book assume that the standard C header files such as STDIO.H are designed to work with C++ programs.

If you are using C header files not conditioned to work with C++ compilers, and you cannot alter the C header files, you can still specify the extern "C" linkage by surrounding the #include directive as follows:

```
extern "C"
{
#include <stdio.h>
}
```

If you must do this, the best approach is to create a new header file with an extern "C" wrapper around the #include directive, as shown in the preceding example. This enables you to avoid cluttering the C++ programs with linkage directives that rightfully belong in header files. All source files that use C functions can do so with a consistent linkage directive.

Restrictions on Linkage Directive

You can specify the linkage directive for one instance of an overloaded function. If you declare the sqrt function for the complex and binary_coded_decimal classes as follows:

```
class complex;
class binary_coded_decimal;

extern complex  sqrt(complex&);
extern binary_coded_decimal sqrt(binary_coded_decimal&);
```

you can also use the standard C sqrt function if you declare it as follows:

```
extern "C" double sqrt(double);
```

In this case, you have two instances of `sqrt` for C++ classes and one from the C library; however, only one version of `sqrt` can be defined in C.

You cannot place linkage specification restrictions because you cannot place them within a local scope; all linkage specifications must appear in the file scope. In particular, the C++ compiler flags the following as an error:

```
// This is an error: cannot have linkage specification in a
// function's scope

main()
{
extern "C" size_t strlen(const char*); // flagged as error
//...

}
```

You can correct this error by moving the linkage specification to the file scope as follows:

```
// This is the right place for linkage specifications, in
// file scope (outside the body of functions)

extern "C" size_t strlen(const char*);

void main()
{
//...

}
```

Linkage to Other Languages

Although you have seen only the `extern "C"` linkage directive, the appearance of `C` within quotation marks should inform you that the linkage mechanism is intended to link C++ programs with functions written in other languages as well. Indeed, the linkage specification mechanism is designed for this purpose, but C++ compilers are required to support only two linkages: `"C"` and `"C++"`. You have seen examples of C linkage; C++ is the default linkage for all C++ programs.

Using the ANSI Standard C Library

By now you know how to use C functions in C++ programs. If your C compiler's standard header files are designed to work with a C++ compiler, you can use the C functions by simply including the appropriate header files in your C++ program. If you are a C programmer, you also know that C relies on its library to provide capabilities such as I/O, memory management, and mathematical functions. Every C program of any significance uses functions such as `printf`, `scanf`, and `gets` that are declared in the STDIO.H header file. In addition to the I/O functions, the standard C library has many more functions such as those for string manipulation and those that return date and time in various formats. The following sections summarize the capabilities of the ANSI C library and demonstrate their use in sample C++ programs.

Overall Capabilities of the ANSI C Library

From Chapter 3, "An Overview of ANSI Standard C," you know that the standard defines not only the C programming language but the contents of the library as well. Even the header files and the prototypes of the functions are specified by the standard. Because most C compilers are beginning to conform to the ANSI standard for C, the standard C library is a good place to look for functions that may be useful in your C++ programs.

The ANSI standard specifies more than 140 functions for the C library, but many of these functions, not yet available in most C compilers, are for handling international character sets. Table 14.1 lists most of the functions in the standard C library, grouped according to capability. The sections following the table further describe each function category and how each might be used in C++ programs.

Table 14.1. Capabilities of the standard C library.

Category of Function	Function Names
Standard I/O	`clearerr, fclose, feof, ferror, fflush, fgetc, fgetpos, fgets, fopen, fprintf, fputc, fputs, fread, freopen, fscanf, fseek, fsetpos, ftell, fwrite, getc, getchar, gets, printf, putc,`

Category of Function	Function Names
	putchar, puts, remove, rename, rewind, scanf, setbuf, setvbuf, sprintf, sscanf, tmpfile, tmpnam, ungetc, vfprintf, vprintf, vsprintf
Process control	abort, assert, atexit, exit, getenv, localeconv, longjmp, perror, raise, setjmp, setlocale, signal, system
Memory allocation	calloc, free, malloc, realloc
Variable-length argument list	va_start, va_arg, va_end
Data conversions	atof, atoi, atol, strtod, strtol, strtoul
Mathematical functions	abs, acos, asin, atan, atan2, ceil, cos, cosh, div, exp, fabs, floor, fmod, frexp, labs, ldexp, ldiv, log, log10, modf, pow, rand, sin, sinh, sqrt, srand, tan, tanh
Character classification	isalnum, isalpha, iscntrl, isdigit, isgraph, islower, isprint, ispunct, isspace, isupper, isxdigit, tolower, toupper
String and buffer manipulation	memchr, memcmp, memcpy, memmove, memset, strcat, strchr, strcmp, strcoll, strcpy, strcspn, strerror, strlen, strncat, strncmp, strncpy, strpbrk, strrchr, strspn, strstr, strtok
Search and sort	bsearch, qsort
Time and date	asctime, clock, ctime, difftime, gmtime, localtime, mktime, strftime, time

Standard I/O Functions

The standard I/O functions, declared in the STDIO.H header file, include some of the most commonly used functions in the C library, such as `printf` and `scanf`. Almost all C programs use at least one of these functions. You can continue to use these functions in C++. However, as explained in Chapter 8, "C++ Classes for Standard

I/O," most C++ compilers include the `iostream` class library, which provides a cleaner, object-based mechanism for I/O in C++ programs.

Process Control Functions

This broad category of the standard C library includes the signal-handling functions that manage error conditions and utility functions that terminate a process, communicate with the operating system, and set up numeric and currency formats, depending on the locale for which your program is customized. These functions are declared in the following header files:

- LOCALE.H declares `localeconv` and `setlocale`.
- SIGNAL.H declares `raise` and `signal`.
- SETJUMP.H declares `longjmp` and `setjmp`.
- STDLIB.H declares `abort`, `atexit`, `exit`, `getenv`, `perror`, and `system`.
- ASSERT.H declares `assert`.

The following section provides a summary of these functions and their uses.

Environment Variables

The term *process* refers to an executing program—when you run a program, you create a process. The *environment* of a process includes the information necessary to execute the process. The exact interpretation of the environment differs from one operating system to another. In UNIX and MS-DOS, the environment consists of an array of null-terminated strings, with each string defining a symbol of the form:

```
VARIABLE=value
```

where the symbol appearing on the left side of the equality is an environment variable. In a UNIX system, you can see the environment variables using either of the commands `printenv` or `env`. In MS-DOS, type `SET` at the DOS prompt to see a list of environment variables.

Environment variables are used to pass information to processes. For example, under UNIX, the full-screen editor `vi` uses the `TERM` environment variable to determine the type of terminal on which the text is to be displayed. You, the user, indicate the terminal type in the `TERM` environment variable, and the `vi` editor picks up this setting by determining the value of `TERM`. Your programs can exploit environment variables as well. For instance, in UNIX systems, the `TZ` environment variable indicates your time zone. You can get the value of this environment variable by calling the `getenv` function, one of the utility routines defined in the STDLIB.H header file.

Exception Handling Using *setjmp* and *longjmp*

In C, you can use `setjmp` and `longjmp` to handle exceptional conditions. You can save the *state* (or the *context*) of the process by calling `setjmp` and then calling `longjmp` with the saved context to revert to a previous point in your program. (The terms *state* and *context* have the same meaning and refer to the information needed to reconstruct the process exactly as it is at a particular point in its flow of execution.) ANSI C requires a compiler to define an array data type named `jmp_buf` that can hold the information needed to restore a calling environment. This data type is defined in the SETJMP.H header file. To understand the mechanics of `setjmp` and `longjmp`, consider the following C code:

```
/*-------------------------------------------------------------*/
/*  Illustrates use of "setjmp" and "longjmp" to
 *  handle exceptions
 */

#include <setjmp.h>
jmp_buf last_context;

void process_commands(void);
/*-------------------------------------------------------------*/
void main(void)
{
/* Establish a context to which you can return */
    if (setjmp(last_context) == 0)
    {
        process_commands();
    }
    else
    {
/* This part executed when longjmp is called.
 * Place code for handling error here...
 */

    }
}
/*-------------------------------------------------------------*/
```

```
void process_commands(void)
{
    int error_flag;
/* ... */
/* In case of error, return to last context */
    if(error_flag) longjmp(last_context, 1);
}
```

The setjmp function saves the current context in the last_context variable and returns 0. In this case, the if statement in main is satisfied, and process_commands() is called. Assume the integer error_flag is set to 1 when any error occurs in the process_commands function. Then you can handle the error by testing this flag and by calling the longjmp function with two arguments. The first argument is the jmp_buf array, which contains the context to which you want to return. When the calling environment reverts to this saved state, and longjmp returns, it will be exactly like returning from the call to setjmp, which originally saved the last_context buffer. The second argument to longjmp specifies the value to be returned by the function. It should be nonzero so that the if statement in main branches to the else clause when the return is induced by a longjmp.

You can use the combination of setjmp and longjmp to jump unconditionally from one C function to another without using the conventional return statement. Essentially, setjmp marks the destination of the jump and longjmp acts as a nonlocal goto that executes the jump.

It is tempting to use setjmp and longjmp to handle exceptions in C++, but the calls to constructors and destructors create some problems. All objects initialized up to the point of the error must be destroyed before calling longjmp to jump to an error handling section of the program. This can be done only if you keep track of all objects created in your program. Still, at least one major C++ class library, the *NIH Class Library* (NIH stands for National Institutes of Health), uses setjmp and longjmp to handle exceptions. Nevertheless, you may not have to devise your own exception handling scheme using setjmp and longjmp because the ANSI standard for C++ is expected to include a well-defined method for handling exceptions in C++ programs. Refer to Chapter 13, "Advanced Topics in C++," for further details on this topic.

Customizing Programs to a Locale

The term *locale* refers to the locality, the geographic region, for which certain aspects of your program can be customized. ANSI C groups the locale-dependent aspects of a C program into six categories and defines macros to identify them. Table 14.2 summarizes the locale categories defined in the LOCALE.H header file. You can use the `setlocale` function to selectively set each category shown in Table 14.2 to conform to a selected locale. The locale named `"C"` indicates the minimal environment for C programs. Most compilers support only the locale named `"C"`, but future C compilers may support other locale names as well.

You can obtain the numeric and currency formatting style for the current locale by calling the `localeconv` function, which returns a pointer to a statically allocated `lconv` structure. You will find the `lconv` structure declared in the LOCALE.H header file. This structure includes formatting information such as the decimal point character and the currency symbol for the current locale.

Table 14.2. Locale categories in ANSI standard C.

Locale Category	Parts of Program Affected
`LC_ALL`	The entire program's locale-specific parts (all categories that follow)
`LC_COLLATE`	Behavior of the `strcoll` and `strxfrm` functions, which use the collating sequence of the character set
`LC_CTYPE`	Behavior of the character classification functions
`LC_MONETARY`	Monetary formatting information returned by the `localeconv` function
`LC_NUMERIC`	Decimal point character for the formatted output functions (for example, `printf`) and the data conversion functions, and for the nonmonetary formatting information returned by the `localeconv` function
`LC_TIME`	Behavior of the `strftime` function, which formats time

You can use the locale mechanism to ensure that the output generated by your application program conforms to the standard representation of monetary and numeric information, as practiced in the locality where the program is being used. For instance, you may use `localeconv` to get formatting information in a C++ class designed to represent currency. Unfortunately, most C compilers still support only the `"C"` locale, which does not include any information on formatting monetary information.

Memory Allocation

One advantage that C has over older languages such as FORTRAN is its capability to manage memory at runtime. In FORTRAN, there is no provision for requesting memory at runtime. All data items and arrays must be declared in the program. You must guess the maximum size of an array beforehand, and it is not possible to exceed the maximum without recompiling the program. This is inefficient because you often define large arrays, yet use only a small portion of each.

In C, you can request blocks of memory at runtime and release the blocks when your program no longer needs them. This allows your application to exploit all available memory in the system. Like most other capabilities in C, this comes in the form of four standard functions: `calloc`, `malloc`, `realloc`, and `free`, which are defined in the STDLIB.H header file. `Calloc` and `malloc` are used for allocating memory, `realloc` for adjusting the size of a previously allocated block, and `free` for releasing memory.

C++ not only retains C's ability to allocate memory at runtime but also makes it a part of the language by providing two built-in operators, `new` and `delete`, to handle allocation and deallocation of objects. Of course, many C++ compilers define `new` and `delete` in terms of `malloc` and `free`. If you need to overload the `new` and `delete` operators for one of your C++ classes, you can use `malloc` and `free` to define the overloaded versions of the operators.

Variable-Length Argument Lists

When writing C programs, you have used functions (such as `printf` and `scanf`) that can take a variable number of arguments. In fact, their prototypes use an ellipsis in the argument list to reflect this:

```
int printf(const char *format_string, ...);
int scanf(const char *format_string, ...);
```

ANSI standard C includes the `va_start`, `va_arg`, and `va_end` macros, defined in the STDARG.H header file, that allow you to write functions capable of accepting a variable number of arguments. The only requirement on such functions is that they must accept at least one required argument. You can use these macros in C++ programs as well. As an example, consider a `menu_widget` class with a constructor that accepts a variable number of strings and creates a menu with those strings as labels. The following skeleton C++ program illustrates how you can use the ANSI standard approach to handle a variable number of arguments in a class member function:

```
//-------------------------------------------------------------
//  Demonstrates the use of variable-length argument lists

#include <iostream.h>
#include <stdlib.h>     // For declaration of NULL
#include <stdarg.h>

#define MENU_BAR  1
#define PULL_DOWN 2

typedef char *P_CHAR;

class menu_widget
{
public:
    menu_widget(int style, ...);
// ...
private:
// ...
};

//-------------------------------------------------------------
menu_widget::menu_widget(int style, ...)
{
// Get the first optional parameter using "va_start"
    va_list  argp;        // Used to access arguments
    va_start(argp, style);

// Get items one by one
    char     *item_text;
    int      count = 0;

    cout << "--------------------------------" << endl;
    while((item_text = va_arg(argp, P_CHAR)) != NULL)
    {
        cout << "Item " << count << " = " << item_text << endl;
        count++;
    }
}
//-------------------------------------------------------------
//  Test the use of variable-length argument lists

void main()
{
```

```
    menu_widget m1(MENU_BAR, "File", "Edit", "Utilities", NULL);
    menu_widget m2(PULL_DOWN, "Open", "Close", "New", "Save",
                              "Save As...", "Quit", NULL);
//...
}
```

If you run this program, you get the following output showing that the `menu_widget` constructor is processing a variable number of arguments:

```
--------------------------------
Item 0 = File
Item 1 = Edit
Item 2 = Utilities
--------------------------------
Item 0 = Open
Item 1 = Close
Item 2 = New
Item 3 = Save
Item 4 = Save As...
Item 5 = Quit
```

Data Conversions

The functions in this category—`atof`, `atoi`, `atol`, `strtod`, `strtol`, and `strtoul`—convert character strings into internal representations of variables. They are declared in the STDLIB.H header file.

The conversion routines are ideal for converting command-line arguments from their string representation into the internal format. For example, in a small calculator program, you might want to process an input line of the form:

```
eval 12.43 + 17.52
```

where `eval` is the name of the program that accepts a command line of the form `<value1> <operator> <value2>` and prints the result of the operation. In this example, the program should print 29.95 as the answer. When implementing this program, you can use the `atof` function to convert the second and the fourth command-line arguments (the first argument is always the name of the program) to `double` variables. The code for the addition operator might be written as:

```
#include <stdlib.h>
#include <iostream.h>

void main(int argc, char **argv)
{
```

```
    double op1, op2, result;

    op1 = atof(argv[1]);
    op2 = atof(argv[3]);

    switch(argv[2][0])
    {
// ...
        case '+':
         result = op1 + op2;
// ...
    }
    cout << result << endl;
}
```

This example assumes a decimal calculator. If you want a hexadecimal calculator so that all input and output is in hexadecimal, you can use the `strtoul` function to convert the input arguments to unsigned long integers. This is a typical use of the data conversion functions.

Mathematical Functions

Both C and C++ support basic floating-point data types `float` and `double` and enable you to write arithmetic expressions using these data types. Additionally, the standard C library includes a set of mathematical functions that enables you to evaluate common functions such as *sine* and *cosine*. Most of these functions are declared in the MATH.H header file.

Basic Functions

The trigonometric functions—`cos`, `sin`, `tan`, `acos`, `asin`, `atan`, and `atan2`—evaluate the cosine, sine, and tangent of any angle in radian and compute the inverses of cosine, sine, and tangent. These functions are useful for the transformation of rectangular to polar coordinates that often occurs in graphics programs. Other commonly used mathematical functions are

`sqrt` to compute square roots
`log` to return the natural logarithm of an argument
`log10` to return the base 10 logarithm of an argument
`exp` to compute exponentials

For example, you would call `exp(1.75)` to evaluate e1.75; `fabs` to return the absolute value of a floating-point value; `ceil` to return the nearest integer larger than a given floating-point number; and `floor` to return the nearest integer smaller than its floating-point argument.

Integer Arithmetic

Four functions, declared in STDLIB.H, handle arithmetic using integer arguments: `abs` and `labs` return, respectively, the absolute value of an integer and a long integer; `div` divides one integer by another and returns the integer quotient and an integer remainder; and `ldiv` operates similarly but with long integer arguments.

Generating Random Numbers

If you need to generate random numbers (for a random screen pattern, a game, or a statistical analysis problem, for example), the ANSI C library includes a function named `rand` that can generate a random positive integer in the range `0` to `RAND_MAX`, a constant defined in STDLIB.H. The `rand` function generates random numbers by using a well-defined algorithm. Given the same starting number, `rand` always generates the same sequence of random numbers. In other words, instead of being truly random, the sequence generated by `rand` is a pseudorandom sequence. If the algorithm used to generate the random numbers is good, the sequence will not repeat frequently, and all numbers between `0` and `RAND_MAX` will appear with equal probability. A function named `srand` sets the starting point of the random sequence.

Sometimes you need to select a random sequence of random numbers. For example, you wouldn't want to be dealt the same hand in a card game again and again. ANSI C does not provide a routine to generate a random seed, but you can use the value returned by the `time` function as the argument to `srand` to set a new random seed for `rand`.

Character Classification

The C CTYPE.H header file contains several functions that are useful for classifying and converting characters. The behavior of these functions is affected by the `LC_CTYPE` category of the current locale. Table 14.3 shows a summary of ANSI C functions that can be used to classify and convert characters. These functions are useful when parsing strings. You can use the `isspace` function, for example, to locate a valid whitespace character in a string.

Table 14.3. Summary of ANSI C's character classification functions.

Name	Description
`isalnum`	Returns nonzero if character is alphanumeric
`isalpha`	Returns nonzero if character is alphabetic
`iscntrl`	Returns nonzero if character belongs to the set of control characters
`isdigit`	Returns nonzero if character is a numerical digit
`isgraph`	Returns nonzero if character is printable (excluding the space character)
`islower`	Returns nonzero if character is lowercase
`isprint`	Returns nonzero if character is printable (includes space)
`ispunct`	Returns nonzero if character belongs to the set of punctuation characters
`isspace`	Returns nonzero if character belongs to the set of whitespace characters, which include space, formfeed, newline, carriage return, horizontal tab, and vertical tab
`isupper`	Returns nonzero if character is uppercase
`isxdigit`	Returns nonzero if character is a hexadecimal digit
`tolower`	Converts character to lowercase only if that character is an uppercase letter
`toupper`	Converts character to uppercase only if that character is a lowercase letter

String and Buffer Manipulation

You have already encountered some of ANSI C's string manipulation functions in the `String` class shown in Chapter 10, "Defining Operations on Objects," and Chapter 11, "Using Inheritance in C++." These functions, declared in STRING.H, are primarily for comparing two strings or buffers, copying one string or buffer into another, and searching for the occurrence of a character in a string.

Buffers

A *buffer* is a contiguous block of memory, and *string* refers to an array of characters. By convention, a string in C is marked by a null character—a byte with all zero bits. Because of this, C strings are known as null-terminated strings.

Strings in C and C++

Neither C nor C++ has any built-in data type for strings. Instead, strings are treated as an array of characters with a null character marking the end of the string. You can declare strings as you would any other array objects:

```
char line[81], filename[]="test.1";
```

Here, `line` is a string with room for 81 characters, but because of the terminating null character, `line` can hold no more than 80 characters. The second string, `filename`, is declared without a size, but the initial value of the string provides enough information about the size. The compiler will reserve enough storage for the string and the terminating null character. As shown in Figure 14.1, the `filename` string requires seven bytes of storage.

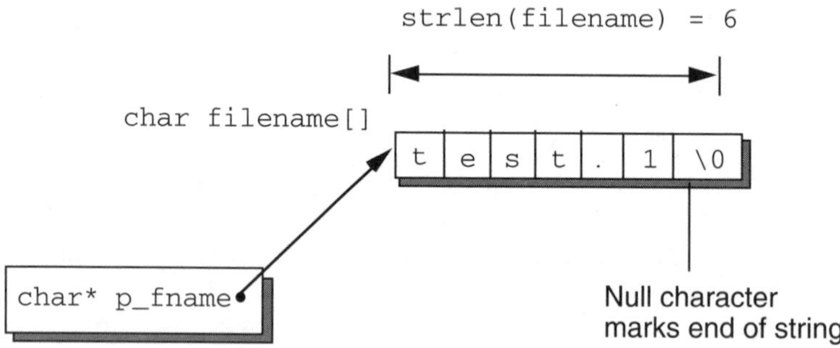

Figure 14.1. A null-terminated string in C and C++.

Because a string is an array of characters, you can also access a string through a `char*` pointer. For example, to access the `filename` string using a pointer named `p_fname`, you would write:

```
char  filename[] = "test.1";
char *p_fname = filename;
```

Once the p_fname pointer is initialized, you can use it to access the filename string as you would through the array named filename. Of course, as shown in Figure 14.1, the p_fname pointer requires some additional storage space. You can also declare and initialize a char* pointer to a string in a single statement. For example, you would write:

```
char *p_str = "Some string";
```

to initialize the p_str character pointer to the string constant Some string. You actually have initialized p_str to the address of the first character of the string Some string.

Length of a String

The length of a C string is the number of characters in the string up to but not including the terminating null character. For example, the filename string in Figure 14.1 is six bytes long, even though seven bytes are needed to store the string. You can use the strlen function to get the length of a C string.

Comparing Strings and Buffers

The string and buffer manipulation category contains five functions for comparing strings and buffers: memcmp, strcmp, strncmp, strcoll, and strxfrm. Each function takes two arguments and returns a zero when the arguments match. The functions return a negative value if the first argument is less than the second and a positive value if the first argument is greater than the second. This means, for strings, that the first argument will appear after the second in a dictionary of words in that character set.

The strcmp function is used for case-sensitive comparisons of two strings. The memcmp and strncmp functions behave like strcmp, but are used for comparing a specified number of characters from the beginning of each string.

The strcoll function is intended to be used for comparing strings using a collating sequence determined by the LC_COLLATE category of the locale. The strxfrm function is a utility routine that transforms a string into a new form so that, if strcmp were used to compare two transformed strings, the result would be identical to that returned by strcoll applied to the original strings.

Concatenating and Copying Strings

The memcpy, memmove, strcat, strcpy, strncat, and strncpy functions are used for concatenating and copying strings and buffers. Each of these functions accepts two arguments. In all cases, the second argument is the source and the first is the destination. When copying or concatenating strings, you must ensure that there is enough room in the destination string to hold the source string. You can do this either by declaring an array of characters with enough room or by allocating memory at runtime.

The memcpy and memmove functions are used for copying one buffer into another. Of these two, the memmove function is guaranteed to work properly, even if the source and destination buffers overlap. Both memcpy and memmove work with nonoverlapping source and destination buffers.

The strcat function appends the second string argument to the first and produces a null-terminated string as the result. The strncat function is similar to strcat, but it copies only a specified number of characters from the second string to the first.

The strcpy function copies the second string argument onto the first one. While strcpy copies the entire string, strncpy will copy only a specified number of characters. Because strncpy does not automatically append a null character to the destination string, you must be alert for instances when the characters being copied do not include a null character.

Search and Sort

The standard C library also includes two very useful functions: qsort (for sorting an array of objects) and bsearch (for searching for an object in a sorted array). These sort and search functions are suitable for in-memory operations when the entire array fits into memory.

Using *qsort* and *bsearch*

Figure 14.2 shows a typical sorting scenario: you have an array of pointers to String objects (see Chapter 11 for the String class), each of which contains a C string, and you want to sort the array by rearranging the pointers so the C strings appear in ascending order. Figure 14.2 shows the original array of pointers and the array after sorting. Although the pointers have been rearranged, the String objects have remained in their original positions. Because the pointers are usually much smaller than the objects, the result is faster sorting—it is faster to shuffle the pointers than to copy the objects. However, memory usage increases because the pointers require extra storage space.

The qsort and bsearch functions are declared in stdlib.h as follows:

```
void *bsearch(const void *key, const void *base, size_t num,
        size_t width,
        int (*compare)(const void *elem1, const void *elem2));
```

```
void qsort(const void *base, size_t num, size_t width,
        int (*compare)(const void *elem1, const void *elem2));
```

As you can see from the prototype, the qsort function expects (as argument) the starting address of the array, the number of elements in it, the size (in bytes) of each element, and a pointer to a function that performs the comparison of any two elements in the array. The bsearch function, in addition, requires a pointer to the value being sought, and the array being searched must already be sorted in ascending order.

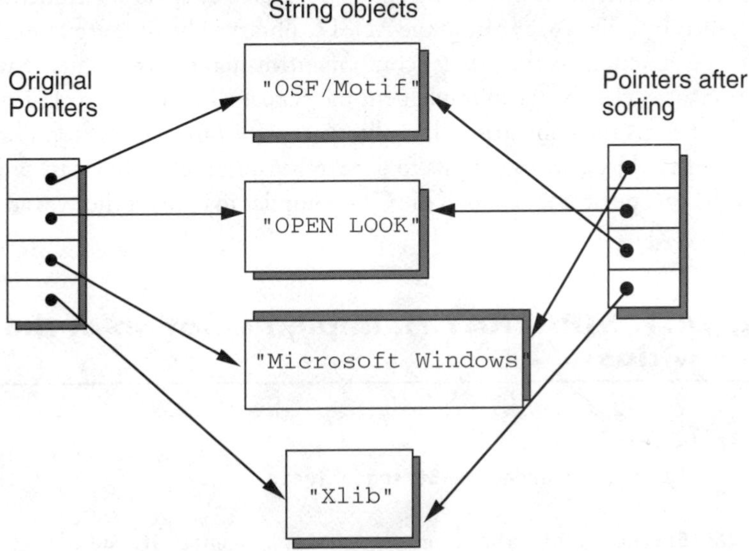

Figure 14.2. Sorting an array of String objects.

The key to using qsort and bsearch is to provide an appropriate comparison function, the last argument to either function. This function will receive, as argument, pointers to the two elements being compared. It must return one of the following integer values:

- A positive value if the first element is greater than the second one
- A zero if the two elements are equal
- A negative value if the first element is less than the second one

You determine the meanings of *less than, greater than,* and *equal.* When sorting String objects, for example, you compare the C string field of the two objects and return a value based on the lexicographic ordering of the strings.

Sorting an Array of *String* Objects

As an example of using qsort, consider the problem of sorting an array of String objects. You must first define a StringArray class that holds an array of pointers to instances of the String class. As shown in Listing 14.1, the StringArray class provides member functions to add new String objects to the array, display the current contents of the array, and sort the array. The STR.H file, which declares the String class, appears in Listing 11.1 in Chapter 11.

For this discussion, the interesting part of StringArray is the sort function. This function sorts by calling qsort from the ANSI C library. The final argument to qsort, the compare function, is the crucial component in making this scheme work. For the StringArray class, you can implement the compare function as a class static function that performs the comparison by calling strcmp from the ANSI C library. You can use String objects as arguments to strcmp because the String class provides a type-conversion operator that allows the C++ compiler to convert the String type to const char* type.

Listing 14.1. STRARRAY.H. Implementation of the StringArray class.

```
//-------------------------------------------------------------
//  File:  strarray.h
//  Implements an array of String objects
//
//  NOTE: The "sort" function sorts the contents of the
//        array by calling the "qsort" function from the
//        standard C library

#if !defined(__STRARRY_H)
#define __STRARRAY_H

#include <stdlib.h>
#include "str.h"

const size_t default_capacity = 16;
    typedef String* StringPtr;

class StringArray
{
public:
// Constructor
    StringArray() : _count(0), _capacity(default_capacity)
```

```
    {
        _strp = new StringPtr[default_capacity];
    }

// Destructor
    ~StringArray();

    void add(const char* s)
    {
// If there is no more room, you should expand the capacity
// by allocating more space.  Here, simply return.
        if(_count == _capacity) return;
        _strp[_count] = new String(s);
        _count++;
    }

// Function to be used with "qsort"
    static int compare(const void* s1, const void* s2)
    {
        return strcmp(**(String**)s1, **(String**)s2);
    }

// The "sort" function simply calls "qsort"
    void sort()
    {
        qsort(_strp, _count, sizeof(String*),
              StringArray::compare);
    }

    void show();

private:
    String** _strp;
    size_t   _count;
    size_t   _capacity;
};

//-----------------------------------------------------------
//  ~ S t r i n g A r r a y
//  Destructor for the StringArray class

StringArray::~StringArray()
```

continues

Listing 14.1. continued

```
//----------------------------------------------------------------
{
int i;
    for(i = 0; i < _count; i++)
        delete _strp[i];
    delete _strp;
}
//Listing 14.1. STRARRAY.H. Implementation of the StringArray class.
//----------------------------------------------------------------
//  s h o w
//  Display the contents of the array

void StringArray::show()
{
    cout << "Contents of String array:" << endl;
    cout << "------------------------" << endl;
    int i;
    for(i = 0; i<_count; i++)
    {
        cout << *_strp[i] << endl;
    }
}

#endif
```

Listing 14.2 displays a sample program that tests the sorting operation of the `StringArray` class. The program sets up an instance of the `StringArray` class, adds some `String` objects to it, and sorts the array. After sorting the array, it displays the contents.

Listing 14.2. Sample sorting program.

```
//----------------------------------------------------------------
//  Sample program to create an array of String objects,
//  add some Strings, and sort the array
#include "strarray.h"

void main()
{
```

```
    StringArray sa;
// Add some strings to the array
    sa.add("OSF/Motif");
    sa.add("OPEN LOOK");
    sa.add("Microsoft Windows");
    sa.add("Xlib");
// Sort the array
    sa.sort();
// Display contents
    sa.show();
}
```

When you run this program, it displays the following as the contents of the sorted array:

```
Contents of String array:
------------------------
Microsoft Windows
OPEN LOOK
OSF/Motif
Xlib
```

As you can see, the array is sorted in ascending order. You can reverse the order of sorting by placing a minus sign in front of the `strcmp` function call in the body of the `compare` function of the `StringArray` class.

Date and Time

The ANSI C library includes a set of functions for obtaining, displaying, and manipulating date and time information. These functions are declared in the TIME.H header file. Figure 14.3 is a pictorial representation of the different formats of date and time in ANSI C and the functions that enable you to convert from one format to another. The core of these functions is the `time` function, which returns a value of the `time_t` type that is defined in the TIME.H header file. This `time_t` value represents the calendar time in encoded form (often called *binary time*). You can convert it to a `tm` structure with the `gmtime` and `localtime` functions. The `gmtime` function accepts a binary time and sets the fields in a `tm` structure to correspond to Greenwich Mean Time (GMT), or Universal Time Coordinated (UTC), as this standard time reference is now called. The `localtime` function sets the fields of the `tm` structure to local time. The `mktime` function converts time from a `tm` structure to a value of `time_t`.

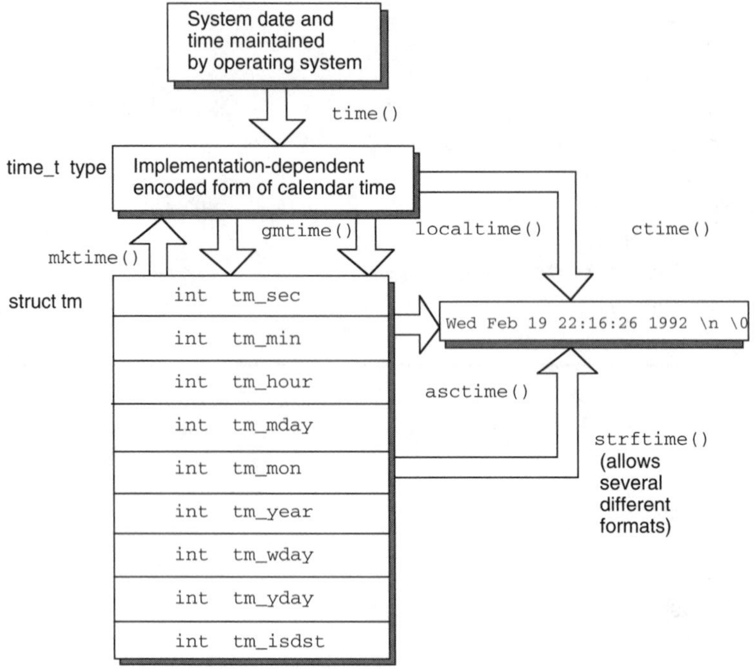

Figure 14.3. Different forms of time in ANSI C.

Printing Date and Time

The `asctime` function converts the value in a `tm` structure to a null-terminated C string that you can print. The `ctime` function converts the output of `time` directly to a string. Thus, you can print the current time from a C++ program as follows:

```
#include <iostream.h>
#include <time.h>

main()
{
    time_t tnow;
// Get the current time in binary form
    time(&tnow);
// Convert the time to a string and print it.
    cout << "Current time = " << ctime(&tnow) << endl;
}
```

A sample output from this program is as follows:

```
Current time = Sat Oct 30 22:16:26 1993
```

A *DateTime* Class

A more concrete example of the time-manipulation functions in C++ is the `DateTime` class, which represents date and time information. As shown in Listing 14.3, the `DateTime` class maintains the calendar time in binary format. Its default constructor calls the `time` function to get the current time. The other interesting member of this class is the addition operator that advances the date by a specified number of days. The addition operator uses the `mktime` function to accomplish this task. The `mktime` function converts calendar time from a `tm` structure into a `time_t` format. Before making this conversion, `mktime` also adjusts all members of the `tm` structure to reasonable values. As you can see from the definition of the `operator+` function in Listing 14.3, you can exploit this feature of `mktime` to advance the `DateTime` values by a number of days.

The `DateTime` class also overloads the << operator so you can use << to print `DateTime` variables on an output stream. This overloading is done with the help of the `print` member function of the `DateTime` class that prints on an `ostream`. The `print` function, in turn, calls `ctime` from the standard C library. Note that the `ctime` function converts a binary time into a formatted C string.

Listing 14.3. DATETIME.H. Defines the `DateTime` class for manipulating calendar time.

```
//--------------------------------------------------------------
//  File:  datetime.h
//
//  A date and time class

#if !defined(__DATETIME_H)
#define __DATETIME_H

#include <time.h>       // ANSI standard "Time" functions
#include <iostream.h>   // For stream I/O

class DateTime
{
public:
```

continues

Listing 14.3. continued

```
DateTime() { time(&_bintime); }
    DateTime(time_t t) : _bintime(t) { }

    friend DateTime operator+(DateTime d, int n)
    {
        struct tm *ltime = localtime(&d._bintime);
        ltime->tm_mday += n;
        time_t t = mktime(ltime);
        return DateTime(t);
    }

    friend DateTime operator+(int n, DateTime d)
    {
        return d+n;
    }

    DateTime operator+=(int n)
    {
        struct tm *ltime = localtime(&_bintime);
        ltime->tm_mday += n;
        _bintime = mktime(ltime);
        return *this;
    }

    void print(ostream& os) { os << ctime(&_bintime);}

private:
    time_t      _bintime;
};

// Stream output operator for DateTime class

ostream& operator<<(ostream& os, DateTime& d)
{
    d.print(os);
    return os;
}

#endif
```

Although the `DateTime` class is far from being complete (it is intended to serve as an example that illustrates how to use ANSI C's time-manipulation functions in a C++ class), you can still use the class for some useful work. Listing 14.4 presents a small program that displays the current date and time and illustrates the use of the addition operators.

Listing 14.4. Sample program to test the `DateTime` class.

```
//---------------------------------------------------------------
//  Test the DateTime class

#include "datetime.h"

void main()
{
    DateTime d1;
    cout << "Current date and time = " << d1 << endl;

// Advance by 45 days
    d1 += 45;
    cout << "45 days later, it will be = " << d1 << endl;

//  Try addition operator...(add another 5 days)
    cout << "50 days later, it will be = ";
    cout << d1+5 << endl;
}
```

A sample output from this program is

```
Current date and time = Fri Sep 10 22:16:26 1993

45 days later, it will be = Mon Oct 25 22:16:26 1993

50 days later, it will be = Sat Oct 30 22:16:26 1993
```

Notice that an extra linefeed appears after each line because the `ctime` function, called by the print member function of `DateTime`, formats the binary time into a string with a newline character at the end. This feature of `ctime`, together with the explicit use of the `endl` manipulator, is responsible for the extra blank lines. To format the time into a string without an extra newline character, you can call the `strftime` function, which is specifically intended for formatting time information.

Compiler-Specific Libraries

Although the standard C library is a good source of portable functions, you should also examine your C++ compiler's offering of nonstandard libraries. In particular, C++ compilers such as Borland C++ 4 include many additional functions in their libraries. Most notable among these functions are the ones for accessing the services of the MS-DOS operating system and those for graphics output.

If you are developing a program specifically for the MS-DOS environment and you do not mind being tied to a particular compiler's library, you should consider making use of the compiler-specific functions. These functions are as easy to use as the standard C functions. In all likelihood, the header files are probably already conditioned to work with the C++ compiler. You only need include the header file and call the function. However, you must know the overall capabilities of the additional functions. You can usually find this information in the documentation that comes with the C++ compiler. Another possible source of information is a book like this one that specifically covers your C++ compiler's library.

Summary

Like C, C++ is built around a sparse core, and all major functions are delegated to support libraries. The core of the language provides a small set of built-in data types, constructs such as `class` and `struct` to define new types, operators to build expressions, and control structures to manage the flow of execution of the program. You must rely on libraries for everything from I/O to string manipulations.

Because C++ is still in a state of evolution, it does not yet have a standard library like ANSI C. Typical C++ compilers include the `complex` class for complex arithmetic and the `iostream` library for I/O. You can, however, use the functions from the standard C library in your C++ programs. To link C++ programs with the C library, you must enclose the declaration of the C functions and data inside an `extern "C" { ... }` linkage specifier. Many C++ compilers, including Borland C++ 4, already provide C header files with declarations enclosed in an `extern "C" { ... }` block. With such header files, using C functions is as easy as including the header files in a C++ program and making the function calls.

The standard C library includes a large assortment of functions that you are guaranteed to find in all standard conforming C compilers. Because C++ does not yet have a standard library, the ANSI C library is a good place to look for functions that may be useful in your C++ classes. This chapter provides a summary description of the ANSI C library and shows you how to use these capabilities in C++ programs and in C++ classes.

15

Building Class Libraries in C++

In Chapter 14, "Using C Libraries in C++ Programs," you were shown how to use existing C libraries in C++ programs. This chapter examines the topics of designing, organizing, and building C++ classes that can provide specific functionality for use in C++ programs. When designing a class library, you must determine the inheritance hierarchy of the classes, the way one class uses the facilities of others, and the kinds of operations the classes will support.

Organizing C++ Classes

If a standard class library for C++ existed, deciding how to organize C++ classes would be easy: you would model your classes after the standard ones. Unfortunately, C++ does not yet have standard classes. The `iostream` class library (described in Chapter 8, "C++ Classes for Standard I/O"), which comes with AT&T's C++ 3.0, may be the only standard class library currently available. Of course, the `iostream` class library serves only I/O. You need much more than the `iostream` classes when developing complete applications in C++. Additionally, even if many standard classes for C++ were available, your particular application may still require you to write new, customized classes. The point is that sooner or later you will face the task of organizing a library of classes that will form the basis of your application. Organization of C++ classes refers to their inheritance hierarchy, as well as the way one class can use the facilities of another. First, consider the question of inheritance hierarchy.

Inheritance Hierarchy Under Single Inheritance

Before AT&T C++ Release 2.0, a class could inherit from only one base class. As shown in Figures 15.1 and 15.2, you can organize the inheritance tree of classes under single inheritance in two distinct ways:

- A single class hierarchy with all classes in the library derived from a single root class (a base class, which is not derived from any other class). The SmallTalk-80 programming language provides this type of class hierarchy. Therefore, this organization of C++ classes is known as the SmallTalk *model* or a single *tree model*.

- Multiple disjoint class hierarchies with more than one root class. This has been referred to as the *forest model* because the library contains multiple trees of class hierarchies.

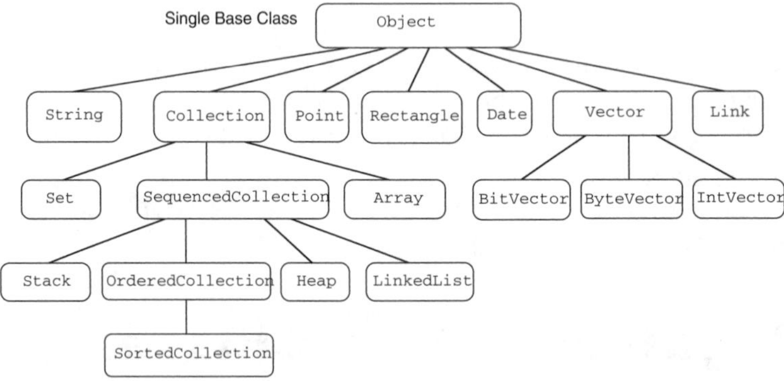

Figure 15.1. A typical single tree organization of C++ classes patterned after SmallTalk-80.

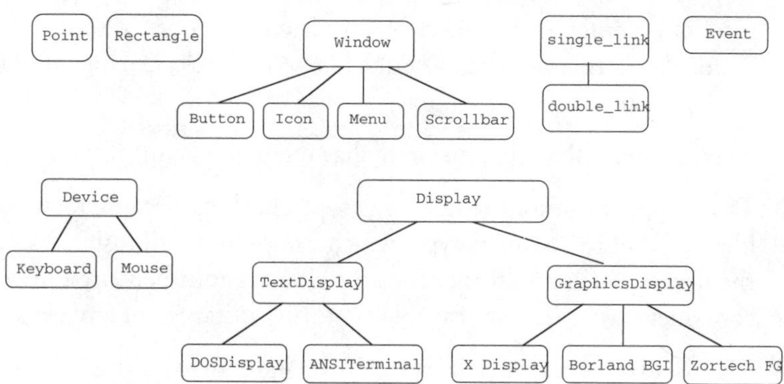

Figure 15.2. A forest of C++ classes for building user interfaces.

Single Class Hierarchy

As Figure 15.1 shows, a library that uses a single class hierarchy starts with a base class, usually named `Object`, which declares a host of virtual functions that apply to all other classes in the library. These virtual functions handle standard operations such as copying, printing, storing, retrieving, and comparing objects. Each derived class defines concrete versions of these functions and thereby provides a standard interface to the library. Several prominent C++ class libraries, including the *NIH Class Library* by Keith Gorlen (NIH stands for National Institutes of Health), use this model of organization. Proponents of the single class hierarchy point out the following benefits of this approach:

- The definition of a single root class ensures that all classes provide the same standard set of `public` interface functions. This enhances consistency and compatibility among classes.

- When all classes are guaranteed to inherit from a single base class, capabilities such as *persistence*, which is the capability for storing and retrieving collections of objects in a disk file, are easier to provide. The single class hierarchy also enables you to easily provide a standard exception-handling mechanism. Again, you can achieve this by placing the exception-handling code in the `Object` class.

- Because every class in the library is an `Object`, you can easily define polymorphic data structures. For example, the following array of pointers:

```
Object *ArrayOfObjPtr[16];
```

can hold pointers to instances of any class in the library, so you can easily define data structures such as linked lists and stacks capable of holding instances of any class in the library.

However, a monolithic class hierarchy has these disadvantages:

- The compiler cannot provide strict type checking because many objects in the library are of the `Object*` type, which can point to an instance of any class in the library. Such pointers to the base class are routinely used in polymorphic container classes that are capable of storing instances of any class in the library.
- The root base class, `Object`, typically includes many virtual functions representing the union of all the virtual functions implemented by the derived classes. This is burdensome if you want to create a derived class because you must provide the definition of all the virtual functions, even though many may not be relevant to that derived class.
- Although a single root `Object` class makes it easy to create a container class capable of storing any other object from the library, you cannot use these containers to store standard C data types such as `float`, `int`, and `char`. If you want to store these types in a container, you must write your own classes that mimic the built-in types of C. For example, you could define `Float` and `Integer` classes that model, respectively, C's `float` and `int` data types.
- Because of the large monolithic class hierarchy, compiling a single program may require processing a large number of header files. This can be a problem on MS-DOS systems, which typically have a limited amount of memory.

Multiple Class Hierarchies

In contrast to the monolithic, single class hierarchy of the Smalltalk-80 library, a C++ class library based on the forest model includes multiple class trees, with each tree providing a well-defined functionality. Figure 15.2, for example, shows several class hierarchies in a C++ class library that provide the objects needed to build window-based user interfaces. Different types of windows are grouped together in the class hierarchy with the `Window` class as the root. Each window has a rectangle represented by the `Rectangle` class, which, in turn, uses the `Point` class to represent the corners of the window. The `Event` class models user input that comes from one of the devices shown in the class hierarchy whose root is the `Device` class. The stand-alone `String` class represents text strings that might appear in windows. You can model the physical display by a class hierarchy with a generic `Display` as the base class. From this generic display, you can further specialize to text or graphics displays. You might categorize text displays into ANSI-standard terminals or IBM PC-compatible displays.

Graphics displays may be based on one of the following: the X Window System, Borland International's Borland Graphics Interface (BGI), or Microsoft Windows.

The main advantages of the forest model of class libraries are:

- Because each class hierarchy is small, you can understand and use the classes easily.
- Virtual functions declared in each root class are relevant to that class tree. It is not difficult, therefore, to implement the derived classes in each hierarchy.

On the other hand, the lack of an overall structure implies that you cannot create the elegant container classes of the Smalltalk model. Thus, the primary disadvantages of the forest model are:

- Because there is no common base class, it is difficult to design container classes such as linked lists, stacks, and queues that can store any type of object. You must devise your own schemes for creating such data structures.
- Anything that requires a library-wide discipline becomes difficult to implement. For example, exception handling and persistence are more difficult to support under the forest model than under a single tree model.

Effects of Multiple Inheritance

The introduction of multiple inheritance in AT&T C++ Release 2.0 changed the implications of organizing C++ class libraries, according to either the single tree model or the forest model. Because multiple inheritance allows a derived class to inherit from more than one base class, you can combine the capabilities of classes in unique ways to suit your needs. A good example is the singly linked list of `String` objects illustrated in Chapter 11, "Using Inheritance in C++." The linked list is constructed by linking instances of a new class named `slink_string`, which is defined from the `String` class and the `single_link` class as follows:

```
class slink_string: public single_link, public String
{
//...
};
```

The `single_link` class is capable of holding a pointer to another instance of `single_link`. In this way, multiple inheritance enables you to combine the capabilities of two classes into a single class. Some ways of applying multiple inheritance to extend the capabilities of C++ class libraries are:

- You can derive a class from two or more classes in a library, even if the class library follows a single tree model of inheritance hierarchy. For example, the

NIH Class Library includes a `Link` class and a `String` class. With multiple inheritance, you can combine these two classes to define a `String` with a `Link` just as you did to define the `slink_string` class in Chapter 11.

- Even with a multiple-class hierarchy, you can add a standard capability such as persistence by defining a new base class and deriving other classes from it. You can do this, although it takes extra work to create a new set of derived classes that incorporate the capability defined in the new base class. With single inheritance, you do not have the opportunity to combine the behavior of two or more classes packaged in a library.

Client-Server Relationship Among Classes

In addition to the inheritance relationship among classes, a class can use the facilities of another class. This is called the *client-server* relationship among classes because the client class, in order to use the capabilities of the server class, calls the member functions of the server class. In C++, the client class needs an instance of the server class to call the member functions of the server. The client class can get this instance in one of the following ways:

- One of the member functions of the client class receives an instance of the server class as an argument.
- A member function of the client class calls a function that returns an instance of the server class.
- An instance of the server class is available as a global variable.
- The client class incorporates an instance of the server class as a member variable.
- A member variable of the client class is a pointer to an instance of the server class.

The last two cases are of interest because they constitute the most common ways of expressing a client-server relationship between two classes. This approach—using a class by incorporating an instance or a pointer to an instance—has been referred to as *composition.* The following sections briefly describe these two approaches of composition.

Class Instance as a Member

In Chapter 6, "C++ and Object-Oriented Programming," Listing 6.4 shows the declaration of several classes intended to represent geometric shapes, such as triangles and rectangles. All geometric shapes are derived from an abstract shape class. In particular, the `rectangle_shape` class is declared as follows:

```
class shape
{
public:
    virtual double compute_area(void) const = 0;
    virtual void draw(void) const{ } = 0;
};

// Define the "rectangle" class

class rectangle_shape: public shape
{
private:
    double x1, y1;  // Coordinates of opposite corners
    double x2, y2;
public:
    rectangle_shape(double x1, double y1, double x2, double y2);
    double compute_area(void) const;
    void draw(void) const;
};
```

A better way to define the `rectangle_shape` class is to use the notion of a point in a plane. For instance, you can first define a `Point` class as follows:

```
//-------------------------------------------------------------------
//  File: point.h
//  Define a point in two-dimensional plane

#if !defined(__POINT_H)
#define __POINT_H

#include <math.h>

typedef double Coord;

class Point
{
public:
```

```
    Point() : _x(0), _y(0) {}
    Point(Coord x, Coord y) : _x(x), _y(y) {}
    Point(const Point& p) : _x(p._x), _y(p._y) {}

    Point& operator=(const Point& p)
    {
        _x = p._x;
        _y = p._y;
         return *this;
    }

    Point operator-(const Point& p) const
    {
        return Point(_x-p._x, _y-p._y);
    }

    Coord xdistance() const { return fabs(_x);}
    Coord ydistance() const { return fabs(_y);}
private:
    Coord _x, _y;
};

#endif
```

Because a rectangle is uniquely defined by any two opposite corners, you can implement the `rectangle_shape` class using two instances of the `Point` class, as follows:

```
//-----------------------------------------------------------
//  File:  rect.h
//  C++ header file with definitions of a rectangle shape


#if !defined(__RECT_H)
#define __RECT_H

#include <stdio.h>
#include <math.h>

#include "point.h"  // For definition of the Point class

class shape
{
public:
    virtual double compute_area(void) const = 0;
```

```
    virtual void draw(void) const = 0;
};

// Define the "rectangle" class

class rectangle_shape: public shape
{
public:
    rectangle_shape(Point& c1, Point& c2) : _c1(c1), _c2(c2){}

    double compute_area(void) const
    {
        Point p = _c1 - _c2;
        return p.xdistance() * p.ydistance();
    }

    void draw(void) const { } // Not defined

private:
    Point _c1, _c2;  // Opposite corners of rectangle
};

#endif  // #if !defined(__RECT_H)
```

`Point _c1` and `_c2` denote two opposite corners of the rectangle. A sample program that uses the `rectangle_shape` class follows:

```
#include <iostream.h>
#include "rect.h"

int main(void)
{
    Point p1(10,10), p2(30,40);
    rectangle_shape r(p1,p2);

    cout << "Area of rectangle = " << r.compute_area();
    cout << endl;

    return 0;
}
```

When you run the program, it displays the expected output:

```
Area of rectangle = 600
```

This is an example of the rectangle_shape class making use of the Point class. Member functions of the rectangle_shape class access the member functions of the Point class through Point instances _c1 and _c2.

Pointer to Class Instance as a Member

An alternative to incorporating Point instances in the rectangle_shape class is to define pointers to the Point class as members of rectangle_shape. Used carefully, this approach enables you to declare the rectangle_shape class without including the definition of the Point class. For instance, you can rewrite the declaration of the rectangle_shape class as follows:

```
//--------------------------------------------------------------
//  File:  rect_p.h
//  C++ header file with definitions of rectangle_shape class
//  This version uses pointers to Point class


#if !defined(__RECT_P_H)
#define __RECT_P_H

#include <stdio.h>
#include <math.h>

class Point;

class shape
{
public:
    virtual double compute_area(void) const = 0;
    virtual void draw(void) const = 0;
};

// Define the "rectangle" class

class rectangle_shape: public shape
{
public:
    rectangle_shape() : _p1(0), _p2(0) {}
    rectangle_shape(const Point& p1, const Point& p2);
    rectangle_shape(const rectangle_shape& r);
    ~rectangle_shape();
```

```
    void operator=(const rectangle_shape& r);

    double compute_area(void) const;

    void draw(void) const { } // Not defined

private:
    Point *_p1, *_p2;    // Pointers to Points
};

#endif  // #if !defined(__RECT_P_H)
```

Notice this declaration of the `rectangle_shape` class does not include the complete declaration of the `Point` class. This effectively hides the specification of the `Point` class from the users of the `rectangle_shape` class. The trick is to not invoke any member functions of the `Point` class within the declaration of the `rectangle_shape` class.

You can place the actual definition of the member functions of `rectangle_shape` in another file and include the declaration of the `Point` class there. For example, the definition of the member functions of the revised `rectangle_shape` class follows:

```
#include "rect_p.h"
#include "point.h"

double rectangle_shape::compute_area(void) const
{
    Point p = *_p1 - *_p2;
    return p.xdistance() * p.ydistance();
}

rectangle_shape::rectangle_shape(const Point& p1, const Point& p2)
{
    _p1 = new Point(p1);
    _p2 = new Point(p2);
}

rectangle_shape::rectangle_shape(const rectangle_shape& r)
{
    _p1 = new Point(*r._p1);
    _p2 = new Point(*r._p2);
}

void rectangle_shape::operator=(const rectangle_shape& r)
{
```

```
    if(this != &r)
    {
        if(_p1 != 0) delete _p1;
        if(_p2 != 0) delete _p2;
        _p1 = new Point(*r._p1);
        _p2 = new Point(*r._p2);
    }
}

rectangle_shape::~rectangle_shape()
{
        delete _p1;
        delete _p2;
}
```

Although `rectangle_shape` is now implemented differently, you can use it as you would use the preceding version. For example, to create a rectangle with corners at (30, 20) and (130, 60), you would write:

```
Point p1(30,20), p2(130,60); // Define the corner points
rectangle_shape r1(p1,p2);   // Create a rectangle
```

This version of the `rectangle_shape` class is much more complicated than the previous one, which uses instances of the `Point` class as member variables. The following explains this complexity:

- The C++ compiler automatically creates and destroys class instances that are member variables of another class. The compiler also handles copy and assignment operations for such class member instances.
- On the other hand, when you use pointers to class instances, you are responsible for creating and destroying these class instances. You also must define the copy constructor and the assignment operator so that these operations work correctly. Therefore, the revised version of the `rectangle_shape` class requires several additional member functions, including a destructor, a copy constructor, and an assignment operator.

As explained in Chapter 12, "Virtual Functions and C++," despite the additional work involved, managing pointers to class instances is necessary when you want to use polymorphism.

Public Interface to C++ Classes

Public interface to the classes in a library is as important as the relationships among the classes. The term *public interface* refers to the public member functions that enable you to access the capabilities of a class. Just as there is no standard C++ class library, there is no standard interface to C++ classes. If you are designing a class library, however, it is good practice to provide a minimal set of member functions. Some member functions are needed to ensure proper operations, others to provide a standard interface to the library. The following sections briefly describe some of the functions needed in each class's interface.

Default and Copy Constructors

Each class in the library should have a *default constructor*—a constructor that takes no argument. The default constructor should initialize any data members that the class contains. For example, the following is the default constructor for the `rectangle_shape` class:

```
class rectangle_shape : public shape
{
public:
    rectangle_shape() : _p1(0), _p2(0) {}
//...
private:
    Point *_p1, *_p2;
};
```

This constructor sets the data members `_p1` and `_p2` to zero.

The default constructor is important because it is called when arrays of class instances are allocated or when a class instance is defined without an initial value. For example, the `rectangle_shape::rectangle_shape()` constructor is called to initialize the `rectangle_shape` objects in the following:

```
rectangle_shape rects[16];
rectangle_shape r;
```

Each class should also include a copy constructor of the form `X(const X&)`, in which `X` is the name of the class. The copy constructor is called in the following cases:

- When an object is initialized with another of the same type, such as:

  ```
  rectangle_shape r2 = r;// where r is a rectangle_shape
  ```

- When an object is passed by value to a function
- When an object is returned by value from a function

As explained in Chapter 10, "Defining Operations on Objects," the copy constructor is necessary for classes that contain pointers as members. If you do not define a copy constructor for a class, the C++ compiler defines one that uses memberwise copy. When a class has pointers as members, memberwise copy will cause pointers in two objects to point to identical areas of the free store.

Copying Objects

Often, it is necessary to make a copy of an object. For instance, Chapter 11 shows how to create a linked list capable of holding `String` objects. A new class, `slink_string`, is created by multiply deriving from `single_link` and `String` classes. This `slink_string` class has links that enable its instances to reside in a `singly_linked_list`. To insert elements into the list, you must be able to create a copy of the object. In the `slink_string` class, this is done by the virtual member function `clone` (see Listings 11.3 and 11.7 in Chapter 11). In the terminology of other C++ libraries such as the NIH Class Library, the `clone` function is equivalent to what is known as the `deepCopy` function because `clone` makes a complete copy of a `slink_string` object, including a copy of the character string allocated by the `String` class. For a class `X`, you can define the `clone` function as follows:

```
X* X::clone() { return new X(*this); }
```

As long as all classes define appropriate copy constructors, the `clone` function will make a duplicate copy of the object on the free store and return a pointer to the copy. When using functions (such as `clone`) that return a pointer to a dynamically created object, you must destroy the object by using the `delete` operator. This will delete the object, provided appropriate destructors are defined for all classes with member variables that are pointers.

Destructors

Defining a destructor is important for classes that include pointers as member variables. The destructor should reverse the effects of the constructor. If the constructor allocates memory by calling `new`, the destructor should deallocate the memory by using the delete operator. As explained in Chapter 12, if the class contains any virtual member functions, you should declare the destructor as virtual.

Assignment Operator

You should define the assignment operator for each class because derived classes do not inherit the assignment operator from the base class. Also, if you do not define the assignment operator, the C++ compiler provides a default one that simply copies each member of one class instance to the corresponding member of another. If a class has member variables that are pointers to other class instances, such memberwise copying will result in multiple pointers that point to a single area of the free store. When defining the assignment operator, you must:

- Handle the special case in which an object is assigned to itself
- Return a reference to the target of the assignment so that statements of the type `x=y=z;` work properly

For an example, see the definition of the `String::operator=` function in Listing 11.2 in Chapter 11.

Input and Output Functions

Each class should also define two functions for I/O:

- An output function that prints a formatted text representation of each member of an object on an output stream
- An input function that can read from an input stream the output generated by the output function and reconstruct the object

These functions allow you to define the << and >> operators so they can accept instances of any class in the library as arguments. For example, you might use the names `print_out` and `read_in`, respectively, for the output and input functions. Each of these functions should take a single argument—the reference to the stream on which the I/O operation occurs. Then, for a class `X`, you would define the output `operator<<` as follows:

```
#include <iostream.h>
//...
ostream& operator<<(ostream& os, const X& x)
{
    x.print_out(os);
```

```
    return os;
}
```

Summary

Organizing a C++ class library involves deciding the inheritance hierarchy of the classes, how one class uses the facilities of other classes, and what public member functions each class supports. There are two trends in picking an inheritance hierarchy for the classes in a library: the single tree model, in which all classes are ultimately derived from a single base class, and the forest model, in which there are multiple disjoint hierarchies of classes. The single tree model of inheritance hierarchy is patterned after the basic classes of the SmallTalk-80 programming language, which does not support multiple inheritance, as does C++. With multiple inheritance, you can mix and match classes from one or more class hierarchies and create custom classes.

Inheritance is not the only relationship among classes. A class also may incorporate instances of other classes as member variables. Although inheritance models the *is-a* relationship among classes, inclusion of class instances captures the *has-a* relationship. The inclusion is in the form of a member variable that is either a class instance or a pointer to a class instance. Defining a class instance as a member variable is simpler than maintaining a pointer to an instance, but the pointer is necessary to exploit polymorphism.

In addition to these relationships among the classes, each class in the library should present a consistent set of member functions so there is a standard public interface to the library. This makes the library easy to use.

16

Using the Borland C++ Class Library

Developing an application in C++ can be easy, provided you can get most of the functionality of the program from existing C++ classes. Programmers embarking on large-scale C++ programming efforts typically begin by designing and developing a library of classes. Then they build the final software products using these classes. Clearly, you can reduce the time spent on software development if an off-the-shelf class library meets the needs of a software project, and if the programmers working on the project can easily use the library. This is where class libraries can be useful.

To help programmers reap the benefits of a class library, Borland C++ comes with a large number of classes that are organized in two broad categories:

- Container classes, known as Borland International Data Structures (BIDS), that provide objects such as linked lists and dynamic arrays and include features to support archiving objects in files.
- ObjectWindows Library (OWL 2.0) classes for building Microsoft Windows applications, including classes that simplify the use of the Graphics Device Interface (GDI).

In addition to these libraries, Borland C++ also comes with a few simple classes that represent new data types, such as `string` and `time`. This chapter provides a tutorial introduction to the BIDS container class library and a few simple classes. In Chapter 18, "Using the ObjectWindows Library (OWL)," you will find a complete coverage of the OWL classes.

Borland C++ 4 includes the full source code for the BIDS and OWL classes. If you want, you can always browse through the source code of these classes to see exactly how they are defined and implemented.

Template-Based Container Classes

Prior to version 3.1, Borland C++ included a hierarchy of container classes, collectively referred to as CLASSLIB, that was derived from a base class named `Object`. The problem with this class library was that only items derived from `Object` could be stored in a container. For example, you cannot store any of the built-in data types such as `float`, `int`, or `double` in the CLASSLIB container classes. The `template` keyword, which is part of AT&T C++ Release 3.0 and supported by Borland C++, provides a much better method of defining container classes that can hold any type of objects including `char`, `float`, `double`, and `int`.

Starting with Borland C++ 3.1, Borland introduced another version of CLASSLIB that uses class templates to define a variety of flexible container classes that can store anything from built-in C++ types such as `int` and `double` to your own class types. Class templates are class definitions parameterized by a data type. Borland calls these class templates the Borland International Data Structures (BIDS). In Borland C++ 3.1, the template-based CLASSLIB was fully compatible with the older `Object`-based CLASSLIB, and you could use either version of CLASSLIB. However, in later versions of Borland C++, the Object-based CLASSLIB has been declared obsolete and you should use the template-based CLASSLIB.

You should know about the Borland C++ class library because your application might need containers such as arrays, lists, and queues capable of holding a variety of objects. When you need such containers, you can save yourself a lot of work by simply using the classes included in Borland C++.

The BIDS container classes offer two levels of abstraction:

- Fundamental Data Structure (FDS)
- Abstract Data Type (ADT)

The FDS class templates are low-level containers that reflect fundamental data storage mechanisms such as vectors and linked lists. The ADT classes represent higher-level data structures such as stacks and queues that are declared using class templates and the FDS classes. You can implement an ADT using any FDS. For example, you can have a stack implemented as a vector or as a linked list. Knowing the internal structure of a specific FDS, you can select the right implementation for an ADT based on whether you want faster code or flexibility of growth at runtime.

Fundamental Data Structure (FDS)

An FDS is a data structure at a lower level of abstraction with close ties to the specific way it is implemented. The class templates representing FDSs fall into one of the following categories:

- Vectors
- Singly-linked lists
- Doubly-linked lists
- Hash Tables
- Binary Trees

Borland calls this category of class templates FDS because each class implies a fundamental way of implementation. For example, a vector is a contiguous sequence of memory locations; the lists, on the other hand, are implemented as a collection of nodes connected by pointers. Vectors allow random access to elements in constant time, whereas time taken to locate an item in a linked list is proportional to the number of nodes traversed before finding the element. Furthermore, a vector is of fixed size and can grow only at the expense of allocating a larger vector and copying the contents of the old vector to the new one. A list, on the other hand, can grow easily with the addition of new nodes. Typically, many classes within the FDS class hierarchy are not meant for use by programmers; these classes have the string `Internal` in their names. Table 16.1 lists the FDS class templates that are meant for use by programmers. Note that `T` denotes any type of object, including built-in types such as `int` and `double` and your own class.

Table 16.1. Fundamental Data Structure (FDS) container classes in Borland C++.

Class Template	Description
BINARY SEARCH TREES	
`TBinarySearchTreeImp<T>`	A binary search tree of objects of type `T`.
`TBinarySearchTreeIteratorImp<T>`	An iterator for binary search trees that stores objects of type `T`.
`TIBinarySearchTreeImp<T>`	A binary search tree of pointers to objects of type `T`.
`TIBinarySearchTreeIteratorImp<T>`	An iterator for binary search trees that stores pointers to objects of type `T`.
DOUBLY-LINKED LISTS	
`TMDoubleListImp<T,Alloc>`	A doubly-linked list of objects of type `T`. The list's storage allocation is managed by the class `Alloc`.
`TDoubleListImp<T>`	A doubly-linked list of objects of type `T`. The list's storage allocation is managed by the class `TStandardAllocator` (declared in header file `<classlib\alloctr.h>`).
`TMSDoubleListImp<T,Alloc>`	A sorted doubly-linked list of objects of type `T`. The list's storage allocation is managed by the class `Alloc`.
`TSDoubleListImp<T>`	A sorted doubly-linked list of objects of type `T`. The list's storage allocation is managed by the class `TStandardAllocator`.
`TMDoubleListIteratorImp<T,Alloc>`	An iterator for a doubly-linked list of objects of type `T`. The list's storage allocation is managed by the class `Alloc`.

`TDoubleListIteratorImp<T>`	An iterator for a doubly-linked list of objects of type `T`. The list's storage allocation is managed by the class `TStandardAllocator`.
`TMIDoubleListImp<T,Alloc>`	A doubly-linked list of pointers to objects of type `T`. The list's storage allocation is managed by the class `Alloc`.
`TIDoubleListImp<T>`	A doubly-linked list of pointers to objects of type `T`. The list's storage allocation is managed by the class `TStandardAllocator`.
`TMISDoubleListImp<T,Alloc>`	A sorted doubly-linked list of pointers to objects of type `T`. The list's storage allocation is managed by the class `Alloc`.
`TISDoubleListImp<T>`	A sorted doubly-linked list of pointers to objects of type `T`. The list's storage allocation is managed by the class `TStandardAllocator`.
`TMIDoubleListIteratorImp<T,Alloc>`	An iterator for a doubly-linked list of pointers to objects of type `T`. The list's storage allocation is managed by the class `Alloc`.
`TIDoubleListIteratorImp<T>`	An iterator for a doubly-linked list of pointers to objects of type `T`. The list's storage allocation is managed by the class `TStandardAllocator`.

HASH TABLES

`TMHashTableImp<T,Alloc>`	A hash table of objects of type `T` with storage allocation managed by the class `Alloc`.

continues

Table 16.1. continued

Class Template	Description
TMHashTableIteratorImp<T,Alloc>	An iterator for a hash table of objects of type T with storage allocation managed by the class Alloc.
THashTableImp<T>	A hash table of objects of type T with storage allocation managed by the class TStandardAllocator.
THashTableIteratorImp<T>	An iterator for a hash table of objects of type T with storage allocation managed by the class TStandardAllocator.
TMIHashTableImp<T,Alloc>	A hash table of pointers to objects of type T with storage allocation managed by the class Alloc.
TMIHashTableIteratorImp<T,Alloc>	An iterator for a hash table of pointers to objects of type T with storage allocation managed by the class Alloc.
TIHashTableImp<T>	A hash table of pointers to objects of type T with storage allocation managed by the class TStandardAllocator.
TIHashTableIteratorImp<T>	An iterator for a hash table of pointers to objects of type T with storage allocation managed by the class TStandardAllocator.
SINGLY-LINKED LISTS	
TMListImp<T,Alloc>	A list of objects of type T. The list's storage allocation is managed by the class Alloc.
TListImp<T>	A list of objects of type T. The list's storage allocation is managed by the class TStandardAllocator.

TMSListImp<T,Alloc>	A sorted list of objects of type T. The list's storage allocation is managed by the class Alloc.
TSListImp<T>	A sorted list of objects of type T. The list's storage allocation is managed by the class TStandardAllocator.
TMListIteratorImp<T,Alloc>	An iterator for a list of objects of type T. The list's storage allocation is managed by the class Alloc.
TListIteratorImp<T>	An iterator for a list of objects of type T. The list's storage allocation is managed by the class TStandardAllocator.
TMIListImp<T,Alloc>	A list of pointers to objects of type T. The list's storage allocation is managed by the class Alloc.
TIListImp<T>	A list of pointers to objects of type T. The list's storage allocation is managed by the class TStandardAllocator.
TMISListImp<T,Alloc>	A sorted list of pointers to objects of type T. The list's storage allocation is managed by the class Alloc.
TISListImp<T>	A sorted list of pointers to objects of type T. The list's storage allocation is managed by the class TStandardAllocator.
TMIListIteratorImp<T,Alloc>	An iterator for a list of pointers to objects of type T. The list's storage allocation is managed by the class Alloc.

continues

Table 16.1. continued

Class Template	Description
TIListIteratorImp<T>	An iterator for a list of pointers to objects of type T. The list's storage allocation is managed by the class TStandardAllocator.
VECTORS	
TMVectorImp<T,Alloc>	A vector of objects of type T. The vector's storage allocation is managed by the class Alloc.
TVectorImp<T>	A vector of objects of type T. The vector's storage allocation is managed by the class TStandardAllocator.
TMCVectorImp<T,Alloc>	A counted vector of objects of type T. The vector's storage allocation is managed by the class Alloc.
TCVectorImp<T>	A counted vector of objects of type T. The vector's storage allocation is managed by the class TStandardAllocator.
TMSVectorImp<T,Alloc>	A sorted vector of objects of type T. The vector's storage allocation is managed by the class Alloc.
TSVectorImp<T>	A sorted vector of objects of type T. The vector's storage allocation is managed by the class TStandardAllocator.
TMVectorIteratorImp<T,Alloc>	An iterator for a vector of objects of type T. The vector's storage allocation is managed by the class Alloc.

`TVectorIteratorImp<T>`	An iterator for a vector of objects of type `T`. The vector's storage allocation is managed by the class `TStandardAllocator`.
`TMIVectorImp<T,Alloc>`	A vector of pointers to objects of type `T`. The vector's storage allocation is managed by the class `Alloc`.
`TIVectorImp<T>`	A vector of pointers to objects of type `T`. The vector's storage allocation is managed by the class `TStandardAllocator`.
`TMICVectorImp<T,Alloc>`	A counted vector of pointers to objects of type `T`. The vector's storage allocation is managed by the class `Alloc`.
`TICVectorImp<T>`	A counted vector of pointers to objects of type `T`. The vector's storage allocation is managed by the class `TStandardAllocator`.
`TMISVectorImp<T,Alloc>`	A sorted vector of pointers to objects of type `T`. The vector's storage allocation is managed by the class `Alloc`.
`TISVectorImp<T>`	A sorted vector of pointers to objects of type `T`. The vector's storage allocation is managed by the class `TStandardAllocator`.
`TMIVectorIteratorImp<T,Alloc>`	An iterator for a vector of pointers to objects of type `T`. The vector's storage allocation is managed by the class `Alloc`.
`TIVectorIteratorImp<T>`	An iterator for a vector of pointers to objects of type `T`. The vector's storage allocation is managed by the class `TStandardAllocator`.

Organization of the FDS Classes

As you study the list of classes in Table 16.1, you will begin to notice a pattern in the names of classes representing a single FDS. The name of each FDS container class reflects how the container's storage and the objects in the container are managed. Each class name starts with a `T` reflecting Borland's convention for naming classes.

The storage management for a class refers to the way memory is allocated for the container. The storage management class should provide the `new` and `delete` operators. The header file `<classlib\alloctr.h>` has examples of storage management classes, including the class `TStandardAllocator`, which simply calls the global `new` and `delete` operators to allocate and release storage. You have to provide a storage management class for the FDS classes that have an `M` as the second letter of the name—these classes are known as *managed* classes. The remainder of the classes use `TStandardAllocator` for memory management and are referred to as *unmanaged* classes.

The name reflects another aspect of the FDS containers: whether a container holds a pointer to an object or the object itself. The classes with names that start with `TI` or `TMI` are meant for storing pointers to objects; all other classes store the object directly. The classes that store pointers are known as *indirect* containers, while the ones that store the objects directly are called *direct* containers.

In addition to storage management and manner of object storage, the FDS containers also provide other behavior, such as keeping the contents sorted. For instance, the vectors and singly- and doubly-linked classes can be sorted. The name of an FDS container class contains the letter `S` if it keeps the contents sorted.

For a category such as singly-linked list, you will find a total of 12 classes in Table 16.1. There are four managed lists, as follows:

- Managed direct list
- Managed indirect list
- Managed direct sorted list
- Managed indirect sorted list

In addition to unmanaged versions of each of the above, bringing the total to eight lists, there are four iterator classes:

- Iterator for managed direct lists
- Iterator for managed indirect lists
- Iterator for unmanaged direct lists
- Iterator for unmanaged indirect lists

As you will see in the next section, iterators allow you to access the contents of a container in a convenient manner.

Iterators

With the FDS containers as well as the ADT containers (described later in this chapter), you need a way to access the contents of a container. The iterator classes provide the ability to do this as easily as indexing through a simple array. The easiest way to see how an iterator works is through an example. Listing 16.1 shows a simple program that illustrates the use of a `TListIteratorImp<T>` to access each element in a list of integers. While the subscript operator ([]) is adequate for accessing an element at a specific index (position) in an array, many other container types such as lists and stacks do not have the notion of an index. The iterators make it possible to access elements from these containers in a simple manner (see example program in Listing 16.1).

Listing 16.1. TSTITER.CPP. Test program to demonstrate iterator.

```
//--------------------------------------------------------------
// File: tstiter.cpp
// Sample program that illustrates the use of iterators

#include <classlib\listimp.h>
#include <iostream.h>

typedef TListImp<int> IntegerList;
typedef TListIteratorImp<int> IntegerListIterator;

void main()
{
    IntegerList l;

    l.Add(1);
    l.Add(2);
    l.Add(3);

// Iterate over list
    IntegerListIterator li(l);

    while(li)
    {
```

continues

Listing 16.1. continued

```
        cout << li++ << endl;
    }
}
```

As you can see from Listing 16.1, the class template `TListImp<T>` is used to declare a list of integers. One way to do this is to write

```
TListImp<int> list1;
TListImp<int> list2;
TListImp<int> list3;
```

However, a better way is to define a new type name using `typedef`, then use that name in subsequent declarations:

```
// Define a type name for a list of integers
typedef TListImp<int> IntegerList;
// ...
// Use the type name to declare a list of integers
IntegerList list1;
//...
IntegerList list2;
IntegerList list3;
```

With this scheme, you can have a more readable name for each new type of list; also, you can change the implementation of the list to another type by changing the `typedef` statement. For example, if you write your own class template for a list and call it `MyList<T>`, you can use that as the basis for the list of integers by simply rewriting the `typedef` statement as

```
typedef MyList<int> IntegerList;
```

without changing any of the list declarations that use the type name `IntegerList`.

When compiled and run, this program prints

```
3
2
1
```

These are all the integer objects in the list. The printed order is the reverse of the order of insertion because the `Add` member function of the list class adds an object to the head of the list.

Vector Classes

There are twelve different vector class templates that can be viewed as two groups, with six classes in each group. The so-called *managed* vector container classes require the programmer to specify a storage management class, while the *unmanaged* vectors use the `TStandardAllocator` class for storage management. The six managed FDS vector classes are

- `TMVectorImp<T,Alloc>` simple direct vector
- `TMCVectorImp<T,Alloc>` counted direct vector
- `TMSVectorImp<T,Alloc>` sorted direct vector
- `TMIVectorImp<T,Alloc>` simple indirect vector
- `TMICVectorImp<T,Alloc>` counted indirect vector
- `TMISVectorImp<T,Alloc>` sorted indirect vector

When you define a specific vector class from any of these templates, you have to provide the type of data, as well as a class that can allocate storage for the vector. Each of these class templates has a counterpart that does not have the `M` as the second letter of the name. These unmanaged vector classes use the `TStandardAllocator` class, declared in `<classlib\alloctr.h>`, as the storage allocator.

In discussing the FDS classes, I use the unmanaged class templates only. However, the discussions apply equally well to the managed class templates.

Simple Direct Vectors

You can create a simple direct vector with the class template `TVectorImp<T>`, in which `T` stands for the type of data that you want to store in the vector. The type `T` should have a default constructor (a constructor without any argument) and a meaningful copy operation. A simple direct vector is like the one-dimensional arrays that you can declare in C++. Like C++ arrays, you can access elements in the array with the subscript operator `[]`.

Listing 16.2 shows a simple program that illustrates the simple direct vector FDS.

Listing 16.2. SDVEC.CPP. Test program to demonstrate simple direct vector FDS.

```
//--------------------------------------------------------------
// File: sdvec.cpp
```

continues

Listing 16.2. continued

```
// Sample program that illustrates simple direct vector

#include <classlib\vectimp.h>
#include <iostream.h>

typedef TVectorImp<int> IntegerVector;

void main()
{
    IntegerVector ivec(10);

    short i;
    for(i = 0; i < 3; i++)
        ivec[i] = i;

// Display the elements
    for(i = 0; i < 3; i++)
    {
       cout << "ivec[" << i << "] = " << ivec[i] << endl;
    }
}
```

Here is the output from the program shown in Listing 16.2:

```
ivec[0] = 0
ivec[1] = 1
ivec[2] = 2
```

Counted Direct Vectors

The counted direct vector container type, `TCVectorImp<T>`, is similar to the simple direct vectors except that there is an `Add` member function for inserting an element into the next available slot in the vector. When you insert elements using the `Add` function, the counted direct vector keeps track of the number of elements in the vector. You can get this count by calling the `Count` function.

If you remove an element from the vector using the `Detach` function, the container is recompacted. You can see this from the output of the program shown in Listing 16.3.

Listing 16.3. CDVEC.CPP. Test program to demonstrate counted direct vector FDS.

```
//-----------------------------------------------------------------
// File: cdvec.cpp
// Sample program that illustrates counted direct vector

#include <classlib\vectimp.h>
#include <iostream.h>

typedef TCVectorImp<int> IntegerCVector;

void main()
{
    IntegerCVector ivec(10);

    ivec.Add(9);
    ivec.Add(7);
    ivec.Add(8);

    cout << "There are " << ivec.Count() <<
            " elements." << endl;

// Display the elements
    cout << "The first three elements are: " <<
            ivec[0] << " " <<
            ivec[1] << " " <<
            ivec[2] << endl;

// Detach the second element
    ivec.Detach((unsigned)1);

// Display elements again
    cout << "After detaching second element: " << endl <<
            "There are " << ivec.Count() <<
            " elements." << endl <<
            "The first two elements are: " <<
            ivec[0] << " " <<
            ivec[1] << endl;
}
```

When compiled and run, the program of Listing 16.3 generates the following output:

```
There are 3 elements.
The first three elements are: 9 7 8
After detaching second element:
There are 2 elements.
The first two elements are: 9 8
```

Sorted Direct Vectors

The class template `TCVectorImp<T>` is an example of a sorted direct vector. These vectors keep their contents in sorted order provided you insert elements using the `Add` function. Because sorting is done by applying the operator < to the elements in the vector, the type `T`, appearing in the template's argument list, must have operator < defined because that operator is used to determine the sorting order of the elements. Listing 16.4 shows an example program that uses a sorted vector to store some integer values.

Listing 16.4. SORTVEC.CPP. Test program to demonstrate sorted direct vector FDS.

```
//-------------------------------------------------------------
// File: sortvec.cpp
// Sample program that illustrates sorted direct vector

#include <classlib\vectimp.h>
#include <iostream.h>

typedef TSVectorImp<int> IntegerSVector;

void main()
{
    IntegerSVector ivec(10);

    ivec.Add(9);
    ivec.Add(7);
    ivec.Add(8);

    cout << "There are " << ivec.Count() <<
            " elements." << endl;

// Display the elements
```

```
    cout << "The first three elements are: " <<
            ivec[0] << " " <<
            ivec[1] << " " <<
            ivec[2] << endl;

// Detach the second element
    ivec.Detach((unsigned)1);

// Display elements again
    cout << "After removing second element: " << endl <<
            "There are " << ivec.Count() <<
            " elements." << endl <<
            "The first two elements are: " <<
            ivec[0] << " " <<
            ivec[1] << endl;
}
```

You can compile and link the program shown in Listing 16.4 with the following command entered at the DOS prompt:

```
bcc -W sortvec.cpp
```

When you run the resulting executable program under Windows, it displays the following output in an EasyWin window:

```
There are 3 elements.
The first three elements are: 7 8 9
After removing second element:
There are 2 elements.
The first two elements are: 7 9
```

As you can see, the sorted vector always keeps its contents in sorted order.

Simple Indirect Vectors

Direct vectors make a copy of each object you add to the vector, which may not be efficient when storing large objects, or may not be possible when storing objects that do not have a copy operator defined. You can use the indirect vectors, and other indirect containers in general, to store pointers to objects.

The `TIVectorImp<T>` class template is an example of a simple indirect vector. Listing 16.5 shows a simple program that illustrates the use of an indirect vector to store pointers to `double` variables.

Listing 16.5. SIVEC.CPP. Test program to demonstrate sorted indirect vector FDS.

```
//-----------------------------------------------------------------
// File: sivec.cpp
// Sample program that illustrates simple indirect vector

#include <classlib\vectimp.h>
#include <iostream.h>

typedef TIVectorImp<double> DoublePtrVector;

void main()
{
    DoublePtrVector dpvec(16, 8);  // Grow in chunks of 8

    double x = 1.1, y = 2.2, z = 3.3;

// Insert some pointers
    dpvec[0] = &x;
    dpvec[1] = &y;
    dpvec[2] = &z;

// Display the first three elements
    int i;
    for(i = 0; i < 3; i++)
    {
       cout << "dpvec[" << i << "] = " << *dpvec[i] << endl;
    }
}
```

The program in Listing 16.5 produces the following output:

```
dpvec[0] = 1.1
dpvec[1] = 2.2
dpvec[2] = 3.3
```

Counted Indirect Vectors

The counted indirect vector stores pointers to objects and keeps a count of the number of filled slots *provided* you insert the pointers into the vector by calling the `Add` function and remove pointers using the `Detach` function. If you remove an element from the middle of a filled area of the vector, a counted indirect vector class such as

TICVectorImp<T> will move the elements to ensure that the vector is filled continuously from index zero onward. Listing 16.6 shows an example of using the TICVectorImp<T> class template.

Listing 16.6. CIVEC.CPP. Test program to demonstrate counted indirect vector FDS.

```
//--------------------------------------------------------------
// File: civec.cpp
// Sample program that illustrates counted indirect vector

#include <classlib\vectimp.h>
#include <iostream.h>

typedef TICVectorImp<float> FloatICVector;

void main()
{
    FloatICVector fvec(16, 4);
    float x = 9.5, y = 7.5, z = 8.5;

    fvec.Add(&x);
    fvec.Add(&y);
    fvec.Add(&z);

    cout << "There are " << fvec.Count() <<
            " elements." << endl;

// Display the elements
    cout << "The first three elements are: " <<
            *fvec[0] << " " <<
            *fvec[1] << " " <<
            *fvec[2] << endl;

// Detach the second element
    fvec.Detach((unsigned)1);

// Display elements again
    cout << "After detaching second element: " << endl <<
            "There are " << fvec.Count() <<
            " elements." << endl <<
```

continues

Listing 16.6. continued

```
                "The first two elements are: " <<
                *fvec[0] << " " <<
                *fvec[1] << endl;
}
```

Here is the output from the program shown in Listing 16.6:

```
There are 3 elements.
The first three elements are: 9.5 7.5 8.5
After detaching second element:
There are 2 elements.
The first two elements are: 9.5 8.5
```

As you can see, after the second element is removed by calling `Detach`, the vector is recompacted by moving the third element to the second slot.

Sorted Indirect Vectors

A sorted indirect vector class is meant for storing pointers to objects. Like its direct counterpart, the sorted indirect vector keeps its contents in sorted order *provided* you insert the pointers into the vector by calling the `Add` function and remove elements using the `Detach` function. To keep the contents sorted, a sorted indirect vector class such as `TISVectorImp<T>` requires that the operator < be defined for the data type `T` that you provide as the class template's argument. Listing 16.7 shows an example program that uses the `TISVectorImp<T>` class template.

Listing 16.7. SORTIVEC.CPP. Test program to demonstrate sorted indirect vector FDS.

```
//--------------------------------------------------------------
// File: sortivec.cpp
// Sample program that illustrates sorted indirect vector

#include <classlib\vectimp.h>
#include <iostream.h>

typedef TISVectorImp<float> FloatISVector;

void main()
{
```

```
    FloatISVector fvec(16, 4);  // Grow by 4 elements at a time
    float x = 9.5, y = 7.5, z = 8.5;

    fvec.Add(&x);
    fvec.Add(&y);
    fvec.Add(&z);

    cout << "There are " << fvec.Count() <<
            " elements." << endl;

// Display the elements
    cout << "The first three elements are: " <<
            *fvec[0] << " " <<
            *fvec[1] << " " <<
            *fvec[2] << endl;

// Detach the second element
    fvec.Detach((unsigned)1);

// Display elements again
    cout << "After detaching second element: " << endl <<
            "There are " << fvec.Count() <<
            " elements." << endl <<
            "The first two elements are: " <<
            *fvec[0] << " " <<
            *fvec[1] << endl;
}
```

The program of Listing 16.7 generates the following output:

```
There are 3 elements.
The first three elements are: 7.5 8.5 9.5
After removing second element:
There are 2 elements.
The first two elements are: 7.5 9.5
```

Lists

Like the FDS vector classes, there are several list class templates: direct and indirect lists in both sorted and unsorted (or simple) varieties. The four combinations—simple direct, simple indirect, sorted direct, and sorted indirect—also come in unmanaged as well as managed versions. These eight list classes, together with four related iterator classes, result in the 12 singly-linked lists in Table 16.1. There are an identical number of doubly-linked list classes also. Because both list types are similar in details, I will describe the singly-linked list classes only.

The simplest list class is the one that you can declare with the template `TListImp<T>`, where `T` denotes the type of object you want to store in the list. To insert objects into the list, call the `Add` function, which makes a copy of the object and inserts the copy at the head of the list. You have to use an iterator class, `TListIteratorImp<T>`, to step through the contents of the list. The iterator steps through the contents of the list from the head to the tail. Thus, the order of retrieval is the reverse of the order of insertion. You can verify this from the output of the example program in Listing 16.8.

If you want to maintain the contents of a list in sorted order, you can use a sorted list class such as `TSListImp<T>`. In this case, the object type `T` should have the operators `<` and `==` defined. Listing 16.8 shows how you would have to define a class so that objects of that class can be stored in a sorted direct list. You can access the list's contents using the same iterator class, `TListIteratorImp<T>`, that you use for an unsorted direct list.

If you want to store large objects in a list, you should use the indirect list classes that store pointers to objects rather than copying the objects. The way you use the indirect list classes is similar to the way the direct lists are used in Listing 16.8, except that when calling `Add`, you have to provide as argument a pointer to an object instead of the object itself.

Listing 16.8. LISTS.CPP. Test program to demonstrate sorted and unsorted list FDS.

```
//-------------------------------------------------------------
// File: lists.cpp
// Sample program that illustrates the list FDS

#include <classlib\listimp.h>
#include <iostream.h>
#include <string.h>

const short CMDLEN = 16;

class Command
{
public:
    Command() : code(0) { cmd[0] = '\0';}
    Command(const char* cs, short _code) : code(_code)
```

```
    {
        short len = strlen(cs);
        if(len < CMDLEN)
            strcpy(cmd, cs);
        else
        {
            strncpy(cmd, cs, CMDLEN-1);
            cmd[CMDLEN-1] = '\0';
        }
    }

    void print(ostream& os) const
    {
        os << code << "     " << cmd;
    }

// Some required operators
    int operator<(const Command& c) const
    { return code < c.code;}

    int operator==(const Command& c) const
    { return code == c.code;}

private:
// Internal details of the command
    char        cmd[CMDLEN];
    short       code;
};

// Prototype for stream insertion operator for commands
ostream& operator<< (ostream& os, const Command& c);

typedef TListImp<Command>             CommandList;
typedef TSListImp<Command>            CommandSList;
typedef TListIteratorImp<Command>     CLIterator;

CommandList   cl;    // unsorted command list
CommandSList  csl;   // sorted command list
//-------------------------------------------------------------
// m a i n
```

continues

Listing 16.8. continued

```
void main()
{
// Create a few Commands
    Command quit("quit", 0);
    Command anim("create_new_animation", 2);
    Command load("load_file", 1);
    Command refresh("refresh", 4);
    Command sound("play_sound_file", 3);

// Add the Commands to the unsorted list
    cl.Add(quit);
    cl.Add(anim);
    cl.Add(load);
    cl.Add(refresh);
    cl.Add(sound);

// Add same commands to the sorted list
    csl.Add(quit);
    csl.Add(anim);
    csl.Add(load);
    csl.Add(refresh);
    csl.Add(sound);

// Go through the unsorted list and display the items
    CLIterator us_cli(cl);

    cout << "------ Unsorted List ------" << endl;

    while(us_cli)
    {
       cout << us_cli++ << endl;
    }

// Now display the contents of the sorted list
    CLIterator s_cli(csl);

    cout << "------  Sorted List  ------" << endl;
    while(s_cli)
    {
       cout << s_cli++ << endl;
    }
```

```
}
//-------------------------------------------------------------
// ostream&  o p e r a t o r < < ( ostream&,  const Command& )
// Stream insertion operator for the Command class

ostream& operator<< (ostream& os, const Command& c)
{
    c.print(os);
    return os;
}
```

Here is the output from the program shown in Listing 16.8:

```
------ Unsorted List ------
3     play_sound_file
4     refresh
1     load_file
2     create_new_anim
0     quit
------  Sorted List  ------
0     quit
1     load_file
2     create_new_anim
3     play_sound_file
4     refresh
```

Binary Tree

The binary tree is another useful FDS container class. A binary tree consists of a collection of nodes; each node can store an object (or a pointer to an object) and has two descendants—a left descendant and a right descendant. A node with no descendants is called a *terminal* or *leaf* node.

When you first add an item to a binary tree, that item is placed in the root node. When you add the next item, that item is compared with the item in the root node. If the item is less than that in the root node, the item is added as the left descendant; otherwise, it becomes the right descendant of the root node. The process of comparing items with nodes and adding each as either a left or right descendant continues as you add subsequent elements to the binary tree. If you pause for a moment and think about this process, you will realize that if we add a sorted list of elements to a binary tree, the three will consist of nodes that have only one type of descendant—left or right, depending on the order in which the elements were sorted. This is a case of the binary tree being completely unbalanced. The algorithm used to search for elements in a binary tree is such that it's best to have a balanced tree with as many left descendants as there are right descendants. Inserting elements in random order tends to result in a well-balanced tree.

Because adding elements to the binary tree involves comparing elements to one another, the objects stored in a binary tree should be of types that have operator == and operator < well defined. This is not a problem for the built-in data types such as `int` and `float`, but class objects that are meant to be stored in a binary tree must provide the ordering operators.

Using the binary tree FDS is simple. Listing 16.9 shows a sample program that inserts a number of integers into a binary tree and uses an iterator to traverse the nodes in the tree.

Listing 16.9. BINTREE.CPP. Test program to demonstrate the binary tree FDS.

```
//--------------------------------------------------------------
// File: bintree.cpp
// Sample program that illustrates the binary tree class.

#include <classlib\binimp.h>
#include <iostream.h>

typedef TBinarySearchTreeImp<int> IntegerBinaryTree;
typedef TBinarySearchTreeIteratorImp<int>
                          IntegerBinaryTreeIterator;

void main()
{
    IntegerBinaryTree itree;

// Add some elements
    itree.Add(9);
    itree.Add(6);
    itree.Add(8);
    itree.Add(7);
    itree.Add(10);

    cout << itree.GetItemsInContainer()  <<
            " items in tree" << endl;
```

```
// Traverse through tree and display the elements
    IntegerBinaryTreeIterator it(itree);

    while(it)
    {
       cout << it++ << endl;
    }
}
```

To build the example program in Listing 16.9, you have to link with the BIDSDBS.LIB (assuming that you are compiling using the small model). For example, to create an EasyWin application, use the following command line from the DOS prompt:

```
bcc -W bintree.cpp c:\bc4\lib\bidsdbs.lib
```

Remember to replace the drive letter and directory names with the appropriate settings for your installation of Borland C++. When you run the resulting program under Windows, it produces the following output:

```
5 items in tree
6
7
8
9
10
```

As you can see, the iterator traverses the nodes of the binary tree in a sorted order.

Abstract Data Type (ADT)

Borland's Abstract Data Type (ADT) template classes offer data types such as stacks and arrays that are built using the FDS containers. The ADT classes also offer containers and, when appropriate, you can select the FDS class that is used to implement a specific container type. For example, you can have a stack implemented as a vector or a list.

The template-based class library in Borland C++ provides the following ADT container types:

- `Array` A one-dimensional indexed data structure.
- `Associations` A pair of objects (the first denotes a key, the second denotes the value associated with that key).

- `Bag` An unordered collection of objects that can have multiple instances of the same object.
- `Deque` A variation of the well-known queue data structure with the property that objects can be inserted and removed at both ends of the queue (a *d*ouble-*e*nded *que*ue, pronounced “deck”).
- `Dictionary` An unordered collection of pairs of associated objects (the first denotes a key, the second denotes the value associated with that key) that provides a member function to look up values using keys.
- `Queue` A FIFO (first-in first-out) data structure that allows you to insert objects at the tail of the queue and remove them from the head.
- `Set` An unordered collection of objects in which only one occurrence of an object is allowed in the set.
- `Stack` A LIFO (last-in first-out) data structure.

There are multiple class templates for each ADT container type. Table 16.2 shows these class templates grouped according to the type.

Some Terms for the Template-Based Containers

The term *managed* class refers to the class templates that accept a storage allocator as an argument for the template. In this chapter, this argument is denoted by the `Alloc` in the template names. When instantiating any managed class template, the programmer has to specify a storage allocator class patterned after the classes shown in the header file `<classlib\alloctr.h>`. The term *unmanaged* class refers to the class templates that use the `TStandardAllocator` class for storage management. This class is declared in `<classlib\alloctr.h>`.

Indirect containers store pointers to objects, while *direct* containers store the objects. When you add an object to a direct container by calling the `Add` function, the container makes a copy of the object and adds it to the container. Thus, direct containers own their contents and the programmer does not have to worry about the objects in the container. However, it is not as straightforward to determine the ownership of the objects referenced through pointers stored in an indirect container. The programmer can specify the ownership of the contents of the indirect container classes by calling the `ownsElements` function, which is a member of the `TShouldDelete` class from which all indirect ADT containers are derived.

Table 16.2. Abstract Data Type (ADT) container classes in Borland C++.

Class Template	Description
ARRAYS (declared in <classlib\arrays.h>)	
`TMArrayAsVector<T,Alloc>`	A managed array of objects of type `T`, implemented as a vector
`TMArrayAsVectorIterator<T,Alloc>`	An iterator for `TMArrayAsVector` classes
`TArrayAsVector<T>`	An unmanaged array of objects of type `T`, implemented as a vector
`TArrayAsVectorIterator<T>`	An iterator for `TArrayAsVector` classes
`TMSArrayAsVector<T,Alloc>`	A managed, sorted vector-based array of objects of type `T`
`TMSArrayAsVectorIterator<T,Alloc>`	An iterator for `TMSArrayAsVector` classes
`TSArrayAsVector<T>`	An unmanaged, sorted array of objects of type `T`, implemented as a vector
`TSArrayAsVectorIterator<T>`	An iterator for `TSArrayAsVector` classes
`TMIArrayAsVector<T,Alloc>`	A managed array of pointers to objects of type `T`, implemented as a vector

continues

Table 16.2. continued

Class Template	Description
`TMIArrayAsVectorIterator<T,Alloc>`	An iterator for `TMIArrayAsVector` classes
`TIArrayAsVector<T>`	An unmanaged array of pointers to objects of type `T`, implemented as a vector
`TIArrayAsVectorIterator<T>`	An iterator for `TIArrayAsVector` classes
`TMISArrayAsVector<T,Alloc>`	A managed, sorted array of pointers to objects of type `T`, implemented as a vector
`TMISArrayAsVectorIterator<T,Alloc>`	An iterator for `TMISArrayAsVector` classes
`TISArrayAsVector<T>`	An unmanaged, sorted array of pointers to objects of type `T`, implemented as a vector
`TISArrayAsVectorIterator<T>`	An iterator for `TISArrayAsVector` classes
`TArray<T>`	A synonym for `TArrayAsVector<T>`
`TArrayIterator<T>`	An iterator for `TArray` classes
ASSOCIATIONS (declared in <classlib\assoc.h>)	
`TMDDAssociation<K,V,Alloc>`	A managed association between a key of type `K` and a value of type `V`
`TDDAssociation<K,V>`	An unmanaged association between a key of type `K` and a value of type `V`
`TMDIAssociation<K,V,Alloc>`	A managed association between a key of type `K` and a pointer to a value of type `V`
`TDIAssociation<K,V>`	An unmanaged association between a key of type `K` and a pointer to a value of type `V`

`TMIDAssociation<K,V,Alloc>`	A managed association between a pointer to a key of type `K` and a value of type `V`
`TIDAssociation<K,V>`	An unmanaged association between a pointer to a key of type `K` and a value of type `V`
`TMIIAssociation<K,V,Alloc>`	A managed association between a pointer to a key of type `K` and a pointer to a value of type `V`
`TIIAssociation<K,V>`	An unmanaged association between a pointer to a key of type `K` and a pointer to a value of type `V`

BAGS (declared in <classlib\bags.h>)

`TMBagAsVector<T,Alloc>`	A managed bag of objects of type `T`, implemented as a vector
`TMBagAsVectorIterator<T,Alloc>`	An iterator for the `TMBagAsVector` classes
`TBagAsVector<T>`	An unmanaged bag of objects of type `T`, implemented as a vector
`TBagAsVectorIterator<T>`	An iterator for the `TBagAsVector` classes
`TMIBagAsVector<T,Alloc>`	A managed bag of pointers to objects of type `T`, implemented as a vector
`TMIBagAsVectorIterator<T,Alloc>`	An iterator for the `TMIBagAsVector` classes
`TIBagAsVector<T>`	An unmanaged bag of pointers to objects of type `T`, implemented as a vector
`TIBagAsVectorIterator<T>`	An iterator for the `TIBagAsVector` classes
`TBag<T>`	A synonym for `TBagAsVector<T>`

continues

Table 16.2. continued

Class Template	Description
`TBagIterator<T>`	A synonym for `TBagAsVector<T>`
DEQUES (declared in <classlib\deques.h>)	
`TMDequeAsVector<T,Alloc>`	A managed deque (double-ended queue) of objects of type `T`, implemented as a vector
`TMDequeAsVectorIterator<T,Alloc>`	An iterator for `TMDequeAsVector` classes
`TDequeAsVector<T>`	An unmanaged deque of objects of type `T`, implemented as a vector
`TDequeAsVectorIterator<T>`	An iterator for `TDequeAsVector` classes
`TMIDequeAsVector<T,Alloc>`	A managed deque of pointers to objects of type `T`, implemented as a vector
`TMIDequeAsVectorIterator<T,Alloc>`	An iterator for `TMIDequeAsVector` classes
`TIDequeAsVector<T>`	An unmanaged deque of pointers to objects of type `T`, implemented as a vector
`TIDequeAsVectorIterator<T>`	An iterator for `TIDequeAsVector` classes
`TMDequeAsDoubleList<T,Alloc>`	A managed deque of objects of type `T`, implemented as a doubly-linked list
`TMDequeAsDoubleListIterator<T,Alloc>`	An iterator for `TMDequeAsDoubleList` classes
`TDequeAsDoubleList<T>`	An unmanaged deque of objects of type `T`, implemented as a doubly-linked list

`TDequeAsDoubleListIterator<T>`	An iterator for `TDequeAsDoubleList` classes
`TMIDequeAsDoubleList<T,Alloc>`	A managed deque of pointers to objects of type `T`, implemented as a doubly-linked list
`TMIDequeAsDoubleListIterator<T,Alloc>`	An iterator for `TMIDequeAsDoubleList` classes
`TIDequeAsDoubleList<T>`	An unmanaged deque of pointers to objects of type `T`, implemented as a doubly-linked list
`TIDequeAsDoubleListIterator<T>`	An iterator for `TIDequeAsDoubleList` classes
`TDeque<T>`	A synonym for `TDequeAsVector<T>`
`TDequeIterator<T>`	A synonym for `TDequeAsVectorIterator<T>`

DICTIONARIES (declared in <classlib\dict.h>)

`TMDictionaryAsHashTable<T,Alloc>`	A managed dictionary of associations, implemented using a hash table
`TMDictionaryAsHashTableIterator<T,Alloc>`	An iterator for the `TMDictionaryAsHashTable` classes
`TDictionaryAsHashTable<T>`	An unmanaged dictionary of associations, implemented using a hash table
`TDictionaryAsHashTableIterator<T>`	An iterator for the `TMDictionaryAsHashTable` classes

continues

Table 16.2. continued

Class Template	Description
`TMIDictionaryAsHashTable<T,Alloc>`	A managed dictionary of pointers to associations, implemented using a hash table
`TMIDictionaryAsHashTableIterator<T,Alloc>`	An iterator for the `TMDictionaryAsHashTable` classes
`TIDictionaryAsHashTable<T>`	An unmanaged dictionary of pointers to associations, implemented using a hash table
`TIDictionaryAsHashTableIterator<T>`	An iterator for the `TMDictionaryAsHashTable` classes
`TDictionary<T>`	A synonym for `TDictionaryAsHashTable<T>`
`TDictionaryIterator<T>`	An iterator for `TDictionary` classes
QUEUES (declared in <classlib\queues.h>)	
`TMQueueAsVector<T,Alloc>`	A managed queue of objects of type `T`, implemented as a vector
`TMQueueAsVectorIterator<T,Alloc>`	An iterator for the `TMQueueAsVector` classes
`TQueueAsVector<T>`	An unmanaged queue of objects of type `T`, implemented as a vector
`TQueueAsVectorIterator<T>`	An iterator for the `TQueueAsVector` classes
`TMIQueueAsVector<T,Alloc>`	A managed queue of pointers to objects of type `T`, implemented as a vector

TMIQueueAsVectorIterator<T,Alloc>	An iterator for the TMIQueueAsVector classes
TIQueueAsVector<T>	An unmanaged queue of pointers to objects of type T, implemented as a vector
TIQueueAsVectorIterator<T>	An iterator for the TIQueueAsVector classes
TMQueueAsDoubleList<T,Alloc>	A managed queue of objects of type T, implemented as a doubly-linked list
TMQueueAsDoubleListIterator<T,Alloc>	An iterator for the TMQueueAsDoubleList classes
TQueueAsDoubleList<T>	An unmanaged queue of objects of type T, implemented as a doubly-linked list
TQueueAsDoubleListIterator<T>	An iterator for the TQueueAsDoubleList classes
TMIQueueAsDoubleList<T,Alloc>	A managed queue of pointers to objects of type T, implemented as a doubly-linked list
TMIQueueAsDoubleListIterator<T,Alloc>	An iterator for the TMIQueueAsDoubleList classes
TIQueueAsDoubleList<T>	An unmanaged queue of pointers to objects of type T, implemented as a doubly-linked list
TIQueueAsDoubleListIterator<T>	An iterator for the TIQueueAsDoubleList classes
TQueue<T>	A synonym for TQueueAsVector<T>
TQueueIterator<T>	Same as TQueueAsVectorIterator<T>

continues

Table 16.2. continued

Class Template	Description
SETS (declared in <classlib\sets.h>)	
`TMSetAsVector<T,Alloc>`	A managed set of objects of type `T`, implemented as a vector
`TMSetAsVectorIterator<T,Alloc>`	An iterator for `TMSetAsVector` classes
`TSetAsVector<T>`	An unmanaged set of objects of type `T`, implemented as a vector
`TSetAsVectorIterator<T>`	An iterator for `TSetAsVector` classes
`TMISetAsVector<T,Alloc>`	A managed set of pointers to objects of type `T`, implemented as a vector
`TMISetAsVectorIterator<T,Alloc>`	An iterator for `TMISetAsVector` classes
`TISetAsVector<T>`	An unmanaged set of pointers to objects of type `T`, implemented as a vector
`TISetAsVectorIterator<T>`	An iterator for `TISetAsVector` classes
`TSet<T>`	Same as `TSetAsVector<T>`
`TSetIterator<T>`	Same as `TSetAsVectorIterator<T>`
STACKS (declared in <classlib\stacks.h>)	
`TMStackAsVector<T,Alloc>`	A managed stack of objects of type `T`, implemented as a vector
`TMStackAsVectorIterator<T,Alloc>`	An iterator for `TMStackAsVector` classes
`TStackAsVector<T>`	An unmanaged stack of objects of type `T`, implemented as a vector
`TStackAsVectorIterator<T>`	An iterator for `TStackAsVector` classes

`TMIStackAsVector<T,Alloc>`	A managed stack of pointers to objects of type `T`, implemented as a vector
`TMIStackAsVectorIterator<T,Alloc>`	An iterator for `TMIStackAsVector` classes
`TIStackAsVector<T>`	An unmanaged stack of pointers to objects of type `T`, implemented as a vector
`TIStackAsVectorIterator<T>`	An iterator for `TIStackAsVector` classes
`TMStackAsList<T,Alloc>`	A managed stack of objects of type `T`, implemented as a list
`TMStackAsListIterator<T,Alloc>`	An iterator for `TMStackAsList` classes
`TStackAsList<T>`	An unmanaged stack of objects of type `T`, implemented as a list
`TStackAsListIterator<T>`	An iterator for `TStackAsList` classes
`TMIStackAsList<T,Alloc>`	A managed list of pointers to objects of type `T`, implemented as a list
`TMIStackAsListIterator<T,Alloc>`	An iterator for `TMIStackAsList` classes
`TIStackAsList<T>`	An unmanaged list of pointers to objects of type `T`, implemented as a list
`TIStackAsListIterator<T>`	An iterator for `TIStackAsList` classes
`TStack<T>`	Same as `TStackAsVector<T>`
`TStackIterator<T>`	Same as `TStackAsVectorIterator<T>`

Arrays

The array class templates declared in `<classlib\arrays.h>` allow you to define one-dimensional arrays to store any type of data. As you can see from the names such as `TArrayAsVector<T>` and `TSArrayAsVector<T>`, the ADT array classes are implemented using the FDS vector classes. You can use the arrays just as you would use C++ arrays. But unlike the built-in C++ arrays, the ADT arrays can provide additional capabilities. They

- Grow at run time, when needed
- Keep a count of elements in the array
- Keep the contents sorted
- Keep the array compact when an element is removed
- Have arbitrary lower and upper indexes
- Have iterator classes that ease access to the array

There are four basic types of arrays: simple direct, simple indirect, sorted direct, and sorted indirect. These four arrays come in two varieties: managed and unmanaged. This results in a total of eight array classes. Each array class also has an associated iterator class that provides easy access to the contents of the array. Thus, there are 16 class templates for defining and using arrays. In Table 16.2 there are 18 entries under the Arrays category; the last two entries are shortened names for templates that appear earlier in the table.

Simple direct arrays such as the one implemented by the template `TArrayAsVector<T>` are as easy to use as C++ arrays that are part of the language. The floating-point array shown in Listing 16.10 shows how you can use the operator `[]` to access the elements of the simple direct array. Simple indirect arrays such as `TIArrayAsVector<T>` behave similarly except that each entry in the array is a pointer to an object of type `T` instead of the object itself.

Sorted arrays keep their contents in sorted order. The class of objects stored in a sorted array is expected to have the operators == and < defined. Listing 16.10 defines a class named `Sprite` that is stored in a sorted indirect array. As you can see, the `Sprite` class defines the operators == and <. These comparison operators compare a member variable named `priority_` that determines the ordering of `Sprite` objects. The array is defined from the class template `TISArrayAsVector<T>` with the following statements:

```
// A sorted, indirect array of sprites
typedef TISArrayAsVector<Sprite> SpriteArray;
typedef TISArrayAsVectorIterator<Sprite> SpriteArrayIterator;
```

The first typedef defines a new type name for an array of Sprites, while the second typedef defines an iterator to traverse the array of Sprite objects. Once these types are defined, creating an array and adding Sprite objects to the array is straightforward:

```
// Create a sorted array of sprites with array indices
// between 0 and 63 and capable of growing 8 elements
// at a time
    SpriteArray sprites(63, 0, 8);

// Create a sprites
    Sprite* s1 = new Sprite("Sprite_1", 200);
// ...

// Insert a sprite into the sorted array
    sprites.Add(s1);
// ...
```

The SpriteArray constructor accepts up to three arguments. The first two numbers are the upper and lower limits of the array indices, while the third number denotes the amount by which the array is capable of growing at runtime, should that become necessary. Notice that to add an element to an array, you have to call the Add function with a pointer to a Sprite as an argument. Because the array simply stores the pointer and does not make a copy of the object, you should make sure that you do not store a pointer to a temporary object such as a local variable in a function. In the example of Listing 16.10, the Sprite objects stored in the indirect array are allocated on the heap by calling the new operator.

By default, the indirect arrays own their contents. This means that you do not have to explicitly free the objects—the array's destructor takes care of deleting all objects by invoking the destructors through the pointers to these objects. This is why Listing 16.10 does not show any calls to the delete operator to free the Sprite objects allocated by new.

With an iterator, you can access the elements of the array as easily as using the operator []. For example, assuming that a stream insertion operator << has been defined for the Sprite class, you would write the following to print out the Sprite objects in the array:

```
// Display the contents of the array
    SpriteArrayIterator si(sprites);

    while(si)
    {
```

```
        cout << *si++ << endl;
    }
```

As you can see, when constructing the iterator, you have to provide the array as an argument to the iterator's constructor; this is how the iterator becomes associated with a specific array. Notice how the `while` statement tests the iterator itself to determine when to stop the loop that traverses through the array. The iterator class defines the following integer cast operator that makes this possible:

```
operator int() const
{
// return zero if no more elements in array
// else return zero
//...
}
```

With the iterator defined, going from one element of the array to the next is as simple as applying the increment operator to the iterator.

Listing 16.10. TSTARRAY.CPP. Test program to demonstrate the array ADT.

```
//-----------------------------------------------------------------
// File: tstarray.cpp
// Sample program that illustrates the array classes

#include <classlib\arrays.h>
#include <iostream.h>
#include <iomanip.h>

class Image   // A dummy image class
{
public:
//...

private:
// This is the image...
    char data[256];
};

class Sprite  // A sprite class with an image and a priority
{
public:
    Sprite() : priority_(0), img(NULL), name_(NULL) {}
```

```
    Sprite(char *n, short prio) : priority_(prio)
    {
        short len = strlen(n);
        name_ = new char[len+1];
        strcpy(name_, n);
        img = new Image;
    }

    ~Sprite()
    {
        if(name_ != NULL) delete[] name_;
        if(img != NULL) delete img;
    }

    short priority() const { return priority_;}
    const char* name() const { return name_;}

    operator==(const Sprite& s) const
    {
        return (priority_ == s.priority());
    }

    operator<(const Sprite& s) const
    {
        return (priority_ < s.priority());
    }

    void print(ostream& os) const
    {
        os << setw(4) << priority_ << " " << name_ << " ";
    }

protected:
    char  *name_;
    short priority_;
    Image *img;
};

ostream& operator<<(ostream& os, const Sprite& s)
{
    s.print(os);
    return os;
```

continues

Listing 16.10. continued

```
}

// A direct array of floats
typedef TArrayAsVector<float> FloatArray;

// A sorted, indirect array of sprites
typedef TISArrayAsVector<Sprite> SpriteArray;
typedef TISArrayAsVectorIterator<Sprite> SpriteArrayIterator;

//-------------------------------------------------------------
// m a i n

void main()
{
// Demonstrate a simple array of floats
    FloatArray farray(10);

    int i;
    for(i = 0; i < 3; i++)
        farray[i] = i + 0.01;

// Display the elements
    for(i = 0; i < 3; i++)
    {
       cout << "farray[" << i << "] = " << farray[i] << endl;
    }

// Create a sorted array of sprites with array indices
// between 0 and 63 and capable of growing 8 elements
// at a time
    SpriteArray sprites(63, 0, 8);

// Create some sprites
    Sprite* s1 = new Sprite("Sprite_1", 200);
    Sprite* s2 = new Sprite("Sprite_2", 50);
    Sprite* s3 = new Sprite("Sprite_3", 100);
    Sprite* s4 = new Sprite("Sprite_4", 500);

// Insert the sprites into the sorted array
    sprites.Add(s1);
    sprites.Add(s2);
```

```
    sprites.Add(s3);
    sprites.Add(s4);

    cout << endl << "A sorted array of sprites" << endl;
    short num = sprites.GetItemsInContainer();
    cout << "There are " << num << " sprites." << endl;

// Display the contents of the array
    SpriteArrayIterator si(sprites);

    while(si)
    {
        cout << *si++ << endl;
    }
}
```

The output of the program shown in Listing 16.10 is as follows:

```
farray[0] = 0.01
farray[1] = 1.01
farray[2] = 2.01

A sorted array of sprites
There are 4 sprites.
  50 Sprite_2
 100 Sprite_3
 200 Sprite_1
 500 Sprite_4
```

Associations

An association is a pair of objects: the first object is the *key* and the second object is the *value*. For instance, an identifying number such as a driver's license number could be a key and the name of a person could be the associated value. To use the association class templates, you have to include the header file `<classlib\assoc.h>`.

To define an association, the type of object used as the key must have a `HashValue` function defined with the following prototype:

```
unsigned HashValue() const
```

Also, the operator == must be defined for the key objects. The reason for requiring the `HashValue` function is that associations are usually used in other container objects such as dictionaries, where they are stored in a hash table. The `HashValue` function maps a key to a hash value that serves as an index for the hash table. The equality operator == is needed because keys are used to look up values from the associations stored in a dictionary, and doing this requires comparing keys to one another.

As you can see from Table 16.2, an association class takes at least two other class types as arguments—the key class and the value class. To associate a direct key with a direct value, you can use the template `TDDAssociation<K,V>`, where `K` denotes the key and `V` the value. The association constructor also takes two arguments—a key and the value. The class template defines the `Key` and `Value` functions to access the key and value respectively.

Associations are not that useful by themselves—they are most commonly used in dictionary containers to organize information. Listings 16.11 and 16.12 illustrate the use of an association class template; this association is later used in a dictionary object. Listing 16.11 shows the definition of a class named ID that is used as a key. Essentially, ID is a four-character identifier. Notice that the `HashValue` function evaluates the exclusive-OR of all four characters in ID to generate the hash value. Listing 16.12 uses the ID class and defines an association using ID objects as key and an integer as the value. For now, the program simply defines and displays a number of associations. In the next section, these associations are stored in a dictionary and looked up using the key.

Listing 16.11. ID.H. A data type used as a key in an association.

```
//-------------------------------------------------------------
// File: id.h
// A class that defines a 4-character identifier

#if !defined (__ID_H)
#define __ID_H

const short IDLEN = 4;
struct ID
{
    ID() { ids[0] = ids[1] = ids[2] = ids[3] = 'X';}

    ID(const char* s)
    {
        short len = strlen(s);
        if(len <= IDLEN)
```

```
            strcpy(ids, s);
        else
            strncpy(ids, s, IDLEN);
    }
    unsigned HashValue() const
    {
        return ids[0]^ids[1]^ids[2]^ids[3];
    }
    operator==(const ID& id) const
    {
        return (((ids[0] == ids[1]) == ids[2]) == ids[3]);
    }
    void print(ostream& os) const
    {
        os << ids[0] << ids[1] << ids[2] << ids[3] << " ";
    }
    char ids[4];
};

ostream& operator<<(ostream& os, const ID& id)
{
    id.print(os);
    return os;
}

#endif
```

Listing 16.12. TSTASSOC.CPP. Test program to demonstrate the association ADT.

```
//----------------------------------------------------------------
// File: tstassoc.cpp
// Sample program that illustrates the association classes

#include <classlib\assoc.h>
#include <iostream.h>
#include <iomanip.h>
#include "id.h"

typedef TDDAssociation<ID,int> Data;
```

continues

Listing 16.12. continued

```
void main()
{
    Data d[6] =
    {
      Data("Naba", 1),
      Data("BOOK", 15),
      Data("OOPC", 8),
      Data("XWSP", 7),
      Data("BCW4", 2),
      Data("ABCD", 4)
    };
    short i;
    for(i = 0; i < 6; i++)
    {
        cout << "(HashValue = " << setw(4) <<
                     d[i].Key().HashValue() <<
                   ")  Key = " << d[i].Key() <<
                   " Value = " << setw(4) <<
                                d[i].Value() << endl;
    }
}
```

When you run the program of Listing 16.12 under Windows, it displays the following output:

```
(HashValue =   44)  Key = Naba  Value =    1
(HashValue =    9)  Key = BOOK  Value =   15
(HashValue =   19)  Key = OOPC  Value =    8
(HashValue =   12)  Key = XWSP  Value =    7
(HashValue =   98)  Key = BCW4  Value =    2
(HashValue =    4)  Key = ABCD  Value =    4
```

Dictionaries

A dictionary is a collection of associations. As the names of dictionary class templates such as `TIDictionaryAsHashTable<T>` imply, the dictionary classes use the hash table as the underlying storage mechanism. Essentially, to store an association in the dictionary, a hash function is used to compute an index from the association's key. A pointer to a linked list is stored at that location, and the association is stored in that linked list. If another association's keys produce the same hash value, that association is simply appended to the linked list. This way, the hash table in the dictionary can store many more associations than the actual number of entries in the hash table.

As with other ADT containers, there are two types of dictionaries: direct and indirect. A direct dictionary stores associations, while an indirect dictionary stores pointers to associations.

Listing 16.13 shows an example program that creates a direct dictionary to store the association defined in Listings 16.11 and 16.12. Associations are added to the dictionary by calling the `Add` member function. As you can see from Listing 16.13, there are two ways to access the contents of the dictionary. The first way is to use an iterator—in this case, the `TDictionaryAsHashTableIterator<T>` iterator. The second way is to call the `ForEach` function, which calls a specified function for each entry in the container. To understand how it works, try running the program shown in Listing 16.13 and examine the source code at the end of the `main` function. Note that you have to include the header file `<classlib\dict.h>` to use the dictionary class templates.

Listing 16.13. TSTDICT.CPP. Test program to demonstrate the dictionary ADT.

```
//--------------------------------------------------------------
// File: tstdict.cpp
// Sample program that illustrates the dictionary class.

#include <classlib\dict.h>
#include <classlib\assoc.h>
#include <iostream.h>
#include <iomanip.h>
#include "id.h"

typedef TDDAssociation<ID,int>              Data;
typedef TDictionaryAsHashTable<Data>        DataDict;
typedef TDictionaryAsHashTableIterator<Data> DataDictIterator;

void disp_item(Data& d, void* junk);
//--------------------------------------------------------------
// m a i n

void main()
{
    DataDict dd;
```

continues

Listing 16.13. continued

```
// Define some associations
    Data disp("Display",     95),
         brow("Browser",    225),
         plot("Plot2D",     135),
         deco("Decode",     315),
         warn("Warning",    125);

// Add the associations to the dictionary
    dd.Add(disp);
    dd.Add(brow);
    dd.Add(plot);
    dd.Add(deco);
    dd.Add(warn);

    short numitems = dd.GetItemsInContainer();
    cout << "There are " << numitems <<
            " items in dictionary." << endl;

// Display all entries using the iterator
    DataDictIterator ddi(dd);

    while(ddi)
    {
        Data d = ddi++;
        cout << d.Key() << " " << d.Value() << endl;
    }

// Demonstrate how to operate on each item of the dictionary
// using the ForEach function
    cout << endl
         << "Displaying the contents using the ForEach function:"
         << endl;
    dd.ForEach(disp_item, NULL);
}
//---------------------------------------------------------------
// d i s p _ i t e m

void disp_item(Data& d, void*)
{
    cout << d.Key() << " " << d.Value() << endl;
}
```

When run, the program of Listing 16.13 produces the following output:

```
There are 5 items in dictionary.
Plot  135
Brow  225
Warn  125
Deco  315
Disp  95

Displaying the contents using the ForEach function:
Plot  135
Brow  225
Warn  125
Deco  315
Disp  95
```

Bags and Sets

Bags and sets are unordered collections of objects or, in the case of indirect containers, collections of pointers to objects. The only difference between a bag and a set is that a bag allows multiple copies of the same object. The simple example program shown in Listing 16.14 illustrates this point by inserting several integers, including a repeating value, into a bag as well as a set. As the output of the program shows, the set does not allow any duplicate entries.

Bags and sets are implemented using the vector data structure. As with other containers, you can insert items into the container with the `Add` function. To access the contents of a bag or a set, you can use an iterator as shown in Listing 16.14. Additionally, you can call the `HasMember` function to check if an item belongs to the bag or set. To get back a pointer to a specific item in the container, use the `FindMember` function.

Listing 16.14. TSTBAG.CPP. Test program to demonstrate Bag and Set ADTs.

```
//-------------------------------------------------------------
// File: tstbag.cpp
// Sample program that illustrates the bag and set classes

#include <classlib\bags.h>
#include <classlib\sets.h>
#include <iostream.h>
```

continues

Listing 16.14. continued

```
// Direct containers of integers
typedef TBag<int> IntBag;
typedef TSet<int> IntSet;

// Bag and Set iterators
typedef TBagIterator<int> IntBagIterator;
typedef TSetIterator<int> IntSetIterator;

//-----------------------------------------------------------
// m a i n

void main()
{
    cout << "Inserting 9 7 9 10 9 8 into both bag and set"
         << endl;

// Create a bag and insert some elements into it.
    IntBag ibag;

    ibag.Add(9);
    ibag.Add(7);
    ibag.Add(9);
    ibag.Add(10);
    ibag.Add(9);
    ibag.Add(8);

// Display the contents of the bag using the iterator
    cout << "Bag has: ";

    IntBagIterator ibi(ibag);

    while(ibi)
        cout << ibi++ << " ";

    cout << endl;

// Repeat the same operations for a set.
// Note that sets do not allow duplicates.
    IntSet iset;
```

```
    iset.Add(9);
    iset.Add(7);
    iset.Add(9);
    iset.Add(10);
    iset.Add(9);
    iset.Add(8);

    cout << "Set has: ";

    IntSetIterator isi(iset);

    while(isi)
        cout << isi++ << " ";

    cout << endl;
}
```

Here is the output of the program shown in Listing 16.14:

```
Inserting 9 7 9 10 9 8  into both bag and set
Bag has: 9 7 9 10 9 8
Set has: 9 7 10 8
```

Queues and Deques

A queue is a *first-in first-out* (FIFO) data structure. Queues are useful as buffers between an originator of data and a recipient. For instance, if data from the keyboard is to be read by a program and the program cannot keep with the speed at which the user is entering text on the keyboard, a queue can be used to store the keystrokes. The program can then retrieve the keystrokes from the queue. The reason for using a queue is that the queue preserves the order in which the data was entered into it. A deque is a *d*ouble-*e*nded *que*ue, meaning you can insert and remove objects at both ends of the queue.

In computer science textbooks, the terms *head* and *tail* or *front* and *back* are used to refer to the two ends of a queue. Data is inserted at the front and retrieved from the back. In Borland C++ documentation, the term *right* is used to refer to the front and *left* means the back. Objects are inserted at the left and retrieved from the right. The deque class templates (in header file `<classlib\deques.h>`) include both `PutLeft` and `PutRight` as well as `GetLeft` and `GetRight` because deques allow insertion and removal at both ends. However, the queue class templates defined in `<classlib\queues.h>` provide only the `Put` and `Get` functions for inserting and removing objects.

Each queue and deque ADT container can be implemented using a vector or a doubly-linked list. For instance, to declare a queue implemented as a vector, you might use the template `TQueueAsVector<T>`, while the `TQueueAsDoubleList<T>` template gives you the corresponding linked list implementation for that queue. In addition to the variations in implementation, there are direct and indirect queue and deque containers with managed or unmanaged storage allocation schemes. Thus, Table 16.2 shows a total of eight queue containers, each with its own iterator class. There is an identical number of deque classes and deque iterators.

You can store any type of object in a queue or deque by using the class templates in the header files `<classlib\queues.h>` and `<classlib\deques.h>` respectively. However, for a queue or deque implemented using a doubly-linked list, operator == has to be defined for the objects being stored in the container. Listing 16.15 shows a sample program that stores `Event` objects in a queue implemented as a doubly-linked list.

As Listing 16.15 shows, the program inserts several `Event` objects using the `Put` function and then accesses each element in the queue with an iterator. Then the program removes the elements from the queue using the `Get` function. If you study the output of the program in Listing 16.15, you will see that the iterator returns the queue's contents back to front (or left to right in Borland's terminology), but the `Get` function returns the elements front to back, which is consistent with the expected behavior of a FIFO data structure.

Listing 16.15. TSTQUEUE.CPP. Sample program to demonstrate the Queue ADTs.

```
//--------------------------------------------------------------
// File: tstqueue.cpp
// Sample program that illustrates the queue ADT.

#include <classlib\queues.h>
#include <classlib\deques.h>
#include <iostream.h>


class Event
{
public:
    Event() : c_(' ') {}
    Event(char _c) : c_(_c) {}
```

```
    char c() const { return c_;}
    void c(const char _c) { c_ = _c;}

    operator==(const Event& e) const
    {
        return (c_ == e.c());
    }


private:
    char c_;
};

typedef TQueueAsDoubleList<Event>         EventQueue;
typedef TQueueAsDoubleListIterator<Event> EventQueueIterator;

void main()
{
    EventQueue evq;
    Event ev('A');

    evq.Put(ev);
    ev.c('B');
    evq.Put(ev);
    ev.c('C');
    evq.Put(ev);
    ev.c('D');
    evq.Put(ev);

// Use the iterator to display contents of the queue
    EventQueueIterator evqi(evq);

    cout << "Traversing the queue with an iterator: " << endl;
    while(evqi)
    {
        cout << evqi++.c();
    }
    cout << endl << endl;

// Retrieve the events one by one
```

continues

Listing 16.15. continued

```
    cout << "Retrieving contents of the queue with Get: "
         << endl;
    while(!evq.IsEmpty())
    {
        Event e = evq.Get();
        cout << e. c();
    }
    cout << endl;
}
```

The program shown in Listing 16.15 generates the following output:

```
Traversing the queue with an iterator:
DCBA

Retrieving contents of the queue with Get:
ABCD
```

The difference in order occurs because the iterator traverses the list from back to front, while the `Get` function returns elements from front to back.

Stacks

A stack is a *last-in first-out* (LIFO) data structure. This means that the last data saved is the first data retrieved. You "push" data onto a stack and you can "pop" the last item you pushed.

Stacks, like the queue classes, have two implementations: vector-based and list-based. Additionally, there are managed and unmanaged versions of both direct and indirect stacks. Together with the iterator classes that help you access the contents of the stack (without having to pop them off the stack), you will find a total of 16 class templates for the stack ADT.

The stack classes provide the functions `Push` and `Pop` for manipulating the stack. Call `Push` to place an object on the stack and `Pop` to remove the object that you inserted last. To access the contents of the stack without actually removing them, use an iterator.

Listing 16.16 shows a sample program that implements a simple four-function calculator. The calculator accepts commands in the reverse Polish notation (RPN), wherein you enter the operands followed by the operator. Thus, to add `1.29` and `3.99`, you would first enter the two numbers and then press the `+` key. The program pushes all operands on the stack and processes each operator by popping two operands from the stack and performing the arithmetic operation. The result is then pushed back on the stack. Pressing the = key pops the result off the stack and displays it. The program displays all the entries in the stack if the user presses t. To quit the program, the user has to press q or enter the string quit.

Listing 16.16. TSTSTK.CPP. An RPN calculator that demonstrates the Stack ADT.

```
//--------------------------------------------------------------
// File: tststk.cpp
// A simple calculator program that shows how to use the
// Stack container

#include <classlib\stacks.h>
#include <iostream.h>
#include <math.h>
#include <string.h>

// A direct stack of doubles
typedef TStackAsVector<double>         DStack;
typedef TStackAsVectorIterator<double> DStackIterator;

//--------------------------------------------------------------
// m a i n

void main()
{
// A simple Reverse Polish Notation (RPN) calculator
// that accepts one "token" per line

    DStack stk(256);

    char input[80];
    cout << "> ";
    cin >> input;
    short len = strlen(input);
    if(len > 4) len = 4;

    while(strnicmp("quit", input, len) != 0)
    {
        double op1 = 0.0, op2 = 0.0, r = 0.0;
```

continues

Listing 16.16. continued

```
        switch(input[0])
        {
            case '=':
                if(!stk.IsEmpty())
                    cout << stk.Pop() << endl;
                break;

            case 't':  // Show the entire stack
            case 'T':
                {
                    DStackIterator si(stk);
                    while(si)
                        cout << si++ << endl;
                }
                break;

            case '+':
            case '-':
            case '*':
            case '/':
                if(!stk.IsEmpty()) op2 = stk.Pop();
                if(!stk.IsEmpty()) op1 = stk.Pop();

                if(input[0] == '+') r = op1 + op2;
                if(input[0] == '-') r = op1 - op2;
                if(input[0] == '*') r = op1 * op2;
                if(op2 > 0.00001 &&
                   input[0] == '/') r = op1 / op2;

                cout << r << endl;

                if(!stk.IsFull()) stk.Push(r);
                break;

            default:
                if(!stk.IsFull())
                    stk.Push(atof(input));
             break;
        }

// Read next input
        cout << "> ";
```

```
        cin >> input;
        len = strlen(input);
        if(len > 4) len = 4;
    }
}
```

Here is a sample session with the calculator program shown in Listing 16.16:

```
> 77000
> 0.05
> t
77000
0.05
> *
3850
> 770
> -
3080
> 4
> /
770
> q
```

The program prompts for input by displaying the > symbol. Everything following the prompt is entered by the user. Also, the lines that do not start with a > are displayed by the program.

Simple Classes

In addition to the container classes, Borland C++ 4 also includes what might be called a set of simple classes. These are non-container classes that include the following:

- `string` An array of characters representing C-style null-terminated string. The `string` class lets you define and manipulate strings without worrying about how the memory for the character array is managed. Include `<cstring.h>` to use the `string` class.

- `TFile` Represents a file. Provides member functions to perform many file operations such as open, close, read from, and write to a file. To use the `File` class, include the header file `<classlib\file.h>`.

- `TDate` Represents a date with day, month, and year. Provides functions to manipulate and display the date. To use the `TDate` class, include the header file `<classlib\date.h>`.
- `TTime` A class that provides access to the current system time and includes basic time manipulation and display functions. Include the `<classlib\time.h>` header file to use the `TTime` class.

The following sections briefly describe these classes.

The *string* Class

Chapters 9 through 11 used the development of a string class as an example illustrating various concepts of object-oriented programming. Borland C++ also comes with a string class. The class is named `string` and is declared in `<cstring.h>`. Internally, the `string` class maintains an array of characters that is shared among multiple `string` objects that have the same value. When any of these `string` objects has to change the contents of the internal character array, the object makes a copy of the shared character array before making any changes. Borland refers to this technique as *copy-on-write* because multiple `strings` share data as long as the data is used in a read-only manner, but whenever a `string` has to "write" to the data it makes a copy of the data before writing.

Using the `string` class is straightforward. Listing 16.17 shows a small program that initializes a string and displays it.

Listing 16.17. TSTSTR.CPP. A sample program that demonstrates the `string` class.

```
//-------------------------------------------------------------
// File: tststr.cpp
// Example program showing how to use the "string" class

#include <cstring.h>
#include <iostream.h>

void main()
{
    try
    {
```

```
        string s;
        s = "Hello, World!";
        cout << s << endl;
    }
    catch(xalloc& xa)
    {
        cout << xa.why() << " : Failed to allocate "
             << xa.requested() << " bytes!" << endl;
    }
}
```

The program looks longer because I have included the exception-handling code to show how to catch exceptions raised by various member functions of the `string` class.

Exceptions from the *string* Class

As explained in Chapter 13, "Advanced Topics in C++," any code that might raise one or more exceptions should be in a `try` block, which is followed by one or more catch blocks. The `catch` block contains the code that gets executed if the exception occurs. In Listing 16.17, the string constructor and the assignment operator (=) might throw a `xalloc` exception. Therefore, these calls are inside a `try` block.

How can you tell that a function is going to throw an exception? The function's prototype provides this information. For instance, the prototypes of the default constructor and operator = for the `string` class, as they appear in `<cstring.h>`, are:

```
// string constructor

string() throw(xalloc);

//...
// Assignment operator
 string _FAR & operator = (const string _FAR &s) THROW_XALLOC;
```

The `throw(xalloc)` that is part of the string constructor's declaration indicates that the constructor may throw a `xalloc` exception. The operator = also throws this exception and this fact is indicated by the THROW_XALLOC macro. At the beginning of the header file `<cstring.h>`, THROW_XALLOC is defined to be `throw(xalloc)` provided you define the macro USE_THROW_SPECIFIERS when compiling the program. According to Borland, use of throw specifiers increases the size of functions, and therefore throw specifiers may not be beneficial to use with inline functions.

The exception `xalloc` is a class derived from `xmsg`; both classes are declared in the header file `<except.h>`. As the `catch` block in Listing 16.17 shows, information about the exception is passed to the exception-handling code through a `xalloc` object. The `why` member function of the `xalloc` object provides some informative message about the exception. The `xalloc` exception is thrown when memory allocation fails; therefore, it is up to you to decide the best way to handle the exception depending on how critically your application depends on that memory allocation.

Capabilities of the *string* Class

You can use the `string` class just as you use null-terminated C strings, but it is much easier to manage `string` objects because you do not have to worry about allocating and deallocating storage for the strings. As for manipulating strings, the `string` class includes member functions that provide capabilities similar to those of the string manipulation functions in the ANSI C library.

Here are some of the major capabilities of the `string` class:

- Constructors — There are over a dozen constructors available to create a string. A few interesting ones are the following:

  `string();` creates a string of zero length.

  `string(const string& s);` copy constructor.

  `string(char c, size_t n);` creates a string with the character `c` repeated `n` times.

  `string(HINSTANCE hinst, UINT id, int len=255);` creates a string from a string resource specified by the `id` (for use in Windows programs).

- Operators — Many string operations such as copying and concatenating that used to require function calls from the ANSI C library are now supported by operators. Here are some important operators:

  `string& operator=(const string& s);` copies from string `s` into this string (it appears on the left-hand side of the assignment).

  `string& operator+=(const string& s);` appends contents of `s` to this string.

`friend string operator+(const string& s, const char* cp);` concatenates string s and the null-terminated C string cp.

`char& operator[](size_t pos);` returns character at the position pos.

`char& operator()(size_t pos);` returns character at the position pos.

`friend int operator==(const string& s1, const string& s2);` returns 1 if the strings s1 and s2 are equal (two strings are equal if they have the same length and if the character arrays contain the same sequence of characters); otherwise returns 0.

`friend int operator<(const string& s1, const string& s2);` returns 1 if s1 is less than s2; returns 0 otherwise.

`friend int operator>(const string& s1, const string& s2);` returns 1 if s1 is greater than s2; 0 otherwise.

- Functions

Member functions of the `string` class provide functionalities similar to those of the ANSI C library's string manipulation functions. Here are some of the member functions:

`void ansi_to_oem();`
`void oem_to_ansi();` converts string from ANSI character set to OEM character set and back. (Used in Windows programs; see Chapter 20, "Displaying Text in Windows," for a discussion of character sets.)

`int contains(const char* cs) const;` returns 1 if the string contains the null-terminated C-style string cs; otherwise returns 0.

`size_t copy(char* cs, size_t n);` copies up to n characters from the string object into the character array cs and returns number of characters that were actually copied.

`const char* c_str() const;` returns a pointer to a null-terminated character array that holds the same characters as the string object.

`size_t find(const string& s);` locates the first occurrence of string s and returns starting position of s in this string. If s is not found, returns the constant NPOS.

`string& insert(size_t pos, const string& s);` inserts string s at position pos in the current string.

`int is_null() const;` returns 1 if the string is empty; returns 0 otherwise.

`size_t length() const;` returns the length of the string.

`istream& read_file(istream& is);` reads from input stream is until the stream reaches end-of-file (EOF) or a null character is read.

`istream& read_line(istream& is);` reads from input stream is until the stream reaches EOF or a newline character is read.

`istream& read_token(istream& is);` reads from input stream is until the stream reaches end-of-file (EOF) or a whitespace character is read.

`string& remove(size_t pos, size_t n);` removes n characters from the string beginning at position pos.

`string& replace(size_t pos, size_t n, const string& s);` replaces n characters at position pos with characters from string s.

`void resize(size_t n);` resizes the character array of the string to n characters, truncating or adding blanks as necessary.

`size_t rfind(const string& s);` locates the last occurrence of string s and returns starting position of s in this string. If s is not found, returns the constant NPOS.

`void to_lower();` converts the string to lowercase.

`void to_upper();` converts the string to uppercase.

There are also several interesting global functions that operate on string objects. Here are a few interesting ones:

`istream& getline(istream& is, string& s);` reads from input stream `is` into the string `s` until the stream encounters end-of-file or a newline is read.

`string to_lower(const string& s);` converts string `s` to lowercase.

`string to_upper(const string& s);` converts string `s` to uppercase.

TFile Class

The `TFile` class supports unbuffered binary read and write operations to disk files. `TFile` offers a number of member functions for manipulating files. It also includes a number of static functions such as `GetStatus` and `Rename` that you can use to query the status of a file or rename it without opening the file.

The `TFile` class makes it easy to open a file, read a block of data from the file into a buffer, and write data from a buffer to a file. Listing 16.18 shows how to do this by reading the first 256 characters from the file C:\CONFIG.SYS and displays it by writing the buffer to `stdout`. Notice how a `TFile` object is initialized with a file handle. In this example, the `fileno` function is used to get the handle corresponding to the C stream `stdout`.

Listing 16.18. TSTFILE.CPP. A sample program that demonstrates the `TFile` class.

```
//--------------------------------------------------------------------
// File: tstfile.cpp
// Sample program to illustrate the TFile class.

#include <classlib\file.h>
#include <iostream.h>
#include <stdio.h>

const size_t BUFSIZE = 256;

void main()
{
// Create a TFile associated with a specific file
    TFile f("c:\\config.sys");
```

continues

Listing 16.18. continued

```
// Read from the file
    char buf[BUFSIZE];
    int n = f.Read(buf, BUFSIZE);

// Associate a TFile with the standard output stream
    TFile sout(fileno(stdout));

// Write the buffer to the output stream
    sout.Write(buf, n);
}
```

Note that you have to link with the BIDSDBS.LIB library to successfully link the program shown in Listing 16.18 (assuming that you are using the small model). The program's output depends on the contents of your system's CONFIG.SYS file.

TDate Class

The `TDate` class lets you define a calendar day and set dates in different ways; also, it provides functions to manipulate and display dates. `TDate` is declared in the header file `<classlib\date.h>`.

To see how easy it is to use the `TDate` class, look at the sample program in Listing 16.19. The program first gets the current date and displays it, adding the weekday by calling the `WeekDay` function and converting it to a string by using the `DayName` function. To determine the date 45 days from now, the program simply adds 45 to the `TDate` object and displays it again.

Listing 16.19. TSTDATE.CPP. A sample program that demonstrates the `TDate` class.

```
//-------------------------------------------------------------
// File: tstdate.cpp
// Sample program to illustrate the TDate class.

#include <classlib\date.h>
#include <iostream.h>

void main()
{
```

```
// Create a TDate with today's date and display the date
    TDate today;
    cout << "Today is: "
         << TDate::DayName(today.WeekDay()) << ", "
         << today << endl;

    cout << "It is day number " << today.Day() << " of "
         << TDate::DaysInYear(today.Year()) << " days" << endl;

// Add 45 days to today's date
    today += 45;
    cout << "45 days from now it will be: "
         << TDate::DayName(today.WeekDay()) << ", "
         << today << endl;
}
```

To successfully link the program of Listing 16.19, you have to link with the BIDSDBS.LIB library (assuming that you are compiling in the small model). The program's output depends on what day you run it, but here is a typical output:

```
Today is: Sunday, October 3, 1993
It is day number 276 of 365 days
45 days from now it will be: Wednesday, November 17, 1993
```

TTime Class

Like the `TDate` class, the `TTime` class provides access to the current system time and allows you to manipulate time in various ways. Listing 16.20 shows an example program that demonstrates how you can use `TTime` to display the current time. Note that the hour and minute returned by the functions `HourGMT` and `MinuteGMT` correspond to the Greenwich Mean Time (GMT) as dictated by the setting of the environment variable TZ, which indicates the time zone and the daylight savings time zone for use in converting a local time to GMT.

Listing 16.20. TSTTIME.CPP. A sample program that demonstrates the `TTime` class.

```
//-------------------------------------------------------------
// date: tsttime.cpp
// Sample program to illustrate the TTime class.
```

continues

Listing 16.20. continued

```
#include <classlib\time.h>
#include <iostream.h>
#include <time.h>

void main()
{
// Create a TTime with today's time and display the time
// in local time as well as in GMT
    TTime now;
    cout << "Time now is: "
         << now << " " << tzname[0] << tzname[1] << " ("
         << now.HourGMT() << ":"
         << now.MinuteGMT() << ":"
         << now.Second() << " GMT)"
         << endl;

// Add 45 days to current time
    now += (long)45 * (long)24 * (long)3600;
    cout << "45 days from now it will be: "
         << now << endl;
}
```

Like the example program for the `TDate` class, you have to link with the BIDSDBS.LIB library to link the program shown in Listing 16.19. The output of the program depends on the exact date and time when you run the program. Here is a typical output:

```
Time now is: October 3, 1993 5:46:35 pm ESTEDT (21:46:35 GMT)
45 days from now it will be: November 17, 1993 4:46:35 pm
```

As you can see, when you display `TTime` objects, both the date and the time appear in the output. To turn off the printing of the date, call the static function `PrintDate` as follows:

```
TTime::PrintDate(0);
```

Summary

You can reduce the time needed to develop C++ programs by using C++ class libraries if the following statements are true:

- The library includes the classes that match your needs.
- The public interface to the classes is well-documented.

Borland C++ 4 includes a template-based container class library with over 200 classes that you can use in your applications. Most of the classes are for organizing objects in collections, with a few classes for modeling data (such as strings and time), and for supporting file I/O. The library includes support for archiving objects in files and restoring them later. This chapter summarizes the container classes and provides a number of example programs to illustrate how you might use these classes.

Another large class library in Borland C++ 4 is the ObjectWindows Library (OWL) with classes that are geared toward making Windows programming easier. The OWL classes are described in Chapter 18 after an introduction to Windows programming in Chapter 17, "Windows Programming with Borland C++."

V

Windows Programming

17

Windows Programming with Borland C++

Windows applications are easy to use and have a rich graphical user interface. Unfortunately for software developers, the ease-of-use comes at the expense of a complex *Application Programming Interface (API)* — the collection of functions that programmers use to write Windows applications. For example, the Windows API contains over 600 functions. Although you can get by with a small fraction of these, you are never quite sure if you are overlooking some function that does exactly what your application needs to do. In addition to coping with the sheer volume of information, you also have to take an entirely different approach when you write Windows applications. Despite these drawbacks, there are definite advantages to writing applications for Windows:

- Windows offers *device independence.* The same Windows application should display its output on any monitor from EGA to VGA and print on any printer from dot-matrix to laser.

- For the developer, Windows offers a variety of predefined user-interface components, including pushbuttons, menus, dialog boxes, lists, and edit windows.
- Windows includes an extensive interface to any graphics device (called Graphics Device Interface, GDI) for drawing graphics and text. In particular, the GDI lets you draw in your own coordinate system.

Until now, C has been the programming language of choice for writing Windows applications. Although C++ has been steadily gaining popularity, calling Windows functions from a C++ program is not as simple as calling, for instance, functions from the standard C library. This is because the compiler has to generate special object code when calling Windows functions, and Windows uses a different method of passing arguments to its functions. In other words, the C++ compiler has to support the requirements imposed by Windows. Like most MS-DOS C++ compilers, Borland C++ 4 supports Windows programming. In particular, Borland C++ 4 comes with OWL 2.0—a library of C++ classes that makes it easier to write Windows applications.

This chapter is designed as a quick introduction to writing Windows programs with Borland C++, OWL, and the container class library that was described in Chapter 16, "Using the Borland C++ Class Libraries." This will not be a complete tutorial. To fully understand this chapter, you need to already be familiar with the basics of object-oriented programming, C++, and Windows programming, and have browsed through Borland's documentation. If you need further information on object-oriented programming or Windows programming, you should consult one of the books listed in the bibliography that appears at the end of this book.

The chapter starts with a small example program—the Windows version of the classic "Hello, World!" program—that illustrates the basics of Windows programming with OWL. Following the example, I describe `AppExpert` and `ClassExpert`—two new tools introduced in Borland C++ 4 that are designed to take care of some routine chores in writing Windows applications.

Isn't Microsoft Windows Already Object-Oriented?

The Microsoft Windows environment was promoted as having an object-oriented architecture, so what do programmers gain by accessing the Windows environment through a layer of C++ classes such as those in the ObjectWindows Library?

Even though Windows supports the concept of certain objects, the data encapsulation and inheritance rely on the programmer's discipline. When you write Windows programs in C, you can access and modify all parts of the structures that represent the objects. Also, anyone who has written a Windows program in C knows that the programmer must attend to myriad details in order for the application and its windows to look and behave properly.

An object-oriented layer in an object-oriented programming language such as C++ can help tremendously, simply by hiding many unnecessary details. Basically, that's what you get when you use C++ classes that support Windows programming. The Windows environment has an underlying object-oriented architecture, but the Windows programming interface is procedural. Using a properly designed set of C++ classes makes the programming interface more object-oriented.

Windows Programming with OWL

The primary purpose of the OWL classes is to provide a complete *application framework* for building Microsoft Windows applications. The collection of classes in OWL are referred to as a framework because they essentially provide all the components for skeletal programs that can be easily fleshed out into complete Windows applications.

Even though the Borland class libraries (OWL and the container classes) include most classes that are necessary to build the user interface and represent various data types, it is easier to build an application if you follow a well-defined architecture (*structural model*) for the application. The *Model-View-Controller (MVC) architecture* prevalent in the Smalltalk-80 programming language is a good candidate architecture for Windows applications.

Model-View-Controller (MVC) Architecture

As Figure 17.1 shows, the MVC architecture separates the application into three separate layers:

1. *Model* refers to the *application layer* where all application-dependent objects reside. For example, in a drawing program, this is the layer that maintains the graphics objects.
2. *View* is the *presentation layer* which presents the application's data to the user. This layer extracts information from the model and displays the information in windows. In a drawing program, this layer uses the list of graphics objects from the model and renders them in a window. Also, the view provides the windows in the application's graphical user interface.
3. *Controller* is the *interaction layer* which provides the interface between the input devices (such as keyboard and mouse) and the view and model layers.

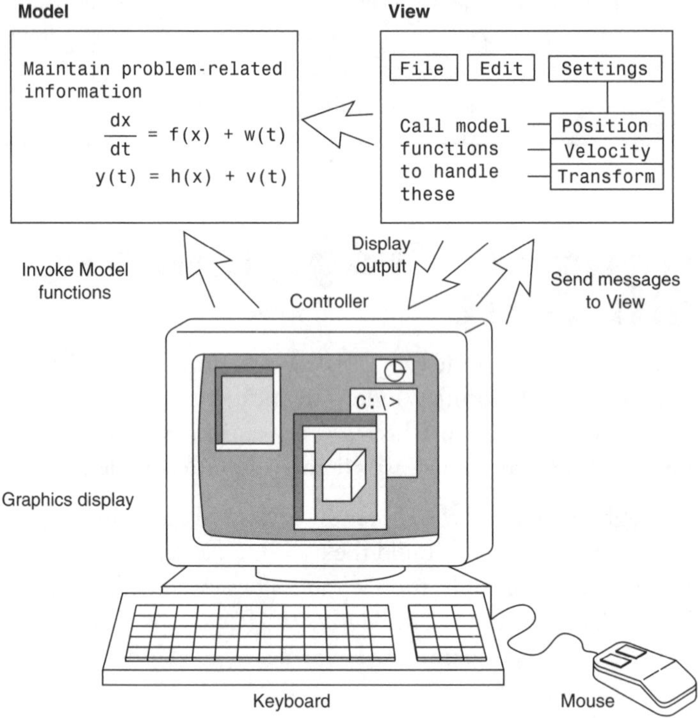

Figure 17.1. MVC architecture of Smalltalk-80.

The MVC architecture does an excellent job of separating the responsibilities of the objects in the system. The application-specific details are insulated from the user interface. Also, the user interface itself is broken down into two parts with the presentation handled by the view and the interaction by the controller.

When building Windows applications using OWL, you do not have to follow the MVC model strictly. For instance, when you use the OWL classes, you will find it difficult to separate the view and controller layers. As shown in Figure 17.2, your application would consist of a model and an associated view-controller pair. Figure 17.2 also shows the usual interactions in Smalltalk-80's MVC architecture. When performing a requested task, the controller accepts input and invokes the appropriate function from the model. When the work is finished, the function in the model sends messages to the view and controller. The view updates the display in response to this message, accessing the model for further information, if necessary. Thus, the model has a view and a controller, but it never directly accesses either of them. The view and controller, on the other hand, access the model's functions and data, when necessary.

MVC Architecture and OWL

OWL supports the MVC architecture through its Document/View model (the term is used here to mean a representation) of applications. OWL's `TDocument` class corresponds to the model of MVC architecture while the `TView` class is the view-controller pair. The `TDocument` class provides the storage for a document's data, and the `TView` class provides the capability to view and manipulate it. The `AppExpert` tool, described later in this chapter, can automatically generate the code for an application that uses a document/view model.

As you will see in the following example, most of the OWL classes contribute to the view and controller pair. You would typically use your own classes as well as the general-purpose classes, such as strings, lists, and arrays, in the application's model layer.

A Windows Application Using OWL

To illustrate how OWL provides a framework for a Windows application, the following sections present an example program that uses OWL to display `Hello, World!` in a window. Even with OWL, you have to attend to many details when writing a Microsoft Windows application. However, to write a more complex Windows application, such as a graphics animation, you would still use the same steps as in this simple example.

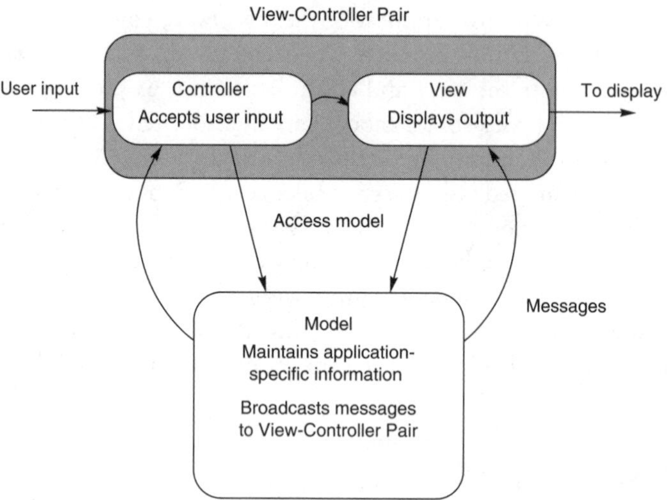

Figure 17.2. Interactions among model, view, and controller in the MVC architecture.

The *HelloApp* Class

All OWL-based Microsoft Windows applications rely on a class derived from the `TApplication` class that models the entire application. Listing 17.1 shows the file HELLO.CPP, which implements the class `HelloApp` that models our sample application. In the `HelloApp` class, you should define at least one member function—`InitMainWindow`—to initialize the main window of the application. When you use the MVC architecture, the following are the basic steps for your application:

1. Create a model for the application. For this application, the model is a class named `HelloModel`, defined in the header file HELLOMDL.H (see Listing 17.2). The model class will hold all application-specific data—in this case, the data is a string to be displayed in a window.

2. Create a view and store a pointer to the model in the view. In this case, the view class is named `HelloView`, and it is declared in the header file `HELLOVW.H` (Listing 17.3). The `HelloView` class is derived from the `TFrameWindow` class of the ObjectWindows library.

3. Derive an application class from `TApplication` and, in the `InitMainWindow` function of the application class, create the model and the view.

4. Write an `OwlMain` function. In that function, create an instance of the application class and call the `Run` function to get the application going. Essentially, the

application class, derived from `TApplication`, provides the functionality of the controller in the MVC architecture.

Listing 17.1. HELLO.CPP. The hello application based on the MVC architecture.

```
//-------------------------------------------------------------
//  File:  hello.cpp
//
//  A Windows application that uses the ObjectWindows Library
//-------------------------------------------------------------
#include "hellovw.h"
#include "hellomdl.h"

class HelloApp: public TApplication
{
public:
// Constructor that simply calls the base class constructor

    HelloApp(LPSTR name) : TApplication(name) {}

    ~HelloApp() { delete m;}

// Function to initialize application's main window
    void InitMainWindow();

private:
    HelloModel *m;
};

//-------------------------------------------------------------
//  H e l l o A p p : : I n i t M a i n W i n d o w

void HelloApp::InitMainWindow()
{
    m = new HelloModel();
    MainWindow = new HelloView(m);
    MainWindow->SetIcon(this, "HELLO_ICON");
    MainWindow->AssignMenu("MainMenu");
    MainWindow->Attr.AccelTable = "MainAccelTable";
}
```

continues

Listing 17.1. continued

```
//-----------------------------------------------------------------
//  O w l M a i n
//
//  Create an instance of the application and "run" it.


int OwlMain(int, char**)
{
    HelloApp hello_world("Hello, World!");
    int status = hello_world.Run();
    return status;
}
```

The *HelloModel* Class

An application's model is supposed to store data unique to the application. In this case, the application is simple enough that the `Hello, World!` string could have been displayed directly from the view class. However, a model class is used here to illustrate how to build a realistic application using the MVC architecture. This application's model, the `HelloModel` class (Listing 17.2), contains the string to be displayed in the window. The string is stored in an instance of a `string` class (declared in the header file `<cstring.h>`) that is created in the constructor of the `HelloModel` class. The view class uses the member function named `get_string` to obtain a pointer to this `string` instance.

Listing 17.2. HELLOMDL.H. Definition of the `HelloModel` class.

```
//-----------------------------------------------------------------
//  File:  hellomdl.h
//
//  The "model" for the "hello" application.  In this case,
//  the model simply stores a string to be displayed in a window

#if !defined(_ _HELLOMDL_H)
#define _ _HELLOMDL_H

#include <cstring.h>
```

```
class HelloModel
{
public:
    HelloModel() { p_str = new string("Hello, World!");}

    ~HelloModel() { delete p_str;}

    string* get_string() { return p_str;}

private:
    string *p_str;
};

#endif
```

The *HelloView* Class

The `HelloView` class, declared in the file HELLOVW.H (Listing 17.3) and implemented in HELLOVW.CPP (Listing 17.4), provides the view for this application. The `HelloView` class is responsible for displaying the message stored in the `HelloModel` class in a window. `HelloView` is derived from the `TFrameWindow` class, which is designed to serve as the main window of an application. The view class stores a pointer to the model; through this pointer the view can access the model as needed.

The most important function of the `HelloView` class is called `Paint`. OWL automatically calls the `Paint` function for a window whenever the window needs repainting. (You will soon see how the painting is done.)

The `About` function is a Windows message response function—the association between a message and its response function is made in the HELLOVW.CPP file (Listing 17.4) by using the `DEFINE_RESPONSE_TABLE1` macro. As you can see in Listing 17.4, the `About` function displays a dialog box with information about the application.

The last line in the body of the `HelloView` class in Listing 17.4:

```
DECLARE_RESPONSE_TABLE(HelloView);
```

is another step that you need to follow to ensure that messages intended for a window get handled properly.

Associating Message Response Functions with Windows Messages

Microsoft Windows works by sending messages to the windows that constitute an application's user interface. OWL uses the idea of *message response functions*. Each message response function is associated with a specific Windows message, and OWL automatically calls that response function when the corresponding Windows message occurs. You include the `DECLARE_RESPONSE_TABLE` macro in the declaration of the window class—a class derived from `TWindow` or `TFrameWindow`. Next, you associate each message response function with a Windows message through a response table enclosed in the `DEFINE_RESPONSE_TABLE1` and `END_RESPONSE_TABLE` macros.

Listing 17.3. HELLOVW.H. Declaration of the `HelloView` class.

```
//-------------------------------------------------------------
//  File:  hellovw.h
//
//  The "view" for the "hello" application.  In this case,
//  the view is a window where the string from the model
//  is displayed.

#if !defined(__HELLOVW_H)
#define __HELLOVW_H

// Include necessary header files

#include <owl\decframe.h>
#include <owl\dialog.h>
#include <owl\applicat.h>
#include <owl\dc.h>
#include "hellores.h"  // Resource identifiers for application

class HelloModel;

class HelloView : public TFrameWindow
{
public:
```

```
    HelloView(HelloModel *a_model);

// Declare functions for handling messages from Windows
    void Paint(TDC& dc, int, TRect &r);
    void About();

protected:
    void EvSize(UINT, TSize&);

private:
    HelloModel *model;
    int         w, h;    // Width and height of window

DECLARE_RESPONSE_TABLE(HelloView);
};

#endif
```

Listing 17.4 shows the implementation of the HelloView class. In this listing you see one of the required steps of Windows programming with OWL: the definition of a message response table. The message response table associates a function table with a Windows message so that Windows calls the specified function in response to the associated message. Because HelloView has two message response functions, EvSize and About, the message response table is defined as follows:

```
DEFINE_RESPONSE_TABLE1(HelloView, TFrameWindow)
    EV_WM_SIZE,
    EV_COMMAND(IDM_ABOUT, About),
END_RESPONSE_TABLE;
```

You start the response table with a DEFINE_RESPONSE_TABLE1 macro that takes two arguments: the name of the class for which the response table is being defined and the name of its base class. An END_RESPONSE_TABLE macro followed by a semicolon marks the end of the response table.

In the response table's body, you list the Windows messages for which this class provides response functions. Each message name is defined by a macro with a name that has an EV_ prefix followed by the standard Windows term for that message. Consequently, EV_WM_SIZE indicates that this class handles WM_SIZE messages sent by Windows when the user resizes a window. The name of the message response function is implicit in this case: EvSize.

The next entry, EV_COMMAND(IDM_ABOUT, About), ensures that the About function is called when the menu item identified by the constant IDM_ABOUT is selected. The About function must be explicitly associated with a menu item because you, as the programmer, may choose to associate any function with a message generated by a menu selection. IDM_ABOUT is a constant defined in the HELLORES.H header file shown in Listing 17.6. Note that each line in the response table, including the last line, must end with a comma.

In Listing 17.4, the Paint function contains the code that displays a message in the application's main window. The Paint function gets the message string from the model by calling the get_string function of the HelloModel class:

```
void HelloView::Paint(TDC& dc, int, TRect&)
{
//...
// Get the message to be displayed
    String* p_string = model->get_string();

// Display the message ...
}
```

The actual rendering of the string is done by calling member functions of the TDC class.TDC provides a *device context* (or DC in Windows terminology). The DC holds information that controls the appearance of drawings created by Windows drawing functions. Notice that the Paint function is called with a reference to a TDC as an argument. In Paint, the TDC is used as follows:

```
    dc.SetTextAlign(TA_BASELINE | TA_CENTER);
    dc.SetBkMode(TRANSPARENT);

// ...

// Draw the string
    dc.TextOut(w/2, h/2, p_string->c_str(), len);
```

Graphics attributes, such as alignment of text and the background mode, are set by calling member functions of the TDC class SetTextAlign and SetBkMode, respectively.

The text string is displayed by calling the TextOut function. In the call to TextOut, w/2 denotes the x-coordinate of the location in the window where the text output starts, h denotes the height of the window, and len is the number of characters in the text string being displayed.

The EvSize member function sets up the variables w and h that denote the width and height of the window, respectively, as follows:

```
// Get window size
    TRect r;
    GetClientRect(r);

    w = r.Width();
    h = r.Height();
```

After getting the width and height of the window, `EvSize` invalidates the entire window—this indicates that the entire window should be repainted in response to a `WM_PAINT` message.

If you want to draw other graphics in the window, you can call other member functions of the TDC class. Chapter 18, "Using the ObjectWindows Library," summarizes the OWL classes for user interface, and Chapter 19, "Graphics Programming with OWL," discusses the drawing functions from the TDC class. Chapter 20, "Displaying Text in Windows," covers the text output functions in detail.

Listing 17.4. HELLOVW.CPP. Implementation of the `HelloView` class.

```
//-------------------------------------------------------------
//  File:  hellovw.cpp
//
//  The "view" layer for the "hello" application
//-------------------------------------------------------------
#include "hellovw.h"
#include "hellomdl.h"

DEFINE_RESPONSE_TABLE1(HelloView, TFrameWindow)
    EV_WM_SIZE,
    EV_COMMAND(IDM_ABOUT, About),
END_RESPONSE_TABLE;

//-------------------------------------------------------------
//  H e l l o V i e w : : H e l l o V i e w
//  Constructor for HelloView class

HelloView::HelloView(HelloModel* a_model) : model(a_model),
                                   TFrameWindow(0, "Hello", 0)
{
}
//-------------------------------------------------------------
```

continues

Listing 17.4. continued

```
//  H e l l o V i e w : : E v S i z e
//  Handle WM_SIZE events

void HelloView::EvSize(UINT, TSize&)
{
// Get window size
    TRect r;
    GetClientRect(r);

    w = r.Width();
    h = r.Height();

// Invalidate window so that the contents are redrawn
    Invalidate(TRUE);
}
//------------------------------------------------------------
//  H e l l o V i e w : : P a i n t
//  Draw contents of window

void HelloView::Paint(TDC& dc, int, TRect&)
{
    dc.SetTextAlign(TA_BASELINE | TA_CENTER);
    dc.SetBkMode(TRANSPARENT);

// Get the message to be displayed
    string* p_string = model->get_string();

// Get number of characters in string
    int len = p_string->length();

// Display string roughly at the center of window
    dc.TextOut(w/2, h/2, p_string->c_str(), len);
}
//------------------------------------------------------------
//  H e l l o A p p : : A b o u t
//  Display the "About..." box

void HelloView::About()
{
    TDialog *p_about = new TDialog(this, "ABOUTHELLO");
```

```
    GetApplication()->ExecDialog(p_about);
}
```

Building the Application

Once you have the header and source files ready, you must compile and link the source files to create a Microsoft Windows application. One method for doing so begins with preparing the source and header files in a DOS window using a text editor. Then run Borland C++ 4 under Windows and define a project that lists all necessary source files and libraries that the application needs. Of course, you could also prepare and edit the source files directly in Borland C++ 4 under Windows. Then you would be able to carry out the entire *edit-compile-link-debug cycle* of software development from within Borland C++ 4.

The companion disk has the project file (HELLO.IDE) that you need to build the example program. The disk also includes all the files needed to build the executable HELLO.EXE. In particular, here are two of the text files that you need:

- HELLO.DEF (Listing 17.5). This file is known as the *module definition* file and is needed to build Microsoft Windows applications.
- HELLORES.H (Listing 17.6). This file defines constants that identify resources such as menu item numbers.

Another important file that you need to build a Windows program is a resource file. For the `HELLO` application, the companion disk has the resource file HELLO.RES. I prepared it using the Resource Workshop program (WORKSHOP.EXE) included with Borland C++.

With the project file HELLO.IDE, you should be able to build HELLO.EXE by selecting Make all from the Project menu. Once the program is successfully built, you can add it to, the Windows Program Manager by selecting New... from the Program Manager's File menu. Once installed in this way, you can run HELLO.EXE by double-clicking its icon in the Program Manager window.

Listing 17.5. HELLO.DEF. Module definition file for HELLO.EXE.

```
NAME            Hello
DESCRIPTION     'Hello from ObjectWindows Library (OWL)'
```

continues

Listing 17.5. continued

```
EXETYPE          WINDOWS
STUB             'WINSTUB.EXE'

CODE      PRELOAD MOVEABLE DISCARDABLE
DATA      PRELOAD MOVEABLE MULTIPLE

HEAPSIZE  8192
STACKSIZE 8192
```

Listing 17.6. HELLORES.H. Resource identifiers for HELLO.EXE.

```
//----------------------------------------------------------
//  File: hellores.h
//
//  Declare the resource IDs for the Hello application
//  In this case, we have only one.

#define IDM_ABOUT 200
```

Testing HELLO.EXE

Once you have successfully compiled and linked the sample application HELLO.EXE, you can run it under Microsoft Windows by typing the following command at the DOS prompt:

```
win hello
```

If you are already running Windows, you can start HELLO.EXE from the Run option in the File menu of the Program Manager.

Figure 17.3 shows the output from the program. If you resize the window, `Hello, World!` should appear centered in the window. Note that the About Hello… dialog also appears in Figure 17.3.

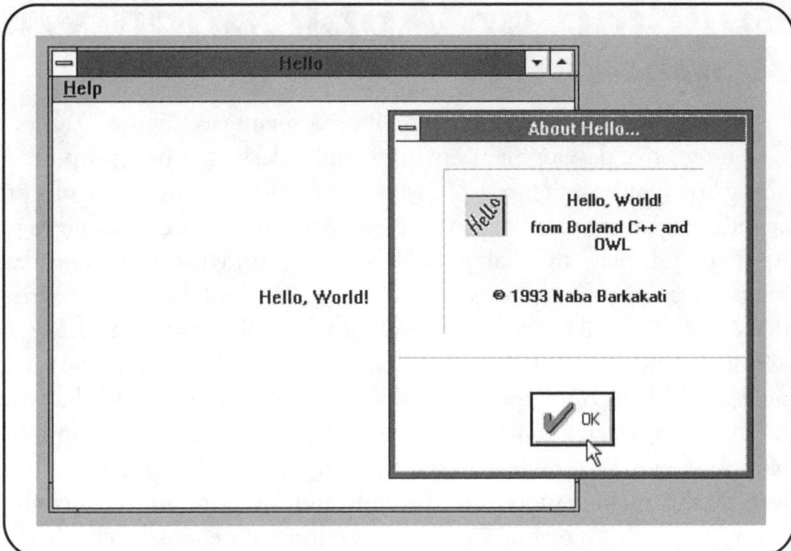

Figure 17.3. Hello, World! from OWL-based HELLO.EXE.

Tools for Building Applications

Now that you have seen an example of a Microsoft Windows application built manually using OWL classes, here are two tools that help build the entire application's framework automatically. The AppExpert and ClassExpert tools, introduced in Borland C++ 4, reduce the programmer's burden by providing a way to generate much of the code that almost all Windows applications share. AppExpert generates the code for a standard set of classes that are necessary for a Windows application. ClassExpert lets you add code to the existing classes as well as declare and define any new classes that your application might need. The best way to learn about AppExpert and ClassExpert is to try them out yourself. The following sections provide an overview of these two new tools.

Building an Application with AppExpert

AppExpert appears as an item in the Project menu (see Figure 17.4) of the Borland C++ interactive development environment. Selecting it brings up the New Project dialog box shown in Figure 17.5, where you must enter the name of a project for the application you are about to generate with AppExpert. After you enter a project name, AppExpert displays the dialog window shown in Figure 17.6. This dialog window offers a host of options through which you can control the features of the application that AppExpert will generate. Borland calls these dialog boxes a *settings notebook.* The left side of the notebook shows a number of topics that denote the categories of options available in AppExpert. The right side shows the options that you can set for the currently selected topic. For instance, Figure 17.6 shows the options for the Application topic. You can select a model for the application and one or more of a set of features that include support for printing and "drag and drop" capability (explained later). You can turn to a new page in the settings notebook by clicking another topic from the list of topics; the right side will show a new page with the options for the selected topic.

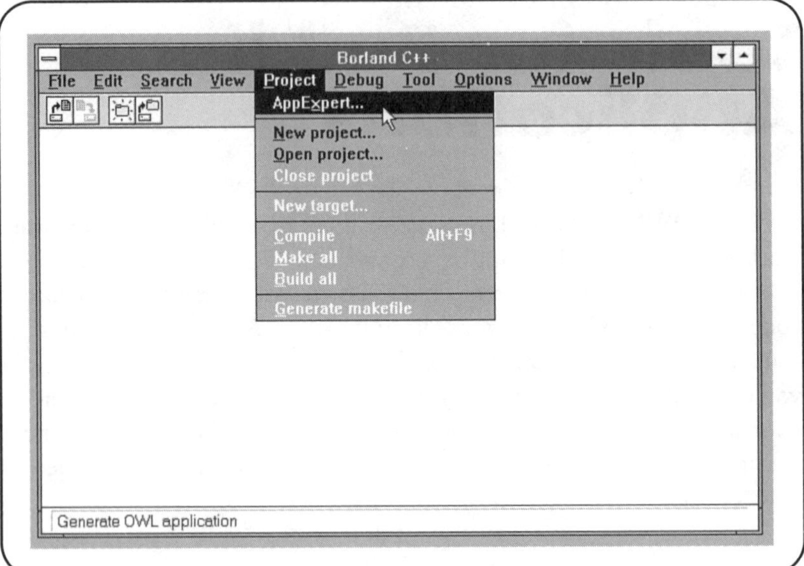

Figure 17.4. Accessing AppExpert from the Project menu.

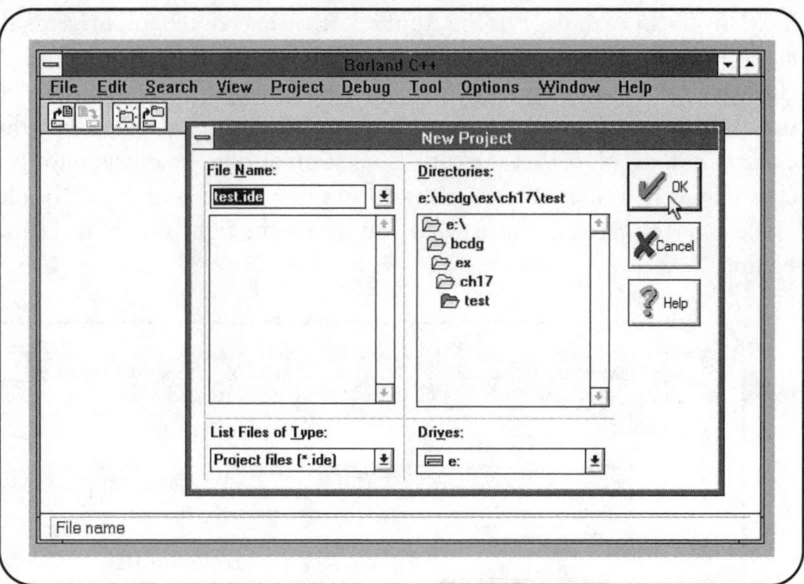

Figure 17.5. Entering a project name for the application to be generated by AppExpert.

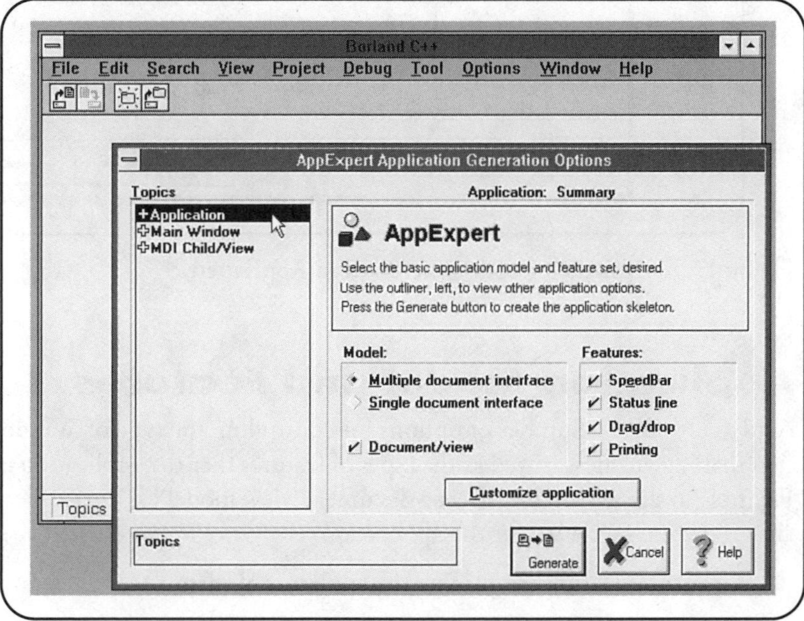

Figure 17.6. Top-level options for the application in AppExpert.

The left side of each page in the AppExpert settings notebook presents the topics in an outline format, with a plus sign (+) before each topic. Clicking the plus sign (+) changes it to a minus sign (-) and reveals an indented list of subtopics. Figure 17.7 shows the result of opening up the Application category and selecting the code generation options. Note that the code generation options enable you to specify certain class names as well as the names and locations of the source and header files that implement the classes. This is what you see on the right side of the settings page in Figure 17.7.

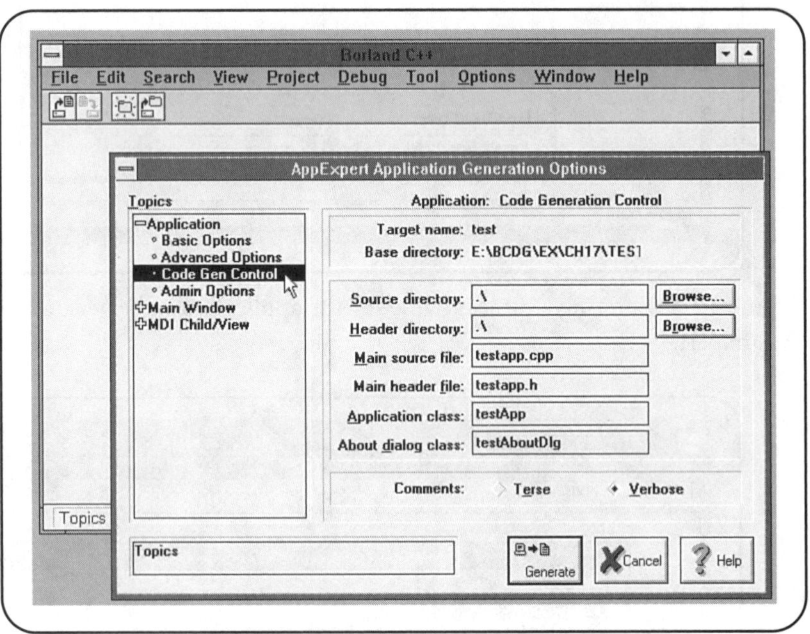

Figure 17.7. Options for code generation in AppExpert.

Application Model and Features

AppExpert offers a number of options for controlling the type of Windows application that it generates, as well as the types of features that the application can have. As Figure 17.6 shows, you can select a document/view model for the application, which creates three C++ classes for the application:

- A document class representing the application's data
- A view class that displays and manipulates the data
- A document manager class that maintains pairs of document and view objects

In addition to selecting the document/view model, you can also specify one of two different styles for the application:

- *Single Document Interface* (SDI) represents a style in which each child window appears by itself outside the main window of the application, overlapping the main window and the sibling windows.
- *Multiple Document Interface* (MDI) limits all child windows to the confines of the application's main window. This is the type of interface you find in most Windows applications, including Borland C++ 4, Microsoft Excel, and Microsoft Word for Windows. In these applications, each open document appears in its own window, but all these windows are managed by a single main window that contains them.

You can also enable or disable one or more of the following features for the application:

- *SpeedBar*: Selecting this option will include support for displaying a bar (also referred to as a *toolbar*) containing a number of pushbuttons with icons like the toolbar that appears under the menubar in Borland C++ 4 (see Figure 17.6).
- *Status line*: This option enables the support for displaying a status message in an area underneath the main window. You can see an example of a status line at the bottom of the main window in the interactive development environment.
- *Drag/Drop*: Selecting this option will allow the generated application to open and display files that are dragged and dropped on it in the File Manager's window. With drag and drop enabled, if you run File Manager and drag the icon of a file (press down the left mouse button and move the mouse without releasing the button) and release the mouse button when the icon is over the generated application's icon, the application should run with the dropped file as the initial file to be displayed.
- *Printing*: If you select this option, the generated application will support printing the documents it displays.

To further customize the application, you can either click the button labeled Customize application or click the plus sign prefix for the Application topic shown in the left side of the AppExpert option window (see Figure 17.6). Of the three subtopics under Application, Basic Options allows you to set the application's name and enable or disable the support for a help file. If you enable support for a help file, AppExpert will automatically generate a help file with a standard format, and include a call to WinHelp to display the help file.

The Code Gen Control options, shown in Figure 17.7, let you specify the directories where the generated source and header files should be placed. Also, you can provide the names of the main source file, main header file, the application class, and the application's dialog class.

The third subtopic under Application, Admin Options, sets the application's version number and also provides a copyright notice and information about the program's author (see Figure 17.8). AppExpert embeds the author information and the copyright notice in all source and header files that it generates. AppExpert also places this information into the VERSIONINFO resource in the resource file (for the test application this will be the TESTAPP.RC file) from which the application extracts and displays this information in the About dialog box.

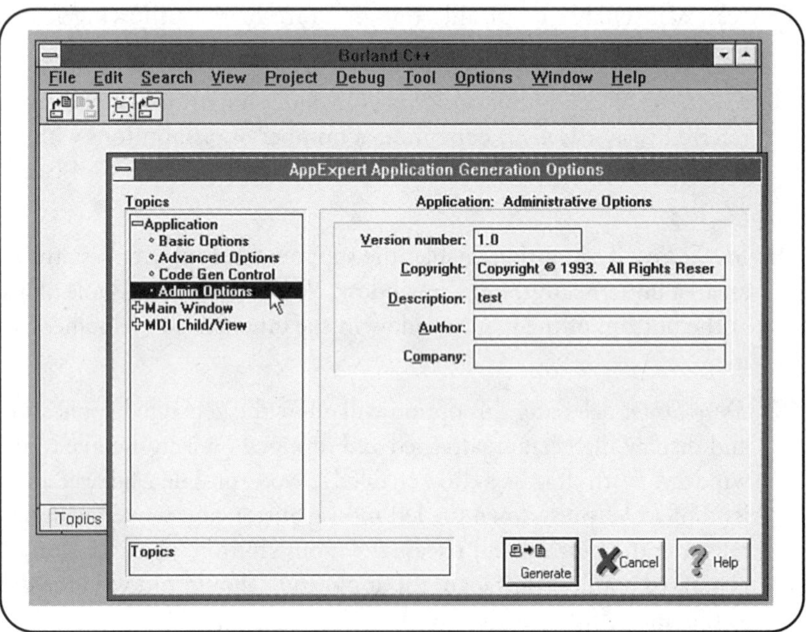

Figure 17.8. Specifying version numbers and author information in AppExpert.

Main Window Styles

The second category of AppExpert options deals with the appearance of the application's main window. The top-level options for this category (see Figure 17.9) allow you to set the window's title and background color. To select a background color, click the button labeled Background color… and pick a color from a color selection dialog box.

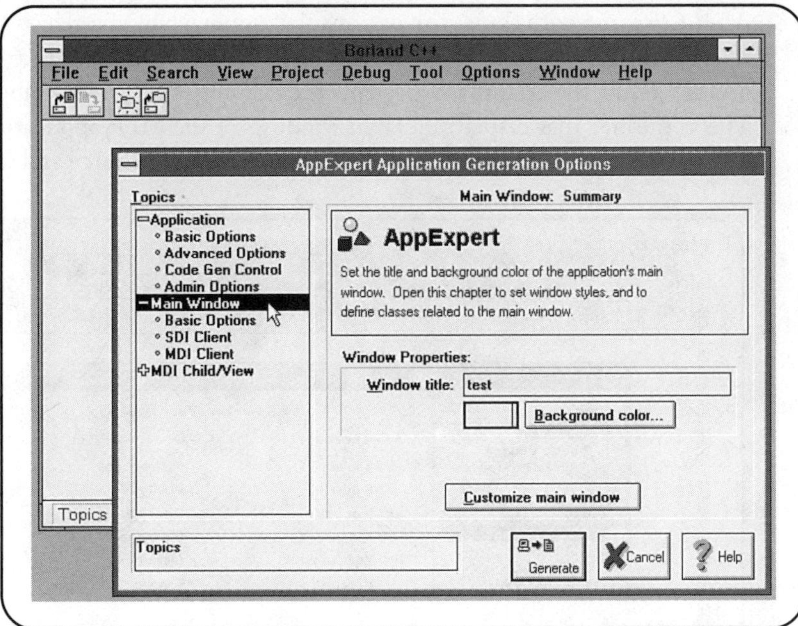

Figure 17.9. Top-level options for the application's main window in AppExpert.

Figure 17.9 also shows the three subtopics under the Main Window topic:

- *Basic Options* enables you to specify the main window's style. Figure 17.10 shows the default settings of the 12 items that you can turn on or off to adjust the style of the window. These style elements correspond to setting the window style using constants such as `WS_CLIPSIBLINGS`, `WS_CLIPCHILDREN`, `WS_VISIBLE`, `WS_MINIMIZE`, `WS_MAXIMIZE`, `WS_CAPTION`, `WS_BORDER`, `WS_DLGFRAME`, `WS_MINIMIZEBOX`, `WS_MAXIMIZEBOX`, `WS_VSCROLL`, and `WS_HSCROLL`, which are defined in the Windows header file `<windows.h>`.
- *SDI Client* category shows the options that apply when you select the Single Document Interface style (see Figure 17.6) for your application. These options define the class that represents the client area of an SDI application. If you have selected a Document/view model for the application, you can also specify the name of the document class and the default extension of files (representing a document's data) that the application can display in the SDI client area.

- *MDI Client* category shows the options that apply when you select the Multiple Document Interface style for your application (see Figure 17.6). These options define the class that represents the client area of an MDI application. This is the area that displays all child windows of the MDI application. You can set the name of the class as well as the names of the source and header files.

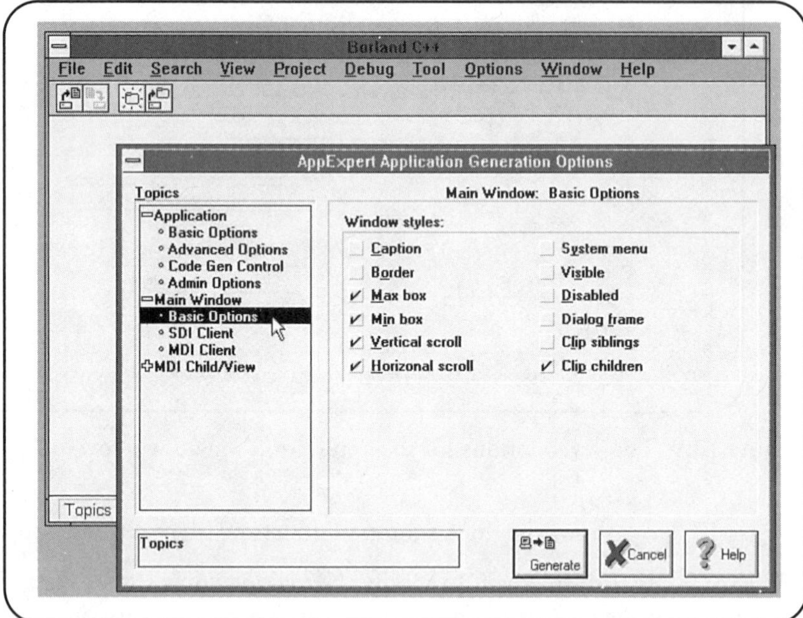

Figure 17.10. Basic options for the application's main window in AppExpert.

MDI Child Window Options

The third set of AppExpert options enables you to specify the name of the class representing the child windows that display documents inside the MDI client window. As the dialog box in Figure 17.11 shows, you can specify the name of the class as well as the names of the header and source files. Clicking the button labeled Customize child and view (or selecting Basic Options from the Topics area) will display another set of options that are similar to those in the SDI Client category under the Main Window topic. These options allow you to specify the document class associated with the MDI child window class and the default file extension of files that the application may display in the MDI child windows.

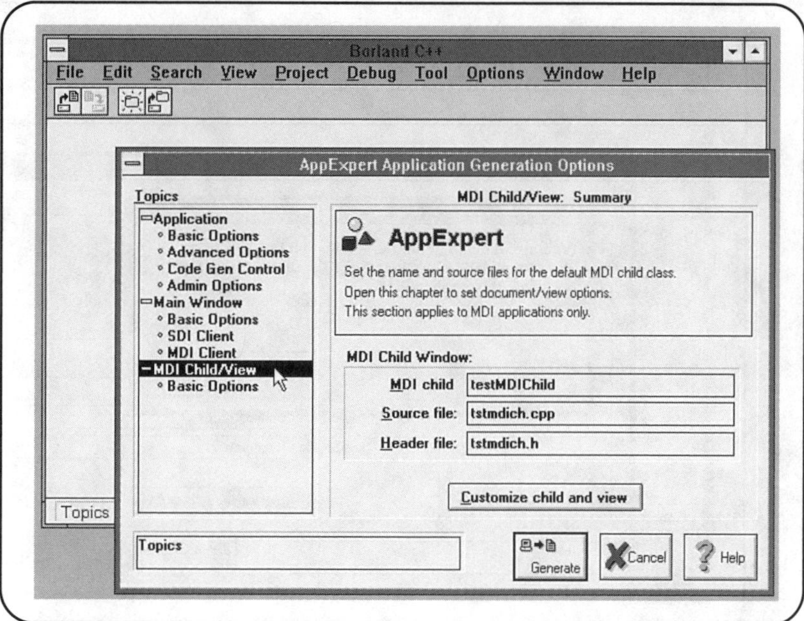

Figure 17.11. Options for the child window class in an MDI application.

Generating the Application

After you have set all the options to customize the application and you want AppExpert to generate the code for the application, click the Generate button that appears at the bottom of the dialog window. AppExpert prompts you for confirmation (see Figure 17.12) and when you click the Yes button (or press Enter), AppExpert will generate all source, header, and support files necessary to build the application.

After AppExpert finishes generating the files, you will return to Borland C++ 4 with a project set up for the new application. Figure 17.13 shows the contents of the project window for an application named TEST that was generated using the default settings in AppExpert. By default, AppExpert generates an MDI application with the Document/view model that allows the user to view and edit text files. The application's main window has a status area and a toolbar with a set of buttons that facilitate opening a file, saving a file, cutting and pasting, searching and replacing, printing, and getting help. AppExpert also generates a standard help file by default.

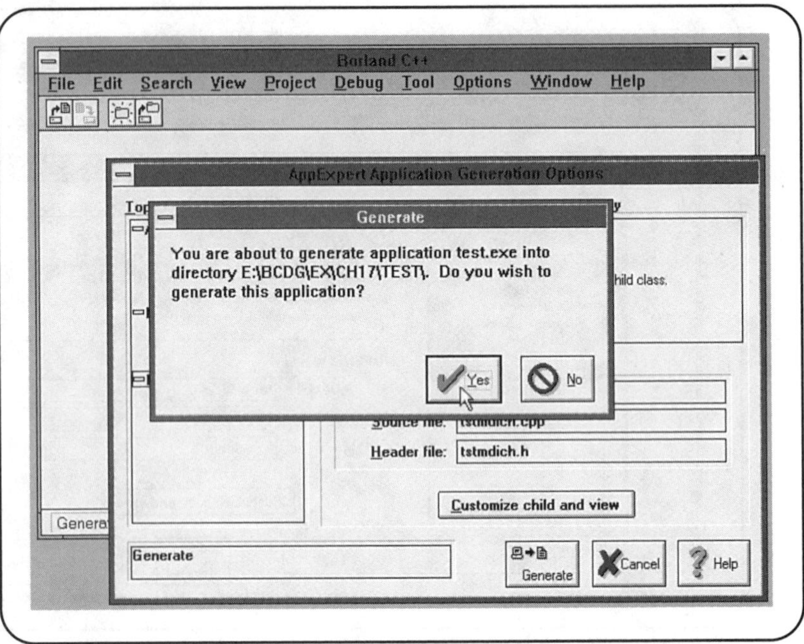

Figure 17.12. Generating code for an application with AppExpert.

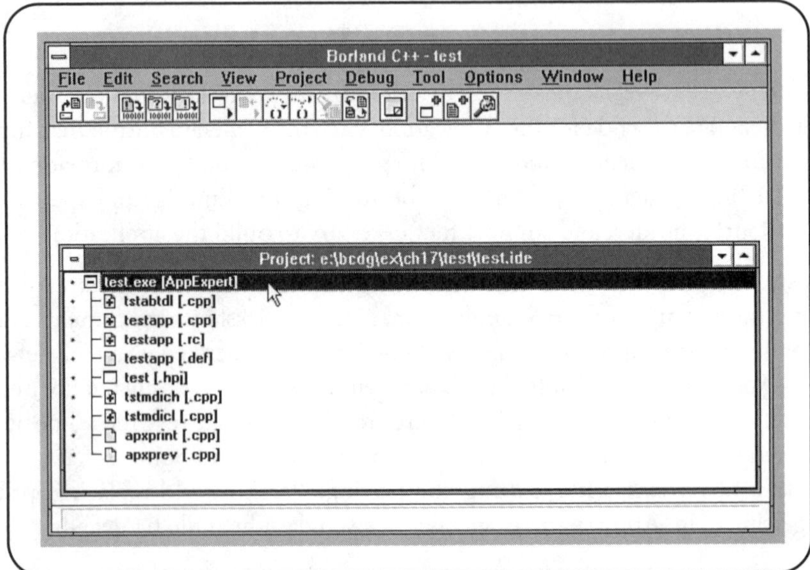

Figure 17.13. The project for a test application generated with the default settings in AppExpert.

For the TEST application, AppExpert generates the following 12 source and header files:

- TESTAPP.CPP and TESTAPP.H are the source and header files for the application class derived from the OWL class `TApplication`.
- TSTABTDL.CPP and TSTABTDL.H are the source and header files for a dialog class derived from the OWL class `TDialog`. This dialog appears when the user selects the About... item from the application's Help menu.
- TSTMDICL.CPP and TSTMDICL.H are the source and header files for the MDI client class derived from the OWL class `TMDIClient`.
- TSTMDICH.CPP and TSTMDICH.H are the source and header files for the MDI child window class derived from the OWL class `TMDIChild`.
- APXPRINT.CPP and APXPRINT.H are the source and header files for the `APXPrintOut` class that provides support for printing in an AppExpert-generated application. The `APXPrintOut` class is derived from the OWL class `TPrintOut`.
- APXPREV.CPP and APXPREV.H are the source and header files for the `PreviewWindow` class that allows the generated application to support a Print Preview capability. The `PreviewWindow` class is derived from the OWL class `TDecoratedFrame`.

Additionally, AppExpert also generates the following support files:

- A help project file (.HPJ) for the help compiler
- A module definition file (.DEF) for the linker
- A resource file (.RC) with the resource definitions
- A number of Rich Text Format files (.RTF) with the help information
- Several bitmap files (.BMP) used for the pushbuttons that are displayed in the toolbar appearing underneath the application's menubar
- Two icon files (.ICO): one icon is used for the application, and the other is used when a MDI child window is minimized

Building the Application

The next logical step is to modify the generated source files to suit your needs and to build the application by compiling and linking the files. To see what AppExpert provides with its default settings, try selecting Make all from the Project menu after

AppExpert finishes generating the files. When the compiling and linking are complete, run the TEST.EXE application by selecting Run from the Debug menu. Figure 17.14 shows the initial screen of the test application. Notice that most of the buttons on the toolbar are greyed out because the application is not displaying any files yet.

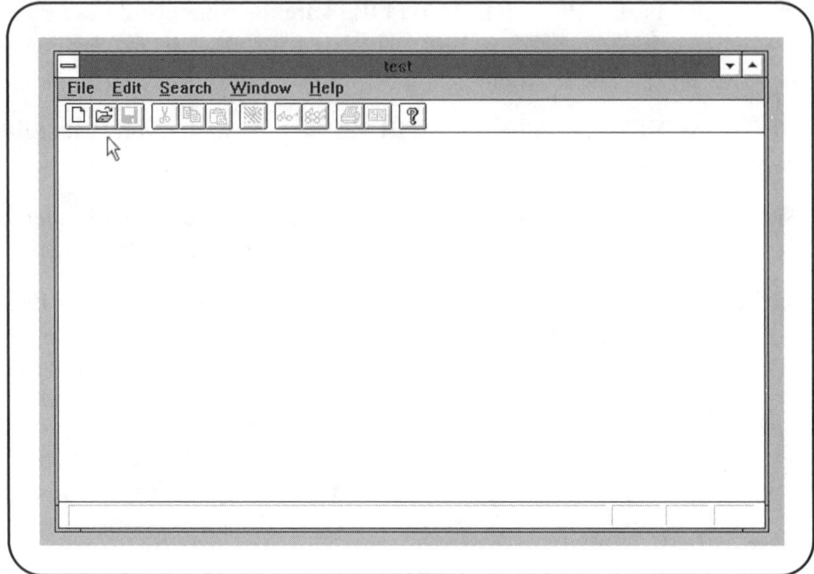

Figure 17.14. Initial screen of the test application.

To see how the new application works, click the File Open pushbutton—this is the second pushbutton on the toolbar with the picture of an open file folder. Figure 17.15 shows the resulting Open dialog box from which you can pick a file to be displayed by the application. You can open more than one file for viewing and editing. As Figure 17.16 shows, they appear in individual windows, all contained within the borders of a main window as determined by the Multiple Document Interface style.

Note that the toolbar icons for printing and print preview (the last two buttons on the toolbar) are enabled because there are files being displayed. Also, the pushbuttons for cutting (the button that shows a pair of scissors) and pasting are also enabled because some text is selected in one of the windows (the selection is highlighted).

The bottom line is that AppExpert can generate a full-fledged text file editor with little effort on your part. The idea behind AppExpert is that you generate the shell or framework for your application and then add code to one or more of the generated files. You may also define new classes that you need for your application. The tool that helps you with these tasks is called ClassExpert.

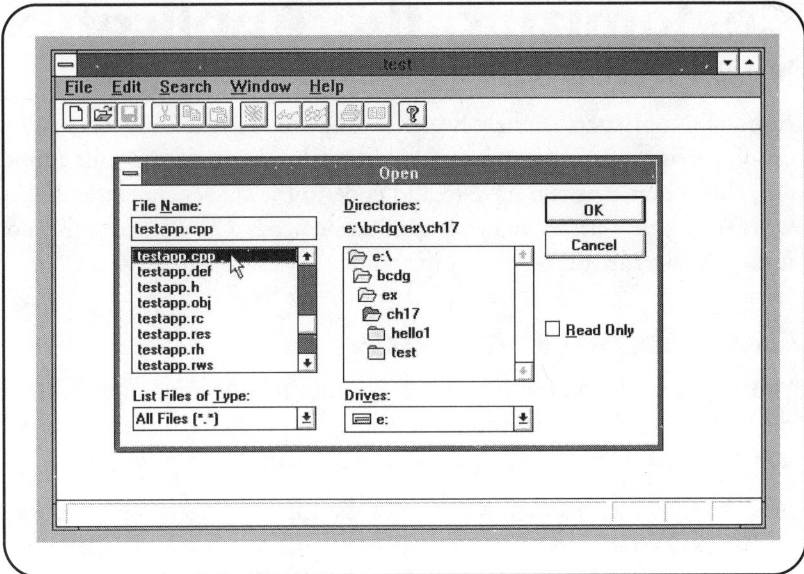

Figure 17.15. The Open dialog in the test application.

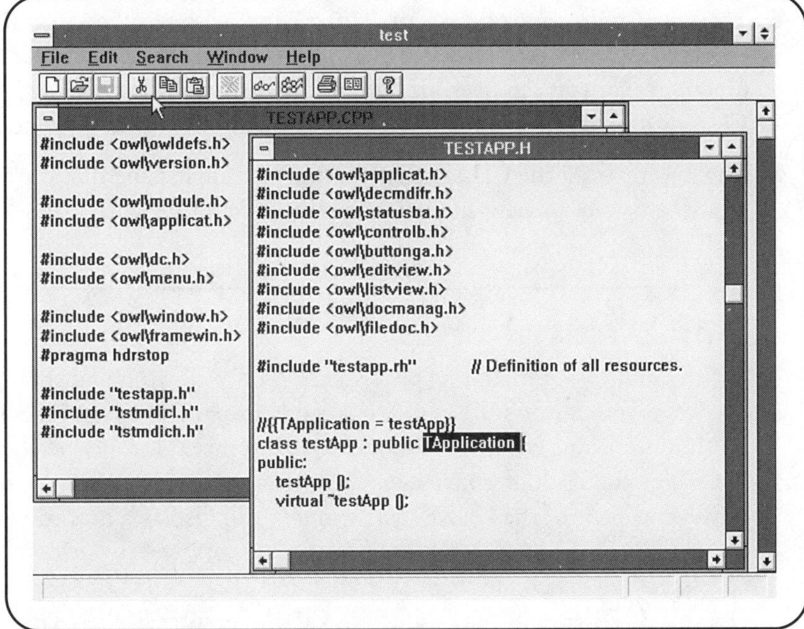

Figure 17.16. Several text files being displayed by the test application.

Customizing the Application with ClassExpert

Although AppExpert can help by generating much of the code that a Windows application needs, you still have to write additional code specific to your application. Usually, this means that you have to add code to the classes generated by AppExpert as well as create new classes that your application needs. ClassExpert is the tool that makes it easy to take care of these customizations.

ClassExpert Window

You can start ClassExpert by selecting it from the View menu or by double-clicking the EXE file's name in the project window. Figure 17.17 shows the ClassExpert window, which is divided into three work areas (panes):

- The upper-left pane shows a list of the application's classes that are derived from OWL classes. The contents of the other two panes depend on the class that is currently selected in this pane. If you double-click a class, the class constructor appears in the lower pane. A single click shows the member function that you last edited.
- The upper-right pane of the ClassExpert window shows the categories of events that the selected class handles. This includes Windows messages, virtual functions that you can override, and notifications of other user actions such as selecting an item from a menu or clicking a button in a dialog window.
- The lower part of the ClassExpert window is a single pane that provides an area where you can view and edit the source files of the currently selected class.

Click the Right Mouse Button for SpeedMenus

Borland C++ 4 includes SpeedMenus—drop-down menus that appear when you position the cursor in a work area and press the *right* mouse button. These drop-down menus are customized for the specific area where you click. For instance, clicking the right mouse button in the Events pane of the ClassExpert window will display a drop-down menu with options to add a handler (for the currently selected event, if any) and edit a dialog or a menu (see Figure 17.19). On the other hand, if you click the right mouse button with the pointer in the Classes pane, the drop-down menu will have options such as creating a new class and viewing class information (see Figure 17.21).

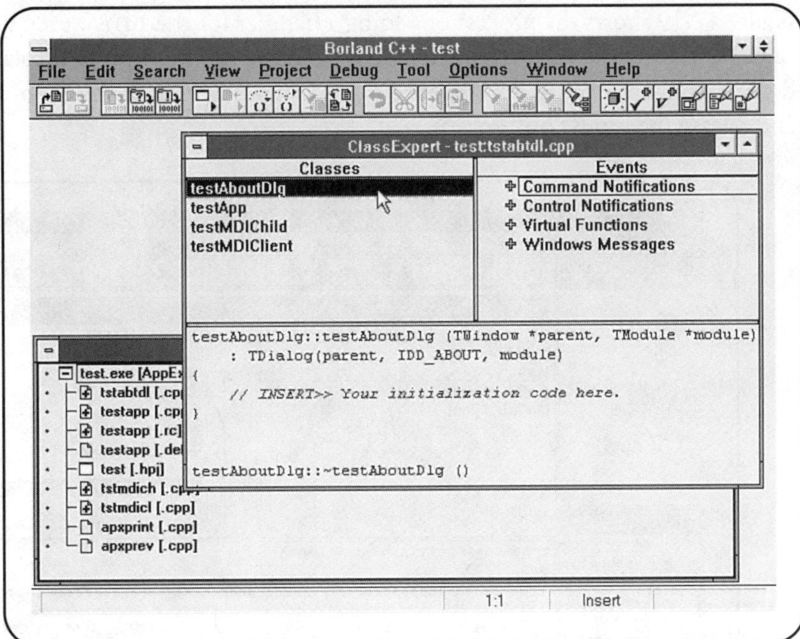

Figure 17.17. The ClassExpert window.

Editing a Class

To edit or view specific member functions of a class, first click the class name in the upper-left pane of the ClassExpert window. Next, select the type of member function you want to edit or view. For instance, to see the virtual function `InitMainWindow` of the `testApp` class, select `testApp` from the Classes pane, click the Virtual Functions category in the Events pane, and scroll down the list to find `InitMainWindow`. You will notice that a check mark appears next to the name, indicating that this function has been defined for the application. (AppExpert does this for you.) Clicking the item labeled `InitMainWindow` shows the function's body in the lower pane of the ClassExpert window (see Figure 17.18).

To view or edit the selected function, click the lower pane; scroll bars will appear, and you will be able to scroll through the source code and edit it.

In addition to editing an existing member function, you can also add new member functions to customize a class. To do this, click an event in the Events pane for which you want to add a handler. With the event highlighted and the cursor in the Events pane, press the right mouse button to bring up the speed menu (drop-down menu).

Figure 17.19 shows the process of adding a handler for the `IdleAction` virtual function. First, click the `IdleAction` item and press the right button to display the drop-down menu. Next move the cursor to the Add handler item in the drop-down menu and release the mouse button.

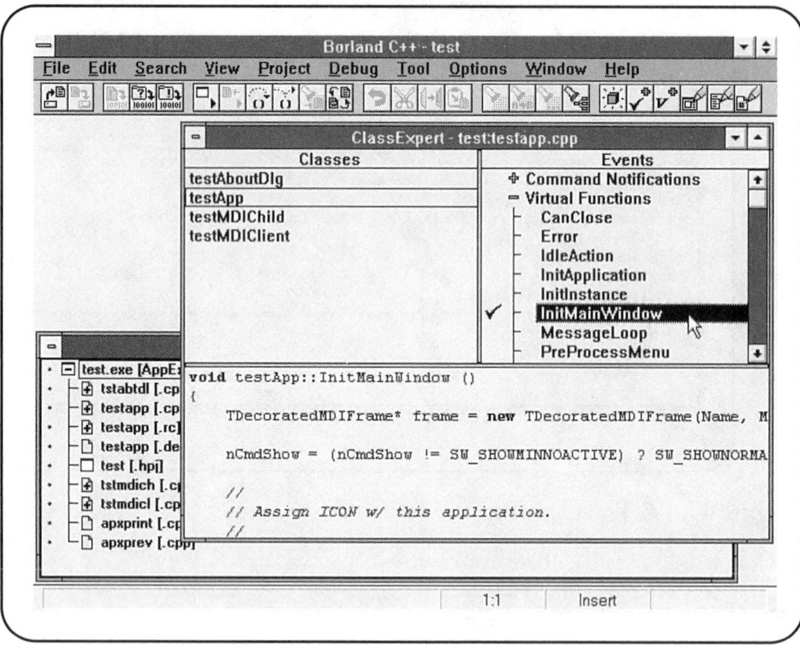

Figure 17.18. Editing a member function with ClassExpert.

Resizing the Panes in the ClassExpert Window

The panes in the ClassExpert window are resizable. Notice the shape of the cursor in Figure 17.20—the cursor takes that shape when you position the cursor on the lines that divide the panes. To enlarge or shrink a pane, position the cursor on the boundary (you will know it is on the boundary when the cursor changes appearance) and drag the boundary line to a new location.

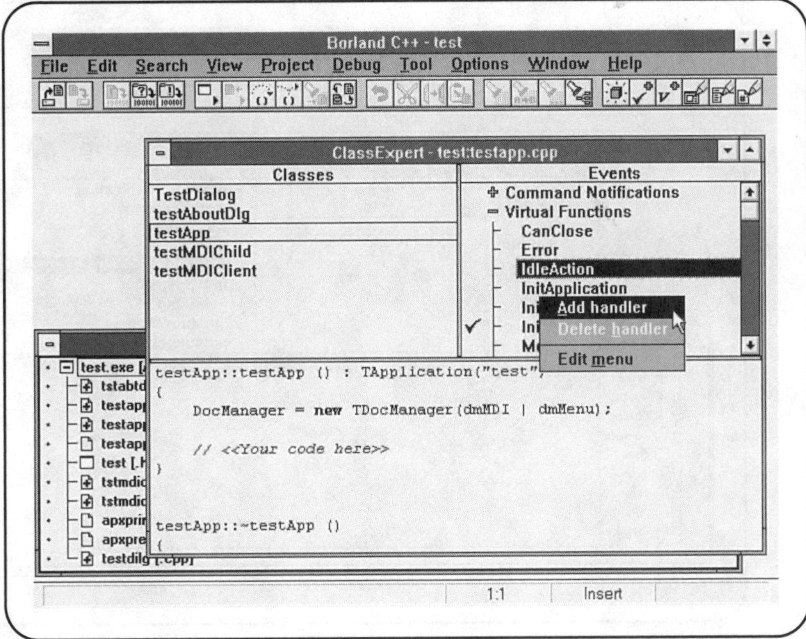

Figure 17.19. Adding a new member function to handle a selected event.

After you add a handler, a check mark appears next to the selected event and the edit pane of the ClassExpert window displays a skeleton handler function with the appropriate name and argument list (see Figure 17.20). The body of the function already includes any necessary calls to base class functions. Notice the comment about inserting your own code into the function's body.

Creating a New Class

In addition to modifying existing classes, you can also add new classes using ClassExpert. To start the process of adding a new class, move the cursor into the Classes pane and click the right mouse button to display the pop-up menu shown in Figure 17.21.

Next, select the Create new class item from the pop-up menu. This will display the dialog box shown in Figure 17.22. As you can see, one of the choices you make is the selection of a base class for the new class. ClassExpert offers a host of OWL classes in the drop-down combo box that appears next to the label, Base class:. The contents of the dialog box are dynamic—they depend on your choice of the base class.

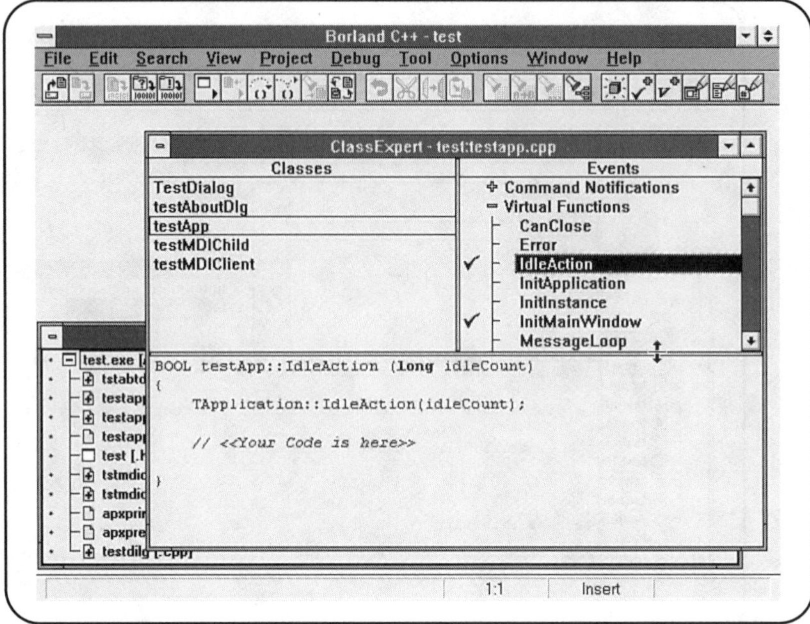

Figure 17.20. Skeleton handler function generated by ClassExpert.

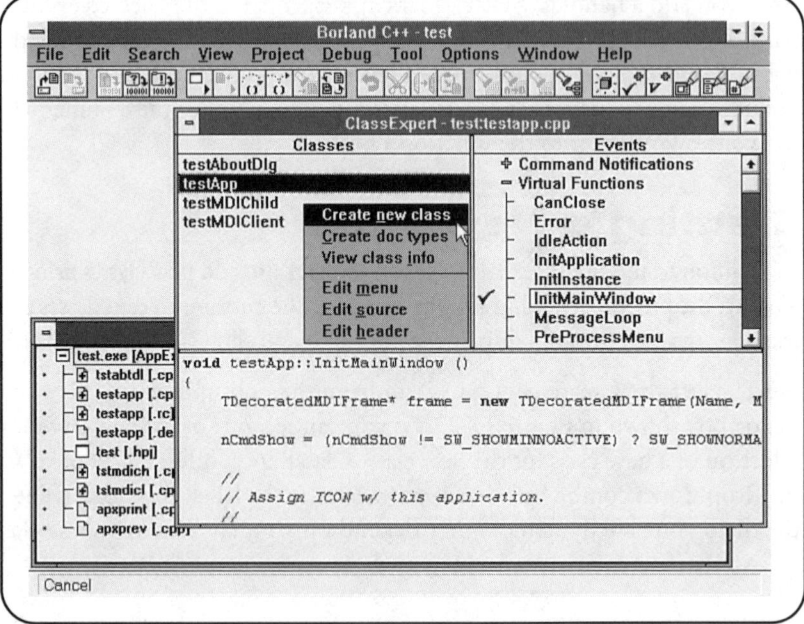

Figure 17.21. Pop-up menu for adding a new class with ClassExpert.

Figure 17.22 shows the contents of the dialog window when you select TDialog as the base class for the new class. For a dialog class, you are expected to enter a dialog ID. You will also have to enter the name of the new class—ClassExpert automatically constructs the name of the source and header files from the class name.

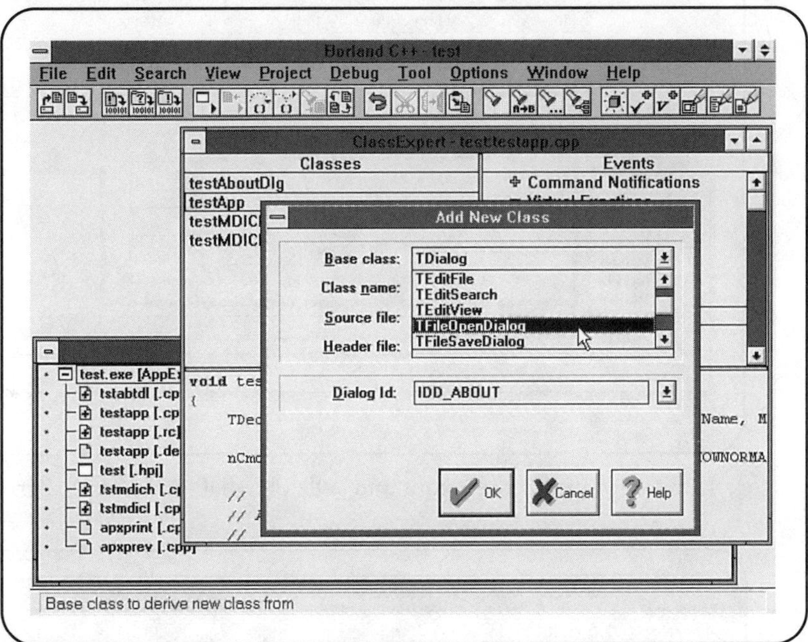

Figure 17.22. Dialog window prompting for information needed to create a new class with ClassExpert.

After you enter a dialog ID and a class name and click the OK button, you will be prompted for the style and layout of the dialog window (see Figure 17.23). Once you indicate the dialog window's layout and style, click the OK button to generate the code for the new class. Figure 17.24 shows the code for the constructor of a new dialog class. You can now fill in the body of the various member functions of the class to complete its implementation.

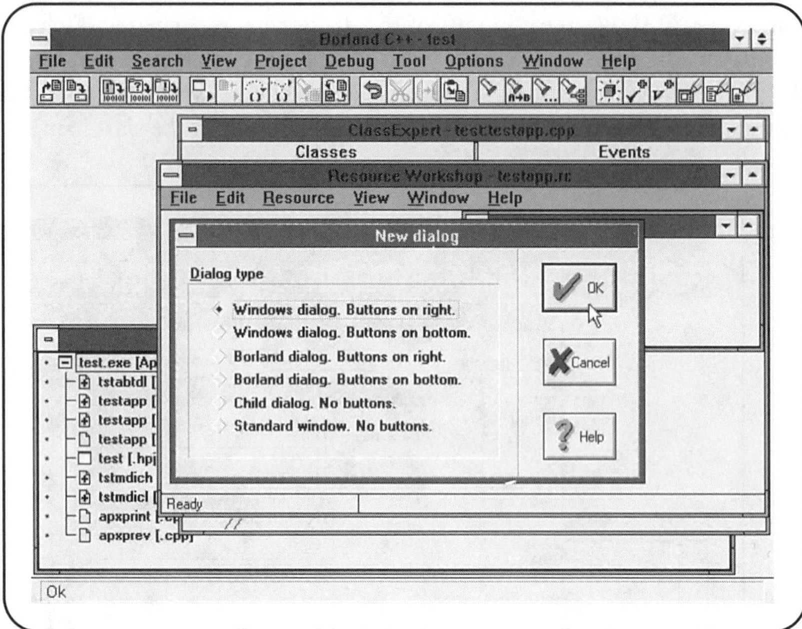

Figure 17.23. Prompt for the layout and style of a dialog in ClassExpert.

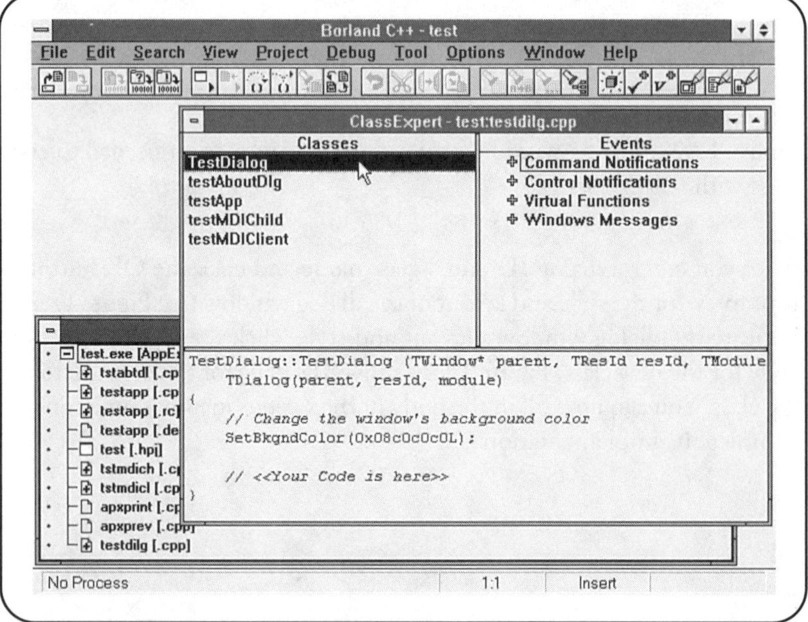

Figure 17.24. ClassExpert-generated code for a new dialog class.

Summary

Borland C++ 4 includes the ObjectWindows Library—a collection of over a hundred classes that provides a framework for building Microsoft Windows applications. This chapter includes a simple example program to illustrate how you use the OWL classes to create Windows programs.

Borland C++ 4 introduces two new labor-saving tools: AppExpert and ClassExpert. AppExpert can automatically generate the source and header files for a Windows application with a selected set of features such as support for printing and drag and drop. ClassExpert lets you customize existing classes and define new classes in a convenient manner. This chapter also provides an overview of AppExpert and ClassExpert,

The OWL classes are summarized in Chapter 18, "Using ObjectWindows Library (OWL)," and are used extensively in the sample applications shown in Chapters 19 through 25.

18

Using the ObjectWindows Library (OWL)

In addition to the general-purpose classes described in Chapter 16, "Using the Borland C++ Class Libraries," Borland C++ also offers a large collection of classes, collectively known as the ObjectWindows Library (or OWL, for short), that help you write applications for the Microsoft Windows environment. An example in Chapter 17, "Windows Programming with Borland C++," illustrates how to use the OWL classes as a framework for Windows programs. This chapter provides an overview of the OWL classes together with a tutorial introduction to some of the more useful classes.

Note that Borland C++ includes the full source code for the OWL classes. Therefore, if you want, you can always browse through the source code of the OWL classes to see exactly how the classes are defined and implemented.

> **What's in a Name? Windows Versus Windows**
>
> This book uses the term *Windows* with an uppercase *W* to refer to *Microsoft Windows*, the graphical operating environment. On the other hand, the lowercase *windows* refers to the rectangular areas of the screen in which applications display their output. Like all graphical operating environments, Windows uses windows extensively.

OWL Classes at a Glance

Figure 18.1 shows an overview of the major class hierarchies in OWL 2.0. Notice that the OWL 2.0 class hierarchy uses multiple inheritance extensively. As explained in Chapter 11, "Using Inheritance in C++," multiple inheritance lets you easily exploit the capabilities of two or more base classes. Most of the OWL classes inherit the event-handling capabilities of the `TEventHandler` class and the persistence (capability to store an object and retrieve it later) afforded by the `TStreamableBase` class. OWL 2.0 also uses multiple inheritance to provide specific functionalities such as support for the Visual Basic Controls (also known as VBX Controls). For this purpose OWL 2.0 provides the `TVbxControl` class, which is derived from the `TControl` class, and a specialized version of the event-handling class known as `TVbxEventHandler`.

The `TWindow` classes represent windows of various types: frame windows that manage one or more child windows, windows where the application displays its graphical or text output, dialog windows that prompt the user for input, and control window objects through which the user controls the application. To support graphics and text output through the Windows Graphics Device Interface (GDI is described further in Chapter 19, "Graphics Programming with OWL"), OWL 2.0 provides the `TGdiBase` class hierarchy with the `TGdiObject` classes. Additionally, the `TGdiBase` hierarchy includes the `TDC` classes that represent the various types of device contexts needed to display output on a device.

Other major class hierarchies include the following: classes for building applications with the document-view model; classes to represent menus and provide clipboard support; and classes for scrolling, printing, and generating exceptions when errors occur in an OWL class. OWL 2.0 also includes classes that represent Windows data types such as `POINT`, `RECT`, and `SIZE`.

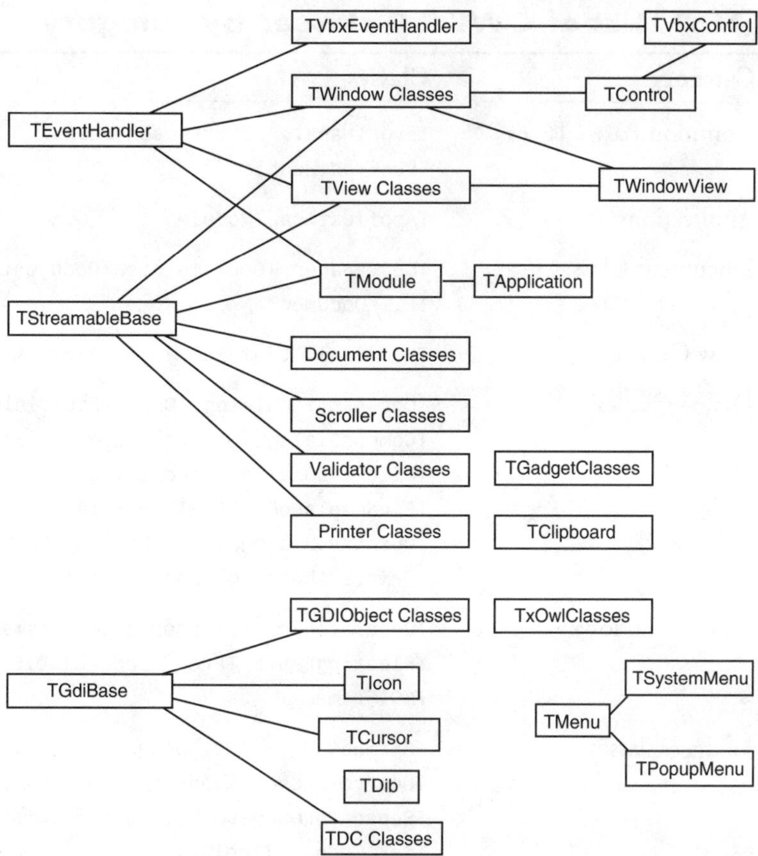

Figure 18.1. Major class hierarchies highlighting the use of multiple inheritance in OWL 2.0.

For another view of OWL, consult Table 18.1, which lists the OWL 2.0 classes by category while Table 18.2 lists them alphabetically. The purpose of these tables is to give you an overall picture of the capabilities of ObjectWindow 2.0. The following sections briefly describe the different categories of OWL classes. The latter part of this chapter provides example programs that illustrate the use of some of the common OWL classes. When you begin to use the OWL classes in your applications, consult Table 18.2 to determine which header file you have to include when you use a specific class.

Table 18.1. List of OWL 2.0 classes by category.

Category	Classes
Common Base Classes	`TEventHandler`, `TStreamableBase`, `TVbxEventHandler`
Applications	`TApplication`, `TModule`
Document Classes	`TDocManager`, `TDocTemplate`, `TDocument`, `TFileDocument`
View Classes	`TEditView`, `TListView`, `TView`, `TWindowView`
Dialog Classes	`TChooseColorDialog`, `TChooseFontDialog`, `TCommonDialog`, `TDialog`, `TFileOpenDialog`, `TFileSaveDialog`, `TFindDialog`, `TFindReplaceDialog`, `TInputDialog`, `TOpenSaveDialog`, `TPrintDialog`, `TPrinterAbortDlg`, `TReplaceDialog`
Frame Windows	`TDecoratedFrame`, `TDecoratedMDIFrame`, `TFloatingFrame`, `TFrameWindow`, `TMDIChild`, `TMDIFrame`
Gadget Classes	`TBitmapGadget`, `TButtonGadget`, `TControlBar`, `TControlGadget`, `TGadget`, `TGadgetWindow`, `TSeparatorGadget`, `TMessageBar`, `TStatusBar`, `TTextGadget`, `TToolBox`
Control Windows	`TButton`, `TCheckBox`, `TComboBox`, `TControl`, `TEdit`, `TEditFile`, `TEditSearch`, `TGauge`, `TGroupBox`, `THSlider`, `TListBox`, `TRadioButton`, `TScrollBar`, `TSlider`, `TStatic`, `TVbxControl`, `TVSlider`
Other Windows	`TClipboardViewer`, `TKeyboardModeTracker`, `TLayoutWindow`, `TMDIClient`, `TPreviewPage`, `TPrintPreview`, `TTinyCaption`
GDI Classes	`TBitmap`, `TBrush`, `TCursor`, `TDib`, `TFont`, `TGdiBase`, `TGdiObject`, `TIcon`, `TPalette`, `TPen`, `TRegion`

Category	Classes
Device Contexts	TClientDC, TCreatedDC, TDC, TDibDC, TDesktopDC, TIC, TMemoryDC, TMetaFileDC, TPaintDC, TPrintDC, TPrintPreviewDC, TScreenDC, TWindowDC
Validator Classes	TFilterValidator, TLookupValidator, TPXPictureValidator, TRangeValidator, TStringLookupValidator, TValidator
Scroller	TScroller, TScrollerBase
Printer Classes	TPrinter, TPrintout
Menu Classes	TMenu, TPopupMenu, TSystemMenu
Clipboard Support	TClipboard, TClipboardFormatIterator
OWL Exception-Handling Classes	TXCompatibility, TXGdi, TXInvalidMainWindow, TXInvalidModule, TXMenu, TXOutOfMemory, TXOwl, TXPrinter, TXValidator, TXWindow
Other Support Classes	List, TBitSet, TCharSet, TCelArray, TColor, TComboBoxData, TCommandEnabler, TDropInfo, TGadgetWindowFont, TInStream, TLayoutMetrics, TListBoxData, TMetaFilePict, TOutStream, TPaletteEntry, TPoint, TProcInstance, TRect, TResId, TRgbQuad, TRgbTriple, TSize, TStatus, TStream

Table 18.2. Alphabetical listing of the classes in OWL 2.0 (multiple base classes are indicated by a + prefix).

Class	Include File*	Base Class	Derivation Type
List	docview.h		
MsgName	eventhan.h		
TApplication	applicat.h	TModule	public

continues

Table 18.2. continued

Class	Include File*	Base Class	Derivation Type
TBitmap	gdiobjec.h	TGdiObject	public
TBitmapGadget	bitmapga.h	TGadget	public
TBitSet	bitset.h		
TBrush	gdiobjec.h	TGdiObject	public
TButton	button.h	TControl	public
TButtonGadget	buttonga.h	TGadget	public
TCelArray	celarray.h		
TCharSet	bitset.h	TBitSet	public
TCheckBox	checkbox.h	TButton	public
TChooseColorDialog	chooseco.h	TCommonDialog	public
TChooseFontDialog	choosefo.h	TCommonDialog	public
TClientDC	dc.h	TWindowDC	public
TClipboard	clipboar.h		
TClipboardFormatIterator	clipboar.h		
TClipboardViewer	clipview.h	TWindow	virtual public
TColor	color.h		
TComboBox	combobox.h	TListBox	public
TComboBoxData	combobox.h		
TCommandEnabler	window.h		
TCommonDialog	commdial.h	TDialog	public
TControl	control.h	TWindow	public
TControlBar	controlb.h	TGadgetWindow	public
TControlGadget	controlg.h	TGadget	public
TCreatedDC	dc.h	TDC	public

Class	Include File*	Base Class	Derivation Type
TCursor	gdiobjec.h	TGdiObject	public
TDC	dc.h	TGdiBase	private
TDecoratedFrame	decframe.h	TFrameWindow	virtual public
+TLayoutWindow	public		
TDecoratedMDIFrame	decmdifr.h	TMDIFrame	public
+TDecoratedFrame	public		
TDesktopDC	dc.h	TWindowDC	public
TDialog	dialog.h	TWindow	virtual public
TDib	gdiobjec.h	TGdiBase	private
TDibDC	dc.h	TCreatedDC	public
TDocManager	docmanag.h	TEventHandler	public
+TStreamableBase	public		
TDocTemplate	docmanag.h	TStreamableBase	public
TDocument	docview.h	TStreamableBase	public
TDropInfo	point.h		
TEdit	edit.h	TStatic	public
TEditFile	editfile.h	TEditSearch	public
TEditSearch	editsear.h	TEdit	public
TEditView	editview.h	TEditSearch	public
+TView	public		
TEventHandler	eventhan.h		
TEventInfo	eventhan.h		
TFileDocument	filedoc.h	TDocument	public
TFileOpenDialog	opensave.h	TOpenSaveDialog	public

continues

Table 18.2. continued

Class	Include File*	Base Class	Derivation Type
TFileSaveDialog	opensave.h	TOpenSaveDialog	public
TFilterValidator	validate.h	TValidator	public
TFindDialog	findrepl.h	TFindReplaceDialog	public
TFindReplaceDialog	findrepl.h	TCommonDialog	public
TFloatingFrame +TTinyCaption	floatfra.h public	TFrameWindow	public
TFont	gdiobjec.h	TGdiObject	public
TFrameWindow public	framewin.h	TWindow	virtual
TGadget	gadget.h		
TGadgetWindow	gadgetwi.h	TWindow	public
TGadgetWindowFont	gadgetwi.h	TFont	public
TGauge	gauge.h	TControl	public
TGdiBase	gdibase.h		
TGdiObject	gdiobjec.h	TGdiBase	private
TGroupBox	groupbox.h	TControl	public
THSlider	slider.h	TSlider	public
TIC	dc.h	TCreatedDC	public
TIcon	gdiobjec.h	TGdiBase	private
TInputDialog	inputdia.h	TDialog	public
TInStream +istream	docview.h public	TStream	public
TKeyboardModeTracker	keymodet.h	TWindow	virtual public
TLayoutMetrics	layoutwi.h		

Class	Include File*	Base Class	Derivation Type
TLayoutWindow	layoutwi.h	TWindow	virtual public
TListBox	listbox.h	TControl	public
TListBoxData	listbox.h		
TListView +TView	listview.h public	TListBox	public
TLookupValidator	validate.h	TValidator	public
TMDIChild	mdichild.h	TFrameWindow	virtual public
TMDIClient virtual	mdi.h	TWindow	public
TMDIFrame	mdi.h	TFrameWindow	virtual public
TMemoryDC	dc.h	TCreatedDC	public
TMenu	menu.h		
TMessageBar	messageb.h	TGadgetWindow	public
TMetaFileDC	dc.h	TDC	public
TMetaFilePict	metafile.h		
TModule +TStreamableBase	module.h public	TEventHandler	public
TOpenSaveDialog	opensave.h	TCommonDialog	public
TOutStream ostream	docview.h public	TStream	public
TPaintDC	dc.h	TDC	public
TPalette	gdiobjec.h	TGdiObject	public
TPaletteEntry	color.h	tagPALETTEENTRY	public
TPen	gdiobjec.h	TGdiObject	public

continues

Table 18.2. continued

Class	Include File*	Base Class	Derivation Type
TPoint	point.h	tagPOINT	public
TPopupMenu	menu.h	TMenu	public
TPreviewPage	preview.h	TWindow	public
TPrintDC	dc.h	TCreatedDC	public
TPrintDialog	printdia.h	TCommonDialog	public
TPrinte	printer.h	TStreamableBase	public
TPrinterAbortDlg	printer.h	TDialog	public
TPrintout	printer.h	TStreamableBase	public
TPrintPreview	preview.h	TLayoutWindow	public
TPrintPreviewDC	preview.h	TPrintDC	public
TProcInstance	point.h		
TPXPictureValidator	validate.h	TValidator	public
TRadioButton	radiobut.h	TCheckBox	public
TRangeValidator	validate.h	TFilterValidator	public
TRect	point.h	tagRECT	public
TRegion	gdiobjec.h	TGdiBase	private
TReplaceDialog	findrepl.h	TFindReplaceDialog	public
TResId	point.h		
TRgbQuad	color.h	tagRGBQUAD	public
TRgbTriple	color.h	tagRGBTRIPLE	public
TScreenDC	dc.h	TWindowDC	public
TScrollBar	scrollba.h	TControl	public
TScroller	scroller.h	TScrollerBase	public
TScrollerBase	scroller.h	TStreamableBase	public
TSeparatorGadget	gadget.h	TGadget	public

Class	Include File*	Base Class	Derivation Type
TSize	point.h	tagSIZE	public
TSlider	slider.h	TScrollBar	public
TStatic	static.h	TControl	public
TStatus	except.h		
TStatusBar	statusba.h	TMessageBar	public
TStream	docview.h		
TStringLookupValidator	validate.h	TLookupValidator	public
TSystemMenu	menu.h	TMenu	public
TTextGadget	textgadg.h	TGadget	public
TTinyCaption virtual	tinycapt.h	TWindow	public
TToolBox	toolbox.h	TGadgetWindow	public
TValidator	validate.h	TStreamableBase	public
TVbxControl +TVbxEventHandler	vbxctl.h public	TControl	public
TVbxEventHandler public	vbxctl.h	TEventHandler	virtual
TView public	docview.h	TEventHandler	virtual
TVSlider	slider.h	TSlider	public
TWindow public	window.h	TEventHandler	virtual
TWindowDC	dc.h	TDC	public
TWindowView +TView	docview.h public	TWindow	public
TXCompatibility	except.h	TXOwl	public

continues

Table 18.2. continued

Class	Include File*	Base Class	Derivation Type
TXGdi	gdibase.h	TXOwl	public
TXInvalidMainWindow	applicat.h	TXOwl	public
TXInvalidModule	module.h	TXOwl	public
TXMenu	menu.h	TXOwl	public
TXOutOfMemory	except.h	TXOwl	public
TXOwl	except.h	xmsg	public
TXPrinter	printer.h	TXOwl	private
TXValidator	validate.h	TXOwl	private
TXWindow	window.h	TXOwl	public

NOTE: All include files are in the OWL subdirectory of the directory where the standard headers are located. For instance, to use any device context class, you should include `<owl\dc.h>`.

Application Class

The `TApplication` class represents a Windows application. As shown in the example in Chapter 17, "Windows Programming with Borland C++," to build a Windows application you need to derive your application class from `TApplication` and override the `InitMainWindow` member function. You would also derive a window class from one of the predefined window types, such as `TFrameWindow`, and create an instance of that window in the `InitMainWindow` member function of the application class. Once the window is displayed, the window's message-handling mechanism takes over the interaction with the user. You must follow a cookbook approach (see Chapter 17 for an example) to handle specific Windows messages.

Prior Experience with Windows API Is Helpful

You can follow a cookbook approach and use the Windows programming classes to develop Microsoft Windows applications. However, to fully exploit the capabilities that these classes offer, you should become familiar with the basics of Windows programming. For example, experience with writing Windows programs in C with the Microsoft Windows Application Programming Interface (API) is helpful, because the ObjectWindows Library provides classes that mimic the organization and the programming interface of the Windows API. This chapter does not cover the Windows API in detail, but rather points out similarities between the Windows programming classes and the API. Consult the *Windows API Reference Manuals* that accompany the Borland C++ compiler for more information.

Menus

The `TMenu` class represents the menu bar in a window. Generally, you would define menus in resource files, and you can initialize a `TMenu` object from the definitions in the resource file using one of the `TMenu`'s constructors. There are two specialized versions of `TMenu` classes: the `TSystemMenu` class represents a window's system menu and the `TPopupMenu` class lets you create a pop-up (drop-down) menu.

Window Classes

The classes in the `TWindow` hierarchy represent different types of windows. `TWindow` is a general-purpose window that can be the main, drop-down, or child windows of an application. The `TWindow` class encapsulates a window handle (the `HWND` type from the Windows API) and provides the member functions necessary to manipulate the window.

The main window of OWL applications is typically a `TFrameWindow` or a `TDecoratedFrameWindow`, which are derived from the `TWindow` class. Two major class hierarchies, dialog and control windows, are also derived from the `TWindow` class.

> **The TWindow Classes and the Windows in Microsoft Windows**
>
> The TWindow class and the Windows window associated with a TWindow object illustrate the relationship between the C++ classes and the Windows API. A window in Windows, represented by a *window handle,* HWND, is an internal data structure that corresponds to an area of the screen where an application's output appears. The Windows API provides many functions that manipulate windows and that accept a window handle as an argument. OWL encapsulates a window handle, HWND, in the TWindow class and defines all necessary member functions to provide the functionality for all window-manipulation functions of the Windows API.

Dialog Classes

Dialog boxes are used in a graphical user interface (GUI) to display messages to the user and prompt for information. A simple dialog box is the window you see when you select the About... option from the Help menu in a Microsoft Windows application. Another example of a dialog box is the window that appears when you select the Open... option from the File menu in many Windows applications. OWL includes a hierarchy of C++ classes that provides several different predefined dialog boxes. Figure 18.2 shows the dialog class hierarchy with the base class, TDialog, which is derived from TWindow. The dialog classes make it very easy to display and use a dialog.

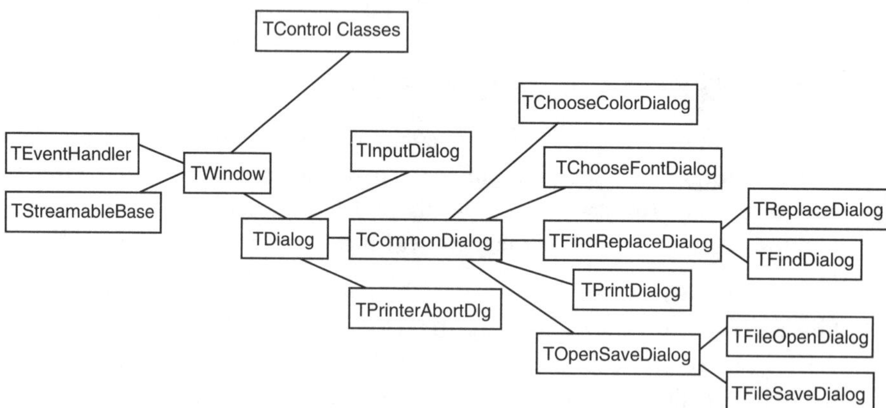

Figure 18.2. Dialog window classes in OWL 2.0.

For instance, with the `TDialog` class, the following is what you would have to write to display the About box in the sample application shown in Chapter 17:

```
TDialog *p_about = new TDialog(this, "ABOUTHELLO");
GetApplication()->ExecDialog(p_about);
```

`ABOUTHELLO` is the name of the dialog box, as defined in the application's resource file. The `ExecDialog` function displays the dialog in a modal manner—the user has to close the dialog box before interacting with the rest of the application. To display a modeless dialog, you have to use the `Create` function of the dialog class.

Other dialog classes in OWL 2.0 include the following:

- `TInputDialog` provides a dialog box that prompts the user for a single text item. The `TInputDialog` class has an associated resource file, `<owl\inputdia.rc>`. If your application uses a `TInputDialog` object, the application's resource file must include `<owl\inputdia.rc>`.
- `TPrinterAbortDlg` displays a dialog box during printing.
- `TFindReplaceDialog` is derived from `TCommonDialog` and provides a modeless dialog box that prompts the user for a string and its replacement. Because this is a *modeless dialog box,* the user can continue to interact with other menu items in the application while `TFindReplaceDialog` is displayed.
- `TOpenSaveDialog` is derived from `TCommonDialog` and displays a list of files and directories from which the user can select a file. The `TOpenSaveDialog` class is further specialized into two classes, `TFileOpenDialog` and `TFileSaveDialog`, which are used to prompt for a filename when opening and saving a file, respectively.
- `TChooseFontDialog` is derived from `TCommonDialog` and provides a dialog box from which the user can select a font.
- `TPrintDialog` is another modal dialog box, derived from `TCommonDialog`, that prompts the user for information necessary for printing.
- `TChooseColorDialog` is derived from `TCommonDialog`. This modal dialog box provides a convenient means to let the user pick a color.

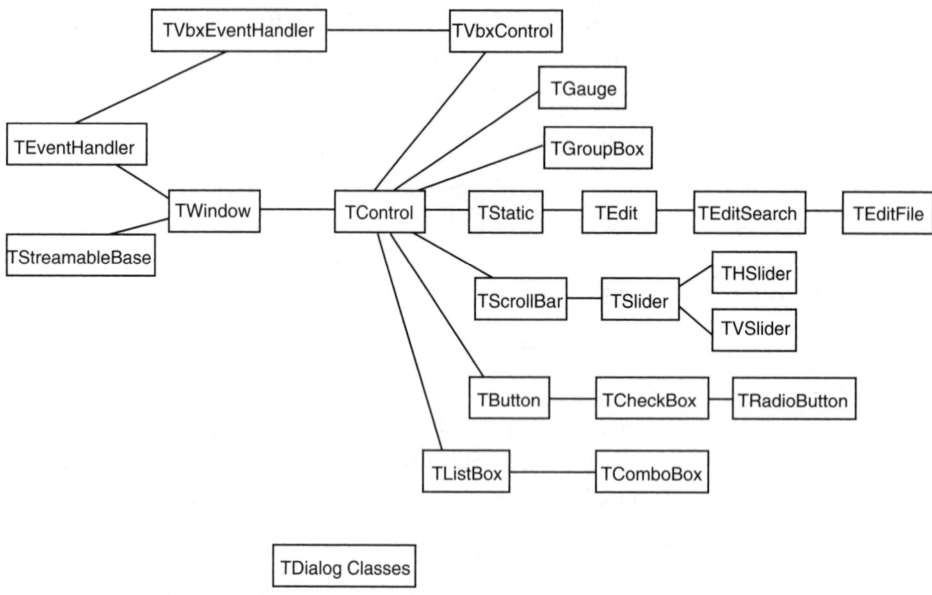

Figure 18.3. Control window classes in OWL 2.0.

Control Classes

Controls refer to user-interface items, such as buttons and scrollbars, that the user manipulates with the mouse to supply input to the application. Controls usually appear inside dialog windows, but you can also place controls such as buttons in your own windows. Figure 18.3 shows the inheritance hierarchy of the control window classes. The sixteen control classes in OWL are derived from the abstract base class `TControl`:

- `TButton` represents a Windows button control, which is used extensively in Windows applications, especially in dialog boxes.
- `TCheckBox` is a special type of `TButton` that displays a check mark if an internal variable is set.
- `TComboBox` is equivalent to a Windows combo box control, which consists of an edit control together with a drop-down listbox for making selections. Usually, the listbox is hidden and a button with an arrow appears next to the edit window. The list appears when the user selects the drop-down arrow. The edit window shows the current selection from the list.

- `TEdit` is a C++ class corresponding to the predefined edit control in Windows that provides a window wherein the user can enter and edit text.
- `TEditFile` enhances the `TEditSearch` class by providing support for opening, editing, and saving the file.
- `TEditSearch` is an enhanced version of the `TEdit` class that adds the capability to search and replace text.
- `TGauge` represents a horizontal or vertical bar showing the current value of a variable (as the value changes), usually used to show the progress of a process.
- `TGroupBox` is a class that, like a Windows group box, draws a frame around a set of radio buttons or check boxes. (Unlike a Windows group box, a `TGroupBox` also manages the group of controls that it contains.)
- `THSlider` is a horizontally oriented `TSlider` control.
- `TListBox` represents a Windows listbox where the application can display a list of items, such as names of files. The user can view the list and select one or more items from it.
- `TRadioButton` is a Windows radio button that the user can turn on or off.
- `TScrollBar` is a Windows scrollbar control that can be oriented either horizontally or vertically.
- `TSlider` is a specialized version of the `TScrollBar` control that provides the capability to display or accept nonscrolling position information.
- `TStatic` provides the functionality of Windows *static controls*, which are text fields used as labels or boxes used as decorative items. The text displayed in a Windows static control cannot be edited by the user.
- `TVbxControl` encapsulates a Visual Basic control and provides a number of member functions such as `GetProp` and `SetProp` that make it easy to access and manipulate the properties of a VBX control.
- `TVSlider` is a vertically oriented `TSlider` control.

Frame Windows

The frame window classes (see Figure 18.4) represent windows that serve as containers for displaying other windows. There are two important classes in this hierarchy—`TMDIChild` and `TMDIFrame`—that are meant to support the Windows *multiple document interface (MDI)*. Applications that follow the MDI style enable you to manage several child windows inside an outer frame window. For example, the Windows Program Manager follows the MDI style when displaying the program groups in various child windows.

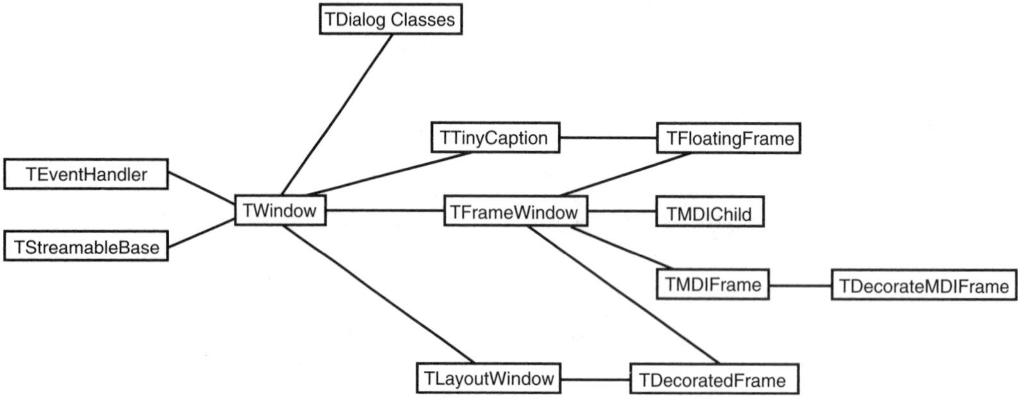

Figure 18.4. Frame window classes in OWL 2.0.

The `TMDIFrame` class, derived from `TFrameWindow`, represents the frame window that serves as the main window in an application that uses MDI. Inside the `TMDIFrame` window, there is a `TMDIClient` window that actually manages the MDI child windows. This must be derived from the `TMDIChild` class. The `TMDIClient` class provides member functions, such as `TileChildren` and `CloseChildren`, that manipulate MDI child windows.

`TDecoratedFrame` is a special type of `TFrameWindow` that contains one or more child windows, such as a status bar and a tool bar, besides the window where the application's output appears. The `TDecoratedFrame` class inherits the capability to manage the layout of these child windows from `TLayoutWindow`. For MDI applications, there is another class—`TDecoratedMDIFrame`—that provides the decoration child windows in a `TMDIFrame` window.

Another specialized version of `TFrameWindow` is the `TFloatingFrame` window, which sports a small caption bar provided by the `TTinyCaption` class. As the name suggests, `TFloatingFrame` windows are useful for implementing features such as a palette of drawing tools in a drawing program.

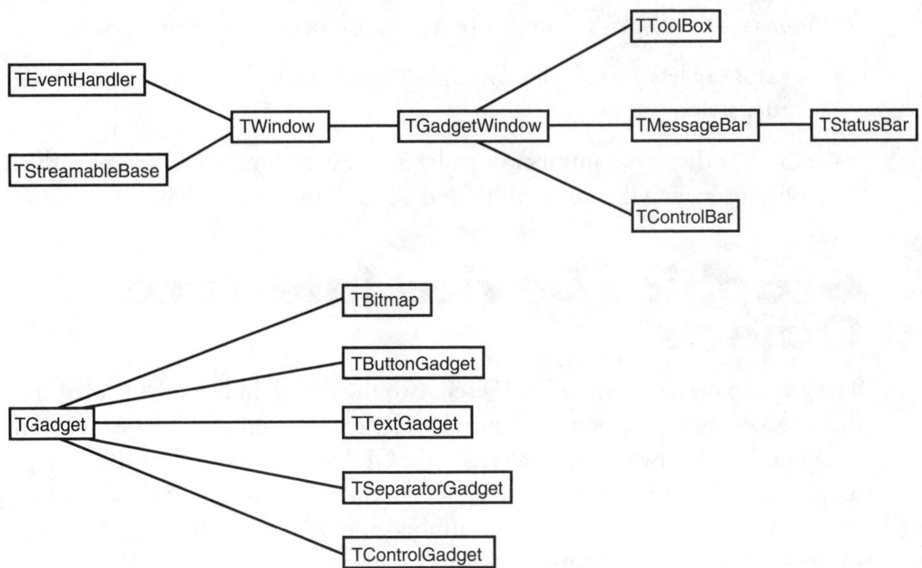

Figure 18.5. Gadget classes in OWL 2.0.

Gadget Classes

Gadgets, derived from the `TGadget` class, are user-interface objects that usually do not have an associated window. One or more of these gadgets are managed and displayed in a window belonging to a `TGadgetWindow`. As the class hierarchies in Figure 18.5 show, control bars and status bars are all derived from the `TGadgetWindow` class and there are gadgets corresponding to many of the control classes such as `TButton` and `TStatic`. The `TGadget` class hierarchy provides the following gadgets:

- `TBitmapGadget` displays an array of one or more bitmap images.
- `TButtonGadget` is a button with a specified bitmap.
- `TControlGadget` creates a `TGadget` object from a `TControl` object. This allows any `TControl` object to be displayed in a `TGadgetWindow` such as a `TControlBar`.
- `TTextGadget` displays a text string.

These gadgets can be placed in any one of the `TGadgetWindow` classes, which include the following:

- `TControlBar` manages a number of gadgets such as `TButtonGadget` and `TSeparatorGadget` and displays them in a single row. In the Borland C++ IDE, such a control bar appears below the menu bar.

- `TMessageBar` displays a single `TTextGadget` object without any border.
- `TStatusBar` lets you display multiple `TTextGadget` objects and control their border styles.
- `TToolBox` displays a number of gadgets in a two-dimensional array with all columns having the same width and all rows the same height.

Graphics Device Interface Objects

The *graphics device interface* (*GDI*) refers to the device-independent set of functions that the Microsoft Windows API provides for graphics output. These GDI functions use a number of drawing tools (referred to as GDI objects) to produce different graphics outputs. OWL 2.0 includes a number of C++ classes that represent these drawing tools. In fact, OWL 2.0 even provides a number of classes that allow other Windows resources such as icons, regions, and device-independent bitmaps (DIB) to be treated like GDI objects. Additionally, the device contexts are also brought under the umbrella of a single class hierarchy based on the `TGdiBase` class (see Figure 18.6).

In Figure 18.6, the `TDib`, `TRegion`, and `TIcon` classes respectively denote a device-independent bitmap, a region, and an icon. The `TDC` class hierarchy represents var-ious device contexts (described in the next section) and the `TGdiObject` classes encapsulate the Windows GDI objects. The `TGdiObject` class serves as the base class for the following GDI classes:

- `TBitmap` represents a bitmap.
- `TBrush` is the C++ class that models a GDI brush that you can use to fill graphics shapes.
- `TFont` is a font encapsulation that you can use to display text.
- `TPen` represents a GDI pen object. You can use the pen to draw the outline of graphics shapes.
- `TPalette` is a GDI color palette.
- `TRegion` represents a region—a combination of elliptical, rectangular, and polygonal areas that can be used for drawing or clipping.

To use these GDI objects, you also need another important item—a device context, described in the next section.

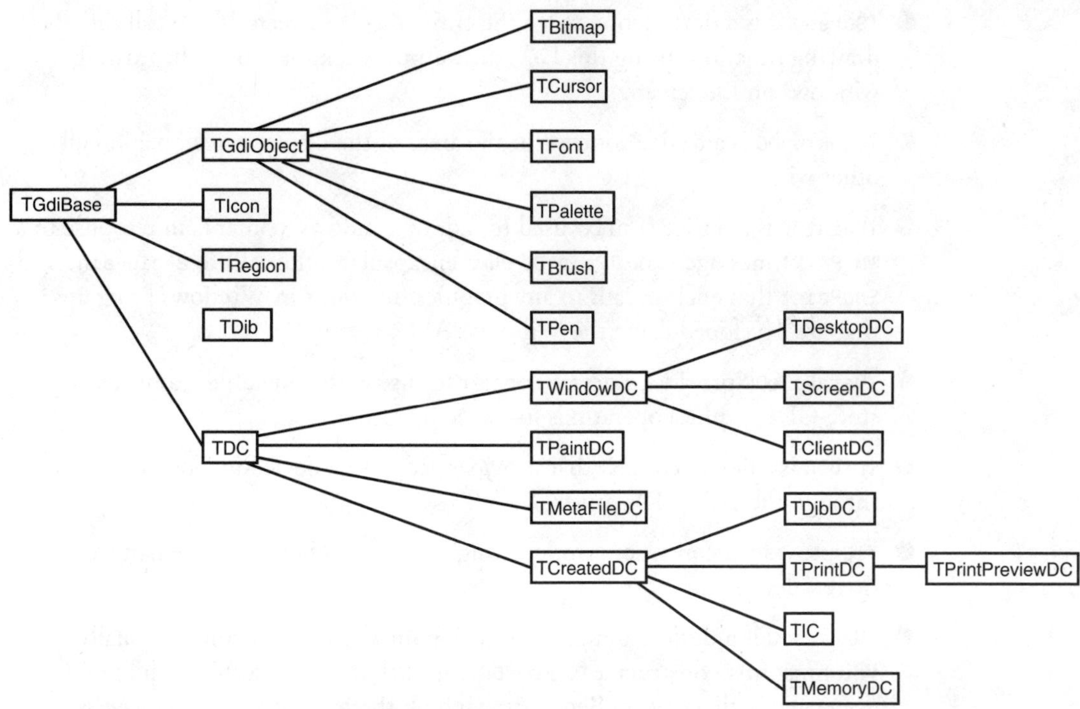

Figure 18.6. GDI and DC classes in OWL 2.0.

Device Context Classes

In Windows, you must obtain a device context (DC) before you can use the GDI functions to display output on a device. The *device context* is an internal data structure that stores graphics attributes, such as background and foreground colors, the pen, and the font. The appearance of graphics and text is controlled by these attributes. Each GDI drawing function in the Windows SDK requires a handle to a DC as an argument. In OWL 2.0, the DC is encapsulated in the C++ `TDC` class with the GDI drawing functions defined as member functions of the `TDC` class.

For specific uses, OWL includes the following classes derived from `TDC`:

- `TWindowDC` provides a device context for the entire window, including the frame.
- `TClientDC` represents a device context associated with the *client area* of a window (the area of a window inside the frame or the area where output appears).

- TScreenDC is a device context for the entire display screen. If you call the drawing functions using this DC, the output will appear over the existing windows on the screen.
- TDesktopDC is a device context for the areas of the display screen behind all other windows.
- TPaintDC is a device context used to redraw windows' contents in response to a WM_PAINT message. The TPaintDC class encapsulates the calls to BeginPaint and EndPaint that enclose calls to any graphics functions in Windows programs that are developed using the Windows API.
- TMetaFileDC provides a device context for use with a metafile—a file used to store GDI graphics operations in a specific format.
- TDibDC is a device context that provides access to a device-independent bitmap through the DIB.DRV driver.
- TIC provides a constructor for creating a device context from the name of a driver, device, and port.
- TMemoryDC is a device context for drawing on a block of memory. Usually, you must first construct a TMemoryDC object that is compatible with the DC associated with a device. Before drawing on the memory DC, you have to select a bitmap into the TMemoryDC.
- TPrintDC is a device context for a printer.
- TPrintPreviewDC is a device context for displaying a preview version of printed output.

TScroller Class

The TScroller class in OWL provides an automated way to scroll the contents of a window. A TScroller can scroll windows that are created with one or both of the styles WS_HSCROLL and WS_VSCROLL. Additionally, a TScroller object can scroll its associated window even if the window does not have any scrollbars.

Other Support Classes

There are many more classes in OWL 2.0 than those mentioned in the overview so far. For instance, there are classes such as TPoint and TRect representing data structures such as POINT and RECT from the Windows API, TClipBoard for exchanging data with the clipboard, and the TXOwl classes for exception-handling.

Validator Classes

OWL 2.0 includes a whole hierarchy of classes, derived from `TValidator`, that gives you a number of ways to validate information that the user enters into an edit control. The `TEdit` class, representing an edit control, has a pointer to a `TValidator` object as a member variable. The `CanClose` function of the `TEdit` class calls member functions such as `Valid`, `IsValid`, and `IsValidInput` of the `TValidator` class to determine if the input entered by the user is acceptable. You can associate a validator with a `TEdit` control by calling its member function `SetValidator` with the pointer to a `TValidator` object as the argument.

The `TValidator` class hierarchy includes the following classes, each designed to validate a specific type of input:

- `TFilterValidator` checks the characters as the user enters them. You have to specify a valid set of characters in the form of a `TCharSet` object.
- `TLookupValidator` compares the value entered by the user against a list of acceptable values. The comparison is performed by calling a virtual function named `Lookup`. You are expected to provide your own `Lookup` function to compare the value with an appropriate set of acceptable values according to your needs.
- `TPXPictureValidator` compares the string entered by the user against a template or *picture*. For instance, if you want the user to enter a seven-digit number with a dash separating the first three digits from the rest, you would use the picture string: `"###-####"`.
- `TRangeValidator` accepts integer values within a range specified by minimum and maximum values.
- `TStringLookupValidator` compares the string entered by the user with a stored list of strings.

Basic Windows Data Types

Three classes—`TPoint`, `TRect`, and `TSize`—serve as basic data types in OWL applications. `TPoint` represents a two-dimensional point with x, y coordinates, `TRect` represents a rectangle, and `TSize` represents relative coordinates. If you have programmed with the Microsoft Windows API, you should recognize `TPoint`, `TRect`, and `TSize` as classes that are similar to their respective POINT, RECT, and SIZE structures.

Three more OWL classes encapsulate data structures used in the Windows API: `TPaletteEntry`, `TRgbQuad`, `TRgbTriple` respectively represent the API data structures

PALETTEENTRY, RGBQUAD, and RGBTRIPLE. As the name implies, TPaletteEntry denotes an entry in a color palette. TRgbTriple is a three-byte representation of color where the three bytes denote the red (R), green (G), and blue (B) intensities of the color. TRgbQuad is a four-byte representation of RGB color, with the first three bytes the same as those in TRgbTriple and the fourth byte reserved for future use.

Exploring the OWL Classes

Previous sections provided an overview of the OWL 2.0 classes. The following sections further explain the usage of these classes through small example programs.

Using the *TControl* Classes

The control classes provide the basic user interface objects such as buttons, edit controls, and list boxes that normally appear in a dialog window. However, you can also use these controls in other types of windows.

TStatic Class

The TStatic class is commonly used to display a text string in a dialog window. To use this class, include the header file <owl\static.h> in your program. You can create an instance of a TStatic control from a description in a resource file, or you can create it by specifying the location, dimension, and text for the TStatic object with the following constructor:

```
TStatic(TWindow*         parent,     // Parent window
        int              id,         // Control ID
        const char far* title,       // Text to be displayed
        int x, int y, int w, int h,// Position and size
        UINT             textlen,    // Number of characters
        TModule*         module = 0);
```

The third argument of the constructor is the null-terminated text string to be displayed in the TStatic control. If you do not know the number of characters in the text string, set the textlen argument to zero; the constructor will determine the number of characters.

Listing 18.1 shows a sample program that uses a TStatic control to display the coordinates of the location where the user last pressed the left mouse button. The program uses another `TStatic` control as a label. Notice how the text displayed in the `TStatic` control is changed in the `EvLButtonDown` function, which Windows calls whenever the user presses the left mouse button with the cursor inside the program's window.

Figure 18.7 shows the program of Listing 18.1 displaying the position of the mouse cursor in a `TStatic` control.

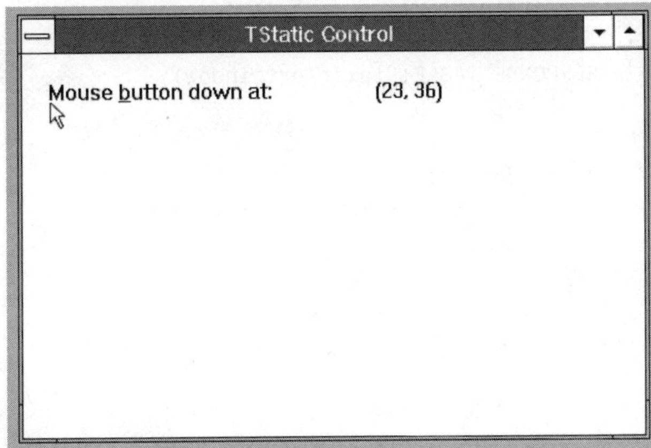

Figure 18.7. Displaying text with a `TStatic` control.

Listing 18.1. STEXT.CPP. Sample program to illustrate the use of `TStatic` control.

```
//---------------------------------------------------------------
// File: stext.cpp
//
// Demonstrate the use of the TStatic objects to display
// static text
//---------------------------------------------------------------
#include <owl\applicat.h>
#include <owl\framewin.h>
#include <owl\static.h>

class StaticTextWindow : public TWindow
{
public:
```

continues

Listing 18.1. continued

```
    StaticTextWindow();
    void EvLButtonDown(UINT modkeys, TPoint& point);

private:
    int     x, y;
    TStatic *clkpos;
    char    pos_string[16];

    DECLARE_RESPONSE_TABLE(StaticTextWindow);
};

// Define the response table
DEFINE_RESPONSE_TABLE1(StaticTextWindow,TWindow)
    EV_WM_LBUTTONDOWN,
END_RESPONSE_TABLE;
//-----------------------------------------------------------------
StaticTextWindow::StaticTextWindow() : TWindow(0, 0, 0),
    x(0), y(0)
{
// Select the window's height and width
    Attr.W = 500;
    Attr.H = 300;

// Set up a few TStatic objects in the window

     new TStatic(this, -1, "Mouse &button down at: ",
                20, 20, 250, 24, 0);

     wsprintf(pos_string, "(%d, %d)", x, y);

     clkpos = new TStatic(this, -1, pos_string, 260, 20,
                         100, 24, 0);

// Change some display attributes of the TStatic object
    clkpos->Attr.Style &= ~SS_LEFT;
    clkpos->Attr.Style |= SS_CENTER;
}
//-----------------------------------------------------------------
// StaticTextWindow:: E v L B u t t o n D o w n
// Process WM_LBUTTONDOWN events
```

```
void StaticTextWindow::EvLButtonDown(UINT, TPoint& point)
{
// Display the location of "mouse button down" in the TStatic
// control
    x = point.x;
    y = point.y;
    wsprintf(pos_string, "(%d, %d)", x, y);
    clkpos->Clear();
    clkpos->SetText(pos_string);
}
//-------------------------------------------------------------------
class StaticTextApp : public TApplication
{
public:
    StaticTextApp() : TApplication() {}
    void InitMainWindow()
    {
        MainWindow = new TFrameWindow(0, "TStatic Control",
                                      new StaticTextWindow, TRUE);
    }
};
//-------------------------------------------------------------------
int OwlMain(int, char**)
{
  StaticTextApp app;
  return app.Run();
}
```

Push Buttons, Check Boxes, Radio Buttons, and Group Boxes

Push buttons are commonly used to enable the user to initiate some action. For instance, a dialog window might have a push button labeled OK that the user can press to indicate acceptance of the settings that the dialog window offers. When the user presses the left mouse button with the cursor on a push button, the button is pushed in, but the button reverts to its original state as soon as the user releases the mouse button. In OWL 2.0, the `TButton` class, declared in the header file `<owl\button.h>`, represents push buttons.

Check boxes and radio buttons are specialized versions of push buttons. Unlike push buttons, these buttons can remain in one of two states: on (set) and off (reset). A check box or a radio button is toggled by a mouse click.

The label for a check box appears next to a square box. When the check box is turned "on" (or checked), a small check mark appears in the box. A radio button has a small circle next to its label. A dot appears in that circle when that radio button is set.

Check boxes and radio buttons are used in groups placed in a group box control (`TGroupBox` class). The difference between check boxes and radio buttons becomes apparent when they are arranged in a group box. From a group of check boxes, the user can click and select more than one check box. However, the user can select only one radio button from a group of radio buttons inside a group box. Thus, you should use check boxes to accept multiple selections from a group, and radio buttons when only one item from a group of related items can be selected. As an example, if you were preparing a dialog box through which an employee selects health insurance coverage, you would use a group of radio buttons to represent the health insurance companies because the employee is allowed to choose only one provider. However, the dialog box might display a number of check boxes showing several specific medical benefits from which the employee can pick one or more.

The `TCheckBox` and `TRadioButton` classes represent check boxes and radio buttons, respectively. To use these classes, include the header files `<owl\checkbox.h>` and `<owl\radiobut.h>`. If you place check boxes and radio buttons in group boxes, you must use the `TGroupBox` class and include the header file `<owl\groupbox.h>`.

Listing 18.2 shows a sample program that lets the user order a serving of ice cream. Figure 18.8 shows the output of the program after the user has selected the items and clicked the button labeled `Order`. As you can see from Listing 18.2, a group box displays the flavors as radio buttons while another group box shows the available toppings in a number of check boxes. The common practice is to use a dialog box to prompt for this type of user input. Typically, the dialog box is created with the Borland Resource Workshop and is initialized from the resource file. This example places the group boxes and the buttons directly in a window.

Creating an instance of a `TGroupBox` is straightforward with the following constructor:

```
TGroupBox(TWindow*         parent,     // Parent window
          int              id,         // Control ID
          const char far* title,      // Title of group box
          int x, int y, int w, int h,// Position and size
          TModule*         module = 0);
```

The `id` is used to associate messages from this `TGroupBox` control with functions that handle the messages. If you do not plan to process any messages from the group box, use -1 as the identifier. The group box appears as a rectangle with the title text placed along the top edge of the rectangle (see Figure 18.8).

The check boxes and radio buttons have similar constructors. Here is the constructor for a TCheckBox:

```
TCheckBox(TWindow*          parent,     // Parent window
          int               id,         // Control ID
          const char far* title,        // Label of check box
          int x, int y, int w, int h,// Position and size
          TGroupBox*        group,      // Group box containing this
                                        // check box
          TModule*          module = 0);
```

Note that the group argument is a pointer to the TGroupBox that contains this check box. Thus, if you plan to place a number of check boxes (or radio buttons) in a group box, you have to first create the group box and provide a pointer to the group box as an argument to the constructor of the check box.

The constructor for the TButton class, used to create the push buttons, is similar to that for the TGroupBox class except for an additional argument:

```
TButton(TWindow*          parent,     // Parent window
        int               id,         // Control ID
        const char far* title,        // Label of button
        int x, int y, int w, int h,// Position and size
        BOOL              isDefault = FALSE, // TRUE = this is
                                      // the default button
        TModule*          module = 0);
```

If the isDefault argument is TRUE, the button has the BS_DEFPUSHBUTTON style, which implies that the button is drawn with a heavy border and the user can select this button by pressing the Enter key. Usually, a push button has an associated control identifier (the id argument in the constructor) because push buttons are used to initiate some action and this requires having a message response function that can be called in response to the message generated by the push button. For instance, in Listing 18.2, the button labeled Order is tied to the take_order function as follows:

- Assign an identifier when creating the button:

```
const int ID_ORDER    = 1;
//...
new TButton(this, ID_ORDER, "Order", 50, 200, 80, 24, TRUE);
```

- Declare the `take_order` function as a member function of the window that contains the button:

```
void  take_order();
```

- Include the `take_order` function in the definition of the message response table with an `EV_COMMAND` macro as follows:

```
// Define the message response table
DEFINE_RESPONSE_TABLE1(ButtonTestWindow, TWindow)
  EV_COMMAND(ID_ORDER, take_order),
//...
END_RESPONSE_TABLE;
```

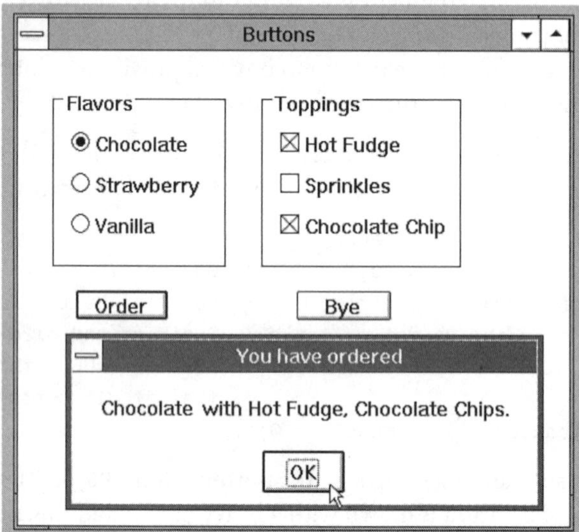

Figure 18.8. Prompting for ice cream flavors and toppings with check boxes and radio buttons.

Listing 18.2. BUTTONS.CPP. Sample program to illustrate the use of push button, check box, radio button, and group box classes.

```
//----------------------------------------------------------------
// File: buttons.cpp
//
```

```
// Sample program to illustrate the use of button, check box,
// radio buttons, and group box.
//-------------------------------------------------------------

#include <owl\applicat.h>
#include <owl\framewin.h>
#include <owl\button.h>
#include <owl\checkbox.h>
#include <owl\radiobut.h>
#include <owl\groupbox.h>

const int ID_ORDER    = 1;
const int ID_BYE      = 2;

const int FWIDTH      = 150;
const int FHEIGHT     = 150;
const int TWIDTH      = 170;
const int THEIGHT     = 150;

static char* flavor_names[3] =
{
    "Chocolate", "Strawberry", "Vanilla"
};

static char* topping_names[3] =
{
    "Hot Fudge", "Sprinkles", "Chocolate Chips"
};

class ButtonTestWindow : public TWindow
{
public:
    TRadioButton* flavors[3];
    TCheckBox*    toppings[3];

    ButtonTestWindow();

// Message handlers for the buttons

    void  take_order();
    void  quit()
```

continues

Listing 18.2. continued

```
    {
        PostQuitMessage(0);
    }

    DECLARE_RESPONSE_TABLE(ButtonTestWindow);
};

// Define the message response table

DEFINE_RESPONSE_TABLE1(ButtonTestWindow, TWindow)
  EV_COMMAND(ID_ORDER, take_order),
  EV_COMMAND(ID_BYE, quit),
END_RESPONSE_TABLE;
//-----------------------------------------------------------------
ButtonTestWindow::ButtonTestWindow() : TWindow(0, 0, 0)
{
// Create the group boxes to display flavor and topping
// selections.
    TGroupBox *gbf = new TGroupBox(this, -1, "Flavors", 30, 30,
                               FWIDTH, FHEIGHT);
    TGroupBox *gbt = new TGroupBox(this, -1, "Toppings",
                               FWIDTH+60, 30, TWIDTH, THEIGHT);
    int i;
    for(i = 0; i < 3; i++)
    {
        flavors[i] = new TRadioButton(this, -1, flavor_names[i],
                            46, 30+34*(i+1), FWIDTH-30, 24, gbf);
        toppings[i] = new TCheckBox(this, -1, topping_names[i],
                       FWIDTH+76, 30+34*(i+1), TWIDTH-30, 24, gbt);
    }

    new TButton(this, ID_ORDER, "Order", 50, 200, 80, 24, TRUE);
    new TButton(this, ID_BYE, "Bye", FWIDTH+90, 200,
                80, 24, FALSE);
}
//-----------------------------------------------------------------
void ButtonTestWindow::take_order()
{
    char buf[256];
// Check which flavor was ordered
    int i, n = 0;
```

```
    for(i = 0; i < 3; i++)
    {
        if(flavors[i]->GetCheck() == BF_CHECKED)
        {
            n = wsprintf(buf, "%s  ",
                            flavor_names[i]);
            break;
        }
    }
    if(i >= 3)
    {
        MessageBeep(MB_ICONEXCLAMATION);
        return;
    }

// Now pick the selected toppings
    int with = 0;
    for(i = 0; i < 3; i++)
    {
        if(toppings[i]->GetCheck() == BF_CHECKED)
        {
            if(with == 0)
            {
                n += wsprintf(&buf[n], "with ");
                with = 1;
            }
            n += wsprintf(&buf[n], "%s, ",
                                      topping_names[i]);
        }
    }
    wsprintf(&buf[n-2], ".");

// Display the order in a message box...
    MessageBox(buf, "You have ordered", MB_OK);
}
//---------------------------------------------------------------
class ButtonTestApp : public TApplication
{
public:
    ButtonTestApp() : TApplication() {}
    void  InitMainWindow();
```

continues

Listing 18.2. continued

```
};
//------------------------------------------------------------------
void ButtonTestApp::InitMainWindow()
{
// Uncomment next line to enable "Borland's Custom Control" look
//    EnableBWCC();

// Uncomment next line to enable Microsoft's 3-D Controls
//    EnableCtl3d();
    MainWindow = new TFrameWindow(0, "Buttons",
                                  new ButtonTestWindow);
}
//------------------------------------------------------------------
int OwlMain(int, char**)
{
    ButtonTestApp app;
    return app.Run();
}
```

In Listing 18.2, you will notice two commented function calls in the body of the `InitMainWindow` function. The call to `EnableBWCC` changes the look of the controls to the 3-D style of the Borland Windows Custom Controls, or BWCC for short. Figure 18.9 shows the result of calling `EnableBWCC()`.

Calling `EnableCtl3d` enables another style of 3-D look for controls such as message boxes. Figure 18.10 shows the output of the program after calling both `EnableBWCC()` and `EnableCtl3d()`.

> **Borland Windows Custom Controls and Microsoft 3-D Controls**
>
> *Borland Windows Custom Controls (BWCC)* are controls with a sophisticated 3-D look that accompany Borland C++. You can conveniently enable the BWCC controls by calling `EnableBWCC()` in the `InitMainWindow` function of your application class. Microsoft also provides a distinctive 3-D appearance for many controls, including message boxes. To enable this look in your OWL application, call `EnableCtl3d()` in `InitMainWindow`.

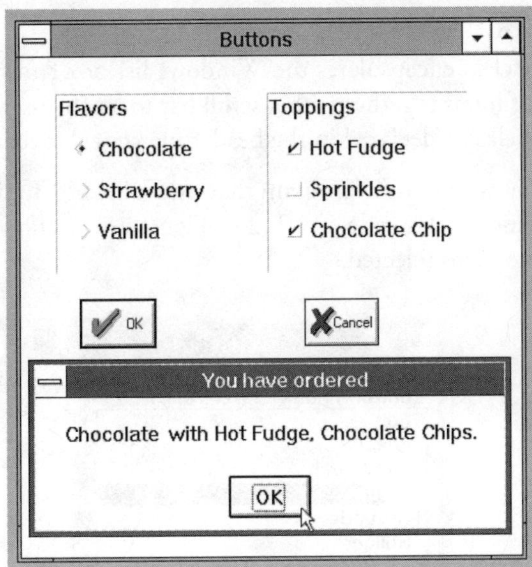

Figure 18.9. The changed look of the controls after calling `EnableBWCC()`.

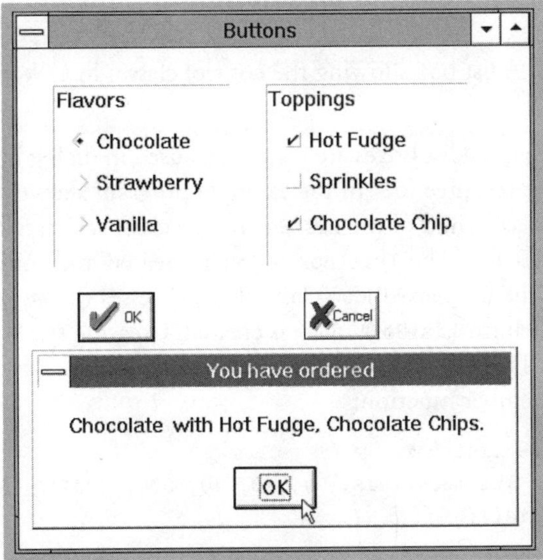

Figure 18.10. The 3-D look of the message box after calling `EnableCtl3d()`.

List Box

The `TListBox` class encapsulates the Windows list box control. Use this control to display a list of items together with a scroll bar to let the user scroll through the list. The `TListBox` class is declared in the header file `<owl\listbox.h>`.

Listing 18.3 shows a sample program that uses a list box to display the names of all the control window classes in OWL 2.0. Figure 18.11 shows the resulting list box with one of the items selected.

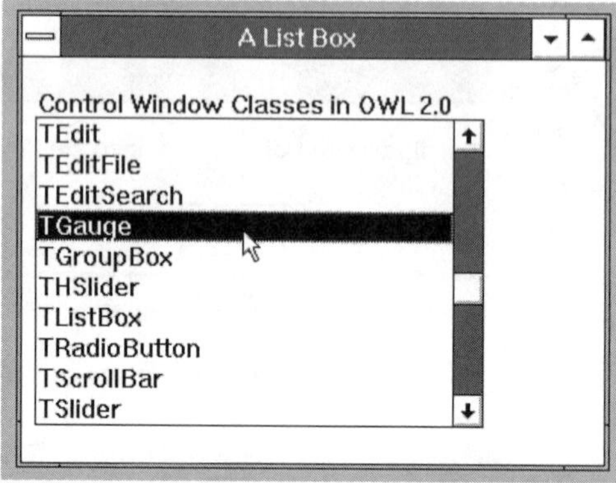

Figure 18.11. A list box showing the control classes in OWL 2.0.

Like other controls, list boxes are most often used in dialog boxes, and their layout is defined in the resource file. In the example program shown in Listing 18.3, the list box is created as a child of the `ListBoxWindow` class, which is derived from the OWL class `TFrameWindow`. The `TListBox` object is created and initialized in the `EvCreate` function (of the `ListBoxWindow` class) that processes the `WM_CREATE` message sent by Windows when the `ListBoxWindow` is created. Creating the `TListBox` object is a two-step process. The first is the invocation of the constructor and the second is a call to the `Create` member function:

```
// Create the list box
    lb = new TListBox(this, -1, 10, 40, 300, 200);
    lb->Create();
```

Once the list box is created, you can insert items into it by calling the `AddString` function of the `TListBox` class. For instance, to insert the string "OWL 2.0", write

```
lb->AddString("OWL 2.0");
```

By default, the list box control sorts its contents in alphabetical order. The default behavior of the list box is controlled by the setting of the `Attr.Style` variable of the `TListBox` class. The `TListBox` constructor adds `LBS_STANDARD` style to this variable with the following statement:

```
Attr.Style |= LBS_STANDARD;
```

The constant `LBS_STANDARD` (defined in `<windows.h>`) is part of the Windows API and it specifies the following behavior for the list box:

- Display a border (`LBS_BORDER`)
- Sort the contents (`LBS_SORT`)
- Notify parent window when user clicks any item (`LBS_NOTIFY`)

Listing 18.3. LSTBOX.CPP. Sample program to illustrate the use of the `TListBox` class.

```
//--------------------------------------------------------------
// File: lstbox.cpp
//
// Sample program to demonstrate the use of TListBox control
//--------------------------------------------------------------
#include <owl\applicat.h>
#include <owl\framewin.h>
#include <owl\static.h>
#include <owl\listbox.h>

class ListBoxWindow : public TFrameWindow
{
public:
    ListBoxWindow(const char *title);
    int EvCreate(CREATESTRUCT far&);

private:
    TListBox   *lb;  // Pointer to List Box

DECLARE_RESPONSE_TABLE(ListBoxWindow);
};
// Define Response table
DEFINE_RESPONSE_TABLE1(ListBoxWindow,TFrameWindow)
    EV_WM_CREATE,
END_RESPONSE_TABLE;
```

continues

Listing 18.3. continued

```
// Items for the list box
static char* control_classes[] =
{
  "TButton",     "TControl",   "TGauge",    "TGroupBox",
  "TListBox",    "TScrollBar", "TStatic",   "TVbxControl",
  "TSlider",     "THSlider",   "TVSlider",  "TEdit",
  "TEditSearch", "TEditFile",  "TCheckBox", "TRadioButton"
};
static numctrls = sizeof(control_classes) /
                  sizeof(control_classes[0]);

//-------------------------------------------------------------
ListBoxWindow::ListBoxWindow(const char *title) :  lb(0),
    TFrameWindow(0, title)
{
// Select the window's height and width
    Attr.W = 400;
    Attr.H = 300;

    new TStatic(this, -1, "Control Window Classes in OWL 2.0",
                 10, 20, 300, 24, 0);
}
//-------------------------------------------------------------
// ListBoxWindow:: E v C r e a t e
// Handle WM_CREATE event. Creates the list box.

int ListBoxWindow::EvCreate(CREATESTRUCT far& cs)
{
    TWindow::EvCreate(cs);

// Create the list box
    lb = new TListBox(this, -1, 10, 40, 300, 200);
    lb->Create();

// Add items to the list box
    int i;
    for(i = 0; i < numctrls; i++)
    {
        lb->AddString(control_classes[i]);
    }
```

```
    return 1;
}
//-----------------------------------------------------------------
class ListBoxApp : public TApplication
{
public:
    void  InitMainWindow();
};
//-----------------------------------------------------------------
void ListBoxApp::InitMainWindow()
{
    MainWindow = new ListBoxWindow("A List Box");
}
//-----------------------------------------------------------------
int OwlMain(int, char**)
{
    return ListBoxApp().Run();
}
```

Combo Box

A combo box is a list box together with an edit control or a static control that displays the current selection from the list box. A combo box can keep the list box hidden, showing only the current selection in the edit control. The list appears when the user clicks a button next to the edit control. Thus, it is convenient to use a combo box to let the user pick one of many items without using a lot of space to display the complete list. Many Windows applications use combo boxes. For example, many Windows word processors use a combo box to let the user select a font.

The OWL class `TComboBox`, derived from `TListBox`, encapsulates the functionality of a Windows combo box control. To use the `TComboBox` class, include the header file `<owl\combobox.h>`.

Listing 18.4 shows a sample program, similar to that for list box, that displays the names of the OWL 2.0 classes derived from `TControl`. Figure 18.12 shows the output of the program. In the figure, the drop-down list box is shown in its visible state. Normally, only the selected item is visible next to the button with an arrow pointing downward.

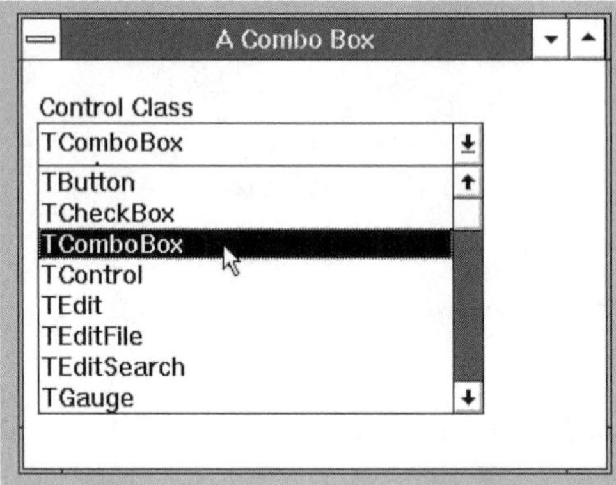

Figure 18.12. A combo box with its drop-down list box showing the control classes in OWL 2.0.

Normally, you would define the layout of a combo box in a resource file and initialize the `TComboBox` object by using a constructor that accepts the resource identifier as an argument. This example creates the combo box with the following constructor:

```
TComboBox(TWindow*  parent,   // Pointer to parent window
          int       id,       // Control identifier
          int x, int y,       // Position in parent window
          int w, int h,       // Size of the control
          DWORD     style,    // Style constants (CBS_xxx)
          UINT      textLen,  // Characters in edit control
          TModule*  module = 0);
```

This constructor calls the `TListBox` constructor and sets the `Attr.Style` variable as follows:

```
Attr.Style = WS_CHILD | WS_VISIBLE | WS_GROUP |
             WS_TABSTOP | CBS_SORT | CBS_AUTOHSCROLL |
             WS_VSCROLL | style;
```

The appearance of the combo box is controlled by the `style` argument that you provide to the constructor. You should use one of the following constants as the style:

- `CBS_SIMPLE` creates a combo box that displays the list box at all times. The edit control displays the current selection in the list box.
- `CBS_DROPDOWN` creates a combo box that is similar to that specified by `CBS_SIMPLE`, except that the list box is not displayed unless the user clicks the button next to the edit control.

- `CBS_DROPDOWNLIST` creates a combo box similar to that created for `CBS_DROPDOWN`, except that the current selection is displayed in a static control instead of an edit control.

These three constants specify the three types of combo boxes that Windows supports.

Once the combo box is created, you can add the strings to the list box by calling the `AddString` member function.

Listing 18.4. COMBOBX.CPP. Sample program to illustrate the use of the `TComboBox` class.

```
//----------------------------------------------------------------
// File: combobx.cpp
//
// Sample program to demonstrate the use of TComboBox control
//----------------------------------------------------------------
#include <owl\applicat.h>
#include <owl\framewin.h>
#include <owl\static.h>
#include <owl\combobox.h>

class ComboBoxWindow : public TFrameWindow
{
public:
    ComboBoxWindow(const char *title);
    int EvCreate(CREATESTRUCT far&);

private:
    TComboBox   *cb;  // Pointer to Combo Box

DECLARE_RESPONSE_TABLE(ComboBoxWindow);
};
// Define Response table
DEFINE_RESPONSE_TABLE1(ComboBoxWindow,TFrameWindow)
    EV_WM_CREATE,
END_RESPONSE_TABLE;

// Items for the Combo box
static char* control_classes[] =
```

continues

Listing 18.4. continued

```
{
  "TButton",     "TControl",   "TGauge",    "TGroupBox",
  "TComboBox",   "TScrollBar", "TStatic",   "TVbxControl",
  "TSlider",     "THSlider",   "TVSlider",  "TEdit",
  "TEditSearch", "TEditFile",  "TCheckBox", "TRadioButton"
};
static numctrls = sizeof(control_classes) /
                  sizeof(control_classes[0]);

//---------------------------------------------------------------
ComboBoxWindow::ComboBoxWindow(const char *title) :
    TFrameWindow(0, title)
{
// Select the window's height and width
    Attr.W = 400;
    Attr.H = 300;

    new TStatic(this, -1, "Control Class",
                10, 20, 300, 24, 0);
}
//---------------------------------------------------------------
// ComboBoxWindow:: E v C r e a t e
// Handle WM_CREATE event. Creates the Combo box.

int ComboBoxWindow::EvCreate(CREATESTRUCT far& cs)
{
    TWindow::EvCreate(cs);

// Create the Combo box
    cb = new TComboBox(this, -1, 10, 40, 300, 200,
                       CBS_DROPDOWNLIST, 25);
    cb->Create();

// Add items to the Combo box
    int i;
    for(i = 0; i < numctrls; i++)
    {
        cb->AddString(control_classes[i]);
    }
```

```
    return 1;
}
//----------------------------------------------------------------
class ComboBoxApp : public TApplication
{
public:
    void  InitMainWindow();
};
//----------------------------------------------------------------
void ComboBoxApp::InitMainWindow()
{
    MainWindow = new ComboBoxWindow("A Combo Box");
}
//----------------------------------------------------------------
int OwlMain(int, char**)
{
    return ComboBoxApp().Run();
}
```

Slider

The slider is a type of scroll bar. You can use a slider control to let the user change the value of a variable between a minimum and maximum value. Figure 18.13 shows a simple horizontal slider. Listing 18.5 shows the program that implements this slider.

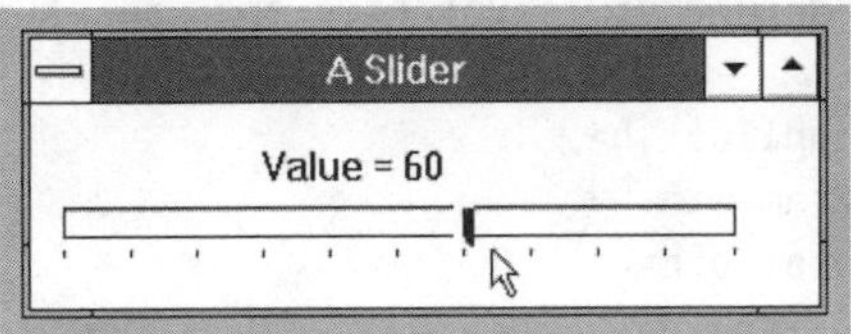

Figure 18.13. A horizontal slider.

The `TSlider` class serves as the base class for two types of slider classes: `THSlider` and `TVSlider` representing horizontal and vertical sliders, respectively. All of these classes are declared in the header file `<owl\slider.h>`, which you must include when you use a slider in your application.

To create the slider, you need a small bitmap defined in a resource file. This bitmap serves as the thumb that slides along the slider (see Figure 18.13). For the program in Listing 18.5, this bitmap is in the resource file HSLIDER.RC (this file appears in this book's companion disk). If you do not provide a bitmap, the `THSlider` constructor uses a bitmap with the identifier `IDB_HSLIDERTHUMB`, which is defined in the resource file `<owl\slider.rc>`.

To create a horizontal slider, use the following constructor:

```
THSlider(TWindow*  parent,  // Pointer to parent window
         int       id,      // Control identifier
         int x, int y,      // Position in parent window
         int w, int h,      // Size of the control
         TResId    thumbID, // ID of bitmap used as thumb
         TModule*  module = 0)
```

The constructor for the vertical slider uses the same argument list. By default, the slider uses 0 and 100 as the minimum and maximum values for the thumb position. Also, the slider displays a set of tick marks and forces the slider to align with the nearest one.

The example program uses a timer to periodically retrieve the position of the slider and display the position in a static control.

Listing 18.5. HSLIDER.CPP. Sample program to illustrate the use of the `THSlider` class.

```
//-------------------------------------------------------------
// File: hSlider.cpp
//
// A sample program that illustrates the use of a TSlider
//-------------------------------------------------------------
#include <owl\applicat.h>
#include <owl\framewin.h>
#include <owl\static.h>
#include <owl\slider.h>

const int PROG_TIMER = 1;

class SliderWindow : public TFrameWindow
{
public:
    SliderWindow(const char *title);
    ~SliderWindow()
```

```
    {
        KillTimer(PROG_TIMER);
    }

    int EvCreate(CREATESTRUCT far&);
    void EvTimer(UINT id);

private:
    TSlider *g;  // Pointer to Slider
    TStatic *curpos;

DECLARE_RESPONSE_TABLE(SliderWindow);
};

// Define Response table
DEFINE_RESPONSE_TABLE1(SliderWindow,TFrameWindow)
    EV_WM_CREATE,
    EV_WM_TIMER,
END_RESPONSE_TABLE;
//-----------------------------------------------------------------
SliderWindow::SliderWindow(const char *title) :
    TFrameWindow(0, title)
{
// Set the window's height and width
    Attr.W = 350;
    Attr.H = 120;

    curpos = new TStatic(this, -1, " ", 100, 16, 100, 24, 16);
}
//-----------------------------------------------------------------
// SliderWindow:: E v C r e a t e
// Handle WM_CREATE event. Creates a horizontal slider.

int SliderWindow::EvCreate(CREATESTRUCT far& cs)
{
    TWindow::EvCreate(cs);

// Create the slider
    g = new THSlider(this, -1, 10, 40, 300, 24, 1);
    g->Create();
```

continues

Listing 18.5. continued

```
// Create a timer
    SetTimer(PROG_TIMER, 1000, NULL);

    return 1;
}
//-----------------------------------------------------------------
// SliderWindow:: E v T i m e r
// Handle WM_TIMER event. Updates the slider.

void SliderWindow::EvTimer(UINT id)
{
    if(id != PROG_TIMER) return;
    int pos = g->GetPosition();

    char buf[20];
    wsprintf(buf, "Value = %d", pos);
    curpos->Clear();
    curpos->SetText(buf);
}
//-----------------------------------------------------------------
class SliderApp : public TApplication
{
public:
    void  InitMainWindow();
};
//-----------------------------------------------------------------
void SliderApp::InitMainWindow()
{
    MainWindow = new SliderWindow("A Slider");
}
//-----------------------------------------------------------------
int OwlMain(int, char**)
{
    return SliderApp().Run();
}
```

Gauge

The `TGauge` class, derived from `TControl`, is useful for displaying the progress of a process or an operation. For instance, a horizontal gauge might be used to show the progress of a disk copy operation. Figure 18.14 shows the appearance of a horizontal gauge. Listing 18.6 presents the program that displays the gauge. This program uses a timer to simulate an operation that is progressing in time and the progress is displayed by periodically updating the position of the gauge.

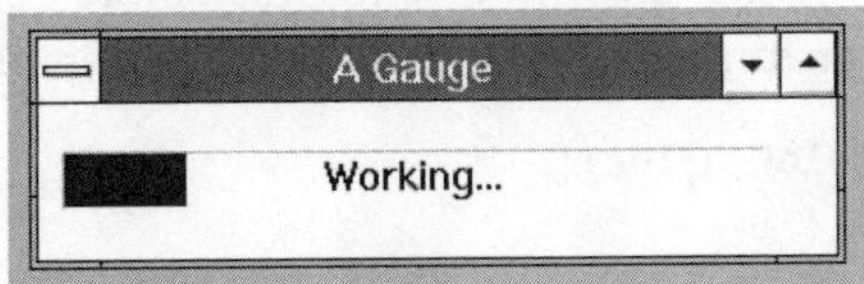

Figure 18.14. A gauge indicating progress.

Use the following constructor to initialize a `TGauge` object:

```
TGauge(TWindow*          parent,     // Pointer to parent
       const char far* title,      // Text inside gauge
       int               id,         // Control ID of gauge
       int X, int Y, int W, int H,// Position and size
       BOOL              isHorizontal = TRUE,
       int               margin = 0,
       TModule*          module = 0);
```

By default, the gauge has a horizontal orientation as you can see from the default value for the `isHorizontal` argument of the constructor.

The `TGauge` class provides several member functions for getting and setting the current value of the gauge. The following code fragment illustrates how you might get and set the value of the gauge:

```
    TGauge *g;  // Pointer to gauge
//...

//Get value of gauge
    int value = g->GetValue();

// Get the range
    int vmax, vmin;
    g->GetRange(vmin, vmax);

// Set a new value.
    value++;
    if(value > vmax)
    {
```

```
// Operation complete.
//...
    }
    g->SetValue(value);
```

By default the gauge fills up with a solid blue color. You can change this color by calling the `SetColor` function, which has the following prototype:

```
void SetColor(TColor color);
```

Listing 18.6. HGAUGE.CPP. Sample program to illustrate the use of the `TGauge` class.

```
//---------------------------------------------------------------
// File: hgauge.cpp
//
// A sample program that illustrates the use of a gauge to
// show progress
//---------------------------------------------------------------
#include <owl\applicat.h>
#include <owl\framewin.h>
#include <owl\gauge.h>

const int PROG_TIMER = 1;

class GaugeWindow : public TFrameWindow
{
public:
    GaugeWindow(const char *title);
    ~GaugeWindow()
    {
        KillTimer(PROG_TIMER);
    }

    int EvCreate(CREATESTRUCT far&);
    void EvTimer(UINT id);

private:
    TGauge *g;  // Pointer to gauge

DECLARE_RESPONSE_TABLE(GaugeWindow);
};
```

```
// Define Response table
DEFINE_RESPONSE_TABLE1(GaugeWindow,TFrameWindow)
    EV_WM_CREATE,
    EV_WM_TIMER,
END_RESPONSE_TABLE;
//------------------------------------------------------------
GaugeWindow::GaugeWindow(const char *title) :
    TFrameWindow(0, title)
{
// Set the window's height and width
    Attr.W = 350;
    Attr.H = 100;
}
//------------------------------------------------------------
// GaugeWindow:: E v C r e a t e
// Handle WM_CREATE event. Creates the gauge.

int GaugeWindow::EvCreate(CREATESTRUCT far& cs)
{
    TWindow::EvCreate(cs);

// Create the gauge
    g = new TGauge(this, "Working...", -1, 10, 20, 300, 24);
    g->Create();

// Create a timer
    SetTimer(PROG_TIMER, 100, NULL);

    return 1;
}
//------------------------------------------------------------
// GaugeWindow:: E v T i m e r
// Handle WM_TIMER event. Updates the gauge.

void GaugeWindow::EvTimer(UINT id)
{
    if(id != PROG_TIMER) return;
    int value = g->GetValue() + 1;

    int vmax, vmin;
    g->GetRange(vmin, vmax);
    if(value > vmax) value = vmin;
```

continues

Listing 18.6. continued

```
    g->SetValue(value);
}
//----------------------------------------------------------------
class GaugeApp : public TApplication
{
public:
    void  InitMainWindow();
};
//----------------------------------------------------------------
void GaugeApp::InitMainWindow()
{
    MainWindow = new GaugeWindow("A Gauge");
}
//----------------------------------------------------------------
int OwlMain(int, char**)
{
    return GaugeApp().Run();
}
```

TEditSearch Class

This section presents a sample program using the `TEditSearch` class as an example of a control that allows the user to enter and edit multiple lines of text. The `TEditSearch` class is derived from `TEdit`, which, in turn, is derived from `TStatic` (see Figure 18.3). The `TStatic` class displays text but does not allow the user to edit it. The `TEdit` class allows editing. The `TEditSearch` class supports search and replace operations in addition to editing.

Listing 18.7 shows a very simple program that displays a `TEditSearch` object inside a `TFrameWindow`. Figure 18.15 shows the resulting window after some text has been entered into it. To build the program, you also need a resource file (EDTSRCH.RC on the companion disk) with the following lines in it:

```
#include <owl\editsear.rh>
#include <owl\inputdia.rh>

#include <owl\inputdia.rc>
#include <owl\editsear.rc>
```

These resources define the menu bar and the pull-down menus that appear in the sample program. The Edit menu offers the following items in the pull-down menu: Undo, Cut, Copy, Paste, Delete, Clear All.

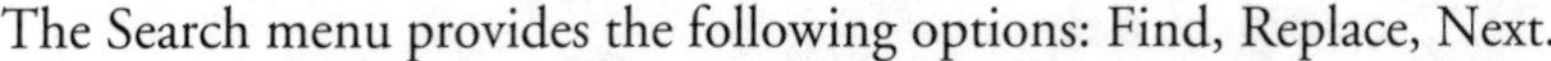

The Search menu provides the following options: Find, Replace, Next.

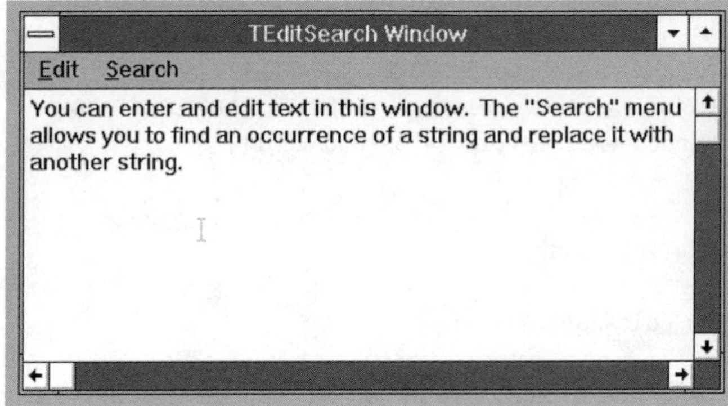

Figure 18.15. A `TEditSearch` window.

Listing 18.7. EDTSRCH.CPP. Sample program to illustrate the use of the `TEditSearch` class.

```
//---------------------------------------------------------------
// File: edtsrch.cpp
//
// A sample program that shows how to use the TEditSearch class
//---------------------------------------------------------------
#include <owl\applicat.h>
#include <owl\framewin.h>
#include <owl\editsear.h>
//---------------------------------------------------------------
class EditApp : public TApplication
{
public:
    EditApp() : TApplication("Edit Search") {}
    void InitMainWindow();
};
//---------------------------------------------------------------
// EditApp::  I n i t M a i n W i n d o w
// A TEditSearch window is used as the program's main window.

void EditApp::InitMainWindow()
{
```

continues

Listing 18.7. continued

```
    MainWindow = new TFrameWindow(0, "TEditSearch Window",
                                        new TEditSearch);
    MainWindow->AssignMenu(IDM_EDITSEARCH);
    MainWindow->Attr.AccelTable = TResId(IDA_EDITSEARCH);
    MainWindow->Attr.Style |= DS_LOCALEDIT;
}
//----------------------------------------------------------------
int OwlMain(int, char**)
{
    return EditApp().Run();
}
```

Using Dialogs

Windows applications use dialog boxes to prompt the user for input. For instance, many Windows applications display a dialog letting you select a file to be opened, or enter the name of a file where data will be saved. Dialog boxes are child windows that contain a variety of controls. Most dialog boxes use list boxes, edit controls, check boxes, radio buttons, and push buttons to let the user enter input and specify options. You have already seen examples of these controls in the previous sections. This section presents a sample program that displays a standard dialog for color selection. This dialog is implemented by the `TChooseColorDialog` class, which is part of a set of nine commonly used dialog classes that are derived from the `TCommonDialog` class: `TChooseColorDialog`, `TChooseFontDialog`, `TFileOpenDialog`, `TFileSaveDialog`, `TFindDialog`, `TFindReplaceDialog`, `TOpenSaveDialog`, `TPrintDialog`, `TReplaceDialog`.

Figure 18.16 shows the appearance of the color selection dialog box implemented by the `TChooseColorDialog` class. Listing 18.8 shows the program that displays the dialog. The entire operation of setting up the dialog and retrieving the user's selection appears in the body of the `CmColor` function in Listing 18.8.

Before displaying the dialog, you have to set up a `TData` object where `TData` is a nested class of `TChooseColorDialog`. In fact, each of the dialog classes derived from `TCommonDialog` has a nested class named `TData`. Here is how the `TData` structure is set up and used to display the `TChooseColorDialog`:

```
    TColor ccol[16];  // Structures for custom colors

// Prepare data structure for the TChooseColorDialog class
    TChooseColorDialog::TData data;
    data.Flags = CC_FULLOPEN;
    data.Color = RGB(0,0,0);
    data.CustColors = ccol;

// Display information about selected color
    if (TChooseColorDialog(MainWindow, data).Execute() == IDOK)
    {
// User's selections are in the "data" object. Use them.
//...
    }
```

You will see examples of other standard dialogs in the example programs in the rest of this book. For instance, Chapter 20, "Displaying Text in Windows," uses a `TChooseFontDialog` to let the user select a font.

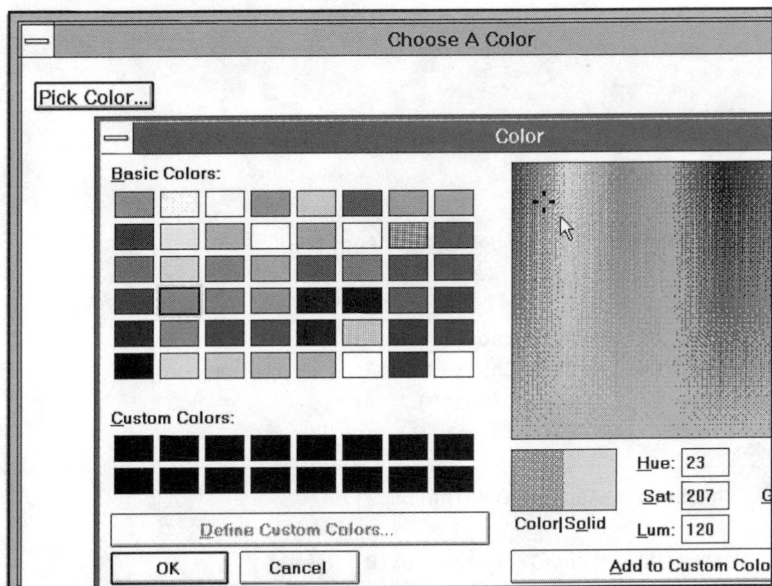

Figure 18.16. The color selection dialog box.

Listing 18.8. COLORDLG.CPP. Sample program to illustrate the use of the `TChooseColorDialog` class.

```
//------------------------------------------------------------
// File: colordlg.cpp
//
// Sample program that demonstrates how to use the
// TChooseColorDialog class.
//------------------------------------------------------------
#include <owl\framewin.h>
#include <owl\applicat.h>
#include <owl\button.h>
#include <owl\color.h>
#include <owl\chooseco.h>

#define CM_COLOR 101

class ChooseColorApp : public TApplication
{
public:
    ChooseColorApp() : TApplication("Choose A Color") {}

private:
    void   InitMainWindow();
    void   CmColor();

DECLARE_RESPONSE_TABLE(ChooseColorApp);
};

// Define the response table for the Application
DEFINE_RESPONSE_TABLE1(ChooseColorApp, TApplication)
  EV_COMMAND(CM_COLOR, CmColor),
END_RESPONSE_TABLE;
//------------------------------------------------------------
void ChooseColorApp::InitMainWindow()
{
    MainWindow = new TFrameWindow(0, Name);

// Display a button that the user can press to bring up the
// color selection dialog
    new TButton(MainWindow, CM_COLOR, "Pick Color...",
                10, 20, 100, 24, TRUE);
}
```

```
//--------------------------------------------------------------
// ChooseColorApp:: C m C o l o r
// Called when user presses the "Pick Color..." button

void ChooseColorApp::CmColor()
{
    char   msg[128];
    TColor ccol[16];

// Prepare data structure for the TChooseColorDialog class
    TChooseColorDialog::TData data;
    data.Flags = CC_FULLOPEN;
    data.Color = RGB(0,0,0);
    data.CustColors = ccol;

// Display information about selected color
    if (TChooseColorDialog(MainWindow, data).Execute() == IDOK)
    {
        wsprintf(msg, "RGB intensities:\r\n\r\n Red: %d\r\n "
                      "Green: %d\r\n Blue: %d",
                       data.Color.Red(), data.Color.Green(),
                       data.Color.Blue());
        MainWindow->MessageBox(msg, Name, MB_OK);
    }
}
//--------------------------------------------------------------
int OwlMain(int, char**)
{
    return ChooseColorApp().Run();
}
```

Building a Tool Bar with Gadgets

A tool bar is a collection of push buttons, usually appearing at the top of an application's main window, that allows the user to quickly initiate an action. Many Windows applications, including Borland C++, have a tool bar. Most of these tool bars include a button that allows the user to quickly bring up the File Open dialog box. Similarly, there is usually a bitmap button on the tool bar to print the document being displayed by the application. The user can perform each of these actions from the menus, but having the buttons on the tool bar makes it faster to do these tasks.

A status bar is another common decoration that appears in the main window of many Windows applications. This is an area at the bottom of a main window where the application displays short help messages, as well as the status of specific keys such as Caps Lock, Num Lock, and Insert.

OWL 2.0 makes it easy to create tool bars and status bars and associate specific message processing functions that are called when the user clicks their buttons. To start with, OWL 2.0 includes the `TDecoratedFrame` and `TDecoratedMDIFrame` classes that let you add a tool bar and a status bar as child windows. OWL also provides the `TControlBar` and `TStatusBar` classes that you can use to directly implement a tool bar and a status bar, respectively. Finally, there are gadget classes that you can use as buttons in the tool bar.

The program in Listing 18.9 demonstrates the ease with which you can add a tool bar and a status bar to your application's main window. Figure 18.17 shows the appearance of the main window created by the program of Listing 18.9.

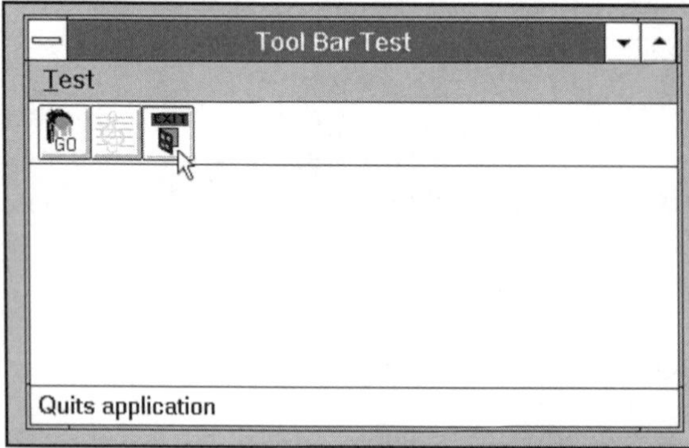

Figure 18.17. A tool bar and a status bar in a main window.

To create the tool bar, you will need the bitmaps for each button. The resource file TOOLBAR.RC (in the companion disk) includes bitmaps for the three buttons that appear in the example program. The steps involved in creating a main window with the tool bar are as follows:

1. Create the frame window. Here is how the example program does it:

```
TDecoratedMDIFrame* frame = new TDecoratedMDIFrame(Name,
                        "MAINMENU", *new TMDIClient, TRUE);
```

2. After creating the frame, create a `TControlBar` as a child of the frame window:

```
// Create a control bar
    TControlBar* cb = new TControlBar(frame);
```

3. Insert button gadgets into the `TControlBar`. Each button gadget has an associated bitmap resource ID and a control ID that tie together a message response function to that button. Here is how the example program inserts the buttons:

```
// Insert buttons into control bar and associate an ID
// with each button

    cb->Insert(*new TButtonGadget(CM_START, CM_START));
    cb->Insert(*new TButtonGadget(CM_SOUND, CM_SOUND));
    cb->Insert(*new TButtonGadget(CM_EXIT, CM_EXIT));
```

4. Insert the `TControlBar` at the top of the frame:

```
// Place the control bar at the top edge of the frame
    frame->Insert(*cb, TDecoratedFrame::Top);
```

Creating the status bar is even easier. All you have to do is create the `TStatusBar` object and add it to the frame window:

```
TStatusBar *sb = new TStatusBar(frame, TGadget::Recessed,
                                TStatusBar::CapsLock |
                                TStatusBar::NumLock |
                                TStatusBar::Overtype);
frame->Insert(*sb, TDecoratedFrame::Bottom);
```

Listing 18.9. TOOLBAR.CPP. Sample program to illustrate the use of the `TControlBar`, `TStatusBar`, and `TButtonGadget` classes.

```
//--------------------------------------------------------------
// File: toolbar.cpp
//
// Sample program to illustrate how to use a TControlBar gadget.
//--------------------------------------------------------------
#include <owl\applicat.h>
#include <owl\buttonga.h>
#include <owl\controlb.h>
#include <owl\statusba.h>
#include <owl\decmdifr.h>
```

continues

Listing 18.9. continued

```
#define CM_START 1

#define CM_SOUND 2

class ToolBarApp : public TApplication
{
public:
    ToolBarApp() : TApplication("Tool Bar Test") {}
    void CmStart();
    void CmSound();

public:
    void InitMainWindow();

DECLARE_RESPONSE_TABLE(ToolBarApp);
};

// Define the response table

DEFINE_RESPONSE_TABLE1(ToolBarApp, TApplication)
    EV_COMMAND(CM_START, CmStart),
    EV_COMMAND(CM_SOUND, CmSound),
END_RESPONSE_TABLE;
//-----------------------------------------------------------------
void ToolBarApp::InitMainWindow ()
{
    TDecoratedMDIFrame* frame = new TDecoratedMDIFrame(Name,
                                "MAINMENU", *new TMDIClient, TRUE);
// Create a control bar
    TControlBar* cb = new TControlBar(frame);

// Insert buttons into control bar and associate an ID
// with each button

    cb->Insert(*new TButtonGadget(CM_START, CM_START));
    cb->Insert(*new TButtonGadget(CM_SOUND, CM_SOUND));
    cb->Insert(*new TButtonGadget(CM_EXIT, CM_EXIT));

// Place the control bar at the top edge of the frame
    frame->Insert(*cb, TDecoratedFrame::Top);
```

```
// Create a status bar
    TStatusBar *sb = new TStatusBar(frame, TGadget::Recessed,
                                    TStatusBar::CapsLock |
                                    TStatusBar::NumLock |
                                    TStatusBar::Overtype);

    frame->Insert(*sb, TDecoratedFrame::Bottom);

    MainWindow = frame;
}
//-----------------------------------------------------------------
// ToolBarApp:: C m S t a r t

void ToolBarApp::CmStart()
{
    MainWindow->MessageBox("Started...", "Control Bar", MB_OK);
}
//-----------------------------------------------------------------
// ToolBarApp:: C m S o u n d

void ToolBarApp::CmSound()
{
    MessageBeep(MB_ICONEXCLAMATION);
}
//-----------------------------------------------------------------
int OwlMain (int, char**)
{
    ToolBarApp   App;
    return App.Run();
}
```

Automatic Scrolling with *TScroller*

The `TScroller` class, derived from `TScrollerBase`, supports scrolling the contents of a window by moving the origin of the viewport. Listing 18.10 shows a program that demonstrates how a `TScroller` object can scroll the contents of a window. Figure 18.18 shows the resulting window.

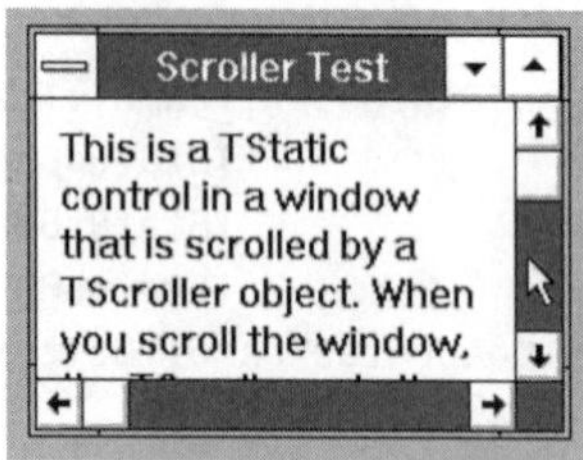

Figure 18.18. Scrolling the contents of a window with a `TScroller`.

The example program displays a `TStatic` control in a frame window. To associate the `TScroller` object with the frame window, you have to set the Scroller member variable to the address of the `TScroller` as follows:

```
// Create the scroller to scroll the contents of this window
    Scroller = new TScroller(this, 8, 16, 25, 10);
```

Once this is done, the `TScroller` will take care of scrolling the contents of the window whenever you use the scroll bar. In fact, the `TScroller` scrolls the contents of the window even if you do not use the scroll bar and simply drag the mouse from inside the client area of the window to outside that area.

The `TScroller` class is defined in the header file `<owl\scroller.h>` and the `TScroller` constructor used in the example program has the following prototype:

```
TScroller(TWindow* window, // Pointer to parent window
          int      xUnit,  // Amount to scroll in x- and y-
          int      yUnit,  // directions (in logical units)
          long     xRange, // Number of x- and y- scroll units
          long     yRange);// in area being scrolled
```

Listing 18.10. SWINDOW.CPP.Sample program to illustrate scrolling the contents of a window with the `TScroller` class.

```
//-------------------------------------------------------------
// File: swindow.cpp
//
// Sample program to illustrate scrolling with a TScroller
//-------------------------------------------------------------
#include <owl\applicat.h>
#include <owl\framewin.h>
```

```
#include <owl\scroller.h>
#include <owl\static.h>
#include <owl\dc.h>

class ScrolledWindow : public TFrameWindow
{
public:
    ScrolledWindow(const char* title);

private:
    TStatic *txt;
};

static char text[] =
"This is a TStatic control in a window that is scrolled by a "
"TScroller object. When you scroll the window, the TScroller "
"sets the viewport origin so that the TStatic control is drawn "
"at a new location and the contents of the window scroll.";

//---------------------------------------------------------------
// ScrolledWindow:: S c r o l l e d W i n d o w
//
// Constructor for a ScrolledWindow that sets scroll styles and
// constructs the Scroller object.
//

ScrolledWindow::ScrolledWindow(const char* title) : txt(0),
    TFrameWindow(0, title)
{
    Attr.W = 200;
    Attr.H = 150;
    Attr.Style |= WS_VSCROLL | WS_HSCROLL;
    new TStatic(this, -1, text, 10, 10, 180, 300, 0);

// Create the scroller to scroll the contents of this window
    Scroller = new TScroller(this, 8, 16, 25, 10);
}
//---------------------------------------------------------------
class ScrolledWindowApp : public TApplication
{
public:
    ScrolledWindowApp() : TApplication("ScrolledWindow") {}
```

continues

Listing 18.10. continued

```
    void InitMainWindow()
    {
        MainWindow = new ScrolledWindow("Scroller Test");
    }
};
//--------------------------------------------------------------
int OwlMain(int, char**)
{
  return ScrolledWindowApp().Run();
}
```

Validating Input Data

OWL 2.0 includes a number of classes that validate information that the user enters into an edit control. The `CanClose` function of the `TEdit` control calls an appropriate function of an associated validator object to determine if the data entered by the user is correct. The validator classes make it easy to check for validity of data in a `TEdit` control.

The example program in Listing 18.11 illustrates the use of the following validator classes:

- `TFilterValidator` checks if keys pressed by the user belong to an acceptable set of characters. For example, the constructor `TFilterValidator("A-Za-z. ")` creates a validator that only accepts the lowercase and uppercase letters, one or more spaces, and one or more periods.
- `TPXPictureValidator` checks that the user-entered string matches a template specified in the program. The example program uses the constructor `TPXPictureValidator("&/&&&#")` to accept the following pattern: a single letter followed by a slash (`/`) that, in turn, is followed by three letters and a digit. The letters are automatically converted to uppercase. This picture validator considers a string such as `W/OSD5` to be valid. Table 18.3 shows the meaning of characters appearing in a picture format used to specify a picture validator.
- `TRangeValidator` accepts numerical values in a specified range.

Table 18.3. Alphabetical listing of the classes in OWL 2.0 (multiple base classes are indicated by a + prefix).

Character	Interpretation by `TPxPictureValidator`
`#`	Accepts a single digit between 0 and 9
`?`	Accepts a lowercase or uppercase letter
`&`	Accepts a letter that the validator automatically converts to uppercase
`@`	Accepts any character
`!`	Accepts any character but forces it to uppercase
`;`	Accepts the next character literally
`*`	Denotes a repetition count
`,`	Denotes alternatives
`[] {}`	Denotes options and groups
`Others`	Accepted literally

The example program displays a window with a push button labeled `Enter Data`. When you click this button, a dialog box with a number of edit controls appears. Each edit field has an associated validator to check the input. If you click the OK button in the dialog box and one of the fields does not contain a valid value, the validator displays an error message. Figure 18.19 shows the error message displayed when you click OK, but the field labeled `Org:` is missing the last digit. Once you correctly enter all the information and click the OK button, the program displays another message box (see Figure 18.20) confirming the values you entered.

The validator classes are declared in the header file `<owl\validate.h>`, which you must include if you use any validator classes in your program.

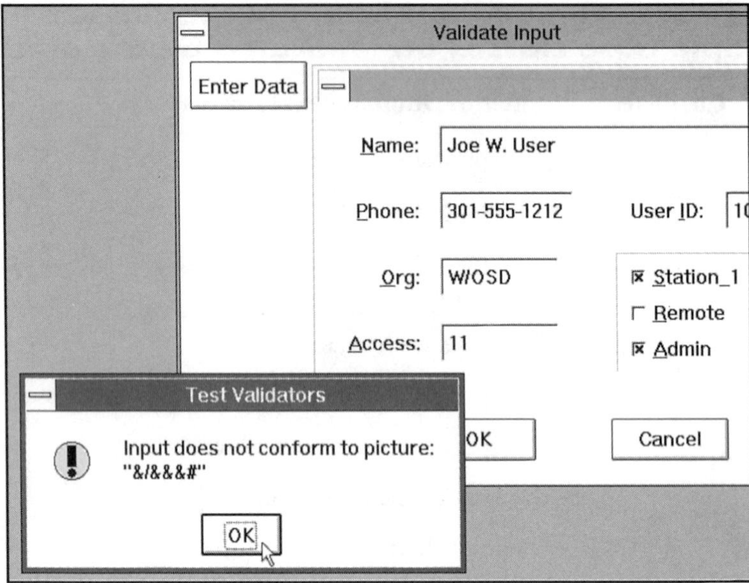

Figure 18.19. Validating user's input with the validator classes.

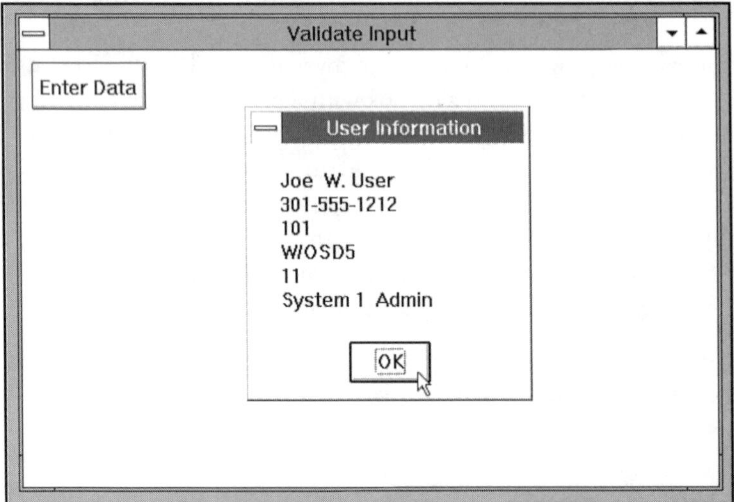

Figure 18.20. Message box confirming information entered by user.

The example program defines a dialog class TUserDlg, derived from TDialog. The TUserDlg object is initialized from a template defined in the resource file validtr.rc (you will find this file in this book's companion disk). The TUserDlg constructor associates an appropriate validator with each TEdit control by calling the SetValidator function of the TEdit class. For instance, the edit control for the Phone: field is validated by a picture validator specified as follows:

```
// The "edit" variable points to the TEdit object
   edit->SetValidator(new TPXPictureValidator("###-###-####"));
```

Notice that the picture, in this case, is a sequence of three digits followed by a dash, another three digits, a dash, and four more digits, which is a 10-digit phone number commonly used in North America.

An interesting feature of the example program in Listing 18.11 is the use of a "transfer" buffer to retrieve the data entered by the user in the TUserDlg dialog box. Essentially, you define a data structure with room for the text entered into the edit controls (for check boxes, you need a Boolean variable, denoted by the Windows API data type BOOL), and store a pointer to this structure in the TransferBuffer member variable of the dialog. By default, the dialog will transfer the contents of its edit controls and check boxes into the transfer buffer. Note that the order of the members in the transfer data structure must correspond to the order in which the corresponding controls are created. Thus, in the example program, the creation of the edit control for the phone number follows that for the name because the UserInfo data structure used for transfers has the phone_num member following the name member.

Listing 18.11. VALIDTR.CPP. Sample program to illustrate validating user input with the validator classes.

```
//--------------------------------------------------------------
// File: validtr.cpp
//
// Sample program to illustrate the use of Validators
//--------------------------------------------------------------
#include <owl\applicat.h>
#include <owl\dialog.h>
#include <owl\framewin.h>
#include <owl\edit.h>
#include <owl\button.h>
#include <owl\checkbox.h>
#include <owl\validate.h>
```

continues

Listing 18.11. continued

```
#define CM_INPUT 201

#define MAXNAMELEN  35
#define MAXPHONELEN 13
#define MAXIDLEN    4
#define MAXORGLEN   8
#define MAXACLEN    3

struct UserInfo
{
  char name[MAXNAMELEN];
  char phone_num[MAXPHONELEN];
  char id[MAXIDLEN];
  char org_code[MAXORGLEN];
  char access[MAXACLEN];
  BOOL Sys1;
  BOOL Remote;
  BOOL Admin;
};

//-------------------------------------------------------------
class TUserDlg : public TDialog
{
public:
    TUserDlg(TWindow* parent, const char* name,
             UserInfo& transfer);
};
//-------------------------------------------------------------
TUserDlg::TUserDlg(TWindow* parent, const char* name,
                   UserInfo& transfer) : TDialog(parent, name),
                                         TWindow(parent)
{
    TEdit* edit;

    edit = new TEdit(this, 101, sizeof(transfer.name));
    edit->SetValidator(new TFilterValidator("A-Za-z. "));

    edit = new TEdit(this, 102, sizeof(transfer.phone_num));
    edit->SetValidator(new TPXPictureValidator("###-###-####"));

    edit = new TEdit(this, 103, sizeof(transfer.id));
```

```
    edit->SetValidator(new TRangeValidator(1, 999));

    edit = new TEdit(this, 104, sizeof(transfer.org_code));
    edit->SetValidator(new TPXPictureValidator("&/&&&#"));

    edit = new TEdit(this, 105, sizeof(transfer.access));
    edit->SetValidator(new TPXPictureValidator("11,12,13,14,15"));

    new TCheckBox(this, 106, 0);
    new TCheckBox(this, 107, 0);
    new TCheckBox(this, 108, 0);

    TransferBuffer = (void far*)&transfer;
}
//--------------------------------------------------------------
class TestWindow : public TFrameWindow
{
public:
    TestWindow(TWindow* parent, const char* title);
    void CmInput();

private:
    UserInfo user_data;

DECLARE_RESPONSE_TABLE(TestWindow);
};

// Define the response table
DEFINE_RESPONSE_TABLE1(TestWindow, TFrameWindow)
    EV_COMMAND(CM_INPUT, CmInput),
END_RESPONSE_TABLE;

//--------------------------------------------------------------
TestWindow::TestWindow(TWindow* parent, const char* title)
           : TFrameWindow(parent, title), TWindow(parent, title)
{
    memset(&user_data, 0, sizeof user_data);
}
//--------------------------------------------------------------
void TestWindow::CmInput()
{
    char user_info[sizeof(UserInfo)+10];
```

continues

Listing 18.11. continued

```
    if (TUserDlg(this,"USERINFO", user_data).Execute() == IDOK)
    {
        strcpy(user_info, user_data.name);
        strcat(user_info, "\n");
        strcat(user_info, user_data.phone_num);
        strcat(user_info, "\n");
        strcat(user_info, user_data.id);
        strcat(user_info, "\n");
        strcat(user_info, user_data.org_code);
        strcat(user_info, "\n");
        strcat(user_info, user_data.access);
        strcat(user_info, "\n");
        strcat(user_info, user_data.Sys1 ? "System 1 " : " ");
        strcat(user_info, user_data.Remote ? "Remote " : " ");
        strcat(user_info, user_data.Admin ? "Admin " : " ");
        MessageBox(user_info, "User Information", MB_OK);
    }
}
//-------------------------------------------------------------------
class ValidatorApp : public TApplication
{
public:
    ValidatorApp() : TApplication("Test Validators") {}

    void InitMainWindow()
    {
        EnableCtl3d();
        MainWindow = new TestWindow(0, "Validate Input");

// Add a button that allows the user to activate a dialog
        new TButton(MainWindow, CM_INPUT, "Enter Data",
                    10, 10, 100, 40);
    }
};
//-------------------------------------------------------------------
int OwlMain(int, char**)
{
    return ValidatorApp().Run();
}
```

Using Frame Windows

Although you have not seen any explicit examples of frame windows, almost all example programs in this chapter use a frame window to display their output. Frame windows serve as containers where the application's windows appear. This section briefly describes two specific frame windows: the `TMDIFrame` class that provides the main window for an MDI application and `TLayoutWindow` that lets you control the layout of child windows inside a main window.

MDI Window Classes

Nowadays most Windows applications support the multiple document interface (MDI) that displays multiple child windows within a main frame window. An MDI application's main window serves as a frame for a client window known as the MDI client window. All other child windows, known as MDI child windows, appear inside the MDI client window. Thus, OWL 2.0 provides three distinct window classes that you can use in an MDI application:

- `TMDIFrame` class for the frame window.
- `TMDIClient` class for the window that appears as a child of the frame window and that holds the MDI child windows.
- `TMDIChild` class for the MDI child windows.

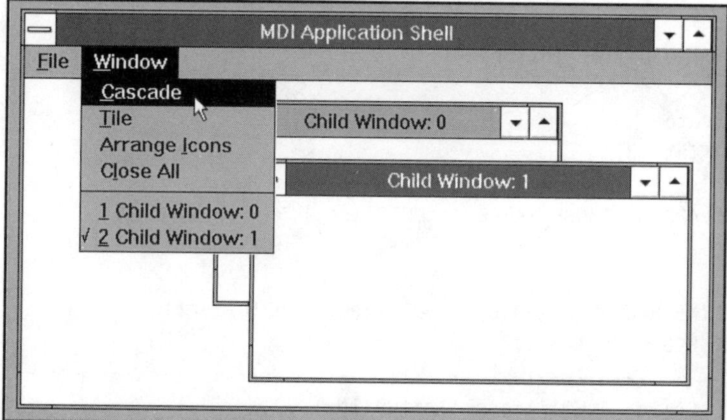

Figure 18.21. The framework of an MDI application.

Listing 18.12 shows a simple MDI application that shows how to use these three classes of windows. Figure 18.21 shows the appearance of the program's main window after two MDI child windows have been created. The menus are defined in a resource file (TSTMDI.RC on the companion disk). As you can see, this simple program provides all the features of a complete MDI application. This ease of programming is possible because all the work is done by the OWL classes `TMDIFrame`, `TMDIClient`, and `TMDIChild`.

Listing 18.12. TSTMDI.CPP. Sample program to illustrate the use of the `TMDIFrame` class.

```
//---------------------------------------------------------------
// File: tstmdi.cpp
//
// Illustrates an MDI application
//---------------------------------------------------------------
#include <owl\applicat.h>
#include <owl\mdi.h>
#include <owl\mdichild.h>
#include <stdio.h>

class AnMDIClient : public TMDIClient
{
public:
    AnMDIClient() : TMDIClient(), id(0) {}

    TMDIChild* InitChild();

private:
    int id;

DECLARE_RESPONSE_TABLE (AnMDIClient);
};

DEFINE_RESPONSE_TABLE1(AnMDIClient, TMDIClient)
END_RESPONSE_TABLE;
//---------------------------------------------------------------
TMDIChild* AnMDIClient::InitChild()
{
  char title[20];
  wsprintf(title, "Child Window: %d", id++);
  return new TMDIChild(*this, title);
}
```

```
//------------------------------------------------------------------
class TMDIApp : public TApplication
{
public:
    TMDIApp() : TApplication("MDI Application Shell") {}
    void InitMainWindow();
};
//------------------------------------------------------------------
void TMDIApp::InitMainWindow()
{
  MainWindow = new TMDIFrame(GetName(), "MDIMENU",
                             *new AnMDIClient);
}
//------------------------------------------------------------------
int OwlMain(int, char**)
{
  return TMDIApp().Run();
}
```

TLayoutWindow

The `TLayoutWindow` is a special type of window that interprets layout metrics associated with child windows and arranges the child windows as specified by their layout metrics. The layout metrics refer to the settings for the x, y position and the width and the height of a child window. The setting of these four values is represented by a `TLayoutMetrics` class, which is declared in `<owl\layoutwi.h>`. The `TLayoutMtrics` class has four public data members representing the x, y positions and width and height:

```
TEdgeConstraint           X;      // can be lmLeft, lmCenter,
                                  //        lmRight
TEdgeConstraint           Y;      // can be lmTop, lmCenter,
                                  //        lmBottom
TEdgeOrWidthConstraint    Width;  // can be lmWidth, lmCenter,
                                  //        lmRight
TEdgeOrHeightConstraint   Height;// can be lmHeight, lmCenter,
                                  //        lmRight
```

As you can see, each member is a type of constraint class denoting some constraints that the specific member must follow. For instance, a constraint might be something like: the left edge of the child window is the same as the left edge of the parent. In this case, you would set the X member of the layout metrics as follows:

```
    TLayoutMetrics lm;
//...
//  Set "left edge same as that of parent"
    lm.X.Set(lmLeft, lmSameAs, lmParent, lmLeft);
```

On the other hand, to set the Height member of the layout metrics to an absolute value of 40 pixels, you have to write:

```
lm.Height.Units = lmPixels;
lm.Height.Absolute(40);
```

Here the first line sets the units of the `Height` constraint and the second line indicates that the `Height` has an absolute value of 40.

Note that the `Set` member function of the constraint class has the following prototype:

```
void Set(TEdge edge,          // Which edge of the child window?
         TRelationship rel, // Constant denoting relationship
         TWindow* otherWin, // Related to this window
         TEdge otherEdge,   // and this edge of the window
         int value = 0)     // Value, if needed
```

The edge can be one of the constants: `lmLeft`, `lmRight`, `lmCenter`, `lmTop`, and `lmBottom`. The `TRelationship` argument can be one of: `lmRightOf`, `lmLeftOf`, `lmAbove`, `lmBelow`, `lmSameAs`, or `lmPercentOf`. The value argument is needed when the indicated relationship requires a value. For example, if you say the top edge of the child window is 10 units below the top edge of the parent, you would set the Y member of the layout metrics as follows:

```
    TLayoutMetrics lm;
//...
//  Set "top edge 10 units below that of parent"
    lm.Y.Set(lmTop, lmBelow, lmParent, lmTop, 10);
```

The best way to understand the use of the `TLayoutWindow` is to study the example program presented in Listing 18.13, which produces the layout shown in Figure 18.22. As the figure shows, the `TLayoutWindow` manages the layout of four child windows. Three of the child windows appear along the top, left, and bottom edge of the parent window. The fourth child window is the larger window in the middle, to the right of the vertical tool bar.

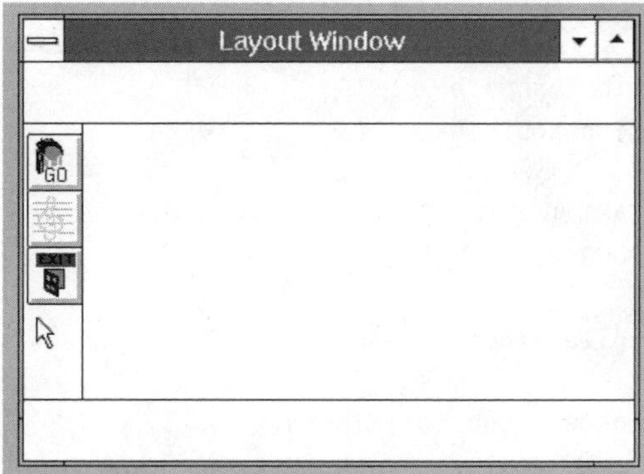

Figure 18.22. Controlling child window layouts with the `TLayoutWindow` class.

The key to setting up the layout is to define the layout metrics for each child window. Once the layout metrics are defined, call the `SetChildLayoutMetrics` function of the `TLayoutWindow` class to set the metrics for each child window. The `SetChildLayoutMetrics` function has the following prototype:

```
void SetChildLayoutMetrics(
    TWindow&        child,    // Child window
    TLayoutMetrics& metrics); // Layout metrics for that window
```

After setting the layout metrics for all child windows, call the `Layout` member function to arrange the child windows according to the constraints specified in each child's layout metrics.

Listing 18.13. LAYOUT.CPP. Sample program to illustrate controlling child window layouts with the `TLayoutWindow` class.

```
//-------------------------------------------------------------
// File: layout.cpp
//
// Sample program that shows how to layout windows in a frame
// using the TLayoutWindow class.
//-------------------------------------------------------------
#include <owl\applicat.h>
#include <owl\framewin.h>
#include <owl\layoutwi.h>
#include <owl\layoutco.h>
#include <owl\color.h>
```

continues

Listing 18.13. continued

```
#include <owl\buttonga.h>
#include <owl\controlb.h>

#define CM_START 1
#define CM_SOUND 2

// A simple child window class

class ChildWindow : public TWindow
{
public:
    ChildWindow(TWindow* parent, int id);
};

// Structure to hold information about the child windows

struct ChildInfo
{
    TWindow*      window;
    TLayoutMetrics lm;
};
const int MaxChildren = 4;

// The layout window that will manage the child windows

class MainLayout : public TLayoutWindow
{
public:
    MainLayout(TWindow* parent);

private:
    ChildInfo  child_info[MaxChildren];
};

//--------------------------------------------------------------
ChildWindow::ChildWindow(TWindow* parent, int id)
    : TWindow(parent)
{
    Attr.Style = WS_CHILD | WS_BORDER | WS_VISIBLE |
                 WS_TABSTOP | WS_CLIPSIBLINGS;
    Attr.Id = id;
```

```
}
//---------------------------------------------------------------
MainLayout::MainLayout(TWindow* parent) : TLayoutWindow(parent, 0)
{
    Attr.Style |= WS_BORDER;

// Create the child windows
    int i;
    for (i = 0; i < MaxChildren; i++)
    {
// Child window 1 will be a TControlBar (created later)
        if(i != 1)
        child_info[i].window = new ChildWindow(this, i+1);
    }

// Add a vertical toolbar as child 1
    TControlBar* cb = new TControlBar(this,
                                        TGadgetWindow::Vertical);

// Insert buttons into control bar and associate an ID
// with each button

    cb->Insert(*new TButtonGadget(CM_START, CM_START,
                                  TButtonGadget::Command, TRUE));
    cb->Insert(*new TButtonGadget(CM_SOUND, CM_SOUND,
                                  TButtonGadget::Command, TRUE));
    cb->Insert(*new TButtonGadget(CM_EXIT, CM_EXIT,
                                  TButtonGadget::Command, TRUE));
    child_info[1].window = cb;

// Define the metrics for each child window
// Here is the layout:
//              ----- Window 0 -----
//              |------------------|
//              |W|                |
//              |i|  Window 3      |
//              |n|                |
//              | |                |
//              |1|                |
//              |------------------|
//              |______Window 2____|
```

continues

Listing 18.13. continued

```
// Window 0: area at top (could be used as a horizontal tool bar)

    child_info[0].lm.X.Set(lmLeft, lmSameAs, lmParent, lmLeft);
    child_info[0].lm.Y.Set(lmTop, lmSameAs, lmParent, lmTop);
    child_info[0].lm.Width.Set(lmWidth, lmSameAs,
                               lmParent, lmWidth);
    child_info[0].lm.Height.Units = lmPixels;
    child_info[0].lm.Height.Absolute(40);

// Window 1: the vertical tool bar on the left

    child_info[1].lm.X.Set(lmLeft, lmSameAs, lmParent, lmLeft);
    child_info[1].lm.Y.Set(lmTop, lmSameAs,
                          child_info[0].window, lmBottom);
    child_info[1].lm.Width.Units = lmPixels;
    child_info[1].lm.Width.Absolute(40);
    child_info[1].lm.Height.Set(lmBottom, lmSameAs,
                               child_info[2].window, lmTop);

// Window 2: the area at the bottom for status messages

    child_info[2].lm.X.Set(lmLeft, lmSameAs, lmParent, lmLeft);
    child_info[2].lm.Y.Set(lmBottom, lmSameAs,
                          lmParent, lmBottom);
    child_info[2].lm.Width.Set(lmWidth, lmSameAs,
                               lmParent, lmWidth);
    child_info[2].lm.Height.Units = lmPixels;
    child_info[2].lm.Height.Absolute(40);

// Window 3: the large "work area" to the right of the tool bar

    child_info[3].lm.X.Set(lmLeft, lmSameAs,
                          child_info[1].window, lmRight);
    child_info[3].lm.Y.Set(lmTop, lmSameAs,
                          child_info[0].window, lmBottom);
    child_info[3].lm.Width.Set(lmRight, lmSameAs,
                               lmParent, lmRight);
    child_info[3].lm.Height.Set(lmBottom, lmSameAs,
                               child_info[2].window, lmTop);

// Set the layout information for each child
```

```
    for (i = 0; i < MaxChildren; i++)
    {
        SetChildLayoutMetrics(*child_info[i].window,
                              child_info[i].lm);
    }

// The following call performs the layout
    Layout();
}
//-----------------------------------------------------------------
class LayoutApp : public TApplication
{
public:
    void InitMainWindow()
    {
        MainWindow = new TFrameWindow(0, "Layout Window",
                                      new MainLayout(0));
        EnableBWCC();
    }
    void CmStart();
    void CmSound();
    void CmExit();

DECLARE_RESPONSE_TABLE(LayoutApp);
};

// Define the response table

DEFINE_RESPONSE_TABLE1(LayoutApp, TApplication)
    EV_COMMAND(CM_EXIT, CmExit),
    EV_COMMAND(CM_START, CmStart),
    EV_COMMAND(CM_SOUND, CmSound),
END_RESPONSE_TABLE;

//-----------------------------------------------------------------
// LayoutApp:: C m S t a r t

void LayoutApp::CmStart()
{
    MainWindow->MessageBox("Started...", "Layout Test", MB_OK);
}
```

continues

Listing 18.13. continued

```
//----------------------------------------------------------------
// LayoutApp:: C m S o u n d

void LayoutApp::CmSound()
{
    MessageBeep(MB_ICONEXCLAMATION);
}
//----------------------------------------------------------------
// LayoutApp:: C m E x i t

void LayoutApp::CmExit()
{
    PostQuitMessage(0);
}
//----------------------------------------------------------------
int OwlMain (int, char**)
{
    return LayoutApp().Run();
}
```

Manipulating Menus

OWL 2.0 provides two classes, `TMenu` and `TSystemMenu`, to represent menus. The `TSystemMenu` class is interesting because you can manipulate the system menu of a window by creating an instance of the `TSystemMenu` class and by using the member functions of that class. This section shows a program (Listing 18.13) that accesses the system menu and replaces the Close menu item with a small bitmap. Figure 18.23 shows the resulting look of the system menu after the modification.

To replace the text in the menu entry with a bitmap, you need a bitmap from a resource file. This example uses a bitmap from the TOOLBAR.RC resource file (you will find the file on the companion disk). As the listing shows, you modify the menu entry using the following steps:

1. Create a `TBitmap` object from the bitmap resource. You need an `HINSTANCE` argument for the `TBitmap` constructor. Here is how the example program does this:

   ```
   TBitmap *bmp_exit = new TBitmap(GetApplication()-
                                   >GetInstance(),
                                   CM_EXIT);
   ```

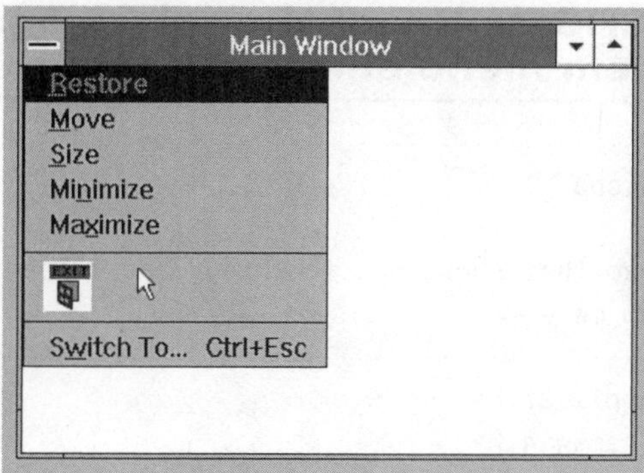

Figure 18.23. Modifying the Close menu item in the system menu using the `TSystemMenu` class.

2. Create a `TSystemMenu` object to access the system menu:

```
TSystemMenu sysmnu(HWindow);
```

3. Modify the specific menu entry with the `TBitmap` created earlier:

```
sysmnu.ModifyMenu(6, MF_BYPOSITION|MF_BITMAP,
                  sysmnu.GetMenuItemID(6), *bmp_exit);
```

   Here the menu item in position 6 is being modified because that is the location of the `Close` menu item in the system menu.

You can access the text string of a menu item by calling the `GetMenuString` function. For instance, you could access the text string of the `Close` menu item with the call:

```
char buf[80];
sysmnu.GetMenuString(6, buf, 70, MF_BYPOSITION);
```

If you simply want to disable the `Close` item in the system menu, you can do so by calling `EnableMenuItem` as follows:

```
sysmnu.EnableMenuItem(6, MF_BYPOSITION|
                      MF_DISABLED|MF_GRAYED);
```

Listing 18.14. CHGMNU.CPP. Sample program that modifies a system menu entry with the `TSystemMenu` class.

```
//------------------------------------------------------------
// File: chgmnu.cpp
//
// Sample program that shows how to change the "Close" item
// in the system menu
//------------------------------------------------------------
#include <owl\applicat.h>
#include <owl\framewin.h>
#include <owl\editsear.h>
#include <owl\dc.h>
#include <owl\menu.h>

class TestApp : public TApplication
{
public:
    TestApp() : TApplication("Menu Test") {}
    void InitMainWindow();
};

class MyFrame : public TFrameWindow
{
public:
    MyFrame(TWindow *parent, char far * title) :  bmp_exit(0),
            TFrameWindow(parent, title) {}
    ~MyFrame() { if(bmp_exit) delete bmp_exit;}
    int EvCreate(CREATESTRUCT&);
private:
    TBitmap  *bmp_exit;
DECLARE_RESPONSE_TABLE(MyFrame);
};

// Define response table for the frame window
DEFINE_RESPONSE_TABLE1(MyFrame, TFrameWindow)
    EV_WM_CREATE,
END_RESPONSE_TABLE;
//------------------------------------------------------------
// MyFrame:: E v C r e a t e
// Handles WM_CREATE messages

int MyFrame::EvCreate(CREATESTRUCT& cs)
```

```
{
    TFrameWindow::EvCreate(cs);

// Change the "Close" item of the System menu into a bitmap
// First create a TBitmap using a bitmap from a resource file
    bmp_exit = new TBitmap(GetApplication()->GetInstance(),
                           CM_EXIT);
// Access the system menu
    TSystemMenu sysmnu(HWindow);

// Replace the text with the bitmap
    sysmnu.ModifyMenu(6, MF_BYPOSITION¦MF_BITMAP,
                      sysmnu.GetMenuItemID(6), *bmp_exit);
    UpdateWindow();

    return 1;
}
//-------------------------------------------------------------
void TestApp::InitMainWindow()
{
  MainWindow = new MyFrame(0, "Main Window");
}
//-------------------------------------------------------------
int OwlMain(int, char**)
{
    return TestApp().Run();
}
```

Summary

Borland C++ 4 includes the ObjectWindows Library Version 2.0 (OWL 2.0) that provides a rich set of C++ classes for developing Microsoft Windows applications. OWL 2.0 organizes the classes into several hierarchies and it exploits multiple inheritance to combine the capabilities of multiple base classes. The bulk of OWL 2.0 classes represent user-interface elements such as controls and dialogs. These classes are derived from two base classes `TEventHandler` and `TStreamableBase` where the `TEventHandler` class provides the event-handling support and the `TStreamableBase` class allows storing objects in a file and retrieving them later.

One major OWL class hierarchy is the TWindow classes. These classes represent windows of various types: frame windows that are meant to manage one or more child windows, windows where the application displays its graphical or text output, dialog windows that prompt user for input, and control window objects through which the user controls the application. To support graphics and text output through the Windows Graphics Device Interface (GDI), OWL 2.0 provides the TGdiBase class hierarchy with the TGdiObject classes. The TGdiBase hierarchy includes the TDC classes that represent the various types of device contexts needed to display output on a device.

Other major OWL class hierarchies include: classes for building applications with a document-view model; classes to represent menus and provide clipboard support; classes for scrolling, printing, and generating exceptions when errors occur in a OWL class. OWL 2.0 also provides classes that represent Windows data types such as POINT, RECT, SIZE, PALETTEENTRY, RGBQUAD, and RGBTRIPLE.

This chapter briefly describes the different categories of OWL classes. The latter part of this chapter provides example programs demonstrating some commonly used OWL classes. The next chapter, "Graphics Programming with OWL," further describes the GDI functions and device contexts.

Graphics Programming with OWL

Chapter 17, "Windows Programming with Borland C++," shows an example of building a Windows application using the OWL classes and Chapter 18, "Using the ObjectWindows Library (OWL)," summarizes the OWL classes used to build the graphical user interface in Windows applications. To display graphics in your application's window, you use functions from the Windows Graphics Device Interface (GDI), which you can access through the `TGdiBase` class hierarchy in OWL. This chapter briefly describes the GDI functions used in drawing graphics. Chapter 20, "Displaying Text in Windows," covers the text output functions.

Windows Graphics Device Interface

GDI refers to the graphics output functions of Windows. GDI is designed to isolate a Windows program from the physical output device such as the display or printer.

The basic idea is that you call GDI functions for all graphics output, and the GDI functions access specific device drivers for the actual graphics output. In addition to producing output on physical devices, GDI also supports output to two pseudo-devices: *bitmaps* and *metafiles*. Bitmaps are rectangular arrays of pixels, and metafiles are stored collections of GDI function calls. Bitmaps are useful for displaying and animating images—tasks that are commonly needed in many Windows applications. Chapter 23, "Understanding Image File Formats," and Chapter 24, "Animating Images," further describe how images are displayed using bitmaps.

Many GDI functions can be important to you when you are writing Windows software. In particular, you need the following categories of GDI functions:

- Vector drawing functions that can draw graphical objects, such as lines, rectangles, and ellipses
- Bitmap manipulation functions to display and manipulate images
- Text output functions to display text in a window
- Palette management functions to exploit the colors supported by a display adapter

The palette is useful in systems with Super VGA or better display adapters that support more than the 16 colors available with standard VGA.

The following sections provide an overview of these functions, but before you can proceed, you have to understand the device context.

Device Context

The device context (DC) is the key to the GDI's support for device-independent graphics in Windows. All GDI functions require a *handle*—an integer identifier—to a DC as an argument. You can think of the DC as a generalized model of a graphics output device. In reality, the DC is a data structure that holds all the information needed to generate graphics output. For instance, the DC contains graphics attributes, including background color, pen, fill style, and font, that control the appearance of graphics and text.

Because a DC represents a graphics device, you have to treat it as a shared resource. When using a DC for graphics output, you should first call an appropriate GDI function to access the DC, use that DC to draw, then immediately release the DC. Note that Windows allows up to five DCs to be open at one time—that's five DCs for the entire Windows system, not per application.

DC in OWL 2.0

In ObjectWindows 2.0, the TDC class encapsulates the Windows DC. The handle to the DC (HDC) is a protected member variable of the TDC class. Specialized versions of the TDC class are available for drawing in a variety of devices and screen areas, including the TClientDC for drawing in the client area of a window, TMemoryDC for drawing on to an in-memory bitmap, and TPrintDC for output to a printer. Figure 18.6 shows the entire TGdiBase class hierarchy, which includes the TDC classes.

All GDI functions appear as member functions of the TDC class. The names of these member functions are the same as the corresponding GDI functions, but the member functions do not need an HDC as an argument. Also, the TDC class includes overloaded versions of the drawing functions that accept several different forms of arguments. As an example, consider the GDI functions MoveTo and LineTo that you can use to draw a line between two points. To draw a line from (x1, y1) to (x2, y2) with the GDI functions, you would write the following:

```
    HDC hdc;
// Assume that the handle to the DC, hdc, is properly set up
    MoveTo(hdc, x1, y1);
    LineTo(hdc, x2, y2);
```

When using OWL classes, you would change the calls to the following form:

```
    TClientDC dc(HWindow);
// Assume that the TClientDC is being created in the member
// function of a TWindow class
    dc.MoveTo(x1, y1);
    dc.LineTo(x2, y2);
```

Additionally, the TDC class in OWL 2.0 also enables you to write these function calls with TPoint objects as argument (TPoint represents a point in the x-y plane):

```
// Assume that the TClientDC is being constructed in the
// member function of a TWindow class
    TClientDC dc(HWindow);
    TPoint start, end;
// Assume that the TPoint objects are appropriately initialized
    dc.MoveTo(start);
    dc.LineTo(end);
```

As you can see, the TDC class offers several flexible ways to call the GDI functions.

The following sections describe the DC as a data type in Windows API. However, the example code shows how to use the DC through the TDC classes in OWL 2.0.

Contents of a DC

The DC contains drawing objects, such as brush, pen, and bitmap, and drawing attributes, such as background color, text color, and font. Table 19.1 summarizes the contents of the DC and provides the default value of each item in it. Note that the constants appearing in the default values column are defined in an include file.

Table 19.1. Contents of a DC and their default values.

Item Name	Default Value	Comments
Background color	White	
Background mode	`OPAQUE`	Background areas in drawings are filled with the background color as opposed to being left untouched.
Bitmap	No default	Used when selecting a bitmap into a memory device context.
Brush	`WHITE_BRUSH`	Defines a fill style.
Brush origin	(0,0)	
Clipping region	Entire client area	Drawing operations affect the area within the clipping region only.
Color palette	`DEFAULT_PALETTE`	
Current pen position	(0,0)	
Device origin	Upper-left corner	
Drawing mode	`R2_COPYPEN`	Specifies how to combine the pen's color with the color that already exists on the drawing surface.
Font	`SYSTEM_FONT`	
Intercharacter spacing	0	
Mapping mode	`MM_TEXT`	One logical unit equals one pixel.
Pen	`BLACK_PEN`	
Polygon fill mode	`ALTERNATE`	
Stretching mode	`BLACKONWHITE`	Used by `StretchBlt` when copying bitmaps from one device to another.

Item Name	Default Value	Comments
Text alignment	TA_LEFT, TA_TOP, and TA_NOUPDATECP	
Text color	Black	
Viewport extent	(1,1)	Viewport refers to a rectangle in the device coordinate system.
Viewport origin	(0,0)	
Window extent	(1,1)	Window refers to a rectangle in the logical coordinate system (the mapping mode maps the window to the viewport).
Window origin	(0,0)	

Getting a DC

Your Windows application will, most likely, acquire a DC in response to the WM_PAINT message because that's when an application's window has to be redrawn. If you use OWL classes and you derive your application's main window from the TWindow class, you can handle all graphics output in a member function named Paint, which has the following prototype:

```
void Paint(TDC& dc,      // Device context for the display
           BOOL erase,   // TRUE = erase the background
           TRect& rect);// Rectangle that needs redrawing
```

OWL calls the Paint function whenever Windows sends a message to the window. As you can see, the function is called with a valid TDC object as an argument, so you do not have to get a DC explicitly. The last argument is a reference to a TRect structure that contains information about the area of the screen that needs to be redrawn.

If you need to update the window as soon as possible without waiting for a WM_PAINT message, you can create an instance of the TClientDC class to get a DC. When the TClientDC object is destroyed, the DC is automatically released. By the way, you also can force an immediate WM_PAINT event by calling the UpdateWindow function.

Persistent DC

When you get the handle to a DC and make changes to the attributes, these changes are lost as soon as you release the DC. However, there is a way to create a private DC for a window so that the contents of the DC persist until the window is destroyed. To do this in a window class `MyWindow` derived from the OWL class `TWindow`, override the `GetWindowClass` function and add the `CS_OWNDC` flag to the class (this is the Windows class representing the type of a window, not a C++ class) style as follows:

```
// Assume that MyWindow: public TWindow

void MyWindow::GetWindowClass(WNDCLASS& wclass)
{
    TWindow::GetWindowClass(wclass);
    wclass.style |= CS_OWNDC;
}
```

Now the window associated with each instance of `MyWindow` class has its own private DC that exists until the window is destroyed. You still have to create a `TClientDC` object to draw with this DC. The penalty you pay for this convenience is about 800 bytes of storage for the DC for each window with the `CS_OWNDC` style.

If you need to store a DC temporarily (perhaps to change some attributes, do some drawing with the changed attributes, and revert back to the original attributes), you can do so by calling `SaveDC`:

```
    TClientDC dc(HWindow);
//...
    int saved_DC_id;
    saved_DC_id = dc.SaveDC();
// Make changes to DC and use it...
// After you are through using the changed DC, restore the DC
    dc.RestoreDC(saved_DC_id);
```

If you simply want to revert a DC back to the state that existed before the last call to `SaveDC`, call the following:

```
dc.RestoreDC(); // No need for exact ID
```

Using a DC for Graphics Output

The primary use of a DC is to draw graphics output. In fact, each GDI function is a member function of the `TDC` class. Here is the typical sequence to follow when using a `TDC` object for graphics output:

1. Create the appropriate `TDC` object. For instance, to draw in the client area of a window, create a `TClientDC` object.
2. Set up the graphics attributes.
3. Call GDI drawing functions that are member functions of the `TDC` class.
4. If you created the `TDC` object by using the `new` operator, destroy the `TDC` object with the `delete` operator.

Setting up the graphics attributes involves selecting drawing objects into the DC. A DC has the following graphics objects:

- *Pen* controls the appearance of lines and borders of rectangles, ellipses, and polygons.
- *Brush* provides a fill pattern used to draw filled figures.
- *Font* specifies the shape and size of textual output.
- *Palette* is an array of colors—the array index identifying each color. For display adapters that can display more than 16 colors, Windows uses a palette to pick the current selection of available colors out of the millions of colors that a display can represent.
- *Bitmap* is used to draw images.
- *Region* is a combination of rectangles, ellipses, and polygons that you can use for drawing or for clipping.

At any time, the DC can have one copy of each type of graphics object. Use the `SelectObject` function to select a graphics object into a DC. For instance, to draw a rectangle filled with a specific fill pattern, you might write

```
// Assume that this code is in the body of the Paint
// function of the application's window and that the
// Paint function has the following prototype:
//   void TestWindow::Paint(TDC& dc, int, TRect&)
//...
// Draw a filled rectangle with specific pen and brush
    dc.SelectStockObject(WHITE_PEN);
    HBRUSH hatch_brush = CreateHatchBrush(HS_DIAGCROSS,
                                          RGB(0, 255, 255));
    dc.SelectObject(hatch_brush);
    dc.Rectangle(20, 10, 80, 50);

// Restore the original objects
```

```
    dc.RestoreObjects();
//...
```

Notice how the call to SelectStockObject selects a stock pen—one of the predefined graphics objects that are always available. The brush, hatch_brush, is created by calling CreateHatchBrush. Once you are finished using the graphics objects, you have to restore the original objects by calling the RestoreObjects function of the TDC class. The RestoreObjects function is not part of the Windows API; this is a function that OWL provides for your convenience.

Determining Device Capabilities with a DC

In addition to drawing with a DC, you also can determine the capabilities of a device through the DC. Specifically, you can call the GetDeviceCaps function to get a value for a specified capability code. For instance, to determine the number of color planes available in the display device, call GetDeviceCaps with the handle to a display device context as follows:

```
int nplanes = dc.GetDeviceCaps(PLANES);
```

where PLANES denotes the capability that you are querying.

You also can use GetDeviceCaps to determine if a device supports enough colors or specific types of graphic operations, such as copying bitmaps or drawing curves for circles and ellipses. For example, in a Windows application you might want to use as many colors as the display adapter supports. If a display adapter supports 256 colors, the DC will support a logical palette. To determine if a DC supports a logical palette, you would write the following:

```
    if(dc.GetDeviceCaps(RASTERCAPS) & RC_PALETTE)
    {
// Yes, device supports logical palette
//...
    }
```

You can test if the device driver associated with a DC is written for Windows 3.0 or later with the following:

```
// For Windows 3.1, the following function returns 0x030a

    if(dc.GetDeviceCaps(DRIVERVERSION) >= 0x300)
    {
// Yes, device driver is for Windows 3.0 or later.
//...
    }
```

GDI Coordinate Systems

The GDI supports the notion of two coordinate systems *physical coordinates* and *logical coordinates.* The physical or device coordinate system is fixed for a device. For a window on the display screen, the physical coordinate system's origin is at the upper-left corner of a window's client area with the positive x-axis extending to the right and the positive y-axis going down.

The logical coordinate system can be one of several, and Windows maps each onto the physical one before displaying any graphics output. All GDI drawing functions accept logical coordinates as arguments. The mapping mode—the way a logical coordinate system is scaled to the physical one—identifies the types of logical coordinate systems that Windows supports. Table 19.2 lists the mapping modes available in Windows GDI.

Table 19.2. Mapping modes in Windows GDI.

Mapping Mode Identifier	Meaning
`MM_ANISOTROPIC`	Logical units along x- and y-axes can be set independently. Use `SetViewportExt` (set viewport extent) and `SetWindowExt` (set window extent) to set up the x- and y- ratios of logical-to-physical units. Note that, in this context, a viewport is a rectangular area in physical coordinate space and a window is a rectangle in logical coordinates. The viewport extent is the width and height of the viewport. The scaling along x- and y-axes is set so that the specified window in logical coordinates is mapped to the viewport in physical coordinates.
`MM_HIENGLISH`	Each logical unit is 0.001 inch with the positive x-axis extending to the right and the positive y-axis going up.

continues

Table 19.2. continued

Mapping Mode Identifier	Meaning
MM_HIMETRIC	Each logical unit is 0.01 millimeter; the x-axis is increasing to the right and the positive y-axis is extending upward.
MM_ISOTROPIC	This mapping mode is like MM_ANISOTROPIC except that the x- and y-axes scalings must be the same.
MM_LOENGLISH	This is like MM_HIENGLISH except each logical unit is 0.01 inch.
MM_LOMETRIC	This is like MM_HIMETRIC except each logical unit is 0.1 millimeter.
MM_TEXT	This is the default mapping mode in which the logical coordinate system is the same as the physical one—each logical unit is one pixel with the x-axis increasing to the right and the y-axis increasing downward.
MM_TWIPS	Each logical unit is 1/20 of a point where a point is 1/72 inch. Thus, in MM_TWIPS mode, each logical unit is 1/1440 inch. The positive x-axis extends to the right and the y-axis increases upward.

Setting a Mapping Mode

Use the SetMapMode function to set a mapping mode. At any time, you can get the current mapping mode with GetMapMode. For example, to set the mapping mode to MM_TWIPS, you would write the following:

```
int old_mapmode = dc.SetMapMode(MM_TWIPS);
```

Specifying the mapping mode may not be enough to draw in a window. After setting a mapping mode such as MM_TWIPS, you have the situation shown in Figure 19.1. As you can see from the figure, a portion of the lower-right quadrant from the logical coordinate space is mapped to the display screen (or the device's work area, in case of devices other than the display). This means that drawings with positive x- and negative y-coordinates are the only ones that get displayed. The reason for this effect is that the logical frame's y-axis increases upward and the physical frame's y-axis increases downward. This is true for all mapping modes except MM_TEXT.

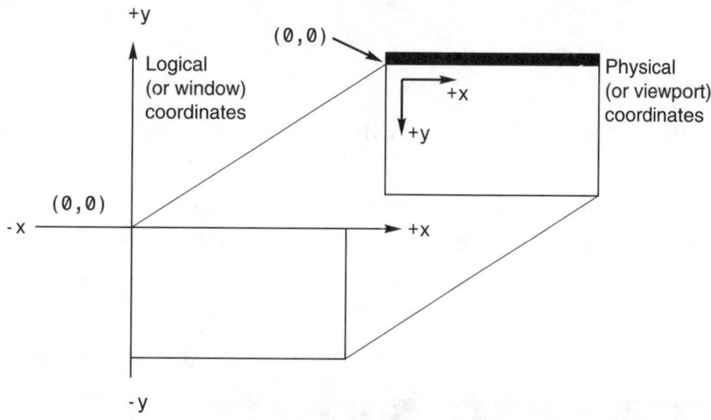

Figure 19.1. Default mapping from logical to physical coordinates.

If you want to work with positive logical coordinates, you have to move the origin of the logical coordinate frame to an appropriate location in the physical space. This way, the positive quadrant (the quadrant where both x- and y-coordinates are positive) of the logical frame is mapped to the visible quadrant of the physical coordinate frame. You can use the SetViewportOrg to relocate the origin of the logical frame. Figure 19.2 illustrates the effect of changing the origin of the logical coordinate axes.

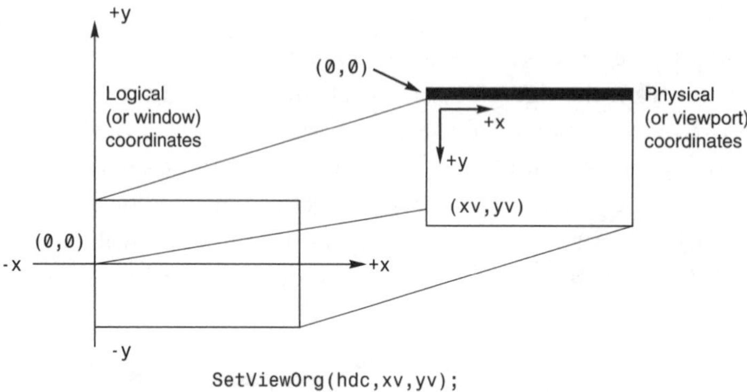

Figure 19.2. Effect of aligning the window origin with a point in the viewport.

You have to follow these steps whenever you are using one of the device-independent modes: `MM_HIENGLISH`, `MM_HIMETRIC`, `MM_LOENGLISH`, `MM_LOMETRIC`, or `MM_TWIPS`. We call these mapping modes device-independent because they express the logical units in absolute measurements, such as millimeters or inches.

Drawing with GDI Functions

The GDI provides a large number of drawing functions, including functions to draw individual pixels, lines, rectangles and polygons, and ellipses. The next few sections briefly summarize the drawing functions.

Drawing Points

You can draw a single point in a specified color with the `SetPixel` function, which you would call as follows:

```
TColor actual_color = dc.SetPixel(x, y, color);
```

This paints the point at the logical coordinates `(x, y)` with the specified color. The color argument to the `SetPixel` function is of type `TColor`. You can specify the color with a 32-bit value whose least significant three bytes represent the red (R), green (G), and blue (B) components of a color. You can specify the color using the `RGB` macro as follows:

```
dc.SetPixel(x, y, RGB(r, g, b));
```

where r, g, and b are integers between 0 and 255 representing the intensity of red, green, and blue components, respectively. Windows uses the nearest available color, and paints the pixel with that color. SetPixel returns the actual color used by Windows.

Although SetPixel can be used to draw an image directly on the display screen, you should use the bitmap manipulation functions to display images in Windows because the bitmap functions are much faster than SetPixel.

Drawing Lines

The GDI functions MoveTo and LineTo are meant for drawing lines. To draw a line from the logical point (x1, y1) to (x2, y2), you would write the following:

```
dc.MoveTo(x1, y1);
dc.LineTo(x2, y2);
```

Windows draws all the pixels starting at (x1, y1) up to, but not including, (x2, y2). The MoveTo and LineTo functions draw lines with the currently selected pen—the MoveTo function moves the pen to a new location without drawing anything, and LineTo draws a line to a specified point with the pen. The pen determines the appearance of the line being drawn. You can either call SelectObject to select a predefined pen into the device context or call CreatePen to create a new pen with a specific style, color, and width. To use the pen, you have to select it into the DC and, when you no longer need the pen, you must call the RestorePen function to restore the original pen back into the DC.

To draw multiple line segments, you should use the Polyline function. You have to store the endpoints of all the line segments in an array. For example, to join the points (x1, y1), (x2, y2), and (x3, y3) with line segments, you would write the following:

```
POINT points[3] =
    {TPoint(x1, y1), TPoint(x2, y2), TPoint(x3, y3)};
dc.Polyline(points, 3);
```

Note that to draw a closed polygon using Polyline, you have to close the figure by specifying the same coordinates for the first and the last points in the array. However, as you will see later, the Polygon function automatically draws a closed figure by connecting the last point to the first.

In addition to straight lines, the TDC class includes the Arc function to draw a curved line that is part of an ellipse. Arc requires four sets of x-y coordinates as its arguments:

```
// Prototype of Arc
BOOL Arc(
    short x1, short y1, // Upper-left corner of bounding box
    short x2, short y2, // Lower-right corner of bounding box
    short xs, short ys, // Defines start point of arc
    short xe, short ye);// Defines end point of arc
```

The points (x1, y1) and (x2, y2) are the opposite corners of a rectangle that encloses the ellipse to which the arc belongs. The starting point of the arc is where a line joining the center of the ellipse and (xs, ys) intersects the ellipse's boundary. The endpoint is defined similarly by the line joining the ellipse's center and (xe, ye). The arc is drawn counterclockwise from the starting point up to, but not including, the endpoint.

Another form of the Arc function takes TRect and TPoint objects as arguments:

```
BOOL Arc(
    connst TRect& r, // Specifies upper-left and lower-right
                     // corners of bounding rectangle
    const TPoint& s, // Defines start point of arc
    const TPoint& e);// Defines end point of arc
```

Drawing Closed Figures

The TDC class provides the following member functions to draw closed figures:

- Rectangle(int x1, int y1, int x2, int y2); draws a rectangle whose upper-left corner is (x1, y1) and lower- right corner is (x2, y2). Note that the right and bottom edges of the rectangle are 1 pixel less than the corner (x2, y2).
- RoundRect(int x1, int y1, int x2, int y2, int x_ellipse, int y_ellipse); draws a rectangle with rounded corners. The rectangle's bounding box is specified by the upper-left corner (x1, y1) and lower-right corner (x2, y2). Each corner is rounded by drawing a small ellipse whose width and height are x_ellipse and y_ellipse, respectively.
- Ellipse(int x1, int y1, int x2, int y2); draws an ellipse bounded by the rectangle whose opposite corners are (x1, y1) and (x2, y2).
- Pie(int x1, int y1, int x2, int y2, int x_start, int y_start, int x_end, int y_end); draws a pie-shaped wedge whose curved edge is a segment of the ellipse bounded by the rectangle defined by the corners (x1, y1) and (x2, y2). The two straight edges of the pie are defined by the line joining the center

of the ellipse and the points (x_start, y_start) and (x_end, y_end). The pie slice starts at the point where the line from the center to (x_start, y_start) intersects the ellipse, and continues counterclockwise to the point where the line from the center to (x_end, y_end) cuts the ellipse.

- Chord(int x1, int y1, int x2, int y2, int x_start, int y_start, int x_end, int y_end); draws a segment of ellipse just like Pie, but unlike Pie, Chord joins the endpoints of the arc with a straight line.
- Polygon(const TPoint* pt, int numpt); draws a polygon by joining the points in the array pt. Polygon automatically joins the first and the last points in the array to form a closed figure.

All drawing functions expect logical coordinates. For each of these closed figures, the Windows GDI draws the outline with the current pen style and fills the inside of the figures with the current brush. There are seven stock brush objects. You create an instance of the brush by calling GetStockObject with one of the following as the argument: BLACK_BRUSH, DKGRAY_BRUSH, GRAY_BRUSH, HOLLOW_BRUSH, LTGRAY_BRUSH, NULL_BRUSH, or WHITE_BRUSH.

You can create your own brush objects by using one of these functions: CreateBrushIndirect, CreateDIBPatternBrush, CreateHatchBrush, CreatePatternBrush, or CreateSolidBrush. CreateSolidBrush is particularly useful for creating a brush of a specified color:

```
HBRUSH red_brush = CreateSolidBrush(RGB(255, 0, 0));
```

The color is specified by an RGB triplet. If you specify a color that is not supported by hardware, Windows uses *dithering* to produce a close approximation of the requested color. More about dithering follows.

Manipulating Rectangles

Rectangles play an important part in the GDI. Accordingly, the GDI includes several functions that manipulate rectangles. OWL provides the TRect class to represent the RECT structure of Windows API, which is defined in the header file <windows.h> as the following:

```
typedef struct tagRECT
{
    int left;    // Upper-left corner of rectangle
    int top;
    int right;   // Lower-right corner of rectangle
```

```
    int bottom;
} RECT;
```

You have already seen the functions `Rectangle` and `RoundRect` meant for drawing rectangles. Table 19.3 lists several other rectangle functions. Most of these are Windows API functions that use the `RECT` structure as argument. However, a few are member functions of `TDC` or `TRect` classes; these are identified in the table.

Table 19.3. GDI functions that manipulate rectangles.

Name	Description
`CopyRect`	Copies from one `RECT` structure to another: `CopyRect(&dest_rect, &src_rect);`
`EqualRect`	Returns `TRUE` if two `RECT` structures are equal: `if(EqualRect(&rect1, &rect2)) { /* Rectangles are equal */ }`
`FillRect`	A member function of the `TDC` class that fills a rectangle up to, but not including, the right and bottom coordinates, with the specified brush: `dc.FillRect(rect, brush);`
`FrameRect`	A member function of the `TDC` class that uses the specified brush (not the pen) to draw a rectangular frame: `dc.FrameRect(rect, brush);`
`Inflate`	A member function of the `TRect` class that increases or decreases the size of a rectangle: `rect.InflateRect(dx, dy);`
`InflateRect`	Increases or decreases the size of a rectangle: `InflateRect(&rect, x, y);`
`Inflate`	A member function of the `TRect` class that increases or decreases the size of the rectangle: `rect.InflateRect(dx, dy);`
`InvertRect`	A member function of the `TDC` class that inverts all the pixels in a rectangle: `dc.InvertRect(rect);`

Name	Description
`Offset`	A member function of the `TRect` class that moves the rectangle along x- and y-axes: `rect.Offset(dx, dy);`
`OffsetRect`	Moves a rectangle along x- and y-axes: `OffsetRect(&rect, x, y);`
`PtInRect`	Returns `TRUE` if a point is in a rectangle: `if(PtInRect(&rect, point)) { /* Point is in rectangle */ }`
`SetRect`	Sets the fields of a `RECT` structure: `SetRect(&rect, left, top, right, bottom);`
`SetRectEmpty`	Sets the fields of a `RECT` structure to zero: `SetRectEmpty(&rect);`
`UnionRect`	Sets the fields of a `RECT` structure to be the union of two other rectangles: `UnionRect(&result_rect, &rect1, &rect2);`

Regions

Regions are areas of the drawing surface. The GDI allows you to define a region as a combination of rectangles, polygons, and ellipses. You can use a region to draw—by filling the region with the current brush—or use it as the *clipping region*—the area where the drawing appears. Table 19.4 lists the GDI functions meant for defining and using regions. Note that to use a region, you must have a handle to it. You can create a region with one of the Windows API functions or through the OWL class TRegion, which represents a region. When using a region as a clipping region, you have to call SetClipRgn to select the region into the DC.

Most functions listed in Table 19.4 are from the Windows API; a few are member functions of the `TDC` class.

Table 19.4. GDI functions that manipulate regions.

Name	Description
CreateRectRgn	Creates a rectangular region using specified coordinates for the opposite corners of the rectangle: `CreateRectRgn(left, top, right, bottom);`
CreateRectRgnIndirect	Creates a rectangular region using the fields of a RECT structure: `CreateRectRgnIndirect(&rect);`
CreateRoundRectRgn	Creates a rectangular region with rounded corners, specified the same way as the RoundRect function
CreateEllipticRgn	Creates an elliptic region: `CreateEllipticRgn(left, top, right, bottom);`
CreateEllipticRgnIndirect	Creates an elliptic region using the fields in a RECT structure: `CreateEllipticRgnIndirect(&rect);`
CreatePolygonRgn	Creates a polygon region: `CreatePolygonRgn(points, npoints, fill_mode);` where fill_mode is ALTERNATE to WINDING
CreatePolyPolygonRgn	Creates a region out of multiple polygons
CombineRgn	Combines two regions into one according to a specified combining mode (which can be one of: RGN_AND, RGN_COPY, RGN_DIFF, RGN_OR, RGN_XOR): `CombineRgn(hresult_rgn, hrgn1, hrgn2, combine_flag);`
EqualRgn	Returns TRUE if two regions are equal: `if(EqualRgn(hrgn1, hrgn2)) { /* regions are equal */}`

Name	Description
`FillRgn`	A member function of the `TDC` class that fills a region with the specified brush: `dc.FillRgn(rgn, brush);`
`FrameRgn`	A member function of the `TDC` class that draws a frame around a region with the specified brush: `dc.FrameRgn(rgn, brush, pt); //pt is a TPoint with width and height of the frame`
`GetRgnBox`	A member function of the `TRegion` class that returns the bounding box (largest rectangle enclosing the region) of the region: `rgn.GetRgnBox(rect);`
`InvalidateRgn`	A member function of the `TWindow` class that marks the specified region for repainting: `InvalidateRgn(hrgn, erase_flag);`
`InvertRgn`	A member function of the TDC class that inverts the pixels in a region: `dc.InvertRgn(rgn);`
`OffsetRgn`	Moves a region by a specified x- and y-offset: `OffsetRgn(hrgn, x, y);`
`PaintRgn`	Fills the region with the current brush: `dc.PaintRgn(rgn);`
`PtInRegion`	Returns `TRUE` if the specified point is in the region: `if(PtInRegion(hrgn, 50, 50)) { /* Point (50,50) is in the region) */ }`
`RectInRegion`	Returns `TRUE` if any part of the specified rectangle is in the region: `if(RectInRegion(hrgn, &rc)) { /* All or part of rectangle rc is in the region. */}`

continues

Table 19.4. continued

Name	Description
`SetRectRgn`	A member function of the `TRegion` class that changes the region to a rectangular shape specified by the `TRect` argument: `rgn.SetRectRgn(rect);`
`ValidateRgn`	A member function of the `TWindow` class that removes the region from the area to be repainted: `ValidateRgn(hrgn);`

Drawing Mode

When you are drawing lines and filled figures, the drawing mode controls the way the pen color is combined with the existing colors. This is referred to as a *raster operation (ROP)*. The GDI defines sixteen ROPs, identified by symbols that start with the R2_ prefix. The default ROP is R2_COPYPEN, which means that the pen simply overwrites whatever exists on the drawing surface. Table 19.5 lists the names of the ROP codes that apply to drawing with the GDI functions. Note that there is another set of ROP codes that applies when copying a bitmap to a DC.

Use the `SetROP2` function to specify a new drawing mode:

```
int previous_ROP = dc.SetROP2(R2_XORPEN);
```

In this case, `SetROP2` sets the ROP code to `R2_XORPEN` and returns the old ROP code, which is stored in the variable named `previous_ROP`.

Table 19.5. Drawing modes in Windows GDI.

Mode Name	Boolean Operation	Comments
`R2_BLACK`	all bits zero	Draws in black, ignoring pen color and existing color
`R2_COPYPEN`	pen	Draws with the pen color (the default drawing mode)
`R2_MASKNOTPEN`	(NOT pen) AND dest	Inverts the bits in the pen color and performs a bitwise-AND with existing color

Mode Name	Boolean Operation	Comments
R2_MASKPEN	pen AND dest	Performs bitwise-AND of pen color and existing color
R2_MASKPENNOT	pen AND (NOT dest)	Inverts existing color and performs bitwise-AND with pen color
R2_MERGENOTPEN	(NOT pen) OR dest	Inverts pen color and performs bitwise-OR with existing color
R2_MERGEPEN	pen OR dest	Performs bitwise-OR of pen color and existing color
R2_MERGEPENNOT	pen OR (NOT dest)	Inverts existing color and performs bitwise-OR with pen color
R2_NOP	dest	Leaves existing color unchanged (hence the name NOP for "no operation")
R2_NOT	NOT dest	Inverts existing color
R2_NOTCOPYPEN	NOT pen	Draws with inverted pen color
R2_NOTMASKPEN	NOT (pen AND dest)	Performs bitwise-AND of pen and existing color and inverts the result
R2_NOTMERGEPEN	NOT (pen OR dest)	Performs bitwise-OR of pen and existing color and inverts the result
R2_NOTXORPEN	NOT (pen XOR dest)	Performs bitwise exclusive-OR of pen and existing color and inverts the result
R2_WHITE	all bits 1	Draws in white color
R2_XORPEN	pen XOR dest	Performs bitwise exclusive-OR of pen color and existing color

Handling Color

Prior to Windows 3.0, the only way to represent a color was to express it in terms of the RGB intensities of the color. To represent the RGB value, the Windows API defines the `COLORREF` type, which is a 32-bit integer value with the RGB intensities stored in the low-order bytes as shown in Figure 19.3. The most significant byte of the `COLORREF` type indicates whether to interpret the value as a color or a palette entry—a topic that is discussed in the next section.

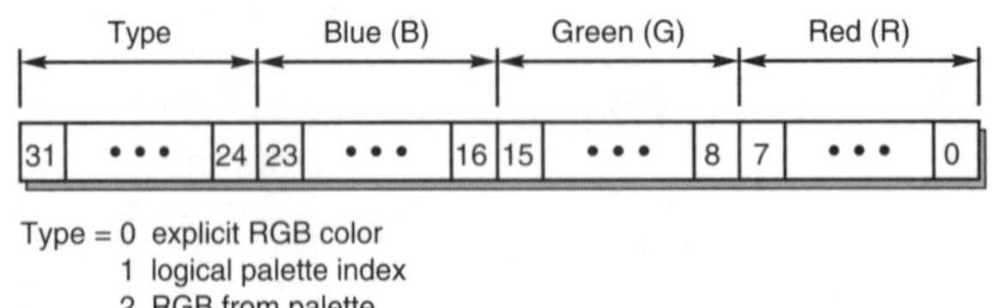

Figure 19.3. Interpreting the contents of a COLORREF value.

You can use the RGB macro to represent an RGB color. For instance, RGB(255, 0, 0) denotes a full-intensity red color. Because each intensity is an 8-bit value, the intensity can range from 0 to 255.

OWL 2.0 includes the `TColor` data type that represents an RGB color. Internally, the `TColor` class maintains the color as a `COLORREF` value.

Windows uses dithering to display colors that may not be supported by the display hardware. The process of dithering displays neighboring pixels in different colors to create unique shades. Because dithering requires a collection of pixels to work, Windows uses dithering only when filling an area—Windows cannot use dithering when drawing points, lines, and text.

System Palette

Display adapters such as VGA, Super VGA, XGA, and 8514/A can generate the necessary signals to display a large number of colors on a color display, but only a small number of these colors are available at any one time. The number of colors that can be displayed at a time is determined by the number of bits of storage allocated for each pixel. In a standard VGA, each pixel has 4 bits of storage—this means the standard VGA can display $2^4 = 16$ simultaneous colors. On the other hand, a Super VGA adapter with enough memory may support a graphics mode in which each pixel can have an 8-bit value. In this case, the display adapter can show $2^8 = 256$ simultaneous colors.

Although the number of simultaneous colors is limited, the display adapter represents each color in terms of the RGB intensities of the color and uses several bits to represent the R, G, and B components. For instance, a VGA display adapter that uses 6 bits per R, G, and B component allows up to $2^6 \times 2^6 \times 2^6 = 262{,}144$ distinct colors. From these you can display any 16 colors if the display adapter supports 4 bits per pixel, or any 256 colors if the adapter supports 8 bits per pixel. The display adapter converts each pixel's contents into a color by interpreting the pixel's value as an index into a table. This table is the *color palette*, whose entries are RGB values.

In keeping with the hardware palette in display adapters, Windows also defines a palette called the *system palette*. This palette has 16 predefined colors for EGA and VGA displays, and 20 predefined colors on displays that support 256 colors or more.

Logical Palette

Starting with version 3.0, Windows supports the notion of a *logical palette* that allows applications to take advantage of the large number of colors available in a system. Provided the display hardware supports more than 20 colors, Windows provides an extended system palette that mimics the hardware palette. Windows automatically sets aside 20 entries in the extended system palette—these are the 20 default colors. When you define a logical palette, Windows maps each color in the logical palette to the extended system palette as follows:

- If a color in the logical palette already exists in the system palette, that color is mapped to the matching color index in the system palette.
- A logical palette color with no match in the system palette is added to the system palette, provided there is room.
- When the system palette becomes full, a logical palette color is mapped to the closest matching color in the system palette.

When there are several applications with logical palettes, Windows maps the logical palette of the topmost window into the system palette.

If you write a Windows application and want to use all 256 colors in a Super VGA adapter, you have to use a logical palette. Otherwise, you can use only the 20 default colors in the system palette.

Creating and Using Logical Palettes

Like a hardware palette, a logical palette is simply a table of RGB colors. Each entry in the table is a `PALETTEENTRY` structure, defined in `<windows.h>` as the following:

```
typedef struct tagPALETTEENTRY
{
    BYTE    peRed;
    BYTE    peGreen;
    BYTE    peBlue;
    BYTE    peFlags;
} PALETTEENTRY;
```

The logical palette itself is a `LOGPALETTE` structure, declared in `<windows.h>` as the following:

```
typedef struct tagLOGPALETTE
{
    WORD         palVersion;      // Windows version
    WORD         palNumEntries;   // Number of palette entries
    PALETTEENTRY palPalEntry[1];  // Array of palette entries
} LOGPALETTE;
```

Here are the steps to follow to create and use a logical palette:

1. Check if the display driver supports logical palettes. Here is how to check:

   ```
   if((dc.GetDeviceCaps(RASTERCAPS) & RC_PALETTE) &&
      (dc.GetDeviceCaps(DRIVERVERSION) >= 0x0300))
   {
   // Supports logical palettes.
   }
   else
   {
   // Does not support logical palettes.
   }
   ```

2. Allocate room for a palette and define the palette entries. For example, here is the C++ code to allocate a logical palette with 16 entries (defined to be shades of red):

   ```
   const int ncolors = 16;
   LPLOGPALETTE lpal = (LPLOGPALETTE) new char[sizeof(LOGPALETTE) +
   (ncolors - 1) * sizeof(PALETTEENTRY)];
   ```

```
lpal->palVersion = 0x0300;
lpal->palNumEntries = ncolors;

int i;
for(i = 0; i < ncolors; i++)
{
    lpal->palPalEntry[i].peRed   = 16*i;
    lpal->palPalEntry[i].peGreen = 0;
    lpal->palPalEntry[i].peBlue  = 0;
    lpal->palPalEntry[i].peFlags = 0;
}
```

The `peFlags` field in each palette entry can be one of the following:

Value	Meaning
0	The entry is a normal palette entry.
PC_EXPLICIT	Treat the low-order 16-bit word as an index to the hardware palette.
PC_NOCOLLAPSE	Do not map this entry to any existing color in the system palette.
PC_RESERVED	This entry will be used for palette animation (this means the entry will be changed often). Do not map colors from other logical palettes with this entry.

3. Create a `TPalette` object using the constructor that accepts a pointer to the `LOGPALETTE` structure as argument:

   ```
   TPalette *pal = new TPalette(lpal);
   ```

4. Call the `SelectObject` function of the `TDC` class to select the new palette into the device context.

   ```
   dc.SelectObject(hpal, 0);
   ```

   A zero for the last argument to `SelectObject` specifies that the palette is to be used as a foreground palette; otherwise, the palette is used for background.

5. Before using the colors in the palette, call the `RealizePalette` member function of the `TDC` class to install the logical palette into the system palette and make the colors available:

```
dc.RealizePalette();
```

6. Before exiting program, call `delete` to free the memory allocated for the logical palette and restore the original palette by calling `RestorePalette`:

```
delete lpal;
dc.RestorePalette();
```

You may want to do this cleanup in the handler for the `WM_DESTROY` event that Windows sends when a window is being closed.

Manipulating Logical Palettes

The Windows GDI provides a number of functions for manipulating logical and system palettes. Table 19.6 summarizes these functions. Most of these GDI functions are available as member functions of the `TDC` or `TPalette` classes.

Table 19.6. Windows functions that manipulate palettes.

Name	Description
`AnimatePalette`	Member function of the `TPalette` class that changes entries in a logical palette resulting in instant changes to colors on the display: `pal.AnimatePalette(start_indx, count, pal_entries);`
`CreatePalette`	Creates a logical palette and returns a handle (that can be used to create a `TPalette`) to the palette
`GetNearestPaletteIndex`	Member function of the `TPalette` class that returns the index of the palette entry that most closely matches a specified `TColor`: `UINT p_indx = pal.GetNearestPaletteIndex(color);`
`GetPaletteEntries`	Member function of the `TPalette` class that retrieves the color values for a specified

Name	Description
	number of entries in a logical palette: `pal.GetPaletteEntries(start_indx, count, pal_entries);`
`GetSystemPaletteEntries`	Member function of the `TDC` class that retrieves the color values for a specified number of entries in the system palette: `dc.GetSystemPaletteEntries(start, num, pal_entries);`
`GetSystemPaletteUse`	Member function of the `TDC` class that returns a flag indicating whether an application can change the system palette: `UINT can_change = dc.GetSystemPaletteUse();`
`RealizePalette`	Member function of the `TDC` class that maps the entries of the currently selected logical palette into the system palette: `dc.RealizePalette();`
`ResizePalette`	Member function of the `TPalette` class that enlarges or reduces the size of a logical palette after it has been created: `pal.ResizePalette(num_entries);`
`SetPaletteEntries`	Member function of the `TPalette` class that changes the color values of a specified number of entries in the logical palette: `pal.SetPaletteEntries(start, count, pal_entries);`
`SetSysColors`	Sets one or more colors in the system palette, identified by constants such as `COLOR_ACTIVEBORDER`, `COLOR_MENU`, and `COLOR_WINDOW`
`SetSystemPaletteUse`	Member function of the `TDC` class that allows the currently active application to

continues

Table 19.6. continued

Name	Description
	change the entries in the system palette: `dc.SetSystemPaletteUse(flag); //flag is one of: SYSPAL_NOSTATIC or SYSPAL_STATIC`
`UpdateColors`	Member function of the `TDC` class that updates the color of the pixels in the client area of a window to reflect the current entries in the system palette: `dc.UpdateColors();`

Handling Palette Messages

If your application uses a logical palette, it should handle three palette-specific Windows messages to ensure that the colors are displayed correctly in the application's windows. First of all, whenever your application's window becomes active, Windows sends a `WM_QUERYNEWPALETTE` message to offer an opportunity to realize the logical palette. The reason is that other applications that also use logical palettes may have loaded different colors into the system palette, and your application needs to reload its colors. The function that handles the `WM_QUERYNEWPALETTE` message should call the `RealizePalette` function to map the logical palette to the system palette. In an OWL program, you declare the message handler for `WM_QUERYNEWPALETTE` as follows:

```
BOOL EvQueryNewPalette();
```

In addition to declaring this member function in the window class, you also have to add the following line to the window's response table:

```
// Assuming window is derived from TWindow
DEFINE_RESPONSE_TABLE1(MyWindow, TWindow)
   EV_WM_QUERYNEWPALETTE,
// Other messages...
END_RESPONSE_TABLE;
```

Then, you might implement the `EvQueryNewPalette` function as follows:

```
    short changed = 0;
```

```
// Assume that "pal" is the TPalette object representing your
// application's logical palette (the one you want to use).

     TClientDC dc(HWindow);
     dc.SelectObject(pal, FALSE);
     int changed = dc.RealizePalette();
     dc.RestorePalette();
     if(changed)
     {
         Invalidate(TRUE);
         UpdateWindow();
     }
```

The `RealizePalette` function returns the number of colors that were changed to accommodate the specified logical palette. You should redraw the contents of the window if any colors change.

The other two palette-related Windows messages are `WM_PALETTEISCHANGING` and `WM_PALETTECHANGED`. These messages matter to an application only if you want to display the best possible colors even when the application's windows are not active. Windows sends the `WM_PALETTEISCHANGING` message to the top-level windows of all applications when the system palette is about to change; the `WM_PALETTECHANGED` message is sent after the system palette has changed. Applications that do not use logical palettes can ignore these messages safely.

If your application has to display the best possible colors when it does not have the input focus, the application should handle the `WM_PALETTECHANGED` message by providing the `EvPaletteChanged` function in the window class. The first step in this function is to ensure that the palette change was not caused by an earlier call to `RealizePalette` made by your application. Here is a code fragment for a function that handles the `WM_PALETTECHANGED` message:

```
// Assume the window class is called MyWindow
void MyWindow::EvPaletteChanged(HWND hWndPalChg)
{
    if(hWndPalChg == HWindow) return;
//...

// Assume that "pal" is the TPalette object representing your
// application's logical palette (the one you want to use).

     TClientDC dc(HWindow);
     dc.SelectObject(pal, FALSE);
```

```
        int changed = dc.RealizePalette();
        if(changed)
        {
            dc.UpdateColors();
        }
        dc.RestorePalette();
}
```

In this case, too, you first realize the logical palette and, if any colors in the system palette change, call `UpdateColors` to refresh the colors quickly in your application's window. Of course, if you want, you also can redraw the contents of the window by invalidating the client area.

Bitmaps

Each pixel in an image corresponds to one or more bits in a bitmap. In a monochrome bitmap, corresponding to a black-and-white image, each bit in the bitmap represents a pixel in the image. For color images, each pixel requires more than one bit in the bitmap to indicate the color of the pixel. Additionally, the mapping of the bits in a pixel to a specific color depends on a color map.

Prior to version 3.0, Windows supported a single bitmap format, now known as the device-dependent bitmap (DDB), that made certain assumptions about the display device. Windows 3.0 introduced a new version, called the device-independent bitmap (DIB) that stores the bitmap information in a device-independent manner—primarily by adding a color palette to the old DDB format. OWL 2.0 provides the `TBitmap` and `TDib` classes to represent DDB and DIB, respectively.

You can think of a bitmap as a canvas in memory where you can draw images. The Windows GDI includes functions such as `BitBlt` and `StretchBlt` that quickly can copy a bitmap to the display device. Bitmaps are very useful in applications that require animating images. For instance, if you have to move a small image around on the display screen, you can store that image in a bitmap and use `BitBlt` to copy the image to the display screen as needed. The following sections summarize the bitmap formats and the bitmap manipulation functions. Chapters 23 and 24 further describe how to interpret image file formats and animate images.

The DDB

The simplest bitmap corresponds to a monochrome image. In this case, each bit in the bitmap represents one pixel in the image. You can derive the bitmap directly from the image by assigning a 1 to each white pixel and 0 to the black ones. Figure 19.4 shows how to write the hexadecimal values representing an 8x8 image. Windows requires that the width (in pixels) of each row of an image be a multiple of 16—each row must have an even number of bytes. Thus, in the example of Figure 19.4, each row is padded with a null byte.

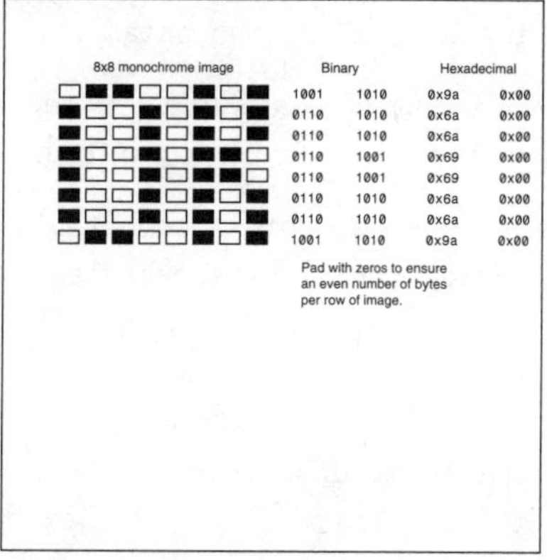

Figure 19.4. Monochrome bitmap format.

Displaying a Bitmap

Once you have the bitmap data, you can display it using the following steps:

1. Define an array of bytes with the bitmap data; write down the hexadecimal values row by row:

```
static BYTE image1[] = //This is the image from Figure 19.4
{
    0x9a, 0x00,  // Pad with zeros to get an even
    0x6a, 0x00,  // number of bytes per row of image
    0x6a, 0x00,
    0x69, 0x00,
    0x69, 0x00,
    0x6a, 0x00,
    0x6a, 0x00,
```

```
        0x9a, 0x00
    };
```

2. Create a `TBitmap` object representing a monochrome bitmap from the bitmap data:

```
// Create the bitmap from the image data
    TBitmap bm(8,       // Width of bitmap (in pixels)
               8,       // Width of bitmap (in pixels)
               1,       // Number of planes
               1,       // Bits per pixel
               image1); // Bitmap data
```

3. Create a memory DC that is compatible with the device where you plan to display the bitmap, and select the bitmap into the memory DC:

```
// Create a memory device context compatible with
// the display device context (represented by the TDC
// object dc)
    TMemoryDC memdc(dc);

// Select bitmap into memory device context
    memdc.SelectObject(bm);
```

4. Transfer the bitmap from the memory DC to the display device context by calling `BitBlt`:

```
// Copy bitmap into the display device context
// (assume that dc is a TClientDC)
    dc.BitBlt(
        10, 10,// Copy to this logical x,y coordinate
        8, 8,  // Width, height of destination rectangle
        memdc, // Copy from this device context (source)
        0, 0,  // Copy from this logical x,y coordinate
        SRCCOPY// One of 256 raster operation codes
        );
```

Stretching a Bitmap

The `BitBlt` function copies a bitmap from one DC to an identical rectangle in another DC. The `StretchBlt` function is another block transfer function that can shrink or stretch a bitmap to fit a specified rectangle in the destination DC. For example, if you want to stretch the 8x8 bitmap of Figure 19.4 to 64x64, you can do so with the following call to `StretchBlt`:

```
dc.StretchBlt(
    10, 10, // Copy to this logical x,y coordinate
    64, 64, // Width, height of destination rectangle
    memdc,  // Copy from this device context (source)
    0, 0,   // Copy from this logical x,y coordinate
    8, 8,   // Width and size of source rectangle
    SRCCOPY // One of 256 raster operation codes
    );
```

Drawing on a Bitmap

Sometimes you may want to prepare a drawing in memory before copying it to a device for displaying or printing. One good time to do this is when you are repeating the same figure. Keeping the drawing in memory and copying it to the device with a call to `BitBlt` is much faster than drawing everything directly on the device. You will find this technique useful for animation as well—the animation looks smoother when you prepare the animated drawing offscreen in memory and copy the drawing to the display.

To prepare a drawing in memory, you have to create a bitmap of a specified size, select it into a memory DC, and draw using that memory DC. The bitmap must be compatible with the device where you plan to display it. Here are the steps to follow:

1. Create a bitmap compatible with the display DC. You have to specify the size of the bitmap:

```
TBitmap bm1(dc,        // compatible with this DC
            64, 64); // width and height in pixels
```

2. Select the bitmap into a memory DC that is compatible with the display DC:

```
TMemoryDC memdc(dc);
memdc.SelectObject(bm1);
```

3. Fill the bitmap with a background color (otherwise the bitmap will have a random bit pattern):

```
// Fill the bitmap with white color
    memdc.SelectStockObject(WHITE_BRUSH);

    memdc.PatBlt(
        0, 0,      // Copy to this logical x,y coordinate
```

```
        64, 64,    // Width and height of rectangle to
                   // be filled with pattern
        PATCOPY); //

    memdc.RestoreBrush(); // Reset the brush
```

4. Draw in the bitmap using GDI drawing functions:

```
// Draw in the bitmap with GDI drawing functions
    memdc.Rectangle(4, 4, 40, 20);
    memdc.TextOut(10, 40, "Hello", 5);
```

5. Display the bitmap by calling `BitBlt` as shown in earlier sections.

ROP Codes

The last argument to the block transfer functions `BitBlt`, `StretchBlt`, and `PatBlt`, is a raster operation (ROP) code that specifies how the source bitmap is combined with the brush pattern and the destination pixels. There are 256 possible ROP codes. The 15 most common are listed in Table 19.7; the logical operations between the source (S), destination (D), and pattern (P) are expressed using the C++ bitwise logical operators: invert(~), AND(&), OR(¦), and exclusive-OR (^).

Table 19.7. Some raster operation codes used by the block transfer functions.

Constant	Operation	Meaning
BLACKNESS	0	Sets all destination pixels to zero (black)
DSTINVERT	~D	Inverts destination pixels
MERGECOPY	P&S	Performs bitwise-AND of source bitmap and brush pattern
MERGEPAINT	~S¦D	Performs bitwise-OR of the inverted source bitmap and the destination pixels
NOTSRCCOPY	~S	Copies inverted source bitmap to the destination
NOTSRCERASE	~(S¦D)	Inverts result of bitwise-OR of the source and destination
PATCOPY	P	Copies brush pattern to the destination

Constant	Operation	Meaning
PATINVERT	P^D	Performs exclusive-OR of the pattern and the destination
PATPAINT	P¦(~S)¦D	Inverts source bitmap and performs bitwise-OR of the result with the pattern and the destination
SRCAND	S&D	Performs bitwise-AND of source bitmap and destination
SRCCOPY	S	Copies source bitmap to the destination
SRCERASE	S&(~D)	Performs bitwise-OR of the source and the inverted destination
SRCINVERT	S^D	Performs exclusive-OR of the source and the destination
SRCPAINT	S¦D	Performs bitwise-OR of the source and the destination
WHITENESS	1	Sets all bits of the destination pixels to 1 (white)

The BITMAP Structure

Device-dependent bitmaps are represented in memory by a BITMAP structure, which is defined in <windows.h> as the following:

```
typedef struct tagBITMAP
{
    int      bmType;        // Always set to zero
    int      bmWidth;       // Width of bitmap (in pixels)
    int      bmHeight;      // Height of bitmap (in pixels)
    int      bmWidthBytes;  // Bytes per row of bitmap data
                            //    (must be even)
    BYTE     bmPlanes;      // Number of bit planes
    BYTE     bmBitsPixel;   // Number of bits per pixel
    void FAR* bmBits;       // Array of bitmap data
} BITMAP;
```

For color bitmaps, each pixel requires multiple bits of data, which may be stored as a number of planes or as groups of bits per pixel. The fields `bmPlanes` and `bmBitsPixel` determine how the bitmap data `bmBits` is interpreted.

When the data is organized as planes, `bmBitsPixel` is set to 1 and the `bmPlanes` field has the number of planes. The `bmBits` array starts with the first line of the image: all the bits of the first plane for the first line followed by the bits for that line from the second plane, and so on.

On the other hand, if the bitmap is meant for a device that stores all bits for a pixel contiguously, the `bmPlanes` field of the `BITMAP` structure is 1, but the `bmBitsPixel` is set to the number of bits used for each pixel. The `bmBits` array then stores the data for the image line by line, with each group of `bmBitsPixel` bits representing the color of consecutive pixels on a line.

The exact storage format for color bitmaps depends on the type of device in which the bitmap is to be displayed. Apart from the device-dependent manner of storing the image data, the `BITMAP` structure has no provision for indicating how the pixel values are mapped to actual colors. The DIB format, described next, corrects this shortcoming of the DDB format.

The DIB

The device-independent format, introduced in Windows 3.0, solves some of the device dependencies of the old-style bitmap format. Here are the specific differences:

- The internal representation of bitmap data is standardized—color bitmaps are stored as multiple bits per pixel with only one plane per pixel. The number of bits per pixel can be one of the following:

  1 for monochrome bitmaps

  4 for 16-color bitmaps

  8 for 256-color bitmaps

  24 for 16,777,216 or 16 million-color bitmaps

- The array of bits stores the image data from the bottom row to the top (in DDB format, the data starts from the top row).
- The DDB format includes information about the resolution of the image.
- The bitmap data for 16- and 256-color bitmaps may be compressed using a run-length encoding (RLE) algorithm.

The DIB format is useful for storing images in files. The Windows PaintBrush application stores bitmaps in DIB format (with the .BMP file extension). Chapter 23, "Understanding Image File Formats," covers the DIB file format and shows how to read and display a device-independent bitmap.

Summary

Windows Graphical Device Interface (GDI) provides the data structures and functions necessary for displaying graphics, text, and images in your application's windows. This chapter provides an overview of the GDI functions. The device context, or DC for short, is the key to device-independent graphics in Windows. The DC holds drawing tools and attributes, such as pen, brush, background color, and font, that affect all graphics and text output.

The Windows GDI also supports drawing to bitmaps. You can define a memory DC with an associated bitmap and either load images or draw in the bitmap with GDI drawing functions. The GDI includes several block transfer functions such as `BitBlt` and `StretchBlt` that can efficiently copy bitmaps from memory to a device.

There are two types of bitmaps: the device-dependent bitmaps (DDB) from Windows versions prior to 3.0 and the device-independent bitmaps (DIB) introduced in Windows 3.0. The DIB format is used to store images in files—the .BMP files created by Windows PaintBrush use the DIB format. Chapter 23 describes how to interpret and display image files of various formats, including the DIB format.

OWL 2.0 provides the `TGdiBase` class hierarchy that represents all data structures such as DC, bitmap, font, brush, and pen needed by the GDI functions. Most of the GDI functions appear as member functions of an appropriate class in the `TGdiBase` hierarchy. In particular, all drawing functions are members of the `TDC` class, which represents a device context.

Displaying Text in Windows

Chapter 19, "Graphics Programming with OWL," describes the graphics output functions available in the Windows GDI. This chapter covers another important category of output functions—text output. Text output is important because text is an integral part of many Windows applications. Although you can get by with OWL classes that provide text-editing capabilities, some Windows applications might use text in captions, annotations, and instructions. With the fonts available in Windows, you can customize the appearance of the text depending on the function. For instance, you might want to use large, bold characters for captions but smaller letters for the annotations. This chapter shows you how to display text in a Windows application.

Simple Text Output

The OWL class `TDC` provides several member functions for displaying text. These functions are similar to the Windows GDI functions with the same names. Here are the three prominent text output functions in the `TDC` class:

- `DrawText(str, nchars, rect, format_flag);` displays `nchars` characters from the text string `str` inside the rectangle defined by a `TRect` object specified by `rect`. The `format_flag` indicates the positioning and formatting of the string.
- `TabbedTextOut(pt, str, nchars, ntabpos, tabpos, tab_origin);` displays `nchars` characters from the string `str` at the logical coordinates specified by the `TPoint` object `pt`. Embedded tabs (`'\t'`) in the string are interpreted according to the tab positions specified (in terms of pixels) in the array of integers `tabpos` with `ntabs` entries. The `tab_origin` argument is the logical x-coordinate where the tabs begin. This function returns TRUE if successful; otherwise it returns FALSE.
- `TextOut(x, y, str, nchars);` displays `nchars` characters from the text string `str` at the logical coordinate (x, y). The positioning of the characters with respect to (x, y) depends on the current text alignment specified by the `SetTextAlign` function.

  You specify the text alignment by calling the `SetTextAlign` function of the `TDC` class. For a `TDC` object named `dc`, a typical call to `SetTextAlign` is as follows:

  ```
  dc.SetTextAlign(TA_BOTTOM | TA_LEFT);
  ```

  where the second argument is a bitwise-OR of flags indicating the location of the text string with respect to the output position. In this case, the text output position is at the top left corner of the string. The vertical alignment can be one of the following:

`TA_BASELINE`	The baseline of the text is aligned with the y-coordinate of the output position.
`TA_BOTTOM`	The bottom of the text is aligned with the y-coordinate of the output position.
`TA_TOP`	The top of the text is aligned with the y-coordinate of the output position.

The horizontal alignment can be one of the following:

`TA_CENTER`	The horizontal center of the text is aligned with the x-coordinate of the output position.
`TA_LEFT`	The left side of the text is aligned with the x-coordinate of the output position.
`TA_RIGHT`	The right side of the text is aligned with the x-coordinate of the output position.

The default alignment is `TA_TOP | TA_LEFT`. Also, by default `TextOut` does not update the current position after the text output. If you want the current position updated, include the `TA_UPDATECP` flag with a bitwise-OR operator in the call to `SetTextAlign`.

In addition to the text alignment, several other attributes in the DC affect text output. By default, the text color is black, but you can set the text color to any RGB value:

```
dc.SetTextColor(RGB(255, 0, 0); // Set text color to red.
```

The background mode determines whether the spaces between the characters are filled in with the current background color. By default, the background mode is `OPAQUE`, which means Windows uses the background color to fill in the spaces between the character strokes. You can set the background mode to `TRANSPARENT` and display the characters without affecting the pixels in between:

```
dc.SetBkMode(TRANSPARENT);
```

Of course, the font is another important attribute that determines the appearance (shape and size) of the text output. By default, Windows displays the text in the system font. As you will see in the next section, however, you can also create and use many other fonts. The easiest way to display text is to use one of the six stock fonts. Like other stock objects, such as brush and pen, the fonts are identified by names. Here are the names of the six stock fonts in Windows:

`ANSI_FIXED_FONT`	This is a fixed-width ANSI character set font (usually Courier).
`ANSI_VAR_FONT`	This is a variable width ANSI character set font (usually MS Sans Serif).
`DEVICE_DEFAULT_FONT`	This is a font that is most suitable for the current device.
`OEM_FIXED_FONT`	This is a fixed-width font that contains the IBM-PC compatible character set. Windows uses this font in all windowed DOS character-mode applications (including `COMMAND.COM`).
`SYSTEM_FIXED_FONT`	This is a fixed pitch ANSI character set font that Windows versions prior to 3.0 used for menus, dialog boxes, message boxes, and captions.
`SYSTEM_FONT`	This is a proportionally spaced ANSI character set font that Windows uses in menus, dialog boxes, message boxes, and captions.

You can use any of these stock fonts just as you use other stock objects: by selecting it into the DC with a call to the `SelectStockObject` function. For example, to use the `ANSI_FIXED_FONT` in an OWL program, you write the following:

```
// Assume that dc is the device context
    dc.SelectStockObject(ANSI_FIXED_FONT);

// Display text using this font
    char msg[] = "Hello, World!";
    dc.TextOut(20, 50, msg, strlen(msg));

// Restore the old font
    dc.RestoreFont();
```

The next few sections discuss how to select and use other fonts.

Using Fonts

The choice of typeface is limited when you use the stock fonts. Windows offers many more typefaces that you can use to create impressive text displays. Before beginning to use the font creation functions, you should understand a few terms related to the use of fonts in Windows.

In Windows, the term *typeface* refers to the appearance of a specific set of characters, regardless of size. A typeface is characterized by features such as serifs that are shared by all characters from the set. A *font*, on the other hand, is a complete set of characters from a typeface with a specific size and style, such as bold or italic. Thus, *Helvetica* is a typeface and *12-point Helvetica Bold* is a font. Another important characteristic of a font is its character set.

Character Set

The *character set* of a font determines the character shape corresponding to each 8-bit character code. The American Standard Code for Information Interchange (ASCII) specifies the characters corresponding to the first 128 character codes. MS-DOS systems define a number of special and line-drawing characters for the last 128 of the 256 character codes that can be represented by an 8-bit value. Unfortunately, the American National Standards Institute (ANSI) defines different characters for the last 128 character codes. Windows primarily supports the ANSI character set in its fonts. However, Windows also supports the extended DOS character set in what is known as an OEM (Original Equipment Manufacturer) font for use in non-Windows applications. Because some characters in the ANSI font are also in the OEM font and vice versa, the Windows API includes two functions for converting from one character set to another: `AnsiToOem` and `OemToAnsi`. Also, the ANSI font includes special accented characters in the last 128 character codes. You have to call `AnsiUpper` and `AnsiLower` to ensure that the case conversions work properly with these characters in the ANSI font.

Font Types

Windows provides two font families: *fixed-width* and *variable-width*. In a fixed-width font, all characters occupy exactly the same width. In a variable-width font, each character takes up only as much space as it needs.

Windows 3.1 supports three types of fonts: *raster, vector,* and *TrueType*. In a *raster* font, each character is defined by a bitmap image. Windows can display these fonts easily because displaying a character involves simply copying the bitmap to the screen.

A vector or *stroke* font defines each character's shape in terms of a series of line segments. Vector fonts can be rotated and scaled easily.

TrueType is a much more sophisticated way of representing fonts. Like PostScript, a TrueType font contains a detailed description of each character. TrueType expresses the character's outline in terms of lines and curves. The font even contains information, known as hints, on displaying each character on various resolution devices. These hints ensure that characters are rendered legibly at all resolutions and in all sizes.

Windows 3.1 includes many fonts—the older vector and raster fonts and a substantial number of new TrueType fonts. To view the available fonts, run the Character Map application (`CHARMAP.EXE`) that comes with Windows. Figure 20.1 shows the window that the `CHARMAP` displays. If you click the font selection box (or on the arrow next to it), a list box appears with the names of available fonts. In Figure 20.1, you can see the character set of the System font.

Font Families

Windows groups all available typefaces into a number of font families. All typefaces with the same general appearance belong to the same family. Here are the characteristics that determine the appearance of a font family:

Stroke Width — This refers to the width of the lines that make up the shape of each character. The stroke width can be fixed or variable.

Pitch This is the separation between characters in a line of text and is controlled by the width of the characters. If all characters in a typeface have the same width, the typeface is said to be of fixed pitch (or monospace). A typeface with a variable pitch is also called proportionally spaced typeface.

Serif The serifs are the small lines that embelish the characters in some typefaces. For instance, look at any character (such as S and A) in the Times Roman font. You will notice the serifs at the end of the lines in the character. Fonts without serifs are referred to as *sans serif* fonts.

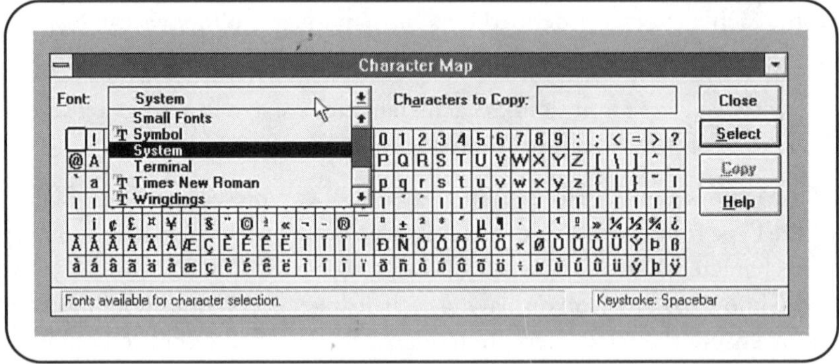

Figure 20.1. Displaying a font with the Character Map application.

Table 20.1 summarizes the font families by names that are defined in the header file WINDOWS.H.

Table 20.1. Font family names.

Name	Description
`FF_DONTCARE`	This name is used by a program when it wants to use a font but it does not care or does not know the font's family.
`FF_ROMAN`	These typefaces have serifs and variable stroke width. Typical examples are Times New Roman, Century Schoolbook, and MS Serif.

Name	Description
FF_SWISS	These typefaces have variable stroke width and do not have any serifs (sans serif). Typical members of this family are Arial, Helvetica, MS Sans Serif, and System.
FF_MODERN	These fonts have constant stroke width. This family includes fonts with or without serifs. Typical examples are Courier, Courier New, and Terminal.
FF_SCRIPT	These fonts resemble cursive handwriting. Examples are Script and Zapf Chancery.
FF_DECORATIVE	These are decorative fonts. Many fonts in this family have characters that do not correspond to any alphabet. Typical examples are Monotype Sorts, WingDings, and Zapf Dingbats.

Getting Information on a Font

When displaying text output, Windows draws each character by painting the pixels in a rectangle matching the size of that character's bitmap. Because you have to specify where Windows should start drawing the characters, you need to know the size of each character's bitmap (at the very least, the maximum width and height of the character bitmaps in a font). The Windows API includes functions that let you obtain such information.

To get aggregate information about a font, call the `GetTextMetrics` member function of a device context object with a `TEXTMETRIC` structure as argument. `GetTextMetric` fills in the fields of the `TEXTMETRIC` structure with information about the font. The `TEXTMETRIC` structure is defined in the header file WINDOWS.H as follows:

```
typedef struct tagTEXTMETRIC
{
    int  tmHeight;           // Height of character(logical unit)
    int  tmAscent;           // Height above baseline
    int  tmDescent;          // Height below baseline
    int  tmInternalLeading;  // Space for diacritical marks
    int  tmExternalLeading;  // Extra space between lines
    int  tmAveCharWidth;     // Average width of characters
                             // in logical units
```

```
    int  tmMaxCharWidth;     // Width of the widest character
    int  tmWeight;           // A value between 0 and 999 that
                             // denotes if font is bold or normal
    Byte tmItalic;           // Nonzero if font is italic
    Byte tmUnderlined;       // Nonzero if font is underlined
    Byte tmStruckOut;        // Nonzero if a line is to be drawn
                             // through every character
    Byte tmFirstChar;        // Character code of first character
    Byte tmLastChar;         // Character code of last character
    Byte tmDefaultChar;      // Character that Windows uses to
                             // display nonexistent characters
    Byte tmBreakChar;        // Character that marks word breaks
    BYTE tmPitchAndFamily;   // Lower 2 bits indicate pitch
                             // Next four bits indicate family
    BYTE tmCharSet;          // Character set of font (usually
                             // ANSI_CHARSET or OEM_CHARSET)
    int  tmOverhang;         // Extra width added when creating
                             // an italic version of the font
    int  tmDigitizedAspectX;// These denote the aspect ratio
    int  tmDigitizedAspectY;// for which font is appropriate
} TEXTMETRIC;
```

Figure 20.2 illustrates the meaning of some of the members of the TEXTMETRIC structure. Keep in mind that the dimensions returned in the TEXTMETRIC structure are in logical units. Thus, these dimensions are in pixel units only if you are using the MM_TEXT mapping mode.

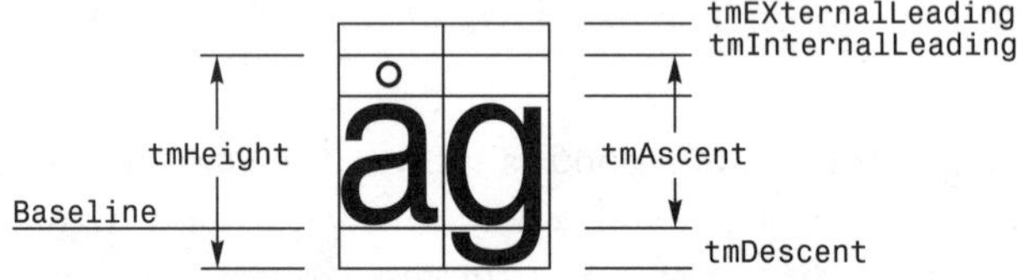

Figure 20.2. Character size information in TEXTMETRIC structure.

Windows 3.1 introduces a new structure, NEWTEXTMETRIC, with four additional fields appended to the older TEXTMETRIC structure. The new fields are meant to hold information about the TrueType fonts. The new structure is used by the EnumFontFamilies function. Because TrueType fonts have many more attributes than the older raster and vector fonts, Windows 3.1 also adds another function, GetOutlineMetrics, and another structure, OUTLINETEXTMETRIC, to provide additional information about the

TrueType fonts. The `OUTLINETEXTMETRIC` structure includes a `TEXTMETRIC` structure and a large number of other fields with detailed information about a TrueType font. You can look up detailed information on the new structure and the `GetOutlineMetrics` function in the online help of Borland C++.

As an example of using the information returned by `GetTextMetrics`, consider the problem of displaying lines of text in a specific font. You need the height of characters to position the lines. Here is how you might set the height of a line of text:

```
    TEXTMETRIC tm;

// Assume dc is the device context
    dc.GetTextMetrics(tm);

    short line_height = tm.tmHeight + tm.tmExternalLeading;
```

While the `GetTextMetrics` function provides information about the height of the characters in a font, you need another function to determine the width of a string displayed in a certain font. Unless the font is monospaced, the width of each character varies; you cannot find the width of a line of text with the general information from `GetTextMetrics`. You have to call either `GetTextExtent` or `GetTextExtentPoint` to determine the width of a string displayed in the current font. Here is how you would use the `GetTextExtent` function to determine the height and width of the string `"Hello"` in logical units:

```
    short slen = strlen("Hello");
// Assume that dc is the device context
    TSize txtsz = dc.GetTextExtent("Hello", slen);
    short line_width = txtsz.cx;
    short line_height = txtsz.cy;
```

These sample code fragments assume you are going to display the text in the currently selected font. If you want to use a specific font, you can follow the procedure outlined in the next section to create and use a font.

Creating a Font

To use a font (other than the stock fonts) in an OWL program, start by creating a `TFont` object that represents a Windows *logical font*—a description of the font you want. This description includes the name of the typeface as well as the font's height, weight, pitch, and family, among several other features.

There are two ways to create a TFont object. The first constructor is similar in appearance to the CreateFont function in the Windows API. For instance, here is an example that creates a bold Helvetica font with characters 60 logical units tall:

```
TFont font = CreateFont(
                    60,                    // height (logical units)
                    0,                     // width (0 means
                                           // Windows chooses width)
                    0,                     // escapement
                    0,                     // orientation
                    FW_BOLD,               // weight
                    0,                     // italic - off
                    0,                     // underline - off
                    0,                     // strikeout - off
                    ANSI_CHARSET,          // character set
                    OUT_DEFAULT_PRECIS,    // output precision
                    CLIP_DEFAULT_PRECIS,   // clipping precision
                    PROOF_QUALITY,
                    VARIABLE_PITCH,        // pitch and family
                    "Helv");               // name of font face
```

Notice that this TFont constructor requires 14 arguments just as the CreateFont function. You can set many of the arguments to zero, but you do have to specify all 14 of the arguments.

If you do not want to specify all these arguments for the TFont constructor, you can use another constructor that relies on the Windows API function CreateFontIndirect, which requires only one argument: a pointer to a LOGFONT structure. The LOGFONT structure has exactly 14 members, one for each of the 14 arguments that CreateFont requires. Thus, you are still going to have to specify many parameters, but you at least can use the second form of the TFont constructor as many times as you need, each time changing the fields of a single LOGFONT structure.

The LOGFONT structure is defined in WINDOWS.H as follows:

```
typedef struct tagLOGFONT
{
    int  lfHeight;
    int  lfWidth;
    int  lfEscapement;
    int  lfOrientation;
    int  lfWeight;
    BYTE lfItalic;
    BYTE lfUnderline;
```

```
    BYTE lfStrikeOut;
    BYTE lfCharSet;
    BYTE lfOutPrecision;
    BYTE lfClipPrecision;
    BYTE lfQuality;
    BYTE lfPitchAndFamily;
    char lfFaceName[LF_FACESIZE];
} LOGFONT;
```

Here is a brief description of each of the fields of the `LOGFONT` structure:

`int lfHeight;`	This is the height (in logical units) of the characters—what you want as the `tmHeight` field of the font's `TEXTMETRIC` structure. If you set this field to zero, Windows selects a font of default height.
`int  lfWidth;`	This is the width of characters in logical units. If this field is zero, Windows selects the font based on the height.
`int  lfEscapement;`	This is an angle measured in tenths of a degree in a counterclockwise direction from the horizontal. It specifies the direction along which `TextOut` is to draw a string of characters. Only certain devices can display text along any arbitrary direction. Most of the time, you can display text only along the horizontal or vertical axes. However, Windows 3.1 can display TrueType fonts along any direction.
`int  lfOrientation;`	This specifies the orientation of the characters with respect to the baseline. The value is an angle, in tenths of a degree, measured counterclockwise from the character's baseline. Windows 3.1 ignores this field.
`int  lfWeight;`	This is the thickness of the lines used to draw the characters. The value can be anywhere between 0 and 1000. Although there are a large number of

	defined symbols to specify many different weights, most fonts support only `FW_NORMAL` and `FW_BOLD` weights. You can set this field to `FW_DONTCARE` if you want Windows to choose a default weight.
`BYTE lfItalic;`	A nonzero value indicates that the font should be italic.
`BYTE lfUnderline;`	A nonzero value indicates that the font should be underlined.
`BYTE lfStrikeOut;`	A nonzero value indicates that the font should be struck out (a horizontal line drawn through the middle of each character).
`BYTE lfCharSet;`	This is the character set of the font. It can be one of `ANSI_CHARSET`, `DEFAULT_CHARSET`, `SYMBOL_CHARSET`, `SHIFTJIS_CHARSET`, `HANGEUL_CHARSET`, `CHINESEBIG5_CHARSET`, or `OEM_CHARSET`.
`BYTE lfOutPrecision;`	This field specifies how Windows should attempt to pick an available font that matches the characteristics of the logical font. Here are a few of the possible values for this field (defined in WINDOWS.H): `OUT_TT_PRECIS`. In case of several matching fonts, this selects the matching TrueType font. `OUT_TT_ONLY_PRECIS`. This selects a TrueType font only. `OUT_DEVICE_PRECIS`. In case of several matching fonts, this selects a font belonging to a specific device (such as printer).

`BYTE lfClipPrecision;`	This specifies how Windows should deal with characters that lie at the edge of the clipping region of the DC. Use `CLIP_DEFAULT_PRECIS` for default clipping, which displays only those parts of the character that lie inside the clipping region.
`BYTE lfQuality;`	This field tells Windows what is more important when selecting a font matching the logical font. If you use the constants `DEFAULT_QUALITY` or `DRAFT_QUALITY`, Windows tries to synthesize any font it can. If you set this to `PROOF_QUALITY`, Windows selects a font closest in size but ensures that size does not exceed the request dimensions.
`BYTE lfPitchAndFamily;`	This field specifies both the pitch and the font family. Use a bitwise-OR of two constant names, one specifying the pitch and the other specifying the font family. The pitch can be one of `DEFAULT_PITCH`, `VARIABLE_PITCH`, or `FIXED_PITCH`. The font family can be one of `FF_DONTCARE`, `FF_ROMAN`, `FF_SWISS`, `FF_MODERN`, `FF_SCRIPT`, or `FF_DECORATIVE`.
`char lfFaceName[LF_FACESIZE];`	This is the name of the typeface you want. Use names such as *Helv*, *Courier*, and *Times New Roman*. In Windows 3.1, the name can be up to 31 characters long (`LF_FACESIZE` is defined to be 32 but that includes room for the terminating null character).

After you create a `TFont` object, you have to select it into the device context before you can use it. This is where Windows selects, from the available set of fonts, one that best matches the parameters of the logical font. Here is how you would use a `TFont` identified by the name `font`:

```
// Assume that dc denotes the device context object.
    dc.SelectObject(font);

// Now display the text string using the selected font.
    dc.TextOut(100, 100, "Test", strlen("Test"));

// Reset font in DC
    dc.RestoreFont();
```

Once a font is selected into a DC, you can call the `GetTextFace` function to find out the name of the actual font being used. And you would call `GetTextMetrics` to find out the relevant size information of the selected font.

Listing All Available Fonts

If you are writing a "drawing program" that allows the user to draw graphics and text, you probably want to offer a way for the user to select a font for the text. You might want to do this through a dialog box where the fonts appear in a combo box. A combo box is a list box next to a single-line edit window. (To see an example of this, select the Fonts... item from the Text menu in the PaintBrush application.) To construct that type of a dialog box, you need the names of all the fonts available under Windows. You can get this information by calling the EnumFontFamilies function, which was introduced in Windows 3.1, to supersede the older EnumFonts function.

When calling the `EnumFontFamilies` function, you have to provide as an argument a pointer to one of your own functions. `EnumFontFamilies` calls this function for each available font; the callback function should include code to do whatever you want to do with the font information (usually add the information to a list box). The callback function's prototype is the following:

```
int CALLBACK enumf_cb(
    const ENUMLOGFONT FAR    *p_elf, // Information about font
    const NEWTEXTMETRIC FAR *p_ntm, // Font dimensions
    int                      ftype,  // Font type
    LPARAM                   lparam);// This is whatever you pass
                          // as last argument to EnumFontFamilies
```

Given a callback function, the general syntax of the call to `EnumFontFamilies` is the following:

```
// Assume that dc is the device context
    dc.EnumFontFamilies("Arial", // Font name or NULL
                     enumf_cb,// Callback function (you provide)
                     lparam); // Last argument to enumf_cb
```

You can call EnumFontFamilies in two different ways:

- To get information on all fonts (of all styles and sizes) of a specific typeface, call EnumFontFamilies with the second argument set to the name of the typeface.
- To enumerate the names of the typefaces, call EnumFontFamilies with the second argument set to NULL.

FontSee—An Example of Enumerating Fonts

This section presents the FontSee application. This application displays a dialog box that lets the user pick a font and see some sample text displayed in that font. To display a list of fonts in the dialog box, I would have had to call the EnumFontFamilies function. I will take the easy way out and use a predefined dialog box offered by the OWL class TChooseFontDialog.

Declaring the Classes for FontSee

The FontSee application has a simple structure. The FontSeeApp class represents the application itself and is derived from the OWL class TApplication. The FontSeeWindow class, derived from TFrameWindow, represents the main window of the application. Listing 20.1 shows the file FONTSEE.H that declares these classes.

Note the TChooseFontDialog::TData member of the FontSeeWindow class is used to pass information to the font-selection dialog box. The TChooseFontDialog::TData is a nested class declared inside the TChooseFontDialog class in the <owl\choosefo.h> header file as follows:

```
// The following is a nested class of TChooseFontDialog
class TData
{
public:
    DWORD       Flags;    // Controls look and feel of dialog
    DWORD       Error;    // Holds error code on return
    HDC         DC;       // Identifies printer whose
                          // fonts are listed (used only if
                          // Flags specifies CF_PRINTERFONTS)
```

```
    LOGFONT      LogFont;  // Attributes of the font
    int          PointSize;// Point size of font in units of
                           // a tenth of a point
    TColor       Color;    // Text color
    char far*    Style;    // List of styles in Font Style list
                           // (see Figure 20.3)
    WORD         FontType; // One of: SIMULATED_FONTTYPE,
                           // PRINTER_FONTTYPE or SCREEN_FONTTYPE
    int          SizeMin;  // Minimum  and maximum point sizes that
    int          SizeMax;  // user can select (used only if
                           // Flags specifies CF_LIMITSIZE)
};
```

The `Flags` member of the data structure control several features of the dialog displayed by the `TChooseFontDialog` object. This field is a bitwise-OR combination of one or more of the following constants (defined in the header file `<commdlg.h>`):

`CF_APPLY`	Enables the *Apply* button.
`CF_ANSIONLY`	Allows only the selection of fonts using the Windows character set. (If you specify this flag, the user will not be able to select a font that contains only symbols.)
`CF_BOTH`	Lists the available printer and screen fonts.
`CF_TTONLY`	Enumerates and allows the selection of TrueType fonts only.
`CF_EFFECTS`	Enables strikeout, underline, and color effects. If you set this flag, you can also set the `Style` and `Color` members of `TData`, and `TChooseFontDialog` sets these members after the user closes the dialog box.
`CF_FIXEDPITCHONLY`	Lists only fixed-pitch fonts.
`CF_FORCEFONTEXIST`	Indicates an error condition if the user attempts to select a font or style that does not exist.
`CF_INITTOLOGFONTSTRUCT`	Uses the `LogFont` member of `TData` to initialize the dialog box controls.
`CF_LIMITSIZE`	Limits font selections to only those with font sizes within the range specified by the `SizeMin` and `SizeMax` members.

CF_NOOEMFONTS	Same as CF_NOVECTORFONTS
CF_NOFACESEL	Does not allow font selections.
CF_NOSTYLESEL	Does not allow style selections.
CF_NOSIZESEL	Does not allow size selections.
CF_NOSIMULATIONS	Does not allow graphics device interface (GDI) font simulations.
CF_NOVECTORFONTS	Does not allow user to select vector-fonts.
CF_PRINTERFONTS	Lists only the fonts supported by the printer associated with the device context (or information context) identified by the DC member of the TData class.
CF_SCALABLEONLY	Allows only the selection of scalable fonts, which include: vector fonts, scalable printer fonts, and TrueType fonts.
CF_SCREENFONTS	Lists only the screen fonts supported by the system.
CF_SHOWHELP	Causes the dialog box to show the Help button.
CF_USESTYLE	Specifies that Style member points to a buffer that contains style data that should be used to initialize the Font Style selection. When the user closes the dialog box, the user-selected style data is returned in this buffer.
CF_WYSIWYG	Allows only the selection of fonts available on both the printer and the display. If this flag is set, the CF_BOTH and CF_SCALABLEONLY flags should also be set.

Of the members of TChooseFontDialog::TData, the LOGFONT structure is the most important because it holds information about the font selected by the user through the font dialog.

Listing 20.1. FONTSEE.H. Declaration of the classes used in the `FontSee` program.

```
//----------------------------------------------------------------
// File: fontsee.h
//
// Declares the classes used in the FontSee sample program
// that displays some sample text in a font selected by the user.
//----------------------------------------------------------------
#if !defined(__FONTSEE_H)
#define __FONTSEE_H

#include <owl\applicat.h>
#include <owl\decframe.h>
#include <owl\dialog.h>
#include <owl\color.h>
#include <owl\point.h>
#include <owl\choosefo.h>
#include <owl\dc.h>

#include <string.h>

// Resource identifiers

#define IDM_ABOUT      200
#define IDM_SELFONT    201

// Declare the main window class

class FontSeeWindow : public TFrameWindow
{
public:
    FontSeeWindow(TWindow *parent, const char far *title);

// Declare functions for handling messages from Windows
    void Paint(TDC& dc, int erase_bg, TRect &r);
    void About();
    void CMSelFont();

private:
    TChooseFontDialog::TData  fd;
    TColor                    font_color;
```

```
DECLARE_RESPONSE_TABLE(FontSeeWindow);
};

// Declare the application class

class FontSeeApp : public TApplication
{
public:
    FontSeeApp(const char far *name) : TApplication(name) {}
    void InitMainWindow();
};

#endif
```

Implementing the Classes in FontSee

Listing 20.2 shows the file FONTSEE.CPP that implements the member functions of `FontSeeApp` and `FontSeeWindows`. These functions constitute the FontSee application.

You might want to study two member functions in detail:

`CMSelFont` is called when the user wants to select a new font (the user indicates this through the Font menu). Notice how this function displays the font selection dialog by calling the `ChooseFont` function.

`Paint` handles `WM_PAINT` messages that Windows sends when the main window has to be redrawn. In `Paint`, you can see how to create fonts of various sizes and use these fonts to display sample text.

Listing 20.2. FONTESEE.CPP. Implementing the FontSee application.

```
//-------------------------------------------------------------
// File: fontsee.cpp
//
// Implements the classes used in the FontSee sample program
// that displays some sample text in a font selected by the user.
//-------------------------------------------------------------
```

continues

Listing 20.2. continued

```
#include "fontsee.h"

// Define the response table for FontSeeWindow
DEFINE_RESPONSE_TABLE1(FontSeeWindow, TFrameWindow)
    EV_COMMAND(IDM_ABOUT,   About),
    EV_COMMAND(IDM_SELFONT, CMSelFont),
END_RESPONSE_TABLE;
//-----------------------------------------------------------------
// FontSeeApp:: I n i t M a i n W i n d o w
// Initialize the main window of the FontSee application

void FontSeeApp::InitMainWindow()
{
    MainWindow = new FontSeeWindow(0, "FontSee");
    MainWindow->SetIcon(this, "FONTSEE_ICON");
    MainWindow->AssignMenu("MainMenu");
    MainWindow->Attr.AccelTable = "MainAccelTable";
    EnableBWCC();
}
//-----------------------------------------------------------------
// FontSeeWindow:: F o n t S e e W i n d o w
// Constructor for the FontSeeWindow

FontSeeWindow::FontSeeWindow(TWindow *parent,
                             const char far *title)
    : TFrameWindow(parent, title)
{
// Set the window position and size
    Attr.X = GetSystemMetrics(SM_CXSCREEN) / 10;
    Attr.Y = GetSystemMetrics(SM_CYSCREEN) / 10;
    Attr.W = Attr.X * 8;
    Attr.H = Attr.Y * 8;

// Initialize the structure
// First zero out the entire structure
    memset(&fd, 0, sizeof(fd));

// Now set the needed fields
    fd.LogFont.lfHeight = 12;
    fd.LogFont.lfWeight = FW_NORMAL;
    fd.LogFont.lfCharSet = ANSI_CHARSET;
    fd.LogFont.lfOutPrecision = OUT_DEFAULT_PRECIS;
```

```
    fd.LogFont.lfClipPrecision = CLIP_DEFAULT_PRECIS;
    fd.LogFont.lfQuality = PROOF_QUALITY;
    fd.LogFont.lfPitchAndFamily = VARIABLE_PITCH;
    strcpy(fd.LogFont.lfFaceName, "Helvetica");
    font_color = GetSysColor(COLOR_WINDOWTEXT);
}
//--------------------------------------------------------------
// FontSeeWindow:: C M S e l F o n t
// Display the Font Selection dialog and get
// the user's choice of font.

void FontSeeWindow::CMSelFont()
{
    fd.Flags = CF_INITTOLOGFONTSTRUCT ¦ CF_BOTH ¦ CF_EFFECTS;
    fd.Color = font_color;

// Activate "choose font" dialog...
    if (TChooseFontDialog(this, fd).Execute() == IDOK)
    {
// Yes, user has chosen font.
// Make sure window gets redrawn with new font
        font_color = fd.Color;
        Invalidate(TRUE);
    }
}
//--------------------------------------------------------------
// FontSelWindow:: P a i n t
// Draw the window's content

void FontSeeWindow::Paint(TDC& dc, int, TRect&)
{
    short   len, x, y, points;
    char    str[256];
    TSize   txtsz;
    int     old_mapmode;
    LOGFONT tmpfont;

    x = 10;
    y = 0;

    tmpfont = fd.LogFont;
    dc.SetTextColor(font_color);
    dc.SetBkColor(GetSysColor(COLOR_WINDOW));
```

continues

Listing 20.2. continued

```
// Set graphics mapping mode to MM_TWIPS. In this mode,
// 1 unit = 1/1440 inch, or 1/20 of a typesetter's point,
// which is approximately equal to 1/72 inch.
    old_mapmode = dc.SetMapMode(MM_TWIPS);

// Display a sample string for point sizes 8, 10, ..., 32
    points = 8;
    while (points <= 32)
    {

// Compute height in twips (20 twips = 1 point)
// Note negative value means height is based on actual
// character height
        tmpfont.lfHeight = -points * 20;
        TFont font(&tmpfont);
        dc.SelectObject(font);

// Prepare the string to be displayed
        wsprintf(str, "ABCabc 123 - %s %d pt",
                 fd.LogFont.lfFaceName, points);
        len = strlen(str);
        txtsz = dc.GetTextExtent(str, len);
        y = y + txtsz.cy + 5;
        dc.TextOut(x, -y, str, len);

// Restore previous font
        dc.RestoreFont();
        points += 2;
    }
// Restore previous mapping mode
    dc.SetMapMode(old_mapmode);
}
//-------------------------------------------------------------
//  FontSeeWindow:: A b o u t
//  Display the "About..." box

void FontSeeWindow::About()
{
    TDialog *p_about = new TDialog(this, "ABOUTFONTSEE");
    GetApplication()->ExecDialog(p_about);
}
```

```
//--------------------------------------------------------------
// O w l M a i n
// The "main" function of the FontSee application
// Create an instance of the application and "run" it.

int OwlMain(int, char**)
{
    FontSeeApp FontSee("FontSee");
    return FontSee.Run();
}
```

Running FontSee

All the files needed to build the FontSee program are in the disk bound into this book. To run the program, start Borland C++ 4 and load the project file FONTSEE.IDE from the Chapter 20 directory.

Press Ctrl+F9 to compile and run the FontSee program. You can pick a new font through the Select menu item in the Font menu. Figure 20.3 shows the font dialog box that appears when you try to a pick a new font. Figure 20.4 shows some sample text displayed in the Arial font at several point sizes.

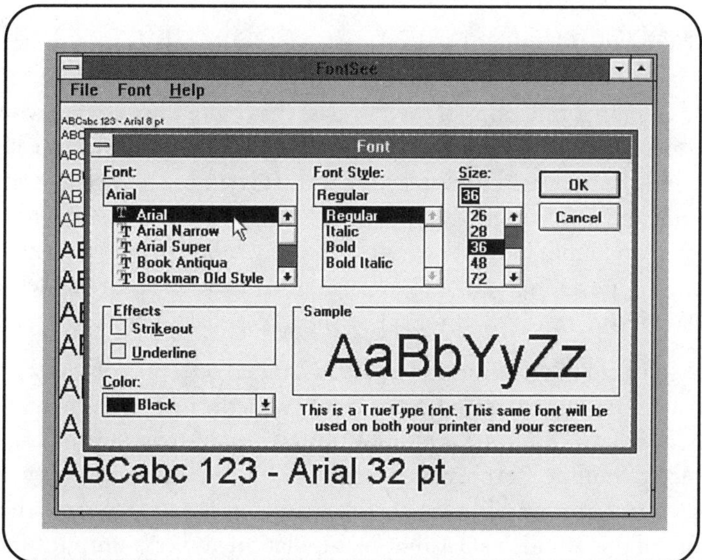

Figure 20.3. The font selection dialog box.

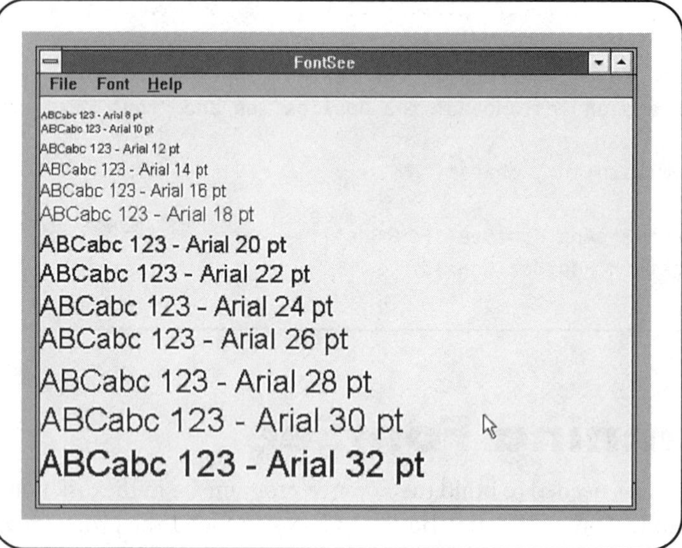

Figure 20.4. Sample text in Arial font at various point sizes.

Summary

The Windows Graphics Device Interface (GDI) includes a number of functions for text output. In Borland's ObjectWindows library (OWL), these functions are available as member functions of the `TDC` class that represents a device context. With these text output functions, you can set the location of text output, the justification of the text, and the font used to display the text. It is simple to display text with the default system font, but you probably want a variety of fonts in any application that uses imaging and animation. The font is like any other Windows object, such as pen or brush. To use a font, you have to create it and select it into the device context before displaying any text in that font. Use the OWL class TFont to create and use a font.

Prior to version 3.1, Windows offered a limited selection of fonts, but the number of available fonts has increased dramatically with the introduction of TrueType fonts in Windows 3.1. TrueType is a sophisticated way of representing fonts, in which each character's outline is expressed in terms of lines and curves. When you use a TrueType font for text output, bitmaps for the characters are prepared on the fly. Fortunately for us, all pre-Windows 3.1 font manipulation and text output functions work with TrueType fonts. However, Windows 3.1 also offers many new functions to deal with TrueType fonts.

This chapter provides an overview of the text display functions and describes how to use fonts in Windows. The sample program, FontSee, lets the user select a font and see sample output in that font at various point sizes. The FontSee program uses the font selection dialog provided by the OWL class `TChooseFontDialog`.

21

Handling Mouse and Keyboard Events

Chapters 19, "Graphics Programming with OWL," and 20, "Displaying Text in Windows," cover the topics of graphics and text output in Windows. Almost all Windows applications also require some input from the user in the form of mouse button presses and keystrokes. The mouse is important for the point-and-click parts of the Windows graphical user interface; the keyboard is indispensable for text entry. Whether it is annotating a figure or typing in a document, most Windows programs have to handle keyboard input to get the job done. This chapter briefly describes how to handle mouse and keyboard inputs under Windows.

Keyboard Messages

Like any other hardware device, Windows handles the keyboard through a device driver. When the user presses and releases a key, the keyboard driver decodes the key and passes the information to Windows. Windows provides the information in the form of keyboard messages to the program currently designated to receive keyboard input. Unlike the mouse, which has a cursor to indicate the window to which the mouse input is directed, Windows needs the concept of the input focus to deliver keyboard input to a specific window.

Input Focus

Windows can send mouse input to a specific window by noting which window contains the mouse cursor. There is no similar way to decide which window should receive keyboard inputs. To solve this problem, Windows uses the concept of *input focus.* The window with the input focus receives all keyboard messages, regardless of the cursor's location. The concept of input focus is tied to that of the *active window* because the active window or a child of the active window always has the input focus. The user makes a window active by clicking the mouse button with the mouse cursor placed inside that window.

Windows sends the `WM_SETFOCUS` message to a window when it becomes active (and receives the input focus) and the `WM_KILLFOCUS` message when the window becomes inactive (and loses the focus). As you will see later, you display or hide the cursor or *caret*—the blinking vertical line that marks the location where text is inserted in a window—in response to the `WM_SETFOCUS` and `WM_KILLFOCUS` messages. Before discussing text entry, let us consider how to handle the keyboard messages.

Handling Keystrokes

Windows places the keystrokes into two categories: *system keystrokes* and *nonsystem keystrokes.* The system keystrokes are those that are important to Windows because they are used for system functions, such as accessing the pull-down menus or switching the active window. Usually, any key pressed in combination with the Alt key is considered a system keystroke. When the user presses and releases a system key, Windows sends a `WM_SYSKEYDOWN` message followed by a `WM_SYSKEYUP` message. Because the system keys are meant for system functions, you do not have to handle these events; Windows takes care of these messages.

Nonsystem keystrokes comprise all other keys besides the system keystrokes. When the user presses and releases any nonsystem key, Windows sends a `WM_KEYDOWN` message followed by a `WM_KEYUP` message. If you want to process these keystrokes in your OWL-based Windows application, you have to provide a member function to handle these messages in the main window class. For example, you declare the member function that handles the `WM_KEYDOWN` messages as follows:

```
void EvKeyDown(
    UINT key,           // Virtual keycode of key pressed
    UINT repeatCount,  // Number of times key was pressed
    UINT flags);        // An 8-bit scan code of the key
                        // as well as other status bits
```

Additionally, you have to include the appropriate message-handler in the response table of that window class as follows:

```
// Assume that the window class is MyWindow, derived from
// TFrameWindow

DEFINE_RESPONSE_TABLE1(MyWindow, TFrameWindow)
    EV_WM_KEYDOWN,
// ...
END_RESPONSE_TABLE;
```

Interpreting the Keystroke Message

In the handler for the `WM_KEYDOWN` message, you have to determine which key was pressed. If you use the Windows API directly, Windows provides this information in an encoded form. However, OWL makes it easier to access such information in message response functions—OWL passes the information through the arguments of the response function. For the `WM_KEYDOWN` message, the three arguments of the `EvKeyDown` function provide a number of details about the keypress, such as the repeat count (the number of keystrokes in the message) and the virtual keycode identifying the key that the user pressed. The *virtual keycode* is a number assigned to each key on a keyboard. Even the mouse buttons are assigned a virtual keycode. Most of the commonly used virtual keycodes have symbolic names that are defined in the header file WINDOWS.H. Table 21.1 shows a list of key names, their numeric keycodes, and the keyboard (or mouse) equivalents.

Table 21.1. Virtual key names.

Symbolic Name	Value (in Hex)	Mouse or Keyboard Equivalent (on U.S. English Keyboard)
`VK_LBUTTON`	01	Left mouse button
`VK_RBUTTON`	02	Right mouse button
`VK_CANCEL`	03	Ctrl+Break key

continues

Table 21.1. continued

Symbolic Name	Value (in Hex)	Mouse or Keyboard Equivalent (on U.S. English Keyboard)
VK_MBUTTON	04	Middle mouse button (for a three-button mouse)
VK_BACK	08	Backspace key
VK_TAB	09	Tab key
VK_CLEAR	0C	5 on numeric keypad with Num Lock off
VK_RETURN	0D	Enter key
VK_SHIFT	10	Shift key
VK_CONTROL	11	Ctrl key
VK_MENU	12	Alt key
VK_PAUSE	13	Pause key
VK_CAPITAL	14	Caps Lock key
VK_ESCAPE	1B	Esc key
VK_SPACE	20	Spacebar
VK_PRIOR	21	Page Up key
VK_NEXT	22	Page Down key
VK_END	23	End key
VK_HOME	24	Home key
VK_LEFT	25	Left Arrow key
VK_UP	26	Up Arrow key
VK_RIGHT	27	Right Arrow key
VK_DOWN	28	Down Arrow key
VK_SELECT	29	*No equivalent key*
VK_EXECUTE	2B	*No equivalent key*
VK_SNAPSHOT	2C	Print Screen key for Windows 3.0 and later

Symbolic Name	Value (in Hex)	Mouse or Keyboard Equivalent (on U.S. English Keyboard)
VK_INSERT	2D	Ins key
VK_DELETE	2E	Del key
VK_HELP	2F	*No equivalent key*
VK_0 to VK_9	30-39	0 through 9 above the letter keys
VK_A to VK_Z	41-5A	A through Z
VK_NUMPAD0	60	0 on numeric keypad
VK_NUMPAD1	61	1 on numeric keypad
VK_NUMPAD2	62	2 on numeric keypad
VK_NUMPAD3	63	3 on numeric keypad
VK_NUMPAD4	64	4 on numeric keypad
VK_NUMPAD5	65	5 on numeric keypad
VK_NUMPAD6	66	6 on numeric keypad
VK_NUMPAD7	67	7 on numeric keypad
VK_NUMPAD8	68	8 on numeric keypad
VK_NUMPAD9	69	9 on numeric keypad
VK_MULTIPLY	6A	Multiply key
VK_ADD	6B	Add key
VK_SEPARATOR	6C	*No equivalent key*
VK_SUBTRACT	6D	Subtract key
VK_DECIMAL	6E	Decimal point key
VK_DIVIDE	6F	Divide key
VK_F1	70	F1 key
VK_F2	71	F2 key
VK_F3	72	F3 key

continues

Table 21.1. continued

Symbolic Name	Value (in Hex)	Mouse or Keyboard Equivalent (on U.S. English Keyboard)
VK_F4	73	F4 key
VK_F5	74	F5 key
VK_F6	75	F6 key
VK_F7	76	F7 key
VK_F8	77	F8 key
VK_F9	78	F9 key
VK_F10	79	F10 key
VK_F11	7A	F11 key
VK_F12	7B	F12 key
VK_F13	7C	*No equivalent key*
VK_F14	7D	*No equivalent key*
VK_F15	7E	*No equivalent key*
VK_F16	7F	*No equivalent key*
VK_F17	80	*No equivalent key*
VK_F18	81	*No equivalent key*
VK_F19	82	*No equivalent key*
VK_F20	83	*No equivalent key*
VK_F21	84	*No equivalent key*
VK_F22	85	*No equivalent key*
VK_F23	86	*No equivalent key*
VK_F24	87	*No equivalent key*
VK_NUMLOCK	90	Num Lock key
VK_SCROLL	91	Scroll Lock key

In the `WM_KEYDOWN` message handler, `EvKeyDown`, you can check for a specific key by testing the `key` field as follows:

```
// Assume MyWindow is the window class
void MyWindow::EvKeyDown(UINT key, UINT repeatCount,
                         UINT flags)
{
//...
// Check if user pressed the F1 function key
    if(key == VK_F1)
    {
// Do whatever you had planned to do in response to the F1 key
//...
    }
}
```

Shift and Toggle Keys

Keys such as Shift, Ctrl, Alt, Caps Lock, and Num Lock are known as *modifier keys* because they modify the meaning of other keys. Shift, Ctrl, and Alt are collectively referred to as *shift keys*, and Caps Lock and Num Lock are called *toggles*. Sometimes you may want to know if any modifier key was down during a specific keystroke. (For instance, was the Shift key down when the user pressed the Q key?) The arguments of the `EvKeyDown` function do not tell you the status of these modifier keys. You have to call the `GetKeyState` function to determine that. For instance, to check if the Shift key is down during the keystroke being processed now, you write

```
// Call GetKeyState inside the keystroke message handler.
    if(GetKeyState(VK_SHIFT) < 0)
    {
// Shift key was down
//...
    }
```

For the shift keys, the return value from `GetKeyState` has the high bit set to 1 if the key is down. For the toggles, `GetKeyState` sets the low order bit of the return value to 1 if the toggle key is down.

The *WM_CHAR* Message

So far you have seen how to handle raw keystrokes through the `WM_KEYDOWN` message. These messages give you information about the user's input at a low level. For instance, on a U.S. English keyboard, if the user holds down the Shift key and types `5` (above the letters), Windows sends a `WM_KEYDOWN` message for the 5 key. It is up to you to call `GetKeyState` to determine if the Shift key was pressed. In such situations, all that you might want is a notification from Windows that the user has entered the % symbol (which is what should happen when the user presses the Shift key and types 5 on a U.S. keyboard). Luckily, Windows provides the WM_CHAR message that directly reports the character entered by the user.

> **WM_KEYDOWN Message Versus WM_CHAR Message**
>
> The WM_KEYDOWN message reports raw keystrokes and WM_CHAR provides information on character input. You should be able to handle most keyboard inputs by handling WM_CHAR messages for all alphanumeric input and WM_KEYDOWN messages for noncharacter keys, such as the cursor keys and the function keys.

If you want to handle WM_CHAR messages in your OWL program, you have to include a member function (in the main window class) to handle these messages. The prototype of this member function is

```
void EvChar(
    UINT key,          // ASCII character code of key pressed
    UINT repeatCount,  // Number of times key was pressed
    UINT flags);       // An 8-bit scan code of the key
                       // as well as other status bits
```

In the EvChar function, you can get the ASCII code of the character in the key argument. Thus, to test for characters such as Backspace, Tab, and the carriage return, include the following code fragment in the EvChar function:

```
void EvChar(UINT key, UINT repeatCount, UINT flags)
{
// This is in the WM_CHAR message handler
//...
    switch(key)
    {
        case '\r':
// Process carriage return key
            break;

        case '\t':
// Process TAB key
            break;
```

```
        case '\b':
// Process BACKSPACE key
            break;

        default:
// Handle all other keys here (perhaps save in a buffer)
    }
```

The Caret

If you have used any Windows word processor, you have seen the caret. If you are going to accept text input and display the text in a window, you have to display the caret. The caret is a systemwide shared resource—there is only one caret in the system. To use the caret, you have to call `CreateCaret` first. Then you can position the caret with a call to `SetCaretPos` and make it visible by calling `ShowCaret`. Finally, when you no longer need the caret, you have to release it by calling `DestroyCaret`.

Using the Caret

If you need the caret, call `CreateCaret` in the handler for the `WM_SETFOCUS` message. Release the caret by calling `DestroyCaret` in the function that handles the `WM_KILLFOCUS` message. You need the caret only if you plan to accept text input and display the text in a window.

When do you create the caret and when do you destroy it? The answer lies in the way Windows delivers keyboard messages—the keyboard input always goes to the window with the input focus. Thus, you should create the caret when your main window receives input focus and destroy it when the focus moves to some other window.

When you first create the caret, it is hidden. You have to call `ShowCaret` to make it visible. Also, when you draw anything in a window in response to any message other than `WM_PAINT`, you have to first hide the caret by calling `HideCaret` and call `ShowCaret` again when drawing is done.

Mouse Messages

In a graphical user interface such as that in Windows, the mouse is even more important than the keyboard because the essence of a graphical interface is to perform actions by pointing and clicking at graphical objects on the screen. Microsoft Windows supports a mouse with up to three buttons (left, middle, and right). However, most Windows applications assume a mouse with a single button because you can never be sure if a system has a mouse with more than one button. The lone button is equivalent to the left mouse of a three-button mouse.

As with the keyboard, Windows delivers all mouse inputs through messages. Unlike the keyboard, there is no confusion over which window gets the mouse input because an on-screen cursor (a small bitmap image) tracks the motion of the mouse. The window with the cursor gets the mouse input. The only exceptions to this rule are the following:

- A window can capture the mouse (described later) and receive all mouse messages irrespective of the cursor's location.
- When a system-modal dialog box is on display, no other window can receive mouse messages.

The types of mouse messages depend on the exact area of the window where the cursor lies. Mouse input with the cursor in the client area (the area inside the frame) of a window generates *client-area mouse messages.* Mouse input with the cursor anywhere else in the window's frame generates *nonclient-area mouse messages.* Because Windows takes care of the nonclient-area messages, most Windows applications handle the client-area messages only.

Drag, Click, and Double-Click

The use of the mouse has spawned several new terms. For instance, you *drag* the mouse by moving it while holding down a button. You *click* by pressing and releasing a mouse button without moving the mouse. A *double-click* means two clicks in rapid succession.

Client-Area Mouse Messages

The area of a window inside the borders is referred to as the client area because that's where the application (which Windows views as a client) can draw. Usually applications are concerned with mouse input in this area. There are 10 client-area mouse messages of interest:

```
WM_LBUTTONDOWN
WM_MBUTTONDOWN
WM_RBUTTONDOWN
WM_LBUTTONUP
WM_MBUTTONUP
WM_RBUTTONUP
WM_LBUTTONDBLCLK
WM_MBUTTONDBLCLK
WM_RBUTTONDBLCLK
WM_MOUSEMOVE
```

As you can surmise from this list, there are three messages (button down, button up, and double-click) per button of a mouse. The tenth event, `WM_MOUSEMOVE`, tells you the location of the mouse cursor; this message is described in the next section.

One of the commonly handled mouse messages is `WM_LBUTTONDOWN`. Windows sends the `WM_LBUTTONDOWN` message when the user presses the left mouse button with the cursor in the client area of a window. A virtual member function, `EvLButtonDown` is already defined as the `WM_LBUTTONDOWN` message handler in the `TWindow` class in OWL. When you derive a new window class from `TWindow` (or one of the classes derived from `TWindow`), and you want to handle `WM_LBUTTONDOWN` messages, all you have to do is declare `EvLButton` as a member function of your window class:

```
void EvLButtonDown(UINT modKeys, TPoint& point);
```

Then define the function where you can get the x- and y-coordinates of the cursor position:

```
// Assume that SampleWindow is the class derived from TWindow
void SampleWindow::EvLButtonDown(UINT modKeys, TPoint& point)
{
//...

// Find the x-y position of mouse cursor
    short xpos = point.x;
    short ypos = point.y;
//...
}
```

The x-y coordinates of the cursor are in pixel units with the origin `(0,0)` at the upper-left corner of the client area. The positive x-axis extends to the right, and the positive y-axis extends down.

You can determine the state of all the mouse buttons as well as that of the Shift and Ctrl keys from the modKeys argument passed to the EvLButtonDown function. Basically, individual bits in the low-order five bits of the modKeys argument hold the state of the buttons and the shift keys. You can test for a specific state by using the bitwise logical operator (&) with a symbolic name. For instance, to test if the Shift key is down, you write the following:

```
void SampleWindow::EvLButtonDown(UINT modKeys, TPoint& point)
{
//...
    if(modKeys & MK_SHIFT)
    {
// Yes, the Shift key is down
// Handle the Shift key + Mouse button event
//...
    }
```

To test for the state of the Ctrl key, use similar code, but replace MK_SHIFT with MK_CONTROL.

You can handle the mouse up messages, WM_LBUTTONUP, in the same way as you handle WM_LBUTTONDOWN. However, the combination of the button down and button up messages become more interesting in combination with WM_MOUSEMOVE messages that are generated when the user moves the mouse.

Handling Mouse Movements

Windows sends WM_MOUSEMOVE messages when the user moves the mouse. To avoid generating too many mouse move messages, Windows does not report every possible position of the mouse. Instead, the WM_MOUSEMOVE messages provide a sampling of the locations that the mouse cursor visits. Yet these reports are good enough to track the position of the mouse.

The most common use of WM_MOUSEMOVE messages is to track the mouse position while the user is moving the mouse and holding down a mouse button. For instance, in a drawing program, the user draws a line with the following sequence of steps:

1. Move the mouse cursor to the startpoint of the line and press the mouse button (usually the left button) down.
2. While holding the button down, move to the endpoint of the line.
3. Release the button.

These actions by the user generate a WM_LBUTTONDOWN message followed by a number of WM_MOUSEMOVE events as the user moves the mouse. Finally, when the user releases the button, Windows generates a WM_LBUTTONUP message. If you are writing the drawing program, start by saving the startpoint of the line in the handler for the WM_LBUTTONDOWN message. In the handler for the WM_MOUSEMOVE event, you track the endpoint and provide some visual feedback by drawing a line from the startpoint to the current endpoint. Finally, upon receiving the WM_LBUTTONUP message, you save the endpoint's location and draw the final version of the line.

While the user is drawing the line, you want to ensure that Windows delivers to your application all mouse events, from the starting WM_LBUTTONDOWN event to the final WM_LBUTTONUP event. One way to ensure this is by capturing the mouse. Essentially, you call the SetCapture function upon receiving the WM_LBUTTONDOWN event and call ReleaseCapture when the WM_LBUTTONUP message arrives. SetCapture and ReleaseCapture are member functions of the TWindow class that call similarly named functions from the Windows API.

Controlling the Cursor Shape

In Windows, whenever the user moves the mouse, a cursor tracks the mouse's motions on the display screen. Applications use the cursor's shape to provide feedback. Most of the time, the cursor is an arrow pointing in the upper-left direction. In a text entry area, however, such as a word processor's window or an input field in a dialog box, the cursor changes to an *I-beam.* The I-beam is a thin vertical line with flourishes at the ends that looks like the capital letter I. In drawing programs a *cross-hair cursor* is often used in the drawing area.

Like the stock pens and brushes that you load into a device context, there are stock cursors in Windows. You may have noticed that many applications display an *hourglass cursor* to indicate a possibly lengthy operation. If you want to do the same in your application, here is what you have to do:

1. Load the hourglass cursor in response to the WM_CREATE message:

```
TCursor *c_wait;
//...
// Assume that SampleWindow is our main window class
void SampleWindow::WMCreate(RTMessage)
{
//...
    c_wait = new TCursor(NULL, IDC_WAIT);
}
```

2. Just before starting the lengthy operation, change the cursor shape by calling the `SetCursor` function:

```
        HCURSOR hc_old = ::SetCursor(*c_wait);

    // Start lengthy operation
    //...

    // Change cursor shape when done
        ::SetCursor(hc_old);
```

You could create the `TCursor` object on the fly when you need to change the cursor, but preparing the cursor beforehand is faster.

As you can see from the sample code, the hourglass cursor is identified by the symbol `IDC_WAIT`. Some of the other commonly used predefined cursors are

`IDC_ARROW`	The left-pointing arrow
`IDC_IBEAM`	The I-Beam cursor
`IDC_CROSS`	A small cross-hair

Setting Cursors Based on Location

The previous example of the hourglass cursor is applicable when you change the cursor shape to let the user know the application may take some time before responding to the user again. You may want to change the cursor shape whenever the cursor enters a specific region in your application's main window (as most word processors do when the cursor moves in and out of the text entry area). To do this, you have to handle the `WM_SETCURSOR` message, which Windows sends when the cursor moves in a window. This gives you a chance to change the cursor shape depending on the location of the mouse.

Assuming that you have loaded the `IDC_IBEAM` cursor, you can handle the `WM_SETCURSOR` message as follows:

```
BOOL SampleWindow::EvSetCursor(HWND /* hWndCursor */,
                               UINT hitTest,
                               UINT /* mouseMsg */)
{
    if(hitTest == HTCLIENT)
    {
// Yes, cursor is in the client area
// Now test to see if cursor is in an area where you want to
// change its shape (this depends on the specific application).
```

```
// Assume that change_cursor is TRUE if the cursor should change
// and that c_ibeam is the pointer to a TCursor object that
// is initialized as the I-Beam cursor.
        if(change_cursor)
            SetCursor(*c_ibeam);
    }
    else
    {
// Cursor is not in the client area—pass the message on.
        DefaultProcessing();
    }
    return TRUE;
}
```

Custom Cursors

Windows 3.0 introduced the `CreateCursor` function, which gives you complete control of the cursor shape. For instance, you might create a cursor that actually displays the cursor coordinates. You could not define a cursor like this beforehand because the cursor has to change as the user moves the cursor in the window. The solution is to create the cursor on the fly by calling `CreateCursor`. To create a cursor, you need two monochrome bitmaps:

- *The* `AND` *mask* is a bitmap that is combined with the existing pixels with the bitwise-AND operation. The `AND` mask should be the cursor's shape drawn in black on a white background.
- *The* `XOR` *mask* is a bitmap to be combined with the existing pixels (after the `AND` mask has been applied) with a bitwise exclusive-OR operation. To get an all-white cursor shape, use an `XOR` bitmap that is the inverse of the `AND` bitmap—the cursor shape drawn in white on a black background.

The `CreateCursor` function expects these two bitmaps as arguments. Here is the prototype of the `CreateCursor` function:

```
HCURSOR CreateCursor(
    HINSTANCE hinst, // Handle to application instance
    int       xhot,  // Horizontal position of hot spot
    int       yhot,  // Vertical position of hot spot
    int       width, // Cursor's width in pixels
    int       height,// Cursor height in pixels
    const void FAR* ANDmask, // Pointer to AND mask
    const void FAR* XORmask);// Pointer to XOR mask
```

The `CreateCursor` function creates a cursor that has the specified width, height, and bit patterns and returns a handle to the cursor if the function is successful. Otherwise, it returns `NULL`.

In an OWL program, you can use a `TCursor` object that represents a custom cursor. Here is the `TCursor` constructor that initializes a custom cursor:

```
TCursor(
    HINSTANCE      hinst, // Handle to application instance
    const TPoint& hot,    // Position of hot spot
    const TSize&  size,   // Cursor's width and height in pixels
    const void FAR* ANDmask, // Pointer to AND mask
    const void FAR* XORmask);// Pointer to XOR mask
```

Much of the work in creating a custom cursor is in defining and initializing the `AND` and `XOR` bitmaps. Chapter 23, "Understanding Image File Formats," shows you how to work with bitmaps.

TextIn—A Text Entry Program

To illustrate the techniques for handling keyboard and mouse messages, the rest of this chapter presents TextIn, a simple program that lets the user enter text in a window. My goal is to let you see some sample code that puts to work most of the functions described earlier in this chapter. TextIn lets you enter text from the keyboard, move the lines of text up and down with the arrow keys, and indicate the text entry point with a click of the mouse. Before you read the code, try running the TextIn program—the companion disk contains the source files and the executable for TextIn. That way you can relate the actions of the program to code that implements those actions.

A *Caret* Class

Although the `TextIn` class is relatively simple, I decided to define a separate class to represent a caret so I can use it in other projects in the future. Listing 21.1 shows the file CARET.H. This declares the `Caret` class that creates and manages a caret. The `Caret` class has the following data members:

- `HWND  hwnd;` identifies the window where the caret is displayed.
- `HFONT hfont;` is the font being used to display text. The caret's dimensions and position depend on the font.

- `HDC hdc;` is a DC used to get information about the font.
- `short active_flag;` indicates whether the caret is active.
- `short cwidth, height;` are the width and height of the caret, respectively.
- `short xref, yref;` denote the starting point of the line of text on which the caret rests.
- `short xpix;` is the x-coordinate of the caret's current position, in pixels.
- `char *line;` is the line of text on which the caret rests.
- `short cpos;` is the character position of the caret.

Listing 21.1. CARET.H. Declaration of the `Caret` class.

```
//--------------------------------------------------------------
// File: caret.h
// Declares the Caret class that models and controls the caret.
//--------------------------------------------------------------
#if !defined(__CARET_H)
#define __CARET_H

#include <owl\dc.h>

class Caret
{
public:
    Caret(HWND _hwnd, HFONT _hfont);

    ~Caret();

    virtual void show() { ShowCaret(hwnd);}
    virtual void hide() { HideCaret(hwnd);}

    void xstart(short x) { xref = x;}
    void ystart(short y) { yref = y;}
    short xstart() { return xref;}
    short ystart() { return yref;}

    void charpos(short cp);
    short charpos() { return cpos;}
```

continues

Listing 21.1. continued

```
    void caret_height(short ch) { cheight = ch;}
    short caret_height() { return cheight;}

    void active()
    {
        if(active_flag) return;
        CreateCaret(hwnd, 0, cwidth, cheight);
        SetCaretPos(xpix, yref);
        ShowCaret(hwnd);
        active_flag = 1;
    }
    void inactive()
    {
     if(!active_flag) return;
     DestroyCaret();
        active_flag = 0;
    }
    short is_active() { return active_flag;}

    char *current_line() { return line;}
    void current_line(char *cl) { line = cl;}

    void font(HFONT hf);

protected:
    HWND  hwnd;
    HFONT hfont;
    TIC   *ic;
    short active_flag;
    short cwidth;
    short cheight;
    short xref;
    short yref;
    short xpix;
    char  *line;
    short cpos;
};

#endif
```

Listing 21.2 shows the file CARET.CPP that implements some of `Caret`'s member functions. Several important member functions such as `show`, `hide`, `active`, and `inactive` are defined directly in the header file CARET.H. In particular, the `active` function creates the caret and `inactive` destroys it. Thus, you should call `active` in response to the `WM_SETFOCUS` message and call `inactive` in response to the `WM_KILLFOCUS` message.

Listing 21.2. CARET.CPP. Implementation of the `Caret` class.

```
//--------------------------------------------------------------
// File: caret.cpp
// Implements the Caret class that models and controls the caret.
//--------------------------------------------------------------
#include "caret.h"

//--------------------------------------------------------------
// Caret:: C a r e t
// Constructs a caret

Caret::Caret(HWND _hwnd, HFONT _hfont) : hwnd(_hwnd),
    hfont(_hfont), xref(0), yref(0), xpix(0),
    line(NULL), cpos(0), active_flag(0), ic(0)
{
    TEXTMETRIC tm;

// Create an information context (to get font dimensions)
    ic = new TIC("DISPLAY", 0, 0, 0);
    ic->SelectObject(hfont);
    ic->GetTextMetrics(tm);
    ic->RestoreFont();

    cwidth = GetSystemMetrics(SM_CXBORDER);
    cheight = tm.tmHeight;
}
//--------------------------------------------------------------
// Caret:: ~ C a r e t
// Destroy a caret

Caret::~Caret()
{
```

continues

Listing 21.2. continued

```
    if(active_flag)
    {
        HideCaret(hwnd);
        DestroyCaret();
    }
    delete ic;
}
//----------------------------------------------------------------
// Caret:: ch a r p o s
// Set the character position

void Caret::charpos(short cp)
{
    cpos = cp;

// Determine width of string up to specified character position
    ic->SelectObject(hfont);
    TSize txtsz = ic->GetTextExtent(line, cpos);
    short width = txtsz.cx;
    ic->RestoreFont();

    xpix = xref + width;

// If caret is active, set its position
    if(active_flag) SetCaretPos(xpix, yref);
}
//----------------------------------------------------------------
// Caret:: f o n t
// Set a new font

void Caret::font(HFONT hf)
{
    TEXTMETRIC tm;

    hfont = hf;
    ic->SelectObject(hfont);
    ic->GetTextMetrics(tm);
    ic->RestoreFont();

    cheight = tm.tmHeight;
}
```

Other TextIn Classes

In addition to the supporting class `Caret`, TextIn relies on the `TextInWindow` class for its main window and the `TextInApp` class to represent the entire application. Listing 21.3 shows the declaration of these classes in the file TEXTIN.H.

As you can see from the declaration of the `TextInWindow` class, the TextIn application maintains a 512-byte buffer that holds any text entered by the user. The text is stored as a single array of bytes with a single newline character (`\n`) marking the end of a line. The `TextInWindow` class has a pointer to a `Caret` object that represents the caret displayed in the window. Most of the other data members are used to track the number of characters and the number of lines in the buffer.

Listing 21.3. TEXTIN.H. Declaration of the classes in TextIn.

```
//---------------------------------------------------------------
// File: textin.h
//
// Declares classes used in the TextIn application that
// lets the user enter text in a window.
//---------------------------------------------------------------
#if !defined(__TEXTIN_H)
#define __TEXTIN_H

#include <owl\applicat.h>
#include <owl\decframe.h>
#include <owl\dialog.h>
#include <owl\color.h>
#include <owl\point.h>
#include <owl\choosefo.h>
#include <owl\dc.h>
#include <owl\gdiobjec.h>

#include <string.h>
#include <stdio.h>

#include "caret.h"

// Resource identifiers
```

continues

Listing 21.3. continued

```
#define IDM_ABOUT      200
#define IDM_SELFONT    201

const int MAXCHR = 512;

// Declare the main window class

class TextInWindow : public TFrameWindow
{
public:
    TextInWindow(TWindow *parent, const char far *title);
    ~TextInWindow()
    {
        if(font != 0) delete font;
        if(c_ibeam != 0) delete c_ibeam;
    }

    void CMSelFont();
    void About();
    void Paint(TDC& dc, int erase_bg, TRect& r);

    int EvCreate(CREATESTRUCT far& createStruct);

    void EvChar(UINT key, UINT repeatCount, UINT flags);
    void EvKeyDown(UINT key, UINT repeatCount, UINT flags);
    void EvLButtonDown(UINT modKeys, TPoint& point);

    BOOL EvSetCursor(HWND hWndCursor, UINT hitTest,
                     UINT mouseMsg);

    void EvSetFocus(HWND /* hWndLostFocus */)
    {
        p_caret->charpos(cpos);
        p_caret->active();
    }
    void EvKillFocus(HWND /* hWndGetFocus*/)
    {
        p_caret->inactive();
    }
    void reposition_caret()
    {
```

```
            p_caret->hide();
            p_caret->inactive();
            p_caret->ystart(linenum * lineheight);
            p_caret->charpos(cpos);
            p_caret->active();
        }

private:
    char                        txtbuf[MAXCHR];
    TChooseFontDialog::TData    fd;
    TColor                      font_color;
    TFont                       *font;
    TCursor                     *c_ibeam;
    Caret                       *p_caret;
    short                       inpos;
    short                       cpos;
    short                       xmargin;
    short                       lineheight;
    short                       linenum;
    short                       count;
    short                       total_lines;

DECLARE_RESPONSE_TABLE(TextInWindow);
};

// Declare the application class

class TextInApp : public TApplication
{
public:
    TextInApp(const char far *name) : TApplication(name) {}
    void InitMainWindow();
};

#endif
```

Listing 21.4 shows the file TEXTIN.CPP that implements the `TextInWindow` and `TextInApp` classes. Note that the `Caret` object is created and initialized in the `WMCreate` member function of the `TextInWindow` class. The `WMCreate` function handles the `WM_CREATE` message that Windows sends when the window is first created.

Code from Chapter 20's FontSee application lets the user select a font in the TextIn application as well. You can see this code in the `CMSelFont` function in Listing 21.4.

You might find the `Paint` function interesting. It displays the text from the buffer one line at a time by looking for the newline character that marks the end of each line (except for the last line, which does not have a newline).

TextIn's text entry capability comes from the `EvChar` function that handles the `WM_CHAR` messages. Code to handle a number of special characters is shown. In particular, look in the `EvChar` function to see how to delete a character in response to a backspace key and how to insert a newline when the user presses the `Enter` key. The deletion of a newline character poses some problems because you have to collapse two consecutive lines into one.

Recall that your application should accept most of the text input through the `WM_CHAR` messages, but it has to handle the `WM_KEYDOWN` messages to respond to special keys such as the arrow keys and function keys. To illustrate this concept, `TextIn` includes the `EvKeyDown` function that responds to `WM_KEYDOWN` messages and handles the up and down arrow keys.

The user can move the text insertion point by positioning the cursor on a character and pressing the left mouse button. This event is handled in the `EvLButtonDown` function that responds to `WM_LBUTTONDOWN` messages.

Listing 21.4. TEXTIN.CPP. Implementation of the classes in `TextIn`.

```
//-------------------------------------------------------------
// File: textin.cpp
//
// Implements several classes used in the TextIn application
// that lets the user enter text in a window.
//-------------------------------------------------------------
#include "textin.h"

// Define the response table for TextInWindow
DEFINE_RESPONSE_TABLE1(TextInWindow, TFrameWindow)
    EV_WM_CREATE,
    EV_WM_CHAR,
    EV_WM_KEYDOWN,
    EV_WM_LBUTTONDOWN,
    EV_WM_SETCURSOR,
    EV_WM_SETFOCUS,
```

```
    EV_WM_KILLFOCUS,
    EV_COMMAND(IDM_ABOUT,   About),
    EV_COMMAND(IDM_SELFONT, CMSelFont),
END_RESPONSE_TABLE;

//-------------------------------------------------------------
// TextInApp:: I n i t M a i n W i n d o w
// Initialize the main window of the TextIn application

void TextInApp::InitMainWindow()
{
    MainWindow = new TextInWindow(NULL, "TextIn");
    MainWindow->SetIcon(this, "TEXTIN_ICON");
    MainWindow->AssignMenu("MainMenu");
    MainWindow->Attr.AccelTable = "MainAccelTable";
    EnableBWCC();
}
//-------------------------------------------------------------
// TextInWindow:: T e x t I n W i n d o w
// Constructor for the TextInWindow

TextInWindow::TextInWindow(TWindow *parent,
                           const char far *title)
    : TFrameWindow(parent, title), inpos(0), cpos(0), linenum(0),
      count(0), font(0)
{
// Set the window position and size
    Attr.X = GetSystemMetrics(SM_CXSCREEN) / 10;
    Attr.Y = GetSystemMetrics(SM_CYSCREEN) / 10;
    Attr.W = Attr.X * 8;
    Attr.H = Attr.Y * 8;

// Initialize the logical font structure
// First zero out the entire structure
    memset(&fd, 0, sizeof(fd));

// Now set the needed fields
    fd.LogFont.lfHeight = 12;
    fd.LogFont.lfWeight = FW_NORMAL;
    fd.LogFont.lfCharSet = ANSI_CHARSET;
    fd.LogFont.lfOutPrecision = OUT_DEFAULT_PRECIS;
    fd.LogFont.lfClipPrecision = CLIP_DEFAULT_PRECIS;
```

continues

Listing 21.4. continued

```
        fd.LogFont.lfQuality = PROOF_QUALITY;
        fd.LogFont.lfPitchAndFamily = VARIABLE_PITCH;
        strcpy(fd.LogFont.lfFaceName, "Helvetica");
        font_color = GetSysColor(COLOR_WINDOWTEXT);

        font = new TFont(&fd.LogFont);
}
//---------------------------------------------------------------
// TextInWindow:: E v C r e a t e
// Handle the WM_CREATE message.

int TextInWindow::EvCreate(CREATESTRUCT far& cs)
{
    int status = TWindow::EvCreate(cs);

// Get dimensions of current font
    TIC ic("DISPLAY", 0, 0, 0);
    TEXTMETRIC tm;
    ic.SelectObject(*font);
    ic.GetTextMetrics(tm);
    ic.RestoreFont();

    lineheight = tm.tmHeight + tm.tmExternalLeading;
    xmargin = tm.tmAveCharWidth;

    strcpy(txtbuf, "Hello...\n123 ");
    count = strlen(txtbuf);
    total_lines = 2;

// Initialize the caret
    p_caret = new Caret(HWindow, *font);
    p_caret->current_line(txtbuf);
    p_caret->xstart(xmargin);
    p_caret->ystart(linenum * lineheight);

// Create an I-Beam cursor for use in the text display area
    c_ibeam = new TCursor(NULL, IDC_IBEAM);
    return status;
}
//---------------------------------------------------------------
// TextInWindow:: C M S e l F o n t
```

```
// Display the Font Selection dialog from COMMDLG.DLL and get
// the user's choice of font.

void TextInWindow::CMSelFont()
{
    TScreenDC sdc;
    fd.Flags = CF_INITTOLOGFONTSTRUCT | CF_BOTH | CF_EFFECTS;
    fd.Color = font_color;
    fd.DC = sdc;

// Activate "choose font" dialog...
    if (TChooseFontDialog(this, fd).Execute() == IDOK)
    {
// Yes, user has chosen font.
        font_color = fd.Color;

// Create the new font
        delete font;
        font = new TFont(&fd.LogFont);

// Get dimensions of characters in this font
        TIC ic("DISPLAY", 0, 0, 0);
        TEXTMETRIC tm;
        ic.SelectObject(*font);
        ic.GetTextMetrics(tm);
        ic.RestoreFont();

        lineheight = tm.tmHeight + tm.tmExternalLeading;
        xmargin = tm.tmAveCharWidth;
        p_caret->xstart(xmargin);
        p_caret->ystart(linenum * lineheight);
        p_caret->font(*font);
        p_caret->charpos(cpos);
        p_caret->hide();
        p_caret->inactive();
        p_caret->active();

// Make sure window gets redrawn with new font
        Invalidate(TRUE);
    }
}
//-------------------------------------------------------------
```

continues

Listing 21.4. continued

```
// TextInWindow:: P a i n t
// Draw the window's content

void TextInWindow::Paint(TDC& dc, int, TRect&)
{
    dc.SetTextColor(font_color);
    dc.SetBkColor(GetSysColor(COLOR_WINDOW));

    dc.SelectObject(*font);

// Display the lines of text
    short line = 0, nch = 0;
    char  *p_c = txtbuf;

    while(line < total_lines-1)
    {
        nch = strcspn(p_c, "\n");
        if(nch <= 0) break;

        dc.TextOut(xmargin, line * lineheight, p_c, nch);
        line++;
        p_c = &p_c[nch+1];
    }
// Display the last line
    nch = strlen(p_c);
    if(nch > 0)
        dc.TextOut(xmargin, line * lineheight, p_c, nch);

// Restore previous font
    dc.RestoreFont();
}
//-------------------------------------------------------------
// TextInWindow:: E v C h a r
// Handle a WM_CHAR message

void TextInWindow::EvChar(UINT key, UINT, UINT)
{
    switch(key)
    {
        case '\b':  // Backspace
// Delete the previous character, if any
```

```
            if(inpos == 0)
                MessageBeep(0);
            else
            {
                inpos—;
                short old_inpos = inpos;
                if(txtbuf[inpos] == '\n')
                {
                    linenum—;
                    total_lines—;
                    short i;
                    for(i = inpos-1; i >= 0; i—)
                        if(txtbuf[i] == '\n') break;
                    cpos = inpos - i;
                    p_caret->current_line(&txtbuf[i+1]);
                }
                cpos—;
// Remove a character
                short i;
                for(i = old_inpos; i < count; i++)
                    txtbuf[i] = txtbuf[i+1];
                count—;
// Redraw window
                reposition_caret();
                Invalidate(TRUE);
            }
            break;

        case '\r':  // Enter key
// Insert a new line
            linenum++;
            total_lines++;
            cpos = -1;
            p_caret->current_line(&txtbuf[inpos]);
            key = '\n';

        default:
// Insert character in buffer and update display
            if(count >= MAXCHR ¦¦
               (key <= VK_ESCAPE &&
                key != '\n'))
            {
```

continues

Listing 21.4. continued

```
                MessageBeep(0);
                return;
            }
            short i;
            if(count > inpos)
            {
                for(i = count; i > inpos; i--)
                    txtbuf[i] = txtbuf[i-1];
            }
            txtbuf[inpos++] = key;
            cpos++;
            count++;
            txtbuf[count] = '\0';
            reposition_caret();
            Invalidate(TRUE);
            break;
    }
}
//-------------------------------------------------------------
// TextInWindow:: E v K e y D o w n
// Handle raw keypresses (for cursor keys).

void TextInWindow::EvKeyDown(UINT key, UINT, UINT)
{
    short caret_has_moved = 0;

    switch(key)
    {
        case VK_UP:
            if(linenum == 0)
                MessageBeep(0);
            else
            {
                linenum--;
                short i;
                for(i = inpos; i >= 0; i--)
                    if(txtbuf[i] == '\n') break;

                if(i > 0)
                    for(i--; i >= 0; i--)
                        if(txtbuf[i] == '\n') break;
```

```
                inpos = i+1;
                cpos = 0;
                p_caret->current_line(&txtbuf[inpos]);
                caret_has_moved = 1;
            }
            break;

        case VK_DOWN:
            if(linenum >= total_lines-1)
                MessageBeep(0);
            else
            {
                linenum++;
                short i;
                for(i = inpos; i < count-1; i++)
                    if(txtbuf[i] == '\n') break;
                inpos = i+1;
                p_caret->current_line(&txtbuf[i+1]);
                cpos = 0;
                caret_has_moved = 1;
            }
            break;
    }

// Reposition caret, if necessary
    if(caret_has_moved)
        reposition_caret();
}
//-----------------------------------------------------------
// TextInWindow:: E v L B u t t o n D o w n
// Handle "mouse button-press" (left button) event.

void TextInWindow::EvLButtonDown(UINT /* modKeys */,
                                 TPoint& point)
{
    short x = point.x;
    short y = point.y;

    if(y > total_lines * lineheight) return;

    short line = y / lineheight;
```

continues

Listing 21.4. continued

```
// See if x coordinate falls on any character of that line
    char *p_c = txtbuf;
    short skipped = 0;

    if(line > 0)
    {
// Skip appropriate number of newlines
        short i, nch;
        for(i = 0; i < line; i++)
        {
            nch = strcspn(p_c, "\n");
            p_c = &p_c[nch+1];
            skipped += nch + 1;
        }
    }
    linenum = line;
    cpos = 0;
    inpos = skipped;

// Find extent of line in current font
    TClientDC dc(HWindow);
    dc.SelectObject(*font);

    short i = 0, wby2prev = xmargin, wby2next = 0,
          wtot = xmargin;

    while(p_c[i] != '\0' && p_c[i] != '\n')
    {
        TSize extent = dc.GetTextExtent(&p_c[i], 1);
        wby2next = extent.cx / 2;
        if(x >= wtot - wby2prev &&
           x <  wtot + wby2next)
        {
            cpos = i;
            inpos += i;
        }
        wby2prev = wby2next;
        wtot += extent.cx;
        i++;
    }

    dc.RestoreFont();
```

```
    p_caret->current_line(p_c);
    reposition_caret();
}
//-----------------------------------------------------------------
//  TextInWindow:: E v S e t C u r s o r
//  Handle WM_SETCURSOR messages

BOOL TextInWindow::EvSetCursor(HWND /* hWndCursor */,
                               UINT hitTest,
                               UINT /* mouseMsg */)
{
    if(hitTest == HTCLIENT)
    {
// Yes, cursor is in the client area
// Change cursor to the I-Beam cursor
        ::SetCursor(*c_ibeam);
    }
    else
    {
// Cursor is not in the client area—pass the message on.
        DefaultProcessing();
    }
    return TRUE;
}
//-----------------------------------------------------------------
//  TextInWindow:: A b o u t
//  Display the "About..." box

void TextInWindow::About()
{
    TDialog *p_about = new TDialog(this, "ABOUTTEXTIN");
    GetApplication()->ExecDialog(p_about);
}
//-----------------------------------------------------------------
// O w l M a i n
// The "main" function of the TextIn application
// Create an instance of the application and "run" it.

int OwlMain(int, char**)
{
    TextInApp TextIn("TextIn");
    return TextIn.Run();
}
```

Running TextIn

The accompanying disk contains the source files, the module definition file (TEXTIN.DEF), the project file (TEXTIN.IDE), and the resource file (TEXTIN.RES) necessary to build TextIn. Use Borland C++ 4 with the project file TEXTIN.IDE to build the application. Once you have built the program successfully, you can run TextIn by pressing Ctrl+F9 in Borland C++ 4. Figure 21.1 shows the TextIn application's window after you select the About TextIn... menu item from the Help menu.

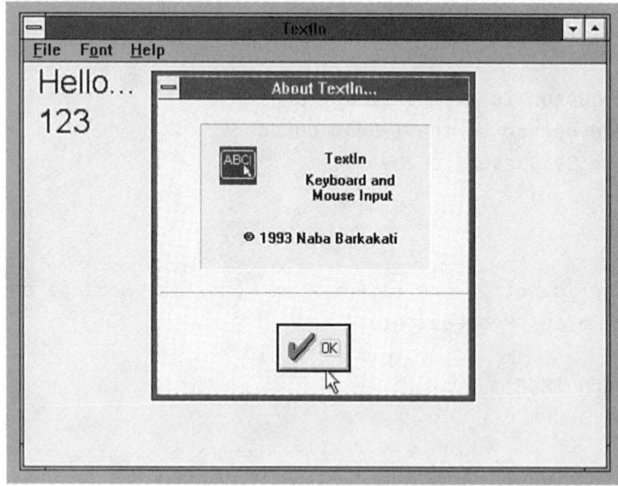

Figure 21.1. The About TextIn window.

Summary

The mouse and keyboard are important input devices in a graphical user interface such as the one provided by Windows. Like everything else in Windows, both keyboard and mouse inputs are sent to an application through messages. For keyboard, there are raw messages such as `WM_KEYDOWN` that report the exact key that is down irrespective of the state of the modifier keys, such as Shift and Ctrl. However, for character input, the `WM_CHAR` message is more suitable because it reports the character entered by the user. The keyboard messages are delivered to the window that has the input focus. The active window, indicated by the user by clicking it, gets the input focus.

Text display requires the use of a caret to mark the location where text appears. The caret is a systemwide resource that must be created upon receipt of the `WM_SETFOCUS` message and destroyed at the receipt of the `WM_KILLFOCUS` message.

The mouse messages usually go to the window that contains the cursor. Most applications handle the `WM_LBUTTONDOWN` message. If an application supports dragging, the application also handles the `WM_MOUSEMOVE` and `WM_LBUTTONUP` messages. The dragging starts with a button down and ends when the button goes up. As soon as the button down message arrives, the application calls `SetCapture` to ensure that Windows sends all future mouse messages to that application only. The capture ends when the application calls `ReleaseCapture` in response to the user's releasing the mouse button.

A rudimentary text entry program, TextIn, illustrates how you can handle keyboard and mouse inputs in an OWL program.

Generating Sound

Generation of sound is a common feature of many Windows applications, especially multimedia applications. The previous chapters cover the basics of graphics programming under Windows. This chapter describes a number of Windows API functions that you can use to generate sound. The first part of this chapter covers a set of Windows API functions that are meant for playing musical notes with the PC's existing speaker. The latter part of the chapter describes the use of Windows 3.1 Media Control Interface (MCI) to play digitized sound waveforms on sound boards such as the SoundBlaster card from Creative Laboratories, Inc.

Sound Under Windows

Compared to the Apple Macintosh, the sound generation capabilities of the IBM-compatible PCs are rather limited. Essentially, all you can do with the PC's speaker is play single notes—you cannot even vary the `volume` (loudness).

One way to improve the sound output under Windows (and DOS) is to install a sound card that can synthesize a wide range of sounds. Some of the popular sound cards are the SoundBlaster, Media Vision, and Microsoft Windows Sound System. These cards convert the `analog` (continuously varying) sound waves into 8-bit or 16-bit numbers, sampling the wave at rates from 4 to 44KHz (44,000 times a second). Higher sampling rates and higher number of bits (16-bit) provide better quality, but you need more disk space to store high quality sound.

Programming for Sound

Like any other device, the sound cards are controlled through drivers. The sound driver provides a standard programming interface for all sound boards. If you look at the SYSTEM.INI file in your system's Windows directory, you might find the following line:

```
sound.drv=sound.drv
```

This tells Microsoft Windows that the sound output is to be performed through the driver named `sound.drv`, which is the default driver for the PC's built-in speaker. The right side of the line may be different if you have a sound card installed in your system. In that case, the right side is the name of the driver that Windows uses to control that sound card.

Once the sound driver is installed, you can use a small set of Windows functions to generate sound. Before I describe how to use these functions, I should point out that Windows 3.1 includes another simpler application programming interface (API), called the multimedia API, for sound cards and other multimedia devices such as CD-ROM drive and video output device. The multimedia API relies on a dynamic link library (DLL), MMSYSTEM.DLL, which provides a high-level set of commands called Media Control Interface (MCI). As a programmer, you can control a multimedia device by sending commands using the `mciSendCommand` function. The latter part of the chapter describes a few of the MCI functions, and the Bibliography section at the end of this book lists sources of information on the MCI functions.

The next few sections cover sound generation under Windows with the PC's built-in speaker or a sound board with a driver that responds to the Windows sound functions. Microsoft recommends that programmers use the MCI functions for controlling sound devices. However, using the old API functions is the only way to guarantee that sound output will work in all PCs because all PCs come with a built-in speaker.

Sound as a Sequence of Notes

Whenever a device is controlled through a driver, the driver presents an abstract model of the device to the programmer. The Windows sound drivers model each sound (a string of notes) as a *`voice`*. You can think of each voice as a queue with a number of notes that are to be played in sequence (see Figure 22.1). At any instant of time, the sound card plays notes from all the voices simultaneously. The PC's speaker can handle only one voice, but most sound cards can handle from 8 to 16 voices.

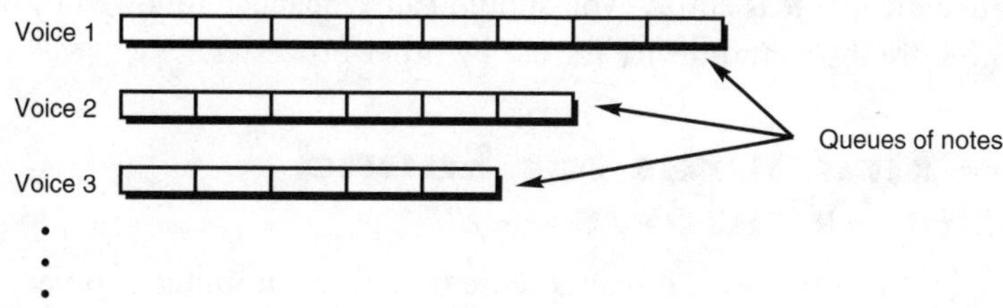

Figure 22.1. Voices in Windows.

To generate sound, you have to follow these steps:

1. Open the sound driver by calling `OpenSound`. If the sound device is not being used by another application, `OpenSound` returns the number of voices available. Otherwise, `OpenSound` returns a negative number. Thus, you start the sound generation code with

   ```
   if(OpenSound() > 0)
   {
   // Sound driver successfully opened. OK to proceed
   }
   ```

2. Call `SetVoiceQueueSize` to set the size of queues for each voice. You have to specify the size in number of bytes. Each note requires 6 bytes of memory. To make room for `n` notes in the first voice's queue, use

   ```
   SetVoiceQueueSize(1, 6*n);
   ```

3. Call `SetVoiceAccent` to set the tempo, volume, and mode (legato, normal, or staccato) of the notes in a voice.

4. Call `SetVoiceNote` to add notes to a voice queue. For each note, you can specify the following characteristics:

   - The note number (between 1 and 84)
   - Duration of the note (1 for a whole note, 2 for a half-note, 4 for a quarter-note, and so on)
   - The number of quarter-note durations to add to the note's duration

5. Call `StartSound` to begin the sound output. You can proceed with other programming tasks while the sound plays. At any time, you can call `CountVoiceNotes` to check how many notes remain in a voice's queue.
6. Once the queue is empty, you should call `StopSound` followed by `CloseSound` to release the sound device for use by other processes.

C++ Structures for Sound Under Windows

For use in C++ programs, it makes sense to define a number of object types to help with sound output. Listing 22.1 shows the header file SOUNDS.H that defines the structures `Note` and `Sound`. `Note` represents a single note and `Music` represents a voice. An important feature of `Music` is the ability to load a simple piece of music from a file into a `Music` object.

Listing 22.1. SOUNDS.H. Declaration of `Note` and `Music` structures.

```
//-------------------------------------------------------------
// File: sounds.h
// Defines arrays of notes for use in Windows programs
//-------------------------------------------------------------

#if !defined __SOUNDS_H
#define __SOUNDS_H

#include <windows.h>

struct Note
{
    Note() : number(1), duration(1), dots(0) {}
    Note(short n, short d, short dt) :
        number(n), duration(d), dots(dt) {}

    short number;   // Note number (range: 1 to 84)
    short duration; // Note duration (1 = whole note,
                    // 2 = half note, 4 = quarter note)
    short dots;     // Number of beats to add to duration
};

struct Music
```

```
{
    Music() : tempo(120), volume(128), mode(S_NORMAL),
              pitch(0), numnotes(0), notes(NULL) {}

    Music(short tmpo, short vol, short m, short po,
          short nn, Note *nt) : tempo(tmpo), volume(vol),
     mode(m), pitch(po), numnotes(nn), notes(nt) {}

    ~Music()
    {
        if(notes != NULL) delete notes;
    }

    short read(char *filename); // Read music from a file

    short tempo;    // Beats (quarter notes) per minute
                    // (default is 120)
    short volume;   // From 0 to 255 (ignored by PC speaker)
    short mode;     // Legato, Normal, Staccato (ignored by
                    // PC speaker)
    short pitch;    // Pitch offset to add to notes
    short numnotes; // Number of notes
    Note  *notes;   // Array of notes
};

#endif
```

Music File Format

To store the music in a file, I adopted a simple text file format. You can decipher the format by reading the source code of the `Music::read` function shown in Listing 22.2. Here are the contents of a sample music file:

```
SPUZZLE.MUSIC          This tune is "Mary had a little lamb"
1                      Version
NUMBER_DURATION_DOT    Format
100          Tempo
128          Volume
NORMAL       Mode
0            Pitch offset
11           Number of notes in this music
43 8 0       First note (Note number, duration, beats to add)
41 8 0       Second note
```

```
39 8 0     and so on...
42 8 0
43 8 0
43 8 0
43 8 0
0  8 0
41 8 0
41 8 0
41 8 0
```

I developed this format for an educational computer game named SPUZZLE (which is why I include an identifying comment referring to SPUZZLE on the first line). The second and third lines specify a version number and the file format. Next comes the characteristics of the music: tempo, volume, and mode. Finally, there are a number of notes followed by the individual notes.

Listing 22.2. SOUNDS.CPP. Implementation of `Music`'s member function.

```
//-------------------------------------------------------------------
// File: sounds.cpp
// Member functions of the Music class
//-------------------------------------------------------------------
#include <string.h>
#include <stdlib.h>
#include <fstream.h>
#include "sounds.h"

//-------------------------------------------------------------------
// M u s i c : : r e a d
// Read music from a file

short Music::read(char * filename)
{
// Open file for reading
    ifstream ifs(filename, ios::in);
    if(!ifs)
    {
// Error reading file. Return 0.
        return 0;
    }
```

```
// Read and interpret the contents of the file
    char line[81];

// First line should have the string SPUZZLE.MUSIC
    ifs.getline(line, sizeof(line));
    strupr(line);
    if(strnicmp(line, "SPUZZLE.MUSIC",
            strlen("SPUZZLE.MUSIC")) != 0) return 0;

// Second line has a version number—just in case the
// contents have to change in the future
    ifs.getline(line, sizeof(line));
    short version = atoi(line);
    if(version != 1) return 0;

// Third line has the format type—it's a string.
// Right now I interpret the "NUMBER_DURATION_DOT" format
    ifs.getline(line, sizeof(line));
    strupr(line);
    if(strnicmp(line, "NUMBER_DURATION_DOT",
       strlen("NUMBER_DURATION_DOT")) != 0) return 0;

// Next few lines...
// Tempo (between 32 to 255)
// Volume (between 0 and 255)
// Mode (a string: NORMAL, LEGATO, or STACCATO)
// Pitch Offset (between 0 and 83)
    ifs.getline(line, sizeof(line));
    tempo = atoi(line);

    ifs.getline(line, sizeof(line));
    volume = atoi(line);

    ifs.getline(line, sizeof(line));
    strupr(line);
    if(strncmp(line, "NORMAL", strlen("NORMAL")))
        mode = S_NORMAL;
    if(strncmp(line, "LEGATO", strlen("LEGATO")))
        mode = S_LEGATO;
    if(strncmp(line, "STACCATO", strlen("STACCATO")))
        mode = S_STACCATO;

    ifs.getline(line, sizeof(line));
```

continues

Listing 22.2. continued

```
    pitch = atoi(line);

// Next comes the number of notes in this piece of music
    ifs.getline(line, sizeof(line));
    numnotes = atoi(line);

// Allocate an array of Note structures
    Note *new_notes = new Note[numnotes];
    if(new_notes == NULL) return 0;

// At this point we have an array of Note structures
// allocated. If there is an existing Note array,
// delete it before loading new value
    if(notes != NULL) delete notes;
    notes = new_notes;

// From this point on each line in the file has the following
// form:
//      Note #(0-83)  Duration (1, 2, 4, 8, ...) Dots (beats)
// example:
//      42  8  0
//      41  8  0
//      39  4  0
// and so on.
    short i;
    char *token;
    for(i = 0; i < numnotes; i++)
    {
        if(ifs.eof())
        {
            numnotes = i;
            break;
        }
     ifs.getline(line, sizeof(line));
// Parse the line...first token
        token = strtok(line, " ");
        notes[i].number = atoi(token);
// Second token
        token = strtok(NULL, " ");
        notes[i].duration = atoi(token);
// Third token
```

```
            token = strtok(NULL, " ");
            notes[i].dots = atoi(token);
        }
        return 1;
    }
```

A Sample Program

Listing 22.3 shows the file PLAYSND.CPP that implements a simple application to let the user open a sound file and play the notes in that file. All the work of the application is done in the `InitMainWindow` function by using the standard file open dialog implemented by the OWL class `TFileOpenDialog`. Once the user selects a file from the list of files displayed in this dialog and clicks the OK pushbutton, `InitMainWindow` calls the `playmusic` function (see Listing 22.3) to open the selected file, interpret the notes, and play them. Then the dialog is displayed again. The user has to press the `Cancel` button to exit the application. Figure 22.2 shows the single dialog box that constitutes the user interface of the PLAYSND.EXE program.

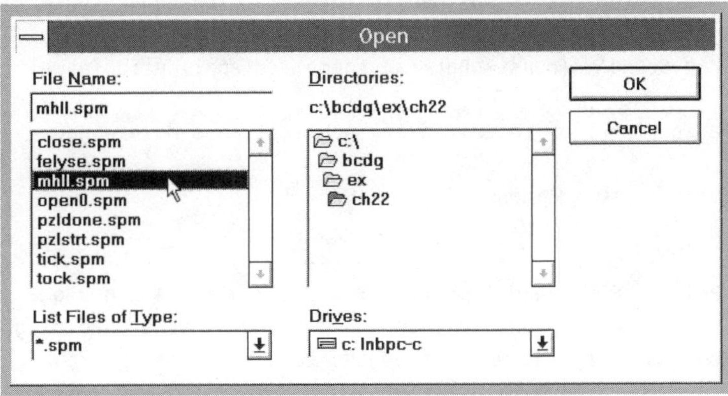

Figure 22.2. The main dialog box of the PlaySound application.

All the files needed to build PLAYSND.EXE are in the companion disk. Open the project file, PLAYSND.IDE, in Borland C++ 4 and select the Make All option from the Project menu to build the program.

Listing 22.3. PLAYSND.CPP. Program that plays notes from a sound file.

```
//------------------------------------------------------------------
//  File:  playsnd.cpp
//
//  A simple program that plays musical notes from files.
//
//------------------------------------------------------------------
#include <owl\frameewin.h> #include <owl\applicat.h>
#include <owl\frameewin.h> #include <owl\opensave.h>
#include <owl\frameewin.h> #include "sounds.h"

static Music m;
static short sound_playing = 0;
void playmusic(Music& m, short wait_till_done);

//------------------------------------------------------------------
class PlaySoundApp: public TApplication
{
public:
// Constructor that simply calls the base class constructor

    PlaySoundApp(const char far *name) : TApplication(name) {}

// Define function to initialize application's main window

    void InitMainWindow();
};
//------------------------------------------------------------------
//  P l a y S o u n d A p p : : I n i t M a i n W i n d o w
//  Everything happens in this function. We display a dialog
//  box and play the music from the selected file.

void PlaySoundApp::InitMainWindow()
{
    EnableCtl3d();

    char name[80] = "*.spm";
    char filter[80] = "*.spm";
    int status = IDOK;
    TOpenSaveDialog::TData data;
```

```
    data.FileName = name;
    data.Filter = filter;
    data.Flags = OFN_HIDEREADONLY ¦ OFN_FILEMUSTEXIST ¦
                 OFN_PATHMUSTEXIST;
MainWindow\ = new  TFrameWindow (0, "PlaySound");

    while(status == IDOK)
    {
        strcpy(name, filter);

// Create and display file selection dialog...
        TFileOpenDialog fd(MainWindow, data);
        status = fd.Execute();

 // Load selected music and play
        if(status == IDOK)
        {
            if(m.read(name)) playmusic(m, 0);
        }
    }
// Quit ...
    StopSound();
    CloseSound();
    PostQuitMessage(0);
}
//------------------------------------------------------------
//  p l a y m u s i c
// Play the notes specified in a Music structure

void playmusic(Music& m, short wait_till_done)
{
    if((m.notes == NULL) ¦¦ (m.numnotes == 0)) return;

// Wait if something is already playing...
    if(!wait_till_done && sound_playing)
    {
        while(CountVoiceNotes(1) > 0);
        sound_playing = 0;
    }

// Turn off anything that might be playing now...
    StopSound();
    CloseSound();
```

continues

Listing 22.3. continued

```
// Open sound driver and play the notes...
    if(OpenSound() > 0)
    {
     SetVoiceQueueSize(1, 6*m.numnotes);
        SetVoiceAccent(1, m.tempo, m.volume,
                       m.mode, m.pitch);
        short i;
        for(i = 0; i < m.numnotes; i++)
            SetVoiceNote(1, m.notes[i].number,
                         m.notes[i].duration,
                         m.notes[i].dots);
        StartSound();
        sound_playing = 1;

// Wait till music is done (if wait_till_done is TRUE)
        if(wait_till_done)
        {
            while(CountVoiceNotes(1) > 0);
            StopSound();
            CloseSound();
        }
    }
}
//-----------------------------------------------------------
//  O w l M a i n
//
//  Create an instance of the application and "run" it.

int OwlMain(int, char**)
{
    PlaySoundApp PlaySound("PlaySound");
    return PlaySound.Run();
}
```

Playing Waveform Sound

If you have a sound card installed in your PC, you probably already know about the waveform files with the .WAV extension. These files contain digitized sound obtained by taking samples of continuously varying sound waveforms. Although music can be synthesized from a collection of notes, there are many complex sounds (such as a baby's cry or a dog's bark) that cannot be broken down into notes. Digitized sound, on the other hand, can represent any type of sound, no matter how complex. All you have to do is generate the sound waveform and take samples at a fast enough rate. Most sound cards are capable of accepting analog sound waveforms, such as those generated by a microphone, and digitizing them. Microsoft Windows includes the software (the Sound Recorder program in the Accessories group under the Program Manager) that you can use to create a .WAV file with a microphone hooked up to the sound card.

The *sndPlaySound* Function

The Windows Media Control Interface makes it very easy to play digitized sounds stored in a .WAV file. You do not have to know how to interpret the contents of the .WAV file. All you have to do is call the `sndPlaySound` function with the name of the .WAV file as one of the arguments and Windows MCI takes care of the details.

> **Restrictions on `sndPlaySound`**
>
> To play a sound waveform file with the `sndPlaySound` function, your system must have a waveform audio device driver installed, and the data format of the sound must be acceptable to the driver. Also, the entire sound waveform must fit in memory.

The `sndPlaySound` function is declared in the header file MMSYSTEM.H as

```
BOOL sndPlaySound(
    LPCSTR sound_name, // Name of sound resource or .WAV file
    UINT   flags);     // Indicates how to interpret sound_name
                       // and how to play the waveform
```

The sndPlaySound function interprets the first argument as the name of a sound listed in the [sounds] section of the WIN.INI file. For instance, here is a typical set of entries in the [sounds] section of a WIN.INI file:

```
[sounds]
SystemAsterisk=chord.wav,Asterisk
SystemHand=chord.wav,Critical Stop
SystemDefault=ding.wav,Default Beep
SystemExclamation=chord.wav,Exclamation
SystemQuestion=chord.wav,Question
SystemExit=chimes.wav,Windows Exit
SystemStart=tada.wav,Windows Start
```

These entries assign a descriptive name to a .WAV file. For instance, if you specify SystemQuestion as the first argument, sndPlaySound plays the waveform in the CHORD.WAV file.

If sndPlaySound cannot find the named sound in the WIN.INI file's [sounds] section, it assumes that the name refers to a waveform file. To locate the file, sndPlaySound searches the current directory followed by the Windows directory and the SYSTEM subdirectory in the Windows directory. Then sndPlaySound searches through the directories listed in the PATH environment variable. If the function cannot find the file, it plays the SystemDefault sound. The sndPlaySound function returns TRUE if it successfully plays a sound; otherwise, it returns FALSE.

The second argument to sndPlaySound tells the function how to interpret the first argument and how to play the sound. This argument is a bitwise-OR combination of one or more of the following constants defined in the header file MMSYSTEM.H:

- SND_SYNC causes the function to play the sound synchronously and return only after the sound ends.
- SND_ASYNC causes the function to play the sound asynchronously and return immediately after beginning the sound. To stop the sound, you must call sndPlaySound with the first argument set to NULL.
- SND_NODEFAULT returns silently without playing the default sound, if sndPlaySound cannot find the specified sound.
- SND_MEMORY indicates that the first argument to sndPlaySound is a pointer to an in-memory image of a waveform sound.
- SND_LOOP causes the sound to play repeatedly until you call sndPlaySound a second time with the first argument set to NULL. Note that the SND_ASYNC flag must accompany the SND_LOOP flag, so you have to specify SND_ASYNC ¦ SND_LOOP to play a waveform repeatedly.

- SND_NOSTOP causes sndPlaySound to return FALSE immediately without playing the requested sound, if a sound is currently playing.

The PlayWave Program

Listing 22.4 shows the file PLAYWAVE.CPP. This implements a simple program allowing the user to open a waveform file and play the digitized sound stored in the file. The playwave program is modeled after the playsnd program. When the program starts up, it displays a standard file open dialog with a list of all .WAV files in the current directory. Once the user selects a waveform file from the list of files displayed in this dialog and clicks the OK pushbutton, the program calls the sndPlaySound function (see Listing 22.4) to open the selected file and play the digitized sound. As the sound plays, the dialog is displayed again. The user has to press the Cancel button to exit the application.

Listing 22.4. PLAYWAVE.CPP. Program that plays digitized sound waveforms.

```
//-------------------------------------------------------------
//  File:  playwave.cpp
//
//  A simple program that plays sound waveform (.WAV) files.
//
//-------------------------------------------------------------
#include <owl\framewin.h> #include <string.h>
#include <owl\framewin.h> #include <owl\applicat.h>
#include <owl\framewin.h> #include <owl\opensave.h>
#include <owl\framewin.h> #include <mmsystem.h>

//-------------------------------------------------------------
class PlayWaveApp: public TApplication
{
public:
// Constructor that simply calls the base class constructor

    PlayWaveApp(const char far *name): TApplication(name) {}

// Define function to initialize application's main window
```

continues

Listing 22.4. continued

```
    void InitMainWindow();
};
//------------------------------------------------------------
//  P l a y W a v e A p p : : I n i t M a i n W i n d o w
//  Everything happens in this function. We display a dialog
//  box and play the digitized sound from the selected file.

void PlayWaveApp::InitMainWindow()
{
    EnableCtl3d();

    char name[80] = "*.wav";
    char filter[80] = "*.wav";
    int status = IDOK;
    TOpenSaveDialog::TData data;

    data.FileName = name;
    data.Filter = filter;
    data.Flags = OFN_HIDEREADONLY ¦ OFN_FILEMUSTEXIST ¦
                 OFN_PATHMUSTEXIST;
MainWindow = new TFrameWindow (0, "PlaySound");

    while(status == IDOK)
    {
        strcpy(name, filter);

// Create and display file selection dialog...
        TFileOpenDialog fd(MainWindow, data);
        status = fd.Execute();

 // Load selected waveform file and play
        if(status == IDOK)
        {
            sndPlaySound(name, SND_ASYNC);
        }
    }
// Quit ...
    PostQuitMessage(0);
}
//------------------------------------------------------------
//  O w l M a i n
```

```
//
//  Create an instance of the application and "run" it.

int OwlMain(int, char**)
{
    PlayWaveApp PlayWave("PlayWave");
    return PlayWave.Run();
}
```

Playing Sound with MCI Command Messages

The `sndPlaySound` function is meant to be a high-level function for playing waveform files. Windows 3.1 also includes two general-purpose media control interfaces:

- *Command Message Interface.* With this interface, you can use the `mciSendCommand` function to send messages (integers that identify various tasks) to the MCI driver for a device.
- *Command String Interface.* With this interface, you can use the `mciSendString` function to send commands in the form of text strings to a multimedia device.

As an example of the command message interface, here is how you can recreate the functionality of the `sndPlaySound` function shown in Listing 22.4. To play a waveform file using the `mciSendCommand` function, you have to replace the single `sndPlaySound` function in Listing 22.4 with the following block of code:

```
// Load selected waveform file and play
        if(status == IDOK)
        {
// Use MCI command interface to play sound
            MCI_OPEN_PARMS mci_open;

// Set up parameters and open waveform audio device
            memset(&mci_open, 0, sizeof(mci_open));
            mci_open.lpstrElementName = name;

            DWORD err = mciSendCommand(0, MCI_OPEN,
                            MCI_WAIT | MCI_OPEN_ELEMENT,
                    (DWORD)(LPMCI_OPEN_PARMS)&mci_open);
            if(err != 0L)
```

```
            {
                char errmsg[MAXERRORLENGTH];
                mciGetErrorString(err, errmsg, sizeof(errmsg));
                MessageBox(0, errmsg, "PlayMCISound",
                           MB_OK | MB_ICONEXCLAMATION);
            }
            else
            {
// Play the sound file...
                MCI_PLAY_PARMS mci_play;
                memset(&mci_play, 0, sizeof(mci_play));
                mciSendCommand(mci_open.wDeviceID, MCI_PLAY,
                    MCI_WAIT, (unsigned long)&mci_play);
            }
        }
```

As you can see, playing a waveform file with the `mciSendCommand` function is more complicated than using the `sndPlaySound` function. However, the `mciSendCommand` interface does offer much more control over the multimedia device. You can, for instance, stop a device as well as pause it or resume it. Although these capabilities may not be important when playing a short segment of digitized sound, such controls are important for other multimedia devices, such as CD-ROM. CD-ROM can be controlled with the `mciSendCommand` function just as you would control a waveform audio device.

Summary

Sound is an integral part of many Windows applications, especially multimedia applications. Until recently, applications for IBM-Compatible PCs had to rely on the simple speaker built into every PC. Nowadays, many PC owners install sound cards capable of generating musical quality sounds, and many applications exploit this capability. Windows provides a device-independent interface to the sound cards through device drivers. Windows 3.1 makes programming the sound cards easier through the Media Control Interface (MCI) of the MMSYSTEM.DLL dynamic link library. This chapter describes how to generate sound using a number of Windows API functions. Two C++ classes, `Note` and `Music`, are used to illustrate how musical notes can be stored in a file, interpreted, and played.

The `sndPlaySound` function and the `mciSendCommand` function can be used to play digitized sound waveforms stored in files with the .WAV extension.

VI

Graphics and Imaging Applications

23

Understanding Image File Formats

Part V, "Windows Programming," shows you various aspects of writing Windows applications with Borland C++. This part of the book presents a few interesting graphics and imaging applications, starting with a discussion of graphics file formats in this chapter.

Many Windows applications, especially multimedia applications, need images because images are used as the central elements of a multimedia graphics application. To use an image in an application, you need the image in an electronic form. You can prepare the images in a paint or drawing program. For conventional hard copy drawings, you have to use a scanner to convert the images into electronic form. Whether drawn with a paint program or scanned from a hard copy, the image is stored in a disk file with its file contents interpreted before you use it in your application. This chapter introduces a number of common image file formats (PCX, BMP, GIF, and TIFF) that describe the layout of the pixels in the file, and also presents a number of C++ classes that can read image files and display images in Windows. The chapter ends with a Windows application, ImageView, that lets you open image files and view them.

Image File Formats

An image is a two-dimensional array of pixels, often called a *raster*. Each horizontal line is called a *scan line* or *raster line*. In the computer, the color of each pixel is represented in one of the following ways:

- If the image is monochrome, the color of each pixel is expressed as a 1-bit value—a 1 or a 0.
- For a true color image, each pixel's color is expressed in terms of red (R), green (G), and blue (B) intensities that make up the color. Typically, each component of the color is represented by a byte—thus providing 256 levels for each color component. This approach requires 3 bytes for each pixel and allows up to 256 x 256 x 256 = 16,777,216 or 16 million distinct combinations of RGB values (colors).
- For a palette-based image, each pixel's value is interpreted as an index into a table of RGB values known as a color palette or colormap. For each pixel, you are supposed to display the RGB value corresponding to that pixel's contents. The number of bits needed to store each pixel's value depends on the number of colors in the color palette. The common sizes of color palettes are 16 (needs 4 bits per pixel) and 256 (needs 8 bits per pixel).

Figure 23.1 shows some of the components of an image. The width and height of the image are expressed in terms of number of pixels along the horizontal and vertical directions, respectively.

Figure 23.1. Elements of an image.

Common Characteristics of Image Files

When storing an image in a file, you have to make sure that you can interpret and display the image later. To ensure that you can read, interpret, and display a stored image, the image file must, at a minimum, contain the following information:

- Dimensions of the image—the width and the height
- Number of bits per pixel
- Type of image—whether pixel values should be interpreted as RGB colors or indexes to a color palette
- Color palette (also known as colormap), if the image uses one
- Image data, which is the array of pixel values

Almost all image files contain this set of information, but each specific file format organizes the information in a different way. Figure 23.2 shows the layout of a typical image file. The file starts with a short header—anywhere from a few to 128 or so bytes. The header contains any information besides the image data and the color palette. Next comes a color palette if the pixel values in the image require a palette. The *image data*—the array of pixel values—appear after the palette. Usually, the pixel array is stored line by line.

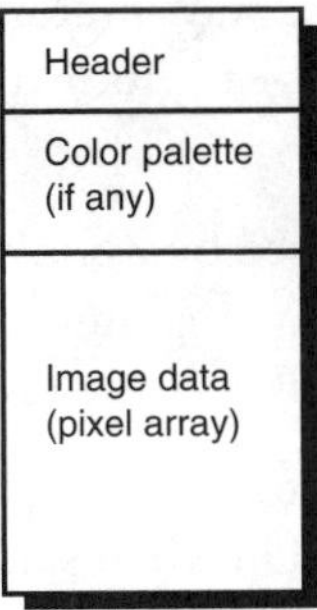

Figure 23.2. Typical image file format.

The array of pixels constitutes the bulk of the image file. For instance, a 256-color, 640x480 image requires 640x480 = 307,200 bytes of storage because each pixel's value occupies 1 byte. Of course, the storage requirements of the image data can be reduced by compressing the data, either by run-length encoding or some other compression scheme.

Note that even though most image files have a layout similar to the one shown in Figure 23.2, there is still room for many possible variations:

- The order of information in the header can vary from one file format to another.
- Some display-dependent image file formats skip the color palette entirely and store only the pixel array.
- The pixel array might be stored from top to bottom or bottom to top.
- If the pixel values are RGB components, the order red, green, and blue may vary.
- The pixel values may be stored in packed format or as bit planes. In the packed format, all bits belonging to a pixel are stored contiguously. When the image is stored according to bit planes, the bits for each pixel are split according to the bit position—the least significant bits of all pixels are stored line by line, then come the bits for the next bit position, and so on.
- The pixel values may be stored in a compressed format.

Some Common Image File Formats

As you can see, there are several ways to store an image in a file, which is why you find so many different types of image file formats. Here are some of the popular image file formats:

- PCX format, originally used by ZSoft's PC PaintBrush, is a popular image file format that many drawing programs and scanners support. PCX files use a run-length encoding (RLE) scheme to store the image in a compressed form.
- Windows BMP format stores an image as a device-independent bitmap, or DIB, a format introduced in Microsoft Windows 3.0. The DIB format includes a color palette and stores the image data in a standard manner to make the image file device-independent. The Windows BMP format can store images with 1 (monochrome), 4 (16 color), 8 (256 color), or 24 (16 million color) bits per pixel. The BMP format is not as efficient as PCX and other formats, but it is relatively easy to interpret a BMP file.
- The 24-bit Truevision Targa file format originated with Truevision's high-performance display adapters for PCs. There are several different types of Targa files; the most popular one is the 24-bit/pixel version that uses 8 bits for

each of the R, G, and B components. This format can store image files with up to 16 million colors. However, the file size for a 24-bit image is very large—a 640x480 24-bit image requires 3x640x480 = 921,600 bytes or almost 1M.

- TIFF or Tagged Image File Format was developed jointly by Microsoft Corporation and Aldus Corporation as a flexible, system-independent file format to store monochrome through 24-bit color images. Most desktop publishing and word processing software can read and use TIFF images. Additionally, all scanners provide control software that can save images in TIFF.
- GIF (pronounced "jif") or Graphics Interchange Format was developed by CompuServe for compact storage of images with up to 256 colors. GIF files store images using the LZW (named after the scheme's authors, Lempel-Ziv and Welsh) compression scheme.

The next part of this chapter describes these five image file formats and shows sample code to interpret and display the images. The description of the image file formats is presented in the context of a C++ class hierarchy designed to represent different types of images.

C++ Classes for Handling Image Files

Because all images have a common set of information, the starting point of the C++ class hierarchy is an abstract base class named `Image`. The `Image` class stores the image in a standard internal format and provides pure virtual functions `write` and `read` to transfer an image to and from disk files. Note that a pure virtual function refers to a virtual function that is set equal to zero:

```
// Functions to load and save images
    virtual int read(const char* filename) = 0;
    virtual int write(const char* filename) = 0;
```

The C++ compiler does not allow you to create instances of a class with pure virtual functions. Thus, to actually use the `Image` class, you have to first derive a class from `Image` and define the `read` and `write` functions in that class. My idea for this design is that each class responsible for handling a specific image type will be derived from `Image`. For instance, a 24-bit Truevision Targa image file (which usually has a .TGA file extension) will be handled by the `TGAImage` class, which will include concrete implementations of the `read` and `write` member functions to load and save a Targa image.

Similarly, classes such as `PCXImage` and `BMPImage` can handle PCX and Windows BMP images, respectively. Figure 23.3 shows the `Image` class hierarchy for the classes needed to handle Targa, PCX, Windows BMP, GIF, and TIFF images.

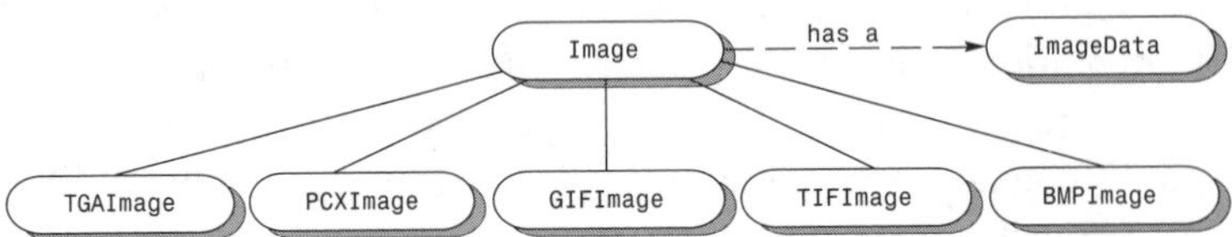

Figure 23.3. Image class hierarchy to handle Targa, PCX, BMP, GIF, and TIFF images.

I have also decided to make the `Image` class dependent on Microsoft Windows by selecting the Windows device-independent bitmap (DIB) format for the internal representation of an image in the `Image` class. This design decision makes it easy to display the image because the `Image` class itself can include a member function that accepts a device context as an argument, converts the internal DIB into a device-dependent bitmap (DDB), and displays the bitmap by calling Windows API functions. Details are explained in subsequent sections.

Another important design decision is to use an `ImageData` class to encapsulate the image's pixel array and then use a pointer to an `ImageData` object in each `Image` class (see Figure 23.3). This is why I made this decision. The DIB format, used for internal representation of images, requires a considerable amount of memory for any reasonably sized color image. When equating one image to another, I did not want to make a complete copy of the image's pixel array; instead, I wanted to copy a pointer to the pixel array and keep a count of how many `Image` class instances are sharing a specific pixel array. When an `Image` is destroyed, the destructor decrements the pixel array's count and destroys the array only when the count is zero, which indicates that the pixel array is not referenced by any `Image` object. This scheme is known as *reference counting*.

ImageData Class

The `ImageData` class represents all data necessary to represent an image—the pixel array as well as other pertinent information about the image. Because I am using a Windows DIB format to represent the image, the definition of the `ImageData` class (see Listing 23.1) is very simple. The most important data in `ImageData` is the pointer (declared with the type `LPVOID`) `p_dib`. This is a pointer to a Windows device-independent bitmap—a block of memory that has the layout shown in Figure 23.4.

The `BITMAPINFOHEADER`, a structure at the beginning of the DIB, contains all relevant information, such as image dimensions and number of bits per pixel, that you need to interpret the image's pixel array. You will see more about the fields of the `BITMAPINFOHEADER` in the `PCXImage` class. In this class, the `read` member function initializes the fields after reading an image in the PCX format and converting it to the internal DIB format.

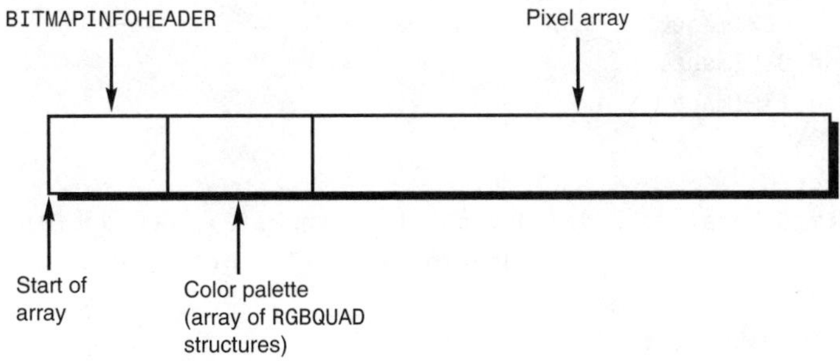

Figure 23.4. Layout of a DIB in memory.

Listing 23.1. IMAGE.H. Header file for the `ImageData` and `Image` classes.

```
//----------------------------------------------------------------
//  File: image.h
//
//  Defines the Image class.
//
//----------------------------------------------------------------
#if !defined(__IMAGE_H)
#define __IMAGE_H

#include <owl\dc.h>
#include <fstream.h>
#include <windowsx.h>

class Image;
class TGAImage;
class BMPImage;
class PCXImage;
class GIFImage;
class TIFImage;
```

continues

Listing 23.1. continued

```
// This class represents the data for an image
class ImageData
{
friend Image;
friend TGAImage;
friend BMPImage;
friend PCXImage;
friend GIFImage;
friend TIFImage;

protected:
    ImageData() : p_dib(0), count(1), hpal(0), hbm_ddb(0),
                  bytes_per_line(0), w(0), h(0) {}

    ~ImageData();

protected:

// This points to a BITMAPINFOHEADER followed by the
// image data.
    LPVOID         p_dib;   // Device independent bitmap
    HPALETTE       hpal;    // Color palette
    HBITMAP        hbm_ddb; // Device dependent bitmap

    unsigned short w, h;    // Width and height
    unsigned short bytes_per_line;

    unsigned short count;
};

// Abstract base class for all images
class Image
{
public:
// Constructors
    Image()
    {
        imdata = new ImageData;
    }
    Image(HBITMAP hbm, unsigned short w, unsigned short h)
    {
```

```
        imdata = new ImageData;
        imdata->hbm_ddb = hbm;
        imdata->w = w;
        imdata->h = h;
    }

    Image(HDC hdc, Image *img, short x, short y,
          unsigned short w, unsigned short h);

// Copy Constructor
    Image(const Image& img);

    virtual ~Image()
    {
        if(--imdata->count <= 0) delete imdata;
    }

// Operators
    Image& operator=(const Image& img);

// Copy the imdata pointer from another image
    void image_data(const Image* img);

// Functions to load and save images
    virtual int read(const char* filename){ return 0;}
    virtual int write(const char* filename){ return 0;}
    virtual int read(ifstream& ifs){ return 0;}
    int write_dib(ofstream& ofs);

// Returns pointer to the Windows Device Independent
// Bitmap (DIB).
    LPVOID get_dib() { return imdata->p_dib;}

// Function to return the handle to the device dependent
// bitmap
    HBITMAP get_ddb() { return imdata->hbm_ddb;}

    unsigned short width()
    {
          if(imdata->p_dib != 0)
            return((LPBITMAPINFOHEADER)imdata->p_dib)->biWidth;
          return imdata->w;
```

continues

Listing 23.1. continued

```
    }
    unsigned short height()
    {
        if(imdata->p_dib != 0)
          return ((LPBITMAPINFOHEADER)imdata->p_dib)->biHeight;
        return imdata->h;
    }

    int image_loaded()
    {
        if(imdata->p_dib == 0) return 0;
        else return 1;
    }

    void detach()
    {
        if(—imdata->count == 0) delete imdata;
        imdata = new ImageData;
    }

// Functions to make palette and convert to DDB
    void make_palette();
    void DIBtoDDB(HDC hdc);
    void DDBtoDIB();

// Function that displays the DIB on a Windows device
// specified by a device context
    void show(HDC hdc, short xfrom = 0, short yfrom = 0,
                       short xto = 0,    short yto = 0,
                       short width = 0, short height = 0,
                       DWORD ropcode = SRCCOPY);
    void show(TDC& hdc, short xfrom = 0, short yfrom = 0,
                       short xto = 0,    short yto = 0,
                       short width = 0, short height = 0,
                       DWORD ropcode = SRCCOPY);

    unsigned int numcolors();
    HPALETTE palette() { return imdata->hpal;}

protected:
    ImageData* imdata;
```

```
};

#endif
```

The `ImageData` class also includes two important member variables:

- `HPALETTE hpal;` is a handle to a Windows color palette—an array of `PALETTEENTRY` structures (defined in `<Windows.h>`) that associate an index with an RGB color. The `make_palette` member function of the `Image` class creates the palette.
- `HBITMAP hbm_ddb;` is the handle to the device-dependent bitmap (DDB) corresponding to the DIB. The `DIBtoDDB` member function of the `Image` class creates the DDB (for a specified device) from the DIB.

Encapsulating the image's data in the `ImageData` class allows sharing of the data between images, but I do not want to give up the ability to directly access and manipulate the image's pixel array from other image classes. One way to provide this access is to declare as `friend` all classes that have to manipulate the private and protected member variables of `ImageData`. In this case, `Image` and its derived classes, such as `PCXImage`, `BMPImage`, `TGAImage`, `GIFImage`, and `TIFImage`, are declared with the `friend` keyword in the `ImageData` class.

Image Class

The `Image` class, declared in the file IMAGE.H (Listing 23.1), is an abstract base class that encapsulates the common features of all images. Because all images are internally maintained in the Windows DIB format, the `Image` class can take care of displaying the image instead of delegating that responsibility to the derived classes. The `show` member function of `Image` displays the image on a device specified by a device context. The Windows API provides a function, `SetDIBitsToDevice`, that lets you directly display a DIB on a device, but this function is comparatively slow. A faster approach is to convert the DIB into a device-dependent bitmap (DDB) and use the `BitBlt` function to display the DDB. The drawback is that creating the DDB requires memory. Consult the listing of the `show` function (Listing 23.2) for complete details of how to display a DIB. The following are the general steps needed to convert the DIB to a DDB and display the DDB:

1. Set up a color palette if the image needs one. DIBs with 1, 4, or 8 bits per pixel use color palettes. The `make_palette` function in Listing 23.2 illustrates how to create a palette. Before converting a DIB to a DDB, you have to realize

the color palette—that means you have to define the color palette and call the Windows API function RealizePalette to ensure that Windows uses the color palette when drawing on that device context.

2. Call the CreateDIBitmap function to get back a handle to a DDB created from the DIB for a specified device. The DIBtoDDB function performs this task by calling CreateDIBitmap as follows:

```
// Note: imdata is a pointer to an ImageData object
//       hbm_ddb is a handle to a bitmap (HBITMAP)
imdata->hbm_ddb = CreateDIBitmap(
             hdc,        // Device context handle
             p_bminfo,   // Pointer to BITMAPINFOHEADER
             CBM_INIT,   // Initialize DDB from DIB
             p_image,    // Pointer to image data
             (LPBITMAPINFO)p_bminfo, // Pointer to a
                         // BITMAPINFO structure
             DIB_RGB_COLORS); // Interpret palette
                         // entries as RGB colors
```

As indicated by the comments, the DIB is specified by three pointers: a pointer to the BITMAPINFOHEADER, a pointer to the image's pixel array, and a pointer to a BITMAPINFO structure with the color palette. In this case, the BITMAPINFO and BITMAPINFOHEADER structures overlap and the image data follows the BITMAPINFOHEADER.

3. Call CreateCompatibleDC to get back a handle to a memory device context (DC) compatible with a specified DC.

4. If the compatible DC is created successfully (the handle is nonzero), select the DDB into the DC by calling the Windows API function named SelectBitmap.

5. Call BitBlt to copy the bitmap from the memory DC to the actual device. Here is a sample call:

```
BitBlt(hdc, xto, yto, wdth, hght,
      memdc, xfrom, yfrom, ropcode);
```

This copies from the memdc device context to hdc. The wdth and hght represent the width and height of the bitmap being copied to the screen.

6. Clean up by deleting the memory DC. The DDB should be deleted also—this is done by the destructor of the ImageData class when the image is no longer needed.

Listing 23.2. IMAGE.CPP. Member functions of the `Image` class.

```
//--------------------------------------------------------------
//  File: image.cpp
//
//  Image manipulation functions
//--------------------------------------------------------------
#include <fstream.h>
#include <string.h>
#include "image.h"

const size_t maxwrite = 30*1024; // Write 30K at a time
//--------------------------------------------------------------
//  I m a g e D a t a : : ~ I m a g e D a t a
//  Destructor for an Image.

ImageData::~ImageData()
{
// If a DIB exists, delete it.
    if(p_dib != 0) GlobalFreePtr(p_dib);

// If a palette exists, free it also.
    if(hpal != 0) DeletePalette(hpal);

// If a DDB exists, destroy it.
    if(hbm_ddb != 0) DeleteBitmap(hbm_ddb);
}
//--------------------------------------------------------------
//  I m a g e : : I m a g e
//  Copy constructor

Image::Image(const Image& img)
{
    img.imdata->count++;
    if(—imdata->count <= 0) delete imdata;
    imdata = img.imdata;
}
//--------------------------------------------------------------
//  I m a g e : : i m a g e _ d a t a
//  Copy the ImageData pointer from another image
```

continues

Listing 23.2. continued

```
void Image::image_data(const Image* img)
{
    img->imdata->count++;
    if(—imdata->count <= 0) delete imdata;
    imdata = img->imdata;
}
//---------------------------------------------------------------
//  I m a g e : : o p e r a t o r =
//  Assignment operator

Image& Image::operator=(const Image& img)
{
    img.imdata->count++;
    if(—imdata->count <= 0) delete imdata;
    imdata = img.imdata;
    return *this;
}
//---------------------------------------------------------------
// I m a g e : : n u m c o l o r s
// Returns the number of colors used. Returns 0 if image uses
// 24-bit pixels.

unsigned int Image::numcolors()
{
    if(imdata->p_dib == 0) return 0;
    LPBITMAPINFOHEADER p_bminfo =
                (LPBITMAPINFOHEADER)(imdata->p_dib);

// If the biClrUsed field is nonzero, use that as the number of
// colors
    if(p_bminfo->biClrUsed != 0)
        return (unsigned int)p_bminfo->biClrUsed;

// Otherwise, the number of colors depends on the bits per pixel
    switch(p_bminfo->biBitCount)
    {
        case 1: return 2;
        case 4: return 16;
        case 8: return 256;
        default: return 0; // Must be 24-bit/pixel image
    }
}
```

```
//---------------------------------------------------------------
// I m a g e : : m a k e _ p a l e t t e
// Create a color palette using information in the DIB

void Image::make_palette()
{
// Set up a pointer to the DIB
    LPBITMAPINFOHEADER p_bminfo =
                        (LPBITMAPINFOHEADER)(imdata->p_dib);
    if(p_bminfo == 0) return;

// Free any existing palette
    if(imdata->hpal != 0) DeletePalette(imdata->hpal);

// Set up the palette, if needed
    if(numcolors() > 0)
    {
        LPLOGPALETTE p_pal = (LPLOGPALETTE) GlobalAllocPtr(GHND,
                                          sizeof(LOGPALETTE) +
                          numcolors() * sizeof(PALETTEENTRY));

        if(p_pal)
        {
            p_pal->palVersion = 0x0300;
            p_pal->palNumEntries = numcolors();

// Set up palette entries from DIB
            LPBITMAPINFO p_bi = (LPBITMAPINFO)p_bminfo;
            int i;
            for(i = 0; i < numcolors(); i++)
            {
                p_pal->palPalEntry[i].peRed =
                        p_bi->bmiColors[i].rgbRed;
                p_pal->palPalEntry[i].peGreen =
                        p_bi->bmiColors[i].rgbGreen;
                p_pal->palPalEntry[i].peBlue =
                        p_bi->bmiColors[i].rgbBlue;
                p_pal->palPalEntry[i].peFlags = 0;
            }
            imdata->hpal = CreatePalette(p_pal);
            GlobalFreePtr(p_pal);
        }
```

continues

Listing 23.2. continued

```
        }
    }
    //--------------------------------------------------------------
    // I m a g e : : D I B t o D D B
    // Create a device dependent bitmap from the DIB

    void Image::DIBtoDDB(HDC hdc)
    {
    // Set up a pointer to the DIB
        LPBITMAPINFOHEADER p_bminfo =
                             (LPBITMAPINFOHEADER)(imdata->p_dib);
        if(p_bminfo == 0) return;

    // If a DDB exists, destroy it first.
        if(imdata->hbm_ddb != 0) DeleteBitmap(imdata->hbm_ddb);

    // Build the device-dependent bitmap.

    // Set up pointer to the image data (skip over BITMAPINFOHEADER
    // and palette).
        LPSTR p_image = (LPSTR)p_bminfo +
                        sizeof(BITMAPINFOHEADER) +
                        numcolors() * sizeof(RGBQUAD);

    // Realize palette, if there is one. Note that this does not do
    // anything on the standard 16-color VGA driver because that
    // driver does not allow changing the palette, but the new palette
    // should work on Super VGA displays.

        HPALETTE hpalold = NULL;
        if(imdata->hpal)
        {
            hpalold = SelectPalette(hdc, imdata->hpal, FALSE);
            RealizePalette(hdc);
        }

    // Convert the DIB into a DDB (device dependent bitmap) and
    // block transfer (blt) it to the device context.
        HBITMAP hbm_old;
        imdata->hbm_ddb = CreateDIBitmap(hdc,
                                         p_bminfo,
```

```
                                        CBM_INIT,
                                        p_image,
                                        (LPBITMAPINFO)p_bminfo,
                                        DIB_RGB_COLORS);

// Don't need the palette once the bitmap is converted to DDB
// format.
    if(hpalold)
        SelectPalette(hdc, hpalold, FALSE);
}
//-------------------------------------------------------------
// I m a g e : : D D B t o D I B
// Create a device independent bitmap from the DDB
// soecified by imdata->hbm_ddb

void Image::DDBtoDIB()
{
// Do nothing if the DDB does not exist or if the DIB exists
    if(imdata->hbm_ddb == 0) return;
    if(imdata->p_dib != NULL) return;

    BITMAP bm;
    GetObject(imdata->hbm_ddb, sizeof(bm), (LPSTR)&bm);

// Set up a BITMAPINFOHEADER for the DIB
    BITMAPINFOHEADER bh;
    bh.biSize        = sizeof(BITMAPINFOHEADER);
    bh.biWidth       = bm.bmWidth;
    bh.biHeight      = bm.bmHeight;
    bh.biPlanes      = 1;
    bh.biBitCount    = (WORD)(bm.bmPlanes * bm.bmBitsPixel);
    bh.biCompression = BI_RGB;

    imdata->w = bm.bmWidth;
    imdata->h = bm.bmHeight;

// Compute bytes per line, rounding up to align at a 4-byte
// boundary
    imdata->bytes_per_line = ((long)bh.biWidth *
                        (long)bh.biBitCount + 31L) / 32 * 4;
```

continues

Listing 23.2. continued

```
    bh.biSizeImage   = (long)bh.biHeight *
                       (long)imdata->bytes_per_line;

    bh.biXPelsPerMeter  = 0;
    bh.biYPelsPerMeter  = 0;

// Determine number of colors in the palette
    short ncolors = 0;
    switch(bh.biBitCount)
    {
        case 1:
            ncolors = 2;
            break;
        case 4:
            ncolors = 16;
            break;
        case 8:
            ncolors = 256;
            break;
        default:
            ncolors = 0;
    }

    bh.biClrUsed        = ncolors;
    bh.biClrImportant   = 0;

// Compute total size of DIB
    unsigned long dibsize = sizeof(BITMAPINFOHEADER) +
                            ncolors * sizeof(RGBQUAD) +
                            bh.biSizeImage;

// Allocate memory for the DIB
    imdata->p_dib = GlobalAllocPtr(GHND, dibsize);
    if(imdata->p_dib == NULL) return;

// Set up palette
    HDC hdc = GetDC(NULL);

// Copy BITMAPINFO structure bh into beginning of DIB.
    _fmemcpy(imdata->p_dib, &bh, (size_t)bh.biSize);
```

```
    LPSTR p_image = (LPSTR)imdata->p_dib +
                    (WORD)bh.biSize +
                    ncolors * sizeof(RGBQUAD);

// Call GetDIBits to get the image and fill the palette indices
// into a BITMAPINFO structure
    GetDIBits(hdc, imdata->hbm_ddb, 0, (WORD)bh.biHeight,
              p_image,(LPBITMAPINFO)imdata->p_dib,
              DIB_RGB_COLORS);

// All done. Clean up and return.
    ReleaseDC(NULL, hdc);
}
//-------------------------------------------------------------
// I m a g e : : s h o w (H D C, ... )
// Display a DIB on a Windows device specified by a
// device context

void Image::show(HDC hdc, short xfrom, short yfrom,
                          short xto,   short yto,
                          short wdth,  short hght,
                          DWORD ropcode)
{

// Set up a pointer to the DIB
    LPBITMAPINFOHEADER p_bminfo =
                           (LPBITMAPINFOHEADER)(imdata->p_dib);
    if(p_bminfo != NULL)
    {
// Set up the palette, if needed
        if(imdata->hpal == 0 && numcolors() > 0) make_palette();

// Convert to DDB, if necessary
        if(imdata->hbm_ddb == 0) DIBtoDDB(hdc);
    }

// "Blit" the DDB to hdc
    if(imdata->hbm_ddb != 0)
    {
        HDC memdc = CreateCompatibleDC(hdc);
        if(memdc != 0)
```

continues

Listing 23.2. continued

```
        {
            HBITMAP hbm_old = SelectBitmap(memdc,
                                          imdata->hbm_ddb);
// If width or height is zero, use corresponding dimension
// from the image.
            if(wdth == 0) wdth = width();
            if(hght == 0) hght = height();

            BitBlt(hdc, xto, yto, wdth, hght,
                   memdc, xfrom, yfrom, ropcode);
            SelectBitmap(memdc, hbm_old);
            DeleteDC(memdc);
        }
    }
}
//----------------------------------------------------------
// I m a g e : : s h o w ( T D C &, ... )
// Display a DIB on a Windows device specified by a
// device context

void Image::show(TDC& dc, short xfrom, short yfrom,
                          short xto,   short yto,
                          short wdth,  short hght,
                          DWORD ropcode)
{

// Set up a pointer to the DIB
    LPBITMAPINFOHEADER p_bminfo =
                         (LPBITMAPINFOHEADER)(imdata->p_dib);
    if(p_bminfo != NULL)
    {
// Set up the palette, if needed
        if(imdata->hpal == 0 && numcolors() > 0) make_palette();

// Convert to DDB, if necessary
        if(imdata->hbm_ddb == 0) DIBtoDDB(dc);
    }

// "Blit" the DDB to hdc
    if(imdata->hbm_ddb != 0)
    {
```

```
        TMemoryDC memdc(dc);
        if(memdc != 0)
        {
            memdc.SelectObject(imdata->hbm_ddb);

// If width or height is zero, use corresponding dimension
// from the image.
            if(wdth == 0) wdth = width();
            if(hght == 0) hght = height();

            dc.BitBlt(xto, yto, wdth, hght,
                      memdc, xfrom, yfrom, ropcode);
            memdc.RestoreBitmap();
        }
    }
}
//---------------------------------------------------------------
// Image::I m a g e
// Construct an image by copying a portion of the bitmap from
// another image

Image::Image(HDC hdc, Image *img, short x, short y,
             unsigned short w, unsigned short h)
{
    imdata = new ImageData;
    if(img == NULL) return;

    unsigned short iw = img->width();
    unsigned short ih = img->height();

    if(x < 0) x = 0;
    if(y < 0) y = 0;

// If width or height is 0, adjust them
    if(w == 0) w = iw;
    if(h == 0) h = ih;

// Make sure width and height are not too large
    if((w+x) > iw) w = iw - x;
    if((h+y) > ih) h = ih - y;

// Save width and height
```

continues

Listing 23.2. continued

```
    imdata->w = w;
    imdata->h = h;

// Create a new bitmap for the new image
    imdata->hbm_ddb = CreateCompatibleBitmap(hdc, w, h);
    if(imdata->hbm_ddb != 0)
    {
        HDC memdcn = CreateCompatibleDC(hdc);
        HDC memdco = CreateCompatibleDC(hdc);
        if(memdcn != 0 && memdco != 0)
        {
            HBITMAP ohbm = SelectBitmap(memdco, img->get_ddb());
         HBITMAP nhbm = SelectBitmap(memdcn, imdata->hbm_ddb);
         BitBlt(memdcn, 0, 0, w, h, memdco, x, y, SRCCOPY);
         SelectBitmap(memdco, ohbm);
            SelectBitmap(memdcn, nhbm);
         DeleteDC(memdco);
         DeleteDC(memdcn);
        }
    }
}
//-------------------------------------------------------------
// Image:: w r i t e _ d i b
// Write out the DIB starting at the current location in
// a stream (assumed to be opened with ios::out ¦ ios::binary)

int Image::write_dib(ofstream& ofs)
{
// If there is no image, return without doing anything
    if(imdata->p_dib == NULL) return 0;

// Check if file is ok
    if(!ofs) return 0;

// Set up BMP file header
    BITMAPFILEHEADER bfhdr;

    bfhdr.bfType = ('M' << 8) ¦ 'B';
    bfhdr.bfReserved1 = 0;
    bfhdr.bfReserved2 = 0;
    bfhdr.bfOffBits = sizeof(BITMAPFILEHEADER) +
```

```
                          sizeof(BITMAPINFOHEADER) +
                          numcolors() * sizeof(RGBQUAD);
    bfhdr.bfSize = (long) height() *
                   (long) imdata->bytes_per_line +
                                   bfhdr.bfOffBits;

// Write the file header to the file
    ofs.write((unsigned char*)&bfhdr, sizeof(BITMAPFILEHEADER));

// Save the file in big chunks.

// Allocate a large buffer to be used when transferring
// data to the file

    unsigned char *wbuf = new unsigned char[maxwrite];
    if(wbuf == NULL) return 0;

    unsigned char huge *data =
                (unsigned char huge*)imdata->p_dib;
    unsigned int chunksize;
    long bmpsize = bfhdr.bfSize - sizeof(BITMAPFILEHEADER);

    unsigned int i;
    while(bmpsize > 0)
    {
        if(bmpsize > maxwrite)
            chunksize = maxwrite;
        else
            chunksize = bmpsize;
// Copy image from DIB to buffer
        for(i = 0; i < chunksize; i++) wbuf[i] = data[i];
        ofs.write(wbuf, chunksize);
        bmpsize -= chunksize;
        data += chunksize;
    }
    delete wbuf;
    return 1;
}
```

BMPImage Class

The `BMPImage` class handles Windows DIB images—usually stored in files with the .BMP file extension, and thus go by the name of BMP images. A BMP image file is the same as the in-memory representation of a DIB, shown in Figure 23.4, with a file header prefix added to the DIB. The header is represented by a `BITMAPFILEHEADER` structure defined in `<windows.h>` as follows:

```
typedef struct tagBITMAPFILEHEADER
{
    UINT    bfType;      // File type. Should be 'BM'
    DWORD   bfSize;      // Size of file in bytes
    UINT    bfReserved1; // 0
    UINT    bfReserved2; // 0
    DWORD   bfOffBits;   // Offset to the start of image data
} BITMAPFILEHEADER;
```

A `BITMAPINFOHEADER` structure follows the file header. The color palette, if any, and the image's pixel array come after the `BITMAPINFOHEADER`.

Listing 23.3 shows the declaration of the `BMPImage` class. As you can see, the `BMPImage` class provides the `read` and `write` member functions and defines one additional member variable:

`BITMAPFILEHEADER bmphdr;` is an instance of a `BITMAPFILEHEADER` structure that is used when reading or writing a BMP image file.

Listing 23.4 shows the file BMPIMAGE.CPP that implements the member functions, `read` and `write`, of the `BMPImage` class.

Listing 23.3. BMPIMAGE.H. Declaration of the `BMPImage` class.

```
//----------------------------------------------------------------
//  File: bmpimage.h
//
//  Defines the BMPImage class representing a Windows BMP image.
//
//----------------------------------------------------------------
#if !defined(__BMPIMAGE_H)
#define __BMPIMAGE_H

#include "image.h"
```

```
class BMPImage: public Image
{
public:
    BMPImage() {}

    ~BMPImage() {}

    virtual int read(const char* filename);
    virtual int write(const char* filename);
    virtual int read(ifstream& ifs);

private:
    BITMAPFILEHEADER bmphdr;
};

#endif
```

Reading a BMP Image

Listing 23.4 shows the file BMPIMAGE.CPP that implements the member functions, `read` and `write`, of the `BMPImage` class. Reading a BMP image into a `BMPImage` object is straightforward because the internal data format of the `Image` class hierarchy is the DIB and because a BMP image file is a file header followed by a DIB. As you can see from the `read` function, reading the BMP image file requires the following steps:

1. Read the file header into the `bmphdr` member of the `BMPImage` class. If `ifs` represents the input file stream, you can read the header as follows:

```
// Read the file header
    ifs.read((unsigned char*)&bmphdr,
                     sizeof(BITMAPFILEHEADER));
```

2. Check that the `bfType` field of the header contains the characters `BM`, which indicates that this is a BMP image.

3. Determine the number of bytes remaining in the file—these are the bytes that make up the DIB stored in the BMP image file. You can position the file pointer at the end of the file and read the byte offset to determine the file size. Subtracting the size of the file header from the length of the file gives you the number of bytes in the DIB that you want to read. Here is how:

```
// Determine size of DIB to read
```

```
// (that's file length - size of BITMAPFILEHEADER)
    ifs.seekg(0, ios::end);
    long bmpsize = ifs.tellg() - sizeof(BITMAPFILEHEADER);
// Reset file pointer...
    ifs.seekg(sizeof(BITMAPFILEHEADER), ios::beg);
```

4. Allocate memory for the DIB by calling the `GlobalAlloc` function:

```
// Allocate space for the bitmap
    imdata->p_dib = GlobalAllocPtr(GHND, bmpsize);
```

5. Read the bytes from the file into this memory. For efficient file I/O, you should read from the file in large chunks. The `BMPImage::read` function reads the image in blocks that are up to 30K in size as defined by the constant `maxread` declared at the beginning of the BMPIMAGE.CPP file (Listing 23.4).

I had to use an intermediate buffer when reading the image because the `read` function of the `ifstream` class (from the C++ `iostream` library) did not work properly with the pointer `imdata->p_dib` that was returned by `GlobalAlloc`.

Listing 23.4. BMPIMAGE.CPP. Member functions of the `BMPImage` class.

```
//---------------------------------------------------------------
//  File: bmpimage.cpp
//
//  Image manipulation functions for Windows BMP images.
//---------------------------------------------------------------
#include <fstream.h>
#include <limits.h>
#include "bmpimage.h"

const size_t maxread  = 30*1024; // Read 30K at a time
const size_t maxwrite = 30*1024; // Write 30K at a time
//---------------------------------------------------------------
//  B M P I m a g e : : r e a d
//  Read and interpret a Windows .BMP image (Device Independent
//  Bitmap).

int BMPImage::read(const char* filename)
{
// If there is an existing image, detach the image data
// before reading a new image
    if(imdata->p_dib != 0) detach();
```

```
// Open file for reading
    ifstream ifs(filename, ios::in | ios::binary);

// Call BMPImage::read(ifstream& ifs) to read in image
    return read(ifs);
}
//-------------------------------------------------------------
// B M P I m a g e : : r e a d ( i f s t r e a m & )
// Read image information from an open file

int BMPImage::read(ifstream& ifs)
{
    if(!ifs)
    {
// Error reading file. Return 0.
        return 0;
    }

// Read the file header
    ifs.read((unsigned char*)&bmphdr, sizeof(BITMAPFILEHEADER));

// Check if image file format is acceptable (the type
// must be 'BM'
    if(bmphdr.bfType != (('M' << 8) | 'B')) return 0;

// Determine size of DIB to read — that's the file size (as
// specified by the bfSize field of the BITMAPFILEHEADER
// structure) minus the size of the BITMAPFILEHEADER
    long bmpsize = bmphdr.bfSize - sizeof(BITMAPFILEHEADER);

// Allocate space for the bitmap
    imdata->p_dib = GlobalAllocPtr(GHND, bmpsize);

// If memory allocation fails, return 0
    if(imdata->p_dib == 0) return 0;

// Load the file in big chunks. We don't have to interpret
// because our internal format is also BMP.

// Allocate a large buffer to read from file
    unsigned char *rbuf = new unsigned char[maxread];
```

continues

Listing 23.4. continued

```
    if(rbuf == NULL)
    {
        detach();
        return 0;
    }

    unsigned char huge *data =
                (unsigned char huge*)imdata->p_dib;
    unsigned int chunksize;
    unsigned int i;

    while(bmpsize > 0)
    {
        if(bmpsize > maxread)
            chunksize = maxread;
        else
            chunksize = bmpsize;
        ifs.read(rbuf, chunksize);

// Copy into DIB
        for(i = 0; i < chunksize; i++) data[i] = rbuf[i];
        bmpsize -= chunksize;
        data += chunksize;
    }
    delete rbuf;

// Compute bytes per line, rounding up to align at a 4-byte
// boundary
    LPBITMAPINFOHEADER p_bi = (LPBITMAPINFOHEADER)imdata->p_dib;
    imdata->bytes_per_line = ((long)p_bi->biWidth *
                         (long)p_bi->biBitCount + 31L) / 32 * 4;

// Ignore OS/2 1.x bitmap files. These files have a header
// size of 12 bytes whereas a Windows 3.1 DIB has a 40-byte
// header.
    if(p_bi->biSize == 12) return 0;

    return 1;
}
//---------------------------------------------------------------
//  B M P I m a g e : : w r i t e
```

```
//  Write a Windows .BMP image to a file (in Device Independent
//  Bitmap format)

int BMPImage::write(const char* filename)
{
// If there is no image, return without doing anything
    if(imdata->p_dib == 0) return 0;

// Open file for binary write operations.
    ofstream ofs(filename, ios::out | ios::binary);
    if(!ofs) return 0;

// Set up BMP file header
    bmphdr.bfType = ('M' << 8) | 'B';
    bmphdr.bfReserved1 = 0;
    bmphdr.bfReserved2 = 0;
    bmphdr.bfOffBits = sizeof(BITMAPFILEHEADER) +
                       sizeof(BITMAPINFOHEADER) +
                       numcolors() * sizeof(RGBQUAD);
    bmphdr.bfSize = (long) height() *
                    (long) imdata->bytes_per_line +
                                    bmphdr.bfOffBits;

// Write the file header to the file
    ofs.write((unsigned char*)&bmphdr, sizeof(BITMAPFILEHEADER));

// Save the file in big chunks.

// Allocate a large buffer to be used when transferring
// data to the file

    unsigned char *wbuf = new unsigned char[maxwrite];
    if(wbuf == NULL) return 0;

    unsigned char huge *data =
                (unsigned char huge*)imdata->p_dib;
    unsigned int chunksize;
    long bmpsize = bmphdr.bfSize - sizeof(BITMAPFILEHEADER);

    unsigned int i;

    while(bmpsize > 0)
```

continues

Listing 23.4. continued

```
    {
        if(bmpsize > maxwrite)
            chunksize = maxwrite;
        else
            chunksize = bmpsize;
// Copy image from DIB to buffer
        for(i = 0; i < chunksize; i++) wbuf[i] = data[i];
        ofs.write(wbuf, chunksize);
        bmpsize -= chunksize;
        data += chunksize;
    }
    delete wbuf;
    return 1;
}
```

Writing a BMP Image

To save a DIB in a BMP format image file requires that you first prepare a header by initializing the fields of the `bmphdr` member variable, which is a `BITMAPFILEHEADER` structure. As shown in the `write` function in Listing 23.4, you can initialize the file header as follows:

```
// Set up BMP file header
    bmphdr.bfType = ('M' << 8) | 'B';
    bmphdr.bfReserved1 = 0;
    bmphdr.bfReserved2 = 0;
    bmphdr.bfOffBits = sizeof(BITMAPFILEHEADER) +
                       sizeof(BITMAPINFOHEADER) +
                       numcolors() * sizeof(RGBQUAD);
    bmphdr.bfSize = (long) height() *
                    (long) imdata->bytes_per_line +
                                    bmphdr.bfOffBits;
```

Once the file header is set up, save the header in the file:

```
// Write the file header to the file
    ofs.write((unsigned char*)&bmphdr, sizeof(BITMAPFILEHEADER));
```

After that, you can write to the file the entire DIB from `imdata->p_dib` in large chunks.

TGAImage Class

The Truevision Targa file format originated with Truevision's display hardware—one of the first video adapters capable of displaying 24-bit RGB color. Although the Targa file format can store images with 1, 8, 16, or 24 bits per pixel, I will focus on the 24-bit format only because it is the most commonly used 24-bit color format for IBM-compatible PCs. Almost any application that deals with 24-bit RGB colors supports the 24-bit Targa file format. For instance, the Targa format is the output format of choice among the popular ray tracing software, such as DKBTrace by David Buck and Aaron Collins.

Listing 23.5 shows the declaration of the `TGAImage` class representing a Targa 24-bit color image. Most Targa files are stored with the .TGA file extension; hence the class name `TGAImage`. Note that the `TGAImage` class defines the `read` member function only. The `read` function reads a Targa 24-bit RGB image and converts it into a Windows device-independent bitmap. I did not develop a `write` function because saving an image in a Targa format is not necessary for multimedia imaging and animation applications.

Like the `BMPImage` class, the `TGAImage` class includes a new member variable, `hdr`—an instance of a `TARGAHeader` structure—defined in Listing 23.5 as follows:

```
struct TARGAHeader
{
    char           offset;
    char           cmap_type;
    char           image_type;
    unsigned short cmap_start;
    unsigned short cmap_length;
    char           cmap_bits;
    unsigned short hoffset;
    unsigned short voffset;
    unsigned short width;
    unsigned short height;
    char           bits_per_pixel;
    char           flags;
};
```

This structure represents the header of a Targa image file. The following are the meanings of the fields of `TARGAHeader`:

- `char offset;` specifies the number of bytes to skip after reading the header. Usually this field is zero.

- `char cmap_type;` indicates the type of colormap being used. For 24-bit color images, this field should be zero.
- `char image_type;` defines the way the image's data is stored (whether it is uncompressed or run-length encoded). A value of 2 indicates an uncompressed RGB color image, which is the only image type that the `TGAImage` class can handle.
- `unsigned cmap_start, cmap_length; char cmap_bits;` specify the colormap, if there is one. There is no colormap for 24-bit RGB color images.
- `unsigned short hoffset, voffset;` specifies the offset between the upper-left corner of the screen and the upper-left corner of the image to be displayed. These fields are usually zero.
- `unsigned short width, height;` are the width and height of the image in pixels.
- `char bits_per_pixel;` indicates the number of bits used to represent the color of each pixel. For 24-bit color images, this field is 24.
- `char flags;` specifies how to interpret the image's data. The `TGAImage` class handles the case when `flags` is 0x20, which implies that the image is stored in a top-down format starting with the first scan line.

Listing 23.5. TGAIMAGE.H. Declaration of the `TGAImage` class.

```
//-------------------------------------------------------------
//  File: tgaimage.h
//
//  Defines the TGAImage class representing Targa True
//  Color images (handles only 24-bit color formats).
//
//-------------------------------------------------------------
#if !defined(__TGAIMAGE_H)
#define __TGAIMAGE_H

#include "image.h"

class TGAImage: public Image
{
public:
```

```
    TGAImage() {}
    TGAImage(Image& img) : Image(img) {}

    ~TGAImage() {}

    virtual int read(const char* filename);
    virtual int write(const char* filename)
    { return 1;} // Do nothing for now

private:
// A structure for the file header
    struct TARGAHeader
    {
        char           offset;
        char           cmap_type;
        char           image_type;
        unsigned short cmap_start;
        unsigned short cmap_length;
        char           cmap_bits;
        unsigned short hoffset;
        unsigned short voffset;
        unsigned short width;
        unsigned short height;
        char           bits_per_pixel;
        char           flags;
    };
    TARGAHeader hdr;
};

#endif
```

The image's pixels come after the file header, one scan line after another. For 24-bit RGB color images, each pixel's color is stored in 3 bytes: first a byte for the blue (B) component, then the green (G), and then the red (R). (Yes, it is opposite of the red-green-blue RGB order that you might have expected.)

The `read` function in Listing 23.6 shows how to load a Targa 24-bit RGB color image into a DIB. The first task is to read the header of the Targa file and initialize the fields of a `BITMAPINFOHEADER` structure. Reading the actual image data is straightforward because Windows 24-bit DIBs use the same layout for image data as does the 24-bit Targa format, except that DIBs expect the image data bottom-to-top with the pixels of the last scan line appearing first. Another important point to note is that the number of bytes in each scan line of a DIB must be a multiple of 4. Thus, you may have to pad the scan lines of the Targa image to meet this requirement of a DIB.

Listing 23.6. TGAIMAGE.CPP. Implementation of the `TGAImage` class.

```
//-----------------------------------------------------------------
//  File: tgaimage.cpp
//
//  Image manipulation functions for 24-bit Targa TrueColor
//  images.
//-----------------------------------------------------------------
#include <fstream.h>
#include "tgaimage.h"
//-----------------------------------------------------------------
//  T G A I m a g e : : r e a d
//  Read a Targa image (only 24-bit TrueColor images handled)

int TGAImage::read(const char* filename)
{
// If there is an existing image, detach the image data
// before reading a new image
    if(imdata->p_dib != 0) detach();

// Open file for reading
    ifstream ifs(filename, ios::in | ios::binary);
    if(!ifs)
    {
// Error reading file. Return 0.
        return 0;
    }

// Read TARGA header
    ifs.read((unsigned char*)&hdr, sizeof(TARGAHeader));

// Check if image file format is acceptable
    if(hdr.cmap_type) return 0;  // We don't handle colormaps

// Allocate memory for the device independent bitmap (DIB)
// Note that the number of bytes in each line of a DIB image
// must be a multiple of 4.
    imdata->bytes_per_line = 3 * hdr.width;
```

```
    if(imdata->bytes_per_line % 4)
        imdata->bytes_per_line = 4 *
                      (imdata->bytes_per_line/4 + 1);

    imdata->p_dib = GlobalAllocPtr(GHND,
                        sizeof(BITMAPINFOHEADER) +
                   (long) imdata->bytes_per_line *
                               (long) hdr.height);

// If memory allocation fails, return 0
    if(imdata->p_dib == 0) return 0;

// Set up bitmap info header
    LPBITMAPINFOHEADER p_bminfo = (LPBITMAPINFOHEADER)imdata->p_dib;
    p_bminfo->biSize = sizeof(BITMAPINFOHEADER);
    p_bminfo->biWidth = hdr.width;
    p_bminfo->biHeight = hdr.height;
    p_bminfo->biPlanes = 1;
    p_bminfo->biBitCount = hdr.bits_per_pixel;
    p_bminfo->biCompression = BI_RGB;
    p_bminfo->biSizeImage = (long)hdr.height *
                            (long)imdata->bytes_per_line;
    p_bminfo->biXPelsPerMeter = 0;
    p_bminfo->biYPelsPerMeter = 0;
    p_bminfo->biClrUsed = 0;
    p_bminfo->biClrImportant = 0;

// Skip "offset" bytes from current position to find image
// data. Usually, offset is zero, in which case this call
// to seekg does nothing.

    ifs.seekg(hdr.offset, ios::cur);

// Load image data into the DIB. Note the DIB image must be
// stored "bottom to top" line order. That's why we position
// data at the end of the array so that the image can be
// stored backwards—from the last line to the first.
    unsigned char huge *data =
                 (unsigned char huge*)imdata->p_dib +
                          sizeof(BITMAPINFOHEADER) +
                    (unsigned long)(hdr.height - 1) *
              (unsigned long)(imdata->bytes_per_line);
```

continues

Listing 23.6. continued

```
// Need a buffer to read each line because the read function of
// the ifstream class does not work with huge pointers

    unsigned char *rbuf = new unsigned char[imdata->bytes_per_line];
    if(rbuf == NULL)
    {
        detach();
        return 0;
    }

    int i, j;
    unsigned short actual_bytes_per_line = 3*hdr.width;

// Pad part of rbuf beyond actual_bytes_per_line with zeros
    if(actual_bytes_per_line < imdata->bytes_per_line)
    {
        for(i = actual_bytes_per_line;
            i < imdata->bytes_per_line;
            i++) rbuf[i] = 0;
    }

// Now read the image data...
    for(i = 0; i < hdr.height; i++, data -= imdata->bytes_per_line)
    {
// Read a line of image data into the buffer
        ifs.read(rbuf, actual_bytes_per_line);

// Copy from buffer into DIB's image data area
        for(j = 0; j < actual_bytes_per_line; j++)
            data[j] = rbuf[j];
    }
    delete rbuf;
// Success!
    return 1;
}
```

PCXImage Class

The PCX file format was developed by ZSoft to store images created by the PC PaintBrush paint program. The name PCX comes from the file extension .PCX that is used for PC PaintBrush files. Here is the PCX file format:

- The file starts with a 128-byte header (described later). The header is followed by encoded scan lines of the image.
- Each scan line in the PCX file is created by first laying out the scan lines of individual bit planes one after another. Then the entire line is encoded using a run-length encoding scheme that works like this: if the two highest-order bits of a byte are set, the low-order six bits indicate how many times the following byte must be repeated. If the two highest-order bits are not both 1, the byte represents the bitmap data.

Examine the `read` function (Listing 23.8) of the `PCXImage` class to understand this better.

PCX File Header

As you can see from the declaration of the `PCXImage` class in Listing 23.7, the PCX file's header is represented by the following `PCXHeader` structure:

```
struct PCXHeader
{
    unsigned char   manufacturer;
    unsigned char   version;
    unsigned char   encoding;
    unsigned char   bits_per_pixel_per_plane;
    short           xmin;
    short           ymin;
    short           xmax;
    short           ymax;
    unsigned short  hresolution;
    unsigned short  vresolution;
    unsigned char   colormap[48];
    unsigned char   reserved;
    unsigned char   nplanes;
    unsigned short  bytes_per_line;
    short           palette_info;
    unsigned char   filler[58];    // Header is 128 bytes
};
```

Here are the meanings of some of the important fields of the PCX file header:

- `unsigned char manufacturer;` is always set to 0x0a for a valid PCX file. You can use this information to verify that a file contains a PCX format image.
- `unsigned char version;` indicates the version of PC PaintBrush that created the image file. If `bits_per_pixel_per_plane*nplanes` is 8 and `version` is greater than 5, the file has a 256-entry color palette (consisting of 256 RGB bytes occupying 256 x 3 = 768 bytes) appended at the end of the image.
- `unsigned char encoding;` should always be 1 to indicate that the image is stored using run-length encoding.
- `unsigned char bits_per_pixel_per_plane;` is the number of bits for each pixel in each bit plane. For instance, a 256-color image would have 1 bit plane with 8 bits per pixel per plane.
- `short xmin, ymin, xmax, ymax;` specify the dimensions of the image. The width is `(xmax - xmin + 1)` and the height is `(ymax - ymin + 1)`.
- `unsigned char colormap[48];` is a 16-entry colormap with a 3-byte RGB value per entry. This colormap is valid if `bits_per_pixel_per_plane*nplanes` is less than or equal to 4.
- `unsigned char nplanes;` is the number of bit planes.

The PCX file header is always 128 bytes long; therefore, you have to pad the structure with enough bytes to make the total size 128 bytes.

Listing 23.7. PCXIMAGE.H. Declaration of the `PCXImage` class.

```
//--------------------------------------------------------------
//  File: pcximage.h
//
//  Defines the PCXImage class representing PCX images.
//
//--------------------------------------------------------------
#if !defined(__PCXIMAGE_H)
#define __PCXIMAGE_H

#include "image.h"

class PCXImage: public Image
{
```

```
public:
    PCXImage() {}
    PCXImage(Image& img) : Image(img) {}

    ~PCXImage() {}

    virtual int read(const char* filename);
    virtual int write(const char* filename)
    { return 1;} // Do nothing for now

private:
// A structure for the file header
    struct PCXHeader
    {
        unsigned char   manufacturer;
        unsigned char   version;
        unsigned char   encoding;
        unsigned char   bits_per_pixel_per_plane;
        short           xmin;
        short           ymin;
        short           xmax;
        short           ymax;
        unsigned short  hresolution;
        unsigned short  vresolution;
        unsigned char   colormap[48];
        unsigned char   reserved;
        unsigned char   nplanes;
        unsigned short  bytes_per_line;
        short           palette_info;
        unsigned char   filler[58];   // Header is 128 bytes
    };
    PCXHeader hdr;
};

#endif
```

Reading a PCX File

Conceptually, reading the PCX file is simple—you read one byte at a time and repeat the following byte a specified number of times when the byte indicates run-length encoding. The early part of the `read` function in Listing 23.8 shows the loop that unpacks the PCX image by undoing the effect of run-length encoding. Written in C++-like pseudocode, the loop looks like this:

```
while (file has not ended)
{
    read a byte
    if(byte & 0xc0) // Are 2 high bits set?
    {
        count = byte & 0x3f;
        copy the byte count number of times
    }
    else
        copy the byte once
}
```

Decoding the run-length encoding is the easy part of reading a PCX image. Because of the design of our `Image` class hierarchy, you also have to convert the PCX image from its bit plane structure to a packed format Windows device-independent bitmap. The code to this conversion is somewhat messy because to store the PCX image as a DIB, you have to combine bits from each bit plane of the PCX image into a packed format representing a pixel's value. Figure 23.5 illustrates the process of converting a PCX image into a Windows DIB format.

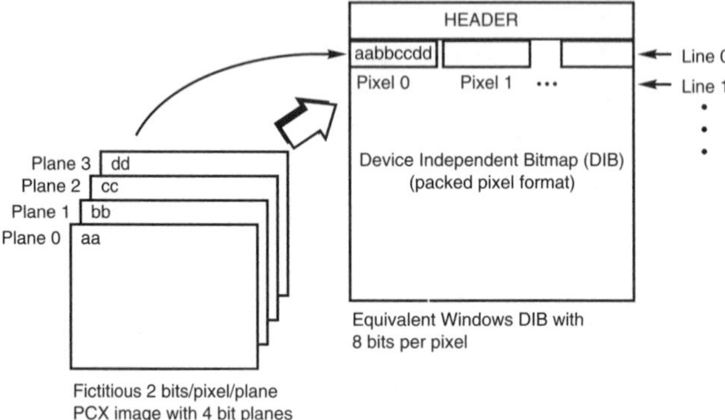

Figure 23.5. Converting a PCX image into a Windows DIB.

The first step in converting the image to a DIB is to initialize the `BITMAPINFOHEADER` that precedes the image in a DIB. The `BITMAPINFOHEADER` structure is defined in `<Windows.h>` as the following:

```
typedef struct tagBITMAPINFOHEADER
{
    DWORD   biSize;          // Size of this structure
    LONG    biWidth;         // Width in pixels
    LONG    biHeight;        // Height in pixels
    WORD    biPlanes;        // Number of planes (always 1)
    WORD    biBitCount;      // Bits per pixel
    DWORD   biCompression;   // One of: BI_RGB, BI_RLE4 or
                             //         BI_RLE8
    DWORD   biSizeImage;     // Number of bytes in image
    LONG    biXPelsPerMeter; // Horizontal resolution
    LONG    biYPelsPerMeter; // Vertical resolution
    DWORD   biClrUsed;       // Number of colors used
    DWORD   biClrImportant;  // How many colors important?
} BITMAPINFOHEADER;
typedef BITMAPINFOHEADER*      PBITMAPINFOHEADER;
typedef BITMAPINFOHEADER FAR* LPBITMAPINFOHEADER;
```

The `read` function of the `PCXImage` class intializes these fields of the `BITMAPINFOHEADER` with information derived from the header of the PCX file.

After setting the `BITMAPINFOHEADER`, the `read` function initializes the color palette that follows the `BITMAPINFOHEADER` in a DIB. The color palette consists of an array of `RGBQUAD` structures, each with the following fields:

```
typedef struct tagRGBQUAD
{
    BYTE    rgbBlue;     // Intensity of blue component (0-255)
    BYTE    rgbGreen;    // Intensity of green component (0-255)
    BYTE    rgbRed;      // Intensity of red component (0-255)
    BYTE    rgbReserved;// Reserved (set to zero)
} RGBQUAD;
```

Each `RGBQUAD` structure defines an RGB color for an entry in the color palette.

Once the color palette is initialized, the `read` function proceeds to convert the PCX bit planes into a packed pixel format image representing a DIB. The pseudocode for this operation looks like the following (a *mask* is a bit-pattern used to extract selected bits from an 8-bit byte or a 16-bit word):

```
Create a mask with the high-order
    "bits_per_pixel_per_plane" bits set
Loop over (all lines in the PCX image)
{
```

```
    Loop over (all bytes in each plane)
    {
        Loop over ("8/bits_per_pixel_per_plane" times)
        {
            Loop over (all planes)
            {
                Pack bits from each plane into a byte
                If all 8 bits are filled, copy byte to
                appropriate location in DIB
            }
            Shift mask to right by
           "bits_per_pixel_per_plane" bits
        }
    }
}
```

To understand this operation, you should carefully study the corresponding loops in the `read` function shown in Listing 23.8. As you can see from the sample programs in the companion disk, the conversion from the PCX format to DIB works perfectly for monochrome, 4-, 8-, and even 24-bit color images.

Listing 23.8. PCXIMAGE.CPP. Implementation of the `PCXImage` class.

```
//--------------------------------------------------------------
//  File: pcximage.cpp
//
//  Image manipulation functions for PCX format images.
//--------------------------------------------------------------
#include <fstream.h>
#include "pcximage.h"
//--------------------------------------------------------------
//  P C X I m a g e : : r e a d
//  Read a PCX image.

int PCXImage::read(const char* filename)
{
// If there is an existing image, detach the image data
// before reading a new image
    if(imdata->p_dib != 0) detach();

// Open file for reading
```

```
    ifstream ifs(filename, ios::in | ios::binary);
    if(!ifs)
    {
// Error reading file. Return 0.
        return 0;
    }

// Read PCX header
    ifs.read((unsigned char*)&hdr, sizeof(PCXHeader));

// Check if image file format is acceptable
    if(hdr.manufacturer != 0x0a) return 0;

// We only handle 1, 4, 8, or 24-bit images
    int bits_per_pixel = hdr.nplanes *
                         hdr.bits_per_pixel_per_plane;

    if(bits_per_pixel != 1 &&
       bits_per_pixel != 4 &&
       bits_per_pixel != 8 &&
       bits_per_pixel != 24) return 0;

    unsigned short image_width = hdr.xmax - hdr.xmin + 1;
    unsigned short image_height = hdr.ymax - hdr.ymin + 1;

// Allocate space where the PCX image will be unpacked.
// Read in PCX image into this area.
    long pcx_image_size = (long) hdr.nplanes *
                          (long) image_height *
                          (long) hdr.bytes_per_line;
    unsigned char huge *image = new unsigned char huge[
                                          pcx_image_size];
    if(image == NULL) return 0;

// Decode run-length encoded image data

    int i, byte, count;
    unsigned long pos = 0L;

    while((byte = ifs.get()) != EOF)
    {
        if((byte & 0xc0) == 0xc0)
```

continues

Listing 23.8. continued

```
            {
                count = byte & 0x3f;
                if((byte = ifs.get()) != EOF)
                {
                    for(i = 0; i < count; i++)
                    {
                        if(pos >= pcx_image_size) break;
                        image[pos] = byte;
                        pos++;
                    }
                }
            }
            else
            {
                if(pos >= pcx_image_size) break;
                image[pos] = byte;
                pos++;
            }
        }

// Allocate memory for the device independent bitmap (DIB)
// Note that the number of bytes in each line of a DIB image
// must be a multiple of 4.

    unsigned short bytes_per_line_per_plane = (image_width *
                         hdr.bits_per_pixel_per_plane + 7) / 8;

    unsigned short actual_bytes_per_line = (image_width *
                                             hdr.nplanes *
                         hdr.bits_per_pixel_per_plane + 7) / 8;
    imdata->bytes_per_line = actual_bytes_per_line;

    if(imdata->bytes_per_line % 4)
        imdata->bytes_per_line = 4 *
                        (imdata->bytes_per_line/4 + 1);

// Make room for a palette
    int palettesize = 16;
    if(bits_per_pixel == 1) palettesize = 2;
    if(hdr.version >= 5 && bits_per_pixel > 4)
    {
```

```
// Go back 769 bytes from the end of the file
        ifs.seekg(-769L, ios::end);
        if(ifs.get() == 12)
        {
// There is a 256-color palette following this byte
            palettesize = 256;
        }
    }
// If image has more than 256 colors then there is no palette
    if(bits_per_pixel > 8) palettesize = 0;

    imdata->p_dib = GlobalAllocPtr(GHND,
                        sizeof(BITMAPINFOHEADER) +
                   palettesize * sizeof(RGBQUAD) +
                   (long) imdata->bytes_per_line *
                              (long) image_height);

// If memory allocation fails, return 0
    if(imdata->p_dib == 0) return 0;

// Set up bitmap info header
    LPBITMAPINFOHEADER p_bminfo = (LPBITMAPINFOHEADER)imdata->p_dib;
    p_bminfo->biSize = sizeof(BITMAPINFOHEADER);
    p_bminfo->biWidth = image_width;
    p_bminfo->biHeight = image_height;
    p_bminfo->biPlanes = 1;
    p_bminfo->biBitCount = hdr.bits_per_pixel_per_plane *
                           hdr.nplanes;
    p_bminfo->biCompression = BI_RGB;
    p_bminfo->biSizeImage = (long)image_height *
                            (long)imdata->bytes_per_line;
    p_bminfo->biXPelsPerMeter = 0;
    p_bminfo->biYPelsPerMeter = 0;
    p_bminfo->biClrUsed = 0;
    p_bminfo->biClrImportant = 0;

// Set up the color palette
    if(palettesize > 0)
    {
        RGBQUAD *palette = (RGBQUAD*) ((LPSTR)imdata->p_dib
                                 + sizeof(BITMAPINFOHEADER));
```

continues

Listing 23.8. continued

```
            int palindex;
            for(palindex = 0; palindex < palettesize; palindex++)
            {
                if(palettesize == 256)
                {
// Read palette from file
                    palette[palindex].rgbRed       = ifs.get();
                    palette[palindex].rgbGreen     = ifs.get();
                    palette[palindex].rgbBlue      = ifs.get();
                    palette[palindex].rgbReserved  = 0;
                }
                if(palettesize == 16)
                {
// 16-color palette from PCX header
                    palette[palindex].rgbRed =
                                  hdr.colormap[3*palindex];
                    palette[palindex].rgbGreen =
                                  hdr.colormap[3*palindex+1];
                    palette[palindex].rgbBlue =
                                  hdr.colormap[3*palindex+2];
                    palette[palindex].rgbReserved  = 0;
                }
                if(palettesize == 2)
                {
// Set up palette for black and white images
                    palette[palindex].rgbRed =
                                  palindex * 255;
                    palette[palindex].rgbGreen =
                                  palindex * 255;
                    palette[palindex].rgbBlue =
                                  palindex * 255;
                    palette[palindex].rgbReserved  = 0;
                }
            }
        }

// Load image data into the DIB. Note the DIB image must be
// stored "bottom to top" line order. That's why we position
// data at the end of the array so that the image can be
// stored backwards—from the last line to the first.
        unsigned char huge *data =
```

```
                    (unsigned char huge*)imdata->p_dib +
                              sizeof(BITMAPINFOHEADER) +
                         palettesize * sizeof(RGBQUAD) +
                       (unsigned long)(image_height - 1) *
                (unsigned long)(imdata->bytes_per_line);

// Define a macro to access bytes in the PCX image according
// to specified line and plane index.

    int lineindex, byteindex, planeindex;

#define bytepos(lineindex,planeindex,byteindex)  \
            ((long)(lineindex)*(long)hdr.bytes_per_line* \
             (long)hdr.nplanes + \
             (long)(planeindex)*(long)hdr.bytes_per_line + \
             (long)(byteindex))

// Construct packed pixels out of decoded PCX image.

    unsigned short onebyte, bits_copied, loc, few_bits,
        k, bbpb = 8/hdr.bits_per_pixel_per_plane;

// Build a mask to pick out bits from each byte of the PCX image
    unsigned short himask = 0x80, mask;
    if(hdr.bits_per_pixel_per_plane > 1)
        for(i = 0; i < hdr.bits_per_pixel_per_plane - 1;
            i++) himask = 0x80 | (himask >> 1);

    for(lineindex = 0; lineindex < image_height;
        lineindex++, data -= imdata->bytes_per_line)
    {
        if(actual_bytes_per_line < imdata->bytes_per_line)
            for(loc = actual_bytes_per_line;
                loc < imdata->bytes_per_line; loc++)
                                        data[loc] = 0;
        loc = 0;
        onebyte = 0;
        bits_copied = 0;
        for(byteindex = 0;
            byteindex < bytes_per_line_per_plane;
            byteindex++)
        {
```

continues

Listing 23.8. continued

```
            for(k = 0, mask = himask; k < bbpb;
                k++, mask >>= hdr.bits_per_pixel_per_plane)
            {
// Go through all scan line for all planes and copy bits into
// the data array
                for(planeindex = 0; planeindex < hdr.nplanes;
                    planeindex++)
                {
                    few_bits = image[bytepos(lineindex,
                               planeindex, byteindex)] & mask;

// Shift the selcted bits to the most significant position
                    if(k > 0) few_bits <<=
                                (k*hdr.bits_per_pixel_per_plane);

// OR the bits with current pixel after shifting them right
                    if(bits_copied > 0)
                            few_bits >>= bits_copied;

                    onebyte |= few_bits;
                    bits_copied += hdr.bits_per_pixel_per_plane;

                    if(bits_copied >= 8)
                    {
                        data[loc] = onebyte;
                        loc++;
                        bits_copied = 0;
                        onebyte = 0;
                    }
                }
            }
        }
    }
    delete image;

// Success!
    return 1;
}
```

GIFImage Class

The Graphics Interchange Format, commonly referred to as GIF (and pronounced "jif"), was developed by CompuServe, Inc. for efficient storage and transmission of raster images. A GIF file is organized into blocks, and there may be more than one graphic image in a file. A GIF file has the following overall structure:

- The file starts with a 6-byte header that may be represented by the following structure:

  ```
  struct GIFHeader
  {
      char  signature[3]; // Should contain: "GIF"
      char  version[3];   // "87a" or "89a"
  };
  ```

  The first three bytes of the header contain the letters `GIF`, and the next three characters denote the version of GIF reader required to decode the file.

- Next comes the logical screen descriptor that provides information about the image, such as the size and number of bits per pixel. The following structure describes the logical screen descriptor:

  ```
  struct LogicalScreenDescriptor
  {
      unsigned short  width;
      unsigned short  height;
      unsigned char   flags;
      unsigned char   bgcolor;
      unsigned char   aspect_ratio;
  };
  ```

  If the most significant bit of the `flags` field is set, the GIF file includes a color table. This color table is called the global color table because it applies to all images contained in the GIF file.

- An array of RGB values denoting the global color table appears next, provided that the presence of the color table is indicated by a 1 in the most significant bit of the `flags` field in the `LogicalScreenDescriptor` structure.

- The rest of the file contains a series of blocks. The first byte of each block identifies the type of the block. One of the most important blocks is the image descriptor block that starts with a comma (0x2c) and contains information about the image about to follow. Here is a structure that represents the information contained in an image descriptor block:

```
struct ImageInfo
{
    unsigned short left;    // Position of image
    unsigned short top;     // (often ignored)
    unsigned short width;   // Size of image
    unsigned short height;
    unsigned char  flags;   // Indicates presence of
                            // color table
};
```

As with the `LogicalScreenDescriptor` structure, a 1 in the most significant bit of the `flags` field in the `ImageInfo` structure indicates that another color table, known as the local color table, follows this block.

If there is a local color table, the table appears next in the GIF file. A single byte follows the local color table. The value in this byte indicates the number of bits needed to represent an actual pixel value of the image. For example, this byte is 8 for a 256-color image because 8 bits can express any value between 0 and 255. This byte determines the initial code size used by the LZW compression algorithm (discussed later).

Next comes the pixel values of the image stored in a sequence of blocks with, at most, 255 bytes in each block. These values are stored in a compressed format encoded using the LZW algorithm with variable-length codes:

- If the GIF file contains multiple images, the sequence of image descriptor and image data blocks is repeated.
- A trailer block containing a single byte with the value 0x3b marks the end of the GIF data stream in the file.

In addition to the image blocks, there are a large number of GIF extension blocks. The `GIFImage` class, shown in Listings 23.9 and 23.10, does not interpret any of these extension blocks. Also, there are two versions of GIF—GIF87a and GIF89a. The `GIFImage` class of Listings 23.9 and 23.10 handle both versions of GIF files.

Listing 23.9. GIFIMAGE.H. Declaration of the `GIFImage` class.

```
//-------------------------------------------------------------
//  File: GIFimage.h
//
//  Defines the GIFImage class representing GIF images.
//
```

```
//  CompuServe requires the following statement in software that
//  uses the GIF image format:
//
//    "The Graphics Interchange Format(c) is the Copyright
//     property of CompuServe Incorporated. GIF(sm) is a
//     Service Mark property of CompuServe Incorporated."
//
//-----------------------------------------------------------------
#if !defined(__GIFIMAGE_H)
#define __GIFIMAGE_H

#include "image.h"

#define HAS_CT       0x80
#define INTERLACED  0x40
#define CTSIZE(x)   (x & 0x07)

#define GIF_IMGSTART ','
#define GIF_EXTSTART '!'
#define GIF_TRAILER  ';'
#define GIF_COMMENT  0xfe

#define GIF_MAXCODE   12
#define GIF_TBLSIZE   4096


class GIFImage: public Image
{
public:
    GIFImage();
    GIFImage(Image& img) : Image(img) {}

    ~GIFImage();

    virtual int read(const char* filename);
    virtual int write(const char* filename)
    { return 1;} // Do nothing for now

    void process_gif(ifstream &ifs,
                     unsigned char huge *image);
    void add_to_image(unsigned char huge *image,
                      unsigned short pixval);
```

continues

Listing 23.9. continued

```
private:
// Structures for GIF blocks
    struct GIFHeader
    {
        char   signature[3]; // Should contain: "GIF"
        char   version[3];   // "87a" or "89a"
    };

    struct LogicalScreenDescriptor
    {
        unsigned short   width;
        unsigned short   height;
        unsigned char    flags;
        unsigned char    bgcolor;
        unsigned char    aspect_ratio;
    };

    struct ImageInfo
    {
        unsigned short left;
        unsigned short top;
        unsigned short width;
        unsigned short height;
        unsigned char  flags;
    };

// This array is used to store decoded GIF image
    unsigned char huge     *gif_image;

    GIFHeader                hdr;
    LogicalScreenDescriptor lsdesc;
    ImageInfo                iminfo;
    unsigned short           interlaced;
    unsigned short           palettesize;
    unsigned short           bits_per_pixel;
    unsigned short           init_code_size;
    unsigned short           code_size;
    unsigned short           clear_code;
    unsigned short           eoi_code;
    unsigned short           max_code;
    unsigned short           free_code;
    unsigned short           curcode;
```

```
    unsigned short          oldcode;
    unsigned short          read_mask;
    unsigned short          data_mask;
    unsigned short          pixel;
    unsigned short          *prefix;
    unsigned char           *suffix;
    unsigned char           *stack;
    unsigned short          istk;    // Stack index
    unsigned short          pass;    // For interlaced images
    unsigned short          x, y;    // Image coordinates
};

#endif
```

Decoding LZW Compressed Data

LZW compression refers to the Lempel-Ziv and Welch compression algorithm that replaces repetitive patterns of data with a value (a *code*) that requires fewer bits than the original data. Actually, the compression scheme used in GIF files is a modified version of the original LZW algorithm with the following enhancements:

- GIF's LZW compression uses variable-length codes using up to a maximum of 12 bits for the codes.
- The LZW compression scheme in GIF uses a unique code (called the *clear code*) that starts the compression process anew whenever the number of bits in the code exceeds 12.

See the "Further Reading" section at the end of this book for references to the original LZW algorithm.

The LZW compression scheme is conceptually simple. The encoder uses a table of strings to keep track of sequences of symbols it encounters in the data stream and to assign a code to each unique string. The code for a string is the index of the string in the table. Initially, the string table contains as many entries as there are symbols. The encoder maintains, in what is known as the current *prefix*, a string of symbols that it is processing at any time. The encoder starts by initializing the prefix to an empty string. Then it enters a loop where it reads the input symbols one at a time into the current *suffix*, which is the most recently read symbol. Next the encoder treats as the *current string* the combination of the current suffix appended to the current prefix and searches the string table for the string. If it finds the string, the encoder appends the current suffix symbol to the prefix and reads the next symbol from the input data stream. If the encoder cannot find the string in the table, it adds the string to the table, sends the code for the current prefix to the output stream, and copies the current suffix symbol to the current prefix. Then the encoder repeats the loop again.

One way to understand LZW compression is to encode a sample input data stream. Assume that the data stream is made up of the four symbols 0, 1, 2, and 3. Thus, the initial string table will contain 0, 1, 2, and 3 as the entries 0 through 3, respectively. According to the GIF specification, codes 4 and 5 are used to represent the clear code and the *end-of-information (EOI) code.* Now consider the 16-symbol input stream `0101010111010100`. Table 23.1 shows the string table, the prefix, the suffix, and the output code as the encoder processes the characters from the input stream.

Table 23.1. LZW encoding according to the GIF convention.

Input data = 0101010111010100

Code	String	Prefix	Suffix	Output
0	0			
1	1			
2	2			
3	3			
4	Clear code			
5	EOI code			
6	01	0	1	0
7	10	1	0	1
8	010	01	0	6
9	0101	010	1	8
10	11	1	1	1
11	110	11	0	10
12	01010	0101	0	9
13	00	0	0	0
		0	<end>	0

As you can see from Table 23.1, the 16 symbols `0101010111010100` are encoded into 9 codes: `0 1 6 8 1 10 9 0 0`. All that remains is to represent each of these values in terms of a specified number of bits—this is the so-called *code size*—and pack the bits into a series of bytes. GIF's LZW encoding scheme starts with the code size set to one more than the number of bits required to represent any symbol in the data stream. For instance, if there are four symbols, you need 2 bits to represent the symbol values (0 through 3). Then the GIF encoder starts with a code size of 3 bits, which means that once the code reaches 8, the encoder has to increase the code size by 1 bit. This process of increasing the code size goes on until the code size is about to reach 13. At that point, the GIF encoder sends a clear code to the output stream and then starts encoding anew with the original code size.

To understand the encoding process, consult Table 23.1 as you study the following C++-like pseudocode that describes the LZW encoding of an input data stream:

```
current_prefix = empty string
while (file has not ended)
{
    current_suffix = next character from input stream
    current_string =  Concatenation of current_prefix
                      and current_suffix
    if(current_string is in string table)
    {
        Append current_suffix to current_prefix
    }
    else
    {
        Add current_string to string table.

        Send code corresponding to current_prefix to
        output stream.

        current_prefix = current_suffix
    }
}
Send current_prefix to output stream.
```

The decoding process is a bit harder to see. Although the encoder's output does not include the string table that was used during the encoding process, there is enough information in the encoded data stream for the decoder to construct the string table on the fly.

Like the encoder, the decoder starts with a string table that is initialized with the basic symbols. In a GIF file, the byte preceding an image descriptor block contains the information needed to initialize the string table. That byte has the number of bits needed to represent the symbols, and the LZW code size is one more than the number of bits.

The decoder reads the first code from the GIF file's image data. This code is guaranteed to be one of the possible symbol values (as opposed to a value that corresponds to a sequence of symbols). The decoder sends the first code directly to the output. It saves the code in a variable. Let us call it `old_code`, for later use.

Next, the decoder begins a loop where it reads a new code from the input. If this code is already present in the string table, the decoder sends to the output the string corresponding to the code and sets as prefix the string corresponding to `old_code`. It sets as suffix the first character of the string corresponding to the current code and adds to the string table (at the next available index) the string constructed by concatenating the prefix and the suffix. If the current code is not in the string table, the decoder picks as prefix the string corresponding to `old_code` and uses as suffix the first character of the prefix. Then the decoder constructs a new string by appending the suffix to the prefix, sends this string to the output, and adds the string to the string table. Finally, the decoder copies the current code to the `old_code` variable and continues with the loop.

The decoding process continues until the decoder reads an EOI code from the input. Also, when the decoder reads a clear code, it clears the string table and resets its internal variables to their initial states.

Reading GIF Files

The key to reading and interpreting a GIF file is in implementing the LZW decompression algorithm. Although the previous section provides a brief description of the decoding process, you have to carefully study the implementation of the `read` and the `process_gif` functions in Listing 23.10 for the details. As you can see from Listing 23.10, the `process_gif` function reads the compressed image data, one block at a time. Then the function extracts the number of bits needed to construct the current code. Once a code is ready, `process_gif` applies the previous section's decoding algorithm to the code. In addition to a prefix and a suffix, `process_gif` uses a stack to construct the string of symbols corresponding to a code.

After the image data is decoded, you have to convert this data into a Windows DIB because that is how images are maintained internally in the `Image` class hierarchy. This conversion process is similar to the one used in the `PCXImage` class. Essentially, the conversion is nothing more than copying the GIF image data into the appropriate bytes of a Windows DIB. You should study the last part of the `read` function (Listing 23.10) for further details.

Listing 23.10. GIFIMAGE.CPP. Implementation of the `GIFImage` class.

```
//-----------------------------------------------------------------
//  File: gifimage.cpp
//
//  Image manipulation functions for GIF format images.
//
//  CompuServe requires the following statement in software that
//  uses the GIF image format:
//
//    "The Graphics Interchange Format(c) is the Copyright
//     property of CompuServe Incorporated. GIF(sm) is a
//     Service Mark property of CompuServe Incorporated."
//
//-----------------------------------------------------------------
#include <fstream.h>
#include <string.h>
#include "gifimage.h"

//-----------------------------------------------------------------
// GIFImage:: G I F I m a g e
// Constructor for the GIFImage class

GIFImage::GIFImage() : palettesize(0), x(0), y(0),
    pass(1), oldcode(0), interlaced(0), pixel(0),
    gif_image(NULL), istk(0), prefix(NULL), suffix(NULL),
    stack(NULL)
{
}
//-----------------------------------------------------------------
// GIFImage:: ~ G I F I m a g e
// Destructor for the GIFImage class

GIFImage::~GIFImage()
{
    if(prefix != NULL) delete prefix;
    if(suffix != NULL) delete suffix;
    if(stack != NULL) delete stack;
    if(gif_image != NULL) delete gif_image;
}
//-----------------------------------------------------------------
```

continues

Listing 23.10. continued

```
//  G I F I m a g e : : r e a d
//  Read a GIF image.

int GIFImage::read(const char* filename)
{
    prefix = new unsigned short[GIF_TBLSIZE];
    suffix = new unsigned char[GIF_TBLSIZE];
    stack = new unsigned char[GIF_TBLSIZE];
    istk = 0;

// If the prefix, suffix, and stack arrays are not allocated
// successfully, do nothing.
    if(prefix == NULL || suffix == NULL || stack == NULL)
        return 0;

// Buffer to hold a block of image data from the GIF file.
    unsigned char buf[256];

// If there is an existing image, detach the image data
// before reading a new image
    if(imdata->p_dib != 0) detach();

// Open file for reading
    ifstream ifs(filename, ios::in | ios::binary);
    if(!ifs)
    {
// Error reading file. Return 0.
        return 0;
    }

// Read GIF header
    ifs.read((unsigned char*)&hdr, sizeof(GIFHeader));
// Check if image file format is acceptable
    if(strncmp(hdr.signature, "GIF", 3) != 0 &&
               hdr.version[0] != '8') return 0;

// Read the logical screen descriptor
    ifs.read((unsigned char*)&lsdesc,
              sizeof(LogicalScreenDescriptor));

// If a global color table is present, read it.
```

```
    RGBTRIPLE *ctbl = NULL;
    if(lsdesc.flags & HAS_CT)
    {
        bits_per_pixel = CTSIZE(lsdesc.flags) + 1;
        palettesize = 1 << bits_per_pixel;
        data_mask = palettesize - 1;
        ctbl = new RGBTRIPLE[palettesize];
        if(ctbl == NULL) return 0;

        ifs.read((unsigned char*)ctbl,
                   palettesize * sizeof(RGBTRIPLE));
    }

// Next comes a series of graphics blocks or special-purpose
// blocks
    int byte = 0, read_an_image = 0;
    while(!read_an_image &&
          (byte = ifs.get()) != GIF_TRAILER)
    {
// Locate an image descriptor and read the image data
        switch(byte)
        {
            case GIF_EXTSTART:
// Skip extension blocks
                {
                    int c = ifs.get();
                    if(c == GIF_COMMENT)
                    {
                        while((c = ifs.get()) != 0)
                            ifs.read(buf, c);
                    }
                    else
                    {
                        int blksize = ifs.get();
                        ifs.read(buf, blksize);
                        while((c = ifs.get()) != 0)
                            ifs.read(buf, c);
                    }
                }
                break;

            case GIF_IMGSTART:
```

continues

Listing 23.10. continued

```
// Read GIF image information
                ifs.read((unsigned char*)&iminfo,
                         sizeof(ImageInfo));
                if(iminfo.flags & INTERLACED)
                {
                    interlaced = 1;
                }

// Allocate memory for the GIF image and read in GIF image
// into this array
                long GIF_image_size = (long) iminfo.width *
                                      (long) iminfo.height;
                gif_image = new unsigned char
                                huge[GIF_image_size];
                if(gif_image == NULL)
                {
                    if(ctbl != NULL) delete ctbl;
                    return 0;
                }

// Read local color table, if any
                if(iminfo.flags & HAS_CT)
                {
                    bits_per_pixel = CTSIZE(iminfo.flags) + 1;
                    palettesize = 1 << bits_per_pixel;
                    data_mask = palettesize - 1;
                    if(ctbl != NULL) delete ctbl;
                    ctbl = new RGBTRIPLE[palettesize];
                    if(ctbl == NULL) return 0;
                    ifs.read((unsigned char*)ctbl,
                             palettesize * sizeof(RGBTRIPLE));
                }
// Next byte is the initial number of bits used for LZW codes
                init_code_size = ifs.get();

                if(init_code_size < 2 || init_code_size > 8)
                {
                    if(ctbl != NULL) delete ctbl;
                    return 0;
                }
                clear_code = 1 << init_code_size;
```

```
                eoi_code = clear_code + 1;
                free_code = clear_code + 2;

// The GIF specification says that, for decompression, the code
// size should be one bit longer than the initial code size.
                code_size = init_code_size + 1;

// Bit mask needed to extract data bits corresponding to the
// code size.
                max_code = 1 << code_size;
                read_mask = max_code - 1;
// Process the encoded data stream from the file.
                process_gif(ifs, gif_image);
                read_an_image = 1;
                break;
            }
        }

// Allocate memory for the device independent bitmap (DIB)
// Note that the number of bytes in each line of a DIB image
// must be a multiple of 4.

    unsigned short actual_bytes_per_line = (iminfo.width *
                                    bits_per_pixel + 7) / 8;

    imdata->bytes_per_line = actual_bytes_per_line;

    if(imdata->bytes_per_line % 4)
        imdata->bytes_per_line = 4 *
                  (imdata->bytes_per_line/4 + 1);

    imdata->p_dib = GlobalAllocPtr(GHND,
                      sizeof(BITMAPINFOHEADER) +
                 palettesize * sizeof(RGBQUAD) +
                 (long) imdata->bytes_per_line *
                            (long) iminfo.height);

// If memory allocation fails, return 0
    if(imdata->p_dib == 0) return 0;

// Set up bitmap info header
    LPBITMAPINFOHEADER p_bminfo = (LPBITMAPINFOHEADER)imdata->p_dib;
```

continues

Listing 23.10. continued

```
    p_bminfo->biSize = sizeof(BITMAPINFOHEADER);
    p_bminfo->biWidth = iminfo.width;
    p_bminfo->biHeight = iminfo.height;
    p_bminfo->biPlanes = 1;
    p_bminfo->biBitCount = bits_per_pixel;
    p_bminfo->biCompression = BI_RGB;
    p_bminfo->biSizeImage = (long)iminfo.height *
                            (long)imdata->bytes_per_line;
    p_bminfo->biXPelsPerMeter = 0;
    p_bminfo->biYPelsPerMeter = 0;
    p_bminfo->biClrUsed = 0;
    p_bminfo->biClrImportant = 0;

// Set up the color palette
    if(palettesize > 0)
    {
        RGBQUAD *palette = (RGBQUAD*) ((LPSTR)imdata->p_dib
                              + sizeof(BITMAPINFOHEADER));

        int i;
        for(i = 0; i < palettesize; i++)
        {
// Load palette from the "ctbl" array (the colors get loaded
// in the wrong order in the ctbl array, hence the apparent
// mismatch of color names in the following statements).
            palette[i].rgbRed       = ctbl[i].rgbtBlue;
            palette[i].rgbGreen     = ctbl[i].rgbtGreen;
            palette[i].rgbBlue      = ctbl[i].rgbtRed;
            palette[i].rgbReserved  = 0;
        }
    }
    if(ctbl != NULL) delete ctbl;

// Load image data into the DIB. Note the DIB image must be
// stored "bottom to top" line order. That's why we position
// data at the end of the array so that the image can be
// stored backwards—from the last line to the first.
    unsigned char huge *data =
                (unsigned char huge*)imdata->p_dib +
                         sizeof(BITMAPINFOHEADER) +
                     palettesize * sizeof(RGBQUAD) +
```

```
                        (unsigned long)(iminfo.height - 1) *
                (unsigned long)(imdata->bytes_per_line);

// Define a macro to access bytes in the GIF image according
// to specified line and byte index.

    int lineindex, byteindex;

#define bytepos(lineindex,byteindex)  \
            ((long)(lineindex) * (long)iminfo.width + \
             (long)(byteindex))

// Construct packed pixels out of decoded GIF image.

    unsigned short onebyte, bits_copied, loc, few_bits, k,
                   bbpb = 8/bits_per_pixel;

    for(lineindex = 0; lineindex < iminfo.height;
        lineindex++, data -= imdata->bytes_per_line)
    {
        if(actual_bytes_per_line < imdata->bytes_per_line)
            for(loc = actual_bytes_per_line;
                loc < imdata->bytes_per_line; loc++)
                                         data[loc] = 0;
        loc = 0;
        onebyte = 0;
        bits_copied = 0;
        for(byteindex = 0; byteindex < iminfo.width;)
        {
            for(k = 0; k < bbpb; k++, byteindex++)
            {
                few_bits = gif_image[bytepos(lineindex,
                                 byteindex)];

// Shift the current value first
                if(k > 0) onebyte <<= bits_per_pixel;

// Then OR the new bits with current pixel
                onebyte |= few_bits;
                bits_copied += bits_per_pixel;

                if(bits_copied >= 8)
```

continues

Listing 23.10. continued

```
                    {
                        data[loc] = onebyte;
                        loc++;
                        bits_copied = 0;
                        onebyte = 0;
                    }
                }
            }
        }
// Delete arrays that are no longer needed
    delete gif_image;
    delete suffix;
    delete prefix;
    delete stack;
    gif_image = NULL;
    suffix = NULL;
    prefix = NULL;
    stack = NULL;

// Success!
    return 1;
}
//-------------------------------------------------------------------
// GIFImage:: p r o c e s s _ g i f
// Processes a LZW data stream from a GIF file. Decoded data is
// placed in "image" array.

void GIFImage::process_gif(ifstream &ifs,
                           unsigned char huge *image)
{
// Buffer to hold a block of image data from the GIF file.
    unsigned char buf[256];

    unsigned short count, input_code, bitpos = 0;
    unsigned long val = 0, tmp;

    for(count = ifs.get(); count > 0; count = ifs.get())
    {
// Read a block of data into the buffer
        ifs.read(buf, count);

// Process the contents of the buffer
```

```
        int i;
        for(i = 0; i < count; i++)
        {
            tmp = buf[i];
            val |= (tmp << bitpos);
            bitpos += 8;

            while(bitpos >= code_size)
            {
                curcode = val & read_mask;
                val >>= code_size;
                bitpos -= code_size;
                if(curcode == eoi_code) return;
                if(curcode == clear_code)
                {
                    free_code = (1 << init_code_size) + 2;
                    code_size = init_code_size + 1;
                    max_code = 1 << code_size;
                    read_mask = max_code - 1;
                    istk = 0;
                    oldcode = 0xffff;
                }
                else
                {
                    if(oldcode == 0xffff)
                    {
// First code, after initialization, is a raw pixel value
                        pixel = curcode & data_mask;
                        add_to_image(image, pixel);
                        oldcode = curcode;
                    }
                    else
                    {
                        input_code = curcode;
                        if(curcode >= free_code)
                        {
// Code is not in table yet. Save last character in stack
                            stack[istk++] = pixel;
                            curcode = oldcode;
                        }
                        while(curcode > data_mask)
                        {
```

continues

Listing 23.10. continued

```
// Save bytes corresponding to compression code in stack for
// later use.
                        stack[istk++] = suffix[curcode];
                        curcode = prefix[curcode];
                    }

                    pixel = curcode & data_mask;
                    stack[istk++] = pixel;

// Add decoded string of bytes to image
                    short j;
                    for(j = istk - 1; j >= 0; j--)
//                    while(--istk)
                    {
                        if(interlaced) add_to_image(image,
                                                    stack[j]);
                        else
                        {
                            image[(long)x + (long)iminfo.width *
(long)y] =
                                                     stack[j];
// Adjust the coordinates, if necessary
                            x++;
                            if(x == iminfo.width)
                            {
                                x = 0;
                                y++;
                            }
                        }
                    }
                    istk = 0;

// Add current information to decompression tables
                    prefix[free_code] = oldcode;
                    suffix[free_code] = pixel;
                    oldcode = input_code;

// Adjust code size, if necessary.
                    free_code++;
                    if(free_code >= max_code)
                    {
```

```
                    if(code_size < GIF_MAXCODE)
                    {
                        code_size++;
                        max_code *= 2;
                        read_mask = max_code - 1;
                    }
                }
            }
        }
    }
  }
 }
}
//---------------------------------------------------------------
// GIFImage:: a d d _ t o _ i m a g e
// Add a pixel to the image

void GIFImage::add_to_image(unsigned char huge *image,
                            unsigned short pixval)
{

    image[x + iminfo.width * y] = pixval;

// Adjust the coordinates
    x++;
    if(x == iminfo.width)
    {
        x = 0;
        if(!interlaced) y++;
        else
        {
            switch(pass)
            {
                case 1:  // Every 8th row, start at row 0
                    y += 8;
                    if(y >= iminfo.height)
                    {
                        y = 4;
                        pass++;
                    }
                    break;
```

continues

Listing 23.10. continued

```
                case 2:  // Every 8th row, start at row 4
                    y += 8;
                    if(y >= iminfo.height)
                    {
                        y = 2;
                        pass++;
                    }
                    break;

                case 3:  // Every 4th row, start at row 2
                    y += 4;
                    if(y >= iminfo.height)
                    {
                        y = 1;
                        pass++;
                    }
                    break;

                case 4:  // Every 2nd row, start at row 1
                    y += 2;
                    break;
            }
        }
    }
}
```

TIFImage Class

The Tagged Image File Format (TIFF) was jointly developed by Aldus Corporation and Microsoft Corporation as a versatile and extensible format for storing raster images. TIFF can handle black-and-white, grayscale, and color images well. TIFF also supports a variety of data compression schemes for the pixel values of an image.

The versatility of TIFF contributes to one of its major problems—very few TIFF readers (including the one shown in the `TIFImage` class) have the capability of decoding all the fields of a TIFF file. Thus, it is quite common for TIFF files created by one application to be nearly useless when loaded into another unrelated application. One reason for the problem in portability of TIFF images is the lack of support for some fields in the TIFF reader. The other reason is that TIFF allows proprietary data field formats and many vendors exploit this feature.

Despite these problems, TIFF is widely supported by desktop publishing and graphics software. Additionally, almost all scanner vendors support the TIFF format.

TIFF File Structure

Like GIF files, a TIFF file uses tagged fields to store the information. The file starts with a header and at least one directory called an Image File Directory (IFD). An IFD contains a number of 12-byte directory entries, each with information on a tagged field. The directory entry for a tagged field identifies the field with a tag (an integer value such as 256 for the `ImageWidth` tag), a constant identifying the data type, the length of the data, and the location of that field's data expressed as an offset from the beginning of the file. If a field's data fits in 4 bytes, the data is placed in the directory entry. Figure 23.6 shows the layout of a TIFF file.

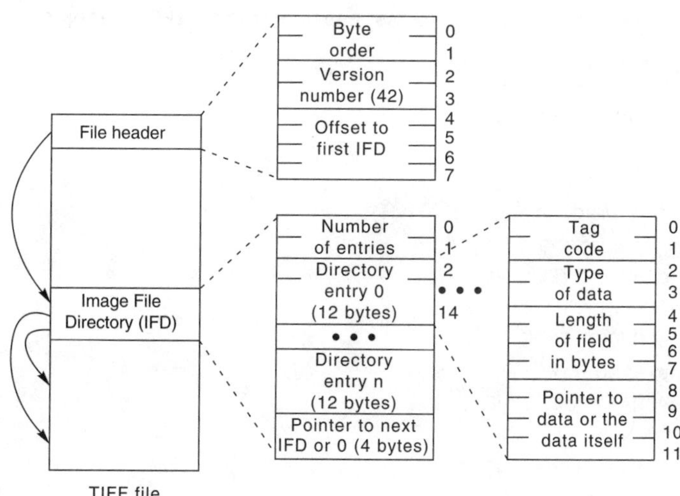

Figure 23.6. TIFF file structure.

The TIFF file header occupies 8 bytes. The first 2 bytes of the file control the interpretation of the data in the rest of the file—these 2 bytes indicate the byte order. These 2 bytes contain the ASCII characters `MM` or `II` to indicate Motorola or Intel byte order, respectively. The Intel byte order is often referred to as the *little-endian byte order*, where the bytes comprising a 16- or 32-bit value are stored in the least-to-most significant byte order. The Motorola or *big-endian byte order* stores the bytes for multibyte integers in the opposite order—from most significant to least significant.

The IFD starts with a 2-byte value that indicates the total number of entries in the directory. The directory entries come next. Each directory entry is a 12-byte structure with information about a tagged field (see Figure 23.6). The IFD ends with a 4-byte value that is either a pointer to the next IFD or a zero marking the end of the last IFD.

Listing 23.11 shows the file TIFIMAGE.H that declares the `TIFImage` class designed to read and interpret a TIFF file. The header file also defines symbolic names for a number of TIFF tags.

Listing 23.11. TIFIMAGE.H. Declaration of the `TIFImage` class.

```
//---------------------------------------------------------------
//  File: TIFimage.h
//
//  Defines the TIFImage class representing TIFF images.
//
//---------------------------------------------------------------
#if !defined(__TIFIMAGE_H)
#define __TIFIMAGE_H

#include "image.h"

#define BYTE_TYPE       1
#define ASCII_TYPE      2
#define SHORT_TYPE      3
#define LONG_TYPE       4
#define RATIONAL_TYPE   5

// TIFF tag types

#define BitsPerSample              258
#define ColorMap                   320
#define Compression                259
#define ImageLength                257
#define ImageWidth                 256
#define PhotometricInterpretation  262
#define PlanarConfiguration        284
#define RowsPerStrip               278
#define SamplesPerPixel            277
#define StripByteCounts            279
#define StripOffsets               273
```

```
class TIFImage: public Image
{
public:
    TIFImage();
    TIFImage(Image& img) : Image(img) {}

    ~TIFImage();

    virtual int read(const char* filename);
    virtual int write(const char* filename)
    { return 1;} // Do nothing for now

// Utility functions to read short and long integers
// from a TIFF file.
    unsigned short get_short(ifstream &ifs)
    {
        if(byteorder[0] == 'I')
            return((ifs.get() & 0xff) |
                   ((ifs.get() & 0xff) << 8));
        else
            return(((ifs.get() & 0xff) << 8) |
                    (ifs.get() & 0xff));
    }

    unsigned long get_long(ifstream &ifs)
    {
        if(byteorder[0] == 'I')
            return((unsigned long)(ifs.get() & 0xff)       |
                   ((unsigned long)(ifs.get() & 0xff) <<  8) |
                   ((unsigned long)(ifs.get() & 0xff) << 16) |
                   ((unsigned long)(ifs.get() & 0xff) << 24));
        else
            return((unsigned long)(ifs.get() & 0xff) << 24) |
                   ((unsigned long)(ifs.get() & 0xff) << 16) |
                   ((unsigned long)(ifs.get() & 0xff) <<  8) |
                   ((unsigned long)(ifs.get() & 0xff));
    }

// Function to read a row from the image file
    unsigned short read_row(ifstream &ifs);

private:
```

continues

Listing 23.11. continued

```
// This array is used to store the decoded TIFF image
    unsigned char huge *TIF_image;

    char              byteorder[2]; // "MM" or "II"
    short             version;      // Always decimal 42
    unsigned long     ifd;          // Offset to directory
    unsigned short    tag;          // Tag code
    unsigned short    type;         // Data type
    unsigned long     length;       // Number of bytes of data
    unsigned long     offset;       // Offset to data (or data)
    RGBTRIPLE         *ctbl;        // Color table
    unsigned short    image_width;
    unsigned short    image_height;
    unsigned short    rows_per_strip;
    unsigned long     byte_count;
    unsigned long     strip_offset;
    unsigned short    numstrips;
    unsigned short    samples_per_pixel;
    unsigned short    bits_per_sample;
    unsigned short    planar_config;
    unsigned short    compression;
    unsigned short    palettesize;
    unsigned short    bits_per_pixel;
    unsigned long     pos;
    unsigned short    bytes_per_line;
    unsigned short    bytes_per_strip_row;
    unsigned short    photometric;
};

#endif
```

Reading a TIFF File

The strategy for reading a TIFF file is to start with the first 2 bytes of the file header. These 2 bytes tell you the byte order, which controls how you interpret the 16- and 32-bit integer values in the TIFF file. The `read` function in Listing 23.12 follows this strategy.

Once you know the byte order, you can read the rest of the header and locate the first IFD from the offset stored there. Next, you should read all the directory entries in the IFD and gather information about each tagged field.

After you have read and collected information on all directory entries in an IFD, you can read the image data. The data is stored in strips of a specified number of rows. The value of the `Compression` tag determines how to decipher the image data. Here are some of the common values for the `Compression` tag:

```
1 = No compression, but the bits are packed tightly into arrays of bytes.
5 = LZW compression as in a GIF file.
32773 = Macintosh PackBits compression (a run-length encoding scheme).
```

The `read` function in Listing 23.12 can handle `Compression` tags 1 and 32773 only. However, you could reuse code from the `GIFImage` class (Listings 23.9 and 23.10) and handle the LZW compression as well.

As you can see from the read function in Listing 23.12, the pseudocode for unpacking the PackBits encoded data is the following:

```
Loop until all bytes are read
{
    Read a byte
    if(byte & 0x80)   // Is most significant bit set?
    {
        if(byte != 0x80) // Byte is not equal to 128
        {
            n = - byte + 1;
            Copy the next byte n times.
        }
        else
        {
            n = byte + 1;
            Copy the next byte n times.
        }
    }
}
```

Once the image data from the TIFF file is available, you have to copy the data into a Windows DIB format. At this point, the steps are identical to those used in copying an unpacked PCX image to a DIB. Thus, for this task, the `read` function of the `TIFImage` class uses the same code fragments as the `read` function of the `PCXImage` class.

Listing 23.12. TIFIMAGE.CPP. Implementation of the `TIFImage` class.

```
//--------------------------------------------------------------
//  File: tifimage.cpp
//
//  Image manipulation functions for TIFF format images.
//
//--------------------------------------------------------------
#include <fstream.h>
#include <string.h>
#include "tifimage.h"

//--------------------------------------------------------------
// TIFImage:: T I F I m a g e
// Constructor for the TIFImage class

TIFImage::TIFImage() : TIF_image(NULL), ctbl(NULL)
{
}
//--------------------------------------------------------------
// TIFImage:: ~ T I F I m a g e
// Destructor for the TIFImage class

TIFImage::~TIFImage()
{
    if(ctbl != NULL) delete ctbl;
    if(TIF_image != NULL) delete TIF_image;
}
//--------------------------------------------------------------
//  T I F I m a g e : : r e a d
//  Read a TIF image.

int TIFImage::read(const char* filename)
{
// If there is an existing image, detach the image data
// before reading a new image
    if(imdata->p_dib != 0) detach();

// Open file for reading
    ifstream ifs(filename, ios::in | ios::binary);
    if(!ifs)
    {
```

```
// Error reading file. Return 0.
        return 0;
    }
// Read the byteorder and version
    ifs.read((unsigned char*)byteorder, 2);
    version = get_short(ifs);

// Check if image file format is acceptable
    if(byteorder[0] != 'I' &&
       byteorder[0] != 'M' &&
       version != 42) return 0;

// Read the first image file directory and decode all the tags.
    ifd = get_long(ifs);

// Set the default values for some important parameters
    image_width = image_height = 0;
    bits_per_sample = 1;
    compression = 1; // assume no compression
    planar_config = 1;
    samples_per_pixel = 1;
    ifs.seekg(ifd, ios::beg);
    unsigned short nptr = get_short(ifs);
    short i;
    for(i = 0; i < nptr; i++)
    {
        tag = get_short(ifs);
        type = get_short(ifs);
        if(type == LONG_TYPE)
        {
            length = get_long(ifs);
            offset = get_long(ifs);
        }
        if(type == SHORT_TYPE)
        {
            length = (unsigned long)get_short(ifs);
            get_short(ifs);
            offset = (unsigned long)get_short(ifs);
            get_short(ifs);
        }

        switch(tag)
```

continues

Listing 23.12. continued

```
            {
                case BitsPerSample:
                    if(length > 1L)
                    {
                        streampos pos = ifs.tellg();
                        ifs.seekg(offset, ios::beg);
                        bits_per_sample = get_short(ifs);
                        ifs.seekg(pos, ios::beg);
                    }
                    else
                        bits_per_sample = offset;
                    break;

                case ColorMap:
                    {
                        streampos pos = ifs.tellg();
                        ifs.seekg(offset, ios::beg);
                        ctbl = new RGBTRIPLE[palettesize];
                        if(ctbl == NULL) return 0;
// Read color table
                        for(i = 0; i < palettesize; i++)
                            ctbl[i].rgbtRed = get_short(ifs);
                        for(i = 0; i < palettesize; i++)
                            ctbl[i].rgbtGreen = get_short(ifs);
                        for(i = 0; i < palettesize; i++)
                            ctbl[i].rgbtBlue = get_short(ifs);
                        ifs.seekg(pos, ios::beg);
                    }
                    break;

                case Compression:
                    compression = offset;
                    break;

                case ImageLength:
                    image_height = offset;
                    break;

                case ImageWidth:
                    image_width = offset;
                    break;
```

```
            case PhotometricInterpretation:
                photometric = offset;
                break;

            case PlanarConfiguration:
                planar_config = offset;
                break;

            case RowsPerStrip:
                if(type == SHORT_TYPE)
                    rows_per_strip = offset & 0xffff;
                else
                    rows_per_strip = offset;
                break;

            case SamplesPerPixel:
                samples_per_pixel = offset;
                break;

            case StripByteCounts:
                if(type == LONG_TYPE)
                    byte_count = offset;
                else
                    byte_count = offset & 0xffff;
                break;

            case StripOffsets:
                if(type == LONG_TYPE)
                    strip_offset = offset;
                else
                    strip_offset = (unsigned short)offset & 0xffff;
                numstrips = (unsigned short)length;
                break;
        }
    }

// Allocate space where the TIFF image will be prepared.
// Read in TIFF image "strips" into this array.

    unsigned short nplanes;
    unsigned short bits_per_pixel_per_plane = bits_per_sample;
    if(planar_config == 1)
```

continues

Listing 23.12. continued

```
        {
            nplanes = 1;
        }
        else
        {
            nplanes = samples_per_pixel;
        }

// We only handle 1, 4, 8, or 24-bit images
        bits_per_pixel = nplanes * bits_per_pixel_per_plane;
        palettesize = 1 << bits_per_pixel;

        if(bits_per_pixel != 1 &&
           bits_per_pixel != 4 &&
           bits_per_pixel != 8 &&
           bits_per_pixel != 24) return 0;

        bytes_per_strip_row = ((long)bits_per_sample *
                               (long)image_width + 7) / 8;
        bytes_per_line = ((long)bits_per_pixel *
                          (long)image_width + 7) / 8;

        long tiff_image_size = (long) nplanes *
                               (long) image_height *
                               (long) bytes_per_line;
        TIF_image = new unsigned char huge[tiff_image_size];

        if(TIF_image == NULL) return 0;

// Now load image data, decoding run-length encoded data, if necessary

        short byte, count, strip;
        pos = 0L;
        if(numstrips == 1)
        {
// All image data is in a single strip
            ifs.seekg(strip_offset, ios::beg);
            for(i = 0; i < image_height; i++)
            {
                if(read_row(ifs) < bytes_per_strip_row)
                    return 0;
```

```
        }
    }
    else
    {
        for(i = 0; i < numstrips; i++)
        {
// First find the strip's offset
            unsigned long offset = strip_offset + i*sizeof(long);
            ifs.seekg(offset, ios::beg);
// Move to the strip's position
            offset = get_long(ifs);
            ifs.seekg(offset, ios::beg);

// Now read rows_per_strip rows
            unsigned short ns;
            for(ns = 0; ns < rows_per_strip; ns++)
            {
                if((i*rows_per_strip + ns) >= image_height)
                    break;
                if(read_row(ifs) < bytes_per_line)
                    return 0;
            }
        }
    }


// Allocate memory for the device independent bitmap (DIB)
// Note that the number of bytes in each line of a DIB image
// must be a multiple of 4.

    unsigned short bytes_per_line_per_plane = (image_width *
                        bits_per_pixel_per_plane + 7) / 8;

    unsigned short actual_bytes_per_line = (image_width *
                                               nplanes *
                        bits_per_pixel_per_plane + 7) / 8;
    imdata->bytes_per_line = actual_bytes_per_line;

    if(imdata->bytes_per_line % 4)
        imdata->bytes_per_line = 4 *
                    (imdata->bytes_per_line/4 + 1);
```

continues

Listing 23.12. continued

```
// If image has more than 256 colors then there is no palette
    if(bits_per_pixel > 8) palettesize = 0;

    imdata->p_dib = GlobalAllocPtr(GHND,
                        sizeof(BITMAPINFOHEADER) +
                   palettesize * sizeof(RGBQUAD) +
                   (long) imdata->bytes_per_line *
                             (long) image_height);

// If memory allocation fails, return 0
    if(imdata->p_dib == 0) return 0;

// Set up bitmap info header
    LPBITMAPINFOHEADER p_bminfo = (LPBITMAPINFOHEADER)imdata->p_dib;
    p_bminfo->biSize = sizeof(BITMAPINFOHEADER);
    p_bminfo->biWidth = image_width;
    p_bminfo->biHeight = image_height;
    p_bminfo->biPlanes = 1;
    p_bminfo->biBitCount = bits_per_pixel_per_plane *
                           nplanes;
    p_bminfo->biCompression = BI_RGB;
    p_bminfo->biSizeImage = (long)image_height *
                            (long)imdata->bytes_per_line;
    p_bminfo->biXPelsPerMeter = 0;
    p_bminfo->biYPelsPerMeter = 0;
    p_bminfo->biClrUsed = 0;
    p_bminfo->biClrImportant = 0;

// Set up the color palette
    if(palettesize > 0)
    {
        RGBQUAD *palette = (RGBQUAD*) ((LPSTR)imdata->p_dib
                              + sizeof(BITMAPINFOHEADER));

        for(i = 0; i < palettesize; i++)
        {
            if(palettesize > 2)
            {
// Load palette from the "ctbl" array if ctbl exists.
                unsigned short factor;
                if(ctbl != NULL)
                {
```

```
                    palette[i].rgbRed       = ctbl[i].rgbtRed;
                    palette[i].rgbGreen     = ctbl[i].rgbtGreen;
                    palette[i].rgbBlue      = ctbl[i].rgbtBlue;
                    palette[i].rgbReserved  = 0;
                }
                else
                {
// Otherwise, define a grayscale palette
                    factor = palettesize - 1 + 2*i;
                    if(photometric == 0)
                        factor = palettesize - 1;
                    palette[i].rgbRed       = factor - i;
                    palette[i].rgbGreen     = factor - i;
                    palette[i].rgbBlue      = factor - i;
                    palette[i].rgbReserved  = 0;
                }
            }
            else  // palettesize == 2
            {
// Set up palette for black and white images
                if(photometric == 0)
                {
                    palette[i].rgbRed       = (1-i) * 255;
                    palette[i].rgbGreen     = (1-i) * 255;
                    palette[i].rgbBlue      = (1-i) * 255;
                    palette[i].rgbReserved  = 0;
                }
                else
                {
                    palette[i].rgbRed       = i * 255;
                    palette[i].rgbGreen     = i * 255;
                    palette[i].rgbBlue      = i * 255;
                    palette[i].rgbReserved  = 0;
                }
            }
        }
    }
    if(ctbl != NULL) delete ctbl;

// Load image data into the DIB. Note the DIB image must be
// stored "bottom to top" line order. That's why we position
// data at the end of the array so that the image can be
```

continues

Listing 23.12. continued

```
// stored backwards—from the last line to the first.
    unsigned char huge *data =
                (unsigned char huge*)imdata->p_dib +
                          sizeof(BITMAPINFOHEADER) +
                     palettesize * sizeof(RGBQUAD) +
                  (unsigned long)(image_height - 1) *
            (unsigned long)(imdata->bytes_per_line);

// Define a macro to access bytes in the TIFF image according
// to specified line and plane index.

    int lineindex, byteindex, planeindex;

#define bytepos(lineindex,planeindex,byteindex)  \
            ((long)(lineindex)*(long)bytes_per_line* \
             (long)nplanes + \
             (long)(planeindex)*(long)bytes_per_line + \
             (long)(byteindex))

// Construct packed pixels out of decoded TIFF image.
    unsigned short onebyte, bits_copied, loc, few_bits,
        k, bbpb = 8/bits_per_pixel_per_plane;

// Build a mask to pick out bits from each byte of the TIFF image
    unsigned short himask = 0x80, mask;
    if(bits_per_pixel_per_plane > 1)
        for(i = 0; i < bits_per_pixel_per_plane - 1;
            i++) himask = 0x80 ¦ (himask >> 1);

    for(lineindex = 0; lineindex < image_height;
        lineindex++, data -= imdata->bytes_per_line)
    {
        if(actual_bytes_per_line < imdata->bytes_per_line)
            for(loc = actual_bytes_per_line;
                loc < imdata->bytes_per_line; loc++)
                                      data[loc] = 0;
        loc = 0;
        onebyte = 0;
        bits_copied = 0;
        for(byteindex = 0;
```

```
                byteindex < bytes_per_line_per_plane;
                byteindex++)
            {
                for(k = 0, mask = himask; k < bbpb;
                    k++, mask >>= bits_per_pixel_per_plane)
                {
// Go through all scan line for all planes and copy bits into
// the data array
                    for(planeindex = 0; planeindex < nplanes;
                        planeindex++)
                    {
                        few_bits = TIF_image[bytepos(lineindex,
                                   planeindex, byteindex)] & mask;

// Shift the selcted bits to the most significant position
                        if(k > 0) few_bits <<=
                                    (k*bits_per_pixel_per_plane);

// OR the bits with current pixel after shifting them right
                        if(bits_copied > 0)
                                few_bits >>= bits_copied;

                        onebyte |= few_bits;
                        bits_copied += bits_per_pixel_per_plane;

                        if(bits_copied >= 8)
                        {
                            data[loc] = onebyte;
                            loc++;
                            bits_copied = 0;
                            onebyte = 0;
                        }
                    }
                }
            }
        }
        if(ctbl != NULL) delete ctbl;
        if(TIF_image != NULL) delete TIF_image;
        ctbl = NULL;
        TIF_image = NULL;

// Success!
```

continues

Listing 23.12. continued

```
    return 1;
}
//------------------------------------------------------------
// TIFImage:: r e a d _ r o w
// Read a row of image data from a TIFF file

unsigned short TIFImage::read_row(ifstream &ifs)
{
    switch(compression)
    {
        case 1:
// Means no compression. Simply read a block of bytes.
            ifs.read((unsigned char*)&TIF_image[pos],
                     bytes_per_strip_row);
            pos += bytes_per_strip_row;
            return bytes_per_strip_row;

        case 32773U:
// Means Macintosh PackBits compression (a form of run-length
// encoding)
            {
                unsigned short n = 0, c, nc;
                while(n < bytes_per_strip_row)
                {
                    c = ifs.get() & 0xff;
                    if(c & 0x80)
                    {
                        if(c != 0x80)
                        {
                            nc = ((~c) & 0xff) + 2;
                            c = ifs.get();
                            while(nc—)
                            {
                                TIF_image[pos++] = c;
                                n++;
                            }
                        }
                    }
                    else
                    {
```

```
                        nc = (c & 0xff) + 1;
                        while(nc--)
                        {
                            TIF_image[pos++] = ifs.get();
                            n++;
                        }
                    }
                }
                return n;
            }

        default:  return 0;
    }
}
```

ImageView—A Windows Image Viewer

Now that you have seen an `Image` class hierarchy for handling BMP, PCX, GIF, TIFF, and Targa image files, it's time for an application that uses these classes. The remainder of this chapter presents `ImageView`, a Windows MDI application that allows the user to open one or more image files for viewing. `ImageView` uses the `Image` class hierarchy developed in an earlier part of this chapter. You can view GIF, TIFF, PCX, BMP, and 24-bit Targa files with `ImageView`.

This book's companion disk includes the complete source code for `ImageView` together with necessary auxiliary files, such as the module definition file (`IMAGEVW.DEF`) and the resource file (`IMAGEVW.RES`). Before reading any more about `ImageView`, you should run the program and see how it works. Then you can read the following descriptions and study the source listings to understand how the program is implemented.

Running *ImageView*

If you have added a new program item for the `ImageView` application in Windows Program Manager, you can start the program by double-clicking on its icon. Otherwise, you have to start the program by selecting Run from the File menu in the

Program Manager and specifying the application's name (`IMAGEVW.EXE`). To view an image, select Open from `ImageView`'s File menu. You will see a file selection dialog box from which you will be able to select an image file. Each image appears in its own window inside `ImageView`'s main window. Figure 23.7 shows the basic features of `ImageView` including a number of images, the About dialog box, and one minimized window.

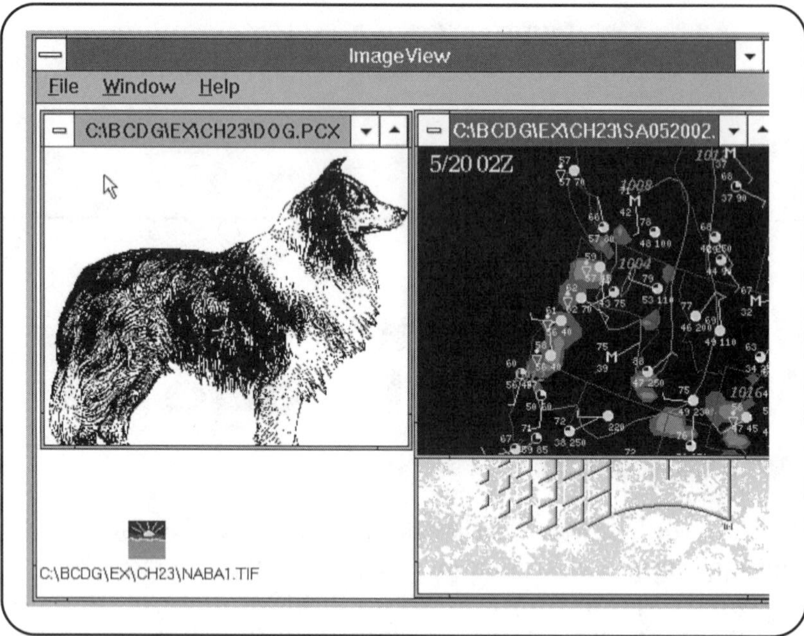

Figure 23.7. Viewing images with `ImageView`.

ImageViewApp Class

The `ImageView` application is built using Borland's OWL classes. As you can see from Listing 23.13, the main source file IMAGEVW.CPP (the one with the `OwlMain` function) looks very much like the main source file of any OWL-based application.

The `ImageViewApp` class, derived from `TApplication`, models the `ImageView` application. Its `InitMainWindow` function creates an instance of an `ImageViewFrame` window, which is the main window of the `ImageView` application. The images are displayed in child windows of `ImageViewFrame`.

Listing 23.13. IMAGEVW.CPP. The main source file of `ImageView`.

```
//----------------------------------------------------------------
//  File:  imagevw.cpp
//
//  A Windows application for viewing images in a variety of
//  formats such as Windows bitmap (.BMP), PC PaintBrush (.PCX),
//  and Targa (.TGA) , Graphics Interchange Format (.GIF), and
//  the Tagged Image File Format (.TIF).
//----------------------------------------------------------------
#include <owl\applicat.h>
#include "imvwwin.h"

class ImageViewApp: public TApplication
{
public:
// Constructor that simply calls the base class constructor

    ImageViewApp(const char far *name) : TApplication(name) {}

// Define function to initialize application's main window
    void InitMainWindow();
};
//----------------------------------------------------------------
//  I m a g e V i e w A p p : : I n i t M a i n W i n d o w

void ImageViewApp::InitMainWindow()
{
    MainWindow = new TMDIFrame("ImageView", "MainMenu",
                               *new ImageViewFrame);

// Assign icon for the application
    MainWindow->SetIcon(this, "IMAGEVIEWAPP_ICON");
    MainWindow->AssignMenu("MainMenu");
    MainWindow->Attr.AccelTable = "MainAccelTable";

    EnableBWCC();
    EnableCtl3d();
}
//----------------------------------------------------------------
//  O w l M a i n
```

continues

Listing 23.13. continued

```
//
//  Create an instance of the application and "run" it.

int OwlMain(int, char**)
{
    ImageViewApp ImageView("ImageView");
    return ImageView.Run();
}
}
```

ImageViewFrame and ImageViewWindow Classes

Listing 23.14 shows the declarations of the `ImageViewWindow` and `ImageViewFrame` classes. The `ImageViewWindow` class has a member variable, `image`, which is a pointer to the `Image` object that it displays. The `ImageViewFrame` class represents the frame window, inside of which one or more `ImageViewWindow` objects display images. As such, the `ImageViewFrame` class does not have any member variables—it only provides member functions, such as `OpenFile` and `About`, that handle menu messages.

Listing 23.14. IMVWWIN.H. Declaration of the window classes in `ImageView`.

```
//-------------------------------------------------------------
// File: imvwwin.h
//
// Classes for an OWL application that lets you open an image
// file and view the image in a window.
//-------------------------------------------------------------
#if !defined(__IMVWWIN_H)
#define __IMVWWIN_H

#include <owl\opensave.h>
#include <owl\applicat.h>
#include <owl\dialog.h>
#include <owl\dc.h>
#include <owl\gdiobjec.h>
#include <owl\mdi.h>
```

```
#include <owl\mdichild.h>
#include "image.h"
#include "bmpimage.h"
#include "pcximage.h"
#include "tgaimage.h"
#include "gifimage.h"
#include "tifimage.h"
#include <strstrea.h>
#include <string.h>

#define IDM_ABOUT      200
#define IDM_OPENFILE   101
#define IDM_SAVE       102
#define IDM_SAVEAS     103

class ImageViewWindow : public TMDIChild
{
public:
    ImageViewWindow(TMDIClient &parent, const char far *title,
                    char far *fname);

    ~ImageViewWindow()
    {
        if(filename != NULL) delete[] filename;
        if(image != NULL) delete image;
    }

    void Paint(TDC& dc, BOOL, TRect&);
    void Save();
    Image *current_image() { return image;}

private:
    char    *filename;
    Image   *image;
};

class ImageViewFrame: public TMDIClient
{
public:
    ImageViewFrame() : TMDIClient() {}

// Declare functions for handling messages from Windows
```

continues

Listing 23.14. continued

```
    BOOL EvQueryNewPalette();
    void EvPaletteChanged(HWND hWndPalChg);

    void OpenFile();
    void SaveFile();
    void SaveAsFile();
    void About();

DECLARE_RESPONSE_TABLE(ImageViewFrame);
};

#endif
```

Remember, the `ImageViewWindow` class contains information about the image it is displaying—in the form of a pointer to an `Image` object as a member variable. The `ImageViewWindow` constructor expects the name of an image file as an argument, which it uses to create and initialize the image. The image file's extension is used to decide what type of image is created: `.BMP` implies a Windows device-independent bitmap file, `.PCX` means PC PaintBrush files, `.GIF` specifies GIF files, `.TIF` specifies TIFF files, and `.TGA` refers to a 24-bit Truevision Targa image. Consult Listing 23.16 for further details of the `ImageViewWindow` constructor.

You should note that the image is displayed in the window by the `Paint` function of the `ImageViewWindow` class. Listing 23.16 shows the simplicity of the `ImageViewWindow::Paint` function—it simply calls the `show` member function of the image object. This shows the benefits of developing a C++ class hierarchy to handle a specific task for managing and displaying images. (You can see the benefits even more clearly with the image animation program in Chapter 24, "Animating Images.")

Listing 23.16. IMVWWIN.CPP. Implementation of the window classes in `ImageView`.

```
//--------------------------------------------------------------
// File: imvwwin.cpp
//
// Member functions of the ImageViewFrame and ImageViewWindow
// classes.
//
//  CompuServe requires the following statement in software that
//  uses the GIF image format:
```

```
//
//    "The Graphics Interchange Format(c) is the Copyright
//     property of CompuServe Incorporated. GIF(sm) is a
//     Service Mark property of CompuServe Incorporated."
//
//--------------------------------------------------------------
#include "imvwwin.h"
//--------------------------------------------------------------
// Define the response table for ImageViewFrame
DEFINE_RESPONSE_TABLE1(ImageViewFrame, TMDIClient)
    EV_WM_QUERYNEWPALETTE,
    EV_WM_PALETTECHANGED,
    EV_COMMAND(IDM_ABOUT,     About),
    EV_COMMAND(IDM_OPENFILE,  OpenFile),
    EV_COMMAND(IDM_SAVE,      SaveFile),
    EV_COMMAND(IDM_SAVEAS,    SaveAsFile),
END_RESPONSE_TABLE;
//--------------------------------------------------------------
// I m a g e V i e w W i n d o w
// Constructor for the ImageViewWindow class

ImageViewWindow::ImageViewWindow(TMDIClient& parent,
    const char far *title, char far *fname) :
    TMDIChild(parent, title)
{
    image = NULL;
    filename = NULL;

// Open the image file. We will decide the file type from
// the file extension:
//   .BMP  = Windows bitmap file
//   .PCX  = PC PaintBrush file
//   .TGA  = 24-bit true color Targa file
//   .GIF  = CompuServe GIF file
//   .TIF  = TIFF file

// Convert filename to uppercase
    strupr(fname);
    char *ext = strrchr(fname, '.');
    size_t len = strlen(fname);
    filename = new char[len+1];
    strcpy(filename, fname);
```

continues

Listing 23.16. continued

```
// Change to an hourglass cursor
    SetCapture();
    ::SetCursor(TCursor(NULL, IDC_WAIT));

// Load file
    if(strcmp(ext, ".BMP") == 0)
    {
        image = new BMPImage;
        image->read(fname);
    }

    if(strcmp(ext, ".PCX") == 0)
    {
        image = new PCXImage;
        image->read(fname);
    }

    if(strcmp(ext, ".TGA") == 0)
    {
        image = new TGAImage;
        image->read(fname);
    }

    if(strcmp(ext, ".GIF") == 0)
    {
        image = new GIFImage;
        image->read(fname);
    }

    if(strcmp(ext, ".TIF") == 0)
    {
        image = new TIFImage;
        image->read(fname);
    }

// Reset cursor to arrow
    ::SetCursor(TCursor(NULL, IDC_ARROW));
    ReleaseCapture();

// Display a message if image format is unknown
    if(image == NULL)
    {
```

```
        MessageBox("Unknown image format!",
                   "ImageView",
                           MB_OK ¦ MB_ICONEXCLAMATION);
    }
}
//------------------------------------------------------------
//  ImageViewWindow:: P a i n t
//  Draw image in the window

void ImageViewWindow::Paint(TDC& dc, BOOL, TRect&)
{
    if(image != NULL)
    {
        image->show(dc);
    }
}
//------------------------------------------------------------
//  ImageViewFrame:: A b o u t
//  Display the "About..." box

void ImageViewFrame::About()
{
    TDialog *p_about = new TDialog(this, "ABOUTIMAGEVIEW");
    GetApplication()->ExecDialog(p_about);
}
//------------------------------------------------------------
// ImageViewFrame:: O p e n F i l e
// Display file dialog and open requested image file

void ImageViewFrame::OpenFile()
{
    char name[80] = "*.bmp";
    char filter[80] = "*.bmp";
    int status = IDOK;
    TOpenSaveDialog::TData data;

    data.FileName = name;
    data.Filter = filter;
    data.Flags = OFN_HIDEREADONLY ¦ OFN_FILEMUSTEXIST ¦
                 OFN_PATHMUSTEXIST;

    strcpy(name, filter);
```

continues

Listing 23.16. continued

```
// Create and display file selection dialog...
    TFileOpenDialog fd(0, data);
    status = fd.Execute();

 // Load selected waveform file and play
    if(status == IDOK)
    {
        ImageViewWindow* iw = new ImageViewWindow(*this,
                                                  name, name);
        iw->Create();
        iw->SetIcon(GetApplication(), "IMAGEVIEWWIN_ICON");
    }
}
//-----------------------------------------------------------------
// ImageViewFrame:: E v Q u e r y N e w P a l e t t e
// Realize palette for the currently active child window

BOOL ImageViewFrame::EvQueryNewPalette()
{
    ImageViewWindow *w = (ImageViewWindow*)GetActiveMDIChild();
    if(w == NULL) return 0;

    HPALETTE hpal = w->current_image()->palette();
    short changed = 0;
    if(hpal)
    {
        TClientDC dc(w->HWindow);
        dc.SelectObject(hpal, FALSE);
        changed = dc.RealizePalette();
        dc.RestorePalette();
        if(changed)
        {
            w->Invalidate(TRUE);
            w->UpdateWindow();
        }
    }
    return changed;
}
//-----------------------------------------------------------------
// ImageViewFrame:: E v P a l e t t e C h a n g e d
// Handle a change in system palette
```

```
void ImageViewFrame::EvPaletteChanged(HWND hWndPalChg)
{
    ImageViewWindow *w = (ImageViewWindow*)GetActiveMDIChild();
    if(w == NULL) return;

    if(hWndPalChg == w->HWindow) return;
    HPALETTE hpal = w->current_image()->palette();
    short changed = 0;
    if(hpal)
    {
        TClientDC dc(w->HWindow);
        dc.SelectObject(hpal, FALSE);
        changed = dc.RealizePalette();
        if(changed)
        {
            dc.UpdateColors();
        }
        dc.RestorePalette();
    }
}
//-------------------------------------------------------------
// ImageViewFrame:: S a v e F i l e
// Saves image (being displayed in currently active child window)
// in .BMP format in a file with the same name as the original,
// except for a .BMP extension.

void ImageViewFrame::SaveFile()
{
    ImageViewWindow *w = (ImageViewWindow*)GetActiveMDIChild();
    if(w != NULL) w->Save();
}
//-------------------------------------------------------------
// ImageViewWindow:: S a v e
// Save image in BMP format

void ImageViewWindow::Save()
{
    char *ext = strrchr(filename, '.');
    if(strcmp(ext, ".BMP") != 0)
```

continues

Listing 23.16. continued

```
    {
// Change to an hourglass cursor
        SetCapture();
        ::SetCursor(TCursor(NULL, IDC_WAIT));

        char bmpfilename[128];
        strcpy(bmpfilename, filename);
        ext = strrchr(bmpfilename, '.');
        strcpy(ext, ".BMP");
        BMPImage ibmp;
        ibmp.image_data(image);
        ibmp.write(bmpfilename);
// Reset cursor to arrow
        ::SetCursor(TCursor(NULL, IDC_ARROW));
        ReleaseCapture();
    }
}
/ / - - - - - - - - - - - - - - - - - - - - - - - - - - - - - - - - -
----------------------------- // ImageV
ewWindow:: S a v e A s F i l e // Display file dialog and
ave image in a selected form


// (Nothing happens for now)

void ImageViewFrame::SaveAsFile(){}
```

Building *ImageView*

You should use the Windows-based interactive development environment of Borland C++ to build the `ImageView` application. The companion disk contains the project file (`IMAGEVW.IDE`) that lists the files necessary to build the application. The disk also includes all files needed to build the executable, `IMAGEVW.EXE`. After you install the code from the companion disk, you should be able to build `IMAGEVW.EXE` by selecting Make all from the Project menu. Once the program is successfully built, you can add it to Windows Program Manager by selecting New… from the Program Manager's File menu.

One of the files that you need to build a Windows program is a resource file. For the `ImageView` application, the resource file, IMAGEVW.RES, is included in the companion disk. I prepared the resource file using the Resource Workshop program included with Borland C++.

Summary

Images are an integral part of many Windows applications and you need lots of images to create an interesting application. Whether you draw images in a paint program or scan from a hard copy, the images are ultimately stored in image files that you have to interpret and use. The basic information in an image file is the same—the dimensions of the image and the pixel array that makes up the image—but there are many ways to organize this information in a file. There are many popular image file formats, such as PCX, GIF, TIFF, Windows BMP, and Truevision Targa. This chapter describes these five popular file formats and presents a C++ class hierarchy that helps you read image files and display images in Microsoft Windows. The next chapter uses the image classes to define sprites that can be animated—moved smoothly—over a background image.

24

Animating Images

Animation is the process of bringing an image to life. We usually associate animation with movement of images and the good examples pioneered by the Walt Disney Company. This chapter includes several C++ classes to model and animate small images known as *sprites.* These sprite animation classes rely on the `Image` classes developed in Chapter 23, "Understanding Image File Formats." This chapter ends with a Windows program that animates a number of sprites on a background image.

Animation Techniques

The Disney movies use a traditional approach to animation in which each frame of the movie has to be prepared individually. This style of animation is commonly known as *frame animation* or *cel animation.* (Cel, short for celluloid, refers to the sheets of acetate on which the images are drawn.) Cel animation is a discipline by itself and is not covered in this chapter.

Sprite Animation

Sprites are used in interactive video games to represent characters and fixtures that are part of the game. When the player moves an input device, such as a joystick, trackball, or mouse, the sprite moves over a background. Essentially, the player plays the video game by manipulating the sprites. Video game machines usually have graphics hardware with built-in support for sprites. In IBM-compatible PCs, the display hardware does not support sprites, so you have to rely on software techniques.

Erase and Redraw Technique

The obvious way to move an image is to erase it at the old location and redraw it at the new location. In a Windows program, you can use the `BitBlt` function for this. If you erase and redraw repeatedly, the image appears to move across the screen. However, a major drawback of this approach is that the display flickers as the image is erased and redrawn.

One way to avoid flickering in erase-and-redraw animation is to use video page flipping, provided the display hardware supports more than one video page. With multiple video pages, you draw the entire screen in the hidden video page while the active page is being displayed. Then you swap the active and hidden video pages to display the updated image. To continue the animation, you simply repeat this process in a loop. Many high-end graphics workstations (Silicon Graphics workstations, for instance) support animation through page flipping—or *buffer swapping* as the technique is known in the workstation world.

Unfortunately, most PC display adapters do not support multiple video pages in the high-resolution video modes. More importantly, Microsoft Windows does not support multiple video pages. So you need some other approach to create flicker-free animation in Windows.

Offscreen Bitmap Technique

Screen flickers occur with the erase and redraw animation because all screen drawing operations are visible. As an image is erased, you see it vanish from the screen. Then the image appears again at a new location. When two video pages are used, the flicker goes away because the screen updates are always done in the hidden page. The fully updated screen appears instantaneously when the video pages are swapped. By this logic, you should be able to avoid the flicker as long as the images are prepared offscreen and the updated screen is redrawn quickly. Luckily, Windows supports drawing on an offscreen bitmap, which can serve as an ideal canvas for preparing the display screen.

Then a single call to BitBlt can transfer the updated images to the display screen quickly. Of course, you have to attend to a myriad of details to prepare the image properly in the offscreen bitmap, but this basic idea works remarkably well for image animation under Windows.

To see how well the offscreen bitmap animation works, all you need to do is run the ANIMATE application (ANIMATE.EXE) from the CH24 directory of the companion disk. The ANIMATE program performs well under Windows even on a lowly 1984-vintage IBM PC-AT (6MHz 80286) equipped with the original IBM EGA display adapter.

C++ Classes for Sprite Animation

To support a Windows application that animates sprites using an offscreen bitmap, you need C++ classes to represent the sprites and to animate them. The animation consists of a fixed background image and zero or more sprites that can be moved around on the background. The following sections define a Sprite class to model a sprite and a SpriteAnimation class to maintain the sprites and the background image.

The *Sprite* Class

Listing 24.1 shows the declaration of the Sprite class. A Sprite has two Image objects:

- The Sprite's image on a black background
- A black silhouette of the Sprite's image on a white background (a mask)

As you can see in the animate function of the SpriteAnimation class (in Listing 24.4), both the image and the mask are needed to allow drawing the Sprite's outline without affecting the background on which the Sprite is drawn. In addition to the image and the mask, a Sprite has an x- and y-position and several other variables to keep track of its motion on the background.

A Sprite object also has a display priority associated with it. This is an integer, stored in the member variable disp_priority, that determines the order in which overlapping sprites are drawn—a Sprite with a higher priority is drawn over one with a lower priority.

Another interesting member variable is dproc of type DRAWPROC, which is declared with this typedef statement:

```
typedef void (_FAR PASCAL *DRAWPROC)(HDC hdc, short x, short y,
                              LPVOID data);
```

As you can see, dproc is a pointer to a function. The function specified by dproc is called whenever the Sprite's image needs to be drawn. You can draw objects—such as a line, rectangle, ellipse, or text—so that a sprite can have much more than a bitmapped image. The moving text in the sample application ANIMATE (in the companion disk) is displayed using this feature of a Sprite.

Listing 24.1. SPRITE.H. Declaration of the Sprite class.

```
//-------------------------------------------------------------
// File: sprite.h
//
// Declares a Sprite class representing a small image that
// can be animated.
//-------------------------------------------------------------
#if !defined(__SPRITE_H)
#define __SPRITE_H

#include <string.h>
#include "image.h"

const unsigned short SPRITE_ACTIVE      = 1;
const unsigned short SPRITE_UPDATE      = 2;
const unsigned short SPRITE_OVERLAP     = 4;
const unsigned short SPRITE_ERASE       = 8;


typedef void (_FAR PASCAL *DRAWPROC)(HDC hdc, short x, short y,
                              LPVOID data);

class Sprite
{
public:
    Sprite() : image(NULL), mask(NULL), disp_priority(1),
            dproc(NULL), dpdata(NULL), status(0), sid(-1),
            image_filename(NULL), mask_filename(NULL)
    {
```

```
        curpos.x = curpos.y = 0;
        lastpos.x = lastpos.y = 0;
    }

    Sprite(HDC hdc, LPSTR imagefilename,
        LPSTR maskfilename, short priority = 1);

    Sprite(Image *img, Image *msk, short priority = 1);

    ~Sprite();

// Read in an image and a mask
    void load_images(HDC hdc, LPSTR imagefilename,
               LPSTR maskfilename);

    operator==(const Sprite& s) const
    {
        return (disp_priority == s.priority());
    }
    operator<(const Sprite& s) const
    {
        return (disp_priority < s.priority());
    }


    int isA() const { return SpriteClass;}

    char far *nameOf() const { return "Sprite";}

    void printOn(ostream& os) const
    {
        os << "Sprite : " << *image_filename << endl;
    }

    short priority() const { return disp_priority;}
    void priority(short dp) { disp_priority = dp;}

    unsigned short width() { return w;}
    unsigned short height() { return h;}
    void width(unsigned wdth) { w = wdth;}
    void height(unsigned hght) { h = hght;}
```

continues

Listing 24.1. continued

```
    short xpos() { return curpos.x;}
    short ypos() { return curpos.y;}
    void xpos(short x)
    {
        lastpos.x = curpos.x;
        curpos.x = x;
    }
    void ypos(short y)
    {
        lastpos.y = curpos.y;
        curpos.y = y;
    }
    void newpos(short x, short y)
    {
        lastpos.x = curpos.x;
        lastpos.y = curpos.y;
        curpos.x = x;
     curpos.y = y;
     reset_moves();
    }

    short lastxpos() { return lastpos.x;}
    short lastypos() { return lastpos.y;}

    void reset_moves()
    {
     xdelta = ydelta = 0;
    }
    short xmove() { return xdelta;}
    short ymove() { return ydelta;}

    void move(short x, short y)
    {
        xdelta += x;
        ydelta += y;
// Mark sprite for update
        status |= SPRITE_UPDATE;
    }

// Functions to manipulate the status of a sprite
    unsigned short needs_update()
```

```
    { return status & SPRITE_UPDATE;}
    unsigned short is_active()
    { return status & SPRITE_ACTIVE;}
    unsigned short is_overlapping()
    { return status & SPRITE_OVERLAP;}
    unsigned short to_be_erased()
    { return status & SPRITE_ERASE;}
    void active() { status |= SPRITE_ACTIVE | SPRITE_UPDATE;}
    void update() { status |= SPRITE_UPDATE;}
    void erase() { status |= SPRITE_ERASE;}
    void overlaps(){ status |= SPRITE_OVERLAP;}
    void update_done(){ status &= ~SPRITE_UPDATE;}
    void unerase() { status &= ~SPRITE_ERASE;}
    void inactive() { status &= ~SPRITE_ACTIVE;}
    void no_overlap() { status &= ~SPRITE_OVERLAP;}

// Convert the device independent bitmaps to device
// dependent bitmaps
    void make_ddb(HDC hdc)
    {
     if(image != NULL) image->DIBtoDDB(hdc);
     if(mask != NULL) mask->DIBtoDDB(hdc);
    }

    void drawproc(DRAWPROC dp, LPVOID data)
    {
     dproc = dp;
        dpdata = data;
    }
    DRAWPROC drawproc() { return dproc;}
    LPVOID data() { return dpdata;}

    HBITMAP hbm_image()
    {
        if(image != NULL) return image->get_ddb();
        else return NULL;
    }
    HBITMAP hbm_mask()
    {
     if(mask != NULL) return mask->get_ddb();
     else return NULL;
    }
```

continues

Listing 24.1. continued

```
    Image* sprite_image() { return image;}
    Image* sprite_mask() { return mask;}

    void id(short _id) { sid = _id;}
    short id() { return sid;}

    static Image* init_image(LPSTR fname);

protected:
    Image          *image;  // The sprite's image
    Image          *mask;   // The mask: a silhouette of image
    unsigned short w, h;    // Width and height of sprite
    short          disp_priority;
    POINT          curpos;
    POINT          lastpos;
    short          xdelta;
    short          ydelta;
    unsigned short status;
    DRAWPROC       dproc;     // Pointer to user-supplied
                              // function to draw
    LPVOID         dpdata;    // Argument for drawproc
    char           *image_filename;
    char           *mask_filename;

    short          sid; // Normally unused, but may be
                        // used to identify Sprite

    enum { SpriteClass = 1};
};

#endif
```

Listing 24.2 shows the file SPRITE.CPP with several member functions of the `Sprite` class. A typical way to create and initialize a `Sprite` is to use the constructor that accepts the names of image and mask files as arguments:

```
Sprite::Sprite(HDC hdc, LPSTR imagefilename,
               LPSTR maskfilename, short priority);
```

This constructor calls the `init_image` function to load the bitmaps corresponding to the image and the mask. The constructor also requires the handle to a device context.

This is necessary because the image and mask bitmaps are converted to a device-dependent format and this step needs a DC.

The `init_image` function (Listing 24.2) loads an image from a file. It uses the filename extension to determine the type of image. The extensions it accepts are

- .BMP for Windows DIB files
- .PCX for PC PaintBrush files
- .TIF for TIFF files
- .GIF for GIF files
- .TGA for 24-bit Truevision Targa files

Listing 24.2. SPRITE.CPP. Implementation of the `Sprite` class.

```
//-------------------------------------------------------------
//  File: sprite.cpp
//  Member functions of the Sprite class.
//
//  CompuServe requires the following statement in software that
//  uses the GIF image format:
//
//    "The Graphics Interchange Format is the Copyright
//     property of CompuServe Incorporated. GIF(sm) is a
//     Service Mark property of CompuServe Incorporated."
//
//-------------------------------------------------------------
#include <fstream.h>
#include <string.h>
#include "sprite.h"
#include "bmpimage.h"
#include "pcximage.h"
#include "tgaimage.h"
#include "gifimage.h"
#include "tifimage.h"

//-------------------------------------------------------------
// S p r i t e : : S p r i t e
// Constructor for a Sprite
```

continues

Listing 24.2. continued

```
Sprite::Sprite(HDC hdc, LPSTR imagefilename,
               LPSTR maskfilename, short priority):
    disp_priority(priority)
{
    image_filename = mask_filename = NULL;

// Read the image and the mask bitmaps
    image = init_image(imagefilename);
    size_t len;
    if(image != NULL)
    {
        w = image->width();
        h = image->height();
        len = strlen(imagefilename);
        image_filename = new char[len+1];
        strcpy(image_filename, imagefilename);
    }

    mask = init_image(maskfilename);
    if(mask != NULL)
    {
        len = strlen(maskfilename);
        mask_filename = new char[len+1];
        strcpy(mask_filename, maskfilename);
    }

// Convert the image and the mask into device dependent bitmaps
    make_ddb(hdc);

// Initialize other member variables
    curpos.x = curpos.y = 0;
    lastpos.x = lastpos.y = 0;
    dproc = NULL;
    dpdata = NULL;
    status = SPRITE_UPDATE | SPRITE_ACTIVE;
}
//-------------------------------------------------------------
// Sprite::S p r i t e ( I m a g e * , I m a g e * ...)
// Construct a Sprite from a image and a mask.

Sprite::Sprite(Image *img, Image *msk, short priority):
    disp_priority(priority)
```

```
{
    image_filename = mask_filename = NULL;

    image = img;
    if(image != NULL)
    {
        w = image->width();
        h = image->height();
    }
    mask = msk;

// Initialize other member variables
    curpos.x = curpos.y = 0;
    lastpos.x = lastpos.y = 0;
    dproc = NULL;
    dpdata = NULL;
    status = SPRITE_UPDATE | SPRITE_ACTIVE;
}
//-----------------------------------------------------------------
// S p r i t e : : ~ S p r i t e
// Destructor for a Sprite

Sprite::~Sprite()
{
    if(image_filename != NULL) delete[] image_filename;
    if(mask_filename != NULL) delete[] mask_filename;
    if(image != NULL) delete image;
    if(mask != NULL) delete mask;
}
//-----------------------------------------------------------------
// S p r i t e : : l o a d _ i m a g e s
// Read in image and mask from files

void Sprite::load_images(HDC hdc, LPSTR imagefilename,
                         LPSTR maskfilename)
{
// Read the image and the mask bitmaps
    image = init_image(imagefilename);
    size_t len;
    if(image != NULL)
    {
```

continues

Listing 24.2. continued

```
            w = image->width();
            h = image->height();
            len = strlen(imagefilename);
            strcpy(image_filename, imagefilename);
        }

        mask = init_image(maskfilename);
        if(mask != NULL)
        {
            len = strlen(maskfilename);
            strcpy(mask_filename, maskfilename);
        }

// Convert the image and the mask into device dependent bitmaps
        make_ddb(hdc);

// Mark sprite as active and in need of update
        status = SPRITE_UPDATE ¦ SPRITE_ACTIVE;
}
//--------------------------------------------------------------
// S p r i t e : : i n i t _ i m a g e
// Read an image from a file

Image* Sprite::init_image(LPSTR fname)
{
    Image *img = NULL;
    if(fname == NULL) return img;

// Read the image file. We will decide the file type from
// the file extension:
//  .BMP  = Windows bitmap file
//  .PCX  = PC PaintBrush file
//  .TGA  = 24-bit true color Targa file
//  .GIF  = CompuServe GIF file
//  .TIF  = TIFF file

// Locate file name extension
    char *ext = strrchr(fname, '.');
    if(ext == NULL) return img;
```

```
// Load file
    if(strnicmp(ext, ".BMP", 4) == 0)
    {
        img = new BMPImage;

        if(!img->read(fname))
        {
            delete img;
            img = NULL;
        }
    }

    if(strnicmp(ext, ".PCX", 4) == 0)
    {
        img = new PCXImage;
        if(!img->read(fname))
        {
            delete img;
            img = NULL;
        }
    }

    if(strnicmp(ext, ".TIF", 4) == 0)
    {
        img = new TIFImage;
        if(!img->read(fname))
        {
            delete img;
            img = NULL;
        }
    }

    if(strnicmp(ext, ".GIF", 4) == 0)
    {
        img = new GIFImage;
        if(!img->read(fname))
        {
            delete img;
            img = NULL;
        }
    }
```

continues

Listing 24.2. continued

```
        if(strnicmp(ext, ".TGA", 4) == 0)
        {
            img = new TGAImage;
            if(!img->read(fname))
            {
                delete img;
                img = NULL;
            }
        }
        return img;
}
```

The *SpriteAnimation* Class

The `SpriteAnimation` class, declared in the file SPRANIM.H (Listing 24.3), manages a number of sprites and a background and provides the capability of animating the sprites. Its main data members are the following:

- `SpriteArray *sprites;` is an array of pointers to sprites that are part of the animation. `SpriteArray` is an instance of the Borland C++ container class `TISArrayAsVector<T>` declared as an array that maintains an array of pointers to Sprite objects (see Chapter 16, "Using the Borland C++ Class Libraries," for more information on the template-based container classes in Borland C++).
- `Image *background;` is the background image that serves as the canvas on which the sprites are animated.
- `HBITMAP hbm_bg;` is the device-dependent bitmap of the background image.
- `HBITMAP hbm_scratch;` is a bitmap that serves as the scratch area where images are prepared before copying to the onscreen window (to be described later).

Additionally, there are a number of handles to device contexts that are kept ready for copying bitmaps to and from various components of the animation.

Listing 24.3. SPRANIM.H. Declaration of the `SpriteAnimation` class.

```
//----------------------------------------------------------
// File: spranim.h
//
```

```
// Classes for animating sprites.
//-------------------------------------------------------------------
#if !defined(__SPRANIM_H)
#define __SPRANIM_H

#include <classlib\arrays.h>
#include "sprite.h"

// A sorted, indirect array of sprites
typedef TISArrayAsVector<Sprite> SpriteArray;
typedef TISArrayAsVectorIterator<Sprite> SpriteArrayIterator;

// A class that manages the animation
class SpriteAnimation
{
public:
    SpriteAnimation(HDC hdc, unsigned short w,
                    unsigned short h,
                    LPSTR filename);
    SpriteAnimation(HDC hdc, unsigned short w,
                    unsigned short h, Image* bg);
    ~SpriteAnimation();

    void init_animation(HDC hdc, unsigned short w,
                                 unsigned short h);
// Add a sprite to the animation
    void add(Sprite* s)
    {
        if(sprites != NULL && s != NULL)
           sprites->Add(s);
    }

// Animate the images
    void animate(HDC hdc, short x, short y);

    void draw_bg(HDC hdc, short x, short y);

    void redisplay_all(HDC hdc, short x, short y);

    void set_refresh(BOOL flag) { refresh = flag;}
```

continues

Listing 24.3. continued

```
// Utility functions
    BOOL rects_overlap(short x1, short y1, short w1, short h1,
                       short x2, short y2, short w2, short h2)
    {
        if((x2 - x1) > w1) return FALSE;
        if((x1 - x2) > w2) return FALSE;
        if((y2 - y1) > h1) return FALSE;
        if((y1 - y2) > h2) return FALSE;
        return TRUE;
    }

    void set_priority(Sprite* s, short prio)
    {
        if(sprites != NULL && s != NULL)
        {
            if(prio != s->priority())
            {
                sprites->Detach(s, TShouldDelete::Delete);
                s->priority(prio);
             sprites->Add(s);
            }
        }
    }
// Returns sprite of highest priority that encloses point (x,y)
    Sprite* sprite_at(short x, short y);

    Image* bgimage() { return background;}
    HBITMAP bg_bitmap() { return hbm_bg;}

// Function to scroll the bitmap by changing top and left
    void xbmp_origin(short x) { left = x;}
    void ybmp_origin(short y) { top = y;}
    short xbmp_origin() { return left;}
    short ybmp_origin() { return top;}

// Functions that draw on the background bitmap
   void bg_rect(short x1, short y1, short x2, short y2)
   { Rectangle(hdc_bg, x1, y1, x2, y2);}
   void bg_line(short x1, short y1, short x2, short y2)
   {
       MoveTo(hdc_bg, x1, y1);
```

```
        LineTo(hdc_bg, x2, y2);
    }
protected:
    SpriteArray    *sprites;
    Image          *background; // The background image
    HBITMAP        hbm_bg;      // Bitmap from "background"
    HBITMAP        hbm_bg_saved;// A copy of hbm_bg
    HBITMAP        hbm_scratch; // Images prepared here before
                                // copying to window
    short          top, left;   // Top left corner and
    short          width;       // dimensions of background
    short          height;      // being displayed
    short          ws, hs;      // Dimensions of scratch
                                // bitmap
    short          bg_image;
    HBITMAP        hbm_sprite;
    HDC            hdc_bg;
    HDC            hdc_sprite;
    HDC            hdc_scratch;
    HBITMAP        old_hbm_bg;
    HBITMAP        old_hbm_sprite;
    HBITMAP        old_hbm_scratch;
    BOOL           refresh;
};

#endif
```

Setting Up a *SpriteAnimation* Object

A `SpriteAnimation` object is designed to manage animation of a number of sprites on a background image. To use `SpriteAnimation`, you have to use this constructor:

```
SpriteAnimation::SpriteAnimation(HDC hdc,
                                 unsigned short w,
                                 unsigned short h,
                                 LPSTR filename);
```

The constructor expects a DC, the width and height of the scratch bitmap, and the name of an image file to be used as the background of the animation. As you can see from Listing 24.4, the constructor loads the background image, sets up a number of bitmaps and DCs, and creates a `SpriteArray` to hold the `Sprite` objects.

Once the `SpriteAnimation` object is created, you can add `Sprites` to the animation by calling the `add` member function of the `SpriteAnimation` class. You have to move the `Sprites` by calling the move function of each `Sprite`. To update the display, call the `animate` function of the `SpriteAnimation` class. A sample application that uses the `SpriteAnimation` class appears later in this chapter.

Animating Sprites

The `animate` member function (see Listing 24.4) of the `SpriteAnimation` class is at the heart of animating sprites on a background image. Before looking into the problem of updating the screen image in an efficient way, consider the problem of redrawing the entire window. If you look at the beginning of the `animate` function in Listing 24.4, you see this line:

```
if(refresh) redisplay_all(hdc, x, y);
```

When the `refresh` flag is set, the `animate` function calls `redisplay_all` to update the entire window. The next section describes how the sprites are drawn on the background.

Updating the Entire Window

In Listing 24.4, you find the source code for the function `redisplay_all` that draws the background and sprites. In a C++-like pseudocode notation, the steps involved in updating the animation are the following:

```
Copy designated portion of background into scratch bitmap
    using BitBlt.

for(all Sprite objects in the animation)
{
    Copy the Sprite's mask to the scratch bitmap using
        BitBlt in the SRCAND mode.

    Copy the Sprite's image to the scratch bitmap using
        BitBlt in the SRCPAINT mode.

    if(Sprite has a dproc)
        Call dproc.
}

Copy the scratch bitmap into the window using BitBlt
    in the SRCCOPY mode.
```

Thus, the basic idea is to copy the background into a scratch bitmap and draw all the sprites on the background. Because the `SpriteAnimation` class stores the sprites ordered by display priority, this step draws the sprites in the correct order.

Figure 24.1 illustrates the process of drawing a sprite on a background. Here are the steps:

1. Combine the sprite's mask bitmap with the background image using a bitwise-AND operation. Remember that the mask is a silhouette of the sprite's image—it is black (all bits 0) on a white (all bits 1) background. This step essentially punches a hole the shape of the sprite in the background image.
2. Combine the sprite's image with the modified background image using a bitwise-OR operation. Because the image is on a white (all bits 1) background, this step fills the hole created in the previous step.

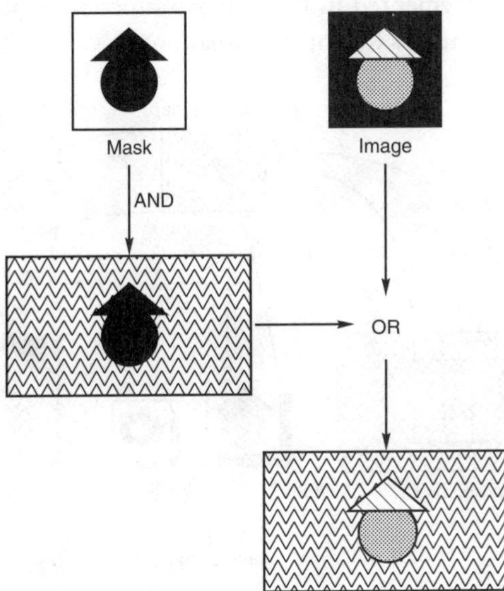

Figure 24.1. Drawing a sprite on a background.

Efficient Animation of Overlapping Sprites

When the whole window does not need to be updated, the `animate` function draws the sprites using an algorithm that updates the window in an efficient manner. Here is the basic algorithm for efficient updates:

1. For a sprite S that needs updating, determine all other sprites that touch sprite S and are also in need of update. Determine the smallest rectangle that encloses all sprites that satisfy these conditions.
2. Find all stationary sprites that also touch the rectangle and mark them as overlapping.
3. From the background image to the scratch bitmap, copy an area corresponding to the rectangle determined in step 1.
4. Draw all overlapping sprites in the scratch bitmap. Set the status of the sprites as updated so they are not included again.
5. Copy the rectangle from the scratch bitmap to the window.
6. Repeat steps 1 through 5 for all sprites.

These steps are implemented in the `animate` function in Listing 24.4. Figure 24.2 depicts the update process for sprite animation.

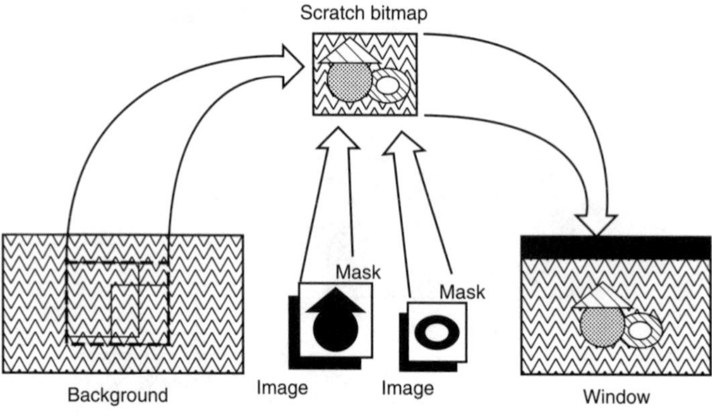

Figure 24.2. Updating the display to animate sprites.

Listing 24.4. SPRANIM.CPP. Implementation of the `SpriteAnimation` class.

```
//-------------------------------------------------------------
// File: spranim.cpp
//
// Member functions of the sprite animation classes.
//-------------------------------------------------------------
#include <stdlib.h>
```

```
#include "spranim.h"

inline short min(short x, short y)
{
    return (((x) < (y)) ? (x) : (y));
}
inline short max(short x, short y)
{
    return (((x) > (y)) ? (x) : (y));
}
//-------------------------------------------------------------------
// S p r i t e A n i m a t i o n
// Constructor for the SpriteAnimation class

SpriteAnimation::SpriteAnimation(HDC hdc,
                                 unsigned short w,
                                 unsigned short h,
                                 LPSTR filename)
{
// Load the background image from the specified file
    background = Sprite::init_image(filename);

    init_animation(hdc, w, h);
}
//-------------------------------------------------------------------
// S p r i t e A n i m a t i o n
// Constructor for the SpriteAnimation class

SpriteAnimation::SpriteAnimation(HDC hdc,
                                 unsigned short w,
                                 unsigned short h,
                                 Image *bg)
{
    background = bg;
    init_animation(hdc, w, h);
}
//-------------------------------------------------------------------
// SpriteAnimation:: i n i t _ a n i m a t i o n
// Initialize the animation

void SpriteAnimation::init_animation(HDC hdc,
                                     unsigned short w,
                                     unsigned short h)
```

continues

Listing 24.4. continued

```
{
// Set up coordinates of rectangle to be displayed
    top = left = 0;
    width = w;
    height = h;
    ws = w;
    hs = h;
    refresh = TRUE;

// Initialize all handles to zero
    sprites = NULL;
    hbm_bg = 0;
    hbm_bg_saved = 0;
    hbm_scratch = 0;
    hbm_sprite = 0;
    old_hbm_bg = 0;
    old_hbm_sprite = 0;
    old_hbm_scratch = 0;
    hdc_bg = 0;
    hdc_sprite = 0;
    hdc_scratch = 0;
    bg_image = 0;

    short bg_small = 0;

    if(background != NULL)
    {
// Create a palette for the background image
        if(background != NULL &&
           background->palette() == 0 &&
           background->numcolors() > 0)
                      background->make_palette();
// Now convert DIB to DDB
        background->DIBtoDDB(hdc);
        hbm_bg = background->get_ddb();
        bg_image = 1;
        if(background->width() < w || background->height() < h)
            bg_small = 1;
    }

    if(!bg_image || bg_small)
    {
```

```
        hbm_bg_saved = hbm_bg;
// Create a blank bitmap to be used as the background
        hbm_bg = CreateCompatibleBitmap(hdc, w, h);
        bg_image = 0;
    }

// Memory device context for the background image
    hdc_bg = CreateCompatibleDC(hdc);
    if(hbm_bg != 0 && hdc_bg != 0)
        old_hbm_bg = SelectBitmap(hdc_bg, hbm_bg);

    if(!bg_image || bg_small)
    {
// Initialize the background bitmap
        HBRUSH hbrbg = CreateSolidBrush(
                            GetSysColor(COLOR_WINDOW));
        HBRUSH oldbr = SelectBrush(hdc_bg, hbrbg);
        PatBlt(hdc_bg, 0, 0, w, h, PATCOPY);
        SelectBrush(hdc_bg, oldbr);
        DeleteBrush(hbrbg);
    }

    if(bg_small)
    {
        HDC hdc_temp = CreateCompatibleDC(hdc);
        HBITMAP hbm_temp = SelectBitmap(hdc_temp, hbm_bg_saved);
        BitBlt(hdc_bg, 0, 0, w, h, hdc_temp,
                    0, 0, SRCCOPY);
        SelectBitmap(hdc_temp, hbm_temp);
        DeleteBitmap(hbm_bg_saved);
        DeleteDC(hdc_temp);
    }

// Create a scratch bitmap of size w x h
    hbm_scratch = CreateCompatibleBitmap(hdc, w, h);

// Memory device context for the scratch bitmap
    hdc_scratch = CreateCompatibleDC(hdc);
    if(hbm_scratch != 0 && hdc_scratch != 0)
    {
        old_hbm_scratch = SelectBitmap(hdc_scratch, hbm_scratch);
    }
```

continues

Listing 24.4. continued

```
// Create a number of other memory device contexts for use
// during the animation. Select a 1x1 bitmap into each
// device context and save the old bitmaps (to be restored
// in the destructor).
    HBITMAP hbm_sprite = CreateCompatibleBitmap(hdc, 1, 1);

    hdc_sprite = CreateCompatibleDC(hdc);
    if(hdc_sprite != 0 && hbm_sprite != 0)
        old_hbm_sprite = SelectBitmap(hdc, hbm_sprite);

// Create a sorted array of sprites with array indices
// between 0 and 63 and capable of growing 8 elements
// at a time
    sprites = new SpriteArray(63, 0, 16);
    sprites->OwnsElements(1);
}
//------------------------------------------------------------
// ~ S p r i t e A n i m a t i o n
// Destructor for the SpriteAnimation class

SpriteAnimation::~SpriteAnimation()
{
// Deselect the bitmaps and destroy them. Also delete
// the DCs.
    if(hdc_scratch != 0 && old_hbm_scratch != 0)
        SelectBitmap(hdc_scratch, old_hbm_scratch);
    if(hbm_scratch != 0) DeleteBitmap(hbm_scratch);
    if(hdc_scratch != 0) DeleteDC(hdc_scratch);

    if(hdc_bg != 0 && old_hbm_bg != 0)
        SelectBitmap(hdc_bg, old_hbm_bg);
    if(hdc_bg != 0) DeleteDC(hdc_bg);

    if(background != NULL) delete background;
    if(!bg_image) DeleteBitmap(hbm_bg);

    if(hdc_sprite != 0 && old_hbm_sprite != 0)
        SelectBitmap(hdc_sprite, old_hbm_sprite);

    if(hdc_sprite != 0) DeleteDC(hdc_sprite);
    if(hbm_sprite != 0) DeleteBitmap(hbm_sprite);
```

```
// Delete the sorted array of sprites—this also deletes the
// sprites currently in the array.
    if(sprites != NULL) delete sprites;
}
//--------------------------------------------------------------
// S p r i t e A n i m a t i o n : : a n i m a t e
// Function that animates the sprites. The selected portion
// of the background is displayed at (x,y) in the window.

void SpriteAnimation::animate(HDC hdc, short x, short y)
{
    if(refresh) redisplay_all(hdc, x, y);

    int i, j, numsprites = sprites->GetItemsInContainer();
    for(i = 0; i < numsprites; i++)
    {
        Sprite* spr = (*sprites)[i];
        if(spr->needs_update())
        {
            short xdel = spr->xmove();
            short ydel = spr->ymove();
            short w = spr->width() + abs(xdel);
            short h = spr->height() + abs(ydel);
            short xold = spr->xpos();
            short xnew = xold + xdel;
            short yold = spr->ypos();
            short ynew = yold + ydel;
            short xfrom = min(xold, xnew);
            short yfrom = min(yold, ynew);
// Mark this sprite as the lone overlapping sprite
            spr->overlaps();

// Find other moving sprites that intersect this sprite
            for(j = 0; j < numsprites; j++)
            {
                Sprite* spr2 = (*sprites)[j];
                if(!spr2->is_overlapping() &&
                spr2->needs_update())
                {
                    short xdel2 = spr2->xmove();
                    short ydel2 = spr2->ymove();
                    short w2 = spr2->width() + abs(xdel2);
```

continues

Listing 24.4. continued

```
                    short h2 = spr2->height() + abs(ydel2);
                    short xold2 = spr2->xpos();
                    short xnew2 = xold2 + xdel2;
                    short yold2 = spr2->ypos();
                    short ynew2 = yold2 + ydel2;
                    short xfrom2 = min(xold2, xnew2);
                    short yfrom2 = min(yold2, ynew2);

                    if(rects_overlap(xfrom, yfrom, w, h,
                       xfrom2, yfrom2, w2, h2))
                    {
// Adjust dimensions of rectangle to be copied
                        short oldw = w;
                        w = max(xfrom2+w2,xfrom+w) -
                            min(xfrom,xfrom2);
                        if(w != oldw) j = 0;
                        short oldh = h;
                        h = max(yfrom2+h2,yfrom+h) -
                            min(yfrom,yfrom2);
                        if(h != oldh) j = 0;
                        if(xfrom2 < xfrom) xfrom = xfrom2;
                        if(yfrom2 < yfrom) yfrom = yfrom2;
                        spr2->overlaps();
                    }
                }
            }
// Adjust xfrom, yfrom, w, and h by comparing with the region
// of background (top, left, width, height) that is currently
// being displayed
            if(rects_overlap(xfrom, yfrom, w, h,
                             left, top, width, height))
            {
                w = min(xfrom+w,left+width) -
                    max(xfrom,left);
                h = min(yfrom+h,top+height) -
                    max(yfrom,top);
                xfrom = max(xfrom,left);
                yfrom = max(yfrom,top);
            }
            else
                continue;
// Check for intersection of the rectangle xfrom, yfrom, w, h
```

```
// with stationary sprites.
            for(j = 0; j < numsprites; j++)
            {
                Sprite* spr2 = (*sprites)[j];
                if((!spr2->needs_update() ¦¦
                    !spr2->is_overlapping()) && spr2->is_active())
                {
                    short w2 = spr2->width();
                    short h2 = spr2->height();
                    short xfrom2 = spr2->xpos();
                    short yfrom2 = spr2->ypos();

                    if(rects_overlap(xfrom, yfrom, w, h,
                                     xfrom2, yfrom2, w2, h2))
                        spr2->overlaps();
                }
            }


// Get a piece of the background into the scratch bitmap

            BitBlt(hdc_scratch, 0, 0, w, h, hdc_bg,
                   xfrom, yfrom, SRCCOPY);
// Loop through all sprites and draw the ones that overlap
            for(j = 0; j < numsprites; j++)
            {
                Sprite* spr2 = (*sprites)[j];
                if(!spr2->is_overlapping()) continue;
                short xdel2 = spr2->xmove();
                short ydel2 = spr2->ymove();
                short w2 = spr2->width() + abs(xdel2);
                short h2 = spr2->height() + abs(ydel2);
                short xold2 = spr2->xpos();
                short xnew2 = xold2 + xdel2;
                short yold2 = spr2->ypos();
                short ynew2 = yold2 + ydel2;
                short xto2 = xnew2 - xfrom;
                short yto2 = ynew2 - yfrom;

// AND sprite's mask onto the scratch bitmap
                HBITMAP hbm = spr2->hbm_mask();
                if(hbm != NULL)
```

continues

Listing 24.4. continued

```
                {
                    SelectBitmap(hdc_sprite, spr2->hbm_mask());
                    BitBlt(hdc_scratch, xto2, yto2, w2, h2,
                           hdc_sprite, 0, 0, SRCAND);

// Now OR sprite's image onto the scratch bitmap
                    SelectBitmap(hdc_sprite, spr2->hbm_image());
                    BitBlt(hdc_scratch, xto2, yto2, w2, h2,
                           hdc_sprite, 0, 0, SRCPAINT);
                }
                else
                {
// Copy the image if there is no mask...
                    if(spr2->hbm_image() != NULL)
                    {
                        SelectBitmap(hdc_sprite,
                                     spr2->hbm_image());
                        BitBlt(hdc_scratch, xto2, yto2, w2, h2,
                               hdc_sprite, 0, 0, SRCCOPY);
                    }
                }
// Call the "draw" function, if any
                if(spr2->is_active() && spr2->drawproc() != NULL)
                    (*(spr2->drawproc()))(hdc_scratch, xto2, yto2,
                        spr2->data());

// Update the sprite's position and change its status bits
                spr2->newpos(xnew2, ynew2);
                spr2->update_done();
                spr2->no_overlap();
            }

// BitBlt the scratch area onto the window
            BitBlt(hdc, x+xfrom-left, y+yfrom-top, w, h,
                   hdc_scratch, 0, 0, SRCCOPY);
        }
    }
}
//--------------------------------------------------------------
// SpriteAnimation:: r e d i s p l a y _ a l l
// Redisplay the background plus all sprites
```

```
void SpriteAnimation::redisplay_all(HDC hdc, short x, short y)
{
// Copy designated portion of background into scratch bitmap
    SelectBitmap(hdc_scratch, hbm_scratch);
    BitBlt(hdc_scratch, 0, 0, ws, hs, hdc_bg, left, top,
           SRCCOPY);

// Draw the active sprites on the scratch bitmap
    int i, numsprites = sprites->GetItemsInContainer();
    for(i = 0; i < numsprites; i++)
    {
        Sprite* spr = (*sprites)[i];
        short xs = spr->xpos() - left;
        short ys = spr->ypos() - top;
        HBITMAP hbm = spr->hbm_mask();
        if(spr->is_active() && hbm != NULL)
        {
// AND the mask
            SelectBitmap(hdc_sprite, spr->hbm_mask());
            BitBlt(hdc_scratch, xs, ys,
                   spr->width(), spr->height(), hdc_sprite,
                   0, 0, SRCAND);
// OR the image
            SelectBitmap(hdc_sprite, spr->hbm_image());
            BitBlt(hdc_scratch, xs, ys,
                   spr->width(), spr->height(), hdc_sprite,
                   0, 0, SRCPAINT);
        }
        if(spr->is_active() && hbm == NULL &&
           spr->hbm_image() != NULL)
        {
// Simply copy the image of the sprite
            SelectBitmap(hdc_sprite, spr->hbm_image());
            BitBlt(hdc_scratch, xs, ys,
                   spr->width(), spr->height(), hdc_sprite,
                   0, 0, SRCCOPY);
        }
        if(spr->is_active() && spr->drawproc() != NULL)
            (*(spr->drawproc()))(hdc_scratch, xs, ys,
                    spr->data());
        spr->update_done();
        spr->no_overlap();
    }
```

continues

Listing 24.4. continued

```
// Copy the scratch bitmap into the window
    BitBlt(hdc, x, y, ws, hs,
           hdc_scratch, 0, 0, SRCCOPY);

    refresh = FALSE;
}
//-------------------------------------------------------------
// S p r i t e A n i m a t i o n : : d r a w _ b g
// Draw the background bitmap

void SpriteAnimation::draw_bg(HDC hdc, short x, short y)
{
    BitBlt(hdc, x, y, width, height, hdc_bg, left, top,
           SRCCOPY);
}
//-------------------------------------------------------------
// S p r i t e A n i m a t i o n : : s p r i t e _ a t
// Returns pointer to Sprite that encloses point (x,y)

Sprite* SpriteAnimation::sprite_at(short x, short y)
{
    int i, numsprites = sprites->GetItemsInContainer();
    Sprite* rs = NULL;

    for(i = numsprites - 1; i >= 0; i—)
    {
        Sprite* spr = (*sprites)[i];
        if(!spr->is_active()) continue;
        short xs = spr->xpos();
        short ys = spr->ypos();
        if(x < xs) continue;
        if(y < ys) continue;

        short ws = spr->width();
        short hs = spr->height();
        if(x > (xs + ws - 1)) continue;
        if(y > (ys + hs - 1)) continue;

        rs = spr;
```

```
        break;
    }
    return rs;
}
```

A Sample Animation Program

This section describes a sample OWL-based Windows program that makes use of the `Sprite` and `SpriteAnimation` classes to animate a number of sprites on a background image. The program is in the companion directory—it should be in the CH7 directory after you install the code on your system. When you run the ANIMATE application, you can see a number of sprites, including one with a text message animated on a complex background image. Figure 24.3 shows a sample output of the program (after you select the About... item from the Help menu).

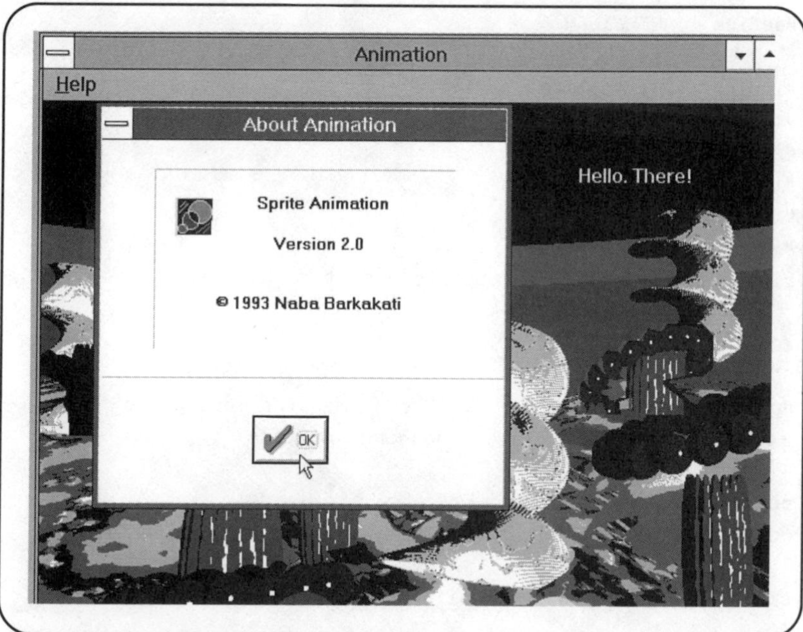

Figure 24.3. Output of the sample animation program.

The *AnimationWindow* Class

The ANIMATE program uses an `AnimationWindow` as its main window. Listing 24.5 shows the declaration of the `AnimationWindow` class, which is derived from `TFrameWindow`.

`AnimationWindow` has a pointer to the `SpriteAnimation` object that manages the animation for the application. The `SpriteAnimation` object is created and initialized in the `WM_CREATE` message handler of the `AnimationWindow` class. An array of pointers to the `Sprite` objects is also maintained in `AnimationWindow` because we have to manipulate the `Sprite` objects using these pointers.

Listing 24.5. ANIMWIN.H. Declaration of the `AnimationWindow` class.

```
//-----------------------------------------------------------
// File: animwin.h
//
// Window classes for a sprite animation application.
//-----------------------------------------------------------
#if !defined(__ANIMWIN_H)
#define __ANIMWIN_H

#include <owl\applicat.h>
#include <owl\framewin.h>
#include <owl\dialog.h>
#include <owl\gdiobjec.h>
#include <owl\dc.h>
#include <owl\point.h>
#include "spranim.h"  // Sprite animation class

#define IDM_ABOUT 200

#define SPRITE_ANIMATE 1 // ID of timer for moving and
                         // drawing sprites

const short AnimBGWidth = 640;
const short AnimBGHeight = 480;

class AnimationWindow : public TFrameWindow
{
public:
```

```
    AnimationWindow(TWindow *parent, const char far *title) :
                    TFrameWindow(parent, title),
                    anim(0), top(0), left(0),
                    width(AnimBGWidth), height(AnimBGHeight)
    {}

    ~AnimationWindow();

    void Paint(TDC& dc, BOOL, TRect&);

    int EvCreate(CREATESTRUCT far &);
    void EvTimer(UINT timer_id);
    BOOL EvQueryNewPalette();
    void EvPaletteChanged(HWND hWndPalChg);
    void About();

private:
    SpriteAnimation  *anim;
    Sprite           **s;
    short            top;   // The point where the background
    short            left;  // is displayed
    short            width;
    short            height;

    void move_sprites();

DECLARE_RESPONSE_TABLE(AnimationWindow);
};

#endif
```

Sprites in the Sample Animation

For this sample application, the file ANIMWIN.CPP includes the definition of the sprites. I have defined a `SpriteInfo` structure to hold the information needed to define a `Sprite`. A static array of `SpriteInfo` structures, called `sprite_data`, defines all the sprites for this application. Notice that the last `SpriteInfo` structure in the `sprite_data` array does not provide any filenames for the image and mask bitmaps. This `Sprite` is used to illustrate the use of a drawing procedure (the `dproc` member variable of a `Sprite`). I use the function `draw_text` (Listing 24.4) to display a text message that can be animated like a bitmapped sprite.

Initializing the Animation

The entire animation is set up in the `EvCreate` function (Listing 24.4) that handles the `WM_CREATE` message sent by Windows to the `AnimationWindow` when the window is created. The initialization involves creating a `SpriteAnimation` object and an array of `Sprite` objects and adding each `Sprite` object to the `SpriteAnimation`.

Animation Strategy

My strategy for this animation is to use a Windows timer event to move the sprites and update the display. Thus, I call `SetTimer` to set up a 50-millisecond timer in the `EvCreate` function. Note that Windows delivers, at most, 18.2 timer events per second or a timer event every 55 milliseconds.

The `WM_TIMER` events are handled by the `EvTimer` function (Listing 24.4). `EvTimer` first checks to ensure that the timer ID matches the one used when the timer was started. Then the sprites are moved. Finally, the display is updated by calling the `animate` function of the `SpriteAnimation` object that manages this animation.

In Listing 24.7, the sprites simply bounce back and forth within the confines of the animation's background. The `move_sprites` function in Listing 24.4 handles the details of the movement algorithm.

Listing 24.7. ANIMWIN.CPP. Implementation of the `AnimationWindow` class.

```
//-------------------------------------------------------------
// File: animwin.cpp
//
// Member functions for the AnimationWindow class.
//-------------------------------------------------------------
#include <stdlib.h>
#include <string.h>
#include "animwin.h"

struct SpriteInfo
{
    SpriteInfo(char* imgfname, char* mskfname,
               short xp, short yp, short xv, short yv,
               short prio) :
               imagefilename(imgfname), maskfilename(mskfname),
               xpos(xp), ypos(yp), xvel(xv), yvel(yv),
               priority(prio) {}
```

```
    char* imagefilename;
    char* maskfilename;
    short  xpos, ypos;     // Initial x-y position
    short  xvel, yvel;     // Initial x- and y-velocity
    short  priority;
};
// Declare an array of sprites to be loaded from image files
static SpriteInfo sprite_data[] =
{
    SpriteInfo("face1.bmp",  "face1m.bmp", 10, 10, 3, 2, 4),
    SpriteInfo("ring.bmp",   "ringm.bmp", 200, 10, -3, 2, 5),
    SpriteInfo("car.bmp",    "carm.bmp",  10, 200, -1, -1, 2),
    SpriteInfo("strange.bmp","strangem.bmp",100, 100, 1, 1, 1),
    SpriteInfo(NULL, NULL, 100, 50, 1, 0, 99)
};
// Total number of sprites
static int numsprites = sizeof(sprite_data) /
                        sizeof(sprite_data[0]);

void _FAR PASCAL _export draw_text(HDC hdc, short x, short y,
                   LPVOID data);

struct TEXT_DATA
{
    LPSTR  text;
    size_t numchars;
};
static TEXT_DATA dt;
static LPSTR msg = "Hello, There!";
//-----------------------------------------------------------------
// Define the response table for AnimationWindow
DEFINE_RESPONSE_TABLE1(AnimationWindow, TFrameWindow)
    EV_WM_CREATE,
    EV_WM_TIMER,
    EV_WM_QUERYNEWPALETTE,
    EV_WM_PALETTECHANGED,
    EV_COMMAND(IDM_ABOUT,     About),
END_RESPONSE_TABLE;
//-----------------------------------------------------------------
// A n i m a t i o n : : E v C r e a t e
// Initialize everything for the animation
```

continues

Listing 24.7. continued

```
int AnimationWindow::EvCreate(CREATESTRUCT far& cs)
{
    int status = TFrameWindow::EvCreate(cs);

// Get a DC for this window
    HDC hdc = GetDC(HWindow);

// Set timers for moving sprites and displaying them
    SetTimer(SPRITE_ANIMATE, 50, NULL);

// Create an instance of the SpriteAnimation class and
// load the images (background plus the sprites)

    anim = new SpriteAnimation(hdc, width, height, "animbg.bmp");

// Create the array of sprites
    s = new Sprite*[numsprites];
    int i;
    for(i = 0; i < numsprites; i++)
    {
        s[i] = new Sprite(hdc, sprite_data[i].imagefilename,
                     sprite_data[i].maskfilename);
        s[i]->priority(sprite_data[i].priority);
        s[i]->newpos(sprite_data[i].xpos, sprite_data[i].ypos);
// Add sprite to animation
        anim->add(s[i]);
    }

// The last sprite is used to display a text string
    s[numsprites-1]->width(100);
    s[numsprites-1]->height(16);
    dt.text = msg;
    dt.numchars = strlen(msg);
    DRAWPROC proc = (DRAWPROC) MakeProcInstance(
                                   (FARPROC) draw_text,
                               GetApplication()->GetInstance());
    s[numsprites-1]->drawproc(proc, &dt);
    s[numsprites-1]->active();
    s[numsprites-1]->update();

// Release the DC
    ReleaseDC(HWindow, hdc);
```

```
    return status;
}
//------------------------------------------------------------
//  ~ A n i m a t i o n W i n d o w
//  Destructor for the animation window.

AnimationWindow::~AnimationWindow()
{
    if(anim != NULL) delete anim;
    if(s != NULL) delete[] s;
    KillTimer(SPRITE_ANIMATE);
}
//------------------------------------------------------------
// A n i m a t i o n W i n d o w : : E v T i m e r
// Handle WM_TIMER events

void AnimationWindow::EvTimer(UINT timer_id)
{
    switch(timer_id)
    {
        case SPRITE_ANIMATE:
            {
                HDC hdc = GetDC(HWindow);
// Move the sprites
                move_sprites();
                anim->animate(hdc, top, left);
                ReleaseDC(HWindow, hdc);
            }
            break;

        default:
            break;
    }
}
//------------------------------------------------------------
//  AnimationWindow:: P a i n t
//  Draw everything in the window

void AnimationWindow::Paint(TDC& hdc, BOOL, TRect&)
{
    if(anim != NULL)
    {
```

continues

Listing 24.7. continued

```
        anim->set_refresh(TRUE);
        anim->animate(hdc, top, left);
    }
}
//---------------------------------------------------------------
// AnimationWindow:: E v Q u e r y N e w P a l e t t e
// Realize palette for the animation's background

BOOL AnimationWindow::EvQueryNewPalette()
{
    if(anim == NULL) return 0;
    if(anim->bgimage() == NULL) return 0;

    HPALETTE hpal = anim->bgimage()->palette();
    short changed = 0;
    if(hpal)
    {
        TClientDC dc(HWindow);
        dc.SelectObject(hpal, FALSE);
        changed = dc.RealizePalette();
        dc.RestorePalette();
        if(changed)
        {
            Invalidate(TRUE);
            UpdateWindow();
        }
    }
    return changed;
}
//---------------------------------------------------------------
// AnimationWindow:: E v P a l e t t e C h a n g e d
// Handle a change in system palette

void AnimationWindow::EvPaletteChanged(HWND hWndPalChg)
{
    if(hWndPalChg == HWindow) return;
    if(anim == NULL) return;
    if(anim->bgimage() == NULL) return;

    HPALETTE hpal = anim->bgimage()->palette();
    short changed = 0;
```

```
    if(hpal)
    {
        TClientDC dc(HWindow);
        dc.SelectObject(hpal, FALSE);
        changed = dc.RealizePalette();
        if(changed)
        {
            dc.UpdateColors();
        }
        dc.RestorePalette();
    }
}
//-----------------------------------------------------------------
//  A n i m a t i o n W i n d o w :: A b o u t
//  Display the "About..." box

void AnimationWindow::About()
{
    TDialog *p_about = new TDialog(this, "ABOUTANIMATION");
    GetApplication()->ExecDialog(p_about);
}
//-----------------------------------------------------------------
// m o v e _ s p r i t e s
// Move the sprites

void AnimationWindow::move_sprites()
{
    int i;
    for(i = 0; i < numsprites; i++)
    {
        if(s[i]->xpos() <= 0 || s[i]->xpos() >= width)
            sprite_data[i].xvel = -sprite_data[i].xvel;

        if(s[i]->ypos() <= 0 || s[i]->ypos() >= height)
            sprite_data[i].yvel = -sprite_data[i].yvel;

        s[i]->move(sprite_data[i].xvel, sprite_data[i].yvel);
    }
}
//-----------------------------------------------------------------
void _FAR PASCAL _export draw_text(HDC hdc, short x, short y,
                   LPVOID data)
```

continues

Listing 24.7. continued

```
{
    TEXT_DATA *td = (TEXT_DATA*)data;
    SetBkMode(hdc, TRANSPARENT);

    SetTextColor(hdc, RGB(255,255,0));
    TextOut(hdc, x, y, td->text, td->numchars);
}
```

The ANIMATE Application

Listing 24.8 shows the main program of the ANIMATE application. Like all OWL-based Windows programs, the ANIMATE application creates an instance of its main window, an `AnimationWindow` object, and starts an event-handling loop by calling the `Run` member function of the application class, `AnimationApp`. All application-specific work is done in the `AnimationWindow` class, described in previous sections.

Listing 24.8. ANIMATE.CPP. Main program of the animation application.

```
//-------------------------------------------------------------
//  File:  animate.cpp
//
//  A Windows application that animates a number of sprites
//  over a background image. Also allows user to move an
//  image around using the mouse.
//-------------------------------------------------------------
#include <owl\applicat.h>
#include "animwin.h"

//-------------------------------------------------------------
class AnimationApp: public TApplication
{
public:
// Constructor that simply calls the base class constructor
    AnimationApp(const char far *name) : TApplication(name) {}

// Define function to initialize application's main window
    void InitMainWindow();
};
```

```
//------------------------------------------------------------------
// A n i m a t i o n A p p : : I n i t M a i n W i n d o w

void AnimationApp::InitMainWindow()
{
    MainWindow = new AnimationWindow(NULL, "Animation");
    MainWindow->SetIcon(this, "ANIMATION_ICON");
    MainWindow->AssignMenu("MainMenu");
    MainWindow->Attr.AccelTable = "MainAccelTable";
}
//------------------------------------------------------------------
//  O w l M a i n
//
//  Create an instance of the application and "run" it.

int OwlMain(int, char**)
{
    AnimationApp Animation("Sprite Animation");
    return Animation.Run();
}
```

Building ANIMATE.EXE

Use Borland C++ 4 to build the ANIMATE application. The companion disk has all the files needed to build the executable, ANIMATE.EXE. In particular, the project file, ANIMATE.IDE, lists the files necessary to build the application. You should be able to build ANIMATE.EXE by selecting Make all from the Project menu. Once the program is successfully built, you can add it to Windows Program Manager by selecting New… from the Program Manager's File menu.

One of the files that you need to build ANIMATE.EXE is the resource file, ANIMATE.RES, which is included in the companion disk. I prepared the resource file using the Resource Workshop program included with Borland C++.

Summary

Images used in Windows multimedia applications are usually animated in some way to support the interactive nature of the application. One of the common tasks in many multimedia applications is to animate (move) small images known as sprites over a background image. The obvious approach of erasing and redrawing sprites produces an undesirable flicker. One way to get around this problem is to draw the images on an offscreen bitmap and copy the final image to the screen using the Windows API function `BitBlt`. This chapter shows the `Sprite` and `SpriteAnimation` classes that allow you to animate sprites over a background image using the offscreen bitmap technique. A sample application, ANIMATE, illustrates how to use the sprite animation classes.

25

A Sample Application

Chapters 22 through 24 discuss techniques for image display, animation, and sound generation. This chapter puts all these techniques to practice in an application that I call ShowMe. You can use ShowMe to build animated product demonstrations (or demos, for short). This chapter shows you how to use ShowMe to build a demo and guides you through the implementation of ShowMe.

Using ShowMe

The source code for the ShowMe application and an executable version of it are on this book's companion disk. The code on the disk is organized by chapter, so the ShowMe application appears in the directory named CH25. You should install the code from the disk, start Windows, and run ShowMe to get a feel for the types of demos that can be created with it.

ShowMe Demo Needs a Sound Card

To fully enjoy the sample demo, you need a sound card installed in your PC. You also need a Windows sound driver capable of playing .WAV sound files. The demo will run on PCs without a sound card, but you won't hear any sound.

Running the Sample Demo

After installing the code from the companion disk, when you run ShowMe under Windows, it automatically runs a demo that promotes this book. The demo uses sequences of animated images and voice annotations (played through a sound card). Figure 25.1 shows the screen at the end of a sequence of animations. The way this demo is designed, ShowMe cycles through the entire demo after waiting for a specified number of seconds. Thus, ShowMe is ideal for the kind of "endless" demos that you can leave running on a PC at a computer show.

To exit from the demo, press the Escape key. ShowMe gives you a chance to exit or resume the demo.

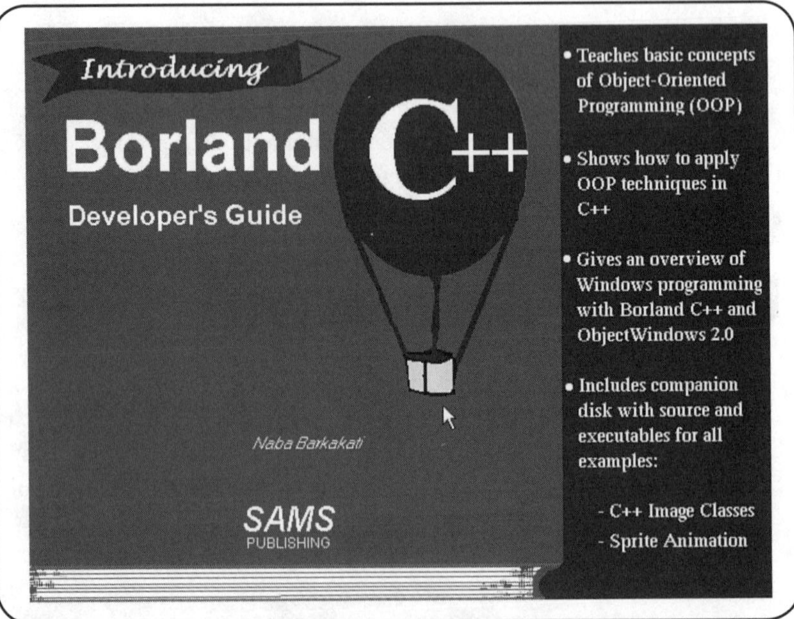

Figure 25.1. Sample ShowMe demo promoting this book.

The ShowMe Scripting Language

ShowMe is essentially a script-driven animated demo maker. The scripts are text files with commands that are interpreted and executed by ShowMe. These commands activate specific capabilities of ShowMe, such as loading a script file, creating an animation, adding a sprite to an animation, moving a sprite, and playing a waveform file containing digitized sound.

ShowMe always starts off by loading a script file named SHOWME.RUN. This is not a limitation, however, because you can use the `load_file` command in the SHOWME.RUN script file to load another script file that actually runs the desired demo. For instance, Listing 25.1 shows the SHOWME.RUN file for the sample demo. The comments in the script file start with the # character. All this file does is load another script file, BDGINTRO.RUN, that actually controls the sample demo.

Listing 25.1. SHOWME.RUN. The initial script file in `ShowMe`.

```
######################################################################
# Input file for the ShowMe application
#
######################################################################

# Load commands from a "run" file

load_file            bdgintro.run
```

ShowMe Commands

To create a demo with ShowMe, you have to prepare a script file with commands from the ShowMe scripting language to control the sequence of events that take place in the demo. Currently, ShowMe's scripting language supports these types of constructs:

- Commands that ShowMe acts upon immediately
- Events that cause commands to be executed at a specified time
- Conditions that activate commands when a specified condition is true

Table 25.1 shows the current list of ShowMe commands, including the arguments expected by each command. Optional arguments appear in square brackets, and required arguments are shown in angular brackets. Note that events and conditions are also specified through commands.

Table 25.1. ShowMe commands.

Command	Description
start	Starts the animation running. You should use it after the animation is ready and the sprites are loaded.
refresh	Redraws the animation.
reset_time [new_time]	Resets the time to a specified new value (a floating-point number). If no new time is specified, ShowMe resets the time to zero.
animation <animation_name> <width> <height>	Starts a new animation with the image from a specified image file as background.
[image_file_name]	The animation's width and height are specified in pixels. The animation is given a name; later on, you have to use this name to refer to the animation.
load_file <script_file_name>	Loads commands from a specified script file. This command provides a way to chain one script file to another. For continuously looping demos, you can load the same script file repeatedly when a specific condition occurs (such as time exceeding a preset value).
sprite <sprite_name> <image_file_name> <mask_file_name> <xpos> <ypos> <priority>	Creates a sprite with the specified image and mask. If you do not have a mask, use NONE as the filename. The sprite is positioned at the specified coordinates in the animation's background. The

Command	Description
	priority of the sprite controls the stacking order of sprites when they overlap. You have to give the sprite a name; later on you can use that name to identify the sprite.
`add <sprite_name> <animation_name>`	Adds a sprite to an animation.
`event <time> <any_ShowMe_command>`	Posts an event scheduled to occur at the specified time. When the time comes, ShowMe executes the command you have specified. Note that this can be any command in this table, including another `event` command. The most common use of the `event` command is to schedule movement of sprites and to start playing sound waveform files.
`condition <cond_name> <expression_string> -> <any_ShowMe_command>`	Specifies a condition to be checked. The exact format of the `<expression_string>` depends on the specific condition being tested. Table 25.2 lists the conditions that you can check. If the condition is true (the value of the associated expression is nonzero), ShowMe interprets and executes the command that follows the `->` in the condition command.
`set <sprite_name> <variable_name> <value>`	Sets the value of the specified variable of the sprite identified by name. Currently, a sprite has the following variables that you can set: `xpos`, `ypos`, `xvel`, `yvel`, `xacc`,

continues

Table 25.1. continued

Command	Description
	`yacc`, and `priority`. The first six variables denote x and y positions, velocities, and accelerations of the sprite. These control the movement of the sprite.
`quit`	Exits ShowMe.
`sound <on_or_off>`	Turns sound on or off. The token following the sound keyword must be `on` or `off`.
`show <sprite_name>`	Makes the named sprite visible.
`hide <sprite_name>`	Hides the specified sprite.
`destroy <animation_name>`	Destroys the animation identified by name.
`swap_anim <animation_name>`	Makes the specified animation the current one. If you have several animations defined, you can switch to a new animation with this command.
`about_showme`	Displays the About ShowMe dialog box.
`play_sound <waveform_file> [flag]`	Plays sound from the specified waveform file. The optional `[flag]` can be `loop` to play the sound continuously, `sync` to play the file synchronously (does not return until sound finishes playing), or `stop` to stop a previously playing sound. By default, the waveform file is played asynchronously (starts playing the sound and returns immediately).

ShowMe Conditions

In ShowMe, a condition involves evaluating an expression and taking a specified action if the expression evaluates to a nonzero value. To specify conditions, you need to know a few more keywords that identify expressions. Table 25.2 summarizes the four keywords used to write expressions in ShowMe condition commands. Optional arguments appear in square brackets and required arguments are shown in angular brackets.

Table 25.2. ShowMe expressions.

Condition	Description
time <operator> <value>	Compares current time with the specified value (a floating-point number) using the specified operator. The <operator> can be one of the following strings: *String* — *Meaning* exceeds — greater than greater_than — greater than gt — greater than less_than — less than lt — less than equals — equal to is — equal to equal_to — equal to eq — equal to ge — greater than or equal to le — less than or equal to
key <operator> <key_code>	Compares the current keystroke with the specified keycode (ASCII code) using the <operator>. See description of the time expression for acceptable operator names.
click on <sprite_name> click in <x1> <y1> <x2> <y2>	The first form checks whether the current mouse click is on the specified sprite. The second form checks whether the mouse click is inside the rectangle whose upper-left corner is (x1, y1) and lower-right corner is (x2, y2).

continues

Table 25.2. continued

Condition	Description
`value <sprite_name> <variable_name> <operator> <value>`	Compares the current value of a sprite's variable with the specified <value>, which can be an integer or a floating-point depending on the type of the sprite's variable. See the description of the `time` expression for acceptable operator names.

A Sample Script File

Now that you have seen the basic command set and the keywords used to write expressions in ShowMe, let me show you how to write a simple demo in ShowMe. Let us re-create an animation somewhat similar to the one shown in Chapter 24, "Animating Images." (Run the ANIMATE application in Chapter 24 to refresh your memory.)

Long Lines in ShowMe Scripts

A single line in a ShowMe script can be as much as 256 characters long. If you end a line with a backslash (\) followed by a new line, ShowMe will merge that line with the next one. You can use this feature to split a long command line into several smaller ones.

The first step is to create an animation using the animation command as follows:

```
# First create the animation (use the bitmap from Chapter 24's
# animation)
animation strange 640 480 ..\ch24\animbg.bmp
```

This animation is named `strange`, it is 640 pixels wide by 480 pixels tall, and it uses the `animbg.bmp` bitmap from Chapter 24 as the background. Notice that comment lines start with a `#`.

Next create a sprite and add it to the animation. Here are the commands to do this:

```
#Create the sprite
sprite ring ..\ch24\ring.bmp ..\ch24\ringm.bmp 10 60 100

# Add the sprite to the animation
add ring strange
```

The sprite is named `ring` and it is placed at (10, 60) in the animation. The sprite's priority is 100, although in the absence of any other sprites, the priority does not matter at all.

To set the sprite in motion, you have to give it a speed. Here is how you can set the x- and y-velocities of the sprite named `ring`:

```
# Set sprite's x and y velocity (in pixels per second)
set ring xvel 30
set ring yvel 40
```

To ensure that the sprite remains inside the animation, you should add a few conditions that reverse the direction of motion whenever the sprite reaches a boundary. For instance, here is how you would set the x-velocity to a negative value whenever the sprite reaches the right boundary of the animation:

```
# Reflect ring off the boundaries...
condition check_ring_xpos1 value ring xpos ge 600 \
        -> set ring xvel -30
```

This condition is named `check_ring_xpos1`, and it checks if the x-position of the sprite is greater than or equal to 600. When the expression is true, this condition sets the x-velocity of the `ring` to -30 pixels per second. You can add more conditions to check for other cases, such as x-position becoming less than zero. Additionally, you can add a few conditions to make a sound whenever the sprite hits the boundaries of the animation.

The final step in the script file is to start the animation. Add the `start` command at the end of the file to get the animation going.

Listing 25.2 shows the complete script file TEST.RUN that implements the bouncing ring on a background image. To run this demo, edit the SHOWME.RUN file and change the first command to

```
load_file   test.run
```

Then run ShowMe to see how your new demo works.

> **File Extension of ShowMe Script Files**
>
> Although a ShowMe script file can have any name, I have been using .RUN as the file extension for ShowMe script files. This lets me refer to the script files as *run* files.

Listing 25.2. TEST.RUN. A sample script file for ShowMe.

```
##################################################################
# File: test.run
#
# A small animated demo.
#
# To run this demo with ShowMe, add the following line in
# the file SHOWME.RUN :   load_file test.run
#
##################################################################

# First create the animation (use the bitmap from Chapter 24's
# animation)
animation strange 640 480 ..\ch24\animbg.bmp

# Now load a sprite
sprite ring ..\ch24\ring.bmp ..\ch24\ringm.bmp 10 60 100

# Add the sprite to the animation
add ring strange

# Set sprite's x and y velocity (in pixels per second)
set ring xvel 30
set ring yvel 40

# Specify the conditions to be checked

# If time exceeds 120 seconds, quit
condition check_time time exceeds 120.0 -> quit

# Reflect ring off the boundaries...
condition check_ring_xpos1 value ring xpos ge 600 \
        -> set ring xvel -30
```

```
condition check_ring_xpos2 value ring xpos le 0 \
        -> set ring xvel 30

condition check_ring_ypos1 value ring ypos ge 440 \
        -> set ring yvel -40

condition check_ring_ypos2 value ring ypos le 0 \
        -> set ring yvel 40

# Make a sound when sprite reflects off boundary
condition check_ring_xsound1 value ring xpos ge 600 \
        -> play_sound ding.wav

condition check_ring_xsound2 value ring xpos le 0 \
        -> play_sound ding.wav

condition check_ring_ysound1 value ring ypos ge 440 \
        -> play_sound ding.wav

condition check_ring_ysound2 value ring ypos le 0 \
        -> play_sound ding.wav

# Start the demo. The animation starts only after
# this command

start
```

The Book Introduction Demo

By now, you should be familiar with ShowMe's capabilities and how you can harness these capabilities with a script file. Now I'll show you the script files that were used to build the sample demo—I call it the Book Introduction (Book Intro, for short) demo because it introduces this book.

I started the script files with the goal of the demo—to introduce the book and point out its major features. I decided to start the demo with a banner saying "Introducing" pulled into the animation by an airplane. Then an announcer introduces the book, its author, and the publisher. As the announcer speaks, the title of the book, the author's name, and the publisher's name appear in that order. Then, the features of the book appear one by one along the right edge of the animation. Eventually, after a specified amount of time elapses, the entire sequence repeats itself.

I implemented the Book Intro demo with two script files:

- BDGINTRO.RUN (Listing 25.3) is the script file that is loaded by a `load_file` command from SHOWME.RUN. This script file sets up the animation, specifies the conditions, and starts the animation.
- BDGLOOP1.RUN (Listing 25.4) is the script file that BDGINTRO.RUN loads whenever a condition is met (for example, time exceeds 45 seconds). This script file resets the time and posts the events that play the sounds and sequence the images.

If you want to create a "looping" demo, this is a good scheme to follow.

Listing 25.3. BDGINTRO.RUN. Script file that sets up the Book Introduction demo.

```
####################################################################
# File: bdgintro.run
#
# An animated demo for the book:
#
#           "Borland C++ Developer's Guide"
#                          by
#                   Naba Barkakati
#            Published by SAMS Publishing
#
# For use with the ShowMe application (Chapter 25)
#
####################################################################

animation bdgintro 640 480 .\bdgintro\bdgbkbg.bmp

sprite balloon .\bdgintro\balloon.bmp  .\bdgintro\balloonm.bmp  \
    264 300 100
sprite naba .\bdgintro\naba.bmp .\bdgintro\nabam.bmp 192 339 100
sprite sams .\bdgintro\sams.bmp .\bdgintro\samsm.bmp 181 396 100

sprite intro_banner .\bdgintro\intro.bmp .\bdgintro\introm.bmp \
    -370 6 99

sprite airplane .\bdgintro\airp.bmp .\bdgintro\airpm.bmp \
    -100 0 99
```

```
sprite item1 .\bdgintro\item1.bmp none 462  18 300
sprite item2 .\bdgintro\item2.bmp none 462 102 300
sprite item3 .\bdgintro\item3.bmp none 462 188 300
sprite item4 .\bdgintro\item4.bmp none 462 290 300

# Add all sprites to the animation
add balloon bdgintro

add naba bdgintro
add sams bdgintro

add intro_banner bdgintro
add airplane     bdgintro

add item1 bdgintro
add item2 bdgintro
add item3 bdgintro
add item4 bdgintro

# Conditions to be checked
condition check_time time exceeds 45.0 \
        -> load_file bdgloop1.run

condition check_airp value airplane xpos ge 270 \
        -> set intro_banner xvel 0

condition check_airp value airplane xpos ge 1200 \
        -> set airplane xvel 0

condition check_balloon value balloon ypos le 4 \
        -> set balloon yvel 0

condition A_Key_pressed key equals 65 -> about x

# Load the file that is used to repeat the demo
load_file bdgloop1.run

# Start the demo. The animation starts only after
# this command

start
```

As you can see from the BDGINTRO.RUN file, the Book Intro animation uses a large number of sprites for effect. Most of the sprites are prepositioned, kept hidden, and shown at a convenient moment. I made the decision to animate only a few sprites when I realized that animating large sprites is slow and it ruins the effect.

To prepare the sprites, I drew the entire scene (as it appears in Figure 25.1) in Paintbrush. After that, I cut out pieces of this drawing and prepared the images and masks needed for the sprites. This allowed me to determine the exact positions of the sprites for the final scene.

To minimize clutter, I placed all the bitmap files and the .WAV files in a separate subdirectory named BDGINTRO. If you examine the BDGINTRO subdirectory (after installing the companion disk), you will see that the sound files and the bitmaps take up over half a megabyte of disk space. This is a common characteristic of multimedia demos because you need a lot of images and sound waveforms for good effect.

Listing 25.4. BDGLOOP1.RUN. Script file that loops through the Book Introduction demo.

```
################################################################
# This file is called to repeat the demo over and over again
#
# Loaded from: bdgintro.run
#
################################################################
# Hide all sprites
hide naba
hide sams

hide item1
hide item2
hide item3
hide item4

set intro_banner xpos -370
set intro_banner ypos 6
set airplane xpos -100
set intro_banner xvel 300
set airplane xvel 300

set balloon xpos 264
set balloon ypos 300
set balloon yvel -100
```

```
play_sound .\bdgintro\aphum.wav loop

# Redraw the animation
refresh

# Set time back to zero...
reset_time

# Post some events...
event 1.4 play_sound last stop
event 1.5 play_sound .\bdgintro\welcome.wav

event 6.5 play_sound .\bdgintro\bynaba.wav
event 6.5 show naba

event 7.8 play_sound .\bdgintro\bysams.wav
event 7.8 show sams

# Display features of the book

event 9.8 play_sound .\bdgintro\item.wav
event 9.8 show item1

event 10.8 play_sound .\bdgintro\item.wav
event 10.8 show item2

event 11.8 play_sound .\bdgintro\item.wav
event 11.8 show item3

event 12.8 play_sound .\bdgintro\item.wav
event 12.8 show item4

event 5.0 play_sound tada.wav
```

Implementing ShowMe

Now that you are familiar with ShowMe as a user, the next few sections show you how I implemented ShowMe. Instead of separating design and implementation, I describe the two topics together in the context of the implementation.

I started by building a framework for ShowMe. My first goal was to get the display up and running. This required definition of the application class `ShowMeApp` and the main window class `ShowMeWindow`. Once these were defined, I added the ability to interpret and execute commands in the `ShowMeWindow` class. Once I got the basic commands working, I added the event-processing and condition-checking commands. As I saw the need, I defined several C++ classes to store information about animations and sprites and to represent events and conditions. The remainder of this chapter covers the three classes: window, event, and condition.

ShowMeApp Class

ShowMe's main application class, `ShowMeApp`, is based on the `TApplication` class from Borland's OWL classes. Listing 25.5 shows the file SHOWME.CPP that defines the `ShowMeApp` class and includes the `OwlMain` function necessary for any OWL-based application. The `OwlMain` function creates an instance of `ShowMeApp` and calls the `Run` member function to begin processing events. ShowMe's main window is displayed when the `Run` calls the `InitMainWindow` function. `InitMainWindow` creates an instance of `ShowMeWindow` and this, in turn, loads the SHOWME.RUN file and gets the demo going.

Listing 25.5. SHOWME.CPP. Definition of the `ShowMeApp` class.

```
//--------------------------------------------------------------
//  File:  showme.cpp
//
//  A program that provides animated product demonstrations.
//--------------------------------------------------------------
#include <owl\applicat.h>
#include "showwin.h"

//--------------------------------------------------------------
class ShowMeApp: public TApplication
{
public:
// Constructor that simply calls the base class constructor

    ShowMeApp(const char far *name) : TApplication(name) {}

// Define function to initialize application's main window
    void InitMainWindow();
};
```

```
//--------------------------------------------------------------
// ShowMeApp::InitMainWindow

void ShowMeApp::InitMainWindow()
{
    MainWindow = new ShowMeWindow(NULL, "ShowMe");
    MainWindow->SetIcon(this, "SHOWME_ICON");
//    MainWindow->AssignMenu("MainMenu");
    MainWindow->Attr.AccelTable = "MainAccelTable";
    EnableBWCC();
    EnableCtl3d();
}
//--------------------------------------------------------------
// OwlMain
//
// Create an instance of the application and "run" it.

int OwlMain(int, char**)
{
    ShowMeApp ShowMe("ShowMe");
    ShowMe.nCmdShow = SW_SHOWMAXIMIZED;
    return ShowMe.Run();
}
```

ShowMeWindow Class

The `ShowMeWindow` class represents the main window of ShowMe. Listing 25.6 shows the file SHOWWIN.H that declares the `ShowMeWindow` class. As you can see, `ShowMeWindow` defines a host of member functions for processing commands (using a scheme to be described later) and a number of member variables to store information on the animations, sprites, events, and conditions that are defined in a ShowMe script file.

Member Variables of *ShowMeWindow*

Of the many private member variables of `ShowMeWindow`, here are the important ones:

- `SpriteAnimation *anim;` denotes the current animation.
- `unsigned long tick_count;` is the current time expressed in terms of timer ticks.
- `AnimArray *anim_info;` is an array of `AnimInfo` (described later) objects with information on all animations.

- `SpriteInfoArray *sprite_info;` is an array of `SpriteInfo` (described later) objects with information on all sprites.
- `EventQueue *event_queue;` is the queue of events.
- `CondArray *conditions;` is an array of `ShowMeCondition` (described later) objects that hold information on the conditions to be tested at each timer tick.
- `short sound_off;` is a flag that controls sound output. Sound is turned off if this flag is true (nonzero).
- `short keydown;` is a flag that is set whenever the user presses a key. This flag is cleared after processing all the events and conditions in the `EvTimer` function.
- `short keycode;` is the ASCII code of the last key that the user pressed.
- `short _clicked;` is a flag that is set whenever the user presses the left mouse button. This flag is cleared after processing all the events and conditions in the `EvTimer` function.
- `short _xclick, _yclick;` are the x- and y-coordinates of the cursor's location at the time of the last mouse button press.

Listing 25.6. SHOWWIN.H. Declaration of the `ShowMeWindow` class.

```
//---------------------------------------------------------------
// File: showwin.h
//
// Declares the ShowMeWindow class that represents the main
// window of the ShowMe application.
//---------------------------------------------------------------
#if !defined(__SHOWWIN_H)
#define __SHOWWIN_H

#include <owl\framewin.h>
#include <classlib\arrays.h>
#include <string.h>
#include <fstream.h>
#include "spranim.h"  // Sprite animation class
#include "showinfo.h" // Information on animation and sprites
#include "event.h"    // ShowMeEvent class
#include "cond.h"     // ShowMeCondition class
```

```
// Container types
typedef TISArrayAsVector<ShowMeEvent>    EventQueue;
typedef TIArrayAsVector<AnimInfo>        AnimArray;
typedef TIArrayAsVector<SpriteInfo>      SpriteInfoArray;
typedef TIArrayAsVector<ShowMeCondition> CondArray;

// Iterators
typedef TISArrayAsVectorIterator<ShowMeEvent>    EvQIterator;
typedef TIArrayAsVectorIterator<AnimInfo>        AnimIterator;
typedef TIArrayAsVectorIterator<SpriteInfo>      SInfoIterator;
typedef TIArrayAsVectorIterator<ShowMeCondition> CondIterator;

#define IDM_HELP    200
#define IDM_ABOUT   201

#define DISPLAY_TIMER      1

const short AnimBGWidth = 640;
const short AnimBGHeight = 480;

class ShowMeWindow: public TFrameWindow
{
public:

    ShowMeWindow(TWindow *parent, const char far *title);

    ~ShowMeWindow();

    void Paint(TDC& dc, BOOL, TRect&);

    void EvLButtonDown(UINT modKeys, TPoint& point);
    void EvLButtonUp(UINT modKeys, TPoint& point);
    void EvMouseMove(UINT modKeys, TPoint& point);
    BOOL EvQueryNewPalette();
    void EvPaletteChanged(HWND hWndPalChg);
    void EvTimer(UINT timerId);
    void EvKeyDown(UINT key, UINT repeatCount, UINT flags);

    void Help()
    {
        WinHelp("SHOWME.HLP", HELP_INDEX, 0);
    }
```

continues

Listing 25.6. continued

```
void process_events();
void handle_conditions();

short anim_count()
{ return anim_info->GetItemsInContainer();}

short sprite_count()
{ return sprite_info->GetItemsInContainer();}

AnimInfo* animation_item(short i)
{ return (*anim_info)[i];}

SpriteInfo* sprite_item(short i)
{ return (*sprite_info)[i];}

short condition_count()
{ return conditions->GetItemsInContainer();}
ShowMeCondition* condition(short i)
{ return (*conditions)[i];}
ShowMeCondition* find_condition(char *name);

AnimInfo* find_anim_info(char *name);
SpriteAnimation* find_anim(char *name);
SpriteInfo* find_sprite_info(char *name);
Sprite* find_sprite(char *name);

void move_sprites();

void load_file(char* filename);
void do_nothing(char*) { }
void make_animation(char* inp);
void load_sprite(char* inp);
void add_sprite(char* inp);
void post_event(char* inp);
void add_condition(char* inp);
void set_value(char* inp);
void del_anim(char* inp);
void swap_anim(char* inp);
void play_sound(char* inp);
void show(char* inp);
void hide(char* inp);
```

```
    void quit(char*) { PostQuitMessage(0);}
    void sound(char* inp)
    {
        if(strnicmp(inp, "on", 3) == 0)
            sound_off = 0;
        if(strnicmp(inp, "off", 3) == 0)
            sound_off = 1;
    }
    void reset_time(char* inp);
    void start(char* inp);
    void About(char*);
    void refresh(char*);

    unsigned long current_ticks() { return tick_count;}
    short xcursor() { return _xcursor;}
    short ycursor() { return _ycursor;}
    short xclick() { return _xclick;}
    short yclick() { return _yclick;}
    short clicked() { return _clicked;}
    void clicked(short clk) { _clicked = clk;}

    SpriteAnimation* cur_anim() { return anim;}

    short key_code() { return keycode;}
    short key_down() { return keydown;}

    static short        init_in_progress;

private:
    SpriteAnimation *anim;        // Current animation
    short           left, top;
    short           timer_id;

    unsigned long   tick_count;

    short           numanim;
    short           numsprite;
    short           numcond;
    AnimArray       *anim_info;    // Array of animations
    SpriteInfoArray *sprite_info;  // Array of sprites
    EventQueue      *event_queue;  // Queue of events
    CondArray       *conditions;   // Conditions to be tested
```

continues

Listing 25.6. continued

```
    short           sound_off;      // TRUE = sound is turned off
    short           keydown;
    short           keycode;
    short           mouse_captured;
    Sprite          *spr_current;
    short           _clicked;
    short           _xcursor, _ycursor; // Mouse position
    short           _xclick, _yclick;   // Location of click

    void kill_timer();

DECLARE_RESPONSE_TABLE(ShowMeWindow);
};

#endif
```

Command Processing in *ShowMeWindow*

Listing 25.7 shows the file SHOWWIN.CPP, which implements the member functions of the `ShowMeWindow` class. One of the primary tasks of `ShowMeWindow` is to interpret and execute the commands that appear in a ShowMe script file. As you have seen from Table 25.1, each command has its own arbitrary syntax. To accommodate all the commands in a uniform manner, I decided to associate each command with a pointer to a member function of the `ShowMeWindow` class. The following `typedef` statement defines the `cmd_handler` type, which denotes a function that processes a ShowMe command:

```
typedef void (ShowMeWindow::*cmd_handler)(char* s);
```

As you can see from the `typedef`, the `cmd_handler` function accepts a string as the sole argument. The idea is that all the commands can be stored in a table that associates the command string with a `cmd_handler` function. To process a command line, all you have to do is extract the command name, search the command table to find the entry whose command name matches the current command, and call the corresponding `cmd_handler` function with the rest of the command line as the argument. The `load_file` function of the `ShowMeWindow` class takes care of processing script files (where the commands appear). In that function, you can see how each command is handled by calling the corresponding `cmd_handler` function.

Because of handling commands through a member function that accepts the entire command line as an argument, each command can have its own syntax (which you might have noticed in Listing 25.1). Also, each command handler has the same general structure—parse the command line and take the appropriate action. The only drawback is the performance penalty involved in parsing and interpreting commands. Because events and conditions store commands that are sometimes parsed at each timer tick, the speed of the animation suffers from this scheme. Nevertheless, I used this simple command-handling scheme in the current implementation assuming that I can develop a more efficient scheme in a future revision of ShowMe.

Animating the Demo

In `ShowMeWindow`, all the work of animating the sprites, processing the events, and handling the conditions occurs in the `EvTimer` function, which Windows calls whenever a `WM_TIMER` event occurs. You need to call `SetTimer` beforehand to set up a timer before the `WM_TIMER` events start to occur. In ShowMe, I have set up a 50-millisecond timer (even though Windows delivers, at most, 18.2 timer events a second or a timer event every 55 milliseconds).

Here is the sequence of processing in the `WMTimer` function:

1. Update the timer tick count by incrementing the `tick_count` variable.
2. Move the sprites according to the currently assigned velocities. The updating is done by calling the `move_sprites` function, which, in turn, calls the `update` function of each `SpriteInfo` in the `sprite_info` array.
3. Handle all conditions by calling the `handle_conditions` function.
4. Call `process_events` to handle any event that is scheduled to occur at this timer tick.
5. Reset the mouse click and keypress indicators. These are set whenever the user clicks the left mouse button or presses a key.
6. Update the display by using the image animation techniques illustrated in Chapter 24.

Listing 25.7. SHOWWIN.CPP. Implementation of the `ShowMeWindow` class.

```
//--------------------------------------------------------------
// File: showwin.cpp
//
// Implementation of the ShowMeWindow class--the main window of
```

continues

Listing 25.7. continued

```
// the ShowMe application.
//--------------------------------------------------------------
#include "showwin.h"
#include <owl\point.h>
#include <owl\dialog.h>
#include <owl\applicat.h>
#include <math.h>
#include <fstream.h>
#include <mmsystem.h>

#define MAXCMDLEN 256

typedef void (ShowMeWindow::*cmd_handler)(char* s);

struct command
{
    char        *cmd;
    cmd_handler handler;
};

static command cmdtable[] =
{
    {"nothing",      ShowMeWindow::do_nothing},
    {"start",        ShowMeWindow::start},
    {"refresh",      ShowMeWindow::refresh},
    {"reset_time",   ShowMeWindow::reset_time},
    {"animation",    ShowMeWindow::make_animation},
    {"load_file",    ShowMeWindow::load_file},
    {"sprite",       ShowMeWindow::load_sprite},
    {"add",          ShowMeWindow::add_sprite},
    {"event",        ShowMeWindow::post_event},
    {"condition",    ShowMeWindow::add_condition},
    {"set",          ShowMeWindow::set_value},
    {"quit",         ShowMeWindow::quit},
    {"sound",        ShowMeWindow::sound},
    {"show",         ShowMeWindow::show},
    {"hide",         ShowMeWindow::hide},
    {"destroy",      ShowMeWindow::del_anim},
    {"swap_anim",    ShowMeWindow::swap_anim},
    {"about_showme", ShowMeWindow::About},
    {"play_sound",   ShowMeWindow::play_sound}
};
```

```
static short numcmd = sizeof(cmdtable) / sizeof(command);
static char *whitespace = " \t\n";

short ShowMeWindow::init_in_progress = 0;

static short first_time = 1;
static short first_load = 1;
static char msg1[] = "Loading SHOWME.RUN ...";
static char msg2[] = "During demo, press [Esc] to exit.";
//---------------------------------------------------------------
// Define the response table for ShowMeWindow
DEFINE_RESPONSE_TABLE1(ShowMeWindow, TFrameWindow)
    EV_WM_QUERYNEWPALETTE,
    EV_WM_PALETTECHANGED,
    EV_WM_TIMER,
    EV_WM_LBUTTONUP,
    EV_WM_LBUTTONDOWN,
    EV_WM_MOUSEMOVE,
    EV_WM_KEYDOWN,
END_RESPONSE_TABLE;
//---------------------------------------------------------------
// ShowMeWindow:: S h o w M e W i n d o w
// Constructor for the ShowMeWindow class

ShowMeWindow::ShowMeWindow(TWindow *parent,
                           const char far *title) :
        TFrameWindow(parent, title),
        left(0), top(0), anim(NULL), anim_info(NULL),
        sprite_info(NULL), event_queue(NULL), tick_count(0L),
        numanim(0), numsprite(0), sound_off(0), numcond(0),
        mouse_captured(0), _xclick(-1), _yclick(-1),
        _xcursor(-1), _ycursor(-1), spr_current(NULL),
        keydown(0), _clicked(0), timer_id(0)
{
    Attr.Style = WS_POPUP | WS_VISIBLE;

// Create the containers for events, sprites, animations,
// and conditions
    event_queue = new EventQueue(63, 0, 16);
    event_queue->OwnsElements(1);
    anim_info = new AnimArray(15, 0, 8);
    anim_info->OwnsElements(1);
```

continues

Listing 25.7. continued

```
        sprite_info = new SpriteInfoArray(63, 0, 16);
        sprite_info->OwnsElements(1);
        conditions = new CondArray(63, 0, 16);
        conditions->OwnsElements(1);
}
//------------------------------------------------------------
// ShowMeWindow:: ~ S h o w M e W i n d o w
// Destructor for a ShowMeWindow

ShowMeWindow::~ShowMeWindow()
{
// Kill the timer
        kill_timer();

// Destroy the containers
        if(anim_info != NULL) delete anim_info;
        if(sprite_info != NULL) delete sprite_info;
        if(event_queue != NULL) delete event_queue;
        if(conditions != NULL) delete conditions;
}
//------------------------------------------------------------
// ShowMeWindow:: E v Q u e r y N e w P a l e t t e
// Realize palette for the animation's background

BOOL ShowMeWindow::EvQueryNewPalette()
{
        if(anim == NULL) return 0;
        if(anim->bgimage() == NULL) return 0;

        HPALETTE hpal = anim->bgimage()->palette();
        short changed = 0;
        if(hpal)
        {
                TClientDC dc(HWindow);
                dc.SelectObject(hpal, FALSE);
                changed = dc.RealizePalette();
                dc.RestorePalette();
                if(changed)
                {
                        Invalidate(TRUE);
                        UpdateWindow();
                }
```

```
    }
    return changed;
}
//-----------------------------------------------------------------
// ShowMeWindow:: E v P a l e t t e C h a n g e d
// Handle a change in system palette

void ShowMeWindow::EvPaletteChanged(HWND hWndPalChg)
{
    if(hWndPalChg == HWindow) return;
    if(anim == NULL) return;
    if(anim->bgimage() == NULL) return;

    HPALETTE hpal = anim->bgimage()->palette();
    short changed = 0;
    if(hpal)
    {
        TClientDC dc(HWindow);
        dc.SelectObject(hpal, FALSE);
        changed = dc.RealizePalette();
        if(changed)
        {
            dc.UpdateColors();
        }
        dc.RestorePalette();
    }
}
//-----------------------------------------------------------------
//  ShowMeWindow:: A b o u t
//  Display the "About..." box

void ShowMeWindow::About(char*)
{
    kill_timer();
    TDialog *p_about = new TDialog(this, "ABOUTSHOWME");
    GetApplication()->ExecDialog(p_about);
    start(NULL);
}
//-----------------------------------------------------------------
//  ShowMeWindow:: P a i n t
//  Draw everything in the window
```

continues

Listing 25.7. continued

```
void ShowMeWindow::Paint(TDC& hdc, BOOL, TRect&)
{
    if(first_load)
    {
        SetBkMode(hdc, TRANSPARENT);
        TextOut(hdc, 100, 100, msg1, strlen(msg1));
        TextOut(hdc,  70, 130, msg2, strlen(msg2));

        first_load = 0;

// Load commands from the "SHOWME.RUN" file
        load_file("SHOWME.RUN");
    }
    if(anim != NULL)
    {
     anim->set_refresh(TRUE);
     anim->animate(hdc, top, left);
    }
}
//--------------------------------------------------------------
// ShowMeWindow:: E v K e y D o w n
// Handle raw keypresses (for the Escape key).

void ShowMeWindow::EvKeyDown(UINT key, UINT, UINT)
{
    keycode = key;
    keydown = 1;

    if(keycode == VK_ESCAPE)
    {
// First kill the timer
        kill_timer();

// Then display a message
        short ret = MessageBox(
                    "Do you really want to quit?",
                    "ShowMe", MB_ICONQUESTION¦MB_YESNO);
        if(ret == IDYES)
            PostQuitMessage(0);
        if(ret == IDNO)
        {
            start(NULL);
```

```
        }
    }
}
//-----------------------------------------------------------------
// ShowMeWindow:: E v T i m e r
// Handle WM_TIMER events

void ShowMeWindow::EvTimer(UINT timerId)
{
    switch(timerId)
    {
        case DISPLAY_TIMER:
// Update the tick count...
            tick_count++;

// Move the sprites
            move_sprites();

// Evaluate all the conditions and take actions
            handle_conditions();

// Process all pending events
            process_events();

// Reset mouse click and key down indicators
            _clicked = 0;
            keydown = 0;

// Update the display
            if(anim != NULL)
            {
                HDC hdc = GetDC(HWindow);
                anim->animate(hdc, top, left);
                ReleaseDC(HWindow, hdc);
            }
            break;
    }
}
//-----------------------------------------------------------------
// ShowMeWindow:: E v L B u t t o n D o w n
// Handle "left" button down events in the ShowMeWindow
```

continues

Listing 25.7. continued

```
void ShowMeWindow::EvLButtonDown(UINT, TPoint& point)
{
    _xclick = point.x;
    _yclick = point.y;
    _clicked = TRUE;
}
//-----------------------------------------------------------
// ShowMeWindow:: E v M o u s e M o v e
// Handle mouse movements in ShowMeWindow

void ShowMeWindow::EvMouseMove(UINT, TPoint& point)
{
    _xcursor = point.x;
    _ycursor = point.y;
}
//-----------------------------------------------------------
// ShowMeWindow:: E v L B u t t o n U p
// Handle mouse button up event in ShowMeWindow

void ShowMeWindow::EvLButtonUp(UINT, TPoint& point)
{
    if(!mouse_captured) return;

    _xclick = point.x;
    _yclick = point.y;
}
//-----------------------------------------------------------
//  ShowMeWindow:: l o a d _ f i l e
//  Load commands from a file

void ShowMeWindow::load_file(char* filename)
{
    char line[MAXCMDLEN];
// Change cursor to an hourglass
    HCURSOR hcursor_old = ::SetCursor(LoadCursor(NULL, IDC_WAIT));

// Open file for reading
    ifstream ifs(filename, ios::in);
    if(!ifs) return;
```

```
// Read and interpret file
    short i, nchr, n, numread;
    char *token, *rest, *inp;
    while(!ifs.eof())
    {
        ifs.getline(line, sizeof(line));
        if(!ifs) break;
        numread = strlen(line);
        if(numread > 0)
        {
            while(line[numread-1] == '\\' && numread < MAXCMDLEN)
            {
                inp = &line[numread-1];
                ifs.getline(inp, MAXCMDLEN-numread);
                numread = strlen(line);
            }
        }

// Skip beginning whitespace
        n = strspn(line, whitespace);
        token = &line[n];

// Comments start with a #
        if(token[0] == '#') continue;
// Find next token
        nchr = strcspn(token, whitespace);
        if(nchr == 0) continue;

        rest = &token[nchr];
        n = strspn(rest, whitespace);
        rest = &rest[n];

        for(i = 0; i < numcmd; i++)
        {
            if(strnicmp(token, cmdtable[i].cmd, nchr) == 0)
            {
                (this->*cmdtable[i].handler)(rest);
                break;
            }
        }
    }
```

continues

Listing 25.7. continued

```
// Reset the cursor shape
    ::SetCursor(hcursor_old);
}
//------------------------------------------------------------
// ShowMeWindow:: m a k e _ a n i m a t i o n
// Create a new animation

void ShowMeWindow::make_animation(char *inp)
{
    if(inp == NULL) return;

// Extract the tokens from the input line
    char *token1 = strtok(inp, whitespace);
    char *token2 = strtok(NULL, whitespace);
    char *token3 = strtok(NULL, whitespace);
    char *token4 = strtok(NULL, whitespace);

    HDC hdc = GetDC(HWindow);
    SpriteAnimation *a = new SpriteAnimation(hdc, atoi(token2),
                                atoi(token3), token4);
    AnimInfo *ai = new AnimInfo(token1, atoi(token2),
                                    atoi(token3), token4, a);
    if(numanim == 0) anim = a;

    anim_info->AddAt(ai, numanim++);
    ReleaseDC(HWindow, hdc);
}
//------------------------------------------------------------
// ShowMeWindow:: l o a d _ s p r i t e
// Loads a sprite from specified files

void ShowMeWindow::load_sprite(char *inp)
{
    if(inp == NULL) return;

// Extract the tokens from the input line
    char *sname = strtok(inp, whitespace);
    char *imgfn = strtok(NULL, whitespace);
    char *mskfn = strtok(NULL, whitespace);
    char *xposv = strtok(NULL, whitespace);
    char *yposv = NULL;
    char *priov = NULL;
```

```
    if(xposv != NULL)
    {
        yposv = strtok(NULL, whitespace);
        if(yposv != NULL)
        {
            priov = strtok(NULL, whitespace);
        }
    }

    short xpos = 0, ypos = 0, prio = 1;
    if(xposv != NULL) xpos = atoi(xposv);
    if(yposv != NULL) ypos = atoi(yposv);
    if(priov != NULL) prio = atoi(priov);

// Create the sprite
    HDC hdc = GetDC(HWindow);
    if(stricmp(mskfn, "none") == 0) mskfn = NULL;
    Sprite *s = new Sprite(hdc, imgfn, mskfn, prio);
    s->newpos(xpos, ypos);
    SpriteInfo *si = new SpriteInfo(sname, s);
    sprite_info->AddAt(si, numsprite++);
    ReleaseDC(HWindow, hdc);
}
//-------------------------------------------------------------
// ShowMeWindow:: a d d _ s p r i t e
// Add a sprite to an animation.

void ShowMeWindow::add_sprite(char *inp)
{
    if(inp == NULL) return;

// Extract the tokens from the input line
    char *token1 = strtok(inp, whitespace);
    char *token2 = strtok(NULL, whitespace);

    AnimInfo *ai = find_anim_info(token2);
    SpriteAnimation *a = ai->anim;
    SpriteInfo *si = find_sprite_info(token1);
    Sprite *s = si->sprite;
// Add the sprite to the animation
    if(s != NULL && a != NULL) a->add(s);
    si->ai = ai;
```

continues

Listing 25.7. continued

```
}
//-------------------------------------------------------------
//  ShowMeWindow:: p r o c e s s _ e v e n t s
//  Process events in the event queue.

void ShowMeWindow::process_events()
{
    if(event_queue == NULL) return;

// Process events up to this time tick
    while(event_queue->GetItemsInContainer() > 0)
    {
        ShowMeEvent* ev = (*event_queue)[0];
        if(keydown && keycode == 32)
        {
// User has pressed the spacebar--move on to next event
        }
        else
            if(ev->tick_count() > tick_count) return;

// Invoke the command specified by this event
        (this->*cmdtable[ev->command_index()].handler)(
                                                ev->command_line());
        event_queue->Detach(0, TShouldDelete::Delete);

        if(keydown && keycode == 32)
        {
// If key was down, reset it and return
            keydown = 0;
        }
    }
}
//-------------------------------------------------------------
//  ShowMeWindow:: h a n d l e _ c o n d i t i o n s
//  Handle all conditions in the "conditions" table

void ShowMeWindow::handle_conditions()
{
    if(conditions == NULL) return;

// Loop through all conditions and handle each one
    short i, num = conditions->GetItemsInContainer();
```

```
    for(i = 0; i < num; i++)
    {
        if(condition(i)->eval())
        {
// Invoke the command specified by this condition
            (this->*cmdtable[condition(i)->command_index()].
                         handler)(condition(i)->command_line());
        }
    }
}
//--------------------------------------------------------------
// ShowMeWindow:: m o v e _ s p r i t e s
// Move the sprites according to current acceleration and
// velocity

void ShowMeWindow::move_sprites()
{
    short i, n = sprite_count();
    for(i = 0; i < n; i++)
    {
        sprite_item(i)->update();
    }
}
//--------------------------------------------------------------
// ShowMeWindow:: f i n d _ a n i m
// Returns a pointer to an animation in the anim_info table

SpriteAnimation* ShowMeWindow::find_anim(char *name)
{
    if(name == NULL) return NULL;
    short i, low = anim_info->LowerBound(),
            hi = anim_info->UpperBound();
    for(i = low; i <= hi; i++)
    {
        if(strncmp(animation_item(i)->_name, name,
                   strlen(name)) == 0)
        return animation_item(i)->anim;
    }
    return NULL;
}
//--------------------------------------------------------------
// ShowMeWindow:: f i n d _ a n i m _ i n f o
```

continues

Listing 25.7. continued

```
// Returns a pointer to the AnimInfo corresponding to the
// named animation

AnimInfo* ShowMeWindow::find_anim_info(char *name)
{
    if(name == NULL) return NULL;

    short i, low = anim_info->LowerBound(),
          hi = anim_info->UpperBound();
    for(i = low; i <= hi; i++)
    {
        if(strncmp(animation_item(i)->_name, name,
                   strlen(name)) == 0)
                     return (animation_item(i));
    }
    return NULL;
}
//-----------------------------------------------------------------
// ShowMeWindow:: f i n d _ s p r i t e _ i n f o
// Returns a pointer to a SpriteInformation that has information
// about a specific sprite (identified by name)

SpriteInfo* ShowMeWindow::find_sprite_info(char *name)
{
    if(name == NULL) return NULL;

    short i, n = sprite_count();
    for(i = 0; i < n; i++)
    {
        if(strncmp(sprite_item(i)->_name, name, strlen(name))
           == 0)
            return sprite_item(i);
    }
    return NULL;
}
//-----------------------------------------------------------------
// ShowMeWindow:: f i n d _ s p r i t e
// Returns a pointer to a sprite in the sprite_info table

Sprite* ShowMeWindow::find_sprite(char *name)
{
    if(name == NULL) return NULL;
```

```
    short i, n = sprite_count();
    for(i = 0; i < n; i++)
    {
        if(strncmp(sprite_item(i)->_name, name, strlen(name))
           == 0)
            return sprite_item(i)->sprite;
    }
    return NULL;
}
//-----------------------------------------------------------------
// ShowMeWindow:: f i n d _ c o n d i t i o n
// Returns a pointer to the named condition from the
// conditions table

ShowMeCondition* ShowMeWindow::find_condition(char *name)
{
    if(name == NULL) return NULL;

    short i, num = conditions->GetItemsInContainer();

    for(i = 0; i < num; i++)
    {
        if(strncmp(condition(i)->name(), name,
                   strlen(name)) == 0)
                         return condition(i);
    }
    return NULL;
}
//-----------------------------------------------------------------
// ShowMeWindow:: p o s t _ e v e n t
// Post an event on the event queue

void ShowMeWindow::post_event(char *inp)
{
    if(inp == NULL) return;

// Extract the tokens from the input line
    char *token1 = strtok(inp, whitespace);
    char *token2 = strtok(NULL, whitespace);
    char *token3 = strtok(NULL, "\0");
```

continues

Listing 25.7. continued

```
// Locate the command (token2) in cmdtable
    short i, nchr;
    for(i = 0; i < numcmd; i++)
    {
        nchr = strlen(token2);
        if(strnicmp(token2, cmdtable[i].cmd, nchr) == 0)
        {
            break;
        }
    }
    if(i == numcmd) return;

// Compute tick count when event should occur
    unsigned long ticks = ((double)ticks_per_sec * atof(token1));
    ticks += tick_count;
    ShowMeEvent *ev = new ShowMeEvent(ticks, i, token3);

    if(ev != NULL &&
       event_queue != NULL) event_queue->Add(ev);
}
//-----------------------------------------------------------------
// ShowMeWindow:: s e t _ v a l u e
// Set the value of a specified variable

void ShowMeWindow::set_value(char *inp)
{
    if(inp == NULL) return;

// Extract the tokens from the input line
    char *token1 = strtok(inp, whitespace);
    char *token2 = strtok(NULL, whitespace);
    char *token3 = strtok(NULL, "\0");

    SpriteInfo *s = find_sprite_info(token1);
    if(s != NULL)
        s->set_value(token2, token3);
}
//-----------------------------------------------------------------
// ShowMeWindow:: h i d e
// Hides a sprite

void ShowMeWindow::hide(char *inp)
```

```
{
    if(inp == NULL) return;

// Extract a token from the input line
    char *token1 = strtok(inp, whitespace);

    SpriteInfo *s = find_sprite_info(token1);
    if(s != NULL)
    {
        if(s->spr() != NULL)
        {
            if(!s->spr()->is_active()) return;
            s->spr()->inactive();
            s->spr()->update_done();
        }
    }
}
//----------------------------------------------------------------
// ShowMeWindow:: s h o w
// Shows a sprite

void ShowMeWindow::show(char *inp)
{
    if(inp == NULL) return;

// Extract a token from the input line
    char *token1 = strtok(inp, whitespace);

    SpriteInfo *s = find_sprite_info(token1);
    if(s != NULL)
    {
        if(s->spr() != NULL)
        {
            if(s->spr()->is_active()) return;
            s->spr()->active();
            s->spr()->move(0,0);
        }
    }
}
//----------------------------------------------------------------
// ShowMeWindow:: s w a p _ a n i m
```

continues

Listing 25.7. continued

```
// Start animating a new SpriteAnimation object

void ShowMeWindow::swap_anim(char *inp)
{
    if(inp == NULL) return;

// Extract the tokens from the input line
    char *token1 = strtok(inp, whitespace);

    SpriteAnimation *a = find_anim(token1);

    if(a != NULL)
    {
        anim = a;
        a->set_refresh(TRUE);
    }
}
//-------------------------------------------------------------
// ShowMeWindow:: d e l _ a n i m
// Destroy an animation

void ShowMeWindow::del_anim(char *inp)
{
    if(inp == NULL) return;

// Extract the tokens from the input line
    char *token1 = strtok(inp, whitespace);

    short i, low = anim_info->LowerBound(),
          hi = anim_info->UpperBound();
    for(i = low; i <= hi; i++)
    {
        if(strncmp(animation_item(i)->_name, token1,
                   strlen(token1)) == 0)
        {
            short j, n = sprite_count();
            for(j = 0; j < n; j++)
            {
                if(strncmp(sprite_item(i)->animinfo()->_name,
                       token1, strlen(token1)) == 0)
                   sprite_item(i)->ai = NULL;
            }
```

```
                if(animation_item(i)->anim == anim)
                        anim = NULL;
                anim_info->Destroy(i);
            }
        }
    }
    //-------------------------------------------------------------
    // ShowMeWindow:: p l a y _ s o u n d
    // Play a waveform sound

    void ShowMeWindow::play_sound(char *inp)
    {
        if(inp == NULL) return;

        if(sound_off) return;

    // Extract the tokens from the input line
        char *wavfn = strtok(inp, whitespace);
        char *type = strtok(NULL, whitespace);

        short flag = SND_ASYNC;
        if(type != NULL)
        {
            if(stricmp(type, "loop") == 0)
                                    flag = SND_ASYNC | SND_LOOP;

            if(stricmp(type, "sync") == 0)
                                    flag = SND_SYNC;

            if(stricmp(type, "stop") == 0)
            {
                wavfn = NULL;
            }
        }

    // Play the sound waveform
        sndPlaySound(wavfn, flag);
    }
    //-------------------------------------------------------------
    // ShowMeWindow:: a d d _ c o n d i t i o n
    // Add a condition to the condition table
```

continues

Listing 25.7. continued

```
void ShowMeWindow::add_condition(char *inp)
{
    if(inp == NULL) return;

// Extract the tokens from the input line
    char *cname = strtok(inp, whitespace);
    char *ename = strtok(NULL, whitespace);

    char *rest = strtok(NULL, "\0");

// Skip beginning whitespace
    short n = strspn(rest, whitespace);
    char *earg = &rest[n];

// Search for a "->" in the rest of the string
    rest = strstr(earg, "->");

    char *cmd = "nothing";
    char *cmdarg = NULL;

// Mark end of "expression argument"
    if(rest != NULL)
    {
        rest[0] = '\0';
        cmd = &rest[2];
// Skip over beginning whitespace
        n = strspn(cmd, whitespace);
        rest = &cmd[n];
        cmd = strtok(rest, whitespace);
        cmdarg = strtok(NULL, "\0");
    }

// Locate the command in cmdtable
    short i, nchr;
    for(i = 0; i < numcmd; i++)
    {
        nchr = strlen(cmd);
        if(strnicmp(cmd, cmdtable[i].cmd, nchr) == 0)
        {
            break;
        }
    }
```

```
    if(i == numcmd) return;

// Create a ShowMeCondition object and save it
    ShowMeCondition *cond = new ShowMeCondition(this, cname,
                                                 ename,
                                                 earg, i, cmdarg);
    if(cond != NULL && conditions != NULL)
                        conditions->AddAt(cond, numcond++);
}
//-------------------------------------------------------------
// ShowMeWindow:: r e s e t _ t i m e
// Reset time to a specified value (or zero, if no value
// is specified)

void ShowMeWindow::reset_time(char *inp)
{
    if(inp == NULL)
    {
        tick_count = 0L;
    }
    else
    {
        tick_count = ((double)ticks_per_sec * atof(inp));
    }
}
//-------------------------------------------------------------
// ShowMeWindow:: s t a r t
// Starts a Windows Timer

void ShowMeWindow::start(char*)
{
// Set up a timer to update the display
    timer_id = SetTimer(DISPLAY_TIMER,
                        DISP_MILLISECONDS, NULL);
    if(!timer_id)
        MessageBox("Failed to start Timer!",
                   "ShowMe: ShowMeWindow",
                   MB_ICONEXCLAMATION | MB_OK);
}
//-------------------------------------------------------------
// ShowMeWindow:: k i l l _ t i m e r
// Kill the timer
```

continues

Listing 25.7. continued

```
void ShowMeWindow::kill_timer()
{
    if(timer_id)
    {
        KillTimer(DISPLAY_TIMER);
        timer_id = 0;
    }
}
//-------------------------------------------------------------
// ShowMeWindow:: r e f r e s h
// Redraw the animation

void ShowMeWindow::refresh(char*)
{
// Update the display
    if(anim != NULL)
    {
        HDC hdc = GetDC(HWindow);
        anim->set_refresh(TRUE);
        anim->animate(hdc, top, left);
        ReleaseDC(HWindow, hdc);
    }
}
```

AnimInfo and *SpriteInfo* Classes

Listing 25.8 shows the file SHOWINFO.H, which declares the `AnimInfo` and `SpriteInfo` classes used to store information about the animations and sprites used in a ShowMe demo.

The `ShowMeWindow` class uses the `AnimInfo` and `SpriteInfo` classes to associate a name with each animation and sprite. Various member functions in `ShowMeWindow` need the capability of locating animations and sprites by name because the scripts identify animations and sprites by name. The member functions can locate the animations and sprites by searching the array of `AnimInfo` and `SpriteInfo` objects in the `ShowMeWindow` class.

The `SpriteInfo` class also uses an array of `NameValue` structures to provide a table that associates the name of a member variable (such as `xpos`) with a pointer to that member variable. As you can see in the implementation of the `SpriteInfo` class (in Listing 25.9), the `NameValue` array is used to set member variables to specified values at run-time.

Listing 25.8. SHOWINFO.H. Declaration of `AnimInfo` and `SpriteInfo` classes.

```
//--------------------------------------------------------------
// File: showinfo.h
//
// Declares the AnimInfo and SpriteInfo classes that store
// information used in the ShowMe application.
//--------------------------------------------------------------
#if !defined(__SHOWINFO_H)
#define __SHOWINFO_H

#include <string.h>
#include "showdefs.h"

class SpriteAnimation;
class Sprite;
class ShowMeWindow;

class AnimInfo
{
public:
friend ShowMeWindow;

    AnimInfo(char *n, short wdth, short hght, char *bgn,
             SpriteAnimation *a);
    ~AnimInfo();

    operator<(const AnimInfo& ai) const
    {
        return strcmp(_name, ai._name);
    }

    operator==(const AnimInfo& ai) const
    {
```

continues

Listing 25.8. continued

```
            return (anim == ai.animim);
        }

        SpriteAnimation* animation() { return anim;}

    protected:
        char            *_name;     // Name of animation
        char            *bgname;    // Name of image file
        unsigned short  w, h;       // Width and height
        SpriteAnimation *anim;      // Pointer to animation
    };

    class SpriteInfo;
    struct NameValue
    {
        NameValue() : name(NULL), type(0), li_value(NULL),
                      factor(1.0) {}

        void set(SpriteInfo *si, char *vs);

        char   *name;
        short  type;
        double factor;
        union
        {
            short  SpriteInfo::*si_value;
            long   SpriteInfo::*li_value;
            float  SpriteInfo::*f_value;
            double SpriteInfo::*d_value;
        };
    };


    class SpriteInfo
    {
    public:
    friend ShowMeWindow;
        SpriteInfo::SpriteInfo(char *n, Sprite *s);
        ~SpriteInfo();

        void set_value(char *n, char *v);
        void update();
```

```
    void animinfo(AnimInfo *_ai) { ai = _ai;}
    AnimInfo* animinfo() { return ai;}

    Sprite* spr() { return sprite;}
    NameValue* name_value(const char* name);

    char *name() { return _name;}

    operator<(const SpriteInfo& si) const
    {
        return strcmp(_name, si._name);
    }

    operator==(const SpriteInfo& si) const
    {
        return (sprite == si.sprite);
    }

protected:
    char      *_name;          // Name of the Sprite
    Sprite    *sprite;
    AnimInfo  *ai;             // Animation where sprite
                               // resides
    short     xpos, ypos;
    double    xvel, yvel;
    double    xacc, yacc;
    NameValue name_table[NUMVAR_SPRITEINFO];
};

#endif
```

Listing 25.9 shows the file SHOWINFO.CPP, which implements the member functions of the `AnimInfo` and `SpriteInfo` classes. An interesting feature of `SpriteInfo` is the way it provides a single function, `set_value`, to set the value of a member variable at run-time. As you can see from Listing 25.9, `SpriteInfo::set_value` searches the array of `NameValue` objects, locates the one with a matching name, and calls that `NameValue` object's set function to set the value (provided as a string). The set function in the `NameValue` class takes care of converting the value into the appropriate internal format (`short`, `long`, `float`, or `double`) depending on the type of the `NameValue`. The constructor of the `SpriteInfo` class sets up the array of `NameValue` objects that constitute its `name_table`.

Listing 25.9. SHOWINFO.CPP. Implementation of `AnimInfo` and `SpriteInfo` classes.

```
//--------------------------------------------------------------
// File: showinfo.cpp
//
// Implements the AnimInfo and SpriteInfo classes that store
// information used in the ShowMe application.
//--------------------------------------------------------------
#include <stdlib.h>
#include <string.h>
#include <math.h>
#include "showinfo.h"
#include "spranim.h"

//--------------------------------------------------------------
// AnimInfo:: A n i m I n f o
// Initialize the AnimInfo class

AnimInfo::AnimInfo(char *n, short wdth, short hght, char *bgn,
                   SpriteAnimation *a) : w(wdth), h(hght),
    anim(a)
{
    _name = new char[strlen(n)+1];
    if(_name != NULL) strcpy(_name, n);
    bgname = new char[strlen(bgn)+1];
    if(bgname != NULL) strcpy(bgname, n);
}
//--------------------------------------------------------------
// AnimInfo:: ~ A n i m I n f o
// Destructor for the AnimInfo class

AnimInfo::~AnimInfo()
{
    if(_name != NULL) delete _name;
    if(bgname != NULL) delete bgname;
    if(anim != NULL) delete anim;
}
//--------------------------------------------------------------
// NameValue:: s e t
// Convert a string to a value and save

void NameValue::set(SpriteInfo *si, char *vs)
{
```

```
    switch(type)
    {
        case SHORT_INT:
            si->*si_value = (double)atoi(vs) * factor;
            break;

        case LONG_INT:
            si->*li_value = (double)atol(vs) * factor;
            break;

        case FLOAT:
            si->*f_value = atof(vs) * factor;
            break;

        case DOUBLE:
            si->*d_value = atof(vs) * factor;
            break;
    }
}
//-----------------------------------------------------------------
// SpriteInfo:: S p r i t e I n f o
// Initialize an instance of the SpriteInfo class

SpriteInfo::SpriteInfo(char *n, Sprite *s) :
    xvel(0), yvel(0), xacc(0), yacc(0),
    sprite(s), ai(NULL)
{
    xpos = s->xpos();
    ypos = s->ypos();

    if(n != NULL)
    {
        _name = new char[strlen(n)+1];
        if(_name != NULL) strcpy(_name, n);
    }

// Initialize the "name table"
    name_table[0].name = "xpos";
    name_table[0].type = SHORT_INT;
    name_table[0].si_value = &SpriteInfo::xpos;

    name_table[1].name = "ypos";
```

continues

Listing 25.9. continued

```
    name_table[1].type = SHORT_INT;
    name_table[1].si_value = &SpriteInfo::ypos;

    name_table[2].name = "xvel";
    name_table[2].type = DOUBLE;
    name_table[2].factor = seconds_per_tick;
    name_table[2].d_value = &SpriteInfo::xvel;

    name_table[3].name = "yvel";
    name_table[3].type = DOUBLE;
    name_table[3].factor = seconds_per_tick;
    name_table[3].d_value = &SpriteInfo::yvel;

    name_table[4].name = "xacc";
    name_table[4].type = DOUBLE;
    name_table[4].factor = seconds_per_tick*seconds_per_tick;
    name_table[4].d_value = &SpriteInfo::xacc;

    name_table[5].name = "yacc";
    name_table[5].type = DOUBLE;
    name_table[5].factor = seconds_per_tick*seconds_per_tick;
    name_table[5].d_value = &SpriteInfo::yacc;
}
//---------------------------------------------------------------
// SpriteInfo:: ~ S p r i t e I n f o
// Destructor for the SpriteInfo class

SpriteInfo::~SpriteInfo()
{
    if(_name != NULL) delete _name;
}
//---------------------------------------------------------------
// SpriteInfo:: s e t _ v a l u e
// Set the value of a variable

void SpriteInfo::set_value(char *n, char *v)
{
    short i;
    for(i = 0; i < NUMVAR_SPRITEINFO; i++)
    {
        if(name_table[i].name == NULL) continue;
```

```
        if(strnicmp(name_table[i].name, n, strlen(n)) == 0)
        {
            name_table[i].set(this, v);
        }
    }
}
//----------------------------------------------------------------
// SpriteInfo:: u p d a t e
// Update a sprite's velocity and position

void SpriteInfo::update()
{
    if(!sprite->is_active()) return;

    xpos += xvel;
    ypos += yvel;
    xvel += xacc;
    yvel += yacc;

    sprite->move(xpos - sprite->xpos(), ypos - sprite->ypos());
}
//----------------------------------------------------------------
// SpriteInfo:: n a m e _ v a l u e
// Return a pointer to the NameValue structure
// corresponding to a named variable

NameValue* SpriteInfo::name_value(const char *name)
{
    if(name == NULL) return NULL;
    short i;
    for(i = 0; i < NUMVAR_SPRITEINFO; i++)
    {
        if(name_table[i].name == NULL) continue;
        if(strnicmp(name_table[i].name, name, strlen(name)) == 0)
        {
            return &name_table[i];
        }
    }
    return NULL;
}
```

ShowMeEvent Class

From Table 25.1, you can see that the syntax for the event command in ShowMe is

```
event <time> <any_ShowMe_command>
```

The post_event function of the ShowMeWindow class (Listing 25.7) processes the event command by creating a ShowMeEvent object and storing it in a PriorityQueue container. Listing 25.10 shows the definition of the ShowMeEvent class, which stores information about the event in the following private member variables:

- unsigned long ticks; is the timer tick when the event occurs.
- short cmdindx; identifies the command to execute. This is the index of the command in the command table defined in the ShowMeWindow class.
- char *orig; is the string to be passed to the command.
- char *cmdarg; is the string through which a copy of the original command string is passed to the command handler. The reason for providing a copy is that the command handler destroys its string argument during parsing.

Listing 25.10. EVENT.H. Definition of the ShowMeEvent class.

```
//------------------------------------------------------------
// File: event.h
//
// Declares the ShowMeEvent class that holds events for
// the ShowMe application.
//------------------------------------------------------------
#if !defined(__EVENT_H)
#define __EVENT_H

#include <string.h>
#include "showdefs.h"

class ShowMeEvent
{
public:
    ShowMeEvent(unsigned long t, short cmd, char *arg) :
        ticks(t), cmdindx(cmd)
    {
     if(arg == NULL)
```

```
    {
        cmdarg = NULL;
        orig = NULL;
    }
    else
    {
           short len = strlen(arg) + 1;
           cmdarg = new char[len];
           if(cmdarg != NULL) strcpy(cmdarg, arg);
           orig = new char[len];
           if(orig != NULL) strcpy(orig, arg);
       }
   }

   ~ShowMeEvent()
   {
       if(cmdarg != NULL) delete cmdarg;
       if(orig != NULL) delete orig;
   }

// The following operators are needed to sort ShowMeEvents
// according to ticks.
   operator<(const ShowMeEvent& sme) const
   {
       return ticks < sme.ticks;
   }

   operator==(const ShowMeEvent& sme) const
   {
       return ((ticks == sme.ticks) &&
               (cmdindx == sme.cmdindx) &&
               (strcmp(orig, sme.orig) == 0));
   }

   short command_index() { return cmdindx;}
   char* command_line()
   {
       if(cmdarg != NULL) strcpy(cmdarg, orig);
       return cmdarg;
   }
   unsigned long tick_count() { return ticks;}
```

continues

Listing 25.10. continued

```
protected:
    unsigned long ticks;    // Time of event
    short         cmdindx; // Command to execute
    char          *orig;    // Clean copy of arguments
    char          *cmdarg; // Arguments for the command
};

#endif
```

Conditions and Expressions

To store the conditions, the `ShowMeWindow` class uses the `ShowMeCondition` class, which, in turn, uses an `Expression` object to store the exact expression to be evaluated by the condition.

Listing 25.11 shows the file COND.H, which declares the `ShowMeCondition` class and the `Expression` class hierarchy. The `ShowMeWindow` class stores information about a condition in the following member variables:

- `char *_name;` is the name that identifies this condition.
- `Expression *expr;` points to the Expression to be evaluated for this condition.
- `short cmdindx;` is the command to execute if the expression evaluates to a nonzero value.
- `char *orig;` is the string to be passed to the command.
- `char *cmdarg;` is the string through which a copy of the original command string is passed to the command handler. The reason for providing a copy is that the command handler destroys its string argument during parsing.

Listing 25.11. COND.H. Declaration of classes for conditions and expressions.

```
//------------------------------------------------------------
// File: cond.h
//
// Declares the ShowMeCondition class that holds a "condition"
// for the ShowMe application. A condition is basically an
```

```
// expression whose value is used to control the sprites
// animated by the ShowMe application. A condition is TRUE if
// its value is nonzero.
//-------------------------------------------------------------
#if !defined(__COND_H)
#define __COND_H

#include <string.h>
#include "showdefs.h"

class ShowMeCondition;
class ShowMeWindow;

class Expression
{
public:
    Expression() : psc(NULL) {}
    Expression(const Expression& expr) : psc(expr.psc) {}
    virtual ~Expression(){}

    virtual short eval() = 0;
    virtual Expression* clone(ShowMeCondition *smc,
                              char *expstr) = 0;
    void set_owner(ShowMeCondition* smc) { psc = smc;}
protected:
    ShowMeCondition *psc;
};

// The TimeExpression class gets the current time and
// performs an operation specified by opcode.

class TimeExpression : public Expression
{
public:
    TimeExpression() : opcode(0), tick_threshold(0L) {}
    TimeExpression(ShowMeCondition *smc, short oc,
                   unsigned long ts) :
        tick_threshold(ts), opcode(oc)
    {
        psc = smc;
    }
```

continues

Listing 25.11. continued

```
    virtual ~TimeExpression() {}

    virtual Expression* clone(ShowMeCondition *smc,
                              char *expstr);
    virtual short eval();

private:
    unsigned long   tick_threshold;
    short           opcode;
};

// The KeyExpression class gets the current keystroke and
// performs an operation specified by opcode.

class KeyExpression : public Expression
{
public:
    KeyExpression() : opcode(0), key(0) {}

    KeyExpression(ShowMeCondition *smc, short oc,
                  short _key) :
        key(_key), opcode(oc)
    {
        psc = smc;
    }

    virtual ~KeyExpression() {}

    virtual Expression* clone(ShowMeCondition *smc,
                              char *expstr);
    virtual short eval();

private:
    short           opcode;
    short           key;

};

// The ClickExpression class gets the current mouse click
// and performs an operation specified by opcode.
```

```
class ClickExpression : public Expression
{
public:
    ClickExpression() : opcode(0), si(NULL),
        x1(0), y1(0), x2(0), y2(0) {}

    ClickExpression(ShowMeCondition* smc, short oc,
                    SpriteInfo* _si,
                    short _x1, short _y1,
                    short _x2, short _y2) : opcode(oc),
        x1(_x1), y1(_y1), x2(_x2), y2(_y2), si(_si)
    {
        psc = smc;
    }

    virtual ~ClickExpression() {}

    virtual Expression* clone(ShowMeCondition *smc,
                              char *expstr);
    virtual short eval();

private:
    short           opcode;
    SpriteInfo      *si;
    short           x1, y1;
    short           x2, y2;
};

// The ValueExpression class gets the value of a variable
// from a sprite and performs an operation specified by opcode.

class ValueExpression : public Expression
{
public:
    ValueExpression() : opcode(0), si(NULL), nmv(NULL),
        l_value(0) {}

    ValueExpression(ShowMeCondition* smc, short oc,
                    SpriteInfo* _si, NameValue* _nmv,
                    char *val);

    virtual ~ValueExpression() {}
```

continues

Listing 25.11. continued

```
    virtual Expression* clone(ShowMeCondition *smc,
                              char *expstr);
    virtual short eval();

private:
    short           opcode;
    SpriteInfo      *si;
    NameValue       *nmv;
    union
    {
        short  s_value;
        long   l_value;
        float  f_value;
        double d_value;
    };
};

class ShowMeCondition
{
public:
    ShowMeCondition(ShowMeWindow *smw, char *cname,
                    char *ename, char* earg,
                    short cmd, char *arg);
    ~ShowMeCondition();

    short command_index() { return cmdindx;}
    char* command_line()
    {
        if(cmdarg != NULL) strcpy(cmdarg, orig);
        return cmdarg;
    }
    short eval()
    {
        if(expr != NULL) val = expr->eval();
        return val;
    }

    char* name() { return _name;}
    ShowMeWindow* owner() { return psm;}

    operator<(const ShowMeCondition& smc) const
    {
```

```
        return strcmp(_name, smc._name);
    }

    operator==(const ShowMeCondition& smc) const
    {
        return ((val == smc.val) &&
                (cmdindx == smc.cmdindx) &&
                (strcmp(orig, smc.orig) == 0) &&
                (strcmp(_name, smc._name) == 0));
    }

protected:
    ShowMeWindow  *psm;     // Need this to access the
                            // conditions table
    char          *_name;   // This condition's name
    Expression    *expr;    // Expression for this condition
    short         val;      // Expression's value
    short         cmdindx;  // Command to execute (if
                            // val is nonzero)
    char          *cmdarg;  // Arguments for the command
    char          *orig;    // Copy of the arguments
};

#endif
```

There is a separate class for each of the expressions listed in Table 25.2:

- `TimeExpression` represents expressions involving the current time.
- `KeyExpression` is an expression that compares a keystroke to a specified ASCII code.
- `ClickExpression` is an expression involving mouse button clicks on a sprite or inside a rectangle.
- `ValueExpression` represents expressions involving the current value of a sprite's variables, such as `xpos` and `ypos`.

As you can see from Listing 25.11, each of these classes is derived from the abstract base class `Expression`. Each `Expression` class is required to provide the following virtual functions:

- `virtual Expression* clone(ShowMeCondition *smc, char *expstr);` creates a copy of the expression, initialized with the parameters in the string `expstr`.

- `virtual short eval();` evaluates the expression and returns a true (nonzero) or false (zero) value.

Listing 25.12 shows the file COND.CPP, which implements the member functions of the `ShowMeCondition` and `Expression` classes. One interesting aspect of the `ShowMeCondition` class is the way in which it initializes the `Expression` object. As you might recall from the sample script file in Listing 25.3, a condition is specified by an expression. The first word of the expression identifies the type of expression. The rest of the string is specific to that expression. Here is the solution employed to handle the creation of the appropriate `Expression` object:

1. Maintain a static table of `exp_list` objects in which `exp_list` is defined as follows:

   ```
   struct exp_list
   {
       exp_list(const char* exprname,
    Expression& _expr):
                name(exprname), expr(_expr) {}

       const char*    name;
       Expression&    expr;
   };
   ```

   The table named `expression_list` at the beginning of Listing 25.12 is an example of such a table. This table associates a name with an instance of an `Expression` class. This table also shows how to initialize a static array of class instances.

2. To create an `Expression` identified by a name, such as `click`, locate it in the table, and call the `clone` member function with the rest of the expression string as an argument. This creates a copy of that `Expression` initialized with the appropriate values. To understand the process, you should study the constructor for the `ShowMeCondition` class shown in Listing 25.12.

Listing 25.12. COND.CPP. Implementation of the `ShowMeCondition` and `Expression` classes.

```
//-------------------------------------------------------------
// File: cond.cpp
//
// Implements the ShowMeCondition class (and other supporting
```

```
// classes) that holds a "condition" for the ShowMe application.
// Each condition is an expression whose value is used to
// control various aspects of the ShowMe application. A
// condition is TRUE if its value is nonzero.
//-----------------------------------------------------------------
#include <math.h>
#include "showwin.h"

TimeExpression     timeEXPR;
KeyExpression      keyEXPR;
ClickExpression    clickEXPR;
ValueExpression    valueEXPR;

struct exp_list
{
    exp_list(const char* exprname, Expression& _expr):
             name(exprname), expr(_expr) {}

    const char*    name;
    Expression&    expr;
};

static exp_list expression_list[] =
{
    exp_list("time",       timeEXPR),
    exp_list("key",        keyEXPR),
    exp_list("click",      clickEXPR),
    exp_list("value",      valueEXPR)
};

static short numexpr = sizeof(expression_list) /
                       sizeof(exp_list);

#define EQ   1
#define GT   2
#define LT   3
#define LE   4
#define GE   5

#define CLICK_ON  1
#define CLICK_IN  2
```

continues

Listing 25.12. continued

```
struct operation
{
    char  *name;
    short opcode;
};

static operation oplist[] =
{
    {"exceeds",       GT},
    {"less_than",     LT},
    {"greater_than",  GT},
    {"equals",        EQ},
    {"is",            EQ},
    {"equal_to",      EQ},
    {"eq",            EQ},
    {"gt",            GT},
    {"ge",            GE},
    {"lt",            LT},
    {"le",            LE}
};
static short numops = sizeof(oplist) / sizeof(oplist[0]);

static char *whitespace = " \t\n";

//-------------------------------------------------------------
// ShowMeCondition:: S h o w M e C o n d i t i o n
// Constructor for the ShowMeCondition class

ShowMeCondition::ShowMeCondition(ShowMeWindow *smw, char *cname,
                char *ename, char* earg,  short cmd, char *arg) :
    psm(smw), cmdindx(cmd), val(0)
{
    if(cname != NULL)
    {
        _name = new char[strlen(cname)+1];
        if(_name != NULL) strcpy(_name, cname);
    }

    if(arg != NULL)
    {
        short len = strlen(arg) + 1;
```

```
        cmdarg = new char[len];
        if(cmdarg != NULL) strcpy(cmdarg, arg);
        orig = new char[len];
        if(orig != NULL) strcpy(orig, arg);
    }
    else
    {
        cmdarg = orig = NULL;
    }

// Locate expression in exp_list
    short i;
    for(i = 0; i < numexpr; i++)
    {
        if(strnicmp(expression_list[i].name, ename,
                    strlen(ename)) == 0)
        {
// Create an Expression object by cloning this one
            expr = expression_list[i].expr.clone(this, earg);
        }
    }
}
//-----------------------------------------------------------------
// ShowMeCondition:: ~ S h o w M e C o n d i t i o n
// Destructor for the ShowMeCondition class

ShowMeCondition::~ShowMeCondition()
{
    if(_name != NULL) delete _name;
    if(expr != NULL) delete expr;
    if(cmdarg != NULL) delete cmdarg;
    if(orig != NULL) delete orig;
}
//-----------------------------------------------------------------
// TimeExpression:: clone
// Create a new TimeExpression using values in the string
// expstr.

Expression* TimeExpression::clone(ShowMeCondition *smc,
                                  char *expstr)
{
```

continues

Listing 25.12. continued

```
    if(expstr == NULL) return NULL;

// Extract tokens from expstr
    char *token1 = strtok(expstr, whitespace);
    char *token2 = strtok(NULL, whitespace);

    short i, oc;
    for(i = 0; i < numops; i++)
    {
        if(strnicmp(oplist[i].name, token1,
                                 strlen(token1)) == 0)
        {
            oc = oplist[i].opcode;
            break;
        }
    }

    if(i == numops) return NULL;
    unsigned long ts = ((double)ticks_per_sec * atof(token2));
    return (new TimeExpression(smc, oc, ts));
}
//-----------------------------------------------------------------
// TimeExpression:: e v a l
// Evaluate a time expression

short TimeExpression::eval()
{
    ShowMeWindow *psm = psc->owner();

// Get current time ticks
    unsigned long curtick = psm->current_ticks();
    switch(opcode)
    {
        case GT: return curtick > tick_threshold;
        case LT: return curtick < tick_threshold;
        case GE: return curtick >= tick_threshold;
        case LE: return curtick <= tick_threshold;
        case EQ: return curtick == tick_threshold;
    }
    return 0;
```

```
}
//----------------------------------------------------------------
// KeyExpression:: clone
// Create a new KeyExpression using values in the string
// expstr.

Expression* KeyExpression::clone(ShowMeCondition *smc,
                                  char *expstr)
{
    if(expstr == NULL) return NULL;

// Extract tokens from expstr
    char *opnm = strtok(expstr, whitespace);
    if(opnm == NULL) return NULL;
    char *keyval = strtok(NULL, whitespace);
    if(keyval == NULL) return NULL;

    short i, oc;
    for(i = 0; i < numops; i++)
    {
        if(strnicmp(oplist[i].name, opnm,
                                 strlen(opnm)) == 0)
        {
            oc = oplist[i].opcode;
            break;
        }
    }
    if(i == numops) return NULL;
    return (new KeyExpression(smc, oc, atoi(keyval)));
}
//----------------------------------------------------------------
// KeyExpression:: e v a l
// Evaluate a time expression

short KeyExpression::eval()
{
    ShowMeWindow *psm = psc->owner();

    if(!psm->key_down()) return 0;
    short keycode = psm->key_code();
```

continues

Listing 25.12. continued

```
    switch(opcode)
    {
        case GT: return keycode >  key;
        case LT: return keycode <  key;
        case GE: return keycode >= key;
        case LE: return keycode <= key;
        case EQ: return keycode == key;
    }
    return 0;
}
//----------------------------------------------------------------
// ClickExpression:: clone
// Create a new ClickExpression using values in the string
// expstr.

Expression* ClickExpression::clone(ShowMeCondition *smc,
                                   char *expstr)
{
    if(expstr == NULL) return NULL;

// Extract tokens from expstr
    char *token1 = strtok(expstr, whitespace);
    char *token2;
    SpriteInfo *si = NULL;
    short oc = 0;
    if(stricmp(token1, "on") == 0)
    {
// Condition is: Click on a sprite. Next token is sprite's name.
        token2 = strtok(NULL, whitespace);
        si = smc->owner()->find_sprite_info(token2);
        oc = CLICK_ON;
    }

    short t=0, l=0, b=0, r=0;
    if(stricmp(token1, "in") == 0)
    {
        oc = CLICK_IN;
// Condition is: Click in a rectangle. Next four tokens are
// coordinates of rectangle's upper left and lower right
// corners.
        token2 = strtok(NULL, whitespace);
        l = atoi(token2);
```

```
        token2 = strtok(NULL, whitespace);
        t = atoi(token2);
        token2 = strtok(NULL, whitespace);
        r = atoi(token2);
        token2 = strtok(NULL, whitespace);
        b = atoi(token2);
    }
    return (new ClickExpression(smc, oc, si, l, t, r, b));
}
//-----------------------------------------------------------------
// ClickExpression:: e v a l
// Evaluate a time expression

short ClickExpression::eval()
{
    ShowMeWindow *psm = psc->owner();

    if(psm->clicked())
    {
        short x = psm->xclick();
        short y = psm->yclick();
        short l,t,r,b;
        if(opcode == CLICK_ON)
        {
            if(psm->cur_anim() == NULL) return 0;
            if(si->animinfo() == NULL) return 0;
            if(si->animinfo()->animation() == NULL) return 0;
            if(psm->cur_anim() != si->animinfo()->animation())
                                                return 0;
            if(si->spr() == NULL) return 0;
            if(!si->spr()->is_active()) return 0;

            l = si->spr()->xpos();
            t = si->spr()->ypos();
            r = l + si->spr()->width();
            b = t + si->spr()->height();
        }
        else
        {
            l = x1;
            t = y1;
            r = x2;
```

continues

Listing 25.12. continued

```
            b = y2;
        }
        if(x > l && x < r && y > t && y < b) return 1;
    }
    return 0;
}
//-----------------------------------------------------------------
// ValueExpression:: V a l u e E x p r e s s i o n
// Constructor for a ValueExpression

ValueExpression::ValueExpression(ShowMeCondition* smc, short oc,
                      SpriteInfo* _si, NameValue* _nmv,
                      char *val) :
    opcode(oc), si(_si), nmv(_nmv)
{
    psc = smc;
    switch(_nmv->type)
    {
        case SHORT_INT:
            s_value = atoi(val);
            break;

        case LONG_INT:
            l_value = atol(val);
            break;

        case FLOAT:
            f_value = atof(val);
            break;

        case DOUBLE:
            d_value = atof(val);
            break;
    }
}
//-----------------------------------------------------------------
// ValueExpression:: clone
// Create a new ValueExpression using values in the string
// expstr.
```

```
Expression* ValueExpression::clone(ShowMeCondition *smc,
                                   char *expstr)
{
    if(expstr == NULL) return NULL;

// Extract tokens from expstr
    char *sprnm = strtok(expstr, whitespace);
    char *varnm = strtok(NULL, whitespace);
    char *opnm = strtok(NULL, whitespace);
    char *val = strtok(NULL, whitespace);

    SpriteInfo *si = smc->owner()->find_sprite_info(sprnm);
    if(si == NULL) return NULL;

    NameValue *nmv = si->name_value(varnm);
    if(nmv == NULL) return NULL;

    if(opnm ==  NULL) return NULL;
    short i, oc;
    for(i = 0; i < numops; i++)
    {
        if(strnicmp(oplist[i].name, opnm,
                               strlen(opnm)) == 0)
        {
            oc = oplist[i].opcode;
            break;
        }
    }
    if(i == numops) return NULL;

    if(val == NULL) return NULL;

    return (new ValueExpression(smc, oc, si, nmv, val));
}
//--------------------------------------------------------------
// ValueExpression:: e v a l
// Evaluate a value expression

short ValueExpression::eval()
{
    ShowMeWindow *psm = psc->owner();
    if(nmv == NULL) return 0;
```

continues

Listing 25.12. continued

```
    if(psm->cur_anim() == NULL) return 0;
    if(si->animinfo() == NULL) return 0;
    if(si->animinfo()->animation() == NULL) return 0;
    if(psm->cur_anim() != si->animinfo()->animation())
                                        return 0;
    if(si->spr() == NULL) return 0;
    if(!si->spr()->is_active()) return 0;

    switch(nmv->type)
    {
        case SHORT_INT:
            if(opcode == EQ) return si->*(nmv->si_value) == s_value;
            if(opcode == GT) return si->*(nmv->si_value) > s_value;
            if(opcode == GE) return si->*(nmv->si_value) >= s_value;
            if(opcode == LT) return si->*(nmv->si_value) < s_value;
            if(opcode == LE) return si->*(nmv->si_value) <= s_value;

        case LONG_INT:
            if(opcode == EQ) return si->*(nmv->li_value) == l_value;
            if(opcode == GT) return si->*(nmv->li_value) > l_value;
            if(opcode == GE) return si->*(nmv->li_value) >= l_value;
            if(opcode == LT) return si->*(nmv->li_value) < l_value;
            if(opcode == LE) return si->*(nmv->li_value) <= l_value;

        case FLOAT:
            if(opcode == EQ) return si->*(nmv->f_value) == f_value;
            if(opcode == GT) return si->*(nmv->f_value) > f_value;
            if(opcode == GE) return si->*(nmv->f_value) >= f_value;
            if(opcode == LT) return si->*(nmv->f_value) < f_value;
            if(opcode == LE) return si->*(nmv->f_value) <= f_value;

        case DOUBLE:
            if(opcode == EQ) return si->*(nmv->d_value) == d_value;
            if(opcode == GT) return si->*(nmv->d_value) > d_value;
            if(opcode == GE) return si->*(nmv->d_value) >= d_value;
            if(opcode == LT) return si->*(nmv->d_value) < d_value;
            if(opcode == LE) return si->*(nmv->d_value) <= d_value;
    }
    return 0;
}
```

Other Files

In addition to the source and header files you have seen so far, ShowMe needs a few more files:

- SHOWDEFS.H (Listing 25.13) is the header file with a common set of macros used by several source files.
- SHOWME.RES is the resource file for ShowMe. You will find SHOWME.RES on the companion disk.

Listing 25.13. SHOWDEFS.H. Common definitions for ShowMe.

```
//-----------------------------------------------------------------
// File: showdefs.h
//
// Common identifiers and macro definitions for the ShowMe
// applications.
//-----------------------------------------------------------------
#if !defined(__SHOWDEFS_H)
#define __SHOWDEFS_H

#define SHORT_INT      1
#define LONG_INT       2
#define FLOAT          3
#define DOUBLE         4

#define NUMVAR_SPRITEINFO 12

#define DISP_MILLISECONDS 50

const unsigned long ticks_per_sec = (1000.0/
                                     (double)DISP_MILLISECONDS);
const double seconds_per_tick = (double)DISP_MILLISECONDS /
                                1000.0;

#endif
```

Building *SHOWME.EXE*

Borland C++ 4 is used to build the ShowMe application. The companion disk has all the files needed to build the executable file, SHOWME.EXE. In particular, the project file, SHOWME.IDE, lists the source files and libraries necessary to build the application.

After installing the code from the companion disk, you should be able to build SHOWME.EXE by selecting Make all from the Project menu. Once the program is successfully built, you can add it to Windows Program Manager by selecting New... from the Program Manager's File menu.

Summary

This chapter uses the image-animation and sound-generation techniques presented in the previous chapters and blends everything into an application called ShowMe that lets you create stand-alone animated demos. ShowMe supports a simple scripting language that lets you control the demo. Essentially, the scripting language allows you to animate images, play sound files, check for conditions, and specify a sequence of events.

After installing the application from the companion disk and trying it out, you can read this chapter to see how ShowMe is implemented. The disk includes a sample demo that promotes this book. You can use that demo as an example to create other demos. Note that you need a sound board with a Windows sound driver to listen to the voices in the demo.

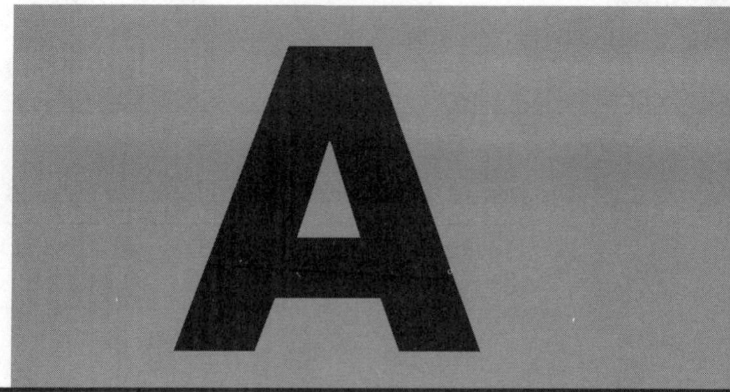

ANSI C Headers

This appendix summarizes the contents of the header files in ANSI standard C.

Macros and Data Types Defined in ANSI C Header Files

Table A.1 provides a list of all macros and data types defined in the standard header files in ANSI C. The header files are then shown in alphabetical order. For each header file, you will find the prototype of each function together with a short description of the function.

Table A.1. Macros and data types in ANSI C library.

Macro or Data Type	Defined In	Description
BUFSIZ	<stdio.h>	Size of buffer used by setbuf
CHAR_BIT	<limits.h>	Maximum number of in a char
CHAR_MAX	<limits.h>	Maximum value of a char
CHAR_MIN	<limits.h>	Minimum value of a char
CLK_TCK	<time.h>	Number of clock ticks per second returned by the clock function
DBL_DIG	<float.h>	Number of significant decimal digits in a double value
DBL_EPSILON	<float.h>	Smallest positive double value x such that 1+x != 1
DBL_MANT_DIG	<float.h>	Number of base FLT_RADIX digits in the mantissa of a double variable
DBL_MAX	<float.h>	Maximum representable finite value that can be stored in a double variable
DBL_MAX_10_EXP	<float.h>	Maximum integer such that 10 raised to that power can be stored in a double variable
DBL_MAX_EXP	<float.h>	Maximum integer such that FLT_RADIX raised to that power can be stored in a double variable
DBL_MIN	<float.h>	Minimum positive floating-point number that can be stored in a double variable
DBL_MIN_10_EXP	<float.h>	Minimum negative integer such that 10 raised to that power can be stored in a double variable
DBL_MIN_EXP	<float.h>	Minimum negative integer such that FLT_RADIX raised to that power minus 1 can be stored in a double variable

Macro or Data Type	Defined In	Description
EDOM	<errno.h>	Constant to indicate invalid argument ("domain error")
EOF	<stdio.h>	A negative integer constant that indicates "end-of-file"
ERANGE	<errno.h>	Constant to indicate unrepresentable result ("range error")
EXIT_FAILURE	<stddef.h>	Status code that can be used with exit to indicate that the program ended with an error
EXIT_SUCCESS	<stddef.h>	Status code that can be used with exit to indicate that the program executed successfully
FILE	<stdio.h>	A data type capable of storing all information necessary to perform file I/O
FILENAME_MAX	<stdio.h>	Maximum length of a file name string
FLT_DIG	<float.h>	Number of significant decimal digits in a float value
FLT_EPSILON	<float.h>	Smallest positive float value x such that 1+x != 1
FLT_MANT_DIG	<float.h>	Number of base FLT_RADIX digits in the mantissa of a float
FLT_MAX	<float.h>	Maximum representable finite value that can be stored in a float
FLT_MAX_10_EXP	<float.h>	Maximum integer such that 10 raised to that power can be stored in a float variable
FLT_MAX_EXP	<float.h>	Maximum integer such that FLT_RADIX raised to that power is representable in a float

continues

Table A.1. continued

Macro or Data Type	Defined In	Description
`FLT_MIN`	`<float.h>`	Minimum positive floating-point number that can be stored in a `float`
`FLT_MIN_10_EXP`	`<float.h>`	Minimum negative integer such that 10 raised to that power can be stored in a `float`
`FLT_MIN_EXP`	`<float.h>`	Minimum negative integer such that `FLT_RADIX` raised to that power minus 1 can be stored in a `float`
`FLT_RADIX`	`<float.h>`	Radix of the exponent representation (usually 2 for binary exponent)
`FLT_ROUNDS`	`<float.h>`	Constant to indicate how floating-point values are rounded (-1=indeterminate, 0=toward 0, 1=to nearest representable value, 2=toward positive infinity, and 3=toward negative infinity)
`FOPEN_MAX`	`<stdio.h>`	Minimum number of files that can be open simultaneously
`HUGE_VAL`	`<math.h>`	A `double` expression that evaluates to a very large value (for use as return value by math functions when computed result is too large)
`INT_MAX`	`<limits.h>`	Maximum value of an `int`
`INT_MIN`	`<limits.h>`	Minimum value of an `int`
`_IOFBF`	`<stdio.h>`	Constant for "full buffering"
`_IOLBF`	`<stdio.h>`	Constant for "line buffering"
`_IONBF`	`<stdio.h>`	Constant for "no buffering"
`L_tmpnam`	`<stdio.h>`	Size of char array large enough to hold temporary file names generated by `tmpnam`

Macro or Data Type	Defined In	Description
LC_ALL	<locale.h>	Constant to indicate the program's entire locale (aspects that depend on the country or geographic region)
LC_COLLATE	<locale.h>	Constant to indicate behavior of strcoll and strxfrm
LC_CTYPE	<locale.h>	Constant to indicate behavior of all character handling routines
LC_MONETARY	<locale.h>	Constant to indicate behavior of monetary formatting information returned by localeconv
LC_NUMERIC	<locale.h>	Constant to indicate behavior of decimal point format information returned by localeconv
LC_TIME	<locale.h>	Constant to indicate behavior of strftime function
LDBL_DIG	<float.h>	Number of significant decimal digits in a long double value
LDBL_EPSILON	<float.h>	Smallest positive long double value x such that 1+x != 1
LDBL_MANT_DIG	<float.h>	Number of base FLT_RADIX digits in the mantissa of a long double
LDBL_MAX	<float.h>	Maximum representable finite value that can be stored in a long double
LDBL_MAX_10_EXP	<float.h>	Maximum integer such that 10 raised to that power is representable in a long double
LDBL_MAX_EXP	<float.h>	Maximum integer such that FLT_RADIX raised to that power minus 1 can be stored in a long double

continues

Table A.1. continued

Macro or Data Type	Defined In	Description
LDBL_MIN	<float.h>	Minimum positive floating-point number that can be stored in a long double
LDBL_MIN_10_EXP	<float.h>	Minimum negative integer such that 10 raised to that power is representable in a long double
LDBL_MIN_EXP	<float.h>	Minimum negative integer such that FLT_RADIX raised to that power minus 1 can be stored in a long double
LONG_MAX	<limits.h>	Maximum value of a long int
LONG_MIN	<limits.h>	Minimum value of a long int
MB_CUR_MAX	<stdlib.h>	Number of bytes in a multibyte character for the current locale (always less than MB_LEN_MAX)
MB_LEN_MAX	<limits.h>	Maximum number of bytes in a multibyte character
NDEBUG	*not defined*	If defined, assert will be ignored
NULL	<locale.h> <stddef.h> <stdio.h> <stdlib.h> <string.h> <time.h>	Implementation-defined null pointer constant
RAND_MAX	<stdlib.h>	Maximum integral value returned by the rand function
SCHAR_MAX	<limits.h>	Maximum value of a signed char
SCHAR_MIN	<limits.h>	Minimum value of a signed char
SEEK_CUR	<stdio.h>	Constant to indicate "relative to current position"

Macro or Data Type	Defined In	Description
SEEK_END	<stdio.h>	Constant to indicate "relative to end-of-file"
SEEK_SET	<stdio.h>	Constant to indicate "relative to start-of-file"
SHRT_MAX	<limits.h>	Maximum value of a short int
SHRT_MIN	<limits.h>	Minimum value of a short int
SIG_DFL	<signal.h>	Constant to indicate default handling of a signal
SIG_ERR	<signal.h>	Constant to indicate error return from the signal function
SIG_IGN	<signal.h>	Constant to indicate that a signal should be ignored
SIGABRT	<signal.h>	Signal to indicate abnormal termination
SIGFPE	<signal.h>	Signal due to divide by zero, overflow, or other floating-point errors
SIGILL	<signal.h>	Signal due to illegal instruction
SIGINT	<signal.h>	Signal raised when a specified attention key is pressed by the user (for example, Ctrl-C)
SIGSEGV	<signal.h>	Signal generated when accessing a storage location at an invalid address
SIGTERM	<signal.h>	Signal sent to program to terminate it
TMP_MAX	<stdio.h>	Minimum number of unique names that can be obtained by calling the tmpnam function
UCHAR_MAX	<limits.h>	Maximum value of an unsigned char

continues

Table A.1. continued

Macro or Data Type	Defined In	Description
`UINT_MAX`	`<limits.h>`	Maximum value of an `unsigned int`
`ULONG_MAX`	`<limits.h>`	Maximum value of an `unsigned long int`
`USHRT_MAX`	`<limits.h>`	Maximum value of an `unsigned short int`
`clock_t`	`<time.h>`	Data type capable of holding value of time returned by the `clock` function
`errno`	`<errno.h>`	Global variable to indicate the cause of the last error
`div_t`	`<stdlib.h>`	Data structure that can hold the value returned by `div`
`fpos_t`	`<stdio.h>`	A data type capable of recording all information necessary to specify each unique position in a file
`jmp_buf`	`<setjmp.h>`	An array type capable of holding information necessary to restore a calling environment
`struct lconv`	`<locale.h>`	Structure to hold strings to be used in formatting numeric and monetary values
`ldiv_t`	`<stdlib.h>`	Data structure that can hold the value returned by the `ldiv` function
`offsetof`	`<stddef.h>`	Macro of the form `offsetof(structure_type, member)` that returns a size_t value which is the offset in bytes, of the member from the beginning of the structure
`ptrdiff_t`	`<stddef.h>`	Signed integral data type which can hold the result of subtracting one pointer from another

Macro or Data Type	Defined In	Description
sig_atomic_t	<signal.h>	A data type that can be accessed as a single entity even in the presence of hardware and software interrupts
size_t	<stddef.h> <stdlib.h>	An unsigned integral data type which is the result of the sizeof operator
stderr	<stdio.h>	Pointer to FILE data associated with the standard error stream
stdin	<stdio.h>	Pointer to FILE data associated with the standard input stream
stdout	<stdio.h>	Pointer to FILE data associated with the standard output stream
time_t	<time.h>	Data type capable of representing value of time returned by the time function
struct tm	<time.h>	Data structure for holding components of a calendar time
va_list	<stdarg.h>	Data type suitable for holding information needed by the macros va_start, va_arg, and va_end
wchar_t	<stddef.h> <stdlib.h>	An integral data type which can hold the entire range of values necessary to represent the largest extended character set supported by the compiler

Header Files in ANSI C

<assert.h>

```
void assert(<expression>);
```

Abort process if expression is false.

`<ctype.h>`

`int isalnum(int c);`

True if `c` is alphanumeric.

`int isalpha(int c);`

True if `c` is a letter.

`int iscntrl(int c);`

True if `c` is a control character.

`int isdigit(int c);`

True if `c` is a decimal digit.

`int isgraph(int c);`

True if `c` is any printable character except space.

`int islower(int c);`

True if `c` is a lowercase letter.

`int isprint(int c);`

True if `c` is a printable character.

`int ispunct(int c);`

True if `c` is a punctuation character.

`int isspace(int c);`

True if `c` is a space character.

`int isupper(int c);`

True if `c` is an uppercase letter.

`int isxdigit(int c);`

True if `c` is a hexadecimal digit.

`int tolower(int c);`

Convert `c` to lowercase if it is uppercase.

`int toupper(int c);`

Convert `c` to uppercase if it is lowercase.

<errno.h>

Defines the macros `EDOM`, `ERANGE`, and `errno` (see Table A.1).

<float.h>

Defines macros that specify various properties of floating-point data types: `float`, `double`, and `long double`. Consult Table A.1 for a complete list of these macros.

<limits.h>

Defines macros that specify various properties of integer data types: `char`, `int`, and `long`. Consult Table A.1 for a complete list of these macros.

<locale.h>

```
struct lconv *localeconv(void);
```

Gets information on formatting monetary and numeric values.

```
char *setlocale(int category, const char *locale_name);
```

Sets a new locale.

<math.h>

```
double acos(double x);
```

Computes arc cosine of `x`.

```
double asin(double x);
```

Computes arc sine of `x`.

```
double atan(double x);
```

Computes arc tangent of `x`.

```
double atan2(double y, double x);
```

Computes arc tangent of `y/x`.

```
double ceil(double x);
```

Returns the smallest integer value that is not less than `x`.

```
double cos(double x);
```

Computes cosine of angle `x` (radians).

```
double cosh(double x);
```

Computes the hyperbolic cosine of `x`.

```
double exp(double x);
```

Computes the exponential of x (e^x).

```
double fabs(double x);
```

Computes absolute value of x.

```
double floor(double x);
```

Returns the largest integer value that is not greater than x.

```
double fmod(double x, double y);
```

Divides x by y with an integer quotient and returns the remainder.

```
double frexp(double x, int *expptr);
```

Breaks down x into mantissa and exponent of two.

```
double ldexp(double x, int exp);
```

Reconstructs x out of mantissa and exponent of two (compute $x*2^{exp}$).

```
double log(double x);
```

Computes the natural logarithm of x.

```
double log10(double x);
```

Computes logarithm to the base 10 of x.

```
double modf(double x, double *intptr);
```

Breaks x into fractional and integer parts.

```
double pow(double x, double y);
```

Computes x raised to the power y (x^y).

```
double sin(double x);
```

Computes sine of angle x (radians).

```
double sinh(double x);
```

Computes the hyperbolic sine of x.

```
double sqrt(double x);
```

Computes the square root of x.

```
double tan(double x);
```

Computes tangent of angle x (radians).

```
double tanh(double x);
```

Computes the hyperbolic tangent of x.

<setjmp.h>

```
void longjmp(jmp_buf env, int value);
```

Returns by restoring a saved context (non-local `goto`).

```
int setjmp(jmp_buf env);
```

Saves the current context for use by `longjmp`.

<signal.h>

```
int raise(int signum);
```

Creates an exception condition corresponding to the specified signal number.

```
void (*signal(int signum, void (*handler)(int sigarg)))(int);
```

Sets up the function named `handler` as the function to be called when the signal specified by `signum` occurs.

<stdarg.h>

```
void va_start(va_list arg_ptr, prev_param);
```

Sets `arg_ptr` to beginning of argument list.

```
<type> va_arg(va_list arg_ptr, <type>);
```

Gets next argument of specified type.

```
void va_end(va_list arg_ptr);
```

Resets `arg_ptr`.

<stddef.h>

Defines the macros and data types `NULL`, `offsetof`, `ptrdiff_t`, `size_t`, and `wchar_t`.

<stdio.h>

```
void clearerr(FILE *file_pointer);
```

Clears error indicator of stream specified by `file_pointer`.

```
int fclose(FILE *file_pointer);
```

Closes the file specified by `file_pointer`.

```
int feof(FILE *file_pointer);
```

Checks if end of file occurred on a stream.

```
int ferror(FILE *file_pointer);
```

Checks if any error occurred during file I/O.

```
int fflush(FILE *file_pointer);
```

Writes out (flush) buffer to file.

```
int fgetc(FILE *file_pointer);
```

Gets a character from a stream.

```
int fgetpos(FILE *file_pointer, fpos_t *current_pos);
```

Gets the current position in a stream.

```
char *fgets(char *string, int maxchar, FILE *file_pointer);
```

Reads a string from a file.

```
FILE *fopen(const char *filename, const char *access_mode);
```

Opens a file for buffered I/O.

```
int fprintf(FILE *file_pointer, const char *format_string,...);
```

Writes formatted output to a file.

```
int fputc(int c, FILE *file_pointer);
```

Writes a character to a stream.

```
int fputs(char *string, FILE *file_pointer);
```

Writes a string to a stream.

```
size_t fread(void *buffer, size_t size,  size_t count, FILE
*file_pointer);
```

Reads unformatted data from a stream into a buffer.

```
FILE *freopen(const char *filename, const char *access_mode, FILE
*file_pointer);
```

Reassigns a file pointer to a different file.

```
int fscanf(FILE *file_pointer, const char *format_string,...);
```

Reads formatted input from a stream.

`int fseek(FILE *file_pointer, long offset, int origin);`

Sets current position in file to a new location.

`int fsetpos(FILE *file_pointer, const fpos_t *current_pos);`

Sets current position in file to a new location (use with `fgetpos`).

`long ftell(FILE *file_pointer);`

Gets current location in file.

`size_t fwrite(const void *buffer, size_t size, size_t count, FILE *file_pointer);`

Writes unformatted data from a buffer to a stream.

`int getc(FILE *file_pointer);`

Reads a character from a stream.

`int getchar(void);`

Reads a character from `stdin`. Same as `fgetc(stdin)`.

`char *gets(char *buffer);`

Reads a line from `stdin` into a buffer.

`void perror(const char *string);`

Prints error message corresponding to last system error.

`int printf(const char *format_string,...);`

Writes formatted output to `stdout`.

`int putc(int c, FILE *file_pointer);`

Writes a character to a stream.

`int putchar(int c);`

Writes a character to `stdout`.

`int puts(const char *string);`

Writes a string to `stdout`.

`int remove(const char *filename);`

Deletes a named file.

```
int rename(const char *oldname, const char *newname);
```

Renames a file.

```
void rewind(FILE *file_pointer);
```

Rewinds a file.

```
int scanf(const char *format_string,...);
```

Reads formatted input from `stdin`.

```
void setbuf(FILE *file_pointer, char *buffer);
```

Sets up a new buffer for the stream.

```
int setvbuf(FILE *file_pointer, char *buffer,
        int buf_type, size_t buf_size);
```

Sets up new buffer and control the level of buffering on a stream.

```
int sprintf(char *p_string, const char *format_string,...);
```

Writes formatted output to a string.

```
int sscanf(const char *buffer, const char *format_string,...);
```

Reads formatted input from a string.

```
FILE *tmpfile(void);
```

Opens a temporary file.

```
char *tmpnam(char *file_name);
```

Gets temporary file name.

```
int ungetc(int c, FILE *file_pointer);
```

Pushes back character into stream's buffer.

```
int vfprintf(FILE *file_pointer, const char *format_string, va_list
arg_pointer);
```

Writes formatted output to a file (allows variable length argument list).

```
int vprintf(const char *format_string, va_list arg_pointer);
```

Writes formatted output to `stdout` (allows variable length argument list).

```
int vsprintf(char *p_string, const char *format_string,
        va_list arg_pointer);
```

Writes formatted output to a string (allows variable length argument list).

<stdlib.h>

`void abort(void);`

Aborts a process by calling `raise(SIGABRT)`.

`int abs(int n);`

Gets absolute value of an integer.

`int atexit(void (*func)(void));`

Sets up function to be called when process terminates.

`double atof(const char *string);`

Converts string to floating point value.

`int atoi(const char *string);`

Converts string to an integer value.

`int atol(const char *string);`

Converts string to a long integer value.

`void *bsearch(const void *key, const void *base, size_t num, size_t width, int (*compare)(const void *elem1, const void *elem2));`

Performs binary search.

`void *calloc(size_t num_elems, size_t elem_size);`

Allocates an array and initializes all elements to zero.

`div_t div(int numer, int denom);`

Divides one integer by another and returns quotient and remainder.

`void exit(int status);`

Terminates process after flushing all buffers.

`void free(void *pointer);`

Frees a block of memory.

`char *getenv(const char *varname);`

Gets definition of environment variable whose name is `varname`.

`long labs(long n);`

Finds absolute value of long integer `n`.

```
ldiv_t ldiv(long numer, long denom);
```

Divides one long integer by another (returns quotient and remainder).

```
void *malloc(size_t num_bytes);
```

Allocates a block of memory.

```
int mblen(const char *s, size_t n);
```

Returns the number of bytes in a single multibyte character.

```
size_t mbstowcs(wchar_t *pwcs, const char *mbs, size_t n);
```

Converts a sequence of multibyte characters in `mbs` into a sequence of codes of `wchar_t` type.

```
int mbtowc(wchar_t *pwchar, const char *s, size_t n);
```

Converts the multibyte character in `s` to `wchar_t` type.

```
void qsort(void *base, size_t num, size_t width, int (*compare)(const
void *elem1, const void *elem2));
```

Uses the quicksort algorithm to sort an array.

```
int rand(void);
```

Gets a random integer between 0 and `RAND_MAX` (also defined in `<stdlib.h>`).

```
void *realloc(void *pointer, size_t newsize);
```

Reallocates (adjusts the size of) a block of memory.

```
void srand(unsigned seed);
```

Sets a new seed for the random number generator (`rand`).

```
double strtod(const char *string, char **endptr);
```

Converts string to a floating point value.

```
long strtol(const char *string, char **endptr, int radix);
```

Converts string to a long integer using a given radix.

```
unsigned long strtoul(const char *string, char **endptr, int radix);
```

Converts string to unsigned long integer using a specified radix.

```
int system(const char *string);
```

Executes a command in `string` by passing it to the command processor of the underlying operating system.

```
size_t wcstombs(char *mbs, const wchar_t *pwcs, size_t n);
```

Converts a sequence of codes of `wchar_t` type into a sequence of multibyte characters.

```
int wctomb(char *s, wchar_t wchar);
```

Converts a character of `wchar_t` type into a multibyte equivalent.

<string.h>

```
void *memchr (const void *s, int c, size_t n);
```

Searches for first occurrence of a character in a buffer.

```
int memcmp (const void *s1, const void *s2, size_t n);
```

Compares two buffers.

```
void *memcpy (void *dest, const void *src, size_t n);
```

Copies the `src` buffer into the `dest` buffer.

```
void *memmove (void *dest, const void *src, size_t n);
```

Moves a number of bytes from one buffer to another.

```
void *memset (void *s, int c, size_t n);
```

Sets `n` bytes of buffer `s` to the character `c`.

```
char *strcat(char *string1, const char *string2);
```

Appends `string2` to `string1`.

```
char *strchr(const char *string, int c);
```

Searches string for the first occurrence of the character `c`.

```
int strcmp(const char *string1, const char *string2);
```

Compares `string1` and `string2` according to alphabetical order.

```
int strcoll(const char *string1, const char *string2);
```

Compares `string1` with `string2` using a locale-specific collating sequence.

```
char *strcpy(char *string1, const char *string2);
```

Copies `string2` to `string1`.

```
size_t strcspn(const char *string1, const char *string2);
```

Finds first occurrence of a character from `string2` in `string1`.

`char *strerror(int errnum);`

Gets error message corresponding to specified error number.

`size_t strlen(const char *string);`

Determines the length of a string (excluding the terminating null character).

`char *strncat(char *string1, const char *string2, size_t n);`

Appends `n` characters from `string2` to `string1`.

`int strncmp(const char *string1, const char *string2, size_t n);`

Compares first `n` characters of two strings.

`char *strncpy(char *string1, const char *string2, size_t n);`

Copies first `n` characters of `string2` to `string1`.

`char *strpbrk(const char *string1, const char *string2);`

Locates first occurrence of any character from `string2` in `string1`.

`char *strrchr(const char *string, int c);`

Finds last occurrence of character `c` in `string`.

`size_t strspn(const char *string1, const char *string2);`

Locates the first character in `string1` that is not in `string2`.

`char *strstr(const char *string1, const char *string2);`

Finds the first occurrence of `string2` in `string1`.

`char *strtok(char *string1, const char *string2);`

Gets tokens from `string1` (`string2` has the token separators).

`size_t strxfrm(char *string1, char *string2, size_t maxchr);`

Transforms `string2` to `string1` using transformation rule appropriate for current locale.

`<time.h>`

`char *asctime(struct tm *time);`

Converts time from `struct tm` to string of the form `Sat Dec 4 10:15:55 1993`.

```
clock_t clock(void);
```

Gets elapsed processor time in clock ticks.

```
char *ctime(const time_t *time);
```

Converts binary time to string.

```
double difftime(time_t time2, time_t time1);
```

Computes the difference between two times in seconds.

```
struct tm *gmtime(const time_t *time);
```

Gets Greenwich Mean Time (GMT) in a `tm` structure.

```
struct tm *localtime(const time_t *time);
```

Gets the local time in a `tm` structure.

```
time_t mktime(struct tm *timeptr);
```

Converts time from `struct tm` to `time_t`.

```
size_t strftime(char *str, size_t maxsize, const char *format_string,
const struct tm *timeptr);
```

Converts time from `struct tm` to string using specified format.

```
time_t time(time_t *timeptr);
```

Gets current time in a binary format.

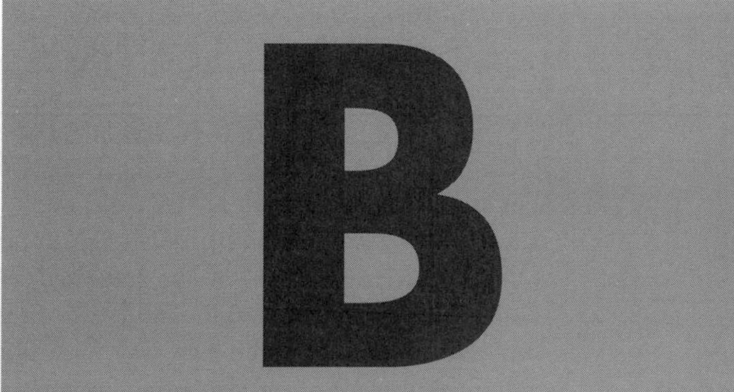

Bibliography

C++ and object-oriented programming (OOP) are steadily gaining popularity, and the number of books and articles on these topics reflect this trend. Here is a list of resources that will help you learn more about C++ and object-oriented programming. The list, organized by category, also includes a number of references for other topics such as Microsoft Windows programming and ANSI Standard C. This bibliography is by no means exhaustive; it's just a sample of the numerous books and journals that cover C++ and object-oriented programming.

C++ and Object-Oriented Programming

Most books on C++ cover object-oriented programming. One recent book, *Data Abstractions and Object-Oriented Programming in C++,* by Keith Gorlen, Sanford Orlow, and Perry Plexico, does a good job of teaching data abstraction and OOP using C++. Much of the book focuses on showing how to exploit reusable software components from class libraries such as the NIH Class Library developed by the authors.

For an official description of C++, you want a copy of *The C++ Programming Language,* Second Edition, by Bjarne Stroustrup, the inventor of C++. Another source of official description of C++ is *The Annotated C++ Reference Manual,* (often referred to as the *ARM*) by Margaret Ellis and Bjarne Stroustrup. The annotations in this book can help you understand the motivation behind the choices made during the design and improvement of the C++ programming language.

The book by Mark Mullin, *Object-Oriented Program Design with Examples in C++,* is worth noting because it covers object-oriented techniques with a single, large-scale program example in C++. Jerry Smith's book, *Reusability & Software Construction: C & C++,* is another that covers the design and implementation of a single program; in this case, a window-based text editor.

There are a host of other books by authors such as Lippman, Pohl, Dewhurst, Swan, and Weiskamp that cover the C++ programming language. Some offer insights into OOP, but focus mainly on teaching the C++ language without much emphasis on object-orientation.

To keep up with recent developments on how others are using C++ and how the ANSI standard for C++ is progressing, you should consult journals such as *The C++ Report,* published by SIGS Publications, New York, NY.

Dewhurst, Stephen C. and Kathy T. Stark. *Programming in C++*, Prentice Hall, Englewood Cliffs, NJ, 1989.

Ellis, Margaret A. and Bjarne Stroustrup. *The Annotated C++ Reference Manual*, Addison-Wesley Publishing Company, Reading, MA, 1990.

Gorlen, Keith E., Sanford M. Orlow, and Perry S. Plexico. *Data Abstractions and Object-Oriented Programming in C++*, John Wiley & Sons, Ltd., Chichester, West Sussex, England, 1990.

Lippman, Stanley B. *C++ Primer,* 2nd Edition, Addison-Wesley, Reading, MA, 1991.

Mullin, Mark. *Object-Oriented Program Design with Examples in C++*, Addison-Wesley, Reading, MA, 1989.

Pohl, Ira. *C++ for C Programmers*, The Benjamin/Cummings Publishing Company, Redwood City, CA, 1989.

Smith, Jerry D. *Reusability & Software Construction: C & C++*, John Wiley & Sons, Inc., New York, NY, 1990.

Stroustrup, Bjarne. *The C++ Programming Language,* Second Edition, Addison-Wesley Publishing Company, Reading, MA, 1991.

Swan, Tom. *Learning C++*, Sams Publishing, Carmel, IN, 1992.

Weiskamp, Keith and Bryan Flamig. *The Complete C++ Primer*, Academic Press, Inc., San Diego, CA, 1990.

Object-Oriented Design and Programming

As a topic, object-oriented programming is still in the evolutionary stage—its very definition is a subject of debate among experts. Still, the basic concepts of OOP have been covered in many books and journal articles.

Bertrand Meyer's book, *Object-Oriented Software Construction,* has a good description of the object-oriented approach. For a high-level overview of object-oriented concepts, terminology, and software, consult the recent books by Setrag Khosafian and Razmik Abnous (*Object Orientation: Concepts, Languages, Databases, User Interfaces*) and by Ann Winblad, Samuel Edwards, and David King (*Object Orientation: Concepts, Languages, Databases, User Interfaces*).

Other good sources of information on recent developments in OOP include the proceedings of the annual *Object-Oriented Programming Systems, Languages, and Applications* (OOPSLA) conference sponsored by the Association for Computing Machinery and the *Journal of Object-Oriented Programming* published bimonthly by SIGS Publications, Inc. of New York, NY.

Object-Oriented Analysis, Design, and Programming

Object-Oriented Programming (OOP) refers to the implementation of programs using objects, preferably in an object-oriented programming language such as C++. Although this book focuses on OOP using C++, the analysis and design phases of the software development process are even more important than the language used. *Object-Oriented Analysis (OOA)* refers to methods of specifying the requirements of the software in terms of real-world objects, their behavior, and their interactions.

> *Object-Oriented Design (OOD)*, on the other hand, turns the software requirements into specifications for objects and derives class hierarchies from which the objects can be created. OOD methods usually use a diagramming notation to represent the class hierarchy and to express the interaction among objects.

Despite a recent surge in books and articles on object-oriented design, this topic remains an elusive one to grasp. Because no single approach works for all problems, most descriptions of object-oriented design are, of necessity, a collage of case studies and extrapolations based on the experience of programmers in the field. You have to work through many examples before you can arrive at a set of guidelines for the software design approach that best suits a specific problem. Here is a selection of reading material to help you achieve that goal. Although this is a short list, each of these sources will, in turn, provide you with numerous other references on object-oriented design.

Grady Booch first described object-oriented design in his 1983 book on the Ada programming language. In his 1990 book, *Software Engineering with Ada,* he presents a more refined description of the incremental and iterative nature of object-oriented software design.

Brad Cox, the originator of the *Objective-C* language, describes his view of object-oriented programming in his 1986 book, *Object-Oriented Programming: An Evolutionary Approach.* He promotes the idea of packaging software in modular units that he calls *Software-ICs* (software integrated circuits).

Bertrand Meyer, author of an object-oriented language named *Eiffel,* describes object-oriented design as supported by the Eiffel language in his book *Object-Oriented Software Construction.* One of his ideas is the notion of *programming by contract*—the idea that for correct operation, a software module and its consumers must, in some way, formally express the rights and obligations of each side.

The recent book by Rebecca Wirfs-Brock, Brian Wilkerson, and Lauren Wiener, *Designing Object-Oriented Software,* presents a detailed example of object-oriented design using a "responsibility-driven" approach. The idea is to identify the classes, their responsibilities, and their collaborators. In this approach, you lay out the design on a set of index cards, called CRC cards, where CRC stands for Class, Responsibility, and Collaboration. This seems to be a promising step-by-step approach to object-oriented design of software.

The September 1990 issue of *Communications of the ACM*—the flagship magazine of the Association for Computing Machinery—is a special issue on object-oriented design. Consult this issue for a good assortment of articles on the object-oriented approach. In another article in the May 1989 issue of this journal, "An Object-Oriented Requirements Specification Method," Sidney Bailin presents a method for specifying the requirements for object-oriented software.

Notational schemes are another important tool because they let you express your design in a concise, yet descriptive manner. Although Booch, Meyer, and Cox have used some form of notation in their books, there is no universally accepted convention. For a sampling of some proposed notational schemes, see the recent journal articles.

Another interesting idea is to mix conventional function-oriented design with object-oriented concepts in a hybrid design strategy. Larry Constantine, one of the pioneers of structural techniques, discusses such an approach in a *Computer Language* article called "Objects, Functions, and Program Extensibility."

For a description of SmallTalk-80's Model-View-Controller (MVC) architecture, see Adele Goldberg's recent article in *Dr. Dobb's Journal,* "Information Models, Views, and Controllers." For another good discussion of the MVC model as well as some other examples of practical applications of object-oriented methods, see the compendium of essays edited by Lewis Pinson and Richard Wiener, *Applications of Object-Oriented Programming.*

Beck and Cunningham's article in *Proceedings of OOPSLA 1989,* "A Laboratory for Teaching Object-Oriented Thinking," describes the use of index cards to record initial class designs. This tool is used by Wirfs-Brock and colleagues in their responsibility-driven design approach.

The recent book by James Rambaugh and his colleagues at the General Electric Research and Development Center at Schenectady, New York is another recommended source of material on object-oriented modeling and design. This book covers the entire development life cycle—analysis, design, and implementation—using a graphical notation and methodology developed by the authors.

Bailin, Sidney. "An Object-Oriented Requirements Specification Method," *Communications of the ACM,* Vol. 32, No. 5, May 1989, pages 608-623.

Beck, K. and H. Cunningham. "A Laboratory for Teaching Object-Oriented Thinking," *Proceedings of OOPSLA 1989,* New Orleans, LA, October 1989, pages 1-6.

Booch, Grady. *Object-Oriented Design with Applications,* The Benjamin/Cummings Publishing Company, Redwood City, CA, 1991.

Booch, Grady. *Software Engineering with Ada*, The Benjamin/Cummings Publishing Company, Redwood City, CA, 1991.

Communications of the ACM, Special Issue on Object-Oriented Design, Volume 33, No. 9, September 1990, pages 38-159.

Constantine, Larry L. "Objects, Functions, and Program Extensibility," *Computer Language*, Vol. 7, No. 1, January 1990, pages 34-54.

Cox, Brad. *Object-Oriented Programming—An Evolutionary Approach*, Addison-Wesley Publishing Company, Reading, MA, 1986.

Goldberg, Adele. "Information Models, Views, and Controllers," *Dr. Dobb's Journal*, July 1990, pages 54-61.

Khosafian, Setrag and Razmik Abnous, *Object Orientation: Concepts, Languages, Databases, User Interfaces*, John Wiley & Sons, Inc., New York, NY, 1990.

Meyer, Bertrand. *Object-Oriented Software Construction*, Prentice Hall International (U.K.) Ltd., Hertfordshire, Great Britain, 1988.

Pinson, Lewis J. and Richard S. Wiener, Editors. *Applications of Object-Oriented Programming*, Addison-Wesley Publishing Company, Reading, MA, 1990.

Rambaugh, James, Michael Blaha, William Premerlani, Frederick Eddy, and William Lorensen. *Object-Oriented Modeling and Design*, Prentice Hall, Englewood-Cliffs, NJ, 1991.

Winblad, Ann L., Samuel D. Edwards, and David R. King. *Object-Oriented Software*, Addison-Wesley Publishing Company, Reading, MA, 1990.

Wirfs-Brock, Rebecca, Brian Wilkerson, and Lauren Wiener. *Designing Object-Oriented Software*, Prentice Hall, Englewood Cliffs, NJ, 1990.

ANSI Standard C

There are many books on C and all recent books cover the ANSI standard for C. If you are familiar with C as defined in Kernighan and Ritchie's original book, *The C Programming Language,* First Edition, and want to learn about the changes wrought by the ANSI standardization of C, you can get the second edition of Kernighan and Ritchie's book. Other good references to ANSI Standard C are the books by authors such as Plauger (*Standard C*) and Kochan (*Programming in ANSI C*).

Kernighan, Brian W. and Dennis M. Ritchie. *The C Programming Language*, First Edition, Prentice Hall, Inc., Englewood-Cliffs, NJ, 1978.

Kernighan , Brian W. and Dennis M. Ritchie. *The C Programming Language*, Second Edition, Prentice Hall, Inc., Englewood-Cliffs, NJ, 1988.

Kochan, Stephen G. *Programming in ANSI C*, Hayden Books, Carmel, IN, 1988.

Plauger, P.J. and Jim Brodie. *Standard C*, Microsoft Press, Redmond, WA, 1989.

Borland C++ and Windows Programming

Like C++, Microsoft Windows programming is a favorite topic of computer book authors. Among the available books, the books by Myers and Doner, Conger, and Schulman are very useful.

Loren Heiny's book shows examples of graphics programming for Windows using Borland C++ and OWL. Brian Myers and Chris Doner provide very good tutorial coverage of graphics programming with the Windows API and Microsoft C. Although Myers and Doner do not cover Windows programming with Borland C++, you can readily adapt the information from their book for use in your Borland C++ programs. For reference information on Windows API functions, you will find James Conger's recent book handy. Charles Petzold's classic book is another good tutorial on the Windows programming in C with the Windows API.

There are a host of books on Windows programming with Borland C++. Ted Faison's book covers programming with OWL and Borland's container class library in detail. Peter Norton and Paul Yao focus exclusively on Windows programming with OWL.

Popular programming journals are a good source of information on programming with Windows Multimedia Control Interface (MCI). Chapter 15 of the book by Brian Myers and Chris Doner shows a sample application, written in C, that plays sound waves using the MCI commands of the MMSYSTEM.DLL. James Conger's book includes a concise description of the older Windows API functions for generating sound.

There are a number of books devoted to the SoundBlaster board. You will find these books useful if you are looking for a description of the hardware and learning how to set up the board and use the utilities that come with the board. The programming information is primarily oriented toward DOS programmers.

Conger, James L. *The Waite Group's Windows API Bible*, Waite Group Press, Mill Valley, CA, 1992.

Faison, Ted. *Borland C++ 3.1 Object-Oriented Programming, Second Edition*, Sams Publishing, Carmel, IN, 1992.

Heimlich, Rich, David Golden, Ivan Luk, and Peter Ridge. *SoundBlaster: The Official Book*, Osborne McGraw-Hill, Berkeley, CA, 1993.

Heiny, Loren. *Windows Graphics Programming with Borland C++*, Wiley, New York, 1992.

Myers, Brian and Chris Doner. *Programmer's Introduction to Windows 3.1*, SYBEX, Alameda, CA, 1992.

Norton, Peter, and Paul Yao. *Borland C++ Programming for Windows*, Bantam, New York, 1992.

Petzold, Charles. *Programming Windows*, Microsoft Press, Redmond, WA, 1992.

Schulman, Andrew, David Maxey, and Matt Pietrek. *Undocumented Windows*, Addison-Wesley, Reading, MA, 1992.

Stolz, Axel. *The SoundBlaster Book*, Abacus, Grand Rapids, MI, 1992.

Imaging and Animation

For information on displaying and manipulating Windows DIB files (the ones commonly known as the BMP files), consult the book by Brian Myers and Chris Doner (listed in the previous section).

Steve Rimmer has written several books that explain many popular file formats, such as MacPaint, PCX, GIF, TIFF, Truevision Targa, and Microsoft Windows BMP. Rimmer's books include source code in C and 80x86 assembly language to interpret image files. He also provides code to display images on display adapters such as EGA, VGA, and Super VGA.

David Kay and John Levine have recently written a book on graphics file formats. Their book describes a large number of image file formats including PCX, TIFF, JPEG, Windows DIB, Truevision Targa, GIF, MacPaint, and Macintosh PICT. This would be the book to consult if you have questions about any of the image file formats described in this chapter.

Craig Lindley's books also cover a number of image file formats, most notably, PCX, TIFF, and GIF. Additionally, one of his books describes the public domain ray tracing program, DKBTrace, which you can use to create computer-generated imagery.

For information on LZW data compression techniques, consult the articles by Ziv and Lempel, by Welch, and by Nelson.

If you are interested in cell animation, you might want to try out the animation studio software from The Walt Disney Company. It runs under DOS and includes the tools necessary to create the cells for an animation.

For a general discussion of animation, consult Chapter 21 of the classic graphics textbook by Foley, van Dam, Feiner, and Hughes.

The Animation Studio, Walt Disney Computer Software, Inc., Burbank, CA, 1991.

Foley, James D., Andries van Dam, Steven K. Feiner, and John F. Hughes. *Computer Graphics Principles and Practice,* Second Edition, Addison-Wesley Publishing, Reading, MA, 1990.

Kay, David C., and John R. Levine. *Graphics File Formats*, Windcrest/ McGraw-Hill, Blue Ridge Summit, PA, 1992.

Lindley, Craig A. *Practical Image Processing in C*, Wiley, New York, 1991.

———. *Practical Ray Tracing in C*, Wiley, New York, 1992.

Nelson, M.R. "LZW Data Compression," *Dr. Dobb's Journal*, October 1990.

Rimmer, Steve. *Bit-Mapped Graphics*, Windcrest/McGraw-Hill, Blue Ridge Summit, PA, 1990.

———. *Supercharged Bit-Mapped Graphics*, Windcrest/McGraw-Hill, Blue Ridge Summit, PA, 1992.

Welch, T. "A Technique for High-Performance Data Compression," *Computer*, June 1984.

Ziv, J., and A. Lempel. "A Universal Algorithm for Sequential Data Compression," *IEEE Transactions on Information Theory*, May 1977.

Index

Symbols

A

B

C

D

E

F

H

I

J

K

L

M

Q

R

S

T

U

V

X

Y

Z

Disk Install

→

What's on the Disk

The disk contains the complete source code, executable files, and support files for the programs developed in the book. The programs include the following:

- ImageView—A Windows application for viewing images in a variety of formats such as Windows bitmap (.BMP), PC PaintBrush (.PCX), Targa (.TGA), Graphics Interchange Format (.GIF), and Tagged Image File Format (.TIF).
- Animate—A Windows application that animates a number of sprites over a background image. Also enables you to move an image around using the mouse.
- ShowMe—An application that provides animated product demonstrations.

Installing the Floppy Disk

The software included with this book is stored in a compressed form. You cannot use the software without first installing it to your hard drive. The installation program runs from within Windows.

> The programs on this disk require approximately 4M of disk space.

1. From File Manager or Program Manager, choose **R**un from the **F**ile menu.
2. Type **`<drive>INSTALL`** and press Enter, where _`<drive>` is the letter of the drive that contains the installation disk. For example, if the disk is in drive B:, type **`B:INSTALL`** and press Enter.

Follow the on-screen instructions in the installation program. The files will be installed in the \BCDEV directory, unless you chose a different directory during installation. When the installation is complete, be sure to read the file README.TXT. This file contains information on the files and programs that were installed.